The Shariatisation of Indonesia

Studies in Islamic Law and Society

VOLUME 52

The titles published in this series are listed at *brill.com/sils*

The Shariatisation of Indonesia

The Politics of the Council of Indonesian Ulama (Majelis Ulama Indonesia, MUI*)*

By

Syafiq Hasyim

BRILL

LEIDEN | BOSTON

The Library of Congress Cataloging-in-Publication Data is available online at https://catalog.loc.gov
LC record available at https://lccn.loc.gov/2022051724

Typeface for the Latin, Greek, and Cyrillic scripts: "Brill". See and download: brill.com/brill-typeface.

ISSN 1384-1130
ISBN 978-90-04-52570-2 (hardback)
ISBN 978-90-04-53489-6 (e-book)

This book is printed on acid-free paper and produced in a sustainable manner.

Contents

Acknowledgements IX
A Note on Transliterations XII
Abbreviations XIII

1 **The Politics of Shariatisation in Indonesia** 1
1.1 Introduction 1
1.2 Shariatisation from Local and Global Perspectives 6
1.3 Shariatisation and Islamisation in Indonesia 14
1.4 Theoretical Framework 26
1.5 Methodology, Sources of Research and Structure of the Book 38

2 **MUI and the History of the Sharia Trajectory in Indonesia** 43
2.1 Introduction 43
2.2 The Shariatisation of MUI and Indonesia's State Ideology 44
2.3 Discourse on Indonesia's State Ideology and MUI's Response 48
2.4 The Institutionalisation of the Ulama 53
2.5 The Genesis of MUI 56
2.6 Leadership of MUI Senior Ulama 72
2.7 The Reform Era: The Changing Role of MUI 78
2.8 Internal Dynamism 87

3 **A Living Organisation: Pre-existing Conditions and the Organisational Vehicle of Shariatisation** 93
3.1 Introduction 93
3.2 Internal Causes of Shariatisation 95
3.2.1 *From Pancasila to Islam* 95
3.2.2 *From* Khādim al-Ḥukūma *to* Khādim al-Umma 100
3.2.3 *From* Payung *to* Tenda Besar 105
3.3 Institutional Vehicles for Shariatisation 108
3.3.1 *The Fatwa Commission* 109
3.3.1.1 The Soul of MUI 109
3.3.1.2 Fatwa Issuance Methodology 112
3.3.1.3 New Conservatism 118
3.3.2 *Lembaga Pengkajian Pangan, Obat-obatan dan Kosmetika (LPPOM, the Institute for Foods, Drugs and Cosmetics Assessment)* 123

3.3.2.1 Pioneer of the Halal Movement in Indonesia 123
3.3.2.2 National, Regional and International Networks 128
3.3.2.3 Certification and Labelling 133
3.3.2.4 Auditing Lawfulness of Goods 136
3.3.3 *Dewan Syariah Nasional* (*DSN, The National Sharia Board*) 140
3.3.3.1 History of DSN 140
3.3.3.2 Institutionalising the Sharia Economy and Finance 142
3.3.3.3 Issuing Fatwa on Economic and Finance Issues 148
3.3.4 *Komisi Hukum dan Perundang-Undangan* (*The Law and Legislation Commission*) 152
3.3.4.1 Special Legal Envoy 152
3.3.4.2 Drafting Sharia 156
3.4 Conclusion 160

4 Sharia Activism: Opportunity Structure, Frame, and Mobilisation 162
4.1 Introduction 162
4.2 The Legal and Political Structure of Indonesia 163
4.2.1 Reformasi *as an Open Stage* 165
4.2.2 *Divided National Elites* 170
4.2.3 *Friends of Shariatisation* 175
4.2.4 *A Weak State* 186
4.3 Framing Shariatisation 191
4.3.1 *Al-Amr bi al-Maʿrūf wa al-Nahy ʿan al-Munkar* 194
4.3.2 *Ukhuwwa Islāmiyya* 198
4.3.3 *Sharia Is the Solution* 200
4.4 The Mobilisation of Sharia 203
4.4.1 *National Congress* 203
4.4.2 *The Meeting of Ulama* 207
4.4.3 *Congress of the Indonesian Islamic Community* 214
4.4.4 *Media and Publications* 221
4.5 Conclusion 228

5 Regional Shariatisation: The Presence of MUI in Aceh, Bulukumba and Cianjur 230
5.1 Introduction 230
5.2 Aceh 234
5.2.1 *The Ulama Advisory Council* (*MPU*) *as Public Sharia Body* 238

5.2.2 *Belief and Public Morality* 242
5.2.3 *Qanun Jinayat* 246
5.3 Bulukumba, South Sulawesi 248
5.3.1 *Perda Syariah as Public Morality* 252
5.4 Cianjur, West Java 258
5.4.1 Perda Akhlakul Karimah 263
5.4.2 Jilbabisasi, Aliran Sesat *and* Gerakan Pemurtadan 265
5.5 Conclusion 269

6 MUI's Discourse and Its Relevance for Shariatisation: Case Studies of Fatwa 271
6.1 Introduction 271
6.2 Deviant Groups and Islamic Worship 273
6.2.1 Takfir 273
6.2.2 *Worship* 293
6.2.3 *Public Morality* 306
6.2.4 *Proper Islam: Halal Lifestyle and Sharia Economy* 318
6.2.4.1 *Halal* Lifestyle 319
6.2.4.2 Sharia Economy 326
6.3 Compliance and Social Resistance 337

7 The Dilemma of Electoral Politics and the Politics of the *Umma*: MUI's Trajectory of Shariatisation in the Era of Joko Widodo's Presidency 342
7.1 Introduction 342
7.2 MUI and Electoral Politics 343
7.2.1 *The MUI Fatwa on General Elections* 346
7.2.2 *The 2012 Jakarta Gubernatorial Election: MUI and a Muslim Leader as a Must* 349
7.2.3 *The 2014 Presidential Elections: MUI and the Polarisation of Indonesian Muslims* 352
7.2.4 *The 2017 Jakarta Gubernatorial Election as a Stage of Islamist Mobilisation* 355
7.2.5 *The 2019 Presidential Elections: Jokowi's Reconciliation with MUI through Ma'ruf Amin* 360
7.3 The *Umma* and Islamic Discourse in Indonesian Conceptualisation 363
7.3.1 *The Politics of the* Umma *and MUI* 366
7.3.2 *The Jokowi Administration* 369
7.3.3 *Localising the Identity Politics of the* Umma 372

7.3.4 *Populist Shariatisation: Contesting Social and Economic Justice for the* Umma 377

7.4 MUI and Its Political Dilemma 382

7.4.1 *Ma'ruf Amin's Vice Presidency and MUI Moderatism* 385

7.4.2 *The 2020 MUNAS-MUI and Aligning with the Government* 388

7.4.3 *Shariatisation in the Public Sphere under the Jokowi Administration* 390

7.4.4 *Halal Certification for Covid-19 Vaccines* 394

7.5 Conclusion 396

8 Concluding Reflections 398

References 421

Index 448

Acknowledgements

First of all, I want to express my deepest love and gratitude to my family—to my wife Diah, and sons Rama and Shakti, and my daughter Naraya Qirani—for their sincere understanding and company in the process of transforming this PhD dissertation into a book. My deepest thanks go to my parents: my late father, Mudzakir, who taught me from a very young age when attending Islamic boarding school about the importance of loving knowledge, as well as having an open and tolerant attitude towards difference and diversity among people of different backgrounds, and my mother, who has given me strong emotional support throughout my life. My thanks go to my younger sisters, Zulfa and Umi Salama, and also my younger brother Luqman Hakim, who always prays for the health of my family.

As this project started as a PhD dissertation, I express my great thanks to my first supervisor, Birgit Krawietz, whose provided criticism and constructive advice on writing a dissertation which is not only enjoyable for expert readers, but also for non-expert readers. Without her suggestions, I would have ignored the importance of an international audience. Furthermore, her comments and suggestions on benefitting from a broader perspective beyond the boundary of Islamic studies were most valuable. I am greatly indebted to Vincent Houben for his patience in advising me to switch my activist writing style to a more academic one. His broad and deep knowledge of the history of Indonesia enabled me to structure my overlapping and unsystematic knowledge and experience of the country into a more comprehensible and well-argued dissertation. I also thank Nico Kaptein for his generous support for my studies both at Leiden University, the Netherlands, and at the BGSMCS, Freie Universität, Berlin, Germany.

The weekly Berlin Graduate Muslim Cultures and Societies (BGSMCS) colloquium has enriched me with an understanding of other traditions, from activist scholarship to pure academic scholarship. Gudrun Kraemer is the first person to enlighten me about the importance of positioning myself clearly as an academic or activist when I first presented my dissertation outline. I have followed her invaluable advice until now.

I am very grateful to all of my cohorts at the BGSMCS for their openness and willingness to exchange ideas and sources on various disciplines. My boundless thanks go to my countless Indonesian friends, particularly in Berlin and also in other cities of Germany. I cannot name them all. All of them are my extended family. I will never forget their company and closeness that gave me and my family a great experience living in Berlin during my PhD studies.

I owe thanks to Meiwita Budhiharsana (former representative of the Ford Foundation Jakarta) and David Hulse (the current representative of the Ford Foundation, Jakarta), both members of the organisation that provided me grant for my fieldwork in Indonesia. My special thanks go to the Friederich Ebert Stiftung (FES) in Jakarta that provided me with the airline ticket from Indonesia to Berlin at the beginning of my studies in 2009. I would specially like to thank Michel Gilsenan (New York University), Amina Wadud, and Irwan Abdullah (University of Gadjah Mada, Yogyakarta). Without their encouragement and recommendations, my presence in the BGSMCS would not have become a reality. My sincere thanks go to Robert Hefner (Boston University), Greg Fealy (Australian National University), Tim Lindsey (Melbourne University), Khaled Masʿud (Leiden University and Pakistan), Abdullahi al-Naʿim (Emory University), Abdulkader Tayob (University of Cape Town), Ebrahim Moosa (Duke University), and Claudia Derichs (University of Humboldt) for their openness in responding to my emails and discussing my dissertation with me.

Turning to my fieldwork in Indonesia, I express my deep respect to Sahal Mahfudh (Former General Chairman of MUI), Ma'ruf Amin (Former General Chairman of MUI and Indonesian Vice-President 2019–2024), Slamet Effendi Yusuf (Former Chairman of MUI), Amidhan (Former Chairman of MUI), Asrori M. Karni, Solahudin al-Ayyubi, Mohammad Asrorun Niam Sholeh, Akbar, and Ucup (librarian at the MUI office library in Jakarta). My special gratitude goes to Ichwan Sam (Former Secretary General of MUI) and Zainut Tauhid. Both of them provided great access to MUI information and people. Without their sincere help, I would not have been able to attend some important MUI events. I want to thank to Said Aqil Siradj (General Chairman of Nahdlatul Ulama 2010–2021), Asʿad Ali (Vice General Chairman of Nahdlatul Ulama), Din Syamsuddin (Former General Chairman of Muhammadiyah) and the late Bahtiar Effendy (from the Faculty of Political Science of State Islamic University, Jakarta) for their time for my interviews. My thanks go to Muslim Ibrahim (Former Chairman of Aceh Ulama Council, MPU), KH. Sanusi Baco (Former Chairman of MUI of South Sulawesi) and KH. Hafidz Ustman (Former Chairman of MUI of West Java), KH. Abdul Halim (Former Chairman of Cianjur MUI), and Tjamirudin (Former Chairman of MUI Branch of Bulukumba) who welcomed me. Unforgettable memories came from my interviews with Partabai Pobokori (Former Mayor of Bulukumba, South Sulawesi) in his official residence in Makassar, the NGO activists and scholars of Aceh, Syarifah Rahmatillah, Soraya Kamaruzaman, Saifuddin Bantansyah (University of Syiah Kuala), and Syarizal (IAIN ar-Raniri) in Banda Aceh—many thanks for their information. A special thanks goes to my nephew, Irwan Asnawi, who took me on long motorcycle rides during my fieldwork in Makassar and Bulukumba: such long journeys and wonderful fieldwork.

I should also thank Leonard Sebastian, who gave me opportunity to revise this manuscript through a one-year fellowship (2018–2019) at the Indonesian Programmeme at RSIS-Nanyang Technological University (Singapore). My great thanks go to Yew Foong, coordinator of the Indonesia Studies Programme of ISEAS-Yusof Ishak Singapore; its generous fellowship since 2020 made it possible for me to continue my revisions to this manuscript.

Finally, I should express my deepest gratitude to the German Research Foundation, Deutsche Forschungsgemeinscaft, for being a principal funder of my PhD studies at the BGSMCS, FU, Berlin.

A Note on Transliterations

I use the transliteration system based on IJMES (*International Journal of Middle East Studies*) Arabic terms and names. For Indonesian names and loan-terms adopted from Arabic, I follow contemporary standard Indonesian spelling. Arabic terms written in Arabic with Indonesian transliteration have been rewritten in the dissertation in accordance with the transliteration of the *Journal of Islamic Studies*. Common words such as zakāt, halal, ulama and sharia are written in neither italics nor with full Arabic transliteration. The citation and reference system follows the Chicago style that mentions the author and date of the text in the body of the dissertation and also in the footnotes. Sources that refer to online and print media are cited in the footnotes. Indonesian and foreign terms are written in italics, but not names of political parties, Islamic organisations, laws, or regulations. All Indonesian and Arabic sources are written in their respective languages and then translated. Indonesian and Arabic personal names are written in the Indonesian style, as the Western surname convention does not often fit Indonesian and Arabic naming practices.

Abbreviations

AAOIFI	Accounting and Auditing Organisation for Islamic Financial Institutions
ABI	Aksi Bela Islam (Action to Defend Islam)
ABRI	Angkatan Bersenjata Republik Indonesia (Indonesian Armed Forces)
AD	Angkatan Darat (Army)
AJMI	Aceh Judicial Monitoring Institute
AKKBB	Aliansi Kebangsaan dan Kebebasan Beragama dan Berkeyakinan (Alliance for Nationhood, Faith and Religious Freedom)
AMAP	Aliansi Masyarakat Antipornografi (Anti-pornography Social Alliance)
APBN	Anggaran Pendapatan dan Belanja Negara (State Revenue and Expenditure Budget)
BAKORPAKEM	Badan Koodinasi dan Pengawasan Kepercayaan Masyarakat (Coordinating Agency for Society's Beliefs)
BPJPH	Badan Penyelenggara Jaminan Produk Halal (State Agency for Halal Product Assurancce)
BKKSP	Badan Kerja Sama Pondok Pesantren Indonesia (Collaboration Body for Indonesian Islamic Boarding Schools)
BMAU	Badan Musyawarah Alim Ulama (Ulama Advisory Body)
BMI	Bank Muamalat Indonesia (Indonesian Muamalat Bank)
BRR	Badan Rehabilitasi dan Rekonstruksi Aceh (National Agency for Rehabilitation and Reconstruction of Aceh)
DDII	Dewan Dakwah Islamiyah Indonesia (Council of Islamic Propagation of Indonesia)
DI/TII	Darul Islam/Tentara Islam Indonesia (Indonesian Islamic Army)
DMI	Dewan Masjid Indonesia (Indonesian Council of Mosques)
DPH	Dewan Pimpinan Harian (Executive Committee)
DPR RI	Dewan Perwakilan Rakyat Republik Indonesia (National Parliament of Indonesia)
DPRA	Dewan Perwakilan Rakyat Aceh (Local Parliament of Aceh)
DPS	Dewan Pengawas Syariah (Sharia Supervisory Board)
DSN	Dewan Syariah Nasional (National Sharia Board)
FUI	Forum Umat Islam (Islamic People's Forum)
FUI	Forum Ukhuwah Islamiyyah (Islamic Brotherhood Forum)
FURKON	Forum Umat Islam Penegak Keadilan dan Konstitusi (Muslim Society Forum for Justice and Constitution Enforcement)

FPI	Front Pembela Islam (Islam Defenders Front)
GAM	Gerakan Aceh Merdeka (Independent Aceh Movement)
GARIS	Gerakan Reformis Islam (Islamic Reform Movement)
GBHN	Garis-garis Besar Haluan Negara (Guidelines of National Development)
GUM	Gerakan Umat Islam (Islamic Society Movement)
GUPPI	Gabungan Usaha Perbaikan Pendidikan Islam (Consortium for the Improvement of *Islamic Education*)
HAM	Hak Asasi Manusia (Human Rights)
HTI	Hizbut Tahrir Indonesia (Indonesia's Liberation Party)
IAIN	Institute Agama Islam Negeri (State Institute for Islamic Studies)
ICIP	International Centre for Islam and Pluralism
ICMI	Ikatan Cendekiawan Muslim Indonesia (Indonesian Association of Muslim Intellectuals)
IKADI	Ikatan Dai Indonesia (Indonesian Association of Muslim Preachers)
ILO	International Labour Organisations
IMF	International Monetary Fund
IPB	Institute Pertanian Bogor (The Bogor Agricultural Institute)
JAI	Jamaah Ahmadiyah Indonesia (Indonesian Ahmadiyah Congregation)
JAKIM	Jabatan Kemajuan Islam Malaysia (Department of Islamic Development Malaysia)
JAT	Jamaah Ansharut Tauhid (the Community of Helpers for the Union of God)
JIL	Jaringan Islam Liberal (Liberal Islam Network)
JMI	Jabatan Mufti Islam (National Mufti of Brunei)
JPH	Jaminan Produk Halal (Halal Product Assurance)
KAKANDEPAG	Kepala Kantor Departemen Agama (The Head of Religious Affairs Office)
KKG	Kesetaraan dan Keadilan Gender (Gender Equality and Equity)
KISDI	Komite Islam untuk Solidaritas Dunia Islam (Islamic Committee for International Solidarity)
Komnas Perempuan	Komisi National Perempuan (National Commission on Violence Against Women)
KPPSI	Komite Persiapan Penegakan Syariat Islam (Committee for Preparation of Sharia Implementation)

KUHP	Kitab Undang-Undang Hukum Pidana (Indonesian Criminal Code)
KUHAP	Kitab Undang-Undang Hukum Perdata (Indonesian Civil Code)
KUII	Kongres Umat Islam Indonesia (Congress of the Indonesian Islamic Community)
LBH	Lembaga Bantuan Hukum (Legal Aid Institute)
LDII	Lembaga Dakwak Islam Indonesia (Indonesian Institute for Islamic Propagation)
LFN	Lembaga Fatwa Negara (State Council of Fatwa)
LKS	Lembaga Keuangan Syariah (Sharia Finance Institution)
LPII	Lembaga Pengkajian dan Pengembangan Islam (Institute for the Study and Development of Islam)
LPPOM	Lembaga Pengkajian Pangan, Obat-obatan dan Kosmetika (Institute for Foods, Drugs and Cosmetics Assessment)
MAWI	Majelis Agung Waligereja Indonesia (Indonesian Council of Bishops)
MMI	Majelis Mujahidin Indonesia (Indonesian Mujahidin Council)
MONAS	Monumen Nasional (National Monument)
MPR	Majelis Permusyawaratan Ulama (People's Consultative Assembly of Indonesia)
MPU	Majelis Permusyawaratan Ulama (Ulama Advisory Council)
MPUA	Majelis Permusyawaratan Ulama Aceh (Acehnese Ulama Advisory Council)
MUI	Majelis Ulama Indonesia (Council of Indonesian Ulama)
MUIPDIA	Majelis Ulama Indonesia Propinsi Daerah Istimewa Aceh (Council of Indonesian Ulama of Special Aceh Province)
MUPDIA	Majelis Ulama Propinsi Daerah Istimewa Aceh (Ulama Council of Special Aceh Province)
MTA	Majelis Tafsir Al-Qur'ān (Qur'ān Exegesis Council)
MUD	Majelis Ulama Daerah (Council of Regional Ulama)
MUN	Majelis Ulama National (National Ulama Council)
MUNAS MUI	Musyawarah National Majelis Ulama Indonesia (National MUI Congress)
MUKERNAS	Musyawarah Kerja Nasional (National Work Consultation)
MUI	Majelis Ulama Indonesia (Council of Indonesian Ulama)
MUUI	Majelis Ukhuwah Umat Islam (Council of Muslim Community Solidarity)
MUIS	Majelis Ugama Islam Singapore (Islamic Religious Council of Singapore)
MUNAS	Musyawarah National (National Meeting)

NKRI	Negara Kesatuan Republik Indonesia (Unitary State of the Indonesian Republic)
NU	Nahdlatul Ulama (The Awakening of Muslim Scholars)
PPPP	Pedoman Penghayatan dan Pengamalan Pancasila (Guidance in Reflection on and Application of Pancasila)
PAKEM	Pengawas Aliran Kepercayaan Masyarakat (Monitoring Agency for Society's Belief)
PAN	Partai Amanah Nasional (National Mandate Party)
PARMUSI	Persaudaraan Muslimin Indonesia (Indonesian Muslim Brotherhood)
PBB	Partai Bulan Bintang (Crescent Star Party)
PBR	Partai Bintang Reformasi (Reform Star Party)
PDII	Pusat Dakwah Islam Indonesia (Indonesian Centre for Islamic Propagation)
PDIP	Partai Demokrasi Indonesia Perjuangan (Indonesian Democracy Party for Struggle)
Perda Syariah	Peraturan Daerah Berdasar Syariah (sharia bylaw)
PERSIS	Persatuan Islam (Federation of Islam)
PERTI	Persatuan Tarbiyah Islamiyah Indonesia (Union for Islamic Education)
PGI	Persekutuan Gereja-Gereja Indonesia (Communion of Churches in Indonesia)
PKI	Partai Komunis Indonesia (Indonesian Communist Party)
PK	Partai Keadilan (Justice Party, the forerunner of the PKS)
PKS	Partai Kesejahteraan Sejahtera (Prosperous Justice Party)
POLRI	Polisi Republik Indonesia (Indonesian police)
PPP	Partai Persatuan Pembangunan (United Development Party)
PUSA	Persatuan Ulama Seluruh Aceh (All Acehnese Ulama Association)
RAKERNAS	Rapat Kerja Nasional (National Working Meeting)
RUU	Rancangan Undang-Undang (draft law)
RUUAPP	Rancangan Undang-Undang Anti Pornografi dan Pornoaksi (Draft Law on Anti-Pornography and Pornographic Behaviour)
SDSB	Sumbangan Dermawan Sosial Berhadiah (State Sponsored Lottery)
SI	Syarikat Islam (Association of Islam)
SILMUI	Silaturahmi dan Musyawarah Umat Islam (Solidarity Meeting for the Muslim Community)
SJH	Sistem Jaminan Halal (Halal Assurance System)
SKB	Surat Keputusan Bersama (Joint Decree)
SKP	Sekretariat Kerjasama Kepercayaan (Secretariat for Cooperation on Beliefs)

TMI	Taman Mini Indonesia (Mini-Indonesia Theme Park)
TPFKM	Tim Pencari Fakta Kasus Maluku (Maluku Fact Finding Team)
TPM	Tim Pembela Muslim (Muslim Lawyers Team)
TPT	Tim Penanggulangan Terorisme (Counter-Terrorism Team)
UUD	Undang-undang Dasar (Constitution)
UUS	Unit Usaha Syaria (Sharia Business Unit)
YDDP	Yayasan Dana Dakwah dan Pembangunan (Dakwah Development Fund Foundation)
WHC	World Halal Council

CHAPTER 1

The Politics of Shariatisation in Indonesia

1.1 Introduction

The Majelis Ulama Indonesia (MUI, the Council of Indonesian Ulama) has brought about a rising shift of sharia from the private to the public sphere since the last two decades, which has been regarded as evidence of MUI's attempts to promote shariatisation in Indonesia. This perception stems from MUI's increasing authority as an organisation that strives for the normative regulation of Muslim behaviour in the formally non-theocratic (secular) country of Indonesia. Although MUI has promoted sharia norms since its inception in 1975, the collapse of the authoritarian Suharto regime in 1998 gave this ulama organisation more resonance in endorsing the implementation of discourses on Islamic public morality, halal lifestyle, pure Islam, and so forth through shariatisation in the social and legal fields.

This book seeks to interrogate this perception that MUI's mission is to shariatise Indonesian society, given its official support of Indonesia not as a theocratic Islamic state but rather as the Unitary State of the Indonesian Republic, or Negara Kesatuan Republik Indonesia (NKRI).[1] Three key questions drove the research: firstly, "Is MUI striving for the shariatisation of Indonesian society, and if so in what ways?;" secondly, "How does shariatisation impact the legal and public spheres of Indonesia, given that both MUI and the national consensus hold that Indonesia's state ideology is Pancasila?;"[2] and thirdly, "What kind of political climate does shariatisation engender, and what is the position

1 In his speech on 17 August 2007, the President of the Republic of Indonesia, Susilo Bambang Yudhoyono, stated that the most appropriate form for the Indonesian state is the Unitary State of the Republic of Indonesia (NKRI). The four primary pillars that constitute the basic values and consensus underlying the Republic of Indonesia are: Pancasila, the 1945 Constitution, Unity in Diversity and the Unitary State of the Republic of Indonesia (NKRI).

2 *Panca* means five and *Sila* means principles; the five principles are belief in one God, just and civilised humanity, unity of Indonesia, democracy and social justice. For more recent discussions of the ideology of Pancasila see Eka Darmaputra's *Pancasila and the Search for Identity and Modernity in Indonesian Society: A Cultural and Ethical Analysis* (Leiden & Boston: Brill, 1988). Also Douglas Ramage, *Politics in Indonesia, Democracy, Islam and the Ideology of Tolerance* (London & New York: Routledge, 2005). Benyamin Fleming, *Public Religion And the Pancasila-Based State of Indonesia: An Ethical And Sociological Analysis* (New York: Peter Lang, 2006).

 | DOI:10.1163/9789004534896_002

of the state of Indonesia and society with regard to shariatisation?" These are the three main research questions, which will be further investigated under derivative questions in the following chapters.

The shariatisation of Indonesia is defined here as the various initiatives aimed at invigorating and incorporating the norms of sharia into the legal and public spheres of Indonesia. This definition is inspired by the theory of sharia evolution introduced by Muḥammad Saʿīd al-ʿAshmāwī, an Egyptian scholar who describes sharia in five stages. The first stage of sharia, implemented in the era of the Prophet Muḥammad, referred not to Islamic legal rules but rather the path of God with its aspects of worship, ethical code, and social relations. The second stage referred to precepts mentioned in the Qurʾān implemented in society as legal rules. In the third stage, sharia expanded its meaning to cover legal rulings in the Qurʾān and the traditions of the Prophet Muḥammad. In the fourth and final stage, sharia includes the whole body of Islamic law, which has developed over the course of Islamic history. Thus the fourth definition covers the opinions and interpretations of legal scholars.[3] In this book, shariatisation not only refers to the adoption of sharia norms in the legal sphere—the legislation and positivisation of sharia—but also the public sphere in general.

A further question, then, to be addressed here is: "How are shariatisation and Islamisation connected?" With regard to the definition above, both have more in common than they have differences. What distinguishes them is their focus: shariatisation has a narrower but deeper focus than Islamisation. If Islamisation is culturalisation, or the assimilation of the culture of Islam, lacking a prescribed order, then shariatisation is structuralisation, or the cultivation of Islam through its political and legal structure, following a prescribed order. Islamisation offers alternative ideas but does not dictate the law and order of public life, whereas shariatisation enforces law and order with the idea that adherence to sharia offers a better future for the world. Shariatisation thus represents a more concrete process than Islamisation. This was evident in the Islamisation of science projects in Indonesia, promoted by Muslim scholars such as A.M. Saefudin (b. 1940), Jujun Suryasumanteri (b. 1940), and Dawan

3 Arskal Salim, *Challenging the Secular State: The Islamization of Law in Modern Indonesia* (Honolulu: University of Hawaii Press, 2008), pp. 13–14; Muhammad Saʿīd Al-ʿAshmāwī, "The Sharia: The Codification of Islamic Law," in *Liberal Islam: A Source Book*, ed. Charles Kurzman (Oxford & New York: Oxford University Press, 1998), 49–58; Bassam Tibi, *The Sharia State: Arab Spring and Democratization* (New York: Routledge, 2013), p. 51; Asʿad Abu Khalil, "Against the Taboos of Islam: Anti Conformist Tendencies in Contemporary Arab/Islamic Thought," in *Between the State and Islam*, ed. Charles Butterworth and William Zartman (Cambridge: Cambridge University Press, 2001), 110–34, p. 125.

Rahardjo (1942–2018) as well as many others from the 1990s to early 2000s, which has now disappeared from public debate.[4]

Often shariatisation is defined as equivalent to legal Islamisation, which is a more appropriate description of the legislation of sharia or the positivisation of sharia.[5] Shariatisation is more than just dealing with both issues, but rather an attempt to introduce the Islamic belief system as a way to impose law and order in the public sphere. This is evident from MUI's ambition to mainstream the Sunnī belief system as incumbant upon all Indonesian Muslims. In other words, shariatisation can be grasped as having a broader context than legal Islamisation. Rather than codifying the norms of sharia as positive legal rules, shariatisation (*tashrīʿ*) can take shape formally and informally in numerous fields and may vary in its level of depth and significance in the legal and public spheres. It depends heavily on the theological concepts, opportunities, and movement models being used in a particular context. The nuances of shariatisation span the domains of theology and culture as well as that of politics and, more importantly, law. Shariatisation paths can be both proactively and reactively forged into the legal and public spheres, and proactive shariatisation is deeply internally established to constitute a sharia-based state through the incorporation of Islamic legal norms into the national legal system. Proactive shariatisation means that shariatisation is projected to respond to external issues at the national, transnational and global level as a means of expressing Islamic identity and is more strategic, whereas reactive shariatisation is more tactical and short-term oriented. Shariatisation takes shape at two levels: at the level of discourse and level of movement or activism. Actors initiating shariatisation can be individuals, groups, or the state in bringing about partial and universal incorporation of sharia in the legal and public spheres in Indonesia. The use of the term "shariatisation" itself is beginning to find common use in academia.[6]

---

4 Books published on the Islamisation of science projects include Jujun Suparjan Suriasumantri Saefuddin and M. Ahmad, *Desekularisasi Pemikiran: Landasan Islamisasi* (Bandung: Mizan, 1987); Hanna Djumhana Bastaman, *Integrasi Psikologi Dengan Islam: Menuju Psikologi Islami* (Yogyakarta: Pustaka Pelajar & Yayasan Insan Kamil, 1995); M. Rahardjo, *Islam Dan Transformasi Budaya* (Jakarta: LSAF, 2002), Kuntowijoyo and A.E. Priyono, *Paradigma Islam: Interpretasi Untuk Aksi* (Bandung: PT Mizan Publika, 2008), Ziauddin Sardar and A.E. Priyono, *Jihad Intelektual: Merumuskan Parameter-Parameter Sains Islam* (Jakarta: Risalah Gusti, n.d.), and Amin Rais, *Cakrawala Islam: Antara Cita dan Fakta* (Bandung: Mizan, 1987).

5 Tim Lindsey, "Monopolising Islam? The Indonesian Ulama Council and State Regulation of the 'Islamic Economy,'" *Bulletin of Indonesian Economic Studies* 48, no. 2 (2012): 253–74; Arskal Salim, *Challenging the Secular State: The Islamization of Law in Modern Indonesia* (Honolulu: University of Hawaii Press, 2008).

6 The use of the term shariatisation in the context of studies on Indonesia has been mentioned in Lissi Rasmussen, *Bridges Instead of Walls: Christian Muslim Interaction in Denmark,*

Islamisation is oriented towards change of a political establishment from the secular to an Islamic system, while shariatisation is aimed at incorporating the norms of sharia into the legal and public spheres.[7] Shariatisation holds that the state is only a medium that enables sharia to be implemented in the legal and public spheres, while the state political system itself remains secular, whereas Islamisation views the state as the fundamental entity of political Islam, which should first be established before sharia can be enacted as the basic legal code. However, shariatisation often has a deeper impact on Muslim societies than Islamisation does. In the experience of Pakistan, for instance, Islamisation has failed to gain ground in the Muslim community because it is promoted by the state and modern sectors of society such as industrial elites and business circles, while shariatisation is more attractive because it is associated with non-Westernised social forces and is also society-driven. Although shariatisation does not desire the creation of a formal Islamic state, Farzana Shaikh, referring to the case of Pakistan, states that this is an advantage: shariatisation is thus a movement that appeals to the vernacular groups of Pakistan that want sharia to be implemented at the micro level in the legal and public spheres.[8] Olivier Roy puts forward a similar argument about neo-fundamentalism, employing the term to describe the type of Islamist movement that strives for the implementation of sharia without instrumentalising an Islamic state as its vehicle.[9] He states that in neo-fundamentalist discourse the application of sharia does not depend on any political policy, body of positive law, or state entity. A key characteristic of this movement is its ability to create a space for power in order to manipulate or circumvent sharia. Sharia is never prevented from inclusion through induction, commentaries, and interpretation. Roy argues that the idea of the incompleteness of

---

Indonesia and Nigeria (Minneapolis: Lutheran University Press, 2007), p. 112; Lindsey, "Monopolising Islam?"; Shaikh Farzana, "From Islamisation to Shariatisation," *Third World Quarterly* 29, no. 3 (2008): 593–609; Olivier Roy, *The Failure of Political Islam* (Cambridge, MA: Harvard University Press, 1996), p. 30.

7 John L Esposito, "Introduction: Modernising Islam and Reislamisation in Global Perspective," in *Modernizing Islam: Religion and the Public Sphere in Europe and the Middle East*, ed. John L Esposito (New Brunswick & New Jersey: Rutgers University Press, 2003), 1–14, p. 7; Fariba Adelkhah, "Reislamization in the Public Sphere," in *Public Islam and the Common Good*, ed. Armando Salvatore and Dale Eickleman (Leiden & Boston: Brill, 2006), 103–1.

8 Shaikh Farzana, "From Islamisation to Shariatisation," *Third World Quarterly* 29, no. 3 (2008): 593–609, p. 595.

9 The concept of neofundamentalism was introduced by Oliver Roy to describe the type of Islamist movement that strives to re-establish sharia without using an Islamic state as its vehicle. Roy, *The Failure of Political Islam*, p. ix.

the sharia also allows for innovation in the process of shariatisation.[10] In the neo-fundamentalist movement, sharia can be applied in various state forms because the state entity is no longer considered as the paramount space for the implementation of sharia law. In this framework, all Muslim peoples are living under the system of the global *umma*. Generally, under shariatisation the geographical boundaries of state borders are viewed as artificial constructs. In such cases, the phenomenon of the shariatisation can be called "Islamisation without an Islamic state."[11]

Taking into consideration the nuances distinguishing the concepts of shariatisation and Islamisation above, in this book I have made the choice to use the term shariatisation. This term was chosen as a result of its prevalence: shariatisation and its derivatives are widely used in the written and oral discourse of MUI such as books, leaflets, magazines and conference proceedings, and in the speech of its leaders, in accordance with MUI's aim of imposing sharia through the process of legislation. Besides that, the use of this term relates to the reason why MUI does not use the term *fiqh* (or *fiqhiyya*), which is probably closer to its agenda. Although the term *fiqh* itself is rarely found in both the written and practical discourse of MUI, however, this book speculates that behind the frequent mention of the term sharia or shariatisation, in line with *fiqh*, is the ulama council's aim of encouraging the obedience of Indonesian Muslims. MUI seems to be aware that the term sharia or shariatisation can attract more interest in Indonesian Muslim society than *fiqh* because the order of sharia is undisputed while that of *fiqh* is not. It is also based on MUI's general conceptualisation that sharia is divine law and therefore unchangeable, while *fiqh* is a result of interpretation of God's will, which is changeable.

This book describes the role of MUI in the shariatisation in Indonesia since its establishment in 1975. It uncovers the history of MUI's establishment, the role of MUI in post-Suharto Indonesia, the transition era from an authoritarian to a reform regime, the making of activities and discourse, and the political role of MUI in shariatisation. During this changeover, the people of Indonesia—the largest Muslim country in the world—re-contested their fundamental issues and rights regarding identity and representation, which had been sensitive

10 Ibid, p. 10.

11 Asef Bayat, "Un-Civil Society: The Politics of 'the Informal People,'" *Third World Quarterly* 18, no. 1 (1997): 53–74; Asef Bayat, *Making Islam Democratic: Social Movements and the Post-Islamist Turn* (Redwood City, CA: Stanford University Press, 2007), p. 147.

and restricted under the Suharto era.[12] Most importantly, "Islamist" groups[13] have actively used this transition to voice their aspirations and agenda, calling for Indonesia to be more closely aligned with sharia law. The coverage of MUI's role in the pre-reform era helps reveal the continuity and discontinuity of MUI discourses and practices between the pre- and post-reform eras of Indonesia.

1.2 Shariatisation from Local and Global Perspectives

Locating MUI in the setting of the shariatisation movement in Indonesia is a challenging task, particularly when viewed through the framework of the nation-state. Firstly, MUI is not a judiciary body but an organisation of ulama that issues fatwa and other kinds of Islamic advice. Secondly, MUI itself has accepted the Pancasila state as the final form of the Indonesian state. Discussing the role of MUI in the shariatisation of Indonesia means discussing its influence on the legal and public spheres through its issuance of fatwa and *tawṣiyya* (Islamic recommendations), referred to here as the discourse of MUI, and its activism. As Indonesia is not a theocratic Islamic country, shariatisation is not aimed at the establishment of a sharia state. This, then, leads to the question: "How should MUI be located in the context of shariatisation from a domestic and a global perspective?"

MUI was originally established in 1975 to bolster the Indonesian Muslim community's adherence to Islam.[14] Although it is not an official state body, it has a pivotal influence in delivering religious prescriptions for both the state and society on ways to contextualise Islam within the framework of

12 Dwight Y King, *Half-Hearted Reform: Electoral Institutions and the Struggle for Democracy in Indonesia* (Westport: Greenwood Publishing Group, 2003); Dewi Fortuna Anwar, "The Habibie Presidency: Catapulting Towards Reform," in *Soeharto's New Order and Its Legacy: Essays in Honour of Harold Crouch*, ed. Edward Aspinal and Greg Fealy (Canberra: ANU E Press, 2010); Donald L. Horowitz, *Constitutional Change and Democracy in Indonesia* (Cambridge: Cambridge University Press, 2013). During the period 1998–2012, Indonesia was governed by four presidents; (1) Baharuddin Joesoef Habibie, 1998–1999, (2) Abdurrahman Wahid, 1999–2000, (3) Megawati Sukarno Putri, 2000–2004, (4) Susilo Bambang Yudoyono, 2004–2009, 2009–2014.

13 Bobby S Sayyid, *A Fundamental Fear: Eurocentrim and the Emergence of Islamism* (London & New York: Zed Books, 1997), p. 17.

14 MUI, *20 Tahun Majelis Ulama Indonesia*, ed. H.S. Prodjokusumo (Jakarta: Sekretariat Majelis Ulama Indonesia, 1995); Muhammad Atho Mudzhar, *Fatwa of the Council of Indonesian Ulama: A Study of Islamic Legal Thought in Indonesia 1975–1988* (Jakarta: INIS, 1993); Wahiduddin Adams, *Pola Penyerapan Fatwa Majelis Ulama Indonesia (MUI) Dalam Peraturan Perundang-Undangan 1975–1997* (Jakarta: Departemen Agama, 2004).

Indonesia's nation-state, as its authority to pass fatwas is recognised by other Islamic organisations. In this regard, both state and society can consult the Council on purely Islamic (sharia) or related issues. In the Suharto era, MUI's influence in the legal and public spheres was limited, as by law Pancasila was defined as the ideological foundation of the Indonesian state, political parties, and mass-based organisations. In the Suharto era, MUI played its role of subjugating the norms of Islam into the framework of the nation-state of Indonesia by attempting to convince the Islamic public that sharia could be harmonised into Pancasila. MUI also acted as the main Islamic organisation to promote national security, religious harmony and national development programmemess during the period of this authoritarian regime. One key way for MUI to remain close with the state was to provide legitimacy to government policies, initiatives, and directives by transforming them into religious language that was acceptable and understandable to the general Muslim populace.[15] MUI became the state mouthpiece for interpreting Islam within the context of Indonesia, often called Indonesian Islam, which is characterised as a form of Islam that is moderate in nature and appreciative of the vernacular culture and value of Indonesian society.[16]

However, MUI's role in the post-reform era changed in keeping with the larger social and political shifts of the new Indonesia. President Baharuddin Jusuf Habibie (1998–1999), who replaced Suharto, although only president for one year, opened up liberalisation and democratisation in certain aspects of national politics and law, including the right for political parties and mass-based organisations to claim Islam as their sole ideology.[17] The new policies also influenced the MUI's change in organisational orientation from a nationalist-religious body to an increasingly Islamist one, thus altering the

15 Donald J. Porter, *Managing Politics and Islam in Indonesia* (London & New York: Routledge Curzon, 2004); Mudzhar, *Fatwa of the Council of Indonesian Ulama*; Nadirsyah Hosen, "Behind the Scenes: Fatwas of Majelis Ulama Indonesia," *Journal of Islamic Studies* 2, no. 15 (2004): 147–79.

16 Azyumardi Azra, *Islam in the Indonesian World, an Account of Institutional Formation* (Bandung: Mizan, 2006); Azyumardi Azra, "Distinguishing Indonesian Islam: Some Lessons to Learn," in *Islam in Indonesia: Contrasting Images and Interpretations*, ed. Jajat Burhanudin and Kees van Dijk (Amsterdam: Amsterdam University Press, 2013), 63–74; Martin van Bruinessen, "Indonesian Muslims and Their Place in the Larger World of Islam," in *Indonesia Rising: The Repositioning of Asia's Third Giant*, ed. Anthony Reid (Singapore: Institute of Southeast Asian Studies, 2012), 117–40.

17 Harold Crouch, *Political Reform in Indonesia after Soeharto* (Singapore: ISEAS, 2010); Luthfi Assyaukanie, *Islam and the Secular State in Indonesia* (Singapore: ISEAS, 2009).

alignment of its services from state-orientated to *umma*[18]-oriented.[19] At this point, the changing circumstances of MUI met the interests of Islamist groups that wanted sharia to become a significant part of the legal system and practice of Indonesia. MUI began to become closer to Islamist groups, as can be seen in its fatwa and religious recommendations justifying the agenda and programmemes of Islamist groups desiring the implementation of sharia law. This is also evident from MUI's reluctance to criticise the phenomena of sharia bylaws promoted by Islamist groups in many regions of Indonesia. In addition, MUI seems to have assumed the position of the loyal provider of discourse promoting the expansion of sharia from the private realm to the legal and public spheres of Indonesia.[20] As a democratic society whose state neutrality is its benchmark, the imposition of such Islamic provisions into the legal rules and order of Indonesia can be seen as disturbing. However, MUI, since the reform era in 1998, has viewed this issue differently. As a country with a large Muslim majority, MUI tolerates this expansion and agrees that sharia should be part of the national legal discourse and practice, as evidenced by statements from MUI figures such as Sahal Mahfudh, Amin, and Ridwan.[21] In this regard, the presence of sharia in the legal practice and discourse of Indonesia can be regarded as a possible solution to the country's economic stagnation; as the popular slogan states, "Islam is the solution" (*al-Islām hūwa al-ḥall*).[22]

---

18 *Umma* means the Muslim community but also denotes the global community of Muslim believers. Every Muslim is therefore an integral part of the *umma*. Ziauddin Sardar, *Reading the Qur'an:The Contemporary Relevance of the Sacred Text of Islam* (Oxford & New York: Oxford University Press, 2011), pp. 246–7; Endang Turmudi, *Struggling For The Umma: Changing Leadership Roles of Kiai in Jombang East Java* (Canberra: ANU E Press, 2006); Peter G. Mandeville, *Transnational Muslim Politics: Reimagining the Umma*, vol. 2002 (London & New York: Routledge, 2002).

19 Piers Gillespie, "Current Issues in Indonesian Islam: Analysing the 2005 Council of Indonesian Ulama Fatwa No. 7 Opposing Pluralism, Liberalism and Securalism," *Journal of Islamic Studies* 2, no. 18 (2007): 202–40, p. 212; Syafiq Hasyim, "The Council of Indonesian Ulama (Majelis Ulama Indonesia, MUI) and Religious Freedom," Irasec's Discussion Papers 12, 2011.

20 MUI, *Himpunan Fatwa MUI Sejak 1975* (Jakarta: Erlangga, 2011), p. 863.

21 Interview with Sahal Mahfudh, Jakarta, 2011; Interview with Ma'ruf Amin, Jakarta, 2010; Interview with Cholil Ridwan, Jakarta, 2010.

22 The slogan *Islām hūwa al-ḥall* is popularly used by Indonesian Islamist groups such as the HTI, MMI and PKS. This can be seen from MUI's focus on *al-masā'il al-qānūniyya* (religious questions which are related to the Constitution) as a priority that attracted the attention of most MUI members at the Ulama Meeting in Padang, West Sumatera, in 2009. See M. Imdadun Rahmat, *Arus Baru Islam Radikal, Transmisi Revivalisme Islam Timur Tengah Ke Indonesia* (Jakarta: Erlangga, 2005), p. xi; MUI, *Ijma' Ulama: Keputusan Ijma' Ulama Komisi Fatwa Se-Indonesia III* (Jakarta: Majelis Ulama Indonesia, 2009), pp. 91–101.

The increasing promotion of sharia norms in the public and legal spheres of Indonesia cannot be separated from the global phenomenon of Islamic revivalism or Islamism. International discourse recognises that Islamism has a multiplicity of expressions, but this overview is limited to only three: namely al-Ikhwān al-Muslimūn (the Muslim Brotherhood) of Egypt in 1928, the Iranian Revolution in 1979, and the Jama'at-i Islami movement in Pakistan. The definition of Islamism here refers to the analyses used by some social scientists who have observed the phenomenon. William Shepard states that "Islamism" is a tendency to view Islam as an ideology.[23] Bobby Sayyid refers to those placing her or his Muslim identity at the centre of her or his political enterprise as Islamist.[24] In a similar tone, Muhammed Ayoob employs the term Islamism to describe Islamic identity as the ultimate goal of a Muslim's struggle.[25] These three models of Islamism are presented here because of their broad influence in other countries, including Indonesia. Fred R. Von Der Mehden has indicated that the thoughts of Sayyid Quṭb, Ḥasan al-Bannā and some others have been frequently quoted in prominent national media of Indonesia such as *Prisma*, *Tempo*, and *Panji Masyarakat*.[26] Gilles Kepel's claim that these movements have a direct impact on the Islamisation projects of many Islamic countries is therefore accurate, and many Muslim countries treat the Muslim Brotherhood of Egypt as the model for Islamisation.[27] Bassam Tibi argues that al-Bannā was the first person to introduce the concept of a sharia state.[28] Al-Bannā also planted the intellectual seeds of nascent socio-religious and mass-oriented Islamic movements in the societies of the Arab Middle East and North Africa. Despite his politics, viewed as controversial by some Arab countries and the Islamic world in general, al-Bannā succeeded in becoming a profound ideological influence on Muslim activists and scholars.[29] The prolific ascendency of many Islamist groups throughout the entire Islamic world, including Indonesia, can be traced to the spread and circulation of Ḥasan al-Bannā's

23 William F Shepard, "Islam and Ideology: Towards A Typology," *International Journal of Middle East Studies* 19 (1987): 307–66, p. 308.

24 Sayyid, *A Fundamental Fear*, p. 17.

25 Mohammed Ayoob, *The Many Faces of Political Islam, Religion and Politics in the Muslim World* (Michigan: Michigan University Press, 2008), p. 2.

26 Fred R. von der Mehden, *Two Worlds of Islam: Interaction Between Southeast Asia and the Middle East* (Florida: University Press of Florida, 1993), p. 87.

27 Gilles Kepel, *Muslim Extremism in Egypt: The Prophet and Pharaoh* (Berkeley & Los Angeles: University of California Press, 1986), p. 9.

28 Bassam Tibi, *The Sharia State: Arab Spring and Democratization* (New York: Routledge, 2013), p. 52.

29 Abu Ibrahim Rabi', *Intellectual Origins of Islamic Resurgence in the Modern Arab World* (Albany: University of New York Press, 1996), p. 64.

tenets. Indonesia began to translate al-Bannā's works in the 1970s and the books have been used as training manuals for Indonesian Islamists and propagators since the 1980s. Partai Keadilan Sejahtera (PKS, the Prosperous Justice Party), for instance, has adopted the thoughts of al-Bannā into its constitution.[30] Some underground organisations—such as Jema'ah Tarbiyah, discussed in the next section—employ his tenets to bind its members emotionally to the struggle for sharia.

Besides al-Bannā, Indonesian Muslims also welcome the thoughts of Sayyid Quṭb. Barbara Zollner reveals that Quṭb's writings contain the ideological inspiration for radical Islamic activism or even militancy; Quṭb's commentary on the Qur'ān, *Fī Ẓilāl al-Qur'ān* and, even more so, his book *Maʿālim fī al-Ṭarīq* are ideological and theological guidebooks that provided the basic thinking for Islamist groups that first emerged in the 1970s and eventually transformed into today's jihadist networks in and beyond Egypt.[31] Salwa Ismail lists three of Quṭb's most popular ideas in Islamism: first, the restoration of *ḥākimiyya* (God's governance), second, the reassessment of the modern day as *jāhiliyya* (a state of ignorance) and third, the central concept of *jihād* (struggle) for sharia.[32] Indonesian Islamism has shared these three ideas to some degree. In Indonesia, Quṭb's books, alongside al-Bannā's works, are widely translated and distributed as manuals for Islamist movements. Both al-Bannā and Quṭb have a privileged place in the hearts and minds of Islamist activists from the Indonesian Sunnī denomination.[33] PKS's response to the Egyptian military coup toppling Mohammed Morsi from his position as President of Egypt in August 2013 indicated the party's strong support of the Muslim Brotherhood.[34]

---

30 M. Imdadun Rahmat, *Ideologi Politik PKS: Dari Masjid Kampus Ke Gedung Parlemen* (Yogyakarta: PT LKiS Pelangi Aksara, 2008), pp. 101–29.

31 Barbara Z.E. Zollner, *The Muslim Brotherhood: Hasan al-Hudaybi and Ideology* (London & New York: Routledge, 2009), p. 51.

32 Salwa Ismail, *Rethinking Islamist Politics: Culture, the State and Islamism* (London & New York: I.B. Tauris, 2006), p. 84.

33 Several current day prominent Muslim scholars who have inherit the intellectual legacy of the Muslim Brotherhood are Yūsuf al-Qaraḍāwī of Egypt, Muṣṭafā al-Sibāʿī of Syria, Saʿīd Ḥawwā of Syria, Ḥasan Turābī of Sudan, and Rashīd al-Ghanūshī of Tunisia (Rabi', *Intellectual Origins of Islamic Resurgence*, p. 63).

34 M. Imdadun Rahmat, *Ideologi Politik PKS: Dari Masjid Kampus Ke Gedung Parlemen* (Yogyakarta: PT LKiS Pelangi Aksara, 2008); Yon Machmudi, *The Rise of Jemaah Tarbiyah and the Prosperous Justice Party (PKS)* (Canberra: ANU E Press, 2008). "PKS Minta Pemerintah Dukung Mohammed Morsi", Tempo, 26 June 2012, https://nasional.tempo.co/read/413106/pks-minta-pemerintah-dukung-mohammed-morsi, viewed on 22 July 2022; on PKS support for the *Ikhwani* party, see also "PKS: Kudeta Militer Presiden Morsi, Kemunduran Demokrasi," Liputan, 4 July 2013, https://www.liputan6.com/news/read/630184/pks-kudeta-militer-presiden-morsi-kemunduran-demokrasi, viewed on 22 July 2022.

This Indonesian Ikhwāni party stated that the military coup was a handicap for democratisation in Egypt, mobilised a protest on the issue, and also persuaded the government to strongly support the Muslim Brotherhood and criticise the coup.

The second model of Islamism is the Iranian Revolution, the influence of which was tangible in neighbouring countries and also more distant ones such as Indonesia and Malaysia.[35] The Shīʿa presence in Indonesia can be dated back to the arrival of Islam in the archipelago. Jalaluddin Rakhmat (an important figure of the Indonesian Shīʿa community), who refers to the Persian theory on the coming of Islam in Indonesia, states that Shīʿism has been present in Indonesia since the first wave of Islam arrived in the country.[36] However, Indonesian Muslims have a unique understanding of Shīʿism and the Iranian Revolution. Although the majority Sunnī Indonesian Muslims have tried to reject Shīʿism as an Islamic sect, they nevertheless take the spirit of the revolution as a lesson to be learned, and as the first model of an Islamist anti-state movement. The Iranian Revolution also reverberated in other countries, and as Vali Nasr says: "The Iranian Revolution both strengthened existing Islamist tendencies and redirected their energies towards goals articulated in the Iranian Revolution that had not hitherto featured prominently in South Asian Islamist discourse".[37] The revolution has greatly contributed to transforming the Islamist discourse, installing a new pattern of religious-political activism and reshaping a new set of power relations between the state and society. The Shīʿa resonance in Malaysia could be seen through the use of Iranian Revolution discourse as "a model of Islamic revival and viability of an Islamic state" in the country.[38] The success of Khomeini in leading the revolt against the regime of Reza Shah Pahlevi in particular was understood as a new enlightenment by Indonesian Muslims.[39] Indonesian and Malaysian admiration of

35 J.S. Levy and M. Froelich, "Causes of the Iran-Iraq War," in *Regionalization of Warfare* (New Brunswick, NJ: Transaction Books, 1985), 127–43, p. 134; Fred R. Von der Mehden, *Two Worlds of Islam: Interaction Between Southeast Asia and the Middle East* (Florida: University Press of Florida, 1993), p. 87.

36 Aboebakar Atjeh, *Aliran Syi'ah Di Nusantara* (Jakarta: Islamic Research Institute, 1977); Pradana Boy Zulian and Bachtiar Bachtiar, "Indonesia: Complex Experience of Religious Diversity Governance," in *Routledge Handbook on the Governance of Religious Diversity* (New York: Routledge, 2021), 267–81, p. 269.

37 Vali Nasr, "The Iranian Revolution and Changes in Islamism in Pakistan, India and Afghanistan," in *Iran and the Surrounding World: Interactions in Culture and Cultural Politics* (Seattle: University of Washington Press, 2002), pp. 327–8.

38 Shanti Nair, *Islam in Malaysian Foreign Policy* (New York: Routledge, 1997), p. 130.

39 Yudi Latif, *Indonesian Muslim* (Singapore: Institute of Southeast Asian Studies, 2008), p. 360; Adrian Vickers, *A History of Modern Indonesia* (Cambridge: Cambridge University Press, 2013), p. 183.

the Iranian Revolution reflects a possibility that ideas and practice between Sunnī and Shīʿa groups might be exchanged. In this regard, although Sunnī and Shīʿa Islamist movements have different ideological and theological underpinnings, both share similar models of (re)Islamisation from above.[40]

The third model of Islamism is Jamaʾat-i Islami. Vali Nasr states that this Islamic party reflects multifaceted relations between a religious-political leadership, the politicisation of Islam, the sacralisation of politics, and adaptation to modernity.[41] The Jamaʾat-i Islami did not topple the established political system of Pakistan, but instead has preferred to struggle for its political and legal agenda from within the prevailing system.[42] With this preference, even though the party has failed to rule the state of Pakistan, it has been able to take part in shaping the national history; Pakistan has become a country that applies sharia in its legal system. The party has triggered the emergence of social and political movements, not only in Pakistan but in many other Muslim countries,[43] and has not only influenced Islamic revivalism from Morocco to Malaysia but has also inspired the expression of revivalist thinking in Southwest Asia and South Asia since 1941. In Indonesia, besides its general *paradigm*, the reverberation of Jamaʾat-i Islami can be seen from the appreciation some groups of Indonesian Muslims have for the thoughts of Mawdudi. Greg Barton has compared Abu al-ʿAla al-Mawdudi's role as a thinker with that of Indonesian Islamist scholar and politician Mohammad Natsir,[44] who struggled for a sharia-based state through his banned-political party, Masyumi,[45] and then Dewan Dakwah Islamiyah Indonesia (DDII, the Council of Indonesian Islamic Propagation). Mehden states that Hamka, the Indonesian Muslim reformist, suggested that Indonesians read Mawdudi or even Ali Shariati.[46]

The main motivation behind the increase of shariatisation movements can generally be ascribed to the great disenchantment of Muslim societies with

40 Gilles Kepel, *Muslim Extremism in Egypt*, p. 12.

41 Seyyed Vali Reza Nasr, *The Vanguard of the Islamic Revolution: The Jamaʿat-i Islami of Pakistan* (London: I.B. Tauris, 1994), p. xiv.

42 Ibid., p. xv.

43 Ibid, p. xiv.

44 Greg Barton, *Gus Dur: The Authorized Biography of Abdurrahman Wahid* (Jakarta: Equinox Publishing, 2002), p. 130; Von der Mehden, *Two Worlds of Islam*, p. 88; Bernhard Platzdasch, *Islamism in Indonesia: Politics in the Emerging Democracy* (Singapore: Institute of Southeast Asian Studies, 2009), p. 31.

45 Masyumi is an Islamic political party that was established as a melting pot of many Islamic organisations in Indonesia. Natsir led this party from 1949 to 1958. The DDII is an Islamic civil society organisation established by the former followers of Masyumi after this party was banned in 1960. Platzdasch, *Islamism in Indonesia*, pp. 31–7.

46 Von der Mehden, *Two Worlds of Islam*, p. 88.

the performance of existing secular systems, either in their home countries or in the West.[47] Thus the secular system becomes their first target for change. Islamist groups believe that the established secular ideologies of the modern world will inevitably collapse due to their inability to provide the answer to the predicament of Islamic identity, the dislocation of peoples, and discrimination in many Muslim countries. Therefore, the emergence of Islamisation cannot be understood except by recourse to the hegemony of Western modernity under the context of expansionist colonialism and also through the experiences of Muslims in witnessing the failures of modern states and societies, social dislocation because of rapid development and urbanisation, and also the desire to reaffirm the faith and religion.[48]

The augmentation of numerous Islamist movements in Indonesia with their provocative jargon and agenda also follows the pattern of countering a secular system. MUI is central here due to its position as a predominant producer of fatwa and advice and as a *tenda besar* (large tent, or umbrella organisation) accommodating diverse Islamic organisations in Indonesia. Many Islamist organisations and individuals are supportive of MUI's position. The Front Pembela Islam (FPI, the Islam Defender Front),[49] for instance, on many occasions acts as the staunch supporter of MUI fatwa and *tawṣiyya*. The Hizbut Tahrir Indonesia (HTI, Liberation Party of Indonesia), whose Indonesian chapter was established in 1984 in Bogor, West Java, had gone along with MUI's discourse and activism in support of the supremacy of Islamic authority. The spokeperson of HTI, Ismail Yusanto, was active in the period of 2005–2010. The Majelis Mujahidin Indonesia (MMI, Indonesian Mujahidin Council), an umbrella organisation of Indonesian Islamist groups located in Yogyakarta, is very committed to the 2005 MUI fatwa against liberalism, secularism and pluralism. Greg Fealy states their movements attempt to offer an alternate model for reshaping the state and Muslim society of Indonesia due to the apparent

47 Kepel, *Muslim Extremism in Egypt*; Sayyid, *A Fundamental Fear*; David Emmanuel Singh, "Integrative Political Ideology of Mawlana Mawdudi and Islamisation of the Muslim Masses in the Indian Subcontinent," *South Asia: Journal of South Asian Studies* XXIII, no. 1 (2010): 129–48.

48 Esposito, "Introduction: Modernising Islam and Reislamisation in Global Perspective", p. 2; Rabi', *Intellectual Origins of Islamic Resurgence*, p. 249.

49 The FPI is a radical Islamic organisation, often involved in violent actions, which was established soon after the resignation of Suharto in 1998, assumed by many to be established with the fully backing of the Indonesian military. See studies on the FPI such as: Jajang Jahroni, *Defending the Majesty of Islam: Indonesia's Front Pembela Islam, 1998–2003* (Bangkok: Asian Muslim Action Network, 2008); Noorhaidi Hasan, *Laskar Jihad Laskar Jihad* (Ithaca: SEAP Publications, 2006), pp. 14–6; Greg Fealy, "Islamic Radicalism in Indonesia: The Faltering Revival?," *Southeast Asian Affairs*, no. 1 (2004): 104–21.

failure of the secular democratic system in offering prosperity and justice, and as the best way to restore Muslim society and the state to the true path of God.[50] A similar stance in supporting MUI has been adopted by other Islamist political parties, such as the PKS,[51] Partai Persatuan Pembangunan (PPP, United Development Party), and Partai Bulan Bintang (PBB, Crescent Star Party).[52] To some degree, the first and second largest Islamic organisations, NU and Muhammadiyah, also back the MUI.

1.3 Shariatisation and Islamisation in Indonesia

Shariatisation and Islamisation are often understood as intertwined phenomena and thus the terms have been interchangeably used. In the context of Indonesia, both are seen to refer to the revival of Islamic identity marked by the presence of sharia in the legal and public spheres. This section seeks to provide an overview of some case studies on the increasingly prevalent phenomena of fashioning shariatisation and Islamisation in the legal and public spheres of Indonesia in general and on the role of MUI in particular. One striking case study refers to the role of the Jema'ah Tarbiyah, an Islamic assembly for education, and that of the PKS. Yon Machmudi, in his 2008 work *The Rise of Jemaah Tarbiyah and the Prosperous Justice Party* (*PKS*), states that these two groups have made a significant contribution to the Islamisation of Indonesia.[53] The Jema'ah Tarbiyah emerged in the 1980s.[54] Its name literally means "education congregation", *jema'ah* being an Indonesian Arabic expression for congregation and *tarbiyah* meaning education. The group used the term *tarbiyah* not only to refer to education in the usual sense, but also as a movement to educate Muslims about Islam as *al-dīn wa al-dawla* (unity of religion and state). Although the Jema'ah Tarbiyah attracted a large membership amongst students from some state universities such as the University of Indonesia, the University of Gadjah Mada, the Bandung Institute of Technology and many others, the organisational structure of this group was barely visible in the public domain. Some experts therefore labelled it as a clandestine Islamist organisation. However, its lack of visibility was not without cause,

50 Fealy, "Islamic Radicalism in Indonesia: The Faltering Revival?" p. 116.

51 Masdar Hilmy, *Islamism and Democracy in Indonesia* (Singapore: ISEAS, 2010), pp. 135–68.

52 PBB is a small Islamist party and did not pass the electoral threshold in the last three general elections.

53 Machmudi, *The Rise of Jemaah Tarbiyah and the Prosperous Justice Party* (*PKS*), p. xvii.

54 Greg Fealy, *Voices of Islam in Southeast Asia: A Contemporary Sourcebook* (Singapore: Institute of Southeast Asian Studies, 2006), p. 48.

as its main mission was to establish a sharia-based state in Indonesia. This agenda was clearly in opposition to the national ideology of the Pancasila state. It is therefore understandable that during the Suharto era this group was oppressed by the state and also by mainstream Islamic organisations such as NU and Muhammadiyah.

Interestingly, one of the Jema'ah Tarbiyah's principles was to educate and re-Islamise those who were already Muslims, as they regarded existing Muslims outside their group as being still in a state of ignorance on their true teachings of their religion (*jāhiliyya*).[55] The Jema'ah Tarbiyah believes that Islam is an all-encompassing system (*shāmil*), which must be the only guidance for life (*manhaj al-ḥayā*) and provide for all the spiritual and worldly needs of human beings. Islam covers law, civilisation, culture, the political system and governance.[56] The Islamisation model of Jema'ah Tarbiyah is strategically undertaken through the establishment of small group discussions (*ḥalaqa*) on Islam in several university campuses, as mentioned above. It seems that the Jema'ah Tarbiyah adopted the ideology and practices of the Muslim Brotherhood.

Indonesia's Islamist political party, PKS, stemmed from and was set up by this group, and can thus be said to be a political transformation of the Jema'ah Tarbiyah. Although not all members of the Jema'ah Tarbiyah agreed to the establishment of the PKS, most agreed that a political party should be built as a "legal vehicle," according to Indonesian law, for their agenda to Islamise or re-Islamise society and the state.[57] The party has tried to combine a pragmatic and idealist approach towards a model of Islamisation, but it has never rejected allegations of a "hidden agenda" to establish a sharia-based state. To encourage the acceptance of sharia implementation, the PKS has sought to change its negative image among Indonesians, even among Muslims. It has explained that implementing sharia is not just about imposing a set of Islamic laws but rather a means to promote all positive aspects of human values and behaviour. For the PKS, (Islamic) universal morality and values must take priority in solving the Indonesian political and economic crises.[58] Sharia can

55 This idea on restoring the concept of *jāhiliyya* to refer to the ignorance of modern society was adopted from Sayyid Quṭb. See Ismail, *Rethinking Islamist Politics*, p. 84.

56 Machmudi, *The Rise of Jemaah Tarbiyah and the Prosperous Justice Party* (*PKS*), 2008, p. 66.

57 The party was originally established under the name Partai Keadilan (PK, Justice Party) in 1998. It assumed the name Partai Keadilan Sejahtera (PKS, Prosperous Justice Party) in 2002. Members of Jema'ah Tarbiyah were divided into two between those who accepted and those who did not accept the party. See Machmudi, *The Rise of Jemaah Tarbiyah and the Prosperous Justice Party* (*PKS*), pp. 72–73.

58 Ibid, p. 196.

be implemented in new areas to combat issues such as corruption, collusion and nepotism,[59] which have been traditionally part of the secular domain, and the PKS claims that clean governance, justice and prosperity will be the main achievements resulting from a sharia framework. The implementation of Islamic law must be aimed at achieving prosperity, security, justice and peace in the world. In more simple daily interactions, the PKS instructs its members to participate in maintaining public facilities, such as transportation, parks, roads and toilets as part of implementing sharia. Finally, it can be argued that the shariatisation of Indonesia in the PKS framework can be seen as equivalent to the formal inclusion of all profane activities within the realm of Islamic values, as can be justified by religious doctrine.[60]

A general overview on the Islamisation of Indonesia can be found in Arskal Salim's research.[61] In his study, Salim tries to situate the legal Islamisation in Indonesia on three levels: the first is the process of having sharia acknowledged by the Indonesian Constitution; the second is its nationalisation; and the third is its localisation. With regard to the first, Salim admits that the efforts to have sharia acknowledged as part of the state Constitution have been undertaken on several occasions in modern Indonesian history. Salim describes how various attempts at shariatisation, from the early period of Indonesian independence up to the early reform era, were made using different methods and strategies, for instance through the political lobbying of the Indonesian parliament to pass specific national laws in support of legal Islamisation. Yet different interpretations of sharia emerged between Islamist political parties during the Indonesian reform era in the National People's Assembly meeting in 2002. From this, Salim concludes that there is a lack of agreement amongst different factions of Indonesian Islamist groups over a solid, unified definition of sharia, even though they have long struggled for this goal.

Salim takes the institutionalisation of *zakāt* (Islamic almsgiving) as his example for the nationalisation of sharia. As he sees it, the enactment of Act No. 38/1999 on Islamic Almsgiving Administration can be seen as a form of nationalisation of sharia because it represents a serious attempt to interpret the *zakāt* payment in accordance with the nature of Indonesian Islam. This law, for instance, includes various details relating to *zakāt* payment which are not found in the tradition of Islamic jurisprudence. Salim states that the

59 The phrase corruption, collusion, and nepotism, known as *kolusi, korupsi dan nepotisme* or KKN, was a popular phrase that emerged with the reform era in 1998 to criticise such self-serving political practices from the Suharto regime.

60 Machmudi, *The Rise of Jemaah Tarbiyah and the Prosperous Justice Party* (PKS), p. 196.

61 Arskal Salim, *Challenging the Secular State: The Islamization of Law in Modern Indonesia* (Honolulu: University of Hawaii Press, 2008), pp. 88–92.

nationalisation of sharia in this case was a successful attempt by Muslims to raise the status of Islam in the legal and public domains of Indonesia, but he emphasises that "the enactment of the Administration Law in Indonesia is politically dissonant for non-Muslims who feel discriminated against by some of its provisions."[62] Non-Muslim groups' criticism of this law is understandable, since Indonesia is not officially an Islamic state.

Lastly, Salim's study describes the localisation of sharia, meaning its implementation as part of provincial or district law. Salim employs the case study of the enactment of sharia in Aceh since 2000. The struggle to implement sharia in Aceh was a long one with the goal of establishing Aceh province with particular authority in religious matters.[63] Many victims fell during the long conflict between the Indonesian army and the Gerakan Aceh Merdeka (GAM, Free Aceh Movement). Salim recognises the pre-eminent role played by the ulama in Acehnese society in struggling for the implementation of sharia once Indonesia became a self-governing entity in 1945, and describes how the Acehnese ulama consistently attempted to localise sharia, noting the establishment of the Acehnese Council of Muslim scholars as a turning point in the history of the shariatisation in Aceh.[64] He also discusses how the structuring of the ulama into a consultative council following the right of implementation of sharia law in Aceh province in 2002 was less powerful than it seemed on the surface. Finally, he focuses on the increased implementation of sharia in Aceh following the 2004 tsunami, which he views as a trigger for the accelerated enactment of sharia in the region. He states that the Acehnese interpreted the tsunami as a message from God warning against sinful deeds and encouraging peace among conflicting groups and a return to religion as the path to salvation, concluding that the tragedy was seens as a message that the Acehnese people should comply with sharia rules and that provincial governments should enforce them in earnest.[65] Neither Machmudi nor Salim examined the role of MUI as a discourse provider for the shariatisation of Indonesia, however.

How then can the role of MUI be understood? Since its inception in 1975, the organisation has attracted the attention of various researchers and scholars. The first serious study of MUI was Atho Mudzhar's examination of its nature as a fatwa-giver from the perspectives of socio-political surroundings,

62 Ibid, p. 139.
63 Ibid, p. 143.
64 Ibid, p. 144–5.
65 Ibid, p. 163.

societal reactions and Islamic legal methods.[66] Mudzhar's pioneering study investigated MUI fatwas in terms of their content, methodology and resonance in the public sphere, and attempted to cover the historical and political development of Islam and Islamic law from the pre-colonial era of Indonesia up to the Suharto regime as a foundation for understanding the organisation's role, especially as a fatwa institution. His examination covered the period of 1975–1988, and it is a far-reaching historical and political account of the early development of MUI. Mudzhar has tried to take a balanced stance in seeing the intricate relationships between the political motives behind MUI's establishment, especially its endorsement by the Suharto regime, and the need for Muslim society to have a body of ulama. He sees its inception as an expression of mutual benefit for both the state and Muslim society. With regard to the state, he concludes that the establishment of MUI was part of Suharto's desire to use the ulama's power to secure his own, while with regard to Muslim society, the establishment of MUI could be used by the ulama as means to combat atheism and communism.[67]

In his examination of Islamisation-inclined MUI fatwa, Mudzhar evaluated eight clusters of Islamic legal opinions consisting of ritual, marital and cultural affairs, food, Muslims' attendance at Christmas celebrations, some issues on health, family planning and Muslim minorities. The fatwa prohibiting Muslims from attending Christmas celebrations was the most controversial issue in that era, and Hamka resigned from his position as General Chairman of MUI as a result.[68] It stated that Muslims are prohibited from attending Christmas celebrations, and are also therefore forbidden from participating in any related activity.[69] In examining the fatwa, Mudzhar drew on the traditional Indonesian Christian practice of inviting Muslims to official Christmas celebrations: those who were invited were reluctant to decline for fear they might be judged intolerant. This was the basis for the MUI fatwa. Although Mudzhar acknowledges the Christmas fatwa to be based on solid Islamic arguments, the government of Indonesia considered it a threat to Indonesian tolerance and pluralism.[70]

Mudzhar categorises the distribution of MUI Islamic edicts according to the degree of government influence. Out of the twenty-two fatwas he examines, eleven fall into the category of neutral and minimal government influence, while the other eleven fall into the category of fatwas with strong government

66 Mudzhar, *Fatwa of the Council of Indonesian Ulama*.
67 Ibid, pp. 149, 48.
68 Mujīburraḥmān, *Feeling Threatened: Muslim-Christian Relations in Indonesia's New Order* (Amsterdam: Amsterdam University Press, 2006), p. 95.
69 Mudzhar, *Fatwa of the Council of Indonesian Ulama*, p. 101.
70 Ibid, p. 104.

influence.[71] He also claims that some of MUI's fatwas related to cultural affairs were independent of government influence, and that the influence of the fatwas did not correspond to the role of MUI in general. In addition to this, he states that MUI has been relatively successful in obtaining greater acceptance from Muslim society, Islamic organisations and the government of Indonesia; at the same time, the role of the fatwa has declined. He also notes that the influence of the fatwas was closely related to the leadership of MUI.[72]

Mudzhar's conclusions can thus be summarised in three key points. First, the production of fatwas appears to be driven by a desire to support government policy; this does not mean that the Islamic edicts produced do not contain religious arguments, however. Second, the issuance of MUI's fatwas is also aimed at responding to and coping with the challenges of modernity. Third, the issuing of fatwas is associated with inter-religious relations.[73]

A similar study on MUI has been conducted by Wahiduddin Adams.[74] Adams' work, covering the period 1975–1997, focuses on discerning the role of fatwas as a source of inspiration for certain state regulations of Indonesia. Through this study, Adams wanted to uncover the relation between MUI's legal opinion and the drafting of national regulations. His theoretical framework follows the approach of legal science, especially that developed by Dutch scholar van Apeldoorn, who argued that the formulation of national regulations was inspired by religion. The compiling of the *Burgerlijk Wetboek* is taken as an example of the influence of the Christian tradition on the legal code of the Dutch.[75] Adams starts his account by drawing on the notion of fatwa, *ijtihād* (independent Islamic legal reasoning), and legislation in Islamic law, and refers to explanations of fatwa and *ijtihād* ranging from al-Ghazālī (b. 1058), Ibn Qayyim al-Jawziyya (b. 1292), Ibn Qāsim al-ʿIbbādī, (b. 1586) and al-Shawkānī (b. 1760), up to Wahba al-Zuḥaylī (b. 1932).[76] Elucidation on various forms and degrees of the fatwa and *ijtihād* methodology is presented to show how these discourses are developed and advanced in Islam. In the context of Indonesia, for instance, Adams indicates how the attempts to produce fatwa and conduct *ijtihād* are undertaken not only by individual Muslim scholars, but also collectively by a number of Muslim scholars from various disciplines (Islamic and general studies). He shows the role of fatwa and *ijtihād* not only in the local

71 Ibid, p. 122.

72 Ibid, p. 125.

73 Ibid, pp. 119–120.

74 Wahiduddin Adams, *Pola Penyerapan Fatwa Majelis Ulama Indonesia (MUI) Dalam Peraturan Perundang-Undangan 1975–1997* (Jakarta: Departemen Agama, 2004).

75 Ibid, p. 21.

76 Ibid, pp. 20–41.

Indonesian context, but also as sources for national legislation in many Islamic countries such as Saudi Arabia, Pakistan, Egypt and others.[77]

Through his study, Adams justifies the hierarchical system of Indonesian law and describes Islam's position within it. He believes that the legal system of Indonesia implicitly and explicitly provides a place of Islam to intervene. Islam becomes an integral part of developing the country's national legal system.[78] Garis-Garis Besar Haluan Negara (GBHN, the Guidelines of National Development) refers to Islam as a sub-system of Indonesian law.[79] From this, Adams considers that the infiltration of Islam into the draft of any national law is tolerable and justifiable. In the fourth chapter of his study, he tries to demonstrate the influence of MUI fatwas on the national legislation of Indonesia, and locates MUI's Islamic legal opinions as responses to the drafting of national laws. MUI's fatwas are not only seen as an influencing factor but also as a result, influenced by the legislation process. In his concluding remarks, Adams proposes some models for the way fatwas have penetrated into the drafting of national regulations and law. First, for draft laws related to religious matters, fatwas were proposed by MUI through the Ministry of Religious Affairs. Second, for draft laws with potentially negative effects on society but with a potentially positive effect on government income, MUI would forward its fatwas to non-state institutions with close connections with the regime. For example, in the last period of the Suharto era, MUI proposed its fatwas through Ikatan Cendekiawan Muslim Indonesia (ICMI, the Association of Indonesian Muslim Intellectuals).[80] In this assessment, MUI's fatwas are viewed as issued in a reactive and not proactive manner.

More research on the role of MUI in *ijtihād* was undertaken by Nadirsyah Hosen, who looked into the method of handing down a fatwa, its sources, and the relationship between these Islamic legal opinions at the national and local levels.[81] For this purpose, Hosen drew on the historical background and especially the role of the MUI Fatwa Commission. He emphasises that fatwa development depends on the Commission's chairman and members. His observations on the background and qualifications of the Fatwa Commission members between 1975 and 1998 yield a number of interesting points. Firstly,

77 Ibid, pp. 58–82.

78 Ibid, p. 95.

79 GBHN were the national development guidelines followed during the Suharto era. This model is no longer used.

80 Adams, *Pola Penyerapan Fatwa Majelis Ulama Indonesia* (MUI) *Dalam Peraturan Perundang-Undangan 1975–1997*, pp. 203–204.

81 Nadirsyah Hosen, "Behind the Scenes: Fatwas of Majelis Ulama Indonesia," *Journal of Islamic Studies* 2, no. 15 (2004): 147–79.

the commission members include both academics and traditionally qualified ulama. Most of the members have both university and *pesantren* (traditional Islamic boarding school) qualifications. Secondly, a number of members are graduates of Middle East universities.[82] Thirdly, the presence of five female members on the Fatwa Commission represents a higher proportion than that found in the NU or the Muhammadiyah.[83] Fourthly, many of the committee members originate from various Islamic organisations, not limited to the NU and the Muhammadiyah, including those such as Al-Irsyad[84] and Persatuan Tarbiyah Islamiyah (PERTI, the Union for Islamic Education). Fifthly, Hosen emphasises that Commission members represent a broad range of recognised, respected expertise in relevant disciplines of Islam, such as Islamic law, the Qur'ān, the *ḥadīth* and Islamic theology.[85] By revealing the qualifications of its diverse membership, Hosen seeks to prove that MUI has long paved the way of undertaking an *ijtihad kolektif* (collective *ijtihād*).[86]

MUI has used the method of collective *ijtihād* since its establishment in 1975, but only officially acknowledged this in 1986. However, according to Hosen, the method of *ijtihād* employed by the Fatwa Commission before 1997 was mainly a conventional analytical approach based on the primary four sources of Islam—the Qur'ān, the traditions of the Prophet, *ijmāʿ* (consensus of the ulama) and *qiyās* (analogical reasoning)—as developed by scholars of Islamic jurisprudence and Islamic legal theory among the four schools of Islamic law (*al-madhāhib al-arbaʿa*).[87] Hosen notes some changes in fatwa methodology, as the Fatwa Commission does not strictly follow one school's methods but allows the all the schools of Islamic law to form the basis for an Islamic legal

82 There is no a precise record of the number of Fatwa Commission members who have graduated from Middle Eastern universities in this era. However, they include the following figures: Ibrahim Hosen, (b. 1917, the former Commission Chairman from the al-Azhar University), Ali Mustafa Yaqub (the King Saud University of Medina), Huzaemah Tahido Yanggo (b. 1946, from al-Azhar University), Said Aqil Husen al-Munawwar (from the University of Medina), Satria Effendi M. Zein, (from the University of Medina), Muslim Nasution (from the King Saud University of Medina), and many others.

83 The quite significant presence of female members of the Fatwa Commission did not reflect a higher attention to issues of women's rights.

84 Al-Irsyad was an Islamic organisation established by Ahmad Surkati in 1914. Members of al-Irsyad are Indonesian descendants of Ḥaḍramīs (from Haḍramawt in Yemen). See Natalie Mobeni-Kasheh, *The Hadrami Awakening: Community and Identity in the Netherlands East Indies, 1900–1942* (Cornell: Cornell South East Asia Publication, 2004), pp. 52–70.

85 Robert B. Cribb and Audrey R. Kahin, *Historical Dictionary of Indonesia* (Lanham & Maryland: Scarecrow Press, 2004), p. 340.

86 The definition of the collective *ijtihād* will be discussed in Chapter 3 of this book.

87 Nadirsyah Hosen, "Behind the Scenes: Fatwas of Majelis Ulama Indonesia."

opinion. In his view, MUI's attempts to open itself up to the consideration of all schools of Islamic thought can be seen as a "reform" of the Islamic jurisprudence approach used by traditional Muslim scholars and Islamic groups in Indonesia, which strictly followed one school in both method and opinion. Hosen concludes that the collective Islamic independent legal reasoning of MUI cannot be classified as the highest level of *ijtihād* as undertaken by the main scholars of Islamic jurisprudence and legal theory in the medieval period of Islam.[88] He also suggests that MUI should decrease its dependence on methodology developed during the classical period, as the current social, political and economic challenges to MUI are different from those faced in the previous era. He concludes that in order to reform the methodology of Islamic law, new concepts are needed in view of the extensive changes that have taken place in Indonesia.[89]

MUI's involvement in the politics of the post-Suharto era is continued by Nur Ichwan in his journal article, "Ulama, State and Politics: Majelis Ulama Indonesia After Suharto."[90] Ichwan examines the influence of fatwa and *tawṣiyya* in the political process of Indonesia, and concludes that the post-Suharto transitional era has seen the establishment of organisations that strengthen civil society, including MUI. The article concludes with a strong argument that the increasing independence of MUI after Suharto's resignation has given the organisation more space to participate in discussing the future of Indonesian Islam in the public arena.

Unlike the studies of Mudzhar, Adams, Hosen and Ichwan, Piers Gillespie focuses on MUI's belief-policing role by examining MUI Fatwa No. 7/2005 prohibiting Muslims from embracing pluralism, liberalism and secularism as a case study.[91] This Islamic legal opinion attracted much attention from Muslims and non-Muslims in Indonesia, and was the most controversial fatwa issued by MUI since the reform era. Gillespie indicates that the conservative inclinations of MUI, embodied in Fatwa No.7/2005, developed as a result of public dissatisfaction with the reform period. It also intersects with the increasing prominence of a number of Islamist politicians and public figures as they articulated the need for a greater role for Islam in Indonesia after the New Order era. MUI and its member organisations asserted that the only way

88 Ibid, p. 178.

89 Ibid, p. 179.

90 Moch Nur Ichwan, "'Ulamā', State and Politics: Majelis Ulama Indonesia after Suharto," *Islamic Law and Society* 12, no. 1 (2005): 45–72.

91 Piers Gillespie, "Current Issues in Indonesian Islam: Analysing the 2005 Council of Indonesian Ulama Fatwa No. 7 Opposing Pluralism, Liberalism and Securalism," *Journal of Islamic Studies* 2, no. 18 (2007): 202–40.

to escape from the multidimensional crisis affecting the country was through the implementation of sharia bylaws.[92] The impact of this assertion was a strident call to formalise sharia, as can be seen in regions as diverse as Aceh, South Sulawesi, Banten and Central Java.

Gillespie notes that the specific reason cited by MUI in issuing Fatwa No.7/2005 was to oppose the dominance of neo-modernist discourse during the last twenty-five years,[93] and says that, "the growth of liberalism and the myriad of new interpretations of Indonesian cultural life in Indonesia during the first five years of the twenty-first century was a source of much resentment for conservative Muslims in Indonesia."[94] Moreover, he argues that MUI and its Islamist collaborators expressed their deep disappointment in what they perceived to be the offensive dissemination of liberal Islamic thought usually identified with Jaringan Islam Liberal (JIL, the Liberal Islam Network). Gillespie says this has revived the long-held notion of a 'conspiracy' among the conservative groups. This situation ran parallel to increasing suspicions amongst Indonesian Muslims, who viewed the emergence of Islamic liberalism as an attempt by US and Jewish groups to subvert Islam. Although the issuing of Fatwa No. 7/2005 led to political upheaval and turbulence in the context of Indonesian pluralism, it did not lead to any decline in Indonesian Muslims' desire to uphold the country's secular and liberal political system.[95]

In this work, Gillespie reaches two conclusions. Firstly, MUI's sharp criticism of Westerners and Indonesian Islamic liberals, along with neo-modernist concepts of pluralism and liberalism, does not decrease the use of these concepts as a means of understanding the diversity within Indonesian Islam. Secondly, despite the weak theological arguments with which MUI and its conservative allies defended Fatwa No. 7/2005, this cannot be used as a pretext to ignore or dismiss their criticism. Gillespie argues that liberal Islamic groups have treated this group as ignorant polemicists.[96] However, he adds that it is important to consider several challenges that will always be present, and that will reshape and redefine MUI's role in the context of modern Indonesian society. Openness from MUI is needed in the context of the changes facing Indonesian Muslims, and it needs new concepts and approaches to provide direction for Indonesian Muslim society with regard to societal and political issues. In his final conclusion, Gillespie stated that this umbrella Islamic

92 Ibid, p. 203.
93 Ibid, p. 232.
94 Ibid, p. 237.
95 Ibid, pp. 238–9.
96 Ibid, p. 240.

organisation "will continue to shoulder the historical baggage of an Islamic organisation that for many years sided with the New Order regime policies rather than aligning itself more closely with the Indonesian *umma*."[97] He views MUI's dilemma as a state-funded Islamic organisation that requires funding to defend the interests of the *umma* but is bound by the government's spending decisions. Thus MUI will always remain caught between criticisms and accusations directed at it by the *umma* and an "uneasy and difficult relationship with the government when it disagrees with its policies."[98]

More recent works on MUI have been written by both Tim Lindsey and Mun'im Sirry. Lindsey focuses on MUI's tendency to monopolise interpretations of Islam related to the issue of the Islamic economy, and states that it has become more conservative since the downfall of Suharto, especially on social and moral issues.[99] He considers MUI to have been successful in convincing the state to pass bills supported by the Council on the sharia economy, halal certificates for foods, and other issues. The establishment of the Dewan Syariah Nasional (DSN, the National Sharia Board) and its role in sharia finance institutions is real evidence of MUI influence in the shariatisation of Indonesia's finance and economy. Through the Dewan Pengawan Syariah (DPS, Sharia Supervisory Board), The DSN wields complete authority over every single product of the sharia finance system. Lindsey calls this the key to the Islamicity of Indonesia's Islamic financial institutions.

A similar role is also played by MUI in the field of inspecting and issuing halal labels. In this regard, MUI fatwas, which were originally non-binding edicts, have become as enforceable as state regulations. In influencing the administration of national *ḥajj* (pilgrimage), neither MUI members nor fatwas are highly considered. Lindsey concludes that the influence of MUI in the three above-mentioned domains proves the function of MUI fatwas as quasi-legislation for lawmaking.[100]

Unlike most experts, who view MUI fatwas as creating controversy and stirring up intolerance and violence to a certain extent, Mun'im Sirry argues that the fatwas create space for creative and fruitful public discourse.[101] The MUI fatwa on banning Muslims from expressing Christmas greetings has opened up debates and controversy among Muslim scholars. The MUI fatwa banning secularism, liberalism and pluralism also created an intense public debate

97 Ibid, p. 240.
98 Ibid, p. 240.
99 Tim Lindsey, "Monopolising Islam?"
100 Ibid, p. 265.
101 Mun'im Sirry, "Fatwas and Their Controversy: The Case of the Council of Indonesien Ulama," *Journal of Southeast Asian Studies* 44, no. 1 (2013): 100–117.

between the so-called liberal Islamic groups and MUI supporters. Sirry states that the debates and controversies arising from such fatwas indicate a healthy public discourse, which is more useful than physical contestation. Finally, he draws three conclusions. Firstly, there is a strong alignment between MUI conservative and radical Islamic groups. Secondly, MUI's controversial fatwas reflect the political climate of the current regime. Thirdly, the critical engagement between those who agree and disagree with MUI fatwas is a form of mechanism enabling them to stabilise their position.[102]

This book is focused on looking at the role of MUI—through its fatwas, recommendations, publications, congress, networking and many other forms of activism—in its attempts to implement sharia in the legal and public spheres of Indonesia at the level of discourse and practice. Thus, although different foci and approaches are applied, this book intends to deepen understanding and fill in the gaps in the case of matters left unexplored or referred to in less detail in the works mentioned above. Last but not least, this study is also expected to highlight the significance of Indonesian Islam in the context of Islamic studies on non-Arabic-speaking countries. In this regard, Islamic studies in Western universities are often dominated by the study of Islam in the Middle East and neglect the existence of non-Arabic-speaking countries, especially Islam in Asia. Yet focusing the study of Islam on the Middle East not only creates a monolithic view that Islam is identical with the religious practice in that region, but is also unfair to the Muslim community as a whole since there are so many who live outside of the Middle East and speak non-Arabic languages. In fact, most of the world's Muslim population resides outside the Middle East. Indonesia is not only the largest Muslim country in the world, but also has a long history of Islamic studies. Moreover, Indonesian Islam is an essential part of Islamic studies as Islam in this country is understood and practised differently from the way it is in the religion's heartland, Saudi Arabia. In relation to the focus of this book, for instance, the influence of a fatwa body such as MUI on the processes of the nation-state is very different from that of fatwa councils in the Middle East. Fatwa bodies and their discursive and practical results can work with the agenda of a secular state on one hand and as a religion on the other. The case of Indonesian Islam, with its particular characteristics, is expected to show an alternative expression of the religion. The study of Islam in Indonesia therefore produces two key contributions: first, it is a reminder of the diversity and pluralism of the Muslim world; and second, it shows the particularity of Indonesian Islam that is compatible with the progress of the modern world.

102 Ibid, p. 100.

1.4 Theoretical Framework

The shariatisation of Indonesia reflects a multifaceted and diverse image that not only represents the various discourses on the normativity of Islam, purification, moral control and normalisation, but also the attempts to include sharia norms into the legal and public spheres of Indonesia. In looking at the role of MUI in this process, various interdisciplinary and multidisciplinary theoretical approaches taken from the larger bodies of sociology, anthropology, discourse analysis and also Islamic and religious studies are employed for this study.

Firstly, the sociological theory on "public Islam": this approach is valuable in illuminating the phenomenon of sharia's presence in Indonesia's legal and public spheres. The concept of public Islam itself has strong roots in the larger theoretical discourse on the public sphere which has been introduced by theoreticians like Jurgen Habermas, Oskar Negt and Alexander Kluge, Craig Calhoun, Nancy Fraser, Samuel N. Eisenstandt.[103] In the 1990s, the concept of the public sphere began to be used as a means to portray the way Islam was carving out its space in the modern world. Armando Salvatore and Dale Eickelman, for instance, define public Islam as "the highly diverse invocations of Islam as ideas and practices that religious scholars, self-ascribed religious authorities, secular intellectuals, Ṣūfī orders, mothers, students, workers, engineers, and many others make to civic debate and public life."[104]

On this basis, shariatisation is understood as one model employed by contemporary Islamic movements in fashioning the norms of Islam as part of public contestation and debate. Salvatore states that the uprising of public Islam is a form of strategy of public conversation that absorbs "a disciplining programme"—"shariatisation"—for the benefit of Muslims.[105] In following this argument, the concept of public Islam situates the project of MUI shariatisation as not only a spatial struggle for expressing the ideas and practices of

103 Armando Salvatore, "The Reform Project in the Emerging Public Spheres," in *Islam and Modernity Key Issues and Debates*, ed. Muhammad Khalid Masud, Armando Salvatore, and Martin van Bruinessen (Edinburgh: Edinburgh University Press, 2009), 185–205, p. 186; Armando Salvatore and Dale F Eickelman, "Public Islam and the Common Good," in *Public Islam and the Common Good*, ed. Armando Salvatore and Dale F. Eickelman (Leiden & Boston: Brill, 2006), xi–xxv; Robert W. Hefner, "Public Islam and the Problem of Democratization," *Sociology of Religion* 62, no. 4 (2001): 491–14; Miriam Hoexter, Shmuel Noah Eisenstadt, and Nehemia Levtzion, eds., *The Public Sphere in Muslim Societies* (New York: SUNY Press, 2002), p. 2.

104 Salvatore and Eickelman, *Public Islam and the Common Good*, p. xii.

105 Salvatore, "The Reform Project in the Emerging Public Spheres", p. 196.

Islam, but also "a way of envisioning alternative political realities."[106] Following Henri Lefebvre, the greatest French sociologist on urban space,[107] the publicisation of sharia is a form of MUI attempt to produce a space for implementing sharia in Indonesia. To approach the traditions of Islamic discourse more closely, Salvatore and Eickelman also associate public Islam with the concept of *maṣlaḥa* (public interest, a term used in the discourse of Islamic legal theory). Both argue that public interest is deeply rooted in Islam, especially as related to the notion of commanding right and forbidding wrong.[108] This is the concept that leads Islam to engage in the wider public sphere, which is not only related to Muslim issues but also to non-Muslim ones. Furthermore, public Islam, as Salvatore and Eickelman argue, relates to the concept that the *umma* can never be led astray, or in Arabic *lā tajtamiʿ ummatī ʿalā al-ḍalāla*.[109] In short, the use of the concept of the public sphere here is useful to highlight how and why sharia presents in legislation and the daily life of Indonesian Muslims.

To prove specifically how MUI's discourse and activism influence the process of "lawmaking" in Indonesia, I follow Lucinda Peach's theory on legislating morality or religion. Peach defines lawmaking as "the procedures by which several types of public policy enactments and regulations are made legally binding and enforceable on citizens through the coercive power of the state."[110] Peach also categorises lawmaking as not only the product of legislation but also of other rules such as executive decisions, policies and so forth. From her perspective, MUI's role in the process of lawmaking is not like that of official lawmakers who are directly involved, such as members of government and other public officials, legislators, presidents, governors, mayors, city and town council members, and also members of the judiciary. MUI's position here is as a kind of pressure group, whilst the definition of lawmaker only encompasses it when perpetuating or proposing specific legal discourse and practice to the lawmakers of Indonesia. Through its works and activities as a fatwa-giver, MUI can influence the lawmaking of Indonesia.

106 Salvatore and Eickelman, *Public Islam and the Common Good*, p. xii.

107 Henri Lefebvre, *The Production of Space* (Oxford & Cambridge MA: Blackwell Publishing, 1991).

108 Salvatore, "The Reform Project in the Emerging Public Spheres", p. 196; Michael Cook, *Forbidding Wrong in Islam: An Introduction* (Cambridge: Cambridge University Press, 2003); Michael Cook, *Commanding Right and Forbidding Wrong in Islamic Thought* (Cambridge: Cambridge University Press, 2004); Felicitas Opwis, "Maslaha in Contemporary Islamic Legal Theory," *Islamic Law and Society* 12, no. 2 (2005): 82–223.

109 Salvatore and Eickelman, *Public Islam and the Common Good*.

110 Lucinda J. Peach, *Legislating Morality: Pluralism and Religious Identity in Lawmaking* (Oxford & New York: Oxford University Press, 2002), p. 13.

The function of MUI in the shariatisation of legal discourse and practice of Indonesia, still referring to Peach, can be evidenced through the content or effect of the law. Peach states that "the contribution of religion may be evident on the face of a particular law, such as by language that makes explicit references to religion, religious institutions, or distinctively religious themes."[111] She continues that "the presence of an explicitly theological rationale may also be inferred from the absence of an adequate secular rationale or purpose for the law or in the consequences of the law for particular groups of religious believers and nonbelievers." In short, "religious influence may also be evident if the language of a law is directly traceable to the teachings or pronouncements of a particular religion."[112]

To further discern the position of MUI fatwas in relation to shariatisation, Peach categorises the range of possible types of religious influence on lawmaking into three forms: authority, justification and guidance. Firstly, authority means that religion—scripture and the advice of religious clerics—provides inspiration, motivation and orientation for lawmakers in stipulating, drafting and deciding a law. She states, "motivation will usually be evident in the face of a law, even if no specific scriptural authority or religious language is explicitly used."[113] In this regard, Peach uses the example of a law forbidding the sale or consumption of pork as being influenced by biblical prohibitions against eating swine. Secondly, justification or rationale means that the influence of religion is apparent in its function as legitimising the reasons for lawmaking. She provides the example of a legislator's justification for voting against the death penalty on the basis that killing is prohibited in the Ten Commandments. However, this kind of influence is not always visible in the content of the law. Thirdly, guidance means that religion is used by lawmakers "to provide a source of guidance or moral principles and norms to assist in making a legal decision."[114] Peach remarks that the guidance of religion heralds the enactment of the law, while it does not always "provide[s] the actual content of the lawmaker's decision."[115]

The influence of religion in the process of lawmaking confirms the fact that the legal traditions of various religions, beliefs and customary laws are a natural influence on the lawmaking of the Indonesian state. From the perspective of legal pluralism, state law can therefore either accommodate or

111 Ibid, p. 14.
112 Ibid, p. 14.
113 Ibid, p. 15.
114 Ibid, p. 15.
115 Ibid, p. 15.

keep its distance from the various legal traditions of Indonesia. In a situation where the state is weak and fragile, the roles of non-state law-making agencies such as MUI and its allies can become increasingly dominant. Paul Schiff Berman states that "in places in where the state is weak or non-existent, the non-state lawmaking communities tend to have great powers."[116] He continues, "non-state norms can create forceful obligation in and of themselves, even harden into formal law."[117]

In describing MUI's organisational capacity for encouraging mobilisation, contesting opportunity and maximising the incorporation of sharia into the legal discourse and practice of Indonesia, it is also important to consider the theory surrounding social movement organisations. Social movement theory was popularised by a circle of sociologists in the 1960s to depict social contentions as a means to social transformation.[118] The theory is useful for describing and conceptualising how MUI, with its institutional capacity as a non-juridical institution, has been able to mobilise resources, offer and frame ideas, and use political structural opportunities to develop opportunities for the presence of sharia in the legal norm and public sphere of Indonesia.

The theoretical elements of social movement organisation have been adopted as a way of analysing such elements as the political structural opportunity, resource mobilisation, and framing. It also represents a new trend among scholars by using broader interdisciplinary approaches to study social activism.[119] Firstly, the notion of political opportunity structure, developed by Charles Tilly, Doug McAdam and Sidney Tarrow, concentrates on the centralisation of the state as an important target for instigating social movements. Some scholars equate political opportunity structure with the "political context" that enables a movement to emerge. Tilly argues that social movements will emerge when windows of opportunity open providing access to the polity. What he means here by political opportunity are the more stable features of political institutions, such as bureaucratic agencies, formal mechanisms regulating access to political authorities, and the capacity of state agents to

116 Paul Schiff Berman, *Legal Pluralism: A Jurisprudence of Law Beyond Borders* (Cambridge: Cambridge University Press, 2012), p. 42.

117 Ibid, p. 43; Warwick Tie, *Legal Pluralism: Toward a Multicultural Conception of Law* (London: Ashgate/Dartmouth, 1999).

118 Klandermans Bert and Conny Roggeband, *Handbook of Social Movements Across Disciplines* (New York, Dordrecht, Heidelberg, London: Springer, 2009), p. 1.

119 Davis S. Meyer, "Opportunities and Identities: Bridge Building in the Social Movements," in *Social Movements, Identity, Culture and the State*, ed. David S. Meyer, Nancy Whittier, and Belinda Robnett (Oxford, New York: Oxford University Press, 2002), p. 5; Bert and Roggeband, *Handbook of Social Movements Across Disciplines*, p. 11.

implement changes. In the context of Indonesia, the openness of political opportunity structure took shape in the form of political and legal deregulation policy during the transition era in 1998, when Islamic organisations were first allowed to employ Islam as the ideological basis of their organisations. Included are some regulations and rulings that paved the way for the increasing inclusion of sharia in Indonesian state law, such as Act No. 22/1999 and Act No. 32/2004 that govern Regional Autonomy and Decentralisation. These laws were employed by MUI and other Islamist groups to provide a legal foundation for their efforts in mobilising the movement for shariatisation.

The second notion of social movement organisation theory is the concept of the mobilising structure. This concept refers to such formal and informal organisations and networks that facilitate routine communication and coordination among groups of people.[120] Shariatisation here can be categorised as a kind of collective Islamic contention that involves vigorous participation by various Islamic organisations and individuals, where MUI functions as the leading agency and facilitator, and as well as communicator between the groups. So far, MUI has shown its ability to build and facilitate intensive communication between Islamic organisations as a result of its position as a "large tent" for other Islamic groups. In this regard, the existence of such an organisation becomes an important part of the movement.[121] In addition, most scholars accept that without some effort to establish formal and informal organisations, no movement can mobilise a sustained flow of resources and energy towards enacting social change. Further, Jackie Smith and Tina Fetner say that "the mobilising structures concept emphasises the fact that most social movements combine diverse sets of actors, some of which are explicitly organised around movement goals and others that are organised for other social purposes."[122]

The third analytical category of the social movement organisation theory is framing. This is needed because the use of both political (and non-political) opportunity structures and mobilisation of resources remains insufficient to account for the collective action of the above-mentioned shariatisation. Framing theory was firstly introduced by Todd Gitlin[123] in his study on the role of media in social change in America. William Gamson, Bruce Fireman

120 Klandermans and Roggeband, *Handbook of Social Movements Across Disciplines*, p. 28.
121 Ibid.
122 Ibid, pp. 30–31.
123 Todd Gitlin, *The Whole World Is Watching: Mass Media in the Making & Unmaking of the New Left* (California: University of California Press, 1980).

and Stefan Rytna in their volume *Encounter with Unjust Authority*[124] placed a greater emphasis on the use of this concept from the media to political actors, especially concerning their role in framing injustices to mobilise collective action.[125] The framing approach was widely recognised in the study of social movement organisation theory in the mid-1990s.

Framing is a means of mediating between the two pillars of social movement organisation theory, namely political context and resource mobilisation frameworks. Through framing, the meanings and definitions of such contentions can be shared with others. Framing is about socio-cultural perceptions and the construction of shared understandings that justify, dignify, and motivate collective action. The framing processes draw on and modify the available cultural stock, such as images of justice and injustice, as well as the repertoires of contention and models of action. They are about building a consensus for action, but building consensus can be a competitive and even conflictive process. There are four framing functions: "defining problems, designing causes, making moral judgments and suggesting remedies."[126] David A. Snow and Robert D. Benford reveal the importance of framing in social contention because it helps to imbue a conceptual void and analytic purchase on understanding the interpretive work engaged in by movement actors and others within the movement field of action.[127] The use of framing is important to package the ideology that MUI wants to exercise,[128] and because this notion helps to attract support from and establish a shared identity amongst Muslims regarding their desire to enact sharia law. The notion of framing is also relevant to explain the issues of injustice, marginalised position, infringements and other related Muslim grievances as reasons for the implementation of an Islamic legal system. Without this framing, it would be difficult to attract solidarity, support and active participation from members of the movement (movement society).

---

124 William A. Gamson, Bruce Fireman, and Steven Rytina, *Encounters with Unjust Authority* (Chicago: Dorsey Press, 1982).

125 John A. Noakes and Hank Johnston, "Frames Of Protest: A Road Map To A Perspective," in *Frames Of Protest: Social Movements And The Framing Perspective*, ed. Hank Johnston and John A Noakes (Maryland: Rowman & Littlefield, 2005), 1–33, p. 3.

126 Michael T. Maher, "Framing: An Emerging Paradigm or A Phase of Agenda Setting?," in *Framing Public Life: Perspectives on Media and Our Understanding of the Social World*, ed. Stephen D. Reese, Oscar H. Gandy, and August E. Grant (New Jersey: Routledge, 2001), 83–94, p. 87.

127 David A Snow and Robert D. Benford, "Clarifying The Relationship Between Framing and Ideology," in *Frames Of Protest: Social Movements And The Framing Perspective*, ed. Johnston Hank and John A. Noakes (Oxford: Rowman & Littlefield, 2005), 205–12.

128 Ibid, p. 209.

As the shariatisation of Indonesia uncovers not only the involvement of pure Islam-based movements but also an expression of political interest, the politicisation of Islam is considered here. The concept of the politicisation of Islam is not a new phenomenon in the tradition of Muslim scholars. It began at the end of the nineteenth century as a reaction by Muslim intellectuals such as Jamaluddin al-Afghani (1838–1897), Muḥammad ʿAbduh (1849–1905), Rashīd Riḍā (1865–1935) and Ḥasan al-Bannā (1906–1949) to the presence of Western imperialism in the Muslim world.[129] This concept applies not only to the current wave of fundamentalism but also to moderate progressive Islamic groups. In the former, Islam is used for the purpose of political Islam, and for the latter, Islam is used to delegitimise the political function of the religion. Thus the politicisation of Islam is flexible and can be modified depending on the situation. Indeed, it is necessary to look carefully at the distinctive features of each Islamic movement.[130]

The utilisation of Islam for political purposes has not only occurred in the reform era of Indonesia, but also during the previous New Order era. During the New Order period, the politicisation of Islam was not just dominated by Islamic organisations such as MUI, but also by the state. For instance, Suharto (1967–1998) politicised Islam in order to shore up his power base by establishing ICMI in the 1990s.[131] During the reform era, the politicisation of Islam has been predominately undertaken by Islamic civil society organisations, as the state has taken a more neutral stance in relation to religion. The politicisation of Islam is thus a relevant and useful theoretical tool for the purposes of this book.

In the context of the shariatisation of Indonesia, the politicisation of Islam has a different impact to that of Islamism. If Islamism promotes the inclusion of sharia provision into the state law as part of their strategy to establish an Islamic state, the politicisation of Islam is undertaken merely to give Islam a higher visibility in the legal discourse and practice of the state and public

129 Muhammad Ibrahim Ayish and Muḥammad ʿIṣām ʿĀyiš, *The New Arab Public Sphere* (Berlin: Frank & Timme GmbH, 2008), pp. 102–3; Hamid Enayat, *Modern Islamic Political Thought* (New York: I.B.Tauris, 2005); Albert Hourani, *Arabic Thought in the Liberal Age 1798–1939* (Cambridge: Cambridge University Press, 1998).

130 John Bunzl, "Introduction in God's Name?" in *Islam, Judaism, and the Political Role of Religions in the Middle East*, ed. John Bunzl (Gainesvile: University Press of Florida: University Press of Florida, 2004), p. 5; Mohammed Ayoob, *The Many Faces of Political Islam, Religion and Politics in the Muslim World* (Michigan: Michigan University Press, 2008), p. 2.

131 Ramage, *Politics in Indonesia, Democracy, Islam and the Ideology of Tolerance*, pp. 77–8; Robert W. Hefner, *Civil Islam: Muslims and Democratization in Indonesia* (New Jersey: Princeton University Press, 2011), pp. 155–6.

sphere through influencing the process of lawmaking of Indonesia. The final goal of this project is to produce a sharia-based state law, not a sharia state, and to increase the piety and religiosity of Indonesian Muslims. In doing so, MUI needs the legitimacy of Islam to obtain a greater bargaining position vis-a-vis the state. Nevertheless, MUI believes that shariatisation does not necessarily become a stepping stone towards the foundation of an Islamic state. In order to strengthen the analytical concept of the politicisation of Islam, Asef Bayat's "post-Islamism" is worth taking into consideration. The term post-Islamism was introduced by Bayat to characterise a growing trend of conservative religiosity, especially among ordinary Muslims, which can be seen in a shift in their orientation from using Islam for the purpose of political Islam towards Islamic piety and religiosity. This phenomenon is a new type of religious commitment and activism expressed by Muslims after the decline of the Islamist agenda which aimed to establish an Islamic state.[132] The energy of Islamism in this regard is channeled towards any activism which can increase Muslim piety and adherence to their religion. This is called active piety, meaning that Muslims not only practise their religion but also preach it and use it to Islamise others.[133] In sum, this phenomenon is a kind of "Islamisation without an Islamic state."[134]

The core spirit of post-Islamism is the advanced metamorphosis of Islamism (its ideas, approaches and practices) from within and without.[135] Post-Islamism covers two important areas. Firstly, it emerges following a set of political and social of conditions where the legitimacy of Islamism is exhausted. Secondly, post-Islamism is also a project, "a conscious attempt to conceptualise and strategise the rationale and modalities of transcending Islamism in social, political and intellectual domains."[136] Post-Islamism is therefore the state of being "in between": it is neither anti-Islam nor un-Islamic nor secular.[137]

Although post-Islamism in Bayat's work rests on the Egyptian and Iranian Islamic experiences, the substance of this approach is also very relevant for examining the shariatisation of Indonesia. In the context of Indonesian

132 Asef Bayat, *Making Islam Democratic: Social Movements and the Post-Islamist Turn* (Redwood City, CA: Stanford University Press, 2007), p. 147.

133 Greg Fealy, "Consuming Islam: Commodified Religion and Aspirational Pietism in Contemporary Indonesia," in *Expressing Islam: Religious Life and Politics in Indonesia*, ed. Greg Fealy and Sally White (Singapore: ISEAS, 2008), 15–39, p. 26.

134 Asef Bayat, *Making Islam Democratic: Social Movements and the Post-Islamist Turn*, 2007, p. 147.

135 Ibid, p. 150.

136 Ibid, p. 11.

137 Platzdasch, *Islamism in Indonesia*, pp. 174–214.

politics, efforts to establish an Islamic state have come to an end; however, the religiosity and piety of Indonesian Muslims is increasingly creeping into the public sphere. It appears that MUI, with its shariatisation agenda, wants to transform Indonesia and its Muslim population, making it more Islamised and pious through shariatisation, but without needing to establish an Islam-based state system. Bayat's statement is similar to the views of Salwa Ismail, who is convinced that the strong characteristics of post-Islamism are confined within the autonomous boundaries of the nation-state and are no longer concerned with the establishment of an Islamic state.[138]

One very important aspect of MUI's shariatisation concerns the role of its fatwa and Islamic recommendations. Ahron Layish argues that the presence of *muftī* (those entitled to pass fatwa) is the most important marker of shariatisation within the history of Islam.[139] No specific approach of Islamic legal theory to deal with MUI fatwa and *tawṣiyya* (Islamic recommendations) is adopted in this book, but rather a combination of analysis based on interdisciplinary or multidisciplinary approaches, not only from the tradition of Muslim scholars but also from Western scholars. In explaining the so-called deviant sects of Islam, the "denomination theory" is employed, which is often used in the context of Western Christian phenomena. Marx Sedgwick also uses it to explain the history of sects in Islam.[140] In this theory, non-mainstream or deviant sects are always understood as a threat to mainstream established Islamic sects. An analytical framework on the orthodox and heterodox is employed to examine how MUI, as a "large tent" of orthodox Indonesian Islamic organisations, regulates and controls the heterodox groups of Indonesian Muslims. Andreas Johanes Köstenberger and Michael J. Kruger argue that the orthodox group is a determining actor.[141] Taal Asad also notes the strong tendency found among the orthodox groups of Islam to channel their thinking to reach heterodox groups.[142]

138 Ismail, *Rethinking Islamist Politics*, p. 161; Cf. Roy, *The Failure of Political Islam*.

139 Aharon Layish, "The Qāḍī's Role in the Islamization of Sedentary Tribal Society," in *The Public Sphere in Muslim Societies*, ed. Miriam Hoexter, Shmuel N. Eisenstadt, and Nehemia Levtzion (New York: State University of New York Press, 2002), 83–108, p. 84.

140 Mark Sedgwick, "Establishments and Sects in the Islamic World," in *New Religious Movements in the Twenty-First Century*, ed. Philip Charles Lucas and Thomas Robbins (New York: Routledge, 2004), 231–56.

141 Andreas Johannes Köstenberger and Michael J. Kruger, *The Heresy of Orthodoxy: How Contemporary Culture's Fascination with Diversity Has Reshaped Our Understanding of Early Christianity* (Wheaton, IL: Crossway, 2010).

142 Talal Asad, *The Idea of an Anthropology of Islam* (Washington, DC: Center for Contemporary Arab Studies, Georgetown University, 1986). See also Talal Asad, "Reflections on Blasphemy and Secular Criticism," in *Religion: Beyond a Concept*, ed. Hent de Vries

To examine the issue of the prevalent visibility of Islamic worship in the public sphere, the sociological perspective on religious piety and religious administration is employed. The concept of the politics of piety, formulated by Saba Mahmood[143] and also Bryan Turner,[144] helps to frame the shariatisation of MUI, implemented through its fatwas, as endorsing the visibility of Islamic rites in the public sphere and thus implementing religious piety. In Mahmood's words, through the politics of piety sharia has enjoyed a "pride of place in the pietists' practice."[145] The theory of administrating religion is useful to see how MUI fatwa and other Islamic advice are used to create a bureaucratisation of religion, as evident for instance in *zakāt* management and also the determination of the dates of Islamic religious celebrations. Sociologically speaking, the administration of such religious worship or rites in the public sphere is legitimate if it is intended to facilitate freedom of religion and does not lead to discrimination; it also has to comply with the norms of public space.[146]

Discourses on the control of the body and normalisation or governmentality form part of the discussion on public morality. These are useful to explain how the discourse of MUI is created and operates to oversee the morality of the Muslim public, as evident in MUI fatwas on abortion, veiling and other issues. In this regard, the commanding right and forbidding wrong referred to by Michael Cook[147] as embodied in *ḥisba* (moral control) is used to explain how MUI creates a discourse to control the morality of the Muslim public. Here the critical analysis of Saadawi[148] and Shahnaz Khan[149] on the control of women's bodies in the Arab countries and Pakistan help explain how MUI fatwa

(Fordham Univ Press, 2009), 580–609, and Kambiz Ghaneabassiri, "Religious Normativity and Praxis Among American Muslims," in *The Cambridge Companion to American Islam* (Cambridge: Cambridge University Press, 2013), 208–27.

143 Saba Mahmood, *Politics of Piety: The Islamic Revival and the Feminist Subject* (New Brunswick, NJ: Princeton University Press, 2011).

144 Bryan S. Turner, *Religion and Modern Society: Citizenship, Secularisation and the State* (Cambridge: Cambridge University Press, 2011).

145 Mahmood, *Politics of Piety*, p. xiv.

146 Winfried Brugger and Michael Mousa Karayanni, eds., *Religion in the Public Sphere: A Comparative Analysis of German, Israeli, American and International Law: A Comparative Analysis of German, Israeli, American and International Law* (Berlin, Heidelberg & New York: Springer, 2007), pp. 316–7.

147 Michael Cook, *Commanding Right and Forbidding Wrong in Islamic Thought* (Cambridge: Cambridge University Press, 2004); Michael Cook, *Forbidding Wrong in Islam: An Introduction* (Cambridge: Cambridge University Press, 2003).

148 Nawal El Saadawi, *The Hidden Face of Eve: Women in the Arab World* (London & New York: Zed Books, 2007).

149 Shahnaz Khan, *Zina, Transnational Feminism, and the Moral Regulation of Pakistani Women* (Vancouver: UBC Press, 2011).

regulate women's bodies in Indonesia. When fatwa are understood as a means of normalising Muslim morality, the discourse of governmentality is referred to as a way of indicating that the function of fatwa is to control and supervise the public morality of the Muslim Indonesian public.[150]

To understand the phenomenon of halalisation and sharia economics, theories on food taboos and also purity and impurity are very useful to explain the underlying reasons why such a person or society need consume pure food and use pure money. Mary Douglas says that "dirt is dangerous." From her perspective, impurity means the defilement of sacred things and places. The body should therefore be cleansed of any kind of impurity.[151] She also stated that uncleanness is dangerous to divinity.[152] From the Islamic perspective, the obligation to consume halal products is intended to free the body from pollution, because worshipping God must be done with a body untainted by any pollution.[153] This is related to the Muslim practice of ritual ablutions before prayer. Johan Fischer's observation on the halalisation of Malaysia is a kind of mirror for the similar project of MUI in Indonesia.[154] Here, the concept of religious purity also applies to the fatwa on sharia economic and financial issues in which the money of Muslim people has to be protected from pollution. All economic and financial practices based on interest or *ribā* are categorised as impure and pollutant. The theory of religious commodification is also relevant here as the practice of halalisation and also sharia banking involve business and economic transactions to some extent, and are not merely motivated by religion.[155]

---

150 Shelley Lynn Tremain, *Foucault and the Government of Disability* (Michigan: University of Michigan Press, 2005); Ghaneabassiri, "Religious Normativity and Praxis Among American Muslims."

151 Mary Douglas, *Purity and Danger: An Analysis of Concepts of Pollution and Taboo* (London & New York: Routledge, 2003), p. 7; Carolyn Rouse and Janet Hoskins, "Purity, Soul Food, and Sunni Islam: Explorations at the Intersection of Consumption and Resistance," *Cultural Anthropology* 19, no. 2 (2004): 226–49, pp. 233–4.

152 Douglas, *Purity and Danger*, p. 8.

153 Rouse and Hoskins, "Purity, Soul Food, and Sunni Islam," p. 232.

154 Johan Fischer, *The Halal Frontier: Muslim Consumers in a Globalized Market* (New York: Palgrave Macmillan, 2011); Johan Fischer, *Proper Islamic Consumption: Shopping Among the Malays in Modern Malaysia* (Copenhagen: NIAS Press, 2008).

155 Vineeta Sinha, *Religion and Commodification: "Merchandizing" Diasporic Hinduism* (New York: Routledge, 2010); Pattana Kitiarsa, ed., *Religious Commodifications in Asia: Marketing Gods* (London & New York: Routledge, 2008); Fealy, "Consuming Islam: Commodified Religion and Aspirational Pietism in Contemporary Indonesia."

The pure Islamic legal theory approach of classical and modern Muslim scholars such as al-Ṭūfī (d. 1316),[156] al-Shāṭibī (d. 1388)[157] and al-Jābirī (d. 2010)[158] and others is not adopted here, but instead is blended with the thoughts of Western scholars. I agree with al-Ṭūfī's concept of *maṣlaḥa* (public interest), which is a courageous solution to the long-unresolved problem as to what should be promoted and prioritised when there is a conflict between the texts of Islam and the public interest. According to him, sharia should not just be read and interpreted using a textual and inter-textual approach, but it should also accommodate the social, cultural and political reality. Al-Ṭūfī prefers using *maṣlaḥa* to ulama consensus and analogy in making Islamic law for two reasons. Firstly, he says, public interest is the place of agreement (*maḥall wifāq*) while the ulama consensus is a place of disagreement (*al-ijmāʿ maḥall al-khilāf*). Secondly, he states that "upholding an agreed thing is better than holding a differed thing," (*al-tamassuk bimā ittufiqa awlā min al-tamassuk bimā ikhtalafa fīhi*), and the texts are diverse and sometimes in conflict with each other. Therefore, he said, following the public interest is the higher good: *fakāna itbāʿuhu awlā*. Al-Ṭūfī provides a promising solution to the problematic issues related to the supremacy of the text, which in most cases has hindered the production of a new interpretation of sharia. In short, the concept of *maṣlaḥa* provides two important aspects for making sharia law: the textual and inter-textual, and the social fact. Thus, in defining *maṣlaḥa*, both the text and the social reality have to be considered. Neither the authority of the text nor the power of social fact can be solely relied on. Al-Shāṭibī explains *maṣlaḥa* as a concept for understanding the two most crucial aspects of Islamic law, namely its texts and context. By using the discursive construct of *maṣlaḥa* introduced by his predecessors, al-Shāṭibī developed a new rational approach to the sources of law in which social realities are taken into consideration for determining suitable legal norms. As a result, adherence to the text of a law, according to al-Shāṭibī, must not be so rigid as to alienate the rationale and higher objective of the sharia.[159] In the case of MUI's fatwa, this notion is useful because almost all MUI fatwas consider two things as final objectives: first, a desire to implement the will of God, and second, the establishment of a

156 Najm al-Dīn Al-Ṭūfī, *Risāla Fī Riʿāya Al-Maṣlaḥa* (Cairo: Dār al-Miṣriyya al-Lubnāniyya, 1993).

157 Abū Isḥāq Al-Shāṭibī, *Al-Muwāfaqāt Fī ʿUlūm al-Sharīʿa* (Beirut: Dār al-Kutub al-Islāmiyya, 1998).

158 Mohammed Abed Al-Jabri, *Democracy, Human Rights and Law in Islamic Thought* (London & New York: I.B. Tauris, 2009).

159 Abū Isḥāq Al-Shāṭibī, *Al-Muwafaqāt Fī Uṣūl al-Sharīʿah*, vol. 2 (Cairo: al-Maktabah al-Tijāriyyah, n.d.), p. 394.

prosperous and a just life for human beings. These two goals also align with the basic tenets of *maṣlaḥa*.

Much benefit has also been gained by referring to the studies of Western scholars such as Felicitas Opwis, Wael B. Hallaq and Frank E. Vogel, amongst many others. Through their studies on Islamic law and Islamic legal theory, the MUI fatwa can be put in a dialogue process with a wider horizon of interdisciplinary and multidisciplinary studies. Felicitas's elaboration on *maṣlaḥa*, for instance, tries to place the discourse within the context of modernity.[160] Wael Hallaq's many voluminous works on Islamic legal theory are very useful as mirrors for illuminating MUI's way of thinking of cases of Islamic jurisprudence and in deciding fatwas, in particular with reference to concepts such as *ijtihād*, *ijmāʿ* (ulama consensus) and also *maṣlaḥa*.[161] Frank Vogel's works on fatwas in Saudi Arabia provide a useful analysis of the use of *maṣlaḥa* in the Saudi context, where it is used by Saudi judges to generate arguments for the national codification of sharia.[162]

In short, various interdisciplinary or multidisciplinary approaches are employed to illuminate the discourse and activism of MUI in increasing the presence of sharia in the legal and public sphere of Indonesia.

1.5 Methodology, Sources of Research and Structure of the Book

This research is a qualitative examination that combines library investigation and fieldwork. Written and oral sources are both very important, and include printed materials such as official documents, records of meetings and discussions, fatwas, monthly magazines, and pamphlets and brochures published by MUI. Included in the written sources are several legal acts which were influenced by MUI fatwas. All the materials used were published between 1998 and 2013. In order to access the written sources, I conducted library research at MUI headquarters in Jakarta during my fieldwork in Indonesia, and also in some

160 Opwis, "Maslaha in Contemporary Islamic Legal Theory"; Felicitas Opwis, *Maṣlaḥah and the Purpose of the Law: Islamic Discourse on Legal Change from the 4th/10th to 8th/14th Century* (Leiden & Boston: Brill, 2010).

161 Wael B. Hallaq, *A History of Islamic Legal Theories: An Introduction to Sunni Usul Al-Fiqh* (Cambridge: Cambridge University Press, 1999); Wael B. Hallaq, *The Origins and Evolution of Islamic Law* (Cambridge University Press, 2005).

162 Frank E. Vogel, *Islamic Law and the Legal System of Saudi: Studies of Saudi Arabia* (Leiden: Brill, 2000), p. 346; Frank E Vogel, "Saudi Arabia: Public, Civil and Individual Shariʿa in Law and Politics," in *Shariʿa Politics: Islamic Law and Society in the Modern World*, ed. Robert W. Hefner (Indiana: Indiana University Press, 2011), 55–93.

libraries in Berlin and at the Royal Netherlands Institute of Southeast Asian and Caribbean Studies at Leiden University, the Netherlands. I attempted to collect all MUI's publications and bring them to Berlin. For the purpose of obtaining information not found in the written sources, I adopted the tradition of oral research: "the collection of materials through the method of an oral exchange or interview with another person or persons about a topic which the interviewer is researching."[163] This meant that I tried to obtain information that could not be found in written materials through interviews. In doing so, I prepared a list of some interviewees who were knowledgeable about the relevant topics, and prepared myself with questions that could not be answered from written sources. With more reserved informants who did not share information easily, I tried to be skillful in my approach. In my interviews with Din Syamsuddin and Ridwan (both important figures of MUI), for example, I required extra time to prepare for the interview. I used a structured interviewing method[164] with a set of topics and research questions that the interview should cover. An outline of the interview should also be prepared by the interviewer to suit the interviewee's background. This model can be also referred to as a focused topical interview.[165] This method was relevant to this research because most informants were senior members of MUI and other Islamic organisations of Indonesia.

I had to be mindful of a number of matters during the interview process. Firstly, high-ranking interviewees, in the case of this research namely the leaders of MUI and other Muslim organisations, "do not like to be controlled by the interviewer."[166] To avoid this problem, a checklist of topics had to be maintained alongside the interview outline. Secondly, most such interviewees asked for a list of questions before they agreed to be interviewed. Thus, before interviewing Ichwan Sam, MUI General Secretary, I sent him a list of questions which he answered when we met. This resulted in a loss of improvisation and spontaneity during the interview process. Thirdly, most high-ranking interviewees want to be interviewed by a high-ranking individual with credibility

163 James H Morrison, "A Global Perspective of Oral History in South in Southeast Asia Theory and Method," in *Oral History in Southeast Asia Theory and Method*, ed. P. Lim Pui Huen, James H. Morrison, and Chua Chong Guan (Singapore: ISEAS, 1998), 1–16, p. 2.

164 Lim How Seng, "Interviewing the Business and Political Elite of Singapore," in *Oral History in Southeast Asia Theory and Method*, ed. P. Lim Pui Huen, James H. Morrison, and Kwa Chong Guan (Singapore: Institute of Southeast Asian Studies, 2000), 55–65, pp. 55–65.

165 Daniel Chew, "Oral History Methodology: The Life History Approach," in *Oral History in Southeast Asia Theory and Method*, ed. P. Lim Pui Huen, James H Morrison, and Kwa Chong Guan (Singapore: Institute of Southeast Asian Studies, 2000), 47–54, p. 47.

166 Seng, "Interviewing the Business and Political Elite of Singapore", p. 62.

and knowledge. These three considerations served as a source of personal reflection during the fieldwork interviews.

I conducted interviews with the elite figures of MUI such as Mahfudh, Din Syamsuddin, Ma'ruf Amin, Ichwan Sam, and representatives of different Islamic organisations in MUI. I also prepared a set of questions for interviews with the MUI chairmen of the organisation's regional branches in three areas: the Islamic province of Aceh, South Sulawesi and West Java. These three regions were chosen due to the strength of shariatisation in these respective provinces. In Aceh, I interviewed the MPU Chairman, human rights activists, academics and also women activists. In the city of Bulukumba, Sulawesi, I was able to conduct interviews with the MUI Chairman of South Sulawesi, Sanusi Baco; the Chairman of the Bulukumba MUI, Tjamiruddin; and also the former Bulukumba Regent, Patabai Pabokori. In Cianjur, West Java, I conducted an interview with the MUI General Chairman of West Java, Hafidz Ustman; the MUI Chairman of the city of Cianjur, Abdul Halim; and some *pesantren* communities. To acquire information on responses and reactions from outside MUI, I conducted interviews with leaders of Islamic organisations such as Saiq Aqil Siradj, As'ad Ali and Masdar F. Mas'udi from Nahdlatul Ulama, and Din Syamsuddin and Fatah Wibisono from Muhammadiyah. To seek independent opinions on the role of MUI, I interviewed Muslim activists and scholars such as Bahtiar Effendy and Djohan Effendi, amongst others.

The book is organised as follows:

Chapter 1 seeks to provide a general introduction to the study by locating Islamisation and shariatisation in the local and global contexts, overviewing some works related to Islamisation and shariatisation, and also the theoretical references used in this writing. This chapter also explains the research process, involving library investigation as well as fieldwork, and the structure of the book.

Chapter 2 introduces MUI and the history of the sharia trajectory in Indonesia. It highlights historical narratives on the presence of Islam in Indonesia, indicating the fact that Islamisation in Indonesia has been debated since the early formation of the state. Discourse on Indonesia's state ideology and MUI's response is also examined in this chapter, as well as the history of ulama institutionalisation in Indonesia and its relation to the establishment of MUI. The characteristics of MUI organisational leadership, in which senior ulama play a key role, and the changing role of MUI in the reform era and its internal dynamism are also discussed.

Chapter 3 focuses on the pre-existing conditions laying the basis for shariatisation, such as the ideological shift from Pancasila to Islam, from *khādim al-ḥukūma* (the custodian of the government) to *khādim al-umma* (the custodian of the Muslim community) and from *payung* (umbrella institution) to *tenda besar* (large tent). In this regard, the vehicles of shariatisation used by MUI are taken into account. The chapter presents four important MUI bodies, namely the Fatwa Commission, the Assessment Institute for Foods, Drugs and Cosmetics (LPPOM), the National Sharia Board (DSN) and the Legal and Legislation Commission.

Chapter 4 highlights how MUI mobilises its resources to drive the shariatisation of legal discourse and practice in Indonesia. It scrutinises the legal, political and cultural structure of Indonesia that provides the opportunity for shariatisation. This chapter also examines how MUI manages its publications and media profile to frame its support for the Islamisation of state law. It looks at how certain ideas are disseminated, topics and priorities decided, and readership and circulation maintained by MUI. The chapter is also concerned with issues that MUI frames as stimulating the discourse for shariatisation, such as *al-amr bi al-maʿrūf wa al-nahy ʿan al-munkar* (commanding right and forbidding wrong). As far as the mobilisation aspect of shariatisation is concerned, this chapter also looks at how MUI uses its regular and non-regular meetings as a stage for consolidating the topic and movement of sharia incorporation, such as Musyawarah Nasional (MUNAS, the National Congress), for strengthening the organisational and public function of MUI.

Chapter 5 examines MUI shariatisation attempts at the regional level in Aceh, Bulukumba (South Sulawesi) and Cianjur (West Java). The discussion in this section is focused on highlighting the establishment of sharia bylaws such the *perda syariah* (sharia regional regulations), the proposed enactment of the *jināya* (Islamic Criminal law) in Aceh, regulating Islamic public morality and *jilbabisasi* (the movement endorsing the wearing of head covering for women), mainstreaming belief, and also Islamic ethics.

Chapter 6 highlights how MUI mobilises its discourse such as fatwa and *tawṣiyya*. Some selected cases of fatwa that display MUI's role in influencing national laws are discussed, covering four major topics: *takfīr* (the declaration that another Muslim is guilty of apostasy), religious practice and public morality, proper Islamic/halal lifestyle, and proper economics. This chapter also covers compliance and social resistance, which is mostly focused on how Indonesian Islamic organisations and scholars respond to the project of shariatisation.

Chapter 7 examines the significant role of MUI in electoral politics and the politics of *umma*, and their dilemma in the presidential era of Jokowi. Three discussions are presented here. The first focuses on MUI and its role in electoral politics such as the 2012 Jakarta gubernatorial elections, the 2014 presidential elections, the 2017 Jakarta gubernatorial elections and the 2019 presidential elections. The second highlights how MUI uses the politics of *umma* in the context of Indonesian conceptualisation. The third uncovers the juxtaposition of MUI with the Jokowi regime and its dilemmatic issues that influence the organisation of MUI and sharatisation in Indonesia in the Jokowi era.

Chapter 8 concludes that MUI shariatisation is still underway. What MUI has achieved now in terms of sharia implementation may either be consolidated or weaken in the future, influenced by many factors. This chapter discusses MUI's future role in the shariatisation of Indonesia by presenting the research findings with theoretical reflections on what has happened and possible future directions.

CHAPTER 2

MUI and the History of the Sharia Trajectory in Indonesia

2.1 Introduction

History is an important part of the human experience, and never arises from or returns to an empty space. It creates a sense of the world that shapes the past and also the future. As Davies says, "the sense of history pretends to be the sense of the world, to ensure continuity between the past and the unfolding future [illusion]."[1] In other words, the world can be sensed through the narrative of history.[2] It is this view of history that provides context for those who envisage the shariatisation of Indonesia as a historical must. It means that any attempt to perpetuate sharia for public and legal order requires historical reference and legitimacy from the past. This is why presenting the history of Islam in Indonesia is viewed as a fundamental necessity, and is perhaps what Sande Cohen, cited in Davies,[3] refers to as an "imaginary obligation" in which the past history of Islam should be readable to make sense of the current situation for its followers. Hence the need to pose the question: "Is MUI heading along the trajectory of shariatisation? If yes, what is MUI's position and how does it relate to the history of Indonesia?" In order to answer these questions, this chapter seeks to shed light on the history or histories of the coming of Islam to Indonesia, and how Indonesian Muslims employ this narrative as part of their religious identity. It will illuminate connections between the past presence of Islam and the current promulgation of shariaritisation in the modern state of Indonesia, and how the current shariatisation project relates to national debates on the state ideology of Indonesia in the early post-independence era and to the establishment of MUI.

1 Martin L. Davies, *Historics Why History Dominates Contemporary Society* (New York: Routledge, 2006), p. 31.

2 Peter Gay, *Freud for Historians* (New York & Oxford: Oxford University Press, 1985), p. 114; Martin L. Davies, *Historics: Why History Dominates Contemporary Society* (New York: Routledge, 2006), p. 34.

3 Davies, *Historics*, p. 29.

 | DOI:10.1163/9789004534896_003

2.2 The Shariatisation of MUI and Indonesia's State Ideology

This section argues that the propagation of shariatisation rests on the historical narrative that Islam is a fundamental identity which is inseparable from the history of Indonesia, its state and society. Identity in its various manifestations is a vital shaper of the actions or agenda of any state and society. It determines the types of actions, projects, and also goals pursued, whether legitimate or illegitimate.[4] By situating Islam as the dominant colour of Indonesia's identity, the endeavour to implement the agenda of shariatisation is understandable. The topic of the Islamic identity of Indonesia is currently a key debate, as the foundation for the question of the legitimacy of embodying this identity within the modern Indonesia state. One path towards understanding this discourse is through a study of the coming of Islam to Indonesia. Discussion of the history of Islam's arrival can affirm a cultural need for shariatisation and as well as denoting Islam as a "long tradition" and "unalienable identity" of this country.[5] Borrowing Sayyid, who uses Richard Rorty's concept of "final vocabularies,"[6] shariatisation is a kind of language or expression used by Indonesian Islamists to instrumentalise the past Islamic heritage for current goals.

There is a tendency amongst Indonesian Muslim historians to nurture a view of Islam as the fundamental identity of the state of Indonesia by presenting a certain historical view of the presence of Islam in this largest Muslim-majority country in the world. In 1986, MUI organised a conference called Amanah Sejarah Umat Islam (The Muslim Community's Historical Mandate),[7] where MUI sought agreement on three matters. The first was agreement on the so-called "Arab theory" which claims that Islam came from the Arab lands to Indonesia in the first century AH (Anno Hegirae), 622 CE.[8] The second was to indicate that the process of Islamisation had begun long before the modern era

4 Frank Bechofer and David McCrone, *National Identity, Nationalism and Constitutional Change* (London: Palgrave Macmillan, 2009), p. 190.

5 Davies, *Historics*, p. 6.

6 Bobby S. Sayyid, *A Fundamental Fear: Eurocentrism and the Emergence of Islamism* (London & New York: Zed Books, 1997), p. 2.

7 Karel Steenbrink, "Indian Teachers and Their Indonesian Pupils: On Intellectual Relation Between Indonesia and India 1600–1800," in *India and Indonesia in the Ancient Regime* (Leiden & New York: Brill, 1988), 129–42, p. 139.

8 Azyumardi Azra, *Islam in the Indonesian World, an Account of Institutional Formation* (Bandung: Mizan, 2006), p. 15; Johan H. Mueleman, "The History of Islam in Southeast Asia: Some Questions and Debates," in *Islam in Southeast Asia: Political, Social, and Strategic Challenges for the 21st Century*, ed. K.S. Nathan and Mohammad Hashim Kamali (Singapore: Institute of Southeast Asian Studies, 2005), 22–44, p. 25; MUI, *15 Tahun Majelis Ulama Indonesia*, ed. H.S. Prodjokusumo (Jakarta: Sekretariat Majelis Ulama Indonesia, 1990), p. 165.

of Indonesia, thus underscoring the significance of Islam for Indonesia.[9] The third was to clarify that the coming of Islam in the first century AH, shortly after the birth of Islam in the Middle East, demonstrates the purity of Indonesian Islam in its early spread to the archipelago. In this regard, using Ernest Gellner's concept,[10] Indonesian Islam can be said to be part of high Islam. The conference concluded that Islam was brought to the archipelago directly from Arabia in the seventh century CE Another similar discussion, titled Sejarah Masuk dan Berkembangnya Islam di Indonesia (The history of the arrival and development of Islam in Indonesia), had been held in Banda Aceh, the capital city of Aceh province, on 10–16 July 1978.[11] This conference had drawn almost identical conclusions to that of 1986. Indonesian Muslim historians who advocate the Arab theory include Hamka (1908–1981), the first general chairman of MUI, as well as Suryanegara[12] and Uka Tjandrasasmita.[13] They affirmed that Islam spread directly to Indonesia from the Arabian Peninsula (Mecca).[14] They referred to Chinese records from the Tang Dynasty[15] that reported an Arab trader community had been discovered on the west coast of Sumatra. They noted with approval that the first propagators of Islam in the archipelago were the Arab traders of the first century AH.[16] This theory, arguing that Islam arrived in Indonesia in the seventh century CE, is yet to be fully accepted by many foreign or Indonesian historians outside MUI. The Arab theory should therefore be viewed as one of various divergent historical narratives regarding the first influx of Islam to Indonesia, as noted by Ricklefs: "Although the spread of Islam is one of the most significant processes of Indonesian history, ...

9 Ahmad Mansur Suryanegara, *Api Sejarah* (Bandung: Salamadani Pustaka Semesta, 2009), p. 99.

10 Michael Lessnoff, "Islam, Modernity and Science," in *Ernest Gellner and Contemporary Social Thought*, ed. Sinisa Malesevic and Mark Haugaard, vol. 2007 (Cambridge: Cambridge University Press, 2007), p. 190.

11 Steenbrink, "Indian Teachers and Their Indonesian Pupils," pp. 129–142.

12 Ahmad Mansur Suryanegara, *Api Sejarah* (Bandung: Salamadani Pustaka Semesta, 2009).

13 Uka Tjandrasasmita, *Arkeologi Islam Nusantara* (Jakarta: Balai Pustaka, 2009).

14 This opinion was delivered in a conference on Masuknya Agama Islam ke Indonesia (The Coming of Islam to Indonesia), held in Medan, North Sumatera, on 17–20 March 1963.

15 The Tang Dynasty was in power from 618 to 907 CE. W. Scott Morton and Charlton M. Lewis, *China: Its History and Culture* (Columbus: McGraw Hill Professional, 2004), pp. 81–97.

16 Hamka (1975) argued that the *Ta Shih* community (Arab) had sent an emissary to China who did not stay in that region but travelled to the island of Java in 674–675. Hamka claimed that the emissary was the Prophet's companion, Muʿāwiya b. Abū Sufyān, the founder of the Umayyad dynasty, who acted as an Arab trader to observe the kingdom of Kalingga and the people of Java.

[it is] also one of the most obscure."[17] Further, the scarcity of adequate historical evidence has given rise to questions surrounding the coming of Islam to Indonesia.[18] However, the three key arguments from the MUI 1986 conference provide strong evidence of the MUI historical narrative of sharia as the pivotal identity of Indonesia.

There are, however, other differing historical narratives such as the Gujarat theory, which suggests that Islam was spread to Pasai from Cambay, in the Indian region of Gujarat, in the thirteenth century. Indonesian Muslim historians such as Ahmad Mansur Suryanegara are critical of this theory and describe it as a fallacy deliberately created by Western scholars.[19] The second theory argues that Islam came to Indonesia from Persia, and was proposed by Hossein Djajadiningrat (d. 1960) and Aboebakar Atjeh (b. 1909). This theory is based on evidence that includes the existence of a similar system of punctuation for the recitation of the Qur'ān used in West Java and in Persia. The third narrative proposes that Islam was brought to Indonesia from China, as promoted by Slamet Muljana (1921–1986). According to this theory, the nine saints of Java[20] who disseminated Islam in the island orginally came from China.[21]

17 M.C. Ricklefs, *A History of Modern Indonesia since c.1200* (Redwood City, CA: Stanford University Press, 2009), p. 3.

18 Ibid.

19 Ahmad Mansur Suryanegara, *Api Sejarah* (Bandung: Salamadani Pustaka Semesta, 2009), p. 99. Suryanegara is a Indonesian Muslim scholar who has strongly promoted the narrative of Islam's arrival in Indonesia in the seventh century. He wrote two volumes on the history of Islam in Indonesia as an attempt to revise historical narratives on the coming of Islam he viewed as misleading, especially those proposed by some Western scholars.

20 *The wali songo* or nine saints were a group of ulama who disseminated Islam in Java. They were (1) Maulana Malik Ibrahim or Sunan Gresik (2) Raden Rahmat or Sunan Ampel (3) Maulana Makdum Ibrahim or Sunan Bonang (4) Syarifuddin or Sunan Drajat (5) Raden Paku or Sunan Giri (6) Raden Sahid or Sunan Kalijaga (7) Ja'far ash-Shadiq or Sunan Kudus (8) Raden Umar Said or Sunan Muria and (9) Syarif Hidayatullah or Sunan Gunung Jati Agus Sunyoto, *Wali Songo: Rekonstruksi Sejarah Yang Disingkirkan* (Jakarta: Transpustaka, 2011); Agus Sunyoto, *Atlas Wali Songo* (Jakarta: Kerjasama Pustaka IIMaN, Trans Pustaka, dan LTN PBNU, 2012).

21 Slamet Muljana, *Hindu-Jawa Dan Timbulnya Negara-Negara Islam Di Nusantara* (Yogyakarta: PT LKiS Pelangi Aksara, 2005), p. 97; Agus Sunyoto, *Wali Songo: Rekonstruksi Sejarah Yang Disingkirkan* (Jakarta: Transpustaka, 2011). This was mentioned by Muljana in his book, *Runtuhnya Kerajaan Hindu Jawa dan Timbulnya Negara-Negara Islam di Nusantara*, ("The Decline of Hindu Kingdom and the Rise of Islamic Kingdoms in the Archipelago"), 1968. This book was banned in 1968 shortly after the so-called communist coup of 1965. President Suharto restricted discussion of the roles and contribution of the Chinese in Indonesia because of China's perceived support for communist political movements. In the Suharto era, Indonesians of Chinese descent were allowed to conduct business, but were not allowed to work as public servants nor be involved in politics.

The fourth narrative is the maritime theory claiming that Islam was spread to the coastal region of the archipelago from maritime countries located in the "Middle East-China ocean highway."[22] This theory argues the disseminators were the early Arab Muslims living in or travelling through these areas. The early contact of Muslim traders with the people of Indonesia occurred in the first and second century AH (seventh to eighth century CE). In the third and fourth centuries AH, the visiting Muslims fraternised with the local people and established local Muslim communities. From the fifth to the ninth centuries AH (twelfth to sixteenth centuries CE), the Islamic communities in the coastal areas were fully established as Islamic states. From the ninth to the thirteenth centuries of AH (sixteenth to twentieth centuries CE), Muslim communities were consolidated and engaged in revolts against colonialism. This thrust of this theory is to reconcile various historical narratives based on internal and external sources regarding the first entrance of Islam to Indonesia.

Presenting these historical narratives on the coming of Islam in Indonesia is important to guard against drawing easy conclusions about the path of Islamisation in the country, namely that it could only have come from the Arab lands, disseminated by Arabs. It is also of critical importance to prevent the politicisation and manipulation of these narratives for the interests of particular Islamic groups in Indonesia. In fact, the coming of Islam does not refer to one single historical narrative but many related to trade, Islamic political rulers, Ṣūfism , and social and cultural encounters and activities. This actually reflects the multiplicity of the current picture of Indonesian Islam, which flourished under the influence of cultural and social traditions from various Muslim countries, as is evident in the presence of its different practices and teachings. Acknowledging the varied models of the early Islamisation process is a more realistic framework within the historical context of Indonesia, rather than just adopting a monolithic model. These multiple historical narratives also highlight the contested nature of the historical narrative of Islam's arrival in Indonesia. There is, as yet, no final and decisive opinion on the time, location and actors behind this early Islamisation process. New discoveries of artefacts and related historical sites in areas of Indonesia are under investigation by scholars from various disciplines, which could lead to new theoretical historical narratives.

Muljana's book was republished in 2005 by the LKIS (Lembaga Kajian Islam dan Sosial, Institute for Social and Islamic Studies), a publishing house in Yogyakarta.

22 N.A. Baloch, "The Advent of Islam in Indonesia and Some Problems Related to the History of Early Muslim Period," *Jurnal Al-Jamiah No. 22 Th. XV-1980/* (Yogyakarta: Perpustakaan UIN Sunan Kalijaga Yogyakarta, July 2, 2008), p. 28.

However, history is repeatedly interpreted and misinterpreted for political ends. Regardless of the multiplicity of Indonesian Islam's histories, using Davies's term, MUI's approach to the narrative on the coming of Islam to Indonesia has been to construct Islam as "historic" of this country.[23] It means that the narrative on the coming of Islam is situated in a context that cannot be divorced from the social, political and cultural aspects of Indonesia. The success of this contestation will depend on how well MUI can establish the Arab theory as the dominant reference for national history.

2.3 Discourse on Indonesia's State Ideology and MUI's Response

Apart from historical claims surrounding past shariatisation, the shariatisation of Indonesia benefits greatly from the still ongoing political discourse of state ideology, and in particular concerning the national debate over the legitimacy of the state ideology of Pancasila, which is still contested politically and culturally in some quarters. The following section discusses the debates and tensions over this ideology in the post-independence era and how MUI positions itself within this discourse.

Soon after the independence of Indonesia from the Dutch was declared on 17 August 1945, problematising the basic state ideology of Indonesia began between those arguing for the adoption of Islam as the ideological basis and those arguing that the Indonesian state should not be based on one particular belief or religion.[24] The former group argued that, as Islam was the religion of the majority, its followers should be granted the privilege to establish a state based on Islam. Mohammad Natsir (d. 1993)[25] stated that the Indonesia's

23 Davies, *Historics*, p. 6.

24 Endang Saifuddin Anshari, *Piagam Jakarta 22 Juni 1945* (Bandung: Pustaka Perpustakaan Salman ITB, 1979), p. 3. This account appears in Anshari's Masters thesis, McGill University, Montreal, Canada. The thesis was translated into Indonesian, entitled *Piagam Jakarta 22 Juni 1945*. The first edition of this book was published in 1981 by Salman Bandung, and it remains a key source for those studying the issue of the Jakarta Charter and the promotion of Islam as the basis of the Indonesian state.

25 Moh. Natsir was a prominent figure in both the history of the Indonesian nation state and Islam in Indonesia. He was born in West Sumatra on 17 July 1908 and died on 6 February 1993 and has been recognised as the main propagator of Islamic state ideology in Indonesia. He was General Chairman of the Masyumi party, and the founder of the Dewan Dakwah Islamiyah Indonesia—Council of Islamic Propagation of Indonesia or DDII, see Thohir Luth, *M. Natsir, Dakwah Dan Pemikirannya* (Jakarta: Gema Insani, 1999), p. 26; M Dzulfikriddin, *Mohammad Natsir Dalam Sejarah Politik Indonesia* (Bandung: Mizan, 2010).

independence from Dutch colonialism was due to the independence movements of Islamic groups that had paved the way for the emergence of Indonesia as an independent state.[26] Natsir said that the independence of Indonesia was not only for the people of Indonesia in general, but for Muslims in particular, and that what this group most strongly desired was to make best use of this independence by establishing an Islamic political entity for the of prosperity and welfare of both their own group and all God's creatures.[27] The pro-Islamic state group claimed that the state of Indonesia was founded because Muslims were willing to be unified under the state of Indonesia, and they demanded the inclusion of sharia into basic national law. In their minds, there was no other gift that could compensate for the sacrifices they had made in striving for Indonesian independence other than to make Indonesia an Islamic state. This aspiration was realised when the Jakarta Charter (*Piagam Jakarta*) was adopted as part of the preamble of the Indonesian Constitution on 22 June 1945. However, it was subsequently rejected by majority Muslim groups and also minority religious groups—Christians, Hindus and Buddhists—who did not support a sharia state.[28] The national consensus finally reached by the founding fathers of Indonesia was that the Indonesian state would not be based on sharia. As a consequence of this, despite the key role played by Muslim communities in striving for national independence, they had to agree to this national deal.[29] Two of the largest Islamic organisations, Nahdlatul Ulama (NU) and Muhammadiyah, agreed that the Pancasila ideology was compatible with and supportive of Islam.[30] This achievement was a huge success for all Indonesians regardless of their religion, ethnicity and gender.

Although the people of Indonesia had achieved a national consensus establishing a nation-state based on Pancasila and the 1945 Constitution of Indonesia, debate on the position of Islam as a basis for the legal system of Indonesia remains a problematic issue still hotly debated in Indonesian

26 Deliar Noer, *The Modernist Muslim Movement in Indonesia, 1900–1942* (Oxford: Oxford University Press, 1973), p. 260.

27 This statement can be seen in Natsir's article, "Indonesische Nationalisme", from *Pembela Islam*, No. 36, 1931.

28 Mujīburraḥmān, *Feeling Threatened: Muslim-Christian Relations in Indonesia's New Order* (Amsterdam: Amsterdam University Press, 2006), pp. 161–163.

29 Eka Darmaputera, *Pancasila and the Search for Identity and Modernity in Indonesian Society: A Cultural and Ethical Analysis* (Leiden & Boston: Brill, 1988), pp. 147–148; Abdullahi Ahmed An-Naʿim, *Islam and the Secular State: Negotiating the Future of Shariʿa* (Cambridge: Harvard University Press, 2009), p. 262.

30 Benyamin Fleming Intan, *Public Religion and the Pancasila-Based State of Indonesia: An Ethical And Sociological Analysis* (New York: Peter Lang, 2006), p. 99; Luthfi Assyaukanie, *Islam and the Secular State in Indonesia* (Singapore: ISEAS, 2009), p. 107.

politics.[31] It seems that the Islamist groups' acceptance of the Pancasila state did not put an end to their dreams of the formation of an Islamic state in Indonesia. This predisposition reappeared in post-reform Indonesia in the eagerness of Islamist groups to revive the incorporation of the Jakarta Charter into the Constitution.[32] Islamic political parties, such as PPP, PBB[33] and PKS, supported by such Islamist groups as HTI, Forum Umat Islam (FUI, the Islamic People's Forum), MMI, and Jama'ah Ansharut Tauhid (JAT, the Community for Helping the Union of God)[34] have requested that Article 29 of the 1945 Constitution of Indonesia be amended to reinstate the Jakarta Charter[35] or, in the case of the PKS, the Piagam Madinah (Medina Charter).[36] The Islamic parties argued that the Muslim acceptance of Pancasila in 1945 was to prevent disintegration in a time of emergency, Muslims being permitted to do what Islam

31 Colin Brown, *A Short History of Indonesia: The Unlikely Nation?* (New South Wales: Allen & Unwin, 2003), p. 152.

32 Steven Drakeley, *The History of Indonesia* (Westport: ABC-CLIO, 2005), p. 170; Nadirsyah Hosen, *Shari'a & Constitutional Reform in Indonesia* (Singapore: Institute of Southeast Asian Studies, 2007).

33 The PBB did not have representatives in the national parliament of Indonesia at the time because it had failed to pass the electoral threshold (2.5 %) determined by State Law No. 10/2008 on General Elections of Indonesia.

34 Jamaah Ansharut Tauhid is a new Islamic organisation founded by Abu Bakar Ba'asyir after his resignation from the MMI.

35 The Jakarta Charter is an Indonesian ideological construct (22 June 1945) that obliged the adherents of Islam to follow sharia. See Arskal Salim, "Zakat Administration in Politics of Indonesian New Order," in *Shari'a and Politics in Modern Indonesia*, ed. Arskal Salim and Azyumardi Azra (Singapore: Institute of Southeast Asian Studies, 2003), 181–92, p. 187; Anshari, *Piagam Jakarta 22 Juni 1945*; Allan A Samson, "Indonesian Islam since the New Order," in *Readings on Islam in Southeast Asia*, ed. Ahmad Ibrahim, Sharon Siddique, and Hussain Yasmin (Singapore: Institute of Southeast Asian Studies, 1985), 165–70, p. 166.

The Medina Charter refers to the first document of peaceful coexistence promoted by the Prophet Muhammad among the Anṣār (Helpers), Muhājirūn (Meccan emigrants), Meccan tribal groups as well as Jewish groups. See Hosen, *Shari'a & Constitutional Reform in Indonesia*, p. 206; Ahmad Sukardja, *Piagam Madinah Dan Undang-Undang Dasar 1945: Kajian Perbandingan Tentang Dasar Hidup Bersama Dalam Masyarakat Yang Majemuk* (Jakarta: Penerbit Universitas Indonesia, 1995); Ludwig W. Adamec, *Historical Dictionary of Islam* (Maryland: Scarecrow Press, 2009), p. 210. This charter is often used as an authority by Islamist groups of Indonesia as a precedent for peaceful coexistence between Muslims and non-Muslims for the present day.

36 Budhy Munawar Rachman and Moh Shofan, *Argumen Islam Untuk Sekularisme* (Jakarta: Grasindo, 2010), p. 128; Robert W. Hefner, "Indonesia: Shariʿa Politics and Democratic Transition," in *Shariʿa Politics: Islamic Law and Society in the Modern World* (Indiana University Press, 2011), 280–303, pp. 297–298.

forbids during such troubled times.[37] However, as the situation in Indonesia had changed and there was no longer any threat to the unity of the Indonesian state, the establishment of a sharia-based state became of major concern to many Indonesian Muslims.

Although we are now in a different era, the supporters of this idea can be considered ideologically close to those who supported the incorporation of the Jakarta Charter into the preamble of the 1945 Constitution back in 1945. This is evident in their rhetoric drawing on the debate surrounding the successful inclusion of the Charter into the preamble of the Indonesian Constitution. Another argument adopted by these groups is that the national consensus regarding Pancasila and the 1945 Constitution of Indonesia that was achieved in 1945 did not reflect a final decision on Indonesia's form of state.[38] These demands reached their apex in the general session of the Majelis Permusyawaratan Rakyat (MPR, People's Consultative Assembly of Indonesia) in 2002 when aspirations to include sharia provisions into the Constitution of Indonesia were declared, but rejected by the MPR.[39] The MPR rejection of the Jakarta Charter can be called the second consensus of the Indonesian people, after the first consensus in 1945, to protect Indonesia's form of state from being transformed into a sharia-based state. Despite this rejection by a majority of the MPR in 2002, the struggle to embed sharia into the state system of Indonesia remains alive and may well manifest itself with different strategies in the near future.

Those advocating a sharia-based state seek to adopt at least two paths to implement sharia in the legal and public sphere of Indonesia: firstly, a legal strategy promoting the inclusion of sharia through existing regulations and secondly, a cultural strategy supporting shariatisation through the mechanisms of the public sphere. With respect to the first strategy, legislation such as State Law No 44/2008 on Pornography, State Law No. 21/2008 on Sharia Banking, and government rulings on halalisation are clear examples. As further evidence, we

37 In Arabic "*al-ḍarūrā tubīḥ al-maḥẓūrā*," literally means a state of emergency can abolish prohibitions. This Islamic legal maxim is often used by Muslim politicians to justify their agenda. In 2001 when Abdurahman Wahid was being impeached by an extraordinary meeting of the general people's assembly of Indonesia, this principle was used to support the presidency of Megawati whom ideological Muslim groups had previously rejected as a presidential candidate in the 1999 general elections.

38 Rachman and Shofan, *Argumen Islam Untuk Sekularisme*, p. 128.

39 Greg Fealy, "Islamisation and Politics in Southeast Asia: The Contrasting Case of Malaysia and Indonesia," in *Islam in World Politics*, ed. Nelly Lahoud and Anthony H Johns (London: Routledge, 2005), 152–69, p. 164; Salim, "Zakat Administration in Politics of Indonesian New Order", p. 186; Hosen, *Shari'a & Constitutional Reform in Indonesia*, p. 94.

can see examples of local governments legislating local sharia bylaws, as in the cases of Aceh, Bulukumba in South Sulawesi, and Cianjur in West Java, elaborated in Chapter 6. This strategy utilises the legal window that opened with the enactment of State Law No. 32/2004 on the regional autonomy (decentralisation) of Indonesia, authorising regional governments to issue their own local regulations or bylaws. Since the reform era, MUI has published fatwas and recommendations that support sharia bylaws. In addition, the propagators of sharia bylaws also use MUI fatwas as theological underpinnings. It can thus be seen that positioning Islam as the ideological foundation of a state does not always take place through promoting the establishment of an Islamic state, but can be transformed into the legal discourse and practice of a nation-state system.

With respect to supporting shariatisation through the mechanisms of the public sphere, Islamist groups, such as HTI, FUI, MMI and JAT have difficulty in achieving public consensus. These groups have declared Pancasila to be a *ṭāghūt* (idolatrous) system.[40] Abu Jibril, from the MMI sharia advisory board, states that those Indonesians who follow Pancasila will go to hell.[41] When the bill on mass organisation was discussed by the Indonesian public over the last five years, HTI spokesperson Ismail Yusanto rejected Pancasila as the *asas tunggal* (sole principle) of the state, as had previously been accepted. This diverse discourse can nowadays be easily found in the public sphere of Indonesia. The political openness of the reform era is one of the root causes that has led to this radicalisation by Islamist movements.

MUI appears to play a key role here. In one sense, the Council stands at a crossroads; on one hand it supports the current Indonesian form of state and ideology, but on the other hand it also supports the aspiration of the above-mentioned Islamist organisations to increase the role of sharia in the legal and public spheres of Indonesia. MUI accepts Pancasila as the state ideology, but not of its own organisation, which since 2000 has upheld Islam as its core ideology. MUI accepts that the Unitary State of the Indonesian Republic is the ultimate form of the Indonesian state and that all Muslim citizens should defend this form.[42] It argues that the harmonisation of *agama* (religion)

40 These Islamic organisations are very active in promoting anti-Pancasila sentiment to the Muslim people of Indonesia. HTI has been banned in Indonesia since 2017.

41 "Abu Jibril: Yang Ikut Pancasila Akan Binasa," *Voa Islam*, 8 June 2011, http://www.voa-islam.com/read/upclose/2011/06/08/15186/abu-jibril-yang-ikut-pancasila-akan-binasa/;#sthash.fV3ClAWb.dpbs viewed on 22 July 2022.

42 MUI, *Himpunan Fatwa MUI Sejak 1975* (Jakarta: Erlangga, 2011), p. 834.

and *kebangsaan* (nationhood) are required.[43] MUI states that religion must be the primary inspiration and guidance when it comes to managing the country, meaning the supremacy of the majority religion—namely Islam and/or mainstream Islam—must be considered within the framework of the Indonesian nation-state. It follows that the establishment of an Islamic state is not a priority for MUI because shariatisation can be implemented within the existing ideology of Indonesia.[44] This is what MUI actually wants to implement for its shariatisation project: positioned as a civil society organisation, yet having real influence and power in the politics of Indonesia, especially in the politics of law-making, it thus occupies a key bargaining position in the state.

2.4 The Institutionalisation of the Ulama

As mentioned in the previous section, the men of Islamic learning, or ulama, have long played an important role in the Islamisation of Indonesia. The institutionalisation of the ulama did not just arise from the creation of MUI in 1975, but dates back to the early presence of Islam in the archipelago. In the historical past of the Muslim world, in the Umayyad (661–749 CE) and the ʿAbbāsid (749–1258 CE) eras, both these Muslim dynasties already had a body of ulama incorporated into their power structure.[45] In general, the establishment of an ulama institution is not only related to efforts to enhance Islamic learning but is also in the interest of rulers, helping sustain and maintain the power of the state over the people.[46] In the general Islamic tradition, the ulama play various roles from social, cultural and theological to political. In the context of political Islam, the ulama are often institutionalised in a body that supports the state, both in the judiciary and justice system and as a religious advisory board.

43 Ibid, p. 386.

44 The phenomenon of sharia bylaws in some local governments will be discussed in Chapter 5.

45 Nikki R. Kiddie, *Scholars, Saints, and Sufis: Muslim Religious Institutions in the Middle East Since 1500* (Berkley, Los Angeles & London: University of California Press, 1972), p. 2. Muhammad Qasim Zaman, "The Ulama and Contestations on Religious Authority," in *Islam and Modernity: Key Issues and Debates* (Edinburgh: Edinburgh University Press, 2009), 206–36.

46 Zouhir Ghazzal, "The 'Ulama': Status and Function," in *A Companion to the History of Middle East*, ed. Youssef M Choueiri (Victoria: Blackwell Publishing, 2005), 71–86, p. 71.

Indeed, the ulama's function, which is closer to a social and cultural entity, can indeed be transformed to become a corporatist body of the state. The solid observance of this model of institutionalisation is, for instance, evident from the position of the *vilayat al-faqeh* (a guardianship of the jurists) system in modern Iran since 1979.[47]

The institutionalisation of the ulama within the context of the Malay peninsula can be observed in the early nineteenth century, from the establishment of a *shaykh al-Islām* (the grand scholar of Islam), *muftī* (juridical advisor) or *hakim* (Indonesian expression for judge) in some court towns and ports of the Malay *negeri* (state system).[48] The *shaykh al-Islām* and *muftī* acted as judges in the sharia courts, especially concerning matters of the personal law of the Muslim people, while the *hakim* was in charge of the criminal courts in which the sharia and customary law were enforced.[49] In the 1970s, the Majlis Kebangsaan Bagi Hal Ehwal Ugama Islam (National Council for Islamic Affairs) was formed in Malaysia. This Council was responsible for the unification of a substantial body of existing statutory Islamic law throughout the Malay state, as well as national policies on religious education, the management of Islamic alms, and determination of a uniform date for the beginning and end of the fasting month. Although, theoretically speaking, the Majlis Kebangsaan was an advisory body, in practical terms it had huge influence on the political policy of Malay *negeri*.[50]

In the context of the pre-modern state of Indonesia, the ulama, mostly in the Islamic sultanates, also played a role as religious advisors and mentors on Islam for Muslim rulers or sultans,[51] as for example in the Acehnese sultanates. The terms *shaykh al-Islām*[52] and *muftī* mentioned in the *Hikayat Aceh* ("The Tale of Aceh") and *Bustan al-Salatin* ("The Garden of Kings") refer to a person

47 John L. Esposito, "Contemporary Islam: Reformation or Revolution?," in *The Oxford History of Islam* (Oxford & New York: Oxford University Press, 1999), 643–90, p. 664.

48 William R. Roff, "The Institutionalisation of Islam in the Malay Peninsula: Some Problems for the Historian," in *Profiles of Malay Culture: Historiography, Religion and Politics* (Jakarta: Ministry of Education and Culture, 1976), 66–73, p. 86.

49 Ibid, p. 87.

50 Ibid, p. 67; Syafiq Hasyim, "Religious Pluralism Revisited: Discursive Patterns of the Ulama Fatwa in Indonesia and Malaysia," *Studia Islamika* 26, no. 3 (2019): 475–509.

51 Amirul Hadi, *Islam and State in Sumatra: A Study of Seventeenth Century Aceh* (Leiden: Brill, 2004), p. 108.

52 The title *shaykh al-islām* was used to refer to Syamsuddin al-Sumatrani (d. 1630), Nuruddin al-Raniri (d. 1658) and ʿAbdul Rauf al-Singkili (d. 1693). Syamsuddin al-Sumatrani was a religious instructor to Sultan Iskandar Muda, who ruled Aceh in the seventh century; see Amirul Hadi, *Islam and State in Sumatra: A Study of Seventeenth Century Aceh* (Leiden: Brill, 2004), pp. 149–150; Peter Riddell, *Islam and the Malay-Indonesian World: Transmission and Responses* (London: C. Hurst & Co. Publishers, 2001), pp. 110–112.

or group of Muslim scholars advising and mentoring the sultan, as well as writing on Islamic issues in response to requests, serving the interests of the sultan.[53] An advisory body of Muslim scholars could also be found in the Javanese Islamic kingdoms. The Sultan of Demak, Raden Patah (1500–1518), bestowed a special position on the *wali songo* or nine saints as his Islamic advisors.[54] Following a different model, the position of Islamic clerics in the state was also maintained under the Dutch. A union of Muslim scholars in the Indonesian archipelago (*Nusantara*) was desired by both by the Muslim community and the Dutch colonial administration. An ulama advisory body was established, tasked with offering inputs and suggestions on matters concerning the Muslim community and Islam. Sayyid Usman (b. 1822) was, for instance, an advisor on Arab affairs for the Dutch colonial administration in 1889.[55]

In the post-colonial era of Indonesia, the ulama remained an important group under the first President of Indonesia Sukarno (d. 1970), who offered a special place for a group of Muslim scholars from NU[56] in his political alliance.[57] He also established the Majelis Ulama Jawa Barat (Ulama Council of West Java) on 12 July 1958 to ward off the threat of Islamic rebellion from

53 Riddell, *Islam and the Malay-Indonesian World: Transmission and Responses*, 2001, p. 160.

54 John Renard, *Tales of God's Friends: Islamic Hagiography in Translation* (California: University of California Press, 2009), pp. 354–8.

55 Azyumardi Azra, "A Hadhrami Religious Scholar in Indonesia: Sayyid 'Uthman," in *Hadhrami Traders, Scholars and Statesmen in the Indian Ocean, 1750s to 1960s*, ed. Ulrike Freitag and William Clarence-Smith (Leiden: Brill, n.d.), pp. 249–263; Peter Riddell, *Islam and the Malay-Indonesian World: Transmission and Responses* (London: C. Hurst & Co. Publishers, 2001), 202. As mentioned in *al-Manār* (an Islamic magazine published by Muhammad 'Abdu and Rashīd Riḍā), an Indonesian person with the initials M.M. asked Rashīd Riḍā about the treatise by Usman titled *Jam'un al-Nafā'is*. M.M. feared this treatise would impede education reform in Batavia because it had been deliberately written by Usman to criticise the Western model of education and organisation which had been adopted in that era. Quoting from the *ḥadīth* narration of Ibn Ḥajr (d. 1449), *man tashabbaha bi qawmin fa hūwa minhum*, meaning whosoever imitates a group becomes part of that group, Usman issued a fatwa prohibiting this imitation. Riḍā responded to M.M. by saying that Usman was not a qualified person of learning able to interpret the *ḥadīth*.

56 Nahdlatul Ulama (NU) was founded in 1926 by Hasyim Asy'ari (d. 1947), Wahab Hasbullah (d. 1971), and other respected traditional ulama in East Java. It is the largest Islamic organisation in Indonesia, and possibly the world, with more than 50 million followers. In the era of Sukarno, when NU was a political party, it had a patron-client relationship with Sukarno Greg Fealy, "Divided Majority, Limit of Indonesian Political Islam," in *Islam and Political Legitimacy*, ed. Shahram Akbarzadeh and Abdullah Saeed (London & New York: Routledge, 2003), 150–68.

57 Muhammad Atho Mudzhar, *Fatwa of the Council of Indonesian Ulama: A Study of Islamic Legal Thought in Indonesia 1975–1988* (Jakarta: INIS, 1993), p. 45.

Darul Islam.[58] Finally, he founded the Majelis Ulama Nasional (Council of National Ulama) in 1962 in Jakarta.[59]

2.5 The Genesis of MUI

A more focused attempt to establish an ulama council began in the Suharto era. Suharto became president in 1967 and sponsored the creation of MUI in 1975; his support was extended after a number of Indonesian Muslim scholars organised the conference known as Mewujudkan Kesatuan Amaliah Sosial Umat Islam dalam Masyarakat dan Partisipasi Alim Ulama dalam Pembangunan Nasional (Achieving the Unification of Muslim Social Duty and the Ulama's Participation in National Development), held by the Pusat Dakwah Islam Indonesia (PDII, Indonesian Centre for Islamic Propagation) on 30 September–4 October 1970.[60] The organisation held a workshop for Indonesian Muslim preachers on 26–29 November 1974, which issued the following joint statement:

> [I]n order to sustain and build the continuity of Muslim participation in national development, the establishment of an ulama council or something similar is needed so the forum that can implement its function (mechanism) effectively and efficiently. The set-up of this mechanism or forum is up to each region, each considering their respective situations

58 *Darul Islam* was an Islamist movement that aimed to establish an Islamic state in Indonesia. DI was led by Kartosuwiryo (1905–1965) and had waged a large rebellion against the state in the late 1940s in West Java. It still has resonance today with Islamist movements in Indonesia. Amelia Fauzi, "Darul Islam Movement (DI), Struggling for an Islamic State of Indonesia," in *Southeast Asia, Historical Encyclopedia, From Angkor Wat to East Timor* (Santa Barbara, CA: ABC-CLIO, 2005), pp. 401–2; Chiara Formichi, *Islam and the Making of the Nation: Kartosuwiryo and Political Islam in Twentieth-Century Indonesia* (Leiden: KITLV Press, 2012); Howard M. Federspiel, *Persatuan Islam: Islamic Reform in Twentieth Century Indonesia* (Singapore: Equinox Publishing, 2009), pp. 189–192; George McTurman Kahin, *Nationalism and Revolution in Indonesia* (Ithaca: SEAP Publications, 2003), pp. 326–331.

59 Wahiduddin Adams, *Pola Penyerapan Fatwa Majelis Ulama Indonesia (MUI) Dalam Peraturan Perundang-Undangan 1975–1997* (Jakarta: Departemen Agama, 2004), p. 109; Deliar Noer, *Administrasi Islam Di Indonesia* (Jakarta: Rajawali, 1998), p. 123; Mudzhar, *Fatwa of the Council of Indonesian Ulama*, p. 47.

60 Pusat Dakwah Islam Indonesia was set up by the Ministry of Religious Affairs on 4 September 1969, see MUI, *15 Tahun Majelis Ulama Indonesia*, ed. H.S. Prodjokusumo (Jakarta: Sekretariat Majelis Ulama Indonesia, 1990), pp. 45–46.

> and conditions and also consensus between ulama and the ruling government.[61]

This mission gained political endorsement from Suharto. In his speech at the workshop he stated:

> [B]uilding community is impossible without harmony and unity. A divided society would not be able to undertake development, especially when the religious community is not solid. On the basis of this, in order to gather together the society of religions to support the rapid and smooth process of national development, I call for a forum (*wadah*) to be established through which ulama and religious leaders or the representatives of existing religious organisations such as MUI, Majelis Ulama Indonesia, the Council of Indonesian Ulama, MAWI, Majelis Agung Waligereja Indonesia, Indonesian Council of Bishops, PGI, Persekutuan Gereja-Gereja Indonesia, Communion of Churches in Indonesia, SKP, Sekretariat Kerjasama Kepercayaan, Secretariat for Cooperation on Beliefs, and many others can sit together, consult and build a joint network in order to develop harmony, mutual understanding and respect among different religious communities.[62]

On this occasion, Suharto advised that a national body of Indonesian ulama would be established, and restated his endorsement a second time when the PDII board members visited him on 24 May 1975.[63] Serious preparations were then made to facilitate MUI's inception. The Ministry of Home Affairs published an instruction to local governments to oversee the prior creation of ulama councils in their respective regions before the establishment of the council at the national level. At the same time, at the central government level, the Panitia Persiapan Musyawarah Nasional Majelis Ulama I (The Preparation Committee for National Congress of Ulama Council I), was established, led by Kafrawi Ridwan, a high state official of the Ministry of Religious Affairs.[64] The task of the preparation committee was to formulate topics and programmes that would be further discussed in the Musyawarah Nasional Majelis Ulama I (MUNAS Ulama I, or National Congress I). The agreed topics and programmes were then more widely discussed with various groups of

61 Ibid, pp. 45–46.
62 Ibid, pp. 45–56.
63 Ibid, p. 47.
64 Ibid.

Muslim scholars and organisations, and also with Suharto to gain his approval. On 1 July 1975, the Ministry of Religious Affairs published a decree appointing the Panitia Musyawarah Nasional Majelis Ulama Seluruh Indonesia I (Committee for the National Consultation Meeting of Indonesian Ulama Council I). The committee's advisory board consisted of Soedirman (the chair, a retired military general), Hamka (d. 1981), Abdullah Syafi'i (d. 1985)[65] and Syukri Ghozali (d. 1984).[66] There were two main objectives of this national consultancy. The first was to initiate the establishment of the Majelis Ulama Tingkat Pusat (National Ulama Council) after its establishment at the regional level. The second was to consolidate national safety and to improve religious harmony. Both of these objectives were presumed by the ruling regime to be a precondition for the success of Indonesian national development.[67]

In order to obtain public support for the establishment of MUI, a series of activities was conducted. On 13 July 1975, for instance, a meeting was held in the official residence of the Minister of Religious Affairs, Mukti Ali, intended as a forum for the sharing of ideas regarding the creation of the ulama council. The Minister of Home Affairs, Amirmachmud,[68] and many Muslim leaders attended this meeting. A press conference regarding the results of the meeting was held on 16 July 1975, attended by Hamka (from the National Committee Advisory Body), Mukti Ali (the Minister of Religious Affairs), and Mashuri (the Minister of Public Information).[69] In the press conference, Mukti Ali stated, "the task of Muslim scholars is not to build a bridge and highway, but to educate the mentality of people who will build this bridge and highway; the ulama are a group who know more about the aspirations of society."[70] He further emphasised, "the Council is not an operational organisation, it has no programme to build mosques or *madrasa* (schools) nor does it have any membership."[71] More specifically, Mashuri argued that the establishment of the Council was to protect Muslim society from the influence of communism. Meanwhile Hamka,

---

65 Abdullah Syafi'i was born in Batavia (the Dutch colonial name for Jakarta). He established the As-Syafi'iyyah Education Foundation in 1972, and was the MUI Chairman in the Hamka era (1975–1981) Herry Mohamad, *Tokoh-Tokoh Islam Yang Berpengaruh Abad 20* (Jakarta: Gema Insani Press, 2006), pp. 73–8.

66 MUI, *15 Tahun Majelis Ulama Indonesia*, p. 47; MUI, *20 Tahun Majelis Ulama Indonesia*, ed. H.S. Prodjokusumo (Jakarta: Sekretariat Majelis Ulama Indonesia, 1995), p. 13.

67 MUI, *15 Tahun Majelis Ulama Indonesia*, p. 47.

68 Amirmachmud was an important figure behind the success of Suharto's obtaining power in Indonesia. Amrimachmud, *H. Amirmachmud Menjawab* (Jakarta: Haji Masagung, 1987).

69 MUI, *15 Tahun Majelis Ulama Indonesia*, p. 48.

70 Ibid.

71 Ibid.

from his theological perspective, emphasised the importance of the Council's establishment for accommodating the interests of the Indonesian Muslim community. In short, with the presence of MUI, the relationship between the ulama and the rulers (*umarāʾ*) was improved.[72]

The National Ulama Congress I took place on 21–27 July 1975 in Wisma Sejahtera, Cipete, Jakarta[73] and its opening ceremony was conducted in the State Palace of Indonesia and attended by more than two hundred participants, most of whom were ulama, high state officials and the Muslim scholars of the Institut Agama Islam Negeri (State Institute for Islamic Studies, IAIN). There were many programmes and agendas discussed and debated during the six-day congress, and overall the event went well. The resource persons of the National Congress were also mostly high state officials like ministers and IAIN lecturers as well as ulama. Indonesian ministers who delivered speeches included Mukti Ali (d. 2004), the Minister of Religious Affairs; Amirmachmud (d. 1995), the Minister of Home Affairs; Maraden Panggabean (d. 2000), the Minister of Defence and Security; Widjojo Nitisastro (b. 1927), the Minister of Economy, Finance and Industry and Head of National Development Planning Agency; and Mashuri Saleh (d. 2001), the Minister of Public Information. Muslim scholars of the IAIN and Muslim organisations who presented papers included Hamka, Akib Suminto, Zarkowi Suyuti, Syukri Ghozali, Abdullah Syafi'i and many others.[74]

Suharto, in his speech at this congress, proposed some important points to frame his perspective of the ideal institutional role for MUI, such as its function as an Islamic body to command right and forbid wrong, a mediating agency to communicate thoughts and activities on the importance of national and regional development programme of Indonesia to Muslim society, and as a motivator, guide and mobilising agency for society in its self-development and future. Suharto also reminded MUI of its main task as a fatwa-provider for both the state apparatus and Muslim society. Hence Suharto advised that the membership of MUI should reflect the diversity of Muslim groups, that it should not get involved in politics, and that it had no direct membership from grassroots society and thus was not a threat to other earlier established Muslim organisations.[75]

72 Ibid.

73 The *Wisma Sejahtera*, a venue for the National Congress, is owned by the Department of Religious Affairs (MORA). This indicates the state's involvement in facilitating the establishment of MUI.

74 MUI, *15 Tahun Majelis Ulama Indonesia*, pp. 49–50.

75 Ibid, pp. 51–52.

MUI was officially established on 26 July 1975 as a forum of ulama and Muslim organisations in Indonesia. Politically speaking, this ulama forum was needed to unify and harmonise the diverse and divergent Muslim organisations into a *wadah tunggal* or single forum. The most appropriate form for the MUI, from the perspective of the ruling regime, was as an intermediary forum representing the ulama and Muslim organisations so they could have a bargaining position with the state. In this framework the forum must be able to unify and accommodate the various interests and agendas of Muslim scholars and organisations, particularly when dealing with issues related to the state.[76] As a forum, MUI was intended to become a clearinghouse for accommodating the aspirations and works of Muslim scholars and organisations. However, it is important to recall here that the term forum during the Suharto era did not refer to a democratic public sphere and people-based medium of association, but merely a state-driven forum. This is actually what Porter depicts as "a range of corporatist initiatives for the capture of target segments of the Muslim constituency, such as mosques, preachers, intellectuals, ulama and women's associations into non-party organisations."[77] MUI was established to provide "an alternative channel of state-Islamic interest intermediation and communication to that of the political parties."[78]

MUI was established to counter the ruling regime's discomfort with the presence of various Islamic organisations and associations as yet unrepresented by a representative body. This was perceived as a threat to the stability of the Suharto regime because their activities and programmes could not be controlled by or guided by the state. The Suharto regime was always on watch, observing the progress of every Muslim organisation and leader. It needed to detect the activities of Islamic organisations and leaders—for example the Islamic insurgences in some areas of Indonesia, such as the Darul Islam movements in West Java, Aceh and Sulawesi—which were inimical to the interests of state integration and security. In order to be well-equipped and prepared with accurate information for control, the creation of MUI as an ulama forum was crucial. Howard Federspiel commented that Suharto indicated that the establishment of MUI was aimed at serving as the chief point of contact with other religious Islamic organisations and leaders.[79] The Suharto government desperately wanted to gain the full support of Muslim organisations and leaders in

76 Ibid, p. 37.

77 Donald J. Porter, *Managing Politics and Islam in Indonesia* (London & New York: Routledge Curzon, 2004), p. 75.

78 Ibid, p. 77.

79 Howard M. Federspiel, *Indonesia in Transition: Muslim Intellectuals and National Development* (New York: Nova Science Publishers, 1998), pp. 90–117.

order to ensure the success of the national development plan. Muslim leaders and organisations with the full encouragement of the ruling regime finally established MUI in 1975, not only driven by religious factors but also by the political motivation of the ruling regime.

In Suharto's speech on 21 July 1975[80] it was mentioned that as a forum, MUI's task was chiefly to consolidate and coordinate the activities of other Muslim organisations rather than to implement its own programmes.[81] Suharto listed several functions for MUI, such as the promotion of ideas, values and the results of national and regional development to the people of Indonesia.[82] In this role, it was hoped MUI would motivate, direct and encourage communities to participate in national development and a better future of themselves. More concretely, Suharto invited the Council to provide advice on inter-religious issues and relations with the state.[83] Indeed, Suharto gained two benefits from this: firstly, MUI acted as a bumper for promoting the consensus of *pembangunan nasional* (national development) which often invoked criticism from Muslim leaders and organisations due to Suharto's authoritarian management of the state; and secondly, MUI became a specific means to impose Suharto's ideas and agendas on Muslim leaders. Nevertheless, the establishment of MUI had the potential to trigger tensions in the community, especially with established Muslim organisations such as Muhammadiyah and NU. In anticipation of this issue, since its inception, MUI was designed merely as a partner of these organisations and had no operational programmes and activities to work practically in the field of health, education, the economy and so on.

In general, Suharto was happy with the establishment of MUI. This can be inferred from Suharto's choice of Taman Mini Indonesia (TMI, Mini-Indonesia Theme Park,) as the venue for the closing ceremony of MUNAS I (National

80 Suharto said: "*hal lain lagi yang dapat diperankan oleh Majelis Ulama adalah menjadi penghubung antara Pemerintah dan Ulama*," meaning that another role that MUI could play was to become a mediator between the government and the ulama. See MUI, *20 Tahun Majelis Ulama Indonesia*, p. 19.

81 Muhammad Atho Mudzhar, *Fatwa of the Council of Indonesian Ulama: A Study of Islamic Legal Thought in Indonesia 1975–1988* (Jakarta: INIS, 1993), p. 54. Practical programmes such as running *pesantren* (traditional boarding schools), *madrasah* (Islamic schools), hospitals, universities, and other related activities had been undertaken by several established Islamic organisations such as Muhammadiyah and Nahdlatul Ulama prior to the creation of MUI.

82 In his speech, Suharto did not specifically address the Muslim community, but the broader community. This was one of the positive elements of Suharto's presidency. He wanted to act as a president for all the people of Indonesia regardless of religion, race, ethnicity and gender.

83 MUI, *20 Tahun Majelis Ulama Indonesia*, p. 19.

Ulama Congress I). This theme park was Suharto's pride and joy because the initiative to build it had come from his wife, popularly called Tien Suharto (her full name being Siti Suhartinah). Suharto was also satisfied because what he had delivered in MUNAS I had been accommodated within the MUI charter, signed by fifty-three ulama, twenty-six of whom were MUI provincial heads, ten individual representatives of national Islamic organisations such as Nahdlatul Ulama, Muhammadiyyah, Syarikat Islam (SI, Association of Islam), Perti, al-Washliyah, Mathla'ul Anwar, Gabungan Usaha Perbaikan Pendidikan Islam (GUPPI, Consortium for the Improvement of *Islamic Education*),[84] Dewan Masjid Indonesia (DMI, Indonesian Council of Mosques), al-Ittihadiyyah and representatives of the Islam and spiritual section of the Indonesian army, air-force, navy, police, and another thirteen ulama not affiliated with any Muslim organisations.[85]

The MUI charter begins with direct injunctions from the Qur'ān, Chapter 3 (Āli ʿImrān), verse 104: "Let there arise out of you a band of people inviting to all that is good, commanding what is right, and forbidding what is wrong: They are the ones to attain felicity,"[86] in addition to two of the Prophet Muhammad's

84 GUPPI was a branch organisation of Golkar established in 1952.

85 More details of their names and places of the origin and organisational background of those participants are as follows: 1. Rahmatullah Shiddiq (Jakarta), 2. A.K. Basuni (West Java), 3. Ismail Yakub (Central Java), 4. Prabuningrat, (Yogyakarta), 5. Maskoen (East Java), 6. Ali Hasjmy (Aceh), 7. Ismail Sulaiman (North Sumatra), 8. Mansour Dawoud Datuk Palimo Kayo (West Sumatra), 9. Said Abdurrahman (Riau), 10. Bafadhal (Jambi), 11. Yusuf Aziz (Bengkulu), 12. Masyhur Azhari (South Sumatra), 13. Soewarno Achmady (Lampung), 14. Moh. Ardani (Kalimantan Barat), 15. Imron Yusuf (Central Kalimantan), 16. Muchtarum (South Kalimantan), 17. Saberani (East Kalimantan), 18. Yoesoef Ontowiryo (North Sulawesi), 19. Muthalib Thohir (Central Sulawesi), 20. Baedhawie (Southeast Sulawesi), 21. Ali Mabham (South Sulawesi), 22. Soulisa (Maluku), 23. Abdul Mu'in Yasin (Papua), 24. Mahrus Umam (Bali), 25. Nuruddin (Nusa Tenggara Barat), 26. Badjideh (Nusa Tenggara Barat), 27. Moh. Dahlan (NU), 28. Basit Wahid (Muhammadiyah), 29. Syafii Wirakusumah (Syarikat Islam), 30. Nurhasan Ibnu Hajar (Perti) 31. Anas Tanjung (Al-Wasliyah), 32. Saleh Su'aidi (Mathla'ul Anwar), 33. Kudratulah (GUPPI), 34. Sukarsono (PTDI), 35. Hasyim Adnan (Dewan Masjid), 36. Zainal Arifin Abbas (Al-Ittihadiyah), 37. Suleiman (Dinas Rohani Islam Angkatan Darat), 38. Nawawi Rambe (Dinas Rohani Islam Angkatan Laut), 39. Djamhani (Dinas Rohani Islam Angkatan Udara), 40. Abdullah Usman (Dinas Rohani Islam Angkatan (POLRI), 41. Hamka (individual). 42. Kudratullah (individual), 43. Thohir Rohili (individual), 44. Syafari (individual), 45. Abdullah Syafii (individual), 46. Rusli Khalil (individual), 47. Abdul Aziz (individual), 48. Mukhtar Luthfi Elanshary (individual), 49. A.K. Basuni (individual), 50. Abdullah Udjong Rimba (individual), 51. Kasman Singodimedjo (individual), 52. Moh. Dahlan (individual), 53. Hasan Basri (individual). See MUI, *15 Tahun Majelis Ulama Indonesia*, pp. 55–56.

86 In Arabic text: "*wa l-takun minkum ummatan yadʿūna ilā al-khayri wa yaʾmurūna bi al-maʿrūf wa yanhawnaʿan al-munkari wa ulāʾika hum al-mufliḥūn.*" This verse is used

sayings, firstly: "The ulama are the heirs of the Prophet,"[87] and secondly: "There are two groups of people whose wellbeing determines the wellbeing of the rest of society: these are the Muslim scholars and the rulers."[88] The following sentence of the charter mentions that MUI was founded on the ideological bases of Pancasila and Article 29 (Verse 1) of the 1945 Indonesian Constitution, meaning that the ulama's role was to guide and educate the *umma* or Muslim community to increase their piety before God and to defend the security of the nation and finally to attack atheism.[89] The ulama's duty was to contribute to the success of Indonesian national development, based on the overall development guidelines.[90] The charter also mentioned the establishment of ulama groups during the Dutch and Japanese colonial eras and the inception of the Majelis Ulama Daerah (MUD, Council of Regional Ulama) in the early years of the Suharto regime throughout the Indonesian provinces as evidence for such ulama institutionalisation. On this basis, there was a need for the establishment of MUI, the nationwide union of ulama of Indonesia, with the objective to implement Islamic brotherhood in order to sustain national cohesion.[91]

It is also worth mentioning here that five of the ten items from Suharto's speech in the National Congress were absorbed into MUI's role for the 1975–1980 period. The first was to offer fatwa and advice related to the problems of Islam and Muslim society for the government of Indonesia and the Muslim community as a manifestation of the doctrine of commanding right and forbidding wrong in order to improve national security. Fatwa could only be issued at the request of the state or the Muslim community, meanwhile advice could be provided whether asked for or not.[92] The second was to strengthen the brotherhood of Islam and to implement harmony among believers for the sake of national unity. The third item was to play a role in representing the Muslim community in the forum of religious dialogue. The fourth was to act as an intermediary agency for ulama and the governing body (*umarāʾ*) and also as an interpreter for the government and Muslim community for the success of the national development programme. Fifthly, MUI was not to get involved

by Indonesian *muballigh* (preacher) as an argument to endorse the activity of Islamic propagation.

87 In Arabic text: *al-ʿulamāʾ waratha al-anbiyāʾ*.

88 In Arabic text: *ṣinfān min al-nās idhā ṣaluḥa ṣaluḥa al-nās wa idhā fasada fasada al-nās: al-ʿulamāʾ wa al-imāra*.

89 MUI, *15 Tahun Majelis Ulama Indonesia*, p. 15.

90 Ibid.

91 Ibid.

92 There were no fatwa requests to MUI from the non-Muslim community in the 1975–1980 period, although this was theoretically allowed in the tradition of Islamic jurisprudence.

in political practice and conduct operational programmes.[93] On the basis of the MUI responsibilities outlined above, it was evident that the ulama council should be primarily focused on playing the role of not only of issuing fatwa, but also of facilitating harmony and solidarity in support of the state agenda.

The Muslim community's response to the inception of MUI was divided into positive and negative camps. This was reflected in editorial reports published by Indonesian national newspapers. The national newspaper *Kompas*,[94] for instance, published opinions from Mahbub Djunaedi[95] and Ayib Bakar.[96] Djunaedi argued the importance of establishing MUI as an ulama organisation acting as an agency to connect the Muslim people of Indonesia and their ruling government. However, he said that MUI's credibility would be measured by their activities. Although viewing MUI in a positive light, Bakar reminded his readers that to preach to a community as ulama with only religious oratory skills was not enough. In addition, ulama should have personal piety.[97] The daily Indonesian newspaper *Pelita* reported that MUI's establishment should be viewed as an effective means of bringing religion to the people and stimulating the national development of Indonesia (7 August 1975).[98] *Tribun* magazine appreciated the way MUI was established, in that it was composed of figures from various Islamic backgrounds. The successful inclusion of all groups within one ulama organisation, said the *Tribun*, indicated a good start for this organisation. These comments appear to indicate that MUI had gained a good level of social acceptance.

Considering the undeniable state presence in the establishment of MUI from the early days and perhaps up to the present, it is not surprising that the organisation has been viewed as a pro-state ulama body. In fact, many people, not only non-Muslims but also Muslims, questioned the neutrality of this council. This public unease over the neutrality of MUI was captured

93 MUI, *15 Tahun Majelis Ulama Indonesia*, pp. 101–102. The term "operational program" was erased from the *Pedoman Dasar* of MUI on the occasion of Munas III in 1985, as a term open to ambivalent interpretations. See also MUI, *20 Tahun Majelis Ulama Indonesia*, p. 63.

94 *Kompas* is currently the largest daily newspaper in Indonesia.

95 Mahbud Djunaedi was born on 27 July 1933 and died in 1995 in Jakarta. He grew up in a NU family environment and studied at the Faculty of Law at the University of Indonesia. He one of the first journalists with a NU historical and cultural background. He was the Chairman of *Persatuan Wartawan Indonesia* (PWI: Indonesia Journalists' Association) and was also on the Central Board of NU.

96 His original name was Abubakar bin Hasan Sahab. He began work as a journalist in the 1970s, and died in 1991.

97 *Kompas*, 30 August 1975.

98 *Pelita* was a Golkar-sponsored newspaper that targeted Muslims as its main readers.

by Hamka, its first appointed general chairman. In an ambiguous statement, Hamka compared the position of MUI to a *kue bika*, an Indonesia cake, which is traditionally cooked in an earthenware pot or *belanga*. To cook *kue bika*, the *belanga* needs to be equally heated from the top and below. In the case of MUI, "heating from below" symbolises the aspirations of society while "heating from the above" symbolises pressure from the state. If MUI failed to accommodate both the aspirations of the Muslim community and the state, this would result in the *kue bika* becoming burnt and inedible, of no use for either the *umma* or the state. In Hamka's metaphor MUI's position was a dilemma.

Several MUI experts such as Atho Mudzhar, Porter, Hosen and Hasyim argue that MUI's dependence on the state is not a matter for doubt.[99] Its pro-regime proclivity, especially in the period from 1975–1998, before President Suharto was deposed, is strong evidence of this. This regime-friendly tendency meant that MUI's role in the Suharto era was viewed as more focused on the issuance of fatwa rather than responding critically to the unjust policies of the Suharto's regime. To some extent, this is a correct assumption, as during the Suharto regime almost all organisations—including MUI—suffered from state intervention. The assertion that MUI as an organisation lacked independent status or freedom from state intervention stems partly from its establishment as a state-led creation. It is true that the idea to establish the organisation came first from Suharto, and it was followed by serious efforts initiated by ministers under the Suharto administration to gain support from the Indonesian ulama and the leaders of Islamic organisations. Amirmachmud (1923–1995) used his authority as the Minister of Home Affairs to send special instruction letters to the governors of the twenty provinces[100] to establish councils of Muslim scholars at the provincial level and also to persuade existing leading Islamic organisation such as Muhammadiyah[101] and NU[102] to join.[103] Mohammad

99 Mudzhar, *Fatwa of the Council of Indonesian Ulama*; Wahiduddin Adams, *Pola Penyerapan Fatwa Majelis Ulama Indonesia* (MUI) *Dalam Peraturan Perundang-Undangan 1975–1997* (Jakarta: Departemen Agama, 2004); Nadirsyah Hosen, "Behind the Scenes: Fatwas of Majelis Ulama Indonesia," *Journal of Islamic Studies* 2, no. 15 (2004): 147–179; Syafiq Hasyim, "The Council of Indonesian Ulama (Majelis Ulama Indonesia, MUI) and Religious Freedom"; Donald J. Porter, *Managing Politics and Islam in Indonesia* (London & New York: Routledge Curzon, 2004).

100 Since the reform era from 1998 onwards, the number of Indonesia's provinces has increased to thirty-three.

101 Muhammadiyah was established in 1912. The founding father of this second largest Islamic organisation was Ahmad Dahlan from Yogyakarta.

102 NU was set up in 1926. The founding father of this largest Muslim organisation was Hasyim Asy'ari from Jombang, East Java.

103 Porter, *Managing Politics and Islam in Indonesia*, 2004, p. 77.

Dahlan and Mukti Ali (1923–2004), who were ministers of religious affairs during the Suharto era, approached religious leaders in order to gain support for the establishment of MUI. Looking at the MUI charter, state intervention in its creation is uncontestable as the charter was signed by high state officials. The charter's content also exhibits the limits of MUI's independence.

MUI's lack of independence derives from the embedded characteristics of this organisation since its inception. Some scholars consider the regular funding supply from the Anggaran Pendapatan dan Belanja Negara (APBN, State Revenue and Expenditure Budget) through the Ministry of Religious Affairs, for instance, to be reason enough to distrust its independence.[104] However, this also depends on the MUI leadership model. Hamka, as MUI general chairman, had the capability to manage the organisation in this ambiguous position. He helped MUI gain regular funding from the state but used this financial support not only to follow state interests in providing religious advice, recommendations and fatwas, but also for MUI's own interests and agenda. In addition, some of the fatwas produced under Hamka's leadership created problems for the ruling regime. This reached its peak with the MUI fatwa prohibiting Muslims from expressing Christmas greetings, which finally forced Hamka to step down from his leadership. Hamka used the establishment of MUI as a means to facilitate the emergence of a free public sphere for Muslim organisations and leaders to discuss and resolve the problem of their *umma*.

However, some groups of Indonesian ulama had plausible reasons for joining MUI. They viewed the establishment of the Council as being mostly based on the mutual interests of both parties—the state and ulama. MUI and the state could thus be viewed as being mutually dependent on one each other. MUI became a public sphere for interaction and negotiation between the state and ulama over the general interests of the *umma*. From this perspective MUI's establishment can be understood as providing space for the ulama to bargain with the state. To understand this, one has to trace the history of MUI's establishment, including the rejection of some Muslim scholars and Muslim leaders of this idea. When the Suharto regime proposed the foundation of MUI, Muslim scholars and clerics did not automatically accept this plan since they feared that the ruling regime would use it as a means to undermine and control the activities of the Indonesian Muslim community. This anxiety was natural, because the ruling regime was suspicious of Islamist movements at the time. However, these concerns were successfully overcome by Muslim religious leaders with ulama such as Hamka using the chance to push the agenda of the

---

104 Tim Lindsey, "Monopolising Islam? The Indonesian Ulama Council and State Regulation of the 'Islamic Economy,'" *Bulletin of Indonesian Economic Studies* 48, no. 2 (2012): 253–74.

umma in contrast to the official view of "*agama dengan bahaya laten tinggi*" (religion with a high latent potential for danger).[105] With MUI, the Indonesian Muslim scholars and clerics and Muslim organisations could negotiate what they wanted with the state.

If MUI were simply to be used as Suharto's political vehicle to hegemonise Muslim discourse, many Muslim scholars would not have accepted his proposal to establish it, but in fact there were many ulama who joined this organisation. There may have been other underlying factors that underpinned their acceptance, such as that which lay behind Hamka's acceptance of the position of MUI Chair. There were two main reasons to join the Council: firstly, MUI was seen as a vehicle to confront the communist ideology that was still pervasive in the 1970s, and secondly, to improve the relationship between Indonesian Muslims and the state.[106]

As a national organisation, MUI's authority stretches from the capital to the regions, and it has branches in almost all provinces, districts, and, in some cases, sub-districts of Indonesia. The MUI headquarters was called the Majelis Ulama Indonesia, while the MUI regional branches at the provincial level were called Majelis Ulama Daerah Tingkat I and at the district level Majelis Ulama Daerah Tingkat II.[107] This hierarchical structure continues to the present. Relations among these different levels of MUI do not follow a hierarchical model, but rather take the form of consultation. This means that the provincial and district MUI are structurally independent from the intervention of the national MUI in Jakarta, even though, to some degree, they are not free from the possible dictation of central MUI and local governmental policies when drawing up a fatwa. Prior to 1983, MUI at the provincial and district level could issue fatwas for their local government and societies. Consequently, Islamic legal edicts issued by the national MUI in Jakarta were different than those issued by MUI at the provincial and district levels. One example of this occurred when the provincial branch of MUI in West Java issued two fatwas. The first was to provide a justification for bank interest, which was intended to balance the inflation rate, and to declare that it did not qualify as prohibited interest (*ribā*). Under the second the MUI branch of West Java province

105 Discussed in *Perlunya Kesatuan Ulama dan Umara* ("The Importance of a Unified Ulama and Government"), a speech given by Alamsjah Ratu Perwiranegara, the Minister of Religious Affairs during Suharto's presidency, on the occasion of MUI's fifteenth anniversary in 1990. See MUI, *15 Tahun Majelis Ulama Indonesia*, p. 18.

106 Deliar Noer, *Administrasi Islam Di Indonesia* (Jakarta: Rajawali, 1998), p. 17; Rusydi Hamka, *Pribadi Dan Martabat Buya Prof. Dr. Hamka* (Jakarta: Pustaka Panjimas, 1981), p. 81.

107 MUI, *20 Tahun Majelis Ulama Indonesia*, p. 39. The Aceh branch of MUI is called Majelis Permusyawaratan Ulama (MPU, The Aceh Ulama Consultancy Body).

disallowed the marriage of pregnant women out of wedlock, even to the man who impregnated her. This legal opinion was based on the Ḥanbalī school of Islamic law, which differed from the majority of Indonesian Muslims who follow the Shāfiʿī school.[108] In 1983, the Central Board of MUI in Jakarta decided that the right to issue fatwas belonged to the national MUI. However, in recent MUI developments there has been a distribution of the authority to issue fatwas between the central and regional MUI.[109]

The MUI structural composition has changed from one period to another, in keeping with the changing social and political circumstances of Indonesia, and the problems and complexities with which MUI must deal. However, for thirty-three years from 1975 to 1998 the structure was relatively stable, and no significant organisational shifts took place. Perhaps the authoritarian characteristics of the Suharto regime influenced MUI's activity. MUI's national board over this period comprised three important bodies: The Dewan Pelindung (the Board of Trustees), the Dewan Pertimbangan (Advisory Board), and the Dewan Pimpinan (the Executive Board).[110] The task of the board of trustees was to give protection and guidance to MUI in the implementation of its programmes. The president of the Indonesian Republic, Suharto, was automatically appointed as the only member of the board of trustees for MUI Central, provincial governors served on the board of trustees for the MUI provincial branches, and mayors served on the board of trustees for the MUI district branches. The board of trustees held the highest position within MUI's structure because of its unlimited authority, including the authority to change the membership of the advisory and executive boards. This arrangement not only applied to MUI, but also to all social and mass-based organisations in Indonesia during the Suharto regime. The task of the MUI advisory board was to issue judgements, advice, guidance, and assistance to the executive board. The chair of the advisory board was the Minister for Religious Affairs for MUI Central and the Kepala Kantor Departemen Agama (Kakandepag, Head of Religious Affairs Office) for the provincial and district branches of MUI.[111] The executive board was responsible for implementing decisions executed in the official meetings and forums of MUI such as the Rapat Kerja Nasional (Rakernas, National Work Meeting), Musyawarah Kerja Nasional (Mukernas, National

108 Asrori S. Karni, Musthafa Helmy, and Ahmadie Thaha, *35 Tahun Majelis Ulama Indonesia* (Jakarta: Komisi Informasi dan Komunikasi Majelis Ulama Indonesia, 2010), p. 66.

109 Discussion of this issue will be further elaborated in Chapter 3.2 on the MUI Fatwa Commission.

110 MUI, *20 Tahun Majelis Ulama Indonesia*, 1995, p. 39.

111 Ibid, pp. 43–44.

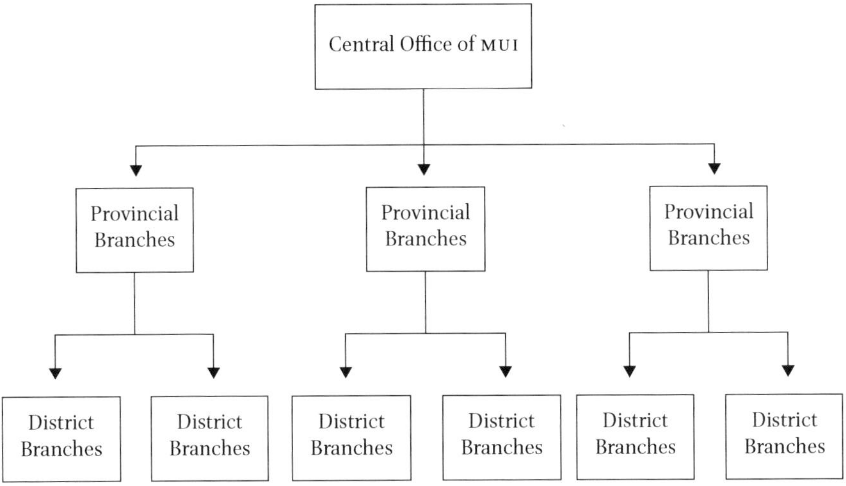

DIAGRAM 1 MUI's nationwide organisational structure
Note: Structure created from data found in MUI publications

Work Consultation) and many others.[112] It was comprised of the general chairman, chairpersons, general secretary and deputy secretaries, treasury and the representatives of the state, Muslim leaders, Muslim organisations and institutions, women and youth associations.[113] The presence of the state is clear at each level and within every important board in MUI's structure.

In its daily operations, MUI is directed by an acting executive board called the Dewan Pimpinan Harian (DPH, Acting Executive Board), which is responsible to the executive board of the Council. In the Suharto era, the DPH of MUI consisted of the general chairman, chairmen, secretary, and treasury and plenary members. The main tasks of the DPH were, first, to lead and implement the activities of MUI; second, to advise and receive proposals from the commissions; third, to initiate collaboration with the government of Indonesia and mutual consultation with other Islamic organisations and institutions in order to deliver guidance and protection to Muslim society; and fourth, to oversee materials and sources for the MUI Rakernas (national work-plan meeting). The leadership model of the daily acting executive leaders was a collegial, not an individual one, based on roles. In this system, all MUI decisions and policies had to be taken collegially through a complete meeting of the members of the daily executive directors. The general chairman has to execute his authority to

112 Ibid, p. 45.
113 Ibid.

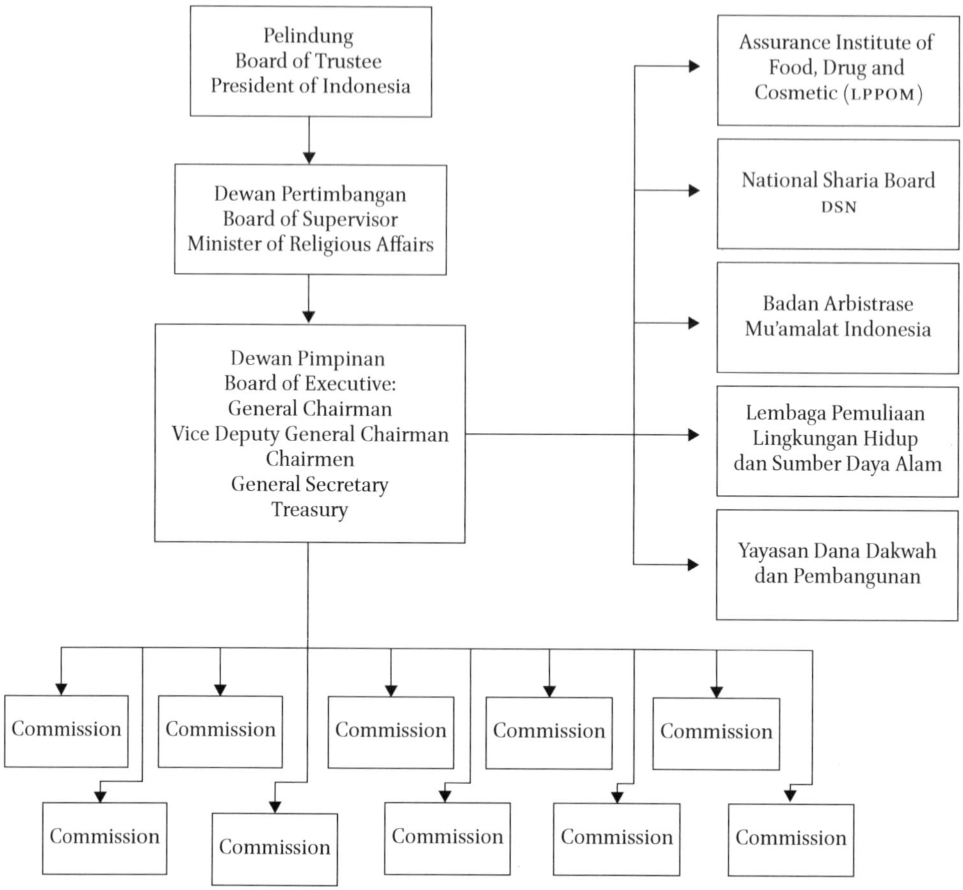

DIAGRAM 2 MUI board structure from 1975–2000
Note: Structure developed on the basis of data on the current MUI member board

decide MUI's policy together with other board members. The general chairman is appointed either through by direct election with a mandate by the provincial branches of MUI or by a special committee, the *formatur* team (with the special authority to select and appoint the leadership). The number of members of this selection committee usually differs from one term to another, depending on a consensus agreed in the National Congress. Considering its important role, being elected to a position on the *formatur* team is a matter for heated competition amongst MUI's functionaries with different ideological and organisational underpinnings. According to MUI regulations, all these positions have a five-year term and are reappointed during the National Congress Meeting or through an internal recall mechanism agreed by MUI.

In addition to the boards, the organisational structure of MUI is also equipped with commissions. The task of the commissions is to conduct analysis and discuss societal problems and the result of their discussions is then submitted to the MUI executive board to be used as basic considerations for making decisions and policy.[114] The number of commissions differs from one period to another. Under Hamka's leadership, MUI's organisational structure was simple, reflecting the needs of MUI as a newly established organisation. It had only five commissions; fatwa, Muslim brotherhood, religious harmony among believers, collaboration between ulama and the *umarāʾ* (the rulers), and general affairs.[115] The most active of the five was the Fatwa Commission.

Under Syukri Ghozali's leadership from 1980 to 1985, additional commissions were added. The new commissions established covered research and development, education and propagation, women's empowerment, and youth development. The number of commissions was increased to respond to the demands of national development.[116] Under Basri's leadership from 1985 to 1998, MUI had eight commissions: Commission I was responsible for strengthening Muslim brotherhood and building relations with other organisations (*Ukhuwah Islamiyah dan Hubungan Antar Organisasi*); Commission II was for Islamic propagation and development (*Dakwah dan Pembangunan*); Commission III was tasked with developing an inter-religious community and foreign relations; Commission IV was responsible for issuing and studying fatwas and law (*Fatwa dan Hukum*); Commission V was responsible for the education, culture and development of ulama; Commission VI was to conduct studies and research on religious issues; Commission VII was responsible for matters pertaining to the organisation; Commission VIII was given the task of dealing with special affairs.[117]

Given the above description, the history of MUI's establishment reveals the multi-faceted nature of the organisation based on a range of political, ideological and theological perspectives. From a political point of view, MUI's establishment was closely linked to both the vested interests of Suharto's agenda of protecting and sustaining his position as president and the interests of Muslim leaders and groups. Although the institutional development of MUI in the Suharto New Order seemed to be under the influence of the ruling regime, MUI always adapted to the changing issues and circumstances. MUI considered

114 MUI, *15 Tahun Majelis Ulama Indonesia*, p. 47.
115 Ibid, p. 125.
116 Ibid, p. 133.
117 Ibid, p. 47.

these developments and changed to remain relevant and significant to the state and also Muslim society. However, in the post-reform era, a significant MUI institutional change took place, which will be elaborated in section 2.7.

2.6 Leadership of MUI Senior Ulama

According to the convention of its member organisations, MUI should be led by credible and senior ulama in order to be respected by other Islamic organisations and the state. In the first five years of MUI, from 1975 to 1980, Hamka served as the first general chairman of MUI. Hamka was born on 17 February 1908 in Maninjau, West Sumatera, and was brought up in a devout Muslim family. His father, Haji Rasul, was acknowledged as an early Muslim reformist after returning from Mecca in 1906. Hamka himself studied Islam and the Arabic language in Sumatera Thawalib, Padang Panjang, West Sumatera. He began work as a teacher of Islamic subjects in 1927 in Perkebunan Tebing Tinggi (a plantation area), Medan, North Sumatera, and in 1929 moved to Padang Panjang, a small region in West Sumatra, to teach.[118] Hamka was active in Muhammadiyah from 1925, and in 1928 became head of the Muhammadiyah chapter in Padang Panjang. In 1953, he was appointed member of the advisory council of Muhammadiyah. Sukarno imprisoned him from 1964 to 1966 because of alleged pro-Malaysia tendencies, and he used this period to write *Tafsīr al-Azhar*.[119] He was recognised as a member of the ulama, a poet, the author of many books, and an editor for magazines.[120]

Hamka was appointed first general chairman of MUI because of his intellectual capability and acceptance by other Muslim scholars in Indonesia. Some speculated that his appointment was linked to his anti-communist sentiments. However, initially Hamka was advised by some of his closest friends not to accept the position as MUI general chairman.[121] At the time it was feared that MUI would only be a "rubber stamp" for Suharto's policies, which could possibly degrade Hamka's credibility as an independent Muslim scholar.[122] There was concern Hamka could lose respect by seemingly lending support to Suharto's regime, which was accused of being hostile to Islam. Hamka, however, finally

118 Karni et al., *35 Tahun Majelis Ulama Indonesia*, p. 58.

119 *Tafsīr al-Azhar* is voluminous exegesis of the Qur'ān, and the most complete work of its kind by an Indonesian scholar.

120 Karni et al., *35 Tahun Majelis Ulama Indonesia*, pp. 59–60.

121 C.W. Watson, *Of Self and Nation: Autobiography and the Representation of Modern Indonesia* (Honolulu: University of Hawaii Press, 2000), p. 113.

122 Ibid.

decided to accept the position of MUI general chairman. There were two reasons Hamka accepted this position. The first was to protect the Muslim community from the latent communist movement, which was perhaps a proxy argument because almost all communists had been killed and or imprisoned during the Suharto era. In order to maintain its power, the Suharto government continued to promote the idea of a continuing communist threat through various strategic means including by campaigning for the restoration of the PKI (the Partai Komunis Indonesia, the Indonesian Communist Party) as the national focus of Indonesian politics. In this case, both Hamka and Suharto's regime shared a common interest in considering communist groups as a threat to Islam and to Indonesia.[123] In the case of East Java, for instance, the war against communist groups was justified under the notion of *jihād* because they were the opponents of Islam.[124] In this regard Hamka can be seen as a natural ally of Suharto's regime. The second reason for Hamka's acceptance of the leadership role was to bridge the gap between the government of Indonesia and the Muslim community after the 1971 general elections and the legislation process of State Law No. 1/1974 on marriage.[125] MUI was a new mechanism for Muslims alongside Suharto's policy on the fusion of Islamic parties into the PPP.[126]

In the era of Hamka's leadership, MUI's function was firstly introduced and implemented by opening strong discussions with other established Muslim organisations, such as NU and Muhammadiyah, and with Muslim scholars and leaders. During this term MUI was perceived as a trusted Muslim organisation among the various groups of Muslim and also non-Muslim groups of Indonesia. This was the result of Hamka's leadership of MUI, and also because some MUI fatwas focused on Islamic jurisprudence and its relative independence from state intervention, political aspects that had not been so much considered in that era.[127] However, Suharto's regime did not trust Hamka completely and kept him in check through members of his own party, Golkar, such as Kafrawi Ridwan (b. 1932), who during Hamka's leadership was given the position of MUI general secretary. Ridwan was a senior official of the Ministry of Religious Affairs. This meant that MUI was led by two important figures with perhaps quite different social and political backgrounds: Hamka, who was seen as a

123 This was clearly stated by Hamka in his speech when he was elected as general chairman of MUI.

124 Robert Cribb, *Indonesian Killing of 1965–1966* (Melbourne: Centre of Southeast Asian Studies Monash University, 1990), p. 16.

125 Karni et al, *35 Tahun Majelis Ulama Indonesia*, pp. 52–53.

126 Vincent J. Houben, "Southeast Asia and Islam," *ANNALS, APPSS*, no. 588 (2003): 149–70.

127 Karni et al., *35 Tahun Majelis Ulama Indonesia*, p. 57.

courageous ulama with a Muhammadiyah background, and Ridwan, who was a member of Suharto's "arty," Golkar. In this context, the presence of Ridwan can be understood as a sort of balance to the leadership style of Hamka and epitomised the congruency of many social groups. Hamka resigned from MUI in 1981 because he held a difference of opinion from the Suharto regime reg"rding" the MUI fatwa prohibiting Muslims from expressing Christmas greetings.[128]

Hamka's efforts to pave the way for MUI as a forum for Indonesian ulama were continued by his successor, Syukri Ghozali. Ghozali was born in 1906 in Salatiga, Central Java. He had received a basic education in *madrasah* and *pesantren*.[129] He began his career as a teacher of Islamic subjects at an elementary Islamic school and then went to Malang to teach high school from 1932–1945. From 1944–1948, he was appointed as one of the deputy chairmen of the NU central board, responsible for education activities, and held a position as a senior official at the Ministry of Religious Affairs. He became prominent at the national level, when he was elected as chairman of the MUI Fatwa Commission in 1975 and then, from 1981–1984, as Hamka's successor as MUI general chairman.[130] His expertise was Islamic jurisprudence and Islamic legal theory,[131] and he also wrote columns in national magazines answering questions from readers regarding Islamic issues.[132]

In his inaugural speech following his election as the general chairman of MUI, Ghozali reasserted the Council's role by stressing that it was not owned by any individual group, such as the ulama, but belonged to all the Muslims of Indonesia. On this occasion, he also recognised the support of the Indonesian government from the centre down to regional levels.[133] During his leadership, Ghozali continued some of Hamka's initiatives, and added his own to establish a new agenda for MUI. Most importantly, revisions aimed at completing the basic statutes of MUI (Indonesian: *Pedoman Dasar dan Pedoman Rumah Tangga*) were conducted during this era.[134] Furthermore, in 1982 MUI's

128 C.W. Watson, *Of Self and Nation: Autobiography and the Representation of Modern Indonesia* (Honolulu: University of Hawaii Press, 2000), p. 113.

129 Further accounts of the history of *madrasah* and *pesantren* can be seen Steenbrink, "Indian Teachers and Their Indonesian Pupils."

130 Mudzhar, *Fatwa of the Council of Indonesian Ulama*, p. 56; Masdar F. Mas'udi and Syafiq Hasyim, "KH. Syukri Ghozali: Arsitek Majelis Ulama Indonesia," in *Tokoh Dan Pemimpin Agama: Biografi Sosial Intelektual*, ed. Saiful Umam and Azyumardi Azra (Jakarta: PPIM, 1998), pp. 33–70.

131 Karni et al., *35 Tahun Majelis Ulama Indonesia*, p. 64.

132 Ibid.

133 Ibid, p. 61.

134 Ibid, p. 66.

provincial chapters were first invited to participate in the National Work Meeting. Ghozali also intensified MUI's function to heighten the spirit of brotherhood between Indonesian Muslims. This was considered important due to the high rivalry among Islamic organisations in Indonesia.

During Ghozali's era, MUI played a moderate role as partner of the ruling regime, while also being the ulama forum responsible for protecting the religiosity of Muslim societies against a background of New Order anti-Muslim policies. Some fatwas issued by MUI were inclined to support Suharto's policies and interests, but, at the same time, the Council was also able to persuade the government of Indonesia not to stereotype Indonesian Muslims. For instance, MUI was quite successful in preventing the government from referring to the hijackers of a Garuda DC 9 aeroplane on 28 March 1981 as *komando jihad* (jihad command), i.e an Islamic terrorist group.[135] In Ghozali's period, MUI's fatwas were centralised, which resulted in the strengthening of the function of MUI as an ulama forum.[136] Syukri Ghozali passed away in 1984 and Hasan Basri was appointed as his successor as MUI general chairman at the third National MUI Congress or MUNAS III in July 1985.

Basri was born on 20 August 1920 in Banjarmasin, South Kalimantan. Unlike his predecessors, who had received special education from traditional Islamic institutions, he obtained most of his education from Muhammadiyah schools, which are more modern using a structured classroom and learning system combining secular and Islamic subjects of studies. Because of this, his knowledge of Islam was related more to general issues of faith.[137] Although Basri can more appropriately be referred to as one of the *zuʿamāʾ* (Muslim leaders) rather than a Muslim scholar, he was highly respected among Indonesian ulama for his calmness and ability to reach compromises between the diverse Islamic organisations of Indonesia. Basri's leadership of MUI did not differ greatly from his predecessor, Ghozali, especially in sustaining a harmonious relation with the state. Like Ghozali, Basri had a good relationship with the ruling regime, which was good capital for him to work closely with other Muslim organisations. In short, Basri's MUI chairmanship was regarded as successful in solidifying social acceptance of the Council and also maintaining a good relationship with the government and other established Muslim organisations.[138] There was almost no ulama and organisation representation

135 MUI, *Majelis Ulama, Ummat Dan Pembangunan*, p. 269.

136 Karni et al, *35 Tahun Majelis Ulama Indonesia*, p. 66.

137 Mudzhar, *Fatwa of the Council of Indonesian Ulama*, pp. 57–58; Karni et al, *35 Tahun Majelis Ulama Indonesia*, pp. 69–70.

138 Mudzhar, *Fatwa of the Council of Indonesian Ulama*, p. 58.

which was not accommodated within MUI's structure, although their numbers differed from one Muslim organisation to another. However, NU, the largest traditionalist Islamic group, for instance, was only given a small portion in MUI's board structure during the Suharto era, particularly when Basri was general chairman, perhaps because NU had been a political ally of the Sukarno regime. Suharto preferred not to include strong numbers of Sukarno's former allies as his main collaborators. In addition, since the 1970s, Suharto had taken the role of Minister of Religious Affairs in his cabinet out of NU hands,[139] a position that had long been given by Sukarno to NU incumbents. MUI followed this pattern in not including many NU leaders into the board structure of the Council because this would not be appreciated by Suharto. Thus, one could say that there was not much internal dispute among the Muslim organisation members of MUI because most of them held a similar compromise position to the Suharto regime.

Nevertheless, MUI's position as an ulama forum grew stronger under Basri's leadership (1985–1998). In this period, MUI did not merely play the role of a forum, but also tried to embrace the position of a strong representative for Muslim scholars and organisations throughout Indonesia. To this end, MUI led the development of Islamic discourse and practice in Indonesia. This could be seen, for instance, from frequent consultative meetings with Muslim scholars and organisations to discuss and solve important religious issues that had a wider impact on the Muslim community of Indonesia, such as determining the start and end of fasting month of Ramaḍān and dates of ʿEid al-Fiṭr and ʿEid al-Aḍḥā, which was handled by MUI with the facilitation of the Ministry of Religious Affairs. The ruling regime had, by this time, become more comfortable in accepting the standardisation of such Islamic practices by MUI. Basri's shortcoming was his failure to provide Suharto with the understanding that the interpretation of Islam was not monolithic, but diverse and different from one Muslim group to another and from one tradition to another. Basri's tendency to compromise with Suharto's ruling regime on this matter was one example of his failure to demonstrate MUI's independence. In this period, the function of MUI changed from being a limited forum of ulama to becoming a forum of Muslim leaders, technocrats and members of the state apparatus. This meant that the role of the ulama in this era was much broader than in the previous periods. The Forum Ukhuwah Islamiyah (FUI, the Islamic

139 Julie Chernov-Hwang, *Peaceful Islamist Mobilization in the Muslim World: What Went Right* (New York: Palgrave Macmillan, 2009), p. 50.

Brotherhood Forum)[140] was introduced during this term as an important vehicle to strengthen MUI's broader role.

MUI also extended itself to cover economic issues by establishing the Yayasan Dana Dakwah dan Pembangunan (YDDP, the Proselytising and Development Fund Foundation) in Jakarta on 29 January 1991. The foundation was established with three objectives: firstly, to collect and organise funding from as many sources as possible to achieve prosperity for the *umma*; secondly, to spiritually and materially support the implementation of MUI programmemes; and thirdly, to deliver guidance for Islamic propagation and mass-based organisations in exploring, developing and using their funding.[141] The foundation developed an early prototype for the establishment of the Bank Muamalat Indonesia (MUI, Muamalat Bank of Indonesia). Although the original idea for a sharia bank came from MUI, its establishment was implemented by Ikatan Cendekiawan Muslim Indonesia (ICMI, Association of Indonesian Muslim Intellectuals)[142] on 30 October 1991. However, proof of MUI's participation in BMI's development can be seen in the Piagam Pendirian Bank Muamalat Indonesia (BMI Establishment Charter), which was signed by the Minister of Religious Affairs as chairman of MUI advisory board, Basri as MUI general chairman, and Prodjokusumo as MUI general secretary.

Basri's chairmanship can be considered quite successful in promoting MUI's relationship with the state. This is evident from his achievement in serving as general chairman for three terms from 1984 to 1998.[143] During this period, there were many things that indicated the close relationship between MUI and the state as well as the Council's dependence. Many fatwas and recommendations were issued during this era, and a high number of these appeared to defend the interests of the ruling regime. This gave others sufficient reason to be suspicious of Basri's leadership. As a result, MUI in this era was not well-respected by many Muslims, and some even referred to MUI as the *"Majelis Ulama Istana"*

---

140 The *Forum Ukhuwah Islamiyah* of MUI is different from *Forum Umat Islam* which is established by a number of Islamic radical organisations as part of political Islam.

141 MUI, *20 Tahun Majelis Ulama Indonesia*, 1995, p. 252.

142 ICMI was founded on 30 December 1990, in Malang, East Java, by several Indonesian Muslim intellectuals. The first General Chairman of ICMI was Baharuddin Joesoef Habibie, who subsequently became president of Indonesia, 1998–1999. This organisation received full support from the Suharto regime because he wanted to shore up political support from the Muslim community. See Robert W. Hefner, *Civil Islam: Muslims and Democratization in Indonesia* (New Jersey: Princeton University Press, 2011), pp. 128–66; Daniel Dhakidae, *Cendekiawan Dan Kekuasaan Dalam Negara Orde Baru* (Jakarta: Gramedia, 2003), pp. 592–608.

143 Adams, *Pola Penyerapan Fatwa Majelis Ulama Indonesia (MUI) Dalam Peraturan Perundang-Undangan 1975–1997*, p. 139.

(Council of Palace Ulama).[144] Basri passed away during the third term of his leadership in November 1998, which was also the same year the reform era began in Indonesia.

2.7 The Reform Era: The Changing Role of MUI

A significant MUI shift emerged in the reform era that began in 1998. This shift can be viewed from two interconnected perspectives, the first being the general circumstances of Indonesian politics, and the second the internal situation of MUI, regarding both its elites and its institutional roles. With respect to the first perspective, the birth of the reform era in 1998 had an important impact on the organisation of MUI. Ali Yafie took over leadership of the organisation after the death of Hasan Basri. Yafie was born on 1 September 1926 in Donggala, Central Sulawesi. He studied religious sciences in the Madrasah As'adiyah in Sengkang, South Sulawesi, and concentrated on the study of Islamic jurisprudence and legal Islamic theory. His appointment was also due to his seniority among the other MUI board members and his role behind the resignation of Suharto, as explained below. In the transitional period after Suharto stepped down in 1998, MUI needed a strong ulama figure as its leader like Yafie. Before joining MUI, he was Deputy Chairman of the NU consultancy board (Syuriah NU) from 1991 to 1992. Yafie resigned from his position due to his disagreement with Abdurrahman Wahid (former general chairman of the NU executive body) over accepting donations from the SDSB (Yayasan Sumbangan Dana Sosial Berhadiah, the Indonesian state-sponsored lottery foundation) to fund NU organisational operations.

Although his leadership lasted only two years, Yafie served during the most difficult period for MUI, particularly in maintaining its relationship with the state, at a time of widespread social protests calling for Suharto to step down. Approaching his resignation on 18 May 1998, Suharto invited a number of prominent Muslim leaders to seek their support and advice on ways to deal with the protest movement against his presidency;[145] Yafie was one of those who attended. During the meeting, Yafie frankly advised Suharto to resign,

144 MUI, *Kumpulan Hasil-Hasil Kongres Umat Islam Indonesia, Umat Islam Menyongsong Era Indonesia Baru* (Jakarta: Dewan Pimpinan Majelis Ulama Indonesia, 1999), p. 43.

145 Other Muslim leaders invited were Abdurrahman Wahid (NU), Nurcholish Madjid (Paramadina Foundation), Emha Ainun Nadjib (artist), Malik Fajar (Muhammadiyah), Cholil Badawi (Muslimin Indonesia), Sutrisno Muhdam (Muhammadiyah), Ma'ruf Amin (NU), Ahmad Bagja (NU), and Yusril Ihza Mahendra. See Karni et al, *35 Tahun Majelis Ulama Indonesia*, p. 101.

telling him that the protestors and activists were seeking *reformasi* (reform), meaning his resignation from the national leadership.[146] Others present had not suspected that Yafie would advise this as Suharto had a good relationship with MUI. Nurcholish Madjid (Cak Nur) (d. 2005), the spokesperson of the group, passed on the statement to journalists, activists and also protestors outside the Palace of Suharto.[147] This was understood as a signal that the Muslim figures who had been invited to the meeting with Suharto supported the reform movement proposed by the students of Indonesia. Yafie's statement disappointed Probosutedjo, Suharto's younger brother and one of Indonesia's wealthiest people, who felt betrayed by MUI's stance.[148] Following this controversial meeting, Suharto finally resigned from his presidency.[149]

The onset of reform era also stimulated change in how MUI viewed the state. This was evident in Kongres Umat Islam Indonesia (KUII, the Indonesian Muslim Community Congress) on 3–7 November 1998 in Jakarta. The KUII was used by MUI and its stakeholders to reflect on their closeness to the ruling regime which was considered a weakness. Therefore, the first step to be undertaken after the fall of Suharto was to create a new image and position for MUI as a neutral and independent organisation that had distanced itself from the Suharto legacy. The KUII was the first attempt of MUI to revise and correct its previous stance through the revitalisation of sharia. The Congress recommended that Indonesian Muslim society must strive to have sharia included into one of the articles of the 1945 Basic Constitution and to remove Pancasila as the sole ideology of mass-based religious and social organisations in Indonesia. The KUII also published a memorandum appealing for Muslim voters not to elect non-Muslims as the president and vice president of Indonesia. This campaign was based on the argument that the majority of the population of Indonesia were Muslims, and therefore the Indonesian president should be a Muslim too.[150] Because Indonesia is not an Islamic state, the arguments

146 I had the chance to interview him about this issue at his private residence, *Bintaro Menteng Residence*, in South Jakarta, on 17 October 2010. Special thanks are due to Hilmi Ali, one of his sons, for accompanying me and arranging this very rare interview.

147 Ann Kull, *Piety and Politics* (Lund: Department of History and Anthropology of Religion Lund University, 2005). Nurcholish Madjid was a Muslim public intellectual who founded the Paramadina Foundation and University of Paramadina, Jakarta. He was famous for his idea on the need of Indonesia to adopt *tajdīd* (Islamic renewal).

148 Interview with Ali Yafie, Jakarta, 2010.

149 Ibid.

150 Muhammad Atho Mudzhar, "Prolog: Fatwa MUI Sebagai Obyek Kajian Hukum Islam Dan Sumber Sejarah Sosial," in *Fatwa Majelis Ulama Dalam Perspektif Hukum Dan Perundang-Undangan*, ed. Nahar Nahrawi et al. (Jakarta: Puslitbang Kehidupan Keagamaan Badan Litbang dan Diklat Kementerian Agama RI, 2012), xxv–xxxix xxxi; MUI, *Kumpulan*

raised by MUI were not purely theological, but rather sociological and political. MUI not only insisted on the Muslim leadership of Indonesia, but also rejected the idea of a woman president. Precluding women from becoming president, according to MUI, had a strong basis in sharia law, despite many other Muslim scholars outside the Council rejecting this legal opinion. This recommendation seemed to have an effective influence on the MPR (People's Consultative Assembly of Indonesia)[151] as it appointed Wahid, popularly known as Gus Dur, to the presidency, even though Megawati Soekarnoputri's party had emerged victorious in the 1999 general elections.[152]

Two other daring recommendations from the 1999 KUII were to remove *aliran kepercayaan* (indigenous beliefs) from the contents of Guidelines of National Development and to ban Islamic groups viewed as deviant such as the Ahmadiyah,[153] Inkar Sunnah (Sunnah rejectionist group)[154] and many others.[155] The last recommendation has been followed by the government of Indonesia in its rejection of the judicial review of State Law No. 01/PNPS/1965 on Religious Defamation and also the publication of the Joint Decree of Three

---

Hasil-Hasil Kongres Umat Islam Indonesia, Umat Islam Menyongsong Era Indonesia Baru, 1999, p. 14.

151 In the 1999 general elections, the Constitution of Indonesia provided the MPR with a mandate to elect the president. In this system, the leader of the political party that obtains the most votes does not automatically become president.

152 Wahid himself bore witness that a woman can become a national leader as agreed by NU on the occasion of its National Congress in Lombok, Province of Nusa Tenggara Barat, in 1997.

153 The Ahmadiyah or Jamaat Ahmadiyah (original Indonesian term used) is an Islamic organisation established in 1889 in India. The group, that follows the teaching of Mirza Ghulam Ahmad, has divided into two groups, Lahore and Qadian, in which the former recognises Mirza Ghulam Ahmad as a *mujaddid* (Islamic reformer) and the latter recognises him as a prophet after Muhammad. The Lahore Ahmadis arrived in Indonesia in 1924 through Yogyakarta and then spread out to other neighbouring cities such as Surakarta. Mathieu Guidère, *Historical Dictionary of Islamic Fundamentalism* (Maryland: Scarecrow Press, 2012), p. 22; Iskandar Zulkarnain, *Gerakan Ahmadiyah Di Indonesia*, vol. 8 (Yogyakarta: PT LKiS Pelangi Aksara, 2005), p. 142. The discussion on the MUI fatwa on the Ahmadiyah is elaborated in Chapter 6.

154 Inkar Sunnah is a group who believe the source of Islam is only the Qur'ān, not including the Sunna (tradition of the Prophet Muhammad). The historical establishment of this group is not clear due to its presence in other Muslim countries such as Malaysia. Intan, *Public Religion And the Pancasila-Based State of Indonesia: An Ethical And Sociological Analysis*, p. 109; Bambang Irawa Hafiludin, Derby Murti Nasution, and Zainal Arifin Aly, *Bahaya Islam Jama'ah, Lemkari, LDII: Pengakuan Mantan Gembong-Gembong LDII, Ust. Bambang Irawan Hafiluddin, Ust. Debby Murti Nasution, Ust. Zaenal Arifin Aly, Ust. Hasyim Rifa'in, Fatwa-Fatwa Ulama Dan Aneka Kasus LDII*. (Jakarta: Gema Insani, 1998). This group will also be discussed further in Chapter 6.

155 MUI, *Kumpulan Hasil-Hasil Kongres Umat Islam Indonesia, Umat Islam Menyongsong Era Indonesia Baru* (Jakarta: Dewan Pimpinan Majelis Ulama Indonesia, 1999).

Ministers—Home Affairs, Religious Affairs and Attorney General—limiting the activities of the Indonesian Ahmadiyah.

Another example of MUI's inclination towards political Islam during this era was the initiative of the Council to organise the event Amanah Umat Islam (The Mandate of Muslim Society). The programme, which was supported by forty Muslim organisations, was designed to focus on three important issues approaching the 1999 general elections. The first was to advise Muslim voters to use their electoral rights responsibly in accordance with the principles of citizenship and morality. The second was that Muslim voters should elect a political party that strove for the aspirations of the Islamic community and Indonesian reform. Thirdly, Muslim voters were advised not to elect political parties whose candidates did not strive for the aspirations and interests of the *umma*.[156] MUI in this term was thus developing a clear tendency to be more engaged in the politicisation of Islam.

The second important step was to benefit from the growing Islamist movement which was emerging during the transition to democracy in Indonesia. This resulted in MUI becoming one of the most important actors in these efforts. Radical Islamist groups of Indonesia viewed the position of the non-political Islam movement which had been followed by most Indonesian Muslims as being unable to accommodate their aspirations to transform the secular state of Indonesia to a sharia-based state. For Indonesian Muslims seeking a sharia-based state, political Islam provides a compatible strategy to achieve this goal through various means, including strategically inserting sharia provisions into Indonesian state law. Although political Islam was not realised in the form of an Islamic empire as in the past, the current phenomenon taking place in Indonesia aligns with the global trend of incorporating sharia into national state law, as visible in other Muslim countries.[157] Many Muslim countries have undergone the process of drafting and amending their state laws in accordance with sharia or so-called constitutional accommodation.[158] This tendency is not only seen in Islamic countries in the Middle East that use sharia as the legal foundation of the state,[159] but also in

156 Ibid.

157 Jan Michiel Otto, ed., *Sharia Incorporated: A Comparative Overview of the Legal Systems of Twelve Muslim Countries in Past and Present* (Amsterdam: Amsterdam University Press, 2010).

158 Clark B. Lombardi, *State Law as Islamic Law in Modern Egypt: The Incorporation of the Sharīʿa Into Egyptian Constitutional Law* (Leiden: Brill Academic Pub, 2006), p. 1; Hefner, "Indonesia: Shariʿa Politics and Democratic Transition," p. 292.

159 For a deeper elaboration on the inclusion of sharia into the state law in Egypt, see Lombardi and Bayat *State Law as Islamic Law in Modern Egypt: The Incorporation of the Sharīʿa into Egyptian Constitutional Law*; *Making Islam Democratic: Social Movements and the Post-Islamist Turn* (Stanford University Press, 2007).

the so-called peripheral Muslim countries, such as Indonesia, Malaysia, and other countries in Southeast and South Asia such as Pakistan and Bangladesh. The Islamisation of the state has become a global trend among Islamic countries throughout the world, from Morocco to Indonesia, and from Saudi Arabia, Pakistan, Egypt, and Kuwait to African Muslim countries.[160]

Although the position of MUI amongst civil society organisations and its non-partisan stance to political parties remained unchanged, it began to turn towards the establishment of sharia-based legal order in Indonesia after the resignation of Suharto. MUI's vision prior to the reform era was to achieve the establishment of a secure, peaceful, just and prosperous society based on Islam, within the framework of the Indonesian Pancasila state. This vision was aligned with the basic philosophy of the organisation at that time, namely Pancasila. Nevertheless, demands from the Muslim community and conservative groups in particular made MUI's role in the political Islam movement increasingly apparent in the public sphere. It was also in the 1998 KUII, for instance, that MUI pushed for the abolition of State Law No. 8/1985 on *Ormas* (*organisasi sosial masyarakat*, social mass and political organisations).[161] B.J. Habibie, the President of Indonesia (1998–1999) granted the abolition of this state law, which meant that MUI and other Muslim organisations could use Islam as their basic ideology, and also had the opportunity to express their Islamic political aspirations. MUI, along with other Islamic organisations, used this opportunity to consolidate its strength, including its political potential, to ensure the success of its objectives.

The National MUI Congress in 2000 decided on a new leadership, with Yafie replaced by Sahal Mahfudh. The new MUI general chairman was expected to bring forth a new image for MUI, as benefiting the Indonesian reform era. Mahfudh was born on 17 December 1937 in Pati and was from a traditional NU ulama family. He studied Islam in several *pesantren* in his hometown. He has a broad interest in Islamic sciences, but mostly focuses on Islamic jurisprudence and Islamic legal theory, and has written books in Arabic, which is very rare amongst Indonesian ulama.[162] His books include *Ḥariqa al-Ḥuṣūl fī Sharḥ Ghāya al-Wuṣūl* and *al-Thamra al-Ḥajaniyya*,[163] as well Indonesian-language books such as *Fiqih Sosial* ("Islamic Jurisprudence on Social Issues"). It seems

160 Noah Feldman, *The Fall and Rise of the Islamic State* (New Jersey: Princeton University Press, 2008); Otto, *Sharia Incorporated.*

161 MUI, *Kumpulan Hasil-Hasil Kongres Umat Islam Indonesia, Umat Islam Menyongsong Era Indonesia Baru*, 1999, p. 10.

162 Many Indonesian ulama write in the local language such as Sundanese, Javanese, or Malay, but using an Arabic script. This is referred to as *Arab Jawi*.

163 *Al-Thamra* means fruit, *al-Hajaniya* is adapted from Kajen, the name of a village in Central Java, where Sahal Mahfudh resides.

the spirit of organisational refinement became a focus for Mahfudh. There was an important change in MUI board structure, being composed now of only the advisory board and the executive board. The executive board has the right to appoint a *pimpinan harian* (acting executive director) of MUI. Most interestingly, senior state officials, who had previously sat on the board of trustees and the advisory board, no longer held these positions. This is an example of MUI's attempt to distance itself from the state. Within the MUI *wawasan* (outlook or *weltanschaung*)[164] formulated in the Mahfudh era, one aspect that MUI strengthens is *ḥurriyya* (freedom), meaning that in conducting its duty, MUI has to be independent from any intervention and influence from others in reaching its decisions and opinions, and must also empower oppressed groups (*mustaḍʿafīn*).[165,166]

While adjusting to the spirit of Indonesia's reform era since 2005, MUI has also tried to reformulate its new role. First, the Council seeks to play a prophetic role that strives to bring social life into line with Islamic teachings. Thus, theoretically speaking, MUI should also open itself up for criticism,

164 MUI's *weltanschaung* is an explanation of the vision, mission, orientation and role of MUI containing the following items: first, *dīniyya* (religiosity), which means that MUI's activities should be based on the values and teaching of Islam. In this way, Islam provides a comprehensive guidance for life. Second is *irshādiyya* (guiding) meaning MUI must attempt to encourage people to "command right and forbid wrong" (*al-amr bi al-maʿrūf wa al-nahyʿan al-munkar*). In a broad sense, all of MUI's activities are planned and intended for the purpose of Islamic propagation. Third, *istijābiyya* (positivity) means MUI must always provide a positive and responsive answer to questions and problems raised by Indonesian Muslim society. Fourth, the principle of *ḥurriyya* (freedom) means that in conducting its duty, MUI must be independent from any intervention and influence from others in reaching its decisions and opinions. Fifth, *taʿāwuniyya* (mutual assistance) means that MUI must conduct its work in the spirit of mutual assistance and help for the sake of goodness and piety in order to empower oppressed groups (*mustaḍʿafīn*). The basis value of this principle is Islamic brotherhood, and on the same basis MUI develops national brotherhood (*ukhuwwa waṭaniyya*) and the brotherhood of humanity (*ukhuwwa bashariyya*). The sixth item is consultancy: the tradition of consultation is promoted by MUI in order to reach a consensus. In this regard, MUI tries to act in a democratic, accommodative and responsive manner in order to respond to the aspirations of Muslim society. Seventh, tolerance (*tasāmuḥ*) mandates that MUI must promote moderation and tolerance in solving the problem of *khilāfiyya* (dissenting opinions) among the different schools of Islamic law. Eighth, the principle of leadership means that MUI, in all its activities, must provide a good model for Muslim society by promoting initiatives which are based on the public interest. Ninth, internationalism (*duwaliyya*) means that as member of the international community, MUI must actively participate in striving for peace and social order in the world in accordance with Islam. See MUI, *Pedoman Penyelenggaraan Organisasi Majelis Ulama Indonesia* (Jakarta: Sekretariat Majelis Ulama Indonesia, 2010), pp. 8–10.

165 Ibid.

166 Ibid.

especially when its proposals are seen as being in opposition to local traditions and culture. Second, MUI seeks to continue its role as a fatwa institution, regardless of whether its opinion is sought by either the state or society. However, in doing so, MUI seeks to accommodate the aspirations of the Muslim communities, which are plural in nature. Third, the Council seeks to provide guidance and services for Muslim society (*al-rāʿī wa khādim al-umma*). In this context, MUI should be prepared and willing to receive requests and also to lend support from and for the *umma*, especially related to fatwa and religious advice. Fourth, MUI seeks to become an institution that commands right and forbids wrong in the proper sense of Islam. The objective of this is to establish Muslim society as the best form of society (*khayr al-umma*) in the world. Fifth, MUI proclaims itself as a pioneer in undertaking renewal (*tajdīd*) of Islamic thought. However, the fatwa and recommendations issued by MUI seem to indicate a turn of the organisation in the direction of Islamic puritanism. Finally, MUI wants to play the role of peacemaker among conflicting groups within Indonesian Muslim communities. For instance, when two Muslim groups have a difference of opinion, MUI seeks to take on a role as a mediator. The method used by the Council in this case is compromise and adjustment (*al-jamʿ wa al-tawfīq*). If this fails, then MUI will decide the stronger opinion of the two (*tarjīḥ*). It is hoped with this that a sense of Muslim brotherhood will be maintained amongst members of the community.[167]

During this era MUI also increased the number and revitalised the function of commissions and institutions. It decided to have around eleven commissions and six autonomous institutions (*lembaga*) and bodies. The commissions are as follows: 1) Islamic brotherhood and organisational relations, (2) Islamic propagation and development, (3) education, social and culture affairs, (4) fatwa (legal opinion), (5) law and legislation, (6) study and research, (7) religious harmony, (8) economy, (9) women's rights, (10) foreign affairs, and (11) information and mass media.[168] The autonomous institutions are as follows: (1) LPPOM or Lembaga Pengkajian Pangan, Obat-obatan dan Kosmetika (Institute for Foods, Drugs and Cosmetics Assessment), (2) the DSN or Dewan Syariah Nasional (National Sharia Board), (3) Badan Arbitrase Nasional Syariah (National Agency of Sharia Arbitration), (4) Badan Penerbit MUI (MUI Publishing House), and (5) YDDP (Yayasan Dana Dakwah Pembangunan,

167 MUI, *Himpunan Keputusan Musyawarah Nasional VIII Majelis Ulama Indonesia* (Jakarta: Majelis Mujahidin Indonesia, 2010), pp. 65.

168 MUI, *Pedoman Penyelenggaraan Organisasi Majelis Ulama Indonesia* (Jakarta: Sekretariat Majelis Ulama Indonesia, 2010); Adams, *Pola Penyerapan Fatwa Majelis Ulama Indonesia (MUI) Dalam Peraturan Perundang-Undangan 1975–1997*, p. 115.

Dakwah Development Fund Foundation).[169] Besides these commissions and institutions, MUI has also set up special task forces on an ad hoc basis to deal with emergencies as they arise, such as Aliansi Masyarakat Anti Pornografi (AMAP, Anti-pornography Social Alliance), Tim Penanggulangan Terorisme (TPT, Counter Terrorism Team), Tim Pencari Fakta Kasus Maluku (TPFKM, Maluku Fact Finding Team) and many others.[170]

However, the state continues to have a presence within MUI through the APBN (State Budget) from which MUI receives 3 billion IDR (Indonesian Rupiah)—approximately 250,000 US dollars—in funding. Although this budget is not enough to cover all MUI expenditure, it is a much larger amount than that received by other Muslim organisations such as Muhammadiyah and NU. Ichwan Sam, the MUI general secretary, has stated that MUI needs to collect around 25 billion IDR (approximately two and a half million US dollars) per year to fund all its activities and programmes.[171] To cover the 22 billion IDR not provided from the APBN, MUI seeks funding support from state ministries, the Central Bank of Indonesia, national enterprises, LPPOM and the DSN. LPPOM alone contributes 20% of the total budget needed by MUI.[172] All these are in accordance with the internal MUI regulations that enable MUI to raise funds from other sources. So far, there are five MUI funding sources: irregular donations from the community; allocations from the central or regional governments; funding from MUI's partnership and collaboration with other groups, such as governmental and non-governmental organisations, both locally and internationally; fundraising efforts, for example through the establishment of foundations, or organising events and activities; and business sources, such as the revenue from MUI's shares in the sharia stock exchange market.[173] It is true that MUI has shares in the Indonesian Muamalat Bank, but this revenue is not significant.[174] However, it must be noted here that among these sources of funding for operational costs, the annual contribution from the state budget and LPPOM are the most regular and reliable. However, unlike during the Suharto era, funding from the state budget is not tied to strong domination by the ruling regime. In fact, many MUI fatwas and recommendations produced in the reform era contradict and challenge the interests of the state.

169 MUI, *Pedoman Penyelenggaraan Organisasi Majelis Ulama Indonesia*, pp. 51–2.

170 Ibid.

171 Interview with Ichwan Sam, Jakarta, 2010.

172 Interview with Zainut Tauhid, Jakarta, 2011.

173 MUI, *Pedoman Penyelenggaraan Organisasi Majelis Ulama Indonesia*, p. 48; Lindsey, "Monopolising Islam? The Indonesian Ulama Council and State Regulation of the 'Islamic Economy'".

174 Interview with Amidhan, Jakarta, 2011.

As a living organisation, MUI's structure will always change in accordance with environmental factors to maintain its relevance in the eyes of the state and the Muslim community. All of the institutional alterations undertaken by MUI have been in response to the impact of social changes during this period. Changes to its structural composition have made this organisation more able to implement its programmes and agendas, especially with regard to the Islamisation of Indonesia's state law. According to social movement organisation theory, organisations that can adjust their structure to meet the demands of their environment will be more successful than those that do not.[175] All the changes can be seen in the following diagram:

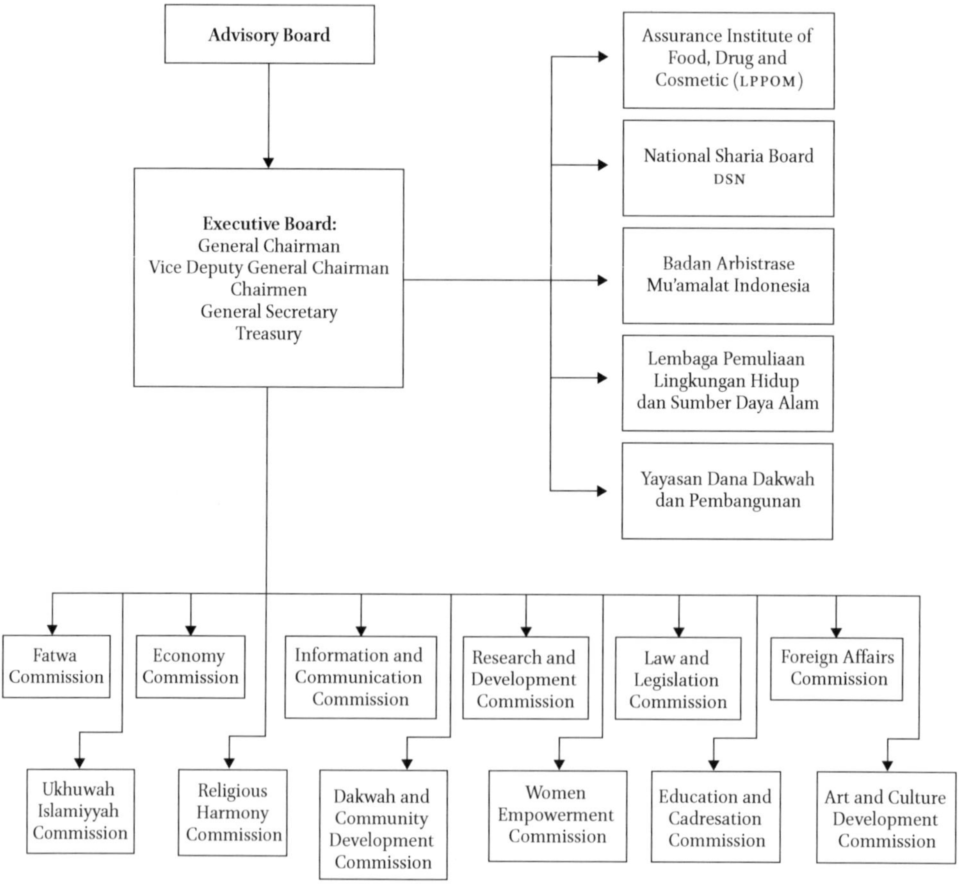

DIAGRAM 3 MUI's board-structure in the reform era

175 Doug McAdam and Richard Scott William, "Organization and Movements," in *Social Movements and Organization Theory*, ed. F. Davis Gerald, Doug McAdam, and Richard Scott William (Cambridge: Cambridge University Press, 2005), 4–40, p. 7.

2.8 Internal Dynamism

MUI is not a homogenous and static organisation. It contains not only those who have aspirations of sharia enforcement, but also those who believe that Indonesia is well positioned currently as a pluralistic and democratic country. This section portrays the various backgrounds of MUI activists and stakeholders, which reflects, to some extent, the dynamism of the Council. The reform era did not just enable the consolidation of MU's internal potential, but also stimulated more vigorous contestation among the different groups of Muslim scholars and organisations within MUI. It was a reminder that MUI is not a homogenous organisation, but rather comprised of many different discourses and points of views on Islam. Although MUI is not a mass-based organisation, because it does not have a grassroots membership, its membership consists of representativeness of various Muslim organisations in Indonesia. Since its establishment, the Council has been supported by Muhammadiyah, NU, Persatuan Islam, Syarikat Islam, Mathla'ul Anwar, Persatuan Tarbiyah Islamiyah, al-Washliyah and many other Islamic organisations. A number of these organisations were founding members of MUI, and as such MUI board membership has been drawn from these organisations up to the present. During the Suharto era, although the MUI executive board was composed of persons from different organisational backgrounds, relations among them were relatively harmonious and unanimous in backing the ruling regime. Suharto had a strong influence over important aspects of MUI such as the appointment of its leaders and board members. Even if MUI members were polarised during the Suharto era, this was not visible due to the strong control of the ruling regime. Suharto's New Order always stressed that as a symbol of the brotherhood of Indonesian Muslim society, the MUI elite must appear united and harmonious because in Indonesian society the ulama and leaders should set a good example for their followers.

Since the beginning of the reform era, some important positions and issues within MUI have been openly decided by its own board members, and are often proportionally decided by the representatives of member organisations. The positions of the general chairman and secretary have traditionally been drawn from either Muhammadiyah or NU ulama. Since the 2005 National Congress, polarised views have begun to emerge within MUI, as can be seen from the grouping of its elites into mainstream and non-mainstream factions. This was promoted by MUI elites who came from non-mainstream Muslim organisations who were frustrated by the domination of the MUI board by the Muhammadiyah and NU mainstream Muslim groups. They therefore proposed that the distribution of power should not be decided by a categorisation of mainstream and non-mainstream, but that each organisation should have one representative within MUI. The non-mainstream faction saw this as a way to engage more Muslim organisations. Most importantly, they cited MUI's identity as a *tenda besar* or large tent for Muslim organisations in Indonesia to justify their argument: "one group, one vote."

Since the beginning of the reform era, MUI has tried to accommodate activists of so-called Muslim fundamentalist groups as MUI's board members. For some MUI leaders, this should be done as part of the Council's role as an umbrella organisation for the Islamic communities and as part of its internal organisational reform.[176] From the perspective of these Islamist activists, their accommodation within MUI should occur because the Council is an open organisation for all Muslims. However, the reason behind their eagerness for inclusion as part of MUI is that the organisation is a strategic hub that can be instrumental in spreading their ideas to both Muslim society and the state. For their ideas to be considered by the *umma* (the Muslim community) and the state, they need to join the MUI board. The openness of the reform era has allowed these groups to be included. They began to sit on the board in 2000, but their bold presence became more visible in 2005–2010.

Ridwan, who was appointed as an executive on MUI's board in 2005, is the most important patron of this group. He was born in Jakarta in 1947 and is a graduate of Medina University, Saudi Arabia. Before joining MUI, he served as Chair of the DDII. During the 2005–2010 period, his role was as the MUI chairman responsible for Islamic propagation or *dakwah*. This is a very important domain due its direct links to the affairs of Muslim society. Ridwan utilised this position to help recruit ulama with similar ideas and commitment to the implementation of sharia law.[177] Muhammad Khathath (the secretary general of Forum Umat Islam), was, for instance, invited to become a member of MUI for the 2005–2010 period due to Ridwan's personal efforts.[178] Besides Khathath, other young actors of the so-called radical faction who succeeded in becoming MUI board members include Adian Husaini and Ismail Yusanto. Husaini was Deputy Chairman of the inter-religious commission and Yusanto was active in the special Islamic propagation commission for the 2005–2010

176 Interview with Slamet Effendi Yusuf, Jakarta, 2010.

177 Interview with Cholil Ridwan, Jakarta, 2011.

178 The Forum Umat Islam (FUI) is an Islamic organisation founded as a confederation of fundamentalist Muslim organisations with one objective: to struggle for the formalisation of sharia law in Indonesia. The FUI founding fathers were Cholil Badawi, Cholil Ridwan and Achmad Khathath (a former HTI activist). Now FUI has at least fifteen chapters. See Ismail Hasani and Bonar Tigor Naipospos, *Wajah Para Pembela Islam* (Jakarta: Pustaka Masyarakat Setara, 2011), p. 137.

period. Yusanto (also as an HTI spokesperson) admits that his position in MUI was not the result of his own ambition, but he was invited by Slamet Effendi Yusuf (NU faction) to join MUI.[179] From Effendi's perspective, he needed to give space to Yusanto and other young militant Islamic activists within MUI in order to control and domesticate them.[180] To some extent, their inclusion is understandable, but it must be acknowledged that MUI has been coloured by their presence.

In addition to the influence of Ridwan, a MUI regulation also permitted this group to find a place on the MUI board. At the National Congress VII, 2005, the composition of the *formatur* team authorised to appoint the general chairman and secretary was dominated by representatives of non-mainstream Muslim organisations and one person from Muhammadiyah. Usually thirteen people made up this committee, including one representative from the MUI advisory board, two representatives from the executive board, five representatives from the regional MUIs, four representatives of Muslim organisations, and one representative of *pesantren* and universities. In this case, the four representatives of Muslim organisations did not include a NU representative. These representatives were led by Nazri Adlani (al-Ittihadiyah), the non-mainstream members of MUI such as Mathla'ul Anwar,[181] Satkar Ulama, al-Ittihadiyah, Dewan Masjid Indonesia (DMI, Indonesian Mosque Board), and some others, who organised a meeting to select the Muslim organisations which would be represented on the *formatur* team. This meeting decided that Ridwan (DDII), Yunahar Ilyas (Muhammadiyah), Fuad Amsyari (ICMI) and Amrullah Achmad (Syarikat Islam) would join the selection team. This was a very interesting development because it was the first time that membership of the selection committee was determined through a voting process rather than a consensus of MUI stakeholders, with the largest Muslim organisations such as Muhammadiyah and NU automatically having one representative each. In the 2005 voting process, NU was, strangely, not represented on the *formatur* team.[182] Due to this selection committee composition, from 2005–2010 MUI accommodated conservative Muslim figures such as Ridwan, Yunahar Ilyas,

179 Interview with Ismail Yusanto, Jakarta, 2011.

180 Interview with Slamet Effendi Yusuf, Jakarta, 2010.

181 The Mathla'ul Anwar is an Islamic social organisation which was established on 19 July 1916 in Menes, Pandeglang, Banten. See Didin Nurul Didin Rosidin, "The Role of Identity of Religious Authority in the Nation State: Egypt, Indonesia and South Africa Compared," in *Varieties of Religious Authority: Changes and Challenges in Twentieth-Century Indonesian Islam*, ed. Azyumardi Azra, Kees van Dijk, and Nico J.G. Kapten (Singapore: Institute of Southeast Asian Studies, 2010), 93–113.

182 Interview with Asrori S. Karni, Jakarta, 2010.

and Amrullah Ahmad on its executive board. They were all new names, none of them having been on the 2000–2005 MUI executive bsoard. Although fewer in number than those representing Muhammadiyah and NU, this group was very active in promoting conservative edicts from MUI, such as fatwas banning liberalism, secularism, pluralism and the Ahmadiyah, without trying to represent the diverse opinions within MUI on such issues. It is fair to say that their presence on the MUI board during this period created an image of MUI as having strongly conservative tendencies. In fact, many people claim that since the reform era, MUI has become a miniature representation of these conservative and radical groups.[183]

Moderate groups within MUI whose actors are mostly recruited from mainstream organisations such as NU and Muhammadiyah have learnt from the aggressive movements of the radical factions during the 2000–2010 board leadership period and have tried to reflect and strengthen their positions in the organisation's structure. They have sought to seriously compete against the fundamentalist factions.[184] This was evident in the selection mechanism following the National Congress of 2010, when the Council determined to include Muhammadiyah and NU as permanent members of the *formatur* team to select MUI board leaders such as the general chairman and secretary general. This decision, implemented in MUI Decree 06/VIII/2010, stated that the composition of MUI's selection team must consider "the growing and developing elements within the lives of Indonesian Muslim communities."[185] This statement means that the selection committee should accommodate the Muhammadiyah and NU majority members. The non-mainstream organisations were thus less well represented in the selection committee in this round. Ridwan (DDII), Amrullah Achmad, Fuad Amsyari and Nazri Adlani—members of a similar team in 2005—were not included in the seventeen-person *formatur* team that selected the MUI board members for the 2010–2015 period. With this structural screen, the mainstream groups ensured they could protect the moderate nature of MUI. It is therefore also important to say here that around 80% of MUI board members from the headquarters down to district levels—provincial and district branches—are recruited from Muhammadiyah and NU.[186]

183 Tim Lindsey, "Monopolising Islam? The Indonesian Ulama Council and State Regulation of the 'Islamic Economy.'"

184 Interview with Solahuddin al-Ayyubi Jakarta, 2010.

185 MUI, *Pedoman Penyelenggaraan Organisasi Majelis Ulama Indonesia*, p. 161.

186 This information was obtained from Ichwan Sam, Secretary General of MUI.

Although the moderate group has signaled success in preserving their positions within the Council, their ability to stem the growing domination of Islamic conservative discourse remains a big question. The moderate group admits that the presence of the radical faction is a threat to the moderate ideals of MUI, but they do not attempt to overcome this discourse. This group knows that the fundamentalist faction is attempting to seize control of MUI for its own purpose and agenda, for instance, by instrumentalising fatwas and Islamic sanctions as a political basis for supporting radicalism and acts of religious hatred and violence promoted by Islamist groups outside MUI, but they are reluctant to criticise this attitude.[187] The fatwa banning secularism, pluralism and liberalism can be seen as one example of this: the fatwa was built on relatively sound Islamic legal and rational arguments, but the fundamentalist faction modified the interpretation to create a blanket ban on pluralism, secularism and liberalism. Such an appropriation occurred in many cases.[188]

However, it would be incorrect to consider the fundamentalist faction as the only primary actor promoting the Council as a conservative ulama organisation. The fatwa commission and all MUI organisational organs, especially through that of Amin and other chairmen, have also greatly contributed in the creation of a sphere for this group to contest and grow the sentiments of Islamic militancy within MUI. In addition, the moderate factions kept silent about their actions. In this regard, their self-proclamation as the moderate faction is meaningless when they still allow the fertilisation of Islamic conservatism in the organisation.

Nevertheless, one cannot overlook constructive efforts being conducted at the level of discourse development by the moderate NU and Muhammadiyah youth wings within MUI to secure the existence of Islamic moderation within fatwas, publication, and activities conducted by MUI. For instance, when suspicions emerged from several Indonesian Islamic and secular NGOs that MUI was promoting a gradual legal Islamisation of Indonesia's state law, the moderate faction of the organisation sought to reject this accusation. This also occurred with the fatwa on Ahmadiyah, which was seen as the trigger for Islamic hatred and violence against the Indonesian Ahmadis and other "deviant" Islamic groups, when moderate groups within MUI tried to clarify that violence against Ahmadiyah had not been recommended by the fatwa and was in fact against the spirit of the fatwa. They argued that the fatwa was intended to

187 Interview with Asrori S. Karni, Jakarta, 2010, and interview with Solahuddin al-Ayyubi, Jakarta, 2010.

188 This issue will be elaborated in Chapter 6.

peacefully return the Ahmadis and other so-called deviant groups to the teachings of mainstream Islam, not through violence but with *al-mawʿiẓa al-ḥasana* (good advice).[189] Therefore, according to these moderate groups, the incidents of violence and rage against the Ahmadis and other groups are an unwished consequence of the fatwa publication, and were no longer MUI's responsibility but that of the Indonesian police.

Although these NU and Muhammadiyah youth wing initiatives are very important for reclaiming MUI as an open organisation, they are still not strong enough to visualise and reflect a moderate Council. It seems that their presence lacks significant support from their elders occupying the high-level MUI positions, such as the leadership board, the Fatwa Commission, the DSN and many others. It seems that the moderate faction has difficulty in expressing their aspirations to the Muslim public because they do not want to be seen as fragmented and polarised. Essentially, it can be said that the dynamics of the Council are more of a reflection of the activities of its elites rather than the interests of the *umma*. Although the moderate group may differ in opinion and perspective on religious discourse within MUI, however, publicly they want to be seen as harmonious and united. All this mirrors the ambiguity and inconsistency of MUI in facing the reform era.

---

189 Interview with Solahuddin al-Ayyubi, Jakarta, 2010, and interview with Slamet Effendi Yusuf, Jakarta, 2010.

CHAPTER 3

A Living Organisation: Pre-existing Conditions and the Organisational Vehicle of Shariatisation

3.1 Introduction

MUI's role in clearing a space for the implementation of sharia in the legal and public spheres of Indonesia was accidental but deliberate, as indicated by such prominent MUI figures as Sahal Mahfudh, Amin, Ichwan Sam, Ridwan, and Slamet Effendi Yusuf. The question that needs to be answered here is: "In what ways has MUI striven to attain this positioning of sharia?" This chapter seeks to illuminate the importance placed by MUI on attaining a designated space for sharia and how MUI employed pre-existing conditions to enable sharia to gain a stronghold in the legal and public spheres of Indonesia. In social movement theory, the concept of the division between internal and external factors is important.[1] The key internal MUI factors to be scrutinised here include its discourse, identity, tradition, and organisational characteristics, in addition to external factors including political opportunities, dominant cultural possibilities and constraints outside MUI. With regard to the shariatisation of the legal and public spheres of Indonesia, both internal and external elements should be examined, as both were important to enable the Council to achieve its goal. This chapter is aimed at addressing the internal factors of MUI. The external aspects are discussed in Chapter 4.

However, before surveying the intentions of the MUI, it is important to note that, by supporting sharia's move from the private to the public sphere, the Council did not intend to position itself as the sole actor of the shariatisation movement, but rather as the promoter and solidarity maker. MUI enjoys a certain advantage—due to its position and extensive experience as fatwa giver and *tenda besar*[2] of Islamic organisations—in creating mainstream discourse, lobbying policymakers, mobilising protests, persuading voters, arguing against the ruling regime, and many other related enterprises. MUI is not only able to

1 Nancy Whittier, "Meaning and Structure in Social Movements," in *Social Movements, Identity, Culture and the State*, ed. David S Meyer, Nancy Whittier, and Belinda Robnett (Oxford, New York: Oxford University Press, 2002), p. 291.

2 *Tenda besar* literally means a large tent or marquee, but in the MUI context it signifies the Council's role as a large accommodating organisation.

DOI:10.1163/9789004534896_004

consolidate its own potentials and resources for mobilising shariatisation, but also those of other Islamic organisations. In fact, many other Muslim organisations have become involved in this movement because of a similar trajectory in striving for the shariatisation of Indonesia. Using Nella Van Dyke and Holly J. McCommon's framework,[3] MUI's shariatisastion is an amalgamation of different Islamic organisations with similar interests to the Council. According to social movement theory,[4] what MUI conducts is shariatisation based on its own ideas and interests, but the presence of similar objectives, targets, and ideologies of many other Muslim organisations enables the Council—through the interpersonal networks of their activists—to unite and embed them. MUI thus comes to take on the role of a collaborator and solidarity maker. This leading role is required to solidify a movement through shared interests and aspirations, finally motivating and mobilising Indonesian Muslims to unite in support of shariatisation. Herbert Feith, an Australian Indonesianist, stated that the role of solidarity maker is often played by intermediary leaders who have the skills to mediate between different levels of society and mass organisations, and also to manipulate integrative symbols.[5] This is precisely what MUI has done for the agenda of shariatisation in Indonesia. MUI has not only underpinned the discourse, but also argued for the Islamic social mobilisation of other groups and organisations to promote the establishment of a new rule of law influenced by sharia. The establishment of a new rule of law is one of the very tangible outcomes of many social contentions in the world,[6] and MUI seeks to achieve a similar target for Indonesia. Using Asef Bayat's theory of post-Islamism on the content and project of such movements, a distinctive model of struggling for sharia can be discovered within MUI.[7] By content, what

3 Nella Van Dyke and Holly J. McCammon, eds., *Strategic Alliances: Coalition Building and Social Movements* (Minneapolis: University of Minnesota Press, 2010), p. xii.

4 Craig J. Jenkins and William Form, "Social Movements and Social Change," in *The Handbook of Political Sociology: States, Civil Societies, and Globalization* (Cambridge: Cambridge University Press, 2005), 331–49, p. 332; Florence Passy, "Social Networks Matter. But How?," in *Social Movements and Networks: Relational Approaches to Collective Action: Relational Approaches to Collective Action*, ed. Mario Diani and Doug McAdam (Oxford: Oxford University Press, 2003), 21–48, p. 21; Christopher Ansell, "Community Embeddedness and Collaborative Governance in the San Francisco Bay Area Environmental Movement," in *Social Movements and Networks: Relational Approaches to Collective Action: Relational Approaches to Collective Action*, ed. Mario Diani and Doug McAdam (Oxford: Oxford University Press, 2003), 123–46, p. 125.

5 Herbert Feith, *The Decline of Constitutional Democracy in Indonesia* (Jakarta: Equinox Publishing, 2006), p. 113.

6 Jenkins and Form, "Social Movements and Social Change", p. 332.

7 Asef Bayat, *Life as Politics: How Ordinary People Change the Middle East* (Amsterdam: Amsterdam University Press, 2010).

is meant here is striving for the acceptance of sharia norms. MUI has learnt what not to do from previous unsuccessful struggles towards this goal; it has tried to be different, and compelled itself to invent new content for the sharia model. By project, what is meant here is that MUI has developed a plan based on rational concepts, strategies and modalities to bring about a new form of shariatisation.

This chapter seeks to illuminate the content or internal causes which are inherent within MUI and some organisational vehicles that support the implementation of sharia in both the legal and public spheres of Indonesia.

3.2 Internal Causes of Shariatisation

There are three pre-existing conditions indicated as internal factors that led MUI to become a more able and effective organisation in promoting sharia. The first is the ideological shift from Pancasila to Islam; the second is the transformation of its service orientation from being the custodian of the government to the custodian of Muslim society; and the third is its eagerness to be recognised by Indonesian Muslims as the *tenda besar* for all Muslim organisations in Indonesia.

3.2.1 *From Pancasila to Islam*

The shift of organisational ideology from Pancasila to Islam since 2000 has provided MUI with greater freedom to favour sharia. Since this change, MUI has had a greater theological legitimacy to persuade other Islamic groups to join this endeavour, particularly those Islamic organisations that believe that extending the space for sharia in the legal and public spheres is a key legitimate part of Islamic doctrine. Historically and politically speaking, MUI was conceived by the Suharto regime to preserve Pancasila as the national ideology of Indonesia. Suharto needed MUI as a partner in fostering a harmonious relationship and a constructive dialogue between Islam and the state. In that era, MUI was often employed as a state instrument to resist any group that sought the implementation of a religion-based ideology, including those seeking a theocratic Islamic state, as this was viewed as being against state interests. Suharto employed this political tactic because he believed he could not promote his ideas without the support of Muslim groups. Evidence of MUI's commitment to Pancasila at this time can be seen in its Establishment Charter:[8]

8 *Piagam Berdirinya Majelis Ulama Indonesia* (Indonesian Ulama Council Establishment Charter) was signed by Hamka and other 52 ulama on 26 July 1975.

> [O]n the basis of the Pancasila and 1945 Constitution, Chapter 29, Article 1, ulama are obliged to educate Muslim society in order to increase piety to God and to strengthen national integrity and to fight against atheism.[9]

During MUI's first five years, from 1975 to 1980, there was no serious challenge to the position of Pancasila as MUI's *asas tunggal* (sole principle). In fact, an even greater emphasis was placed on the Pancasila in MUI's second five-year period (1980–1985).[10] In 1980, during its second National Congress, MUI issued several important recommendations regarding the implementation of Pancasila and its Pedoman Penghayatan dan Pengamalan Pancasila (P4, Guidance on the Reflection on and Application of Pancasila).[11] MUI stated that Pancasila is a way of life to motivate the integration of people from various different ethnicities, religions and gender groups into one nation-state and to create a favourable environment for religious harmony in Indonesia. MUI further stated that the Majelis Permusyawaratan Rakyat (MPR, People's Consultative Assembly of Indonesia) had agreed that the P4 should be disseminated to all Indonesian citizens, including Indonesian Muslims, to strengthen the application and practice of Pancasila in daily life. Pancasila, in this regard, was not only a slogan and rhetorical ideology, but one to be implemented in the realm of Indonesian society. Thus, MUI supported the Indonesian government push to ensure its citizens cultivated and internalised the values of Pancasila as the ideological foundation of their daily lives. MUI was highly supportive of the implementation of P4 and in fact collaborated with some state institutions that were specifically tasked with disseminating these Pancasila implementation guidelines.[12] MUI headquarters and its branches engaged in disseminating Pancasila, not only to the Muslim community but also to the people of Indonesia more generally. At the 1980 National Congress it was revealed that MUI had advised the government to use a book published by the Ministry of Religious Affairs as a key source for the P4 dissemination process.[13]

9 MUI, *20 Tahun Majelis Ulama Indonesia*, ed. H.S. Prodjokusumo (Jakarta: Sekretariat Majelis Ulama Indonesia, 1995), p. 15., 1995), p. 15.

10 MUI, *20 Tahun Majelis Ulama Indonesia*, 1995, p. 88; MUI, *15 Tahun Majelis Ulama Indonesia*, ed. H.S. Prodjokusumo (Jakarta: Sekretariat Majelis Ulama Indonesia, 1990), p. 178.

11 The P4 was established by Suharto to sustain the social and ideological functions of Pancasila. Essentially, it was a series of ideological indoctrination activities to be undergone by all Indonesian citizens, that included reflection, application, and the preservation of Pancasila as the basic foundation of the state.

12 The P4 has not been implemented in Indonesia since the fall of Suharto in 1998.

13 MUI, *20 Tahun Majelis Ulama Indonesia*, p. 88; MUI, *15 Tahun Majelis Ulama Indonesia*, pp. 180–1.

Pancasila's position as MUI's sole ideology remained publicly undisputed during the 1985–1990 period. In fact, it was strengthened by the enactment of Act No. 8/1985 on Social Mass Organisations (Organisasi Masyarakat, or Ormas), following which MUI participated in convincing Muslim organisations to accept Pancasila as their sole ideology. In 1990, during its fourth National Congress, MUI reaffirmed the undisputed position of Pancasila and the 1945 Constitution for its organisation.

However, since the reform era began in 1998, drastic changes have taken place. In 2000, Pancasila was replaced by Islam as the ideological foundation of MUI. This ideological shift was no simple matter but reflected the emergence of a serious new reorientation and political agenda within the organisation. Politically speaking, this tendency has been apparent since the 1990s and was visible from the MUI endorsement for the establishment of ICMI, but MUI was now able to take advantage of the new political structure opportunity, to use it as a vehicle for shariatisation of the legal order of Indonesia. MUI had a hidden agenda of shariatisation within MUI during the New Order but it could not make this explicit at the time. However, MUI's ideological transformation would have been difficult to achieve without the political deregulation under President Habibie through the issuance of MPR Decree No. 18/1998 where the requirement for Pancasila to be the sole ideology of mass organisations (as previously enacted by Act No. 9/1985) was abolished. This was because the 1985 legislation was deemed in conflict with the new Indonesian spirit of democratisation.

MUI's ideological shift was made explicit through the changes to its basic statutes, in particular Article 2 stating that MUI's basic ideology is Islam. This change was made at the seventh National Congress in 2000, two years after the reform era began in 1998.[14] Although some MUI leaders confidently argue that MUI's commitment to the Unitary State of the Indonesian Republic has not changed and reject the inference that this ideological shift reflects a changed MUI focus to promote sharia,[15] in reality they have discarded Pancasila, which is the core symbol of NKRI. More explicitly, both Mahfudh and Amin have stated that the NKRI concept does not completely exclude the application of sharia in the Indonesian legal system. Perhaps this is due to their belief that the ideal Indonesia nationalist state is one that has adopted sharia into its

---

14 MUI, *Pedoman Penyelenggaraan Organisasi Majelis Ulama Indonesia* (Jakarta: Sekretariat Majelis Ulama Indonesia, 2010), p. 17.

15 Interviews with Ma'ruf Amin, Jakarta, 2010, with Ichwan Sam, Jakarta, 2010, and with Sahal Mahfudh, Jakarta, 2011.

national legal system.[16] More evidence of the support of the MUI elites for the incorporation of sharia into Indonesian law can be seen in two further cases. The first is the absence of any regret over the substitution of Islam as its basic ideological foundation. The change was publicly announced to Indonesian Muslims, because it was assumed they would all agree. The second is the increase in MUI's involvement in many activities campaigning for the incorporation of sharia, which would not take place without consent from MUI leaders.

It would seem that adopting Islam as its basic ideology marked a new era and character for MUI. Having this firm, shared ideology had the potential to unify the organisation's various related forces and interests. Using the perspective of Mayer N. Zald's social movement theory, MUI's attempt to introduce sharia norms in both the legal and public spheres of Indonesia was not a solo attempt, but rather a kind of "ideologically structured action."[17] In most cases, the commonality of ideological foundations plays a determinant role in attracting and integrating the varieties of interest, agenda, and programmes that are strived for by those who participate in the movements. Ideology is a tool kit, and suggests how activist groups may operate instrumentally to pursue their beliefs and interests.[18]

More importantly, through this ideological mutation MUI has been able to more easily attract the attention of so-called radical Muslim groups, such as the members of FPI, MMI, HTI, and FUI, who also employ sharia as their ideological compass. Prior to this foundational shift these groups mistrusted MUI, which they viewed as an ally of the secular regime of Indonesia, largely due to its adherence to Pancasila as its guiding principle. From their perspective, a Muslim organisation should adhere to the idea of implementing total Islam. Promoting total Islam—the integration of Islam and state—is, for them, an immutable part of their religion. These groups add that the initiative to establish the tenets of total Islam in Indonesia can be kickstarted by the formalisation of sharia in everyday life. Due to the importance they place on formalising Islam, these groups suspect the commitment of any Muslim organisation that does not strive for the embodiment of Islamic ideology, despite its efforts to achieve prosperity for the *umma*. However, MUI's success embracing these Islamist groups as allies has proven its ability to mobilise collective will to promote the Islamisation of Indonesia's state law. This is in accordance with social

16 Interviews with Sahal Mahfudh, Jakarta, 2011, and with Ma'ruf Amin, Jakarta, 2010.

17 "Ideologically Structured Action: An Enlarged Agenda for Social Movement Research," *Mobilization: An International Quarterly* 5, no. 1 (2000): 1–16.

18 Leo d'Anjou, *Social Movements and Cultural Change: The First Abolition Campaign Revisited* (New York: Transaction Publishers, 1996), p. 42.

movement theory as regards the need for the rich support of various stakeholders and networks to determine the success of the movement.[19]

With Islam as its new ideological foundation, MUI has a greater means at its disposal to promote sharia in the legal and public spheres, including in the legal discourses and practices of Indonesia. These serious MUI attempts to promote sharia as an alternative system for Indonesia is actually in line with similar discussions and attempts—by MUI as well as other Islamic organisations—at many levels of the Indonesian public sphere over the last decade. Through the 1999 KUII, for instance, MUI responded to common aspirations relating to the need for the Indonesian Muslim community to implement their sharia as state law,[20] at the very least by integrating sharia into the compilation of state laws. In doing so, the KUII supported the institutional upgrade of MUI from its current form as a non-state organisation to a Lembaga Fatwa Negara (State Council of Fatwa). As a state organisation, MUI would have more wide-reaching responsibility and its rulings would be legally binding.

The adoption of Islam as MUI's basic ideology can on the one hand be seen as a sign of democratisation, yet on the other hand it indicates that Pancasila has lost much credibility and the concept of the NKRI is a contested one. Indonesia is in fact in the process of reinventing itself, and this creates the space for Islam to step forward as a possible integrative tool. However, without MUI taking the lead role in this movement, the mobilisation of Islam cannot progress well. The state's position in maintaining Pancasila as the basic ideology of Indonesia since the reform era has also led MUI and pro-sharia groups to seek an alternative ideology that can offer a way out of their problems. This is due to their belief that there is no legal system that can provide a better solution than the adoption of sharia into the law of Indonesia. Although this agenda is challenged by some Muslims,[21] as well as other religious and secular groups, MUI remains firm in its belief that sharia can be implemented as the legal norm of Indonesia in such fields as the economy and commodities. MUI's decision to embrace Islam as its ideological foundation is therefore understandable, because in this way it can establish a common ground with other

19 Donatella Della Porta and Mario Diani, *Social Movements: An Introduction* (Oxford: Blackwell Publishing, 2009).

20 MUI, *Kumpulan Hasil-Hasil Kongres Umat Islam Indonesia, Umat Islam Menyongsong Era Indonesia Baru* (Jakarta: Dewan Pimpinan Majelis Ulama Indonesia, 1999), p. 14.

21 It is important to mention here that even though Indonesia is a country with a Muslim majority, not all Muslims support sharia as the basic ideology for their state or their Islamic organisations. The *Nadhiyyin* (Indonesian-Arabic expression for the followers of NU) for instance have supported Pancasila as the basic ideological foundation of their organisation since 1984.

Muslim groups and boost the collective identity of the Muslim community to promote the shariatisation of Indonesia.

3.2.2 *From* Khādim al-Ḥukūma *to* Khādim al-Umma

The second pre-existing condition that has helped fashion the shariatisation of Indonesia is the shift in MUI's devotion from the state to the people. This is famously referred to among the leaders of MUI by the Arabic phrase "*min khādim al-ḥukūma ilā khādim al-umma*," which literally means "from being the custodian of the government to the custodian of the Muslim community." Historically speaking, the position of MUI as the custodian of the government was evidenced through its role as a fatwa-giver on Islamic issues which were inclined to protect the interests of the state rather than those of the Muslim community. However, since the reform era began in 1998, MUI functionaries and activists have revisited this role and its negative image. Accordingly, MUI has moved from promoting state interests to fostering those of the Muslim community. Thus, the role of *khādim al-umma* (the custodian of the Muslim community) is now the new image of MUI in the reform era of Indonesia.[22] Although the term custodian here does not mean serving the people but rather being responsible for Islamic matters affecting the people, nevertheless this change signals MUI's regret over its previous role, which was more inclined to side with the ruling regime than with the interests of the *umma*. During the New Order Era, MUI leaders may have thought they could best protect Islam from Suharto's secular system by cooperating with him. However, by being co-opted to the state machinery, they miscalculated their freedom to manoeuvre and thus were increasingly seen as an arm of the state, pretending to defend Islam but in fact defending the New Order.

This shift in MUI orientation is therefore expected to promote closer relations between the Council and the *umma*.[23] However, this commitment must be implemented into more tangible packages that advocate the interests of the *umma*. By doing this, MUI will have a legitimate basis on which it can reject the frequent accusation of being a collaborator of the state. From the perspective of social movement theory, this new paradigm is quite easy to understand because the success of the MUI's agenda of shariatisation will be determined by the extent to which this organisation aligns with the Muslim community

22 Interviews with Ali Yafie, Jakarta, 2010, and with Nazri Adlani, Jakarta, 2011.

23 Interviews with Ali Yafie, Jakarta, 2010, Nazri Adlani, Jakarta, 2010, and an anonymous informant, Jakarta, 2011.

and networks—with individual Muslims in particular, and collective Muslims in Islamic organisations in general. In this way MUI can begin from a clear position of aligning itself with Muslim grassroots organisations, with the expected return of grassroots support from these organisations. These reciprocal relations will create a stronger movement because both sides—both the organisation and their supporters—are on the same platform.

In order to assess whether the concept of the custodian of the Muslim community is really being implemented or whether it is just rhetoric, it is worth looking at MUI's organisational structure and the broad array of its programmes. In the post-reform era of Indonesia, there are some positive signals from MUI that demonstrate the use of this approach. Since 2000, MUI has, for instance, removed high-ranking state officials from the formal structure of the organisation. The Indonesian president, ministers, and governors no longer sit in key MUI positions such as the head of the board of trustees and the advisory board. This change was accompanied by a change of the board structure itself, in which, since 2000, MUI no longer has three boards—the Dewan Pelindung (board of trustees), Dewan Pertimbangan (advisory board) and Pimpinan (executive board)[24]—but two: the Dewan Penasehat (advisory board) and Dewan Pelaksana (executive board). The position of head of the advisory board was no longer given to a high state official but instead to Ali Yafie (former MUI general chairman from 1998 to 2000). Most interestingly, the Minister of Religious Affairs was also no longer included in the new MUI board structure.[25] However, the Ministry of Religious Affairs still remains the MUI channel for accessing the state budget. This is also true for other Islamic organisations, as the state budget of Indonesia does not allow for direct allocation of funds to non-state bodies. Perhaps the removal of the senior state officials from the board structure was intended to create the image of the Council as one committed to the spirit of the reform era. MUI's commitment to cleansing its board structure of high-ranking state officials continued in the 2005–2010 period.[26] The advisory board members consisted of Tolchah Hasan (b. 1936),[27]

24 MUI, *20 Tahun Majelis Ulama Indonesia*, pp. 43–45.

25 MUI, *Himpunan Fatwa Majelis Ulama Indonesia* (Jakarta: Departemen Agama, 2003), p. 379.

26 The composition of this advisory board was set by the *Surat Keputusan Musyawarah Nasional VII Majelis Ulama Indonesia, No: Kep-07/MUNAS-VII/MUI/VII/2005* (The Letter of National Congress Meeting VII/MUI/, No: Decision-07/MUNAS/MUI/VII/2005.

27 Tolchah Hasan is a senior ulama of NU. He was the Minister of Religious Affairs under President Abdurrahman Wahid, from 1999 to 2001.

Kafrawi Ridwan,[28] Fuad Amsyari (b. 1943),[29] Azwar Anas (b. 1931),[30] and Husein Umar (b. 1940),[31] all of whom are representatives of recognised Muslim organisations and not state officials.[32] Although these efforts do not yet perhaps represent a full implementation of the custodian of the Muslim community concept, nevertheless removing the Indonesian president and high-ranking state officials from MUI board positions was the first sign of MUI's independence of MUI from state intervention. With this change, MUI has not only embraced the freedom to criticise, but also to reject any government policies considered to conflict with the principles of sharia and the interests of the *umma*. This phenomenon, for instance, was evident during Wahid's presidency of 1999–2001 when MUI opposed Wahid's stance on the Islamic legal status of the food additive MSG (monosodium glutamate) known by the brand name Ajinomoto (Islamic legal debates will be further discussed in Chapter 6).[33] MUI deemed that Ajinomoto contained pig fat, whereas Wahid claimed it did not. Here MUI sought to prove its shift from custodian of the state to custodian of the people. In the Suharto era, when the president of Indonesia published a legal or policy statement the Council would deliver a fatwa justifying the state's policies or regulations, with only few exceptions such as the fatwa on Christmas during Hamka's leadership of MUI.

A more concrete statement regarding the new role of MUI as the custodian of *umma* was provided by Mahfudh as follows:

---

28 Kafrawi Ridwan is a retired high official of the Ministry of Religious Affairs. He was the secretary of MUI in the period of Hamka's leadership from 1975 to 1980.

29 Fuad Amsyari obtained a Master of Public Health from Royal Tropical Institute of Amsterdam and a PhD from New York University in 1979. He has been a senior political activist of Partai Bulan Bintang (PBB, the Star-Crescent Islamic Party) that struggles for the implementation of sharia law within the NKRI context. This Islamic party did not obtain sufficient votes to qualify to compete in the 2009 general elections, since it failed to obtain a minimum 2.5% of the national vote.

30 Azwar Anas was born in Padang, West Sumatra, and graduated from the Faculty of Chemical Engineering, Institut Teknologi Bandung (Bandung Technical University) in 1959. He was a member of Suharto's cabinet from 1993–1998.

31 Husein Umar was born on 14 December 1940 in Karangasem, Bali. During his life, he was active in many Islamic organisations such as Pemuda Pelajar Islam (PPI, Youth and Student Association), Himpunan Mahasiswa Islam (HMI, Islamic Student Association), MUI and many others. He was also a senior politician in the PPP and PBB. His last position was general head of Dewan Dakwah Islamiyah Indonesia (DDII).

32 The composition of this advisory board was decided under the *Surat Keputusan Musyawarah Nasional VIII Majelis Ulama Indonesia, No: Kep-06/MUNAS-VIII/2010* (The Letter of National Congress Meeting VII/MUI/, No: Decision-07/MUNAS VIII /2010.

33 Ajinomoto is a Japanese company that produces around 30% of the world's MSG.

> [I]n the previous era, MUI served as an intermediary power agency from the top (the state) to the bottom (*umma*). Now it is not, and its position has been flipped around. Now, MUI is an intermediary agency that brings the interests of the bottom (*umma*) to the top. The difference is fundamental. This is the real change in the model. During my leadership, this is what I have experienced.[34]

This statement seems to suggest that MUI's role as custodian of the *umma* was a conscious decision. Under circumstances whereby MUI is freer to choose between aligning with the interests of the state and the interests of the Muslim community, it prefers to side with the *umma*. This alignment is evident from the way the MUI Fatwa Commission has issued a number of Islamic recommendations and edicts, for instance its fatwa on anti-pornography that was supported by the Muslim majority, as represented in parliament. Furthermore, as MUI Chairman Sahal Mahfudh admits, the Fatwa Commission now issues more courageous fatwa. This is a major difference from Suharto's New Order, when the Fatwa Commission had to consider and consult the state before issuing a fatwa.[35]

Aligning with the Muslim community has increased MUI's credibility in the eyes of many Muslims, particularly with regard to fatwa. Furthermore, Mahfudh claims that Susilo Bambang Yudhoyono (president of Indonesia from 2004 to 2014) often states that all Muslim affairs should refer to MUI's fatwa.[36] From this comment, it would appear that Mahfudh is confident that MUI's new role has positively contributed to an improved MUI image. At a more concrete level, the implementation of *khādim al-umma* can be grasped through several agenda implemented by MUI through its commissions and institutions. The MUI Economy Commission, guided by its motto "to promote sharia-based economy and to shariatise the people's economy," has approached several successful national entrepreneurs and businessmen such as Chairul Tanjung (a successful business tycoon, bank and TV owner), Didi Supriyadi (a businessman) and many others to assist MUI in conceptualising and implementing the empowerment of the people's economy. It is hoped that by recruiting them as MUI Advisory Board members they can guide the Council towards developing small- and medium-scale enterprises.[37] This is a simple means for MUI

---

34 Asrori S. Karni, Musthafa Helmy, and Ahmadie Thaha, *35 Tahun Majelis Ulama Indonesia* (Jakarta: Komisi Informasi dan Komunikasi Majelis Ulama Indonesia, 2010), p. 123.

35 Asrori et al., *35 Tahun Majelis Ulama Indonesia*, p. 124.

36 Interview with Sahal Mahfudh, Jakarta, 2011.

37 Interview with Ma'ruf Amin, Jakarta, 2010.

to create a business network and opportunities. Besides this, through the DSN (Dewan Syariah Nasional, the National Sharia Board), MUI directs the agenda of sharia financial institutions to prioritise small enterprises and retailers. In a similar vein, the Commission on Religious Harmony (Komisi Hubungan Antar Agama) is implementing its alignment with the *umma* through protecting their beliefs, declaring "*aqidah umat terjamin kerukunan bangsa terjalin*:" when a community's faith is guaranteed then national harmony is created.[38] Within this framework, MUI is aiming to help find solutions to such basic problems as religious harmony among Indonesian believers by establishing interfaith dialogue. To support religious harmony and tolerance, some real programmes will also be established by this commission.[39] Furthermore, the Religious Harmony Commission engages with the government of Indonesia in seeking solutions for religious-based disputes and conflicts such as those between Muslims and Christians on the establishment of churches in some areas in Jakarta. MUI has also proposed a road map and code of conduct on religious harmony among Indonesian believers, and its efforts to become more connected to the affairs of the *umma* can also be seen in the programme of the Dakwah and Community Development Commission or DCDC. This commission, for instance, translates the substance of *dakwah* or propagation into the form of social solidarity. In order to reach people at the grassroots level, Islamic propagation must be directed to increase solidarity for the *ḍuʿafāʾ* (weaker members of the community), both at the conceptual and operational level.[40] While the implementation of MUI's role as the custodian of the *umma* is in the early stage of its development, it seems that the organisation is taking serious steps to strengthen it.

However, the concept of the custodian of the Islamic community can also give rise to complex implications, particularly with regard to MUI's religious authority. MUI regards itself as the only Islamic institution given a mandate by the Indonesian *umma*, when in fact it is not. Yet the organisation has taken the dangerous step of employing this claim to legitimise its position as the moral police for the Muslim community through determining the interpretation and practice of Islam.

38 Karni et al, *35 Tahun Majelis Ulama Indonesia*, 2010, p. 148.

39 Interview with Slamet Effendi Yusuf, Jakarta, 2010. Slamet Effendi Yusuf was the chairman of the Commission on Religious Harmony from 2005–2010. The interview was conducted in the MUI Central office, Jakarta, 09 November 2010.

40 Karni et al., *35 Tahun Majelis Ulama Indonesia*, p. 153.

The MUI fatwa banning the *kelompok sesat* (deviant religious groups) of Islam, for instance, is one example.[41] This may seem strange from the perspective of a modern discourse on human rights and religious freedom, in which religion is a private matter. However, assuming the mantle of *khādim al-umma* has given MUI a greater legitimacy in its efforts to consolidate support from different stakeholders and Muslim groups in its aim to Islamise state law. It has created the impression of MUI's devotion to the *umma*, so that whatever is undertaken by MUI is in service to the Muslim community.

3.2.3 *From* Payung *to* Tenda Besar

During the Suharto era, MUI was intended as a *payung* or umbrella institution for all the Islamic organisations. Since the reform era, its status has changed to *tenda besar* or large tent. This change of status is intended to extend its role to a more prominent one in the public sphere. Bahtiar Effendy argued that the notion of *tenda besar* is actually an attempt to turn MUI into a clearing house.[42] As a clearing house, Effendy claimed MUI can play a broader role by reaching out to all elements of the Muslim community in Indonesia. However, in doing so, MUI must revamp its institutional character to accommodate, for example, the different interests and aspirations of its member organisations.

The term *payung*, which was pervasively employed in the Suharto era, was intended to symbolically express the function of MUI as a shelter for all members of the Muslim community in Indonesia in general and Islamic organisations in particular. Since the downfall of Suharto in 1998, however, the term *payung* for MUI has been gradually replaced by the term *tenda besar* to indicate a more permanent shelter. Originally both *payung* and *tenda besar* had similar meanings as a shelter and form of protection, but *tenda besar* indicates a broader shelter than the former. With this new image, MUI is not only expected to play its role as a small shelter umbrella, but also as a greater protector and tent-like space for the entire Muslim community, regardless of their creed, ethnicity and gender, and for Islamic organisations in particular.

---

41 MUI here uses the discourse of blasphemy which was adopted in Act No. 1/PNPS/1965 on *Pencegahan Penodaan Agama* (Prevention of Blasphemy). Through this act, MUI, with its new identity as the custodian of the *umma*, claims to have full authority to represent mainstream Islam. Those Muslims with a faith and practice regarded by MUI as different from those of mainstream groups are therefore judged as "deviant."

42 Interview with the late Bahtiar Effendy in January 2011. He was a graduate of Ohio State University in political sciences and was the Dean of Political Sciences Faculty of State Islamic University. Effendi was also a Muhammadiyah activist and was a MUI board member in the 2005–2010 period.

Further, the cultural and social transformation from *payung* to *tenda besar* also brought with it expectations that MUI would be able to generate not only symbolic but also practical changes. This change signposted that MUI's outreach to the Muslim communities was not shrinking, but rather expanding. The concept of the *tenda besar* was developed to highlight MUI's role as the principal actor promoting the shariatisation of Indonesian law. Acting as an umbrella organisation was no longer sufficient to fulfil MUI's broader and more complex aspirations, issues, problems and challenges. All these need a larger space, which is symbolised by the term *tenda besar*. In proclaiming this function MUI is also claiming to be the only Islamic institution in Indonesia with the authority to consolidate the various potential strengths of the Indonesian umma. However, the *tenda besar* role that MUI plays at the cultural and social level is not recognised within the legal framework of Indonesia. Nevertheless, this concept has been expanded as a cultural and theological assertion, functioning as an effective means for MUI to play its role in mobilising member organisations in particular, and Indonesian Muslims more broadly.

A more tangible implementation of the *tenda besar* concept can be seen in the following two ways. First, all discursive products issued by MUI such as fatwa, recommendations, and other forms of publications must be based on the spirit of sheltering all Indonesian Muslims, regardless of their organisational background, political beliefs and gender. Ideally, all Indonesian Muslims should receive equal treatment, but in reality there is an element of discrimination. Minority Muslim groups, such as the Ahmadiyah, Shīʿa and some Ṣūfī orders with a different interpretation of faith and beliefs from MUI and mainstream Muslim organisations are not considered proper Muslims, and are in fact deemed heretical by MUI. Thus it is evident that the *tenda besar* only protects the beliefs of mainstream Muslim groups. At the practical level, the MUI board structure has tried to accommodate the representatives of all acceptable Muslim organisations in Indonesia, including the Nahdlatul Ulama. This is because it does not want to repeat its pre-reform era history of domination of its leadership boards by the so-called modernist Muslim groups, such as Muhammadiyah, the Parmusi, and Persis. Representatives of the Nahdlatul Ulama, which in Clifford Geertz's perspective[43] is a traditionalist Muslim organisation, were almost completely excluded from MUI largely due to the party's unpopular status with President Suharto. Mas'udi, a prominent NU intellectual, asserts that MUI's establishment during the Suharto era was an attempt by the regime to reduce the legitimacy of NU ulama.[44] The political

43 Clifford Geertz, *The Religion of Java* (Chicago: University of Chicago Press, 1976), p. 366.

44 Interview with Masdar F. Mas'udi, Jakarta, 2011.

relationship between the Suharto regime and NU was a problematic one; the figures of this largest Muslim organisation in Indonesia were not only absent from MUI, but also from the broader structure of the Suharto bureaucracy. There was only one position on the MUI board reserved for a representative of NU, namely the Fatwa Commission, where Syukri Ghozali sat during the early MUI era. Although some Muslim groups claimed that Ghozali's successor, Ibrahim Hosen, was culturally a representative of NU, he never officially declared himself to be affiliated with that organisation.[45] The marginalisation of NU ulama from the structure of MUI was detrimental to the Council, because it meant that NU had no chance to influence state politics. However, on the other hand, NU benefited from this situation because it was positioned as the sole rival to Suharto and MUI. During this period, NU was viewed as the symbol of progressive Islamic civil society, whilst MUI was derided as a rubber stamp, or state collaborator.

Becoming a *tenda besar* does not free MUI from problematic issues. Many Islamic groups and Muslim leaders have eagerly joined MUI in order to increase their Islamic authority, either for their own personal interests or to further the agenda of their particular group—whether it be a political party, organisation, ethnic group or gender. They believe that by seizing positions within the organisation, they will profit by shaping influence in the public sphere.[46] MUI itself needs the presence of politicians—from parties such as PPP, PKB, Partai Demokrat, PDIP, PKS and many others—within its board. Their presence is needed by MUI to represent its interests in parliament, as MUI is not a political party. By appointing representatives of political parties to its boards, MUI can send its message to be discussed in the legislative body.

Another matter issuing from MUI's *tenda besar* status is the internal rivalries among MUI's member organisations, which is evident in the unbalanced distribution of leadership positions among them. Ichwan Sam[47] states that since the reform era, almost 80% of MUI strategic positions have been shared between NU and Muhammadiyah, while the remaining 20%, are distributed amongst other member organisations such as Persis, Parmusi, DDII and some

45 An examination of his historical background and personal thought reveals that Hosen was closer to modernist Islamic organisations than the traditionalists. Information on Hosen can be found in an article written by Wahyu Muryadi, "Mujtahid Dari Ciputat." This article was originally published by *Tempo* magazine on 01 December 1990.

46 Interview with Asroni S. Karni, Jakarta, 2011. Karni is the head of communication for MUI. Solahuddin al-Ayyubi, in an interview in Jakarta in 2011, also discussed MUI's role as *tenda besar*.

47 Ichwan Sam was general secretary of MUI in era of Sahal Mahfudh's leadership from 2000 to 2014.

other small organisations. Although this imbalance has led to criticism, especially from MUI's non-mainstream member organisations, MUI's title as *tenda besar* remains a fair one because its leadership board reflects the broad picture of Indonesian Islam, NU and Muhammadiyah being the two largest Muslim organisations. This is also a re-balancing of MUI's structure from the Suharto era, as discussed above. For MUI to play its role effectively as a *tenda besar*, this ulama council requires the majority support of all Muslim communities and this is more readily achievable when greater numbers of the mainstream Islamic groups are accommodated. Through this approach, MUI has achieved not only a symbolic identity as the representative of the Islamic mainstream, but also strategic and functional allies to assist it in its agenda and programme to promote legal Islamisation in Indonesia.

3.3 Institutional Vehicles for Shariatisation

MUI has a large, strong organisational structure in comparison to other Islamic organisations in Indonesia. It has an office located in Central Jakarta close to the Proklamasi monument.[48] Jokowi (Joko Widodo, president of Indonesia 2014 until the time of writing) promised to support the building of a twenty-storey tower block for the organisation, known as the Menara MUI.[49] The Menara MUI not only indicates an acquaintance between MUI and the state, but also the strong influence of MUI over the state that became the hallmark of the post-reform era. Besides having thirty-three branch offices at the provincial level and more than five hundred at the district level across Indonesia, MUI is also supported by bodies such as commissions and institutions in its internal structures.

This section seeks to examine the profile of MUI bodies that play a prominent role in stimulating the shariatisation of Indonesia, focusing on four. The first is the Fatwa Commission, which is responsible for drawing up fatwas and Islamic recommendations. The second is the Lembaga Pengkajian Pangan, Obat-obatan dan Kosmetika (LPPOM, Institute for Foods, Drugs and Cosmetics Assessment) which is responsible for assessing and ensuring safe and acceptable foods, drinks, medicines and cosmetics for Muslims by issuing halal certificates. The third is the Dewan Syariah Nasional (DSN, National Syariah Board)

48 The Proklamasi monument was built to commemorate the independence of Indonesia.

49 "MUI Bangun Menara dengan Nilai Rp 600 Miliar," Hidayatullah, 27 July 2018, https://hidayatullah.com/berita/nasional/read/2018/07/27/146932/mui-bangun-menara-dengan-nilai-rp-600-miliar.html, viewed on 22 July 2022.

which is responsible for issuing fatwas that relate to sharia banks and sharia finance institutions. The fourth, the Komisi Hukum dan Perundangan (the Law and Legislation Commission), handles legal and legislative issues.

3.3.1 *The Fatwa Commission*

The Fatwa Commission or Komisi Fatwa can be considered as the most important actor among the four above-mentioned MUI bodies due to its uncontested authority in drawing up fatwas. At the level of legal discourse, the Islamic legal opinions of the Fatwa Commission inspire Muslims to practise sharia norms within their social, cultural and political milieu. At the legislative level, lawmakers from the legislative and executive bodies are often inspired by MUI fatwas and recommendations in drawing up draft laws. The Fatwa Commission acts as a powerful MUI engine in warming the machine of shariatisation. However, some Islamic and secular NGOs in Indonesia criticise MUI for intentionally abusing its authority as fatwa-giver to protect some groups and marginalise others.[50] Their criticism is based on several MUI trajectories during the Suharto and reform eras. This section will throw light on the role of the Fatwa Commission in promulgating discourse favourable to shariatisation. Special attention is focused here on the meaning of the Fatwa Commission for MUI, and the logic, methods and procedures that the commission employs in issuing fatwa and other fatwa-like products. This account spans the role of the Fatwa Commission from the Suharto era to the reform era.

3.3.1.1 The Soul of MUI

Throughout MUI's history, the Fatwa Commission has held a central position within the organisation. It can be regarded as the soul of MUI due to its function as the commission charged with issuing Islamic legal opinions. The Commission has been represented in almost all the MUI offices at the national, provincial and district levels since MUI's inception in 1975. Although fatwas issued by the Commission are not legally binding, within the context of the Indonesian legal system they remain the most important conduit by which MUI is able to communicate the importance of sharia enactment to the Indonesian state and the community more broadly. In fact, MUI has employed

50 Setara Institute, *Negara Harus Bersikap, Tiga Tahun Laporan Kondisi Kebebasan Beragama/ Berkeyakinan Di Indonesia 2007–2009* (Jakarta: Setara Institute, 2010), p. 19; Suhadi Cholil et al., *Annual Report on Religious Life in Indonesia 2000* (Yogyakarta: Center for Religious and Cross-cultural Studies (CRCS) Graduate School Gadjah Mada University, 2009), pp. 42–8.

fatwas as a means of expanding its presence and influence amongst the *umma* of Indonesia in general, and high-ranking state officials in particular.

During the Suharto era, many fatwas were issued to justify the policies made by senior officials. This is why David J. Porter argued that the Fatwa Commission was part of MUI's effort to provide more effective support for the New Order regime.[51] During that era, although the Fatwa Commission consisted of prominent ulama representing various Islamic organisations, it was difficult to separate them from the influence of the ruling regime. The prominent features of the Fatwa Commission at that time reflected the characteristics of its mother organisation, MUI, particularly with regards to its dependence on the state. These tendencies were evident in some fatwas and recommendations, such as that supporting Sumbangan Dermawan Sosial Berhadiah (SDSB, the state-sponsored lottery) and others that seemed to consider the interests of the ruling regime more than those of the *umma*. This regimist tendency led to MUI being referred to as the custodian of the ruling regime.[52]

As MUI's independence increased during the reform era, the Fatwa Commission also became more independent of state influence. Now fatwas issued by the Commission are considerably different from those protecting the interests of the ruling regime. The 2001 difference of opinion between MUI and President Wahid (1999–2001) over the Islamic legal status of Ajinomoto is just one of many examples.[53] In 2008, MUI also circulated a fatwa on the Islamic legal status of *Hukum Pelarangan Khitan Perempuan* (the ban on female circumcision) that rejected the regulation issued by the Ministry of Health forbidding the medicalisation of female circumcision. This relatively increased autonomy of MUI makes the Council more confident in its mission for the shariatisation of Indonesian law.

For MUI, a fatwa does not merely function as an Islamic legal opinion for the *mustaftī* (the person requesting the fatwa), but, through the media, it also influences those members of the general public of a similar persuasion to MUI. In many places and situations, the process of legal Islamisation has often been kickstarted by a fatwa. Often, after a fatwa is issued by the Fatwa Commission, MUI leaders then take it to the legal sphere by attracting the attention of lawmakers—through the government or legislatures—because it is through

51 Donald J. Porter, *Managing Politics and Islam in Indonesia* (London & New York: Routledge Curzon, 2004), p. 78.

52 Muhammad Atho Mudzhar, *Fatwa of the Council of Indonesian Ulama: A Study of Islamic Legal Thought in Indonesia 1975–1988* (Jakarta: INIS, 1993), pp. 122–3.

53 Karni et al., *35 Tahun Majelis Ulama Indonesia.*

these bodies that legal initiatives are recognised.[54] However, a fatwa cannot be automatically transformed into state law, but is rather instrumentalised as a source of legislative inspiration or reference using Lucinda Peach's concept on legislating morality and using religious identity in lawmaking.[55] The process leading to the creation of State Law 44/2008 on Pornography and State Law 33/2014 on Halal Product Assurance, for instance, followed this model.

The Fatwa Commission releases fatwas on three types of occasions. The first is during meetings regularly held by the Fatwa Commission.[56] Most fatwas are issued in this way. The second is during the National Congress, where fatwas are usually prepared by the Fatwa Commission and then presented to participants of the National Congress for discussion and approval. The third is during Ijtima Ulama Komisi Fatwa Se-Indonesia (the Ulama Consensus Meeting), which has been held by MUI every two or three years since 1998. No matter the context in which the fatwa is issued, the products of all these events are referred to as MUI fatwas.[57]

To prevent the overlapping of fatwas which could result from the broad organisational structure of MUI, in which each level has its own Fatwa Commission, the authority to issue Islamic edicts is regulated. The Fatwa Commission at MUI headquarters remains the most influential body in providing Islamic legal opinions for national religious matters with a nationwide dimension and also those related to local issues that may resonate with other regions. The Fatwa Commission of MUI provincial branches are tasked with drawing up Islamic legal opinion related to the local cases of each region, but this can only be done after consultation with the MUI Central Board. MUI regional branches can issue their own fatwas when the Islamic edict decided by the MUI Central Board, for whatever reason, cannot be implemented at the regional level. These limits were placed on the authority of MUI provincial Fatwa Commissions in 1983. This safeguarded the strength of the MUI fatwa-making process, but it may also have been related to MUI's role to protect the state's interests,[58] whereby the MUI Central Board in Jakarta needed to control all its branches at the provincial and district levels. All Islamic legal

54 Interviews with Ma'ruf Amin Jakarta, 2010; with Asrorun Niam Sholeh, Jakarta, 2010; and with Wahiduddin Adams, Jakarta, 2010.

55 Lucinda J. Peach, *Legislating Morality: Pluralism and Religious Identity in Lawmaking* (Oxford & New York: Oxford University Press, 2002).

56 Interviews with Asrorun Niam Sholeh, Jakarta, 2010; with Maulana Hasanudin, Jakarta, 2010; and with Ma'ruf Amin, Jakarta, 2010.

57 Interview with Asrorun Ni'am Sholeh, Jakarta, 2010.

58 Karni et al., *35 Tahun Majelis Ulama Indonesia*; MUI, *Himpunan Fatwa MUI Sejak 1975* (Jakarta: Erlangga, 2011), pp. 7–8.

opinions have equal standing and one does not abrogate another, provided it has been formulated on the basis of agreed fatwa guidance and procedure. However, should there be a conflict between fatwas, MUI's national Fatwa Commission and its regional branches will meet to discuss and find the best solution to the problem.

Concerning the fatwa format, the Commission has stated it should consist of five components: the title, general background, dictum, description and appendices, if required. The fatwa opens with the title and decision number. The general background follows containing items such as the grounds and urgency of the fatwa, points for consideration such as *adillat al-aḥkām* (Islamic legal evidences) and prior Fatwa Commission decisions, ulama and expert opinions, and other supporting facts. The dictum section explains the fatwa's substance and provides some recommendations or solutions if needed. Then follows the fatwa description and analysis. The fifth and last section is the list of appendices, if required. The fatwa is signed by the Chairman and the Secretary of the Fatwa Commission. This format is a model of state laws, decrees and other official orders in Indonesia.[59]

3.3.1.2 Fatwa Issuance Methodology

The fatwa issuance methodology is not static, as assumed by those who see MUI as a conservative ulama organisation. The methodology changes over time and it indicates that the fatwa-makers of this organisation do not decide fatwas from an abstract and acontextual space. An important question here is: "What is the MUI methodology for issuing fatwas, and how was it developed?" The way the Fatwa Commission draws up Islamic legal opinions has changed over time. It depends not only on the established discourse of Islamic jurisprudence and sharia, but also relates to the political, legal and cultural circumstances of MUI specifically as well as in Indonesia more broadly. From 1975 to 1980, under the chairmanship of Ghozali, MUI did not yet have an established procedure for issuing a fatwa. MUI's methods for drawing up Islamic legal opinion in that era depended on the two following conditions: the first was the presence of questions that required a response from the Commission,[60] and second was the presence of questions requested by the government, social institutions or from other parts of MUI such as other commissions or branches.

59 This format is not found in fatwa issued by other Islamic organisations such as Muhammadiyah and NU. The fatwa format of NU, for instance, is in the form of a direct legal statement, as is common with Islamic legal edicts issued by fatwa institutions and individuals in Middle Eastern countries.

60 Answering questions is not compulsory for the Fatwa Commission. It has a set of criteria to decide whether or not an answer is warranted to a particular question.

Following this, the Commission would organise a meeting, which was usually attended by the chairman and members of the Commission.[61] When possible the Commission would also invite experts with expertise on issues related to the fatwa.[62] They would normally meet once, but some fatwas needed several meetings before a final decision could be reached. After the discussion was complete, the fatwa was then issued in the form of an Islamic decree.

Although the method of fatwa issuance had not been officially formulated, MUI had clearly adopted the Shāfiʿī school of Islamic law[63] which refers to the Qurʾān, Sunna, *ijmāʿ* (ulama consensus) and *qiyās* (analogical reasoning).[64] This is evident from the standardised format of MUI fatwas that reflected the hierarchy of the four above-mentioned Islamic sources. MUI usually attaches the Qurʾānic reference. If the Qurʾān does not have either an explicit or implicit answer to the question, the fatwa refers to the tradition of the Prophet Muḥammad or Sunna. If the Sunna does not mention anything about this issue, the fatwa employs ulama consensus or *ijmāʿ* as the legal foundation for determining the fatwa. Finally, if there is no ulama consensus, a fatwa can be issued based on *qiyās*. On this basis, fatwas issued by MUI often included a complete set of citations of the arguments relied on from these four sources. If the Fatwa Commission failed to reach an agreement in its deliberations, it would delay issuing the fatwa until a consensus could be achieved. From a *fiqh* discourse perspective, this is termed *mawqūf* (postponement). A *mawqūf* would normally be declared when a place of textual reference (*maʾkhadh*),[65] explicitly dealing with the subject matter could not be found.

The Fatwa Commission published more than twenty fatwa from 1975 to 1980, mostly related to serious problems within Indonesian society, politics and Muslim rituals, such as the ban on narcotics and slaughtering animals with machines, the Islamic legal status of an unwanted child, interfaith marriage, and many other issues. During this era, there were more than fifteen fatwas that specifically related to state laws.[66]

61 MUI, *15 Tahun Majelis Ulama Indonesia*, pp. 106–7.

62 Mudzhar, *Fatwa of the Council of Indonesian Ulama*, p. 68; Wahiduddin Adams, *Pola Penyerapan Fatwa Majelis Ulama Indonesia (MUI) Dalam Peraturan Perundang-Undangan 1975–1997* (Jakarta: Departemen Agama, 2004), p. 116.

63 MUI, *20 Tahun Majelis Ulama Indonesia*, p. 65.

64 Adams, *Pola Penyerapan Fatwa Majelis Ulama Indonesia (MUI) Dalam Peraturan Perundang-Undangan 1975–1997*, p. 116.

65 The term *maʾkhadh*, which is popularly used among traditionalists in Indonesia indicates a textual citation, which is also sometimes called *maqāla* or a treatise.

66 MUI, *Himpunan Fatwa MUI Sejak 1975*, 2011; Mudzhar, *Fatwa of the Council of Indonesian Ulama*, p. 71; MUI, *Himpunan Fatwa Majelis Ulama Indonesia*; MUI, *15 Tahun Majelis Ulama Indonesia*, p. 126. The fatwas included: 1) Fatwa on Friday prayer obligations for

Although the Fatwa Commission had a new Chairman in 1981, Ibrahim Hosen, the fatwa issuance methodology remained relatively similar to that which had existed under Ghozali, until the Fatwa Commission introduced new guidance on issuing fatwas and recommendations in 1986. In this new guidance, two contrasting tendencies were apparent: first, its eclectic methodology, combining the diverse opinions of different *madhhab* provided a solid argument could be built, and second, direct *ijtihād* to the Qur'ān and Sunna.[67] This method, of course, granted greater freedom to implement an independent *ijtihād*, because it did not restrict the scholars to just one school of Islamic thought or *madhhab* but opened up the possibility of a literal understanding of the Qur'ān and Sunna. In following this method, the Fatwa Commission deviated from the traditionalist Muslim groups who argued that *taqlīd* (following only one school of Islamic law) was compulsory because no living Muslims, including the members of the Fatwa Commission, were qualified to conduct Islamic legal reasoning. Traditionalist groups consider there is no Indonesian Muslim scholar who has reached the level of *mujtahid muṭlaq* (unrestricted *mujtahid*), but instead they remained qualified at the level of *mujtahid fī al-madhhab* (*mujtahid* within one of limited schools of Islamic law), therefore, they should follow one of the four established schools of Islamic law in undertaking Islamic legal reasoning.[68] They believed that employing different schools of Islamic law for solving one issue should be avoided because it could potentially lead to the attitude of *tatabbuʿ al-rukhaṣ* (selecting easier religious dispensation) and *talāʿub* (manipulation) in issuing fatwa. NU, for instance, has restricted this use of eclectic methods since its National Congress in 1935.[69]

---

musāfir (travellers) on a ship; 2) Fatwa on the five daily prayers and fasting in regions where there is an imbalance between day and night time; 3) Fatwa on *istiṭāʿa* (capability) to undertake the pilgrimage to Mecca; 4) Fatwa on *miqāt* (the border where Indonesian pilgrims should wear white clothes (*ihrām*) as a symbolic start of the *ḥajj*; 5) Fatwa on anti-menstruation pills; 6) Fatwa on writing the Qur'ān in non-Arabic script; 7) Fatwa on *dūʿa dafʿ al-balāʾ* (a prayer to avoid curses); 8) Fatwa on high-ranking officials setting an example in conducting *ībāda* (acts of worship); 9) Fatwa on *jamāʿa* (groups), *khilāfa* (caliphate) and *bayʿa* (oaths); 10) Fatwa on the trivialisation of religion and misuse of religious texts; 11) Fatwa on living humbly; 12) Fatwa on preparations towards the People's General Assembly meeting; 13) Fatwa on narcotic abuse; 14) Fatwa on repositioning a corpse; 15) Fatwa on Christmas.

67 Interview with Maulana Hasanuddin, Jakarta, 2010. Hasanuddin was Ibrahim Hosen's former secretary and also a member of MUI's Fatwa Commission.

68 Ibn Ṣalāḥ, *Fatāwā Wa Masāʾil Ibn Ṣalāḥ Fī al-Tafsīr Wa al-Ḥadīth Wa al-Uṣūl Wa al-Fiqh Wa Maʿahu Adab al-Muftī Wa al-Mustaftī*, ed. ʿAbd al-Muʿṭī Amīn Qalʿajī (Beirut: Dār al-Maʿrifa, 1986).

69 Mudzhar, *Fatwa of the Council of Indonesian Ulama*, p. 80.

There are two advances to be highlighted in the 1986 fatwa methodology: the first was the introduction of collective *ijtihād* and the second was the adoption of the concept of *maṣlaḥa* (public interest). The adoption of collective *ijtihād* was a rejection of the stagnant position of traditionalist Muslim scholars who argued that the 'door' of *ijtihād*, in accordance with Wael Hallaq, closed after the death of al-Ṭabarī.[70] By promoting the concept of this collective Islamic legal reasoning, the Fatwa Commission placed itself beyond the traditionalist scholars who mostly view *muftī* (fatwa-givers) as Muslim jurists with complete, multi-disciplinary knowledge.[71] The emergence of diverse new disciplines of knowledge in the modern era has, according to MUI, made it impossible for the brain of one single *muftī* to encompass all these disciplines, particularly at a specialised depth, and MUI has therefore stipulated the importance of collective *ijtihād* to handle modern issues. Eickelman envisages a modern *muftī* as just as likely to be an engineer or medical doctor.[72]

Muhammad Qasim Zaman states that the use of collective *ijtihād* and its antecedents from early Islam[73] reflects the spirit of *tajdīd* (Islamic renewal), but it has some crucial issues.[74] In the case of MUI, collective *ijtihād* can open the instrumentalisation of fatwas, for instance to justify the ruling regime's interests as happened in the Suharto era, because it enables different models of interpretations and actors to participate the issuance of a fatwa. Muhammad Qasim Zaman views collective *ijtihād* as a contested space for the so-called traditionalist and modernist camps. The former group fear a tendency of

70 Wael Hallaq, "Was the Gate of Ijtihad Closed?" *International Journal of Middle East Studies* 16, no. 01 (1984): 3–41.

71 See, for instance, requirements for *muftī* to master all disciplines of Islam in Ibn Ṣalāḥ's *Fatāwā Wa Masā'il*, pp. 21–41.

72 Dale F Eickelman, "Clash of Cultures? Intellectuals, Their Public, and Islam," in *Intellectuals in the Modern Islamic World: Transmission, Transformation and Communication*, ed. Stephane A. Dudoignon, Komatsu Hisao, and Kosugi Yasushi (Routledge, 2013), 289–304, p. 301; cf. John L. Esposito, "Contemporary Islam: Reformation or Revolution?," in *The Oxford History of Islam* (Oxford & New York: Oxford University Press, 1999), 643–90.

73 The early antecedent of collective *ijtihād* is evident in Ibn Ṣalāḥ's *Adab al-Muftī wa al-Mustaftī*. He allows a specialist to engage in the process of making a fatwa based on his/her expertise. Ibn Ṣalāḥ, *Fatāwā Wa Masā'il*, p. 28.

74 Muhammad Qasim Zaman, "The Ulama and Contestations on Religious Authority," in *Islam and Modernity: Key Issues and Debates* (Edinburgh: Edinburgh University Press, 2009), 206–36, p. 227; Muhammad Qasim Zaman, "The 'Ulama of Contemporary Islam and Their Conceptions on the Common Good," in *Public Islam and the Common Good*, ed. Armando Salvatore and Dale F. Eickelman (Leiden & Boston: Brill, 2006), 129–56; M.K. Masud, B.M. Messick, and D.S. Powers, *Islamic Legal Interpretation* (Cambridge, Massachusetts, London: Harvard University Press, 1996).

secularising fatwa in the name of *ijtihād*,[75] whereas the latter group firmly believes that collective *ijtihād* is an absolute necessity due to the wider issues—not only religious but also secular—confronting Islam. A related issue of great concern to MUI at the time was that its fatwas were considered as just some of many issued by different fatwa-givers in Indonesia. From the 1980s to the 1990s, other Islamic institutions such as NU, Muhammadiyah, and Persis also issued fatwas, and Indonesian Muslims were free to select amongst them.[76] This contrasts strongly to the current MUI position emerging as the highest authority on fatwas in Indonesia. The instigation of collective *ijtihād* and the concept of *maṣlaḥa* can then be viewed as a reflection of the open-minded approach of MUI in the 1980s.

The accommodation of the above-mentioned notion of public interest in MUI fatwa-making can be seen as progressive on the part of MUI, given the long-standing rejection of Indonesian Muslim jurists of this methodology. The traditionalists view *maṣlaḥa* as a very elastic concept open to abuse by Islamic liberal groups (the MUI fear of liberal groups is discussed later in this chapter). Alternative views of *maṣlaḥa* are not a new phenomenon in the tradition of the Sunnī *ijtihād*; as Frank Vogel states, *maṣlaḥa* has been subject to different opinions among Muslim jurists. Ibn Taymiyya (d. 1328) is one example of those who reject the use of *maṣlaḥa* as an independent root of Islamic law.[77] However, most Muslim jurists recommend the use of *maṣlaḥa* because of its flexibility in generating rational and textual arguments at the same time. Felicitas Opwis argues that *maṣlaḥa* can offer a solution to many legal problems that remain based on the "finite text" of Islam on one hand and grants *mujtahid* to answer questions or problems which are not mentioned in the texts of Islam.[78]

On 30 August 1997, the Fatwa Commission drew up new fatwa guidelines refining its previous methodology. Some reasons behind the publication of these new guidelines were advances in science and technology, as well as the increased religious consciousness of Muslim communities attempting to seek out rational grounds for Islam in facing the modern world.[79] The 1997

75 Zaman, "The Ulama and Contestations on Religious Authority", p. 228.

76 MUI, *20 Tahun Majelis Ulama Indonesia*, pp. 71–2.

77 Frank E. Vogel, *Islamic Law and the Legal System of Saudí: Studies of Saudi Arabia* (Leiden: Brill, 2000), pp. 343–4.

78 Felicitas Opwis, "Maslaha in Contemporary Islamic Legal Theory," *Islamic Law and Society* 12, no. 2 (2005): 82–223, p. 183; Felicitas Opwis, *Maṣlaḥah and the Purpose of the Law: Islamic Discourse on Legal Change from the 4th/10th to 8th/14th Century* (Leiden & Boston: Brill, 2010).

79 MUI, *Himpunan Fatwa Majelis Ulama Indonesia*, p. 1.

guidelines cover some methodological issues, but the emphasis is on the use of public interest and also collective *ijtihād*. It is mentioned that the fatwa must refer to the Qur'ān, Sunna, and not contradict *maṣlaḥa*. MUI also states that collective *ijtihād* must be consulted through consideration of the various opinions of Islamic jurists and experts before publishing a fatwa. This may involve non-Islamic legal experts or *mujtahid* in the traditional sense.

In order to be technically effective and manageable, the 1997 fatwa guidelines introduced a special task force. Each request sent to the Commission seeking a fatwa or answer to an issue related to Islam was handled first by the special task force before going to the desk of the Fatwa Commission.[80] This task force was responsible for registering all questions and problems addressed to the Fatwa Commission. The request should outline the details of the request, such as the name of the sender, the date of the letter and the questions asked. Subsequently the task force would select and categorise the questions into the following groups: questions to be answered by the Fatwa Commission, questions to be addressed by a MUI provincial branch, questions to be answered by the task force itself and lastly questions not requiring an answer from either the Fatwa Commission or the task force.

The task force then distributed the groups of questions as categorised to the MUI Fatwa Commission at different levels so that a fatwa could be issued in response. Considering the large number of questions asked, the Fatwa Commission's chairperson had the authority to decide which questions and problems should be prioritised for immediate response. The Commission's chairperson was also responsible for appointing one or several commission members to compose a working paper related to the questions and problems to be discussed. The meeting met its quorum when attended by more than 50% of its members. From 1985 to 2000, the Fatwa Commission issued around thirty-one fatwas which can be categorised into four themes; Islamic rites, religious sects, social issues, and science and technology. Under the Islamic rites theme, some fatwas issued were on the legal validity of conducting a prayer at a multi-storied mosque, using funds collected from religious alms to finance profitable activities, public morality, and so forth. Under the theme of religious sects, fatwas were issued, for example, on the theological status of Darul Arqam, Sunna-rejecting groups, and on the Angel Gabriel visiting human beings. Under the theme of social issues, fatwas focused on the inclusion of

80 During this period, the task force was composed of Ma'ruf Amin (Chairman), Hasanuddin, Nazri Adlani (member), Ichwan Sam (member), Anwar Ibrahim (member), Ali Musthafa Yacub (member) and Afwan Faizin (member).

Qur'ānic verses in popular songs, the Islamic legal status of massage parlours, transsexual persons, and so forth.

3.3.1.3 New Conservatism

The nature of the Fatwa Commission changed significantly with the commencement of the new political and legal order of Indonesia in 1998. In 2000, Amin replaced Ibrahim Hosen as Chairman of the Fatwa Commission. Amin came from a NU background, where he had held the position of chairman of the Sharia Consultancy Board. Although NU itself, as one of the largest Islamic mass organisations in Indonesia, does not seek to implement sharia as the positive law of Indonesia, Amin himself is a prominent figure in the mission for shariatisation.[81] LPPOM's *Jurnal Halal* portrays Amin's pro-shariatisation view as follows:

> [T]his ulama who is active as an Islamic preacher and in driving the inclusion of sharia into a positive law is always promoting the ideal that Islam is a positive religion, but maintains a strict stance, reminding Muslim society about living in a lawful manner, and promoting the Islamic principle of lawfulness within society such as through halal certification for food, sharia banks for the economy and so forth.[82]

This statement suggests that the shariatisation of Indonesian law was something that was planned and sought by the MUI Fatwa Commission during Amin's leadership. Under his chairmanship, the Fatwa Commission consisted of two deputy chairmen (Amin Suma, State Islamic University Jakarta, and Anwar Ibrahim, Muhammadiyah), a secretary (Maulana Hasanudin, NU) and a deputy secretary (Afifi Fauzi Abbas). In total, twenty-five ulama sat on the Commission, with most of them being recruited from NU and Muhammadiyah and several other organisations.[83]

---

81 Interview with Ma'ruf Amin, Jakarta, 2010.

82 Usman Effendi, "Berbahaya Kalau Lembaga Pemeriksa Halal Terlepas Dari MUI," *Jurnal Halal* (Jakarta, October 2008), p. 28.

83 MUI, *Himpunan Fatwa MUI Sejak 1975* (Jakarta: Erlangga, 2011), p. 381. The NU ulama occupying positions on the Commission included Hasanudin, Agil Hussein al-Munawwar, Hafidz Usman, Irfan Zidni, Nahar Nahrowi, Ali Musthafa Yaqub, Maria Ulfah (female), Mursyidah Thahir (female), Asnawi Latief, Masyhuri Na'im, and Ghazalie Masroeri, who were there due to their expertise in Islamic jurisprudence and Islamic legal theory (hermeneutics). Muhammadiyah ulama on the Council included Faturrahman Djamil and Fattah Wibisono.

One year after the 2000 National Congress, the Fatwa Commission introduced a new method of fatwa issuance which was envisioned to revise the shortcomings of the 1997 method. The 2001 guidelines begin by describing the situation of the modern world in which the progress of science and technology has enabled human beings to achieve happiness but also created new problems that require immediate solutions. The 2001 fatwa guidelines state that leaving problems unresolved for the *umma* was the same as allowing them to become overwhelmed by confusion. This would be an intolerable situation from the perspective of *iʿtiqādī* (based on faith) and *sharʿī* (based on the holy sources of Islam).[84] MUI, as an ulama forum, should be responsible and capable of ensuring that Muslims do not become confused over religious matters.

The 2001 guidelines state that fatwa must not only work for the requester but also for the public good. This clarification seems addressed to the public confusion over whether the MUI fatwa applies to the requester and not to others. What was novel with the 2001 fatwa methodology was that the Fatwa Commission could issue a fatwa of its own accord, as a proactive measure or in anticipation of issues.[85] Traditionally speaking, a fatwa is a response to a request or problem, but now the Fatwa Commission could proactively publish an Islamic legal opinion without requiring a question by a fatwa requester. There are also so-called anticipative fatwas where the Commission issues a fatwa in anticipation of what will happen in the future. The difference between MUI's normal fatwas and these two proactive and anticipative fatwas is that the former are issued in response to actual questions or problems while the latter anticipates questions or problems which are current or will occur in the future.[86] Since the implementation of these proactive and anticipative fatwas, MUI has issued many aimed at controlling the development of Islamic

84 Ibid, p. 382.

85 Ibid, p. 384.

86 Interview with Ma'ruf Amin, Jakarta, 2010, and interview with Asrorun Niam Sholeh, Jakarta, 2010. I had an interesting experience while interviewing Asrorun Niam Sholeh. While conducting the interview, the call for midday prayer began, but he did not request the interview be postponed. Afterwards, I went down to the first floor of the MUI office where I was asked by the front desk staff not to conduct an interview during prayer-time during the next visit. When I told Sholeh about this, he said that I should not worry about it, adding that he and many other young MUI board members, who had moderate views, were often criticised by conservative and fundamentalist groups within MUI for not being committed to implementing the *kāffa* (total) Islam within the internal institutions of the organisation. This reminds me of the opinion of Cholil Ridwan, MUI's representative in charge of the arts and cultural affairs, who said that many members of the MUI elite neglect to implement sharia, even in small things such as performing *salat jama'ah* (collective prayer).

discourse in Indonesia. A number of conservative-leaning fatwas have been published as part of efforts to anticipate problems that will endanger the belief of Indonesian Muslims. One example of this is MUI's fatwa banning liberalism, secularism and pluralism in Indonesia.[87]

Another key characteristic of the 2001 fatwa guidance is its shift to direct referencing of the primary sources of Islamic law. The 1997 fatwa method directly reviews references from the Qur'ān and Sunna, without restricting itself to one specific *madhhab* or Islamic school of law interpretation, thus following a similar model to that of Muhammadiyah scholars.[88] The 2001 fatwa method starts by investigating the opinions of Islamic jurists scattered throughout the *kitab kuning*[89] and only then moving to the Qur'ān and Sunna. This is precisely the method used by NU ulama when determining a fatwa in *Bahsul Masa'il*.[90] For those issues where the basic legal argument is clearly set forth in the Qur'ān and Sunna, referred to as *al-aḥkām al-qaṭʿiyya* (clear rulings, the responsibility of the Fatwa Commission is only to mention the references as they appear in the Qur'ān and Sunna.

This principle is in accordance with the consensus of Islamic jurists who oppose any attempts to reinterpret the established *al-aḥkām al-qaṭʿiyya* concept. This is in keeping with al-Shāfiʿī's pronouncement: "for all things that God has provided a basis for in the Qur'ān and in the explicit sayings of the Prophet, there shall not be any conflict between them for those that understand."[91] Hence any insistence on undertaking a new interpretation would be judged as committing a forbidden interpretation. Regarding *khilāfiyya fī al-madhāhib* (juristic disagreement within the different schools of Islamic

87 This issue is discussed further in Chapter 6.

88 The *Majlis Tarjih* is Muhammadiyah's forum of ulama which is devoted to discussing and issuing fatwa. The *Majlis Tarjih* was first conducted in the 16th Muhammadiyah Congress in 1927 in Pekalongan.

89 The Indonesian term for Arabic Islamic classical literature, which literally means a yellow book. They are so named because many *kitab kuning* are printed on yellow paper. The *kitab kuning* are the main reference employed by traditionalist Muslim scholars such those from NU to determine fatwa. The opposite of the *kitab kuning* are *kitab putih*, which literally means "white books" because they are printed on white paper. In the Indonesian context, *kitab putih* are modern Islamic Arabic-language books. Example of *kitab putih* is *al-Manār* of Muḥammad ʿAbdu and Rashīd Riḍā, *Fiqh al-Sunna* of Sayyid Sābiq, and *al-Fiqh al-Islāmī wa Adillatuhu* of Wahba al-Zuḥaylī.

90 This is an Indonesian-Arabic term for a public fatwa consultation, and a forum for NU ulama to discuss and issue fatwa. The *Bahsul Masail* is regularly conducted by NU and all of its branches. Interview with Maulana Hasanudin, Jakarta, 2010.

91 Al-Shafi'i, *al-Risalah* (Dar al-Kutub al-Ilmiyyah: 1988), p. 323. In Arabic: "[*k*]*ullu mā aqāma allāhu bihi al-ḥujja fī kitābihi aw ʿalā lisāni nabiyyihi manṣūṣan bayyinan lā yaḥillu al-ikhtilāfu fīhi liman ʿalimahu*".

law), also referred to as *taʿāruḍ fī al-madhāhib* (contradictions in the schools of Islamic law), the Fatwa Commission, in the first instance, follows the method of *al-jamʿ wa al-tawfīq* (compile and reconcile). This is often employed by Sunnī-jurists to reach a compromise between two conflicting fatwas. Where this method fails to provide a legal answer, the Fatwa Commission determines its legal opinion by relying on the concept of *tarjīḥ* (preferring the stronger opinion). This involves gauging the strength of the different opinions among the schools of Islamic law (*muqārana al-madhāhib* literally meaning to compare many Islamic schools of law) to decide which argument is the strongest and which has the strongest sources. As an additional tool in this analysis, the Commission also uses the principle of *al-qawāʿid al-fiqhiyya* (Islamic legal maxims).

The 2001 fatwa guidance encourages the use of collective *ijtihād* for questions where the Fatwa Commission is unable to find answers from the different schools of Islamic law. In doing so, the following stages of collective *ijtihād* should be followed. The first is the process of *ilḥāqī*, meaning that questions and problems with no clear answer in credible classical Islamic texts (*al-kutūb al-muʿtabara*)[92] can be solved by referring to questions and problems of a similar nature which are discussed in the texts (*mulḥaq bih*). The second is the process of *istinbāṭī* that literally means developing a legal Islamic opinion from the Qurʾān and Sunna which is utilised when the first approach does not work. Analytical and interpretive frameworks used in this latter approach are *qiyāsī* (analogical reasoning), *istiṣlāḥī* (using public interest into account), *istiḥsānī* (juristic preference) and *sadd al-dharāʾīʿ* (forbidding lawful things that may lead to unlawful ends).[93] In the wider discourse of Islamic law, the use of the analogical reasoning method is largely accepted by most Muslim scholars. Most of the *madhāhib*s (schools of Islamic law) utilise this method, although it is particularly popular amongst followers of the Shāfiʿī school. The notion of *istiṣlāḥī* has similar roots to the concept of public interest or *maṣlaḥa*, although it indicates a preference for collective *ijtihād* based on the spirit of the sharia's intent. Muḥammad ʿĀbid al-Jābirī calls it as "re-rooting the origins of *fiqh* in accordance with the legal intents of sharia."[94]

92 In the context of Indonesian ulama, *al-kutūb al-muʿtabara* are associated with the credible texts used within the Sunni tradition (Mālikī, Ḥanafī, Shāfiʿī and Ḥanbalī).

93 MUI, *Himpunan Fatwa Majelis Ulama Indonesia*, p. 365; MUI, *Himpunan Fatwa MUI Sejak 1975*, 2011. This explanation was also given by MUI in response to a question posed by Abdullah from Jakarta, on 4 July 2009, who asked "What is MUI's method for issuing fatwas?"

94 Mohammed Abed Al-Jabri, *Democracy, Human Rights and Law in Islamic Thought* (London & New York: I.B. Tauris, 2009), p. 91.

MUI considers its method of fatwa issuance to be progressive and modern. However, outside MUI many progressive and modern models of dealing with Islamic law are emerging. MUI views this development as dangerous and in 2005, MUI published a fatwa on the criteria of *maṣlaḥa*. Many people supported this fatwa because they viewed the use of *maṣlaḥa* as a legal concept for consideration would lead to the issuance of more moderate fatwa by MUI. However, this did not occur because this fatwa was also intended to counter the liberal tendency of several Muslim intellectuals and activists, such as those in the JIL and other groups using the notion of *maṣlaḥa*.[95] MUI stated that the adoption of the public interest concept in many publications by JIL and other groups was misleading. MUI categorises these liberal groups as *ifrāṭī* (extremists) or *sesat* (deviant) groups. On this basis MUI felt obliged to respond by drawing up a specific legal opinion on the concept of public interest.[96] MUI's criticism of these groups is evident in the arguments it used in issuing the fatwa. It stated firstly that the concept of *maṣlaḥa* or public interest was often employed by such groups to provide an Islamic legal opinion without following the limits and regulations (in the Arabic phrase, *bilā ḥudūd wa ḍawābiṭ*) agreed by classical ulama of *uṣūl al-fiqh* on how to properly apply this concept. Secondly, it claimed, the misuse of this concept by some groups had led to mistakes in the formulation of fatwa and to confusion within the Muslim community. Thirdly, MUI felt obliged to clarify the proper use of Islamic law by issuing a set of criteria for *maṣlaḥa*. The general content of this fatwa covered three aspects. First, the purpose of the tenet of *maṣlaḥa* according to Islamic law is to support the implementation of the aims of purposive sharia (*maqāṣid al-sharīʿa*), which imply the full protection of religion (*al-dīn*), reason (*al-ʿaql*), life (*al-ḥayā*), property (*al-māl*) and lineage (*al-nasl*). In some works, on Islamic legal theory, these five concepts are popularly referred to as *al-ḍarūriyyāt al-khamsa* (the five necessities). Secondly, MUI argued, the notion of public interest must be applied in accordance with the main textual sources of Islam, namely the Qurʾān and Sunna. The use of this concept to contradict the Qurʾān and Sunna thuscannot be justified as *maṣlaḥa*. Thirdly, a body with the authority to settle the criteria of public interest is an institution that has competency in the domain of sharia, which must issue fatwa in the form of collective *ijtihād*. Although the MUI fatwa on *maṣlaḥa* was intended to

95 The Wahid Institute, International Centre for Islam and Pluralism (ICIP), the Rahima Foundation, Jaringan Intelektual Muda Muhammadiyah (JIMM, Network of Young Muhammadiyah Intellectuals), and many others are viewed by MUI as excessive in their use of *maṣlaḥa* and *maqāṣid al-sharīʿa*.

96 See MUI's answer to the question posed by Abdullah on 04 July 2009, detailed above.

clarify the proper use of *maṣlaḥa*, it did not accommodate the whole array of *maṣlaḥa* discourse in Sunnī Islamic legal theory, such as Najm al-Ṭūfī's concept of *maṣlaḥa*, as used by liberal Muslim thinkers of Indonesia.

However, despite the controversies that have arisen regarding the role of the Fatwa Commission since its establishment, overall it can be said to have taken a far more independent stance from the state since the early days of the reform era. The increased authority of the Fatwa Commission is also evident in the way its fatwas and recommendations have stimulated Islamic public discourse. This means that the Fatwa Commission has been able to insert its fatwas into social, cultural political realms. In this regard, a fatwa is not just issued to simulate discourse, but to provide a religious argument at the practical level.

3.3.2 *Lembaga Pengkajian Pangan, Obat-obatan dan Kosmetika (LPPOM, the Institute for Foods, Drugs and Cosmetics Assessment)*

3.3.2.1 Pioneer of the Halal Movement in Indonesia

The issue of halalness—the lawfulness of goods—is one of the most important and strategic vehicles for fostering the shariatisation of Indonesia. This is because it covers a broad range of issues, related not only to theological discourse, but also to politics and to some extent economic matters. MUI thus feels a sense of responsibility to demand that the state regulates the lawfulness of goods. Although this has long been a concern of MUI, it has only been over the past decade that the Council has begun to take a proactive approach to lobbying the government, particularly with regard to the draft law on halal product assurance. Amin, for instance, stated in LPPOM's *Jurnal Halal* that there would be difficulties in ensuring the permissible nature of goods if this responsibility were not turned over to MUI.[97]

What MUI is striving for with regard to halal issuance rights reflects an issue that is emerging throughout the Muslim world. Mustafa Ceric, the grand *muftī* of Bosnia-Herzegovina, for instance, said that Muslims could conquer the world through the halal movement. Ceric urged the *umma* to take the lead in the world economy by promoting the halal movement, because food represents a basic necessity for all human beings.[98] This appeal makes sense considering that Muslim consumers represent a significant section of the

97 Effendi, "Berbahaya Kalau Lembaga Pemeriksa Halal Terlepas Dari MUI", p. 28.

98 "Former Bosnian Grand Mufti Addresses Middle East Halal Conference", The Global Muslim Brotherhood Daily Watch, 3 January 2013, https://www.globalmbwatch.com/2013/01/03/former-bosnian-grand-mufti-addresses-middle-east-halal-conference-mustafa-ceric-once-urged-muslims-to-conquer-world-through-halalinagural/, viewed on 22 May 2022.

global market: around 1.83 billion people, with an estimated value of $2.3 trillion USD.[99] Indonesia, with the world's largest Muslim population, began to address this issue in the 1990s.

LPPOM is the first Indonesian body with the task of investigating and certifying the permissibility of foods, drugs and cosmetics. Besides being motivated by the importance of halalness in sharia, to which MUI applies a "zero tolerance" principle in rejecting the contamination of commodities by unlawful elements, LPPOM was established following the 1988 controversy over the use of pig fat in some commercial products. *Canopy*, the internal bulletin of Brawijaya University, Malang, East Java, published an article, written by Tri Susanto, revealing that some foods and drinks in public markets contained unlawful materials.[100] This article, which was widely circulated in the public domain, drew an angry response from Muslim consumers. Food and drink sales declined by almost 80% following its publication. If the consumption rate fell any further, this would have had a negative impact on the Indonesian economy, because the food and beverage industries were a vital part of the economy of the country.[101]

On 1 December 1988, MUI and representatives of the Indonesian governments responded to this snowballing problem through a high-level meeting. One of the recommendations to emerge from the meeting was that MUI should establish an institute responsible for reviewing foods, drugs and cosmetics. Finally, on 6 January 1989, LPPOM was established. Its original purpose was to protect Muslim consumers from buying, selling and consuming unlawful commodities, whilst ensuring the political and economic stability of Indonesia.[102] The pioneers of LPPOM within MUI were Hasan Basri (MUI eneral Cchairman, 1985–1998), Amin Aziz (the first executive director of LPPOM, 1989–1994), Aziz Darwis (deputy director), and Peunoh Daly (deputy director). MUI ordered LPPOM to conduct the following tasks: to classify and study the food, drugs and cosmetics available in the Muslim community; to undertake research and formulate concepts with regards to production, commodification and utilisation of food, drugs and cosmetics so that these products complied with Islamic teachings; to study and formulate regulations for restaurants, hotels, animal production facilities and the like regarding the use

99 The report, written by Susan Labadi, can be read at "USA: ISNA Advances the Halal Movement at World Halal Forum—Europe," https://halalfocus.net/usa-isna-advances-the-halal-movement-at-world-halal-forum-europe/, accessed on 21 July 2022.

100 Aisjah Girindra, *Dari Sertifikasi Menuju Labelisasi Halal* (Jakarta: Pustaka Jurnal Halal, 2008), p. 27.

101 Ibid, p. 28.

102 Karni et al., *35 Tahun Majelis Ulama Indonesia*, p. 169.

of ingredients and processes for preparing products; to submit the results of these studies to the MUI Executive Board so the data could be used as a reference in determining the organisation's policy on the processing and commodification of food, drugs and cosmetics; and to organise activities along with the government and private business groups.[103]

LPPOM is an institutional body within MUI with its own executive consisting of a Dewan Penasehat (board of trustees), Dewan Pembina (advisory board) and Dewan Pelaksana (executive board). Unlike MUI, LPPOM still accommodates high-ranking state officials in its structure, and there are at least four ministers included on the board of trustees: the Ministers for Religious Affairs, Health, Trade, and Industry. These positions were probably granted to these ministers due to the close relationship between their portfolios and LPPOM's focus. Another factor may be that LPPOM needs strong support from the state, because the process for issuing halal certification cuts across multiple layers and involves a number of parties with vested interests such as national and international companies, and Muslim and other groups. Furthermore, the Board of Trustees and the Executive Board also have representatives from several Muslim organisations—particularly MUI member organisations such as NU and Muhammadiyah—as well as experts and professionals.

LPPOM mission is to become a credible body for issuing halal certification in Indonesia as well as globally, to provide a feeling of security for Muslim communities and serve as a world centre for halal information, solutions and standards. In order to become so, LPPOM began to conduct and engage in a number of programmes and activities. Six months after its establishment in 1989, for instance, LPPOM held a limited discussion on "*Pengkajian Metodologis Analisa Senyawa Kimiawi Lemak Babi dalam Produk Pangan*" (Methodological Analysis on the Chemical Compound of Lard in Food Products). Although this first meeting did not successfully encapsulate a standardised method for analysing a lard composite within foods, drugs and cosmetics, it was nonetheless an important event because the MUI general chairman publicly spoke about the agreement with the Ministry of Religious Affairs to support LPPOM as an official institute and as a body responsible for publishing guidance and orders, including the requirement to attach halal labels to food, drugs and cosmetic products.[104] The discussion made many recommendations for further action, for instance, regarding the various methods that could be used to prove the presence of lard within foods, medicines and cosmetics. To sharpen the

103 MUI, *20 Tahun Majelis Ulama Indonesia*, pp. 193–94.

104 MUI, *20 Tahun Majelis Ulama Indonesia*, p. 39.

analysis, it was also recommended that LPPOM needed a database of characters, symptoms and indicators of the end processing of foods, medicines and cosmetics, and this entailed a specific methodological analysis as well. The discussion also asked LPPOM to establish a database of fatty acids, which has not yet been published.[105] The last recommendation is that LPPOM should collaborate with national and international institutions working on the same issues.[106] Since its early days, LPPOM was also pro-active in consolidating its ideas in order to influence the legislation of state law on permissible goods. Through this, LPPOM could promote the civilising aspect of Islamic tradition on important legal aspects related to the consumption of foods, medicines and cosmetics because, apart from occupying a central position in the "civilising process," any law, including the state law, is a path for shaping culture and a means for its dissemination. As a consequence, on 1 December 1989 LPPOM organised a seminar to prepare a national law on food protection and security. This seminar received endorsement from the government of Indonesia, represented by the Minister of Health, business and professional groups, and also scientists. The meeting concluded that food security was not only related to material aspects, namely ingredients, but also important in its spiritual aspects, i.e. religion. The conference also asserted that there was a strong demand for proper controls on the production of food. This recommendation also implicitly enhanced the role of the ulama in wider discourses on food, medicines and cosmetics in Indonesia. In addition, LPPOM specifically proposed that ulama be involved in drafting a state law on the security and protection of food, medicines and cosmetics.[107] Pertinent support from the government for the incorporation of ulama was also demonstrated by the presence of B.J. Habibie, the Minister of Research and Technology at the time, at a seminar on "*Pemanfaatan Produk Bioteknologi untuk Menunjang Produksi Pangan, Obat-obatan dan Komestika*" (Utilising Bio-Technological Products to Support Food Production, Medicines and Cosmetics), held by LPPOM on 12 September 1991. Habibie was the most influential minister in the Suharto cabinet and his endorsement of this seminar was a sign that the government also enthusiastically supported the strengthening of LPPOM's role.

105 In following up on the availability of the database, LPPOM initiated a survey and study into halal labelling and alcoholic drinks in malls and markets in Jakarta and Bogor in 1990. From this study, it was found that 16.8% of 150 food products and 160 soft drinks had halal labels attached. 30.76% contained alcohol. See Aisjah Girindra, *Dari Sertifikasi Menuju Labelisasi Halal* (Jakarta: Pustaka Jurnal Halal, 2008), pp. 40–41.

106 Girindra, *Dari Sertifikasi Menuju Labelisasi Halal*.

107 Ibid, p. 40.

The seminar successfully raised some important issues on the contribution of bioscience and technology for human beings in general and Muslims in particular to encourage and persuade producers of foods, medicines and cosmetics to use these halal biotech products. MUI believed that biotech products would be beneficial for business and also for Muslims as the largest consumer community in Indonesia. This was a sign that the Islamic commodification project had become an important part of LPPOM's agenda for the halal movement. The seminar also encouraged scientists and experts in bio-technological issues to undertake more research that could result in more halal food products, drugs and cosmetics being produced. It was said in the conference that the use of biotech products must be based on the ethics of Islam. Finally, the conference recommended MUI to seek out collaboration with universities and research institutes that had programmes on developing bio-technology.[108] This seminar was a foundational event for LPPOM.

As had been recommended in the seminar and due to its limited resources and equipment to conduct laboratory studies into the halal nature of products, LPPOM established a partnership with the Institut Pertanian Bogor (IPB, the Bogor Agricultural Institute). This cooperation began in a de facto manner in 1991 and a cooperation charter was officially signed in 1993, coinciding with the appointment of Aisjah Girindra as the new LPPOM General Director replacing Aziz. Since then, LPPOM has extended its role and operations not only in Indonesia, but also throughout Southeast Asia. The establishment of LPPOM in the provincial branches of MUI such as West Java and Aceh—in addition to the high numbers of applicants for regional certification from Southeast Asian countries—is clear evidence of its progress. Under the agreement, the IPB not only provided laboratory facilities, but also allowed some of its scientists and researchers to assist LPPOM's work. Although the initial drive behind this cooperation was based on religious factors, there are clear economic benefits for both IPB and LPPOM: IPB is able to earn funds to cover the operational costs of its laboratories and pay its researchers, while LPPOM obtains funds from companies that request halal certification for their products. The cost for halal certificates is around IDR 3.5–5 million for each product, and up until now LPPOM has published certificates for 17,328 products. This represents a tremendous increase in just the past few years, as previously, in 2008, the number of products which received certification stood at 10,242.[109] LPPOM's most

108 Ibid, pp. 42–43.

109 Mahmud Farid, Usman Effendi, and Nadia, "Produk Unik Bersertifikat Halal Apa Tujuannya?" *Jurnal Halal*, 2011, p. 8; LPPOM, *Indonesia Halal Directory 2001* (Jakarta: LPPOM MUI, 2011).

recent statistical data on products that are already halal certified are quite promising. For instance, in 2018, there were 204,222 products, and 274,796 products in 2019. This indicates a significant increase in the number of products that MUI has certified as halal.[110]

While seeking support from the national ulama of Indonesia, in 1993, LPPOM held a Mudhakarah Nasional ("National Study"),[111] which was focused on discussing the Islamic legal status of alcohol content within foods and soft drinks. This was a vibrant meeting, as it was able to attract three hundred ulama attendees. The importance of the Mudhakarah Nasional can be seen from the attendance of two important ministers: the Coordinating Minister for Social Welfare, Azwar Anas, and the Minister for Religious Affairs, Tarmizi Tahir.[112] This forum showed that the ulama and government of Indonesia agreed on the need to establish a legitimate halal certifier. It seems that LPPOM was also successful in using this meeting as a means to promote the importance of halal food products, medicines and cosmetics. In the era of Susilo Bambang Yudoyono (the president of Indonesia from 2004–2014, known as SBY), LPPOM gained more support due to the president's backing of MUI as a whole, although towards SBY's last term, Suryadharma Ali, the Minister of Religious Affairs, succeeding in registering State Law No. 33/2014 on Halal Product Assurance. This State Law, then, meant that LPPOM's position as sole halal certifier was transferred to the Badan Penyelenggara Jaminan Produk Halal (BPJPH, Halal Product Assurance Organising Agency). Jokowi came to support the operation of the BPJPH, and although officially LPPOM is no longer a halal certifier at the time of writing, it can still participate in halal certification as the executing agency of halal auditing under the direction of the BPJPH.

3.3.2.2 National, Regional and International Networks

As well as working on the national level, LPPOM has representative offices in the thirty-three provincial branches of MUI.[113] The activities of these branches

110 "Data Statistik Produk Halal LPPOM-MUI Indonesia 2012–2019," https://www.halalmui.org/, 2020.

111 This forum is called a *Mudhakarah* because it is used by participating ulama to exchange Islamic ideas.

112 Working papers presented in this forum were on (1) 'Alcohol: Its Process of Manufacture, Content and Degree' by Aziz Darwis and Tri Susanto, (2) 'The Benefits and Detriment of Alcohol' by Toni Sugiarto, Ali Yafie and Kartono Muhammad and (3) 'The Islamic Legal Status of Alcohol' by Ibrahim Hosen, Aqil Munawar and Latief Muchtar Girindra, *Dari Sertifikasi Menuju Labelisasi Halal*, 2008, p. 47.

113 The presence of LLPOM can be seen in the provincial branches of MUI in West Java, Lampung, Jakarta, Riau Islands, Riau, South Sulawesi, East Java, Bali, North Sumatra, East

are similar to those of the central headquarters of LPPOM in Jakarta, in that they are asked to issue halal certification of goods by companies in their respective regions. LPPOM has also established cooperation with halal institutions abroad that usually work together in issuing halal certificates for products from their own countries, which are exported to Indonesia. LPPOM stipulates that these institutions must be legal entities and have the support of an Islamic centre that provides services to at least forty Muslims. MUI also requires them to have a permanent office, good management, and qualified human resources in their respective countries, and also to have a fatwa body responsible for issuing Islamic legal opinions as well as experts responsible for undertaking the audit necessary for halal certification. Standard operating procedure and credible administration of these bodies are also demanded within this framework. MUI sees the importance of international connections, and therefore requires the foreign halal certifier to be part of a global network, in particular the World Halal Council.[114]

LPPOM's role at the regional and international level is also evident through its active participation in international conferences and events that discuss the topic and present halal goods. LPPOM's participation is a recognition of the reality that foods, drugs and cosmetics follow the flow of globalisation. Many national food industries are, for instance, importing crude materials from abroad, and halal certification must therefore not only be implemented at the domestic level but also involve other countries. International standardisation of the halal nature of foods, medicines and cosmetics was an absolute necessity. To pave the path, on 15–16 August 1990 LPPOM participated in the International Muslim Food and Technology Exhibition (Imfex) in Singapore. At this forum, as the representatives of LPPOM, Aisjah Girindra and Darwis presented the methods for detecting an unlawful compound within foods, drugs and cosmetics.[115] LPPOM also participated in a conference on Health Nutrition held in Rome, Italy, in 1990, and on 18–21 September 1991 attended a similar international conference in Kuala Lumpur, Malaysia. The latter was organised in response to the fact that the Muslim community is the largest

Kalimantan, Bengkulu, Yogyakarta, West Sumatra, Aceh, Central Java, East Nusa Tenggara, Banten, Gorontalo, Central Kalimantan, Maluku, West Kalimantan, South Sumatra, Central Sulawesi, North Sulawesi, West Papua, South Kalimantan, North Maluku, West Nusa Tenggara, Jambi and Bangka Belitung (*Jurnal Halal*, No. 87 Januari-Februari Th. XIV 2011, pp. 54–55).

114 "Daftar Lembaga Sertifikasi Halal," Halal MUI, 2021, https://www.halalmui.org/mui14/main/page/daftar-lembaga-sertifikasi-halal, viewed on 21 July 2022.

115 Girindra, *Dari Sertifikasi Menuju Labelisasi Halal*, p. 41.

consumer group in the world, with almost one billion people residing either in Muslim countries such as Indonesia, Pakistan, and Malaysia or in European countries. The conference agreed on some important issues such as the need for internationalisation on the halal issue; a global definition of permitted food, including the basic ingredients of food products; the process of production in general; the issue of labelling; global and trans-collaboration between different agencies and associations of Muslim consumers; and the need for holding regular international fora.[116]

LPPOM also played an active role in the establishment process of the World Halal Council (WHC) in 1999 in Jakarta. The background to the formation of the WHC was the complicated nature of lawfulness of foods, especially in the borderless market. From an Islamic point of view, the WHC was needed to resolve the different standards in applying the concept of lawfulness to products from Muslim countries. For instance, LPPOM will not automatically accept a halal certificate issued by international certifiers abroad unless they use similar standards in at least two areas: similar methods in the halal investigation process and similarities in the school of Islamic law adhered to by the certifiers. The creation of the WHC was intended to act as a communication forum for international halal certification bodies. Some topics discussed in this forum were, for instance, certification, standardised investigations, and how to establish a homogeneous outlook on halal-related issues. Two LPPOM members were selected as the presidents of this council: the first was Aisjah Girindra, who was appointed in 1999, and the second was Nadratuzzaman Hosen,[117] elected in 2007.

Before July 2011, LPPOM had approved forty-five international certification agencies to grant halal certificates around the world.[118] LPPOM categorises the approved bodies into several clusters as follows: firstly, around forty-five international certification bodies that specialise in cattle slaughtering, located in

116 Ibid, p. 45.

117 Nadratuzzaman Hosen was elected as executive director of LPPOM in 2005. He is the son of Ibrahim Hosen, the former chairman of the Fatwa Commission and was born in 1961. He obtained his BA in Animal Husbandry from IPB, MEc (Master of Agricultural Economics) and his PhD in Institutional Economics from the University of New England, Armidale, Australia. His education background suited his position as the chairman of LPPOM.

118 These procedures and regulations were stipulated in Jakarta on 15 October 2009 and signed by Sahal Mahfudh (MUI General Chairman) and Ichwan Sam (MUI General Secretary).

Asia,[119] Australia,[120] New Zealand,[121] Europe,[122] the United States of America,[123] Latin America,[124] Canada[125] and Africa.[126] The second cluster are those international certification bodies that specialise in food processing. They number around twenty-eight and are present in Asia,[127] Australia,[128] New Zealand,[129]

---

119 Asia: (1) Association of Certification for the Inspection of Food and Supplies (GIMDES), Turkey, (2) Bahagian Kawalan Makanan Halal Jabatan Hal Ehwal Syariah Kementerian Hal Ehwal Ugama, Brunei, (3) Islamic Dawah Council of the Philippines, Inc, (IDCP), (4) Jabatan Kemajuan Islam Malaysia (JAKIM), Malaysia), (5) Majelis Ugama Islam Singapore (MUIS), Singapore, (6) Office Muslim Affairs (OMA), the Philippines, (7) The Central Islamic Committee of Thailand (CICOT), Thailand, (8) Taiwan Halal Integrity Development Association (THIDA).

120 Australia: (1) Australian Federation of Islamic Councils Inc. (AFIC Inc.), (2) Australian Halal Food Authority and Advisers (AHAA), (3) Australian Halal Food Services (AHFS), (4) Global Halal Trade Centre Pty Ltd (GHTC Pty. Ltd), (5) Halal Sidiq Service, (6) Islamic Association of Katanning, (7) Islamic Council of Western Australia, (8) Perth Mosque Incorporated, (9) Supreme Islamic Council of Halal Meat in Australia Inc., (SICHMA), (10) The Adelaide Mosque Islamic Society of South Australian Inc. (11) The Islamic Coordinating Council of Victoria (ICCV), (12) Western Australian Halal Authority (WAHA).

121 New Zealand: (1) Al-Kautsar Halal Food and Inspection (AL-KAHFI).

122 Europe: Halal Feed and Food Inspection Authority (HFFIA), the Netherlands, (2) Halal Food Authority, England, (3) Halal Quality Control, the Netherlands, (4) Total Quality Halal Correct (TQHC), the Netherlands, (5) Halal Certification Services (HCS), Switzerland, (6) European Institute of Halal Certification, Germany, (7) The Muslim Religious Association of Poland, (MRAP), Poland, (8) The Grand Mosque of Paris, France.

123 United State of America: (1) American Halal Foundation (AHC), (2) Halal Food Council, USA, (3) Halal Transaction of Omaha, (4) Islamic Information Centre of America (IICA), (5) Islamic Service of America (ISA), (6) The Islamic Food and Nutrition Council of America (IFANCA).

124 Latin America: Federation of Muslim Association in Brazil, (2) Islamic Dissemination Centre of Latin America (CDIAL), Brazil.

125 Canada: (1) Halal Monitoring Authority (HMA), (2) Islamic Society North of America.

126 Africa: South African National Halal Authority (SANHA).

127 Asia: (1) Association for the Inspection, Certification of Food and Supplies (GIMDES)—Turkey, (2) 2 Islamic Da'wah Council of Philippines, Inc (IDCP)—Philippines, (3) Jabatan Kemajuan Islam Malaysia (JAKIM)—Malaysia, (4) Japan Muslim Association (JMA)—Japan, (5) Majlis Ugama Islam Singapore (MUIS)—Singapore, (6) Taiwan Halal Integrity Development Association (THIDA), (7) The Central Islamic Committee of Thailand (CICOT)—Thailand.

128 Australia: (1) Australian Halal Food Services (AHFS), (2) Global Halal Trade Centre Pty. Ltd (GHTC Pty. Ltd), (3) Supreme Islamic Council of Halal Meat in Australia Inc. (SICHMA), (4) The Islamic Coordinating Council of Victoria (ICCV), (5) Western Australian Halal Authority (WAHA).

129 New Zealand: (1) Asia Pacific Halal Services—New Zealand Pty. 2011 Limited.

Europe,[130] the United State of America,[131] and Latin America.[132] The third cluster is the international certification bodies categorised as part of the flavour industry. There are twelve of these bodies, found in Asia,[133] Australia,[134] Europe[135] and the United States of America.[136] There are also four international certification bodies that specialise in poultry, which are all located in the United States of America.[137]

After having obtained LPPOM's approval, these foreign certification bodies are bound by LPPOM procedures and regulations. For instance, they must be prepared for supervision by a MUI-appointed team that audits their technical capabilities, administration, social responsibility and acceptability, and they must be ready for annual monitoring and evaluation. LPPOM also regulates that the letter of halal assurance granted by the approved international certifiers is recognised only for raw materials produced in the country where the halal certification body is located, except for European countries tied to the European Union treaty. LPPOM states that a halal certificate issued by the approved foreign body cannot be used for retail products. Foreign certifiers are not allowed to delegate their authority to another person or organisation in another other state. The reasoning behind the approval of foreign certifiers is aimed at supporting good management, networking, cooperation, and ethical competition, and enhancing Muslim consumer protection. So far LPPOM has strictly applied these procedures and regulations, as can be seen by their routine evaluation of foreign certification bodies.

---

130 Europe: (1) Halal Control e.k.—Germany, (2) Halal Feed and Food Inspection Authority (HFFIA)—Netherlands, (3) Halal Food Council of Europe (HFCE)—Belgium, (4) Halal Quality Control—Netherlands, (5) Total Quality Halal Correct (TQHC)—Netherlands, (6) Halal Certification Service, (7) European Institute of Halal Certification, (8) The Muslim Religious Association of Poland (MRAP), (9) The Grand Mosque of Paris.

131 United State of America: (1) American Halal Foundation (AHF), (2) Halal Food Council USA, (3) Islamic Information Centre of America (IICA), (4) Islamic Service of America (ISA), (5) The Islamic Food and Nutrition Council of America (IFANCA).

132 Latin America: (1) Federation of Muslims Associations in Brazil.

133 Asia: (1) Islamic Da'wah Council of Philippines, Inc (IDCP)—Philippines, (2) Japan Muslim Association (JMA)—Japan.

134 Australia: (1) Australian Halal Food Services (AHFS), (2) The Islamic Coordinating Council of Victoria (ICCV).

135 Europe: (1) Halal Control e.k.—Germany, (2) Halal Feed and Food Inspection Authority (HFFIA)—Netherlands, (3) Halal Food Council of Europe (HFCE)—Belgium, (4) Halal Quality Control—Netherlands.

136 United State of America: (1) American Halal Foundation (AHF), (2) Halal Food Council USA, (3) The Islamic Food and Nutrition Council of America (IFANCA), (4) Islamic Service of America (ISA).

137 Girindra, *Dari Sertifikasi Menuju Labelisasi Halal*; LPPOM, *Indonesia Halal Directory 2001*.

3.3.2.3 Certification and Labelling

There are two essential parts within LPPOM halal project: certification and labelling. Halal certification is a careful investigation into and discussion on the legal validity of foods, drugs and cosmetics organised by LPPOM and involving the Fatwa Commission, who are responsible for issuing a fatwa on the permissibility of each product. Under LPPOM framework, this fatwa is called a halal certificate. The process of drawing up the halal certificate is almost the same as that of issuing a regular fatwa, except in the case of halal certification it is based on an audit carried out by LPPOM while other fatwas are based on strong arguments from Islamic texts. Halal labelling is the activity of attaching a halal logo to products based on the halal certificate issued by the LLPOM-Fatwa Commission. While the issuance of halal certificates is the authority of LPPOM, the labelling of products is the responsibility of the Badan Pemeriksaan Obat dan Makanan (BPOM, The National Agency of Drug and Food Control) under the Ministry of Health.[138] In accordance with an agreement between MUI and the Ministry of Health, each label published by the Ministry needs to be accompanied by a halal certificate drawn up by LPPOM. However, this does not always take place as planned, and sometimes producers label their products without approval from LPPOM. In order to avoid abuse of the system, since 2007 LPPOM has published a standardised logo for the halal certificate. LPPOM approached the government concerning usage of the logo, but the Ministry of Health did not provide any response until 2008.[139] Perhaps the government was reluctant to accept the label, as the use of a halal certificate from LPPOM was still not a legal requirement for producers. However, now the logo can be seen on each product granted a MUI halal certificate.

From a historical perspective, LPPOM began its activities by granting a halal letter to PT. Cheil Samsung Astra for its monosodium glutamate flavour product in 1991. At this stage, the letter was not yet referred to as a halal certificate due to the lack of mandate from the government of Indonesia. In 1994, after obtaining clear support from the Ministry of Religious Affairs and the Ministry of Health, LPPOM issued twenty halal certificates for commodities produced by PT. Unilever, Indonesia's Wall's factory, and other goods manufactured by companies such as PT. Indofood, McDonalds Indonesia, PT. Siantar Top Industri, PT. Asia Inti Selera, and Holding Groups of Indomilk.[140] These initial forays into the process were viewed positively by producers and gave

138 "Label Halal Kewenangan Siapa?" Halal MUI 2022, https://halalmui.org/mui14/main/detail/label-halal-kewenangan-siapa, accessed on 21 July 2022.

139 Girindra, *Dari Sertifikasi Menuju Labelisasi Halal*, pp. 87–88.

140 Ibid, pp. 55–56.

LPPOM greater confidence to carry out further certification. Since this time, LPPOM has serviced not only local companies but also foreign companies that sell their products to Indonesia.

How does LPPOM award the halal certificate? First, it orders factories or producers wishing to obtain the letter of certification to clearly state that their products do not contain pork or alcohol or any derivative ingredients. LPPOM requires that all products made from animal-based ingredients should be permissible in Islam, for example using animals that were slaughtered following sharia, in accordance with LPPOM standards. The products must not use prohibited ingredients or *najs* (impure) materials such as cadavers, blood, ingredients derived from human organs, faeces and so forth. The cleanliness of storage, food displays, processing venues, and transport of products are also major considerations in obtaining certification. LPPOM regulates that abattoirs should employ a well-trained Muslim butcher who knows how to slaughter animals according to sharia, keeping them separate from pigs and keeping the slaughter yards clean.[141] Technically speaking, besides all these requirements the LLPOM also maintains a Sistem Jaminan Halal (SJH, Halal Assurance System). This system was instituted by LPPOM as a means to assess the readiness of producers to be audited. All companies should have the SJH, which can be granted when they demonstrate a well-documented lawful assurance system, a halal manual, and the presence of standard operating procedures, amongst other necessary steps. Producers who apply for halal certification from LPPOM must complete a form with general information on the producer and the type of product for which they are requesting the certificate. The completed form is then sent back to be assessed and evaluated and, when considered complete, progresses through the LPPOM process. After all steps of the process are completed, LPPOM issues a timetable for the audit process for the products. The results of this audit process are then brought to a meeting of LPPOM auditors, and are then submitted to MUI's Fatwa Commission. The Fatwa Commission will then issue a fatwa when the basic requirements are fulfilled, while it will reject the application if these requirements are not fulfilled. This rejection is usually accompanied by an "audit memorandum" which explains the producers' shortcomings, such as inadequate documentation, the product formula and so forth. By completing an audit memorandum, producers can then submit an application to LPPOM and halal certification will be granted when the MUI Fatwa Commission agrees. The certification lasts two years and certificate renewal should be applied for at least three months before the expiry date. The outline of this process can be seen in following diagram:

141 Ibid, pp. 100–101.

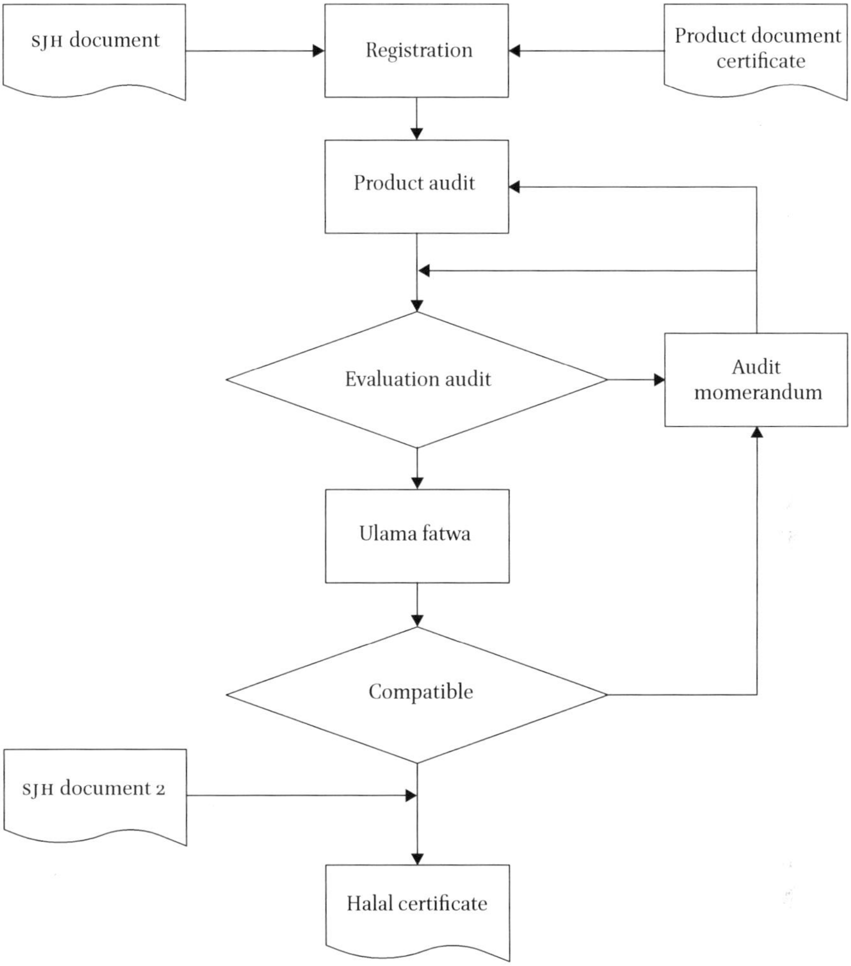

DIAGRAM 4 Procedure of issuing halal certificate within the MUI-LPPOM
Note: LPPOM MUI and AIFDC ICU, *General Guidelines of Halal Assurance System* (Jakarta: LPPOM MUI, 2010)

The labelling is a consequence or a continuation of the certification process. Although this adds costs to production, from LPPOM's perspective, the use of the halal label can be considered a medium of communication between producers and Muslim consumers. With the halal certificate and label, producers are able to inform consumers about the ingredients in their products, and consumers can provide feedback to producers if they are not satisfied with the product.

3.3.2.4 Auditing Lawfulness of Goods

The process of halal audit refers here to the investigative process of examining products based on the principles of sharia law. This process must be undertaken before the halal certificate and label are issued. As a result, all producers who wish to obtain the halal certificate are required to deal with the auditors and the audit process within LPPOM.[142] Without these two elements, LPPOM will not have the scientific, cultural, theological and even legal justification to grant a certificate allowing food consumption. The profile of the audit and auditors in this field reflect the basic elements of LPPOM concerning regulations, as well as the human resources that implement those regulations.

The notion of audits and auditors are modern from the viewpoint of Islamic jurisprudence. The Islamic legal argument for conducting this process is often associated with the discourse of *fiqh* in which ulama are cited as being authorised to rule on whether a product is permitted or not. In the modern era with its associated technological developments, determining whether elements within food and drinks are lawful or not is not a simple issue. It now demands expertise beyond what conventional ulama usually know and understand. LPPOM has sought to fill this gap by hiring skilled scientists as food auditors. By involving the experts, the lawfulness status of such product is more accurate, as it does not only rely on the speculative and literal interpretation of ulama but is also based on scientific and empirical laboratory research.

LPPOM categorises the food audit into three types: a certification audit, a monitoring audit, and an internal audit. The certification audit refers to an audit undertaken in order to prepare for the issuance of the halal certificate. This is the first stage of the certification activity. The monitoring audit is conducted to ensure that the requirements for the halal certificate are properly supported in the production process. This audit is a form of evaluation, because it is undertaken after the producer has received the halal certificate from LPPOM. The internal audit is a routine audit commenced by an internal auditor appointed by the producer or company in question. Each producer or company is obliged by LPPOM to appoint an auditor responsible for maintaining the quality of a product. Although, in principle, the internal auditors are independently appointed by the producers or companies, MUI and Muslim organisations remain able to utilise this opportunity to place their members within large national industries. This takes place because all the auditor training and education is designed and implemented by LPPOM. In recruiting auditors, LPPOM usually first invites member organisations of MUI to send representatives with knowledge and expertise on the issue. The participation

142 Interview with Nazratuzzaman Hosen, Jakarta, 2011.

of these representatives in large industries and companies leads to benefits for the organisations, particularly in obtaining information on potential sources of funding. One example of how this can be utilised is evident in Act No. 40/2007, on *Perseroan Terbatas* Limited Liability Companies, which states that such companies must reserve a portion of their funds for corporate social responsibility (CSR) activities. These three kinds of audit models not only operate in Indonesia, but also in other neighbouring Muslim countries such as Brunei, Malaysia, and Singapore. The shared aspects of the audit process across these countries are due to the communication and exchange of expertise frequently undertaken by the auditors in these areas through conferences, workshops or study visits.

It should be said here that LPPOM's success in investigating halal status greatly depends on the quality of the auditors. This is a point of particular concern for LPPOM, and as a result special training and education sessions are conducted to ensure the capability of auditors. A poor performance by auditors will not only reflect badly on LPPOM but also hinder MUI's broader shariatisation agenda, since it weakens the organisation's image. LPPOM takes this matter very seriously, and auditors must therefore not only have the ability to perform the technical aspects of their work, but must also be Islamic activists who are morally bound to the theological spirit of their religion, particularly the awareness that Muslims are obliged to only consume permitted commodities. Apart from special training and education sessions, LPPOM also states several other requirements that must be met by the auditor. For instance, the auditor must meet the standard of expertise required in the disciplines of food technology, chemicals, medicine, pharmacy, administration and management. Those who have graduated from sharia faculties of Islamic universities, for instance, can only be recruited if they understand sharia matters as well as the other disciplines mentioned above.[143] Furthermore, the auditors should have a sharia outlook, meaning that they should understand the reason why any given thing is lawful or unlawful, the intent of sharia related to the Islamic legal status of lawfulness and unlawfulness, and also the methodological steps used to determine the quality of halal and haram and the Qur'ānic and Sunna arguments in support of this.[144] Those who do not have a background in Islamic studies should understand the main verses of the Qur'ān and the examples of Sunna related this issue. In short, all auditors of LPPOM should know the general rules of *fiqih pangan* (Islamic jurisprudence on food).

143 Interview with Ichwan Sam, MUI Secretary General, Jakarta, 2010.

144 Girindra, *Dari Sertifikasi Menuju Labelisasi Halal*, p. 67.

All the requirements for auditors mentioned above have been outlined in what LPPOM refers to as the code of ethics for auditors, which covers using the audit process as a means of propagating Islam and ensuring that wrong things are forbidden and right things are commanded. This includes the need for auditors to respect the morality of Islam (*al-akhlāq al-karīma*), to protect the image of Islam as a glorious religion, to have good intentions (*niyya*), and to worship God, as a means of implementing social trust. Besides these attitudes, the auditor should take an honest and courageous stance in describing the data and information related to the lawfulness and unlawfulness of products, meaning that absolute impartiality is important. LPPOM also requires the auditor to have a critical and transparent attitude in analysing and providing conclusions, without intimidating producers or companies; to maintain confidentially by not revealing the formulae of products to others; to be competent, and also curious about new developments in their field; to fulfil the requirements for accuracy and certainty in the audit process; and lastly, to reject any and all forms of bribery and not abuse their responsibility, protecting the reputation of LPPOM.[145] As alluded to above, in order to prepare its qualified auditors, LPPOM organises training programmes. The first such training programme was held in 1993, and was aimed at preparing a number of experts to become auditors with LPPOM. There were thirty-six participants in this programme, and many of them had a background in the sciences, such as food science, chemistry, organic and medical sciences and other related fields. This first programme produced a set of basic audit procedures which LPPOM used for its operations.[146] A second training programme was conducted in 1996 to meet the increasing demand for auditors from producers seeking halal certification. There were twenty-five participants in this programme, and LPPOM expanded the scope to its regional branches. Following this, a further training programme was held in 1999, consisting of twenty participants who have since been mobilised as auditors for regional LPPOM branches. Even so, these numbers are still far from sufficient to meet auditing demands, and thus LPPOM continues to recruit auditors on an ongoing basis. It is also worth mentioning here that LPPOM not only organises auditor-training programmes for its own auditors, but also for those from halal-certifying bodies in other countries.

By making public all the procedures and regulations of the audit process, LPPOM wants to demonstrate its serious commitment and also to show the professional nature of its audits. These procedures are also intended to show that both consumers and producers actually demand the role and services

145 Ibid, pp. 68–69.
146 Ibid, p. 66.

provided by LPPOM. It is for this reason that LPPOM sought greater legal support to establish its position as the sole authoritative body providing halal certification for goods in Indonesia.

However, the serious commitment of LPPOM-MUI as the implementing authority for issuing halal certificates was endangered by the proposal of the Ministry of Religious Affairs (MORA) for a new state law that regulates halal in Indonesia. Suryadharma Ali, the Minister of Religious Affairs, argued from the side of legality in which he stated that civil society organisations like MUI cannot ask for public money. In response, MUI stated that MORA was behaving with disrespect.[147] Amidhan, the chairman of MUI and an economist, was disappointed by Suryadharma Ali's move, understanding it as a ploy to divest MUI of its power.[148] There were three options for models to regulate halal certification. The first was that all MUI's authority would be removed, and it would no longer play a part in the halal certification process. The agency responsible for halal certification would be a state body equal to the level of ministries. This proposal was, of course, rejected by MUI. The second option was that LPPOM-MUI would be legally recognised by a new state law as the official agency for halal certification. This option was rejected by MORA, since their aim was to reduce the role of LPPOM. The third option was that MORA would take responsibility for halal certification; this was also rejected by MUI.[149] The model that was finally agreed was that halal certification would be implemented by a special body under the direction of MORA, while fatwa would still be issued by MUI. This became State Law No. 33/2014 on Jaminan Produk Halal (Halal Product Assurance) and was ratified by the government of Indonesia. The emergence of this State Law can be understood in two ways. The first is that it constitutes evidence of MUI's success and contrbution to the state law and general affairs of Indonesia. Without the help of MUI since the 1990s, Indonesia would have no experience in regulating and administrating halal. It is thus fair to say that the state of Indonesia has benefitted from MUI. Second, the law is evidence of the end of MUI's authority, since it transfers their role to BPJPH. The BPJPH is under the administration of Ministry of Religious Affairs. Under the BPJPH, LPPOM is no longer an implementing agency of halal certification. Nevertheless, MUI retains the position of the issuer of fatwa on halal within the BPJPH, and LPPOM can play a role as an institute of halal investigation, like other Islamic organisations, that works under the BPJPH.

147 Interview with Amidhan, Jakarta, 2011.

148 Ibid.

149 Ibid.

However, the birth of BPJPH ended the long monopoly of LPPOM-MUI in issuing halal certification.

3.3.3 *Dewan Syariah Nasional* (*DSN, The National Sharia Board*)

3.3.3.1 History of DSN

The shariatisation of the economic and finance sector has become a strategic path through which MUI is seeking to stimulate shariatisation in the public life of Indonesia. Amin admitted as much when he said that empowering the Muslim community's economic and finance sector would have a strong impact on the Islamic movement.[150] He said that we, as Indonesian Muslims, have nothing to be proud of in our current situation. We have no conceptualisation or *ʿamaliyya* (his Indonesian-Arabic expression for a concrete project) which clearly indicates the progress of our society. Amin suggests that in order to establish a new orientation for Indonesian Muslims, not just at the abstract level of discourse, we need to think about a "movement" (he used the term *ḥaraka*). He advocated empowering and shariatising the people's economy as an alternative method for the Islamic movement, with MUI leading this process.[151]

Historically speaking, a number of movements towards the shariatisation of the economy and financial sector of Indonesia began as early as the 1990s. MUI's initiative to establish the Bank Muamalat Islam (BMI), the first Indonesian sharia-based bank, was evidence of this. On 19–22 August 1990, MUI held a workshop on bank interest and the banking system in Bogor, West Java. This workshop was attended by 165 participants consisting of members of the MUI central board, as well as members of the provincial and district branches, Islamic organisations, academics, professionals and businessmen. The workshop invited four speakers: a representative from the Central Bank of Indonesia (no name mentioned), Ibrahim Hosen (from MUI's Fatwa Commission), Karnaen Purwataatmadja (the former executive director of the Islamic Development Bank, IDB), and Dawam Rahardjo (a Muslim intellectual of Muhammadiyah who specialised in the economic, social and Islamic movements).[152] This was an initial workshop organised by MUI, which raised the issue of possibly setting up a sharia bank that was not based on an interest system.

The results of this workshop received further attention during the National Congress on 22–15 August 1990 in Jakarta. The congress issued a special

150 Interview with Ma'ruf Amin, Jakarta, 2010.

151 Ibid.

152 Karni et al., *35 Tahun Majelis Ulama Indonesia*, p. 157.

recommendation for the establishment of a MUI Banking Team, with the mandate to establish a sharia bank and conduct consultations with a number of important actors and experts. This was around the same time that a "political Islam" movement had begun to emerge in Indonesia; one strong indicator of this was the establishment of ICMI (The Indonesian Association of Muslim Intelllectuals) with the backing of the Suharto government.[153] Many political actors as well as the ruling regime felt obliged to welcome the birth of this Islamic movement in the national arena, which created the opportunity for MUI to speed up the process of establishing a sharia bank. On 1 November 1991, the MUI Banking Team obtained legal support for the establishment of Indonesia Muamalat Bank Ltd.

The team was also supported by a positive response from the executive and legislative arms of the government, as enacted in Act No. 7/1992 on banking issues.[154] Articles 6 and 13 of this Act stipulate that banks may be established on the basis of *bagi hasil* (an Indonesian expression for the sharia profit-sharing principle). In order to provide guidance for the implementation of this law, the government published Government Ordinance No. 72/1992[155] on the profit sharing system. Article 5 of the Ordinance states (Paragraph 1): "Banks which are based on the principle of profit-sharing are obliged to have a sharia advisory board, which has the task of supervising the products of the bank in collecting funds from the community and distributing them, in order to ensure this runs in accordance with the principle of sharia." Paragraph 2 of Article 5 specifies how the Sharia Supervisory Board is to be appointed: "the establishment of the sharia advisory board is undertaken by the related bank after having consulted an institution that serves as a forum for Indonesian ulama." Although Article 5 never explicitly referred to MUI, the Council interpreted the phrase "an institution that serves as a forum for Indonesian ulama" as referring to MUI. This interpretation was also based on the fact that when this Act came into law MUI had been in existence for twenty years and was the only ulama forum in Indonesia. Furthermore, other Muslim organisations such as NU and Muhammadiyah accepted the appointment of MUI as an as an advisory and supervisory body for sharia banks and financial institutions. However, this was not universally accepted and today other groups continue to vigorously protest the way that MUI has claimed this role.

153 Hefner, *Civil Islam: Muslims and Democratization in Indonesia*, p. 139; Hefner, "Islam, State, and Civil Society: ICMI and the Struggle for the Indonesian Middle Class".

154 Hefner, *Civil Islam: Muslims and Democratization in Indonesia*, p. 158.

155 In Indonesia's legal system and practice, government ordinances function as guidelines for the implementation of state law.

On 29–30 July 1997, an ulama workshop on Reksadana Syariah (Sharia Mutual Funds) was organised, and one of the recommendations issued was that MUI should establish an institution to handle fatwa related to problems encountered by sharia finance institutions (Lembaga Keuangan Syariah, LKS). Such an institution was expected to lead, guide and provide advice on Islamic legal edicts needed by sharia finance institutions. MUI appeared to react positively to the recommendation by establishing a special team to form a DSN on 17 October 1997. After two years, MUI issued Decree No. Kep.-754/MUI/II/1999 on 10 February 1999 regarding the creation of the DSN.[156] Five days later, on 15 February 1999, MUI officially established the DSN at an event attended by the former Minister of Religious Affairs, Malik Fadjar (b. 1939). Fadjar's presence at the ceremony was symbolic evidence that the government not only supported the DSN, but also agreed to the shariatisation of the Indonesian economy and financial sector.

The establishment of the DSN does not come as a surprise, politically or socially, as it emerged in response to demands from Indonesian Muslims as well as the ruling regime. MUI's role as a forum of Indonesian ulama, in this regard, is to respond to Muslims who seek the fatwa, guidance and advice of religious scholars on matters pertaining to the economy and their financial affairs. Indonesian Muslims in the business world and the market wish to avoid undertaking business in a way that contradicts the principles of sharia.[157] MUI was well-positioned to enjoy the success resulting from its preparedness in anticipating the needs of Muslim society in this matter. It had already built its capacity in this field by organising conferences and seminars and also through issuing Islamic legal discourse (fatwa and recommendations) on key topics in this area. Thus, when Act No. 7/1992 on Banking was made law, MUI was already well-prepared.

3.3.3.2 Institutionalising the Sharia Economy and Finance

The establishment of sharia banks and sharia financial institutions was a more tangible means of fostering a broader implementation of sharia in the legal and public spheres of Indonesia. Activity in the finance area has a more quantifiable impact and is also closely related to the issue of poverty confronted by many Indonesian Muslims. The establishment of these banks and financial institutions was therefore promoted by MUI as a means of poverty alleviation for Muslims, as well as Indonesians more broadly. Amin states that "the DSN is part of a MUI strategy to boost sharia economics by providing a

156 Interview with Ma'ruf Amin, Jakarta, 2010.

157 Karni et al., *35 Tahun Majelis Ulama Indonesia*, p. 160.

strong impact on the wellbeing of Indonesian Muslims."[158] Amin further stated that the invention of sharia economy was the implementation of the MUI principle pertaining to *fahm al-wāqiʿ* (understanding of the Muslim realm). According to him, "Islam was revealed as a way to reform (*li iṣlāḥ al-wāqiʿ*), cure (*li muʿālaja al-wāqiʿ*), and solve (*li ḥill al-ishkāliyyāt*) the problems of the Muslim realm)."[159] In this regard, the institutionalisation of sharia economy is an important vehicle.

MUI took the view that to achieve greater wellbeing for Indonesian Muslims, sharia banks and financial institutions would need to play a central role.[160] The DSN is a fundamental element in this regard because it deals with the most important institutions of the sharia economy: the banks and financial institutions. It was hoped that if these bodies performed well, this would create a trickle-down effect to improve the economic wellbeing of Indonesian Muslims. Thus the DSN was established with a number of objectives in mind, such as to improve the implementation of sharia law in the economy and financial activities, to issue fatwas on various models of economic and business activities based on sharia considerations, to draw up fatwas on the products of sharia finance industries, and to supervise the implementation of DSN and MUI fatwa.[161]

In addition to strengthening democracy and human rights, the DSN was established as a means to create a more civilised society for Indonesian Muslims, and also for the sake of economic prosperity. MUI had long been conscious of this need, hence the organisation's decision to promote the establishment of sharia banks and financial institutions. MUI does not directly engage in the daily management of these institutions, but nonetheless continues to have a significant role in them. MUI's role here is more as a solidarity maker and, according to social movement theory, will be able to successfully play this role if it can consolidate and mobilise resources—political, financial, and theological—in support of the sharia economic system.

Where does the DSN sit within MUI and how does it interact with the MUI agenda? The DSN organisational structure has changed over time, adjusting to social and political developments in Indonesia as well as the national legal system. From 1999 to 2004, the DSN organisation was directly handled by the MUI General Chairman, Yafie, and the MUI Secretary General, Nazri Adlani. The

158 Interview with Ma'ruf Amin, Jakarta, 2010.

159 Ibid.

160 Ibid.

161 Dewan Syariah Nasional MUI-Bank Indonesia, *Himpunan Fatwa Dewan Syariah Nasional MUI*.

DSN's executive chairman was appointed from one of the MUI Central Board members with Amin (the DSN executive chairman) being the first to serve in this role. During this formative period, the DSN mainly focused on consolidating its internal capabilities by drafting and formalising the basic statutes and operational guidelines. The basic statutes served as a compass of sorts for the DSN and contained the general principles and guidelines of its position, status, authority and mechanisms. The basic statutes, for instance, explain that the DSN is part of MUI that plays a role as a partner for the Ministry of Finance, the Central Bank of Indonesia, and other related bodies to draft regulations on sharia banks and financial institutions.

In a relatively short time, the DSN has been able to play a major role in influencing the legislation process of state law. There have been at least three laws passed in parliament that are directly connected to efforts to strengthen the role of the DSN and the DPS, or Sharia Supervisory Board. The first is Act No. 40/2007 on Perseroan Terbatas (PT, Limited Liability Companies); the second is Act No. 21/2008 on Sharia Banking; and the third is Act No. 40/2008 on Sharia Bonds. Article 40 of Act No. 40/2007 stipulates three major issues for the DPS. First, each limited liability company with core business activities related to sharia finance also needs to recruit a DPS representative. Second, the DPS representatives are appointed under the auspices of the DSN. The number of DPS representatives in each sharia bank and sharia finance institution depends on the financial capacity and the size of the bank. Regardless of number, the person or persons should be experts on Islamic law on human relations and business. This is needed because the operation of sharia-based banks and sharia-based finance institutions are mostly adopted from concepts in this branch of Islamic law.[162] Third, the DPS is responsible for offering advice and guidance to the board of directors of sharia companies and financial institutions.[163] More importantly, the task of the DPS is to observe and ensure the implementation of sharia principles within the daily tasks of the related sharia company or institution. More specifically, Act No. 21/2008, Article 32 regulates that DPS must be present within both sharia banks and conventional banks with Unit Usaha Syariah (UUS, a Sharia Activity Unit) and these representatives should be appointed based on recommendations by the DSN. This indicates the important position of the DSN in this process.

The role of the DSN is legally justified through Article 26 of Act No. 21/2008. This gives the DSN the authority to observe and supervise the implementation

162 Interview with Ichwan Sam, Jakarta, 2010.

163 Karni et al., *35 Tahun Majelis Ulama Indonesia*, p. 161.

of sharia principles in the business activities of sharia companies and industries. This arrangement also grants the DSN the power to force the Central Bank of Indonesia to adopt its fatwas as a source for the bank's regulations.[164] Another important task for the DSN is to issue recommendations, certificates and sharia approval for the establishment of new banks and financial institutions. Through these roles, the DSN not only has the authority to observe and supervise, but also strategically participates in developing the sharia economy and financial sector from an early stage.

A more comprehensive board structure for the DSN emerged in the 2005–2010 period. During this period, the DSN was divided into two divisions: the Plenary Board and the Executive Board. A total of fifty-three people were recruited from among ulama and experts from various disciplines to sit on the Plenary Board, and were tasked with validating fatwas. The Executive Board was divided into three task forces: first, Banking and Pawnbrokers; second, Insurance and Business; and third, Programme and Capital Market. Each taskforce consisted of between three to five members. A total of twenty people, including two representatives each from the Central Bank and the Finance Ministry, sit on the Executive Board.[165] Both the Plenary and Executive Boards of the DSN engage in the process of issuing fatwas.

What is the relationship between the DSN and the DPS? As mentioned above, the main role of the DSN is to issue fatwas on economic and financial issues, while the DPS is tasked with implementing these fatwas into the businesses of the sharia banks and financial institutions.[166] Tim Lindsey states that the appointment of the DPS is a way of assuring the "Islamicity" of the whole sharia economy business process within sharia banks.[167] This is evident from, at least, four practical roles granted to the DPS by the DSN. First, the DPS periodically observes the operation of sharia banks and sharia finance institutions. Second, the DPS delivers advice and suggestions for the innovation and improvement of products of the host sharia bank or financial institution. Third, the DPS must provide at least two reports every year to the DSN regarding the progress of sharia banks and financial products. Fourth, the DPS

164 Tim Lindsey, "Monopolising Islam? The Indonesian Ulama Council and State Regulation of the 'Islamic Economy,'" *Bulletin of Indonesian Economic Studies* 48, no. 2 (2012): 253–74, p. 265.

165 Karni et al., *35 Tahun Majelis Ulama Indonesia*, p. 163.

166 Dewan Syariah Nasional MUI-Bank Indonesia, *Himpunan Fatwa Dewan Syariah Nasional MUI*.

167 Lindsey, "Monopolising Islam?" p. 265.

is responsible for collecting and formulating problems that need to be resolved by the DSN.[168]

All of these roles actually reflect the reality that the DPS is an extension of the DSN. Of course, the DPS can propose some programmes and innovations but the final decision still rests with the DSN.[169] If a new issue emerges, the DPS must pass this on to the DSN to request a fatwa. In addition, if the performance of the DPS within a host bank or institution is considered unsatisfactory, the DSN can issue a recommendation to sack the DPS representative. Within this strong top-down relationship, with the DSN and its mother organisation (MUI) on the one side and the DPS on the other, there is more flexibility and space when it comes to promoting the importance of shariatisation. Up to this point, MUI has taken advantage of this situation to promote its own agenda. This can be seen in a number of events, such as the *Ijtimāʿ Sanawī* (Annual Meeting) where members of the DSN and DPS received updates not only on sharia banking and finance, but also other disciplines that promoted the radical adoption of sharia for their activities.

A recent count of the number of DPS representatives in banks stands at between 250–300. One informant explained that a low-range salary for a DPS representative was around IDR 750,000 to 1,500,000 per month while a higher range salary was between IDR 15 to 20 million per month. The salary is decided by the related host sharia bank or financial institutions, but usually the larger banks and institutions provide larger salaries. It is an unspoken rule within the DSN that positions in the larger banks are generally reserved for members of the MUI elite.

The next question is: "Who is considered as qualified to apply for DPS positions and how does MUI select DPS members?" The DSN requires all those who wish to apply as members of the DPS to meet criteria such as behaving with respect for the morality of Islam (*al-akhlāq al-karīma*), having expertise in the field of *sharīʿa-muʿāmala* (banking and finance), showing committment to developing the sharia-based economy and finance sector, and presenting a capability certificate from the DSN.[170] The DSN regularly organises a special course on sharia banking and finance,[171] intended as preparation to serve within the DPS. The selection process for DPS members includes a "fit and proper test" conducted by the DSN, which MUI refers to as a *silaturahmi*

168 Dewan Syariah Nasional MUI-Bank Indonesia, *Himpunan Fatwa Dewan Syariah Nasional MUI*, pp. 426–9; Lindsey, "Monopolising Islam?"

169 Ibid.

170 Dewan Syariah Nasional MUI-Bank Indonesia, *Himpunan Fatwa Dewan Syariah Nasional MUI*, p. 439. This requirement can be seen in the DSN Directive No. 03/2000.

171 Interview with Abdul Wasiq, Jakarta, 2011.

(courtesy visit). The DSN avoids using the term "fit and proper test" because it is considered disrespectful to the ulama who apply for the positions.[172] In the *silaturahmi*, the applicant is asked a number of questions regarding sharia business, banking, finance, insurance and many other related issues. While these processes are intended to select 'the right person for the right job', many DPS members are still not completely qualified. Many host banks and institutions believe that the ulama are not really needed, while the DPS ulama themselves feel that the banks do not respect them. This can be seen in the salaries that they are offered.[173]

Many have criticised MUI for intentionally and strategically using the DSN as a means to consolidate human and financial resources in order to promote the further shariatisation of Indonesia. On the one hand this criticism holds true, because the authority of the DSN opens up the possibility for financial opportunities and networks for MUI. However, on the other hand, at least up until 2010, the contribution of DPS personnel for both the DSN and MUI has been minimal. The DSN has actually formulated a donation mechanism, but its implementation remains fraught with problems. For example, DPS members have failed to meet collection targets and this issue continues to be a sensitive one within the DSN.[174] The difficulty is due to a common assumption among DPS functionaries who believe their salary is a part of their "*bagian rizki masing-masing*" which literally means part of their livelihood.[175] This metaphorical term was used by Ichwan Sam to describe the sensitivity of DPS members asking for an additional contribution due to the personal nature of their salary, even though they were placed in sharia banking and finance institutions under the auspices of the DSN. Ironically, this issue was not discussed during the *Ijtimā' Sanawī* of 2010 (the 2010 Annual Meeting of the DPS.) It seems that this was intentionally organised by the DSN in order to protect

172 Interviews with Ichwan Sam, Jakarta, 2010, and with Abdul Wasiq, Jakarta, 2011.

173 I obtained this information in an informal conversation with a number of the DPS members during my participatory observations at the *Ijtimāʿ Sanawī* meeting on 13 & 14 December 2010 at the Mercure Hotel, Jakarta.

174 My informant did not mention the exact amount of collected contributions, but from my impression when observing the *Ijtimāʿ Sanawī* of Dewan Syariah Nasional Tahun 2010 (Annual Meeting of the DPS) in Jakarta, was there was a lack of transparency with donations. This meeting itself is an annual forum for the DPS to discuss all issues and problems regarding sharia, finance, and the economy as well as fatwas. Those attending this forum include DPS members and DSN stakeholders such as sharia banks and financial institutions. This meeting is always organised by the DSN under the full sponsorship of the Central Bank of Indonesia.

175 This is a metaphor used by Ichwan Sam (the General Secretary of MUI and DSN) to describe salaries.

the dignity of DPS ulama so they are not depicted as *bakhīl* (penny-pinchers) and to maintain MUI's image as a sincere Islamic organisation. If ulama fight amongst each other over money, this will decrease the level of social and religious respect they enjoy. Although there is no simple answer, the DSN is continuing to work on setting up a donation system mutually beneficial for the DSN and DPS members. Furthermore, the DSN's financial benefits not only come from DPS members but also from the Central Bank, which provides budgetary funds. The DSN will become the ideal vehicle for MUI's Islamisation when it can combine human and financial resources.

3.3.3.3 Issuing Fatwa on Economic and Finance Issues

Unlike LPPOM, which lacks the authority to issue its own fatwa, the DSN has been granted a mandate to issue Islamic legal opinions on issues related to banking, the economy and finance. Those who can request fatwas from the DSN are sharia financial institutions and the regulatory bodies, namely the Central Bank of Indonesia and the Ministry of Finance. Fatwa requests can be sent to the Badan Pengurus Harian (BPH, Executive Board) of the DSN, and if one needs to be issued a taskforce will be set up. The taskforce first conducts a hearing with the fatwa applicant and then seeks clarification and verification from those who are engaged in business with them, as the fatwa seeker is often interconnected with other stakeholders of the DSN. Following this, the DSN then formulates a draft statement of the problem, based on information obtained by the taskforce in the hearing with the applicant. Following this, the task force discusses the issue with other stakeholders before finally drafting a comprehensive explanation of the issue.

The results of the process undertaken by the task force are then submitted to the DSN Executive Board for preliminary discussion prior to drafting the fatwa. Generally speaking, the DSN has its own mechanism in drawing up a fatwa separate from the MUI Fatwa Commission. Besides conducting a sharia examination of the issue by analysing arguments based on the Qur'ān, Sunna and opinions of Muslim scholars (*aqwāl*), the DSN also conducts a hearing with industries and regulatory bodies involved with the fatwa applicant in order to achieve congruence between textual sources and what is actually taking place on the ground. After having consulted references, both textual and contextual sources, the DSN composes a draft solution. They discuss the issue with the regulatory bodies—the Ministry of Finance and the Central Bank—and then compose the fatwa. The draft fatwa is presented at a DSN plenary session in order to discuss and refine the ruling. Finally, the DSN seeks to harmonise the fatwa with existing regulations. Having passed through all steps of this process, the draft is then issued as an official DSN fatwa.[176] The entire process, from the question to the conclusion, actually reflects the implementation of collective *ijtihād* because of the involvement of many groups of Muslim experts and scholars. In addition, the Ministry of Finance and the Central Bank of Indonesia as regulatory bodies also play a direct role in the process of making this fatwa.[177]

Although the procedure differs, the DSN's fatwas are similar in nature to MUI's Islamic legal opinions. This can be seen in the fatwa format and method used by the DSN and the Fatwa Commission, whereby the Qur'ān, Sunna and opinions of previous Muslims scholars are the primary sources of rulings. The DSN fatwa format has sections dealing with social, political and historical contexts, the Islamic textual sources, and the legal decision itself. What marks the fatwa as different is that the DSN's fatwa is legally binding on sharia banks and institutions, while the Fatwa Commission's fatwas are not mandatory, even for the *mustaftī* (fatwa requester).[178]

Since its establishment in 1999 up until December 2010, the DSN has issued seventy-eight fatwas which can be categorised into two groups: fatwas related to sharia banking issues and fatwas related to financial and insurance issues.[179] The two groups can be divided into five sub-groups: first, forty-one fatwas on sharia banking issues; second, five fatwas on sharia stock exchange and capital market issues; third, five fatwas related to sharia insurance; fourth, one fatwa dealing with pawnbrokers; and fifth, two fatwas focusing on sharia accounting issues. In order to better understand the format of the DSN fatwas, it is worth looking at an example of one of the fatwa on saving money. This fatwa follows the standardised format of MUI's fatwas and contains three main parts. Part One looks at social, political and theological considerations, which are used as the basis for drawing up the fatwa. The social need for savings is the need to promote prosperity and investment, and for this banks need to collect funds from the community, for instance through savings. Second, sharia law forbids saving methods that utilise interest. Third, on the basis of these considerations, the DSN saw the need for an Islamic ruling on *muʿāmala sharʿiyya*

176 Karni et al., *35 Tahun Majelis Ulama Indonesia*, p. 164.

177 Ibid.

178 Dewan Syariah Nasional MUI-Bank Indonesia, *Himpunan Fatwa Dewan Syariah Nasional MUI*.

179 This information is based on a Powerpoint presentation by Yuslam Fauzi, "Kontektualisasi dan Aktualisasi Fatwa DSN-MUI," delivered at the DSN *Ijtimāʿ Sanawī*, Jakarta 2010. Fauzi is Managing Director of Bank Syariah Mandiri and chairperson of the Sharia Banking unit.

(Islamic business activities) to be used as a source of guidance on savings services provided by banks. Part Two of the fatwa presents textual arguments, which are based on the Qur'ān and *ḥadīth* as well as the *ijtihād* of classical Muslim scholars following ulama consensus, analogical reasoning, and the principles of Islamic legal maxims. Part Three uses these textual sources to then formulate a fatwa.[180]

Generally speaking, the sharia banks offer an alternative system to conventional banks, although these banks continue to dominate the market: almost 97% of banks operate under conventional non-sharia systems.[181] However, the DSN believes that the success of the sharia economic movement should not be measured by profit but rather from the implementation of sharia within banking operations.[182] Leaders of the DSN argue that this is the difference and the comparative advantage of the sharia system compared to the secular system. In other words, the DSN's concept of sharia banking and financial institutions does not merely seek to increase capital but also to promote Islamic identity. This marks them not just as ordinary businesses but also as part of an Islamic social movement.

While the DSN fatwas are issued to provide benefits for sharia banks and financial institutions in Indonesia, not all of them have met this expectation. Of fifty-seven fatwas on sharia banking issues published from 1999 to 2010, one fatwa—DSN's Fatwa No. 15 on the Distribution Principle of Sharia Finance Institution Revenue—has been identified as a hindrance to the expansion of the sharia banking system. This fatwa declares that sharia banks and financial institutions can use both net revenue sharing and profit sharing in their distribution of revenue. The DSN recommends the usage of the net revenue sharing method because according to Islamic law this is more valid,[183] although Yuslam Fauzi[184] said that this fatwa can lead to asymmetric information, adverse selection and, most importantly, moral hazards. Fauzi identified another six DSN

180 Dewan Syariah Nasional MUI-Bank Indonesia, *Himpunan Fatwa Dewan Syariah Nasional MUI*, pp. 8–13.

181 The Direktorat Perbankan Syariah Bank Indonesia (Sharia Bank Directorate of Indonesia's Central Bank) made this claim in a presentation entitled "Perkembangan Kebijakan dan Masalah Aktual Perbankan Syariah," presented at the *Ijtimāʿ Sanawī* on 13 December 2010 in Jakarta.

182 This statement was delivered by Ma'ruf Amin in his keynote speech at the *Ijtimāʿ Sanawī 2010* in Jakarta.

183 Dewan Syariah Nasional MUI-Bank Indonesia, *Himpunan Fatwa Dewan Syariah Nasional MUI*, p. 83; Lindsey, "Monopolising Islam?" p. 264.

184 Yuslam Fauzi is the general director of Bank Syariah Mandiri and head of Sharia Bank Unit.

fatwas which could potentially affect the growth of sharia banks: first, Fatwa No. 9 on leasing; second, Fatwa No. 22 on parallel investment (Indonesian: *Jual Beli Istisna Paralel*, Arabic: *bayʿ al-istiṣnā*, a contract to purchase something to be manufactured later for a fixed price, according to agreed specifications between the parties); third, Fatwa No. 43 on Investment Certificates for Interbank Profit Sharing; fourth, Fatwa No. 43 on Compensation (*taʿwīḍ*); fifth, Fatwa No. 48 on Rescheduling the Cost-Plus Financing Bill; and sixth, Fatwa No. 54 on Sharia Credit and Debit cards. All these fatwas, Fauzi claimed, could lead to moral hazards, disputes, and unfair returns for consumers, among other problems. Essentially, if the DSN does not revise these fatwas, the progress of sharia banks will be affected. It can be said that the development of sharia banks has stagnated, as can be seen from the fact that only three fatwas were issued by the DSN between 2006 and 2010. This can be seen as proof that the market for sharia banks and financial institutions has not been expanding, because each product offered by these banks would require its own fatwa.

The DSN is aware of this issue and as a result it holds its Annual Meeting, the *Ijtimāʿ Sanawi*, to discuss strategies to deal with such problems. This forum was established by members of the DSN, the DPS and sharia bank practitioners to discuss problems related to sharia, the economy, the financial sector as well as fatwas. Although the form differs slightly from year to year, the overall aims of the event are: first, to update DPS members regarding new DSN fatwa; second, as a forum for regulatory bodies to promote their programmes and new regulations related to the sharia banking system, insurance, the financial sector or issues between the DSN/DPS and host banks and institutions; third, as a forum for *silaturahmi* (Indonesian-Arabic expression for a friendly meeting) between DPS members, sharia banks, and financial institutions in general; and fourth, as a forum for DPS members throughout Indonesia.[185]

Generally speaking, the DSN must respond to problems perceived by sharia practitioners as potential threats that could slow down the development of sharia banks. Finding solutions to these issues can help advance these banks, which in turn will have a positive impact on the distribution of wealth to Indonesian Muslims.

185 Interview with Wahiddudin Adams, Jakarta, 2010. See also Ma'ruf Amin, "Pointers Pidato Ketua DSN-MUI Dalam Acara Pembukaan Ijtima Sanawi (Annual Meeting) DPS Tahun 2010" (Jakarta, 2010). These were some points delivered by Ma'ruf Amin in his keynote speech in the Pembukaan Ijtimāʿ Sanawī (Annual Meeting) DPS Tahun 2010, 12 December 2010.

3.3.4 *Komisi Hukum dan Perundang-Undangan* (*The Law and Legislation Commission*)

3.3.4.1 Special Legal Envoy

Although the Law and Legislation Commission was established after the reform era, its formulation indicates that MUI has a systematic roadmap in attempting a shift of sharia from the private to the public sphere of Indonesia. While it is true that the Fatwa Commission has an important role in supplying Islamic arguments for this change, MUI also needs a special commission that can focus on national legislation. The function of this commission is to deepen and prepare the suitability of the MUI fatwa with the agenda of national legislation. Wahiduddin Adams says, "This body was created as part of the MUI agenda in taking the lead in the shariatisation of national law, which is one of the Council's targets."[186] He further states that, "The main task of the MUI Law and Legislation Commission is first to respond to all law drafts prepared by Indonesian lawmakers and second to propose national law drafts that concern sharia."[187] The establishment of the Law and Legislation Commission took place alongside the national phenomenon of sharia bylaws emerging in provincial and district administrations throughout Indonesia.[188]

After changing its ideology from Pancasila to Islam, MUI never explicitly mentioned the idea of an Islamic state. In a number of statements and publications, MUI maintains that its commitment to the concept of NKRI is non-negotiable. However, its absence from discussions on the possibility to change Indonesia to an Islamic state does not mean that it has nothing to say on the shariatisation of the country more broadly. Of course, as previously mentioned in Chapter 1, MUI's definition of shariatisation is broader than the formation of an Islamic state. This is also supported by statements made by a number of prominent MUI leaders. Mahfudh, for instance, states that ideally speaking the Indonesian state will remain a nation-state based on Pancasila, but within this state system, sharia can be accommodated without being

186 At the time of the interview, 2 November 2010, Wahiduddin Adams was General Director of Legislation at the Ministry of Law and Human Rights and Deputy Chairman of Law and Legislation Commission of MUI.

187 Interview with Wahiduddin Adams, Jakarta, 2010.

188 Robin Bush, "Regional Sharia Regulations in Indonesia: Anomaly or Symptom?" in, *Expressing Islam: Religious Life and Politics*, ed. Greg Fealy and Sally White (Singapore: Iseas, 2008); Dik Roth, "Many Governors, No Provinces: The Struggle for a Province in the Luwu-Tanah Toraja Area in South Sulawesi," in *Renegotiating Boundaries: Local Politics in Post-Suharto Indonesia*, ed. Henk Schulte Nordholt and Gerry van Klinken (Leiden: KITLV Press, 2007), 121–50; Nicholas Parsons and Marcus Mietzner, "Sharia By-Laws in Indonesia: Legal and Political Analysis," *Australian Journal of Asian Law* 11, no. 2 (2009): 190–217.

labelled as a sharia state or law.[189] He also mentions that the shariatisation of Indonesian law should be implemented gradually.[190] Finally, he argues that the acceptance of NKRI does not contradict the aspiration of some Muslim groups who want to incorporate sharia into the state law of Indonesia.

A more obvious stance in support of the shariatisation of Indonesian law can be seen in statements by another leading MUI figure, Amin, who argues that the incorporation of sharia into national legislation is not against the constitution of Indonesia, because the legal system allows for the adoption of legal content from various traditions. These legal sources can be from the Western tradition as well as from the Islamic tradition. Amin argues that all components of Indonesian society have the right to contribute to the formation of such a law and, as a result, he can understand if some Muslim groups are striving to enshrine sharia into state law.[191] In order to promote the Islamisation of Indonesian law, Amin proposes that the first step to be undertaken by MUI is to formalise sharia as part of positive law. However, if this fails MUI can seek to incorporate the substance of sharia—justice, consultancy and so forth—into state law.[192] Amin admits that, up until now, MUI has been working on the second of these options. Both Amin and Mahfudh's views are not particularly unusual, but are shared by many Muslim scholars throughout Indonesia. Hasyim Muzadi (the general chairman of NU, 1999–2010) categorically rejected the establishment of an Islamic state in 2009.[193] However this did not mean that he rejected the imposition of sharia-like provisions into state law in Indonesia. The incorporation of sharia into the Indonesian legal system is not just promoted by scholars from MUI, NU and Muhammadiyah, but also more radically inclined Muslim organisations such as the HTI, MMI, Jama'ah Anshorut Tauhid (JAT, Supporters of the Unity of God)[194] and many others. These radical groups demand the implementation of sharia law through the establishment of an Islamic state, using Islam as the legal and political foundation of Indonesia along with the sharia criminal justice system.

Despite the difference in approaches sought, a common belief between these mainstream as well as Islamist groups is the enactment of sharia-based

189 Interview with Sahal Mahfudh, Jakarta, 2010.

190 Ibid.

191 Interview with Ma'ruf Amin, Jakarta, 2010.

192 Ibid.

193 "Religious Harmony Safe Under Pancasila," *The Jakarta Post*, 10 March 2009, http://www.thejakartapost.com/news/2009/03/10/religious-harmony-safe-under-pancasila039.html, viewed on 22 July 2022.

194 International Crisis Group, "Indonesia: The Dark Side of Jama'ah Ansharut Tauhid (JAT)," Update Briefing (Brussels & Jakarta, 2010).

provisions of Indonesian law. On this basis, MUI's initiative to set up the Law and Legislation Commission is understandable. Besides this, as an ulama institution, MUI's involvement in the shariatisation movement is inevitable. MUI's increased independence from state control since the reform era has also given the Council the confidence to take on a role as a defender of pro-sharia groups in Indonesia. Furthermore, many Islamic organisations that currently support MUI have begun to have a greater influence on the legislation process. For instance, when the KUII, or Indonesian Muslim Community Congress,[195] was organised in 1998, it broadly endorsed the integration of sharia into the state law of Indonesia.[196] Although this was not formulated in a clear statement, it nonetheless showed that the issue of sharia in state law was still unresolved. MUI did not want to overtly promote such a sensitive issue in the immediate aftermath of the fall of the Suharto regime, so it instead took a more gradual approach, one that is backed by the current MUI general chairman.[197]

Demands to incorporate sharia into national law gained pace during the 2005 KUII, particularly as contained in the message of *Deklarasi Jakarta* (Jakarta Declaration).[198] This charter consists of two important points related to the enactment of sharia law in Indonesia. First, sharia should be employed as a solution for all problems facing the Indonesian state and nation. This statement resembles the slogan *al-islām huwa al-ḥall* (Islam is the solution) promoted by many Islamist groups in other Islamic countries, and the transnational nature of these groups may have played a role in seeing its emergence in the KUII. This congress was also the first in the post-reform era, and as a result, participants were very active in using the event as a platform to promote the incorporation of sharia into national law. The 2005 KUII also represented the peak of Islamist groups' influence in MUI. Second, the 2005 KUII demanded that the government revise *Kitab Undang-Undang Hukum Pidana* (KUHP, the Indonesian Criminal Code) to bring it in line with sharia provisions. It motivated the MUI Law and Legislation Commission to become more involved

195 This congress is periodically organised by MUI under the financial support of Ministry of Religious Affairs. A more detailed account of this issue is found in Chapter 4.

196 MUI, *Kumpulan Hasil-Hasil Kongres Umat Islam Indonesia, Umat Islam Menyongsong Era Indonesia Baru*, 1999.

197 Interview with Sahal Mahfudh, Jakarta, 2011.

198 *Deklarasi Jakarta* is a small booklet published by *Badan Pekerja Kongres Umat Islam Indonesia IV* (Organising Committee of Islamic Congress of Islamic Community). The declaration implies several items of the 2005 KUII's recommendation.

in enabling legal concepts to be accommodated within national law as the Muslim public aspired to see sharia law introduced.[199]

Compared to the other bodies within MUI mentioned above, the Law and Legislation Commission does not receive much public attention. However, this does not mean it is any less important. Since its establishment, MUI has attempted to recruit prominent Muslims to the Commission in order to build its profile. Those recruited as Commission members in its first five years, such as chairperson Aisyah Aminy and deputy chair Wahiduddin Adams, had extensive experience in law and legislation issues.[200] Aminy has been a member of the PPP since its inception in 1973. During her term as a parliamentarian, she focused almost entirely on law, legislation and political issues. Meanwhile, Adams, who was born on 17 January 1954 in Palembang, Sumatera, was a legal expert by education and career.[201] He had served as a public servant at the Ministry of Law and Legislation long before his appointment as director-general of legislation at the ministry in 2009.[202] Besides these two individuals, other members of the commission with a background in legal issues include: Muchtar Zarkasyi, Muhda Hadisaputro, Zainudin Ali, Zain Badjebar, Ali Taher Paransong, and many others. The recruitment of these individuals indicates at least two things: first, MUI's serious intent in developing the Commission as a credible body; and second, MUI's high expectations regarding the role of the Commission in preparing a mature concept of influencing the legislation of state law with sharia norms.

Besides the task it plays, the presence of the Law and Legislation Commission has enabled MUI to help prevent any legal disadvantage for Indonesian Muslims caused by the national legislation agenda. Ichwan Sam, the secretary general of MUI, says:[203]

199 MUI, *Dokumentasi Kongres Umat Islam Indonesia IV, Ukhuwah Islamiyah Untuk Indonesia Yang Bermartabat* (Jakarta: Majelis Ulama Indonesia, 2005); MUI, *Kongres Umat Islam Indonesaia IV: Proses Dan Dinamika Permusyawaratan* (Jakarta: BPKUII IV, 2005).

200 Aminy was born in 1931 in Padang Panjang, West Sumatra, and was the first female student to obtain an undergraduate law degree at the Islamic University of Indonesia (UII), Yogyakarta, in 1957. In 1966, she established the Institute for Advocacy of Human Rights (Lembaga Pembela Hak Asasi Manusia, LPHAM). See Majalah Tokoh Indonesia, "BeritaTokoh, Aisyah Aminy," *Majalah Tokoh Indonesia* (Jakarta, 2006).

201 Wahiduddin Adams obtained his B.A. (1979), M.A. (1992), and PhD (2002) in Islamic Law from the State Islamic University.

202 Interview with Wahiduddin Adams, Jakarta, 2011.

203 Interview with Ichwan Sam, Jakarta, 2010.

> MUI has long been aware of the importance of institutionalising legal concerns, and it achieved a good momentum when the Law and Legislation Commission was established in 2000. We need to take a closer look at the process of national legislation in order to remove any possibility of fraud within this process.

The tangible contributions of the commission can be seen in the meeting proceedings and documents from MUI's National Work Meetings as well as internal publications from the commission that discuss proposing counter legal drafts of national laws and revisions of the secular legal system.[204]

Due to the influence of this newly established Commission, from 2000 MUI has introduced a new theme of fatwa called *Masā'il Qānūniyya* (the topics of law) that specifically addresses the various legal issues of Indonesia. The Law and Legislation Commission uses this as a compass in planning programmes, and also drawing up a priority list of the legal agenda regarding the focus in the shariatisation of Indonesian law. As an example, if the Fatwa Commission plans for a fatwa to be focused on a legal study, analysis or counter legal draft document, this is given to the Law and Legislation Commission. In this way, the Commission is not just an implementing body of MUI on the matter of legislation issue, but also benefits other bodies within the organisation. Before the establishment of the Commission, such legal issues were handled by the Fatwa Commission or by the Central Board through the formation of an *ad hoc* team. Such approaches are no longer sufficient as MUI is seeking to become more active in legal issues taking place in Indonesia. By establishing the Law and Legislation Commission, MUI can be involved in legal matters in a systematic and comprehensive manner.

3.3.4.2 Drafting Sharia

The shariatisation of legal discourse and practice of Indonesia has been one of MUI's priorities since the beginning of new reform era, as can be seen in statements delivered by the Council on several important occasions. In 2005 at the KUII, MUI released statements on two important issues closely related to the implementation of sharia. Firstly, the Council asked the parliament to replace the colonial legal system with sharia law. The 'colonial system' referred

---

204 Karni et al., *35 Tahun Majelis Ulama Indonesia*, 2010; Wahiduddin Adams, "Fatwa MUI Dalam Prespektif Hukum Dan Perundangundangan," in *Fatwa Majelis Ulama Dalam Perspektif Hukum Dan Perundang-Undangan*, ed. Nahar Nahrawi et al. (Jakarta: Puslitbang Kehidupan Keagamaan Badan Litbang dan Diklat Kementerian Agama RI, 2012), 3–17, pp. 3–16.

to by MUI here was the Dutch Civil Code (*Burgerlijk Wetboek*). Secondly, the Council strongly advised the parliament and the government to adopt sharia into the draft law on Indonesian Penal and Civil Code (Kitab Undang-Undang Hukum Pidana: KUHP, and Kitab Undang-Undang Hukum Acara Pidana: KUHAP).[205] This second demand was somewhat more realistic in the context of the Indonesian legal system than the first, because wiping out the KUHP and KUHAP from the Indonesian legal system would almost be impossible.

The establishment of the Law and Legislation Commission was an attempt to express a "new Islamic identity" among groups of Indonesian Muslims who wanted to demonstrate their "Muslim-ness" by promoting sharia provision implementation into the state law of Indonesia. These groups eagerly support sharia as an explicit and implicit part of the national legal system. As mentioned earlier, MUI has long been involved in efforts to promote shariatisation, but its role was determined by the ruling regime and the social and political climate in Indonesia. During the Suharto period, these efforts were driven more by the state than by MUI as the Council would not initiate moves to promote shariatisation without state support. Since 1998, however, MUI has taken a much more oppositionist stance towards the state and determined its own position. One of the clearest examples of this was in 2000, when MUI issued a fatwa banning Ajinomoto products which contained pork, despite then-President Wahid's insistence that the products were lawful.[206] This serves as proof of MUI's growing independence during the period.

Thus, MUI has seen the need to strengthen the role of the Commission to support their efforts to promote the Islamisation of state law. Recent prominent cases have only increased the Commission's role, some of which included responses to: an amateur porn-video of Indonesian celebrities uploaded to the Internet,[207] the unresolved case of the Ahmadiyah, and the so-called building of "*gereja liar*" (mostly Protestant churches, built without the permission of their surrounding communities now required under local Indonesian law).[208]

205 MUI, *Kongres Umat Islam Indonesaia IV: Proses Dan Dinamika Permusyawaratan*, 2005, p. 500.

206 Karni et al., *35 Tahun Majelis Ulama Indonesia*, p. 2010.

207 In 2010, most of the Indonesian media was enthralled by the coverage of an amateur porn video case involving Indonesian celebrities Ariel, Luna Maya and Cut Tari which was broadcast on the internet. MUI used this case as ammunition to demand that the government, especially the President, seriously implement the act on pornography. Hertanto Soebijoto, "Kasus Ariel: MUI Akan Surati Presiden," *Kompas*, July 2010, https://surabaya.kompas.com/read/2010/07/06/15513890/kasus.ariel.mui.akan.surati.presiden.

208 This issue has become a widespread phenomenon over the last ten years. A more complete account can be found in *Kontroversi Gereja di Jakarta Kontroversi Gereja Di Jakarta (Yogyakarta: CRCS, 2011)*, a serial monograph published in 2011 by a consortium consisting

MUI considers these issues as proof of weak morality in society and the failure of law enforcement. As a result, MUI has prioritised sharia legislation as an important part of the *umma* agenda and Amin has said that promoting the *taqnīn* (codification) of sharia into the Indonesian legal system is MUI's most urgent priority.[209]

How can the Law and Legislation Commission handle this key MUI mission of incorporating sharia codification into Indonesian state law? To answer this question, it is worth looking at the philosophical background of the Commission. MUI views this body not as an independent entity but rather a legal division of MUI. It provides a legal basis for MUI's rulings, particularly those from the Fatwa Commission. To facilitate the Law and Legislation Commission's role, MUI has delegated a number of tasks to it, such as responsibility for conducting a study and review of laws related to the implementation of sharia in particular, as well as those related to Muslim society more broadly.[210] The Commission has the responsibility for preparing ideas, concepts, and plans for the drafting of state laws and other regulations related to sharia. The commission has also been given the mandate to monitor state laws considered by MUI to contradict the principles of sharia and the interests of the Muslim community.[211] For some of these laws, the Commission has been tasked to propose amendments. Otherwise the Commission will undertake a judicial review of all laws and related regulations viewed as contradicting higher laws, sharia and the interests of Muslim society. Thus the Law and Legislation Commission is expected to guard existing laws and all government regulations which promote sharia as well as promote new laws in this vein. The Law and Legislation Commission also represents MUI in debates on national legislation such as the formation of the Tim Advokasi Majelis Ulama Indonesia (MUI's advocacy team), acting as MUI's representative in the courts.[212] Deputy Chairman Wahiduddin Adams has focused the Commission's attention on two key activities: responding to draft laws or bills (RUU, *rancangan undang-undang*) and preparing counter legal drafts following sharia norms. To this end, the Law and Legislation Commission has conducted studies and legal analysis on several RUU and national regulations.

---

of the Paramadina Foundation, Jakarta, CRCS (the Centre for Religion and Cross-Cultural Studies), MPRK (Magister Perdamaian dan Resolusi Konflik of Gadjah Mada University), and ICRP (the Indonesian Conference on Religion and Peace).

209 Interview with Ma'ruf Amin, Jakarta, 2010.

210 Interview with Ichwan Sam, Jakarta, 2010.

211 Ibid.

212 Karni et al., *35 Tahun Majelis Ulama Indonesia*, p. 139; Adams, *Pola Penyerapan Fatwa Majelis Ulama Indonesia (MUI) Dalam Peraturan Perundang-Undangan 1975–1997*.

From 2005 to 2010, ten bills were studied by the Commission on Film, Pornography, Halal Product Assurance, Sharia Banking, Health, the Management of Pilgrimage, Legal Educational Entities, Religious Court, the law draft on Civil Administration, and Administration of Islamic Almsgiving.[213] Besides reviewing national laws, the Commission has also conducted studies and analysed derivative legal products of state law, such as governmental ordinances, presidential instructions, ministerial decisions, gubernatorial decrees and so forth. The Commission is also an active contributor and participant in forums and discussions on national legislation and sharia and also programmes to promote the products of national legislation, including provisions on sharia.

On the basis of these studies and analyses of the bills and regulations mentioned above, it seems the Commission is not only focusing on the preservation of Islamic laws related to Muslim personal rights such as laws on Islamic almsgiving, the pilgrimage and many others, but also on incorporating sharia into more general public laws on education, health, and civil administration and so on. This is in accordance with the article by Asrorun Ni'am Sholeh (the Secretary of MUI's Fatwa Commission) entitled *Agenda Konsolidasi Regulasi Negara: Pertarungan Nilai dan Ideologi Belum Selesai* ("The Consolidation of State Regulations: the Unfinished Conflict Between Values and Ideology"), which suggests that MUI is also strategically targeting state laws which have no religious content as the object of shariatisation. According to Sholeh, MUI is now facing a real battle fighting against secularist groups that tend to employ these laws as a means to implant their values and ideology into state legislation.[214] Therefore, he concludes, MUI should actively play a more strategic role in initiating, creating, transforming and influencing the policy-making and legislation process of Indonesia's legal system by mobilising all of its resources.[215]

It appears that MUI's shariatisation agenda will become more comprehensive, targeting all Indonesian laws and not just those with a direct relationship with sharia. If this occurs, there may well be clashes between MUI's agenda and the national interests of protecting the state law. Up until now, MUI has continued to support the national ideology and the preservation of the Unitary State of the Indonesian Republic, but it seems this framework is consciously intended by MUI to support the smooth implementation of the Islamisation

---

213 Karni et al., *35 Tahun Majelis Ulama Indonesia*, p. 141; Adams, "Fatwa MUI Dalam Prespektif Hukum Dan Perundangundangan."

214 Asrorun Ni'am Sholeh, "Agenda Konsolidasi Regulasi Negara: Pertarungan Nilai Dan Ideologi Belum Selesai," *Mimbar Ulama Indonesia*, January 2011, p. 32.

215 Ibid.

project of Indonesian state law. MUI has learned from the failures of Islamic fundamentalist groups (MMI, HTI, FPI and FUI) that promoted shariatisation through such radical means as violence and the total implementation of sharia within their communities.

The encouraging comments and opinions of Indonesian lawmakers in the media also indicate that the shariatisation agenda may have a bright future. This can also be seen from the number of MUI initiatives that have been accommodated in state law. Adams mentioned that several such laws, including the State Law on Sharia Banking, the State Law on Pornography and many others, indicate good prospects for the Islamisation of state law as well as the effective work of the Law and Legislation Commission of MUI.[216] Although Indonesia uses a single legal system, Adams argues that this does not necessarily mean different legal systems—such as Islamic, Western, and customary laws—cannot play a role within it. It would seem that MUI's Law and Legislation Commission will continue to play a very active role in the future.

3.4 Conclusion

As a living organisation, MUI's role in the shariatisation of Indonesia, largely implemented by these four bodies, is constantly changing and evolving. It is situated in and adjusts to the circumstances of the Muslim people, the state and society. However, it should be noted here that MUI's internal reform following the Suharto era, from its ideological change to programmematic and concrete agenda of the four bodies, has become the modality for the Council to undergo its project of shariatisation. Besides its institutional capacity, it is crucial to take into account the role of MUI's individual leaders and board members in shaping public discourse on the importance of subjugating national law to the influence of sharia. The shariatisation project benefits from the project attempts of MUI leaders—in theology and politics—in response to the social, legal and political situation surrounding the movement. Following inspiration from Morris and Staggenborg,[217] we can understand MUI leaders as creating enabling conditions for their followers who desire

216 Interview with Ma'ruf Amin, Jakarta, 2010.

217 Aldon D. Morris and Suzanne Staggenborg, "Leadership in Social Movements," in *The Blackwell Companion to Social Movements*, ed. David A. Snow, Sarah A Soule, and Hanspeter Kriesi (Malden: Blackwell Publishing, 2004), 172–96.

the implementation of sharia in the public and legal spheres of Indonesia. In other words, the right combination of organisational capacity and leadership style within MUI can contribute to the success of shariatisation, and also leads to well-prepared MUI responses to it. MUI's ambition to participate in all the issues related to sharia makes this organisation an example and also a reference for other Islamic organisations following a similar agenda.

CHAPTER 4

Sharia Activism: Opportunity Structure, Frame, and Mobilisation

4.1 Introduction

The role played by MUI to facilitate the inclusion of sharia into the legal and public spheres of Indonesia can be described as promoting shariatisation. The question that will be addessed here is: "How is MUI working towards shariatisation, and what activities and strategies does it employ?" In answering this question, the term "sharia activism" is used, as described by Quintan Wictorowicz in referring to Islamic activism, namely "the mobilisation of contention to support Muslim causes."[1] Included in this phrase, Wictorowicz argues, are many aspects of contention such as the *daʿwa* movement, Islamic terrorist groups, and political Islamist groups who want to establish an Islamic state, as well as many other groups in which Islam is commodified to act as the banner of the movement. Mazen Hashem states that Islamic activism can also be regarded as "the orientation of praxis" which results from the dialogue between structure and ideology.[2] Its characteristics are "flux and fixity with pragmatism" when responding to challenges. Referring to Alberto Melucci's new social movements theory, Hashem identifies Islamic activism as activism established on the basis of "interplay of aims, resources, and obstacles and connected with Islamic ideology."[3] Thomas Olesen defines Islamic activism as "activism where Islam forms the ideological basis of an organization."[4]

Besides referring to the analytical perspectives of social movement organisation theory, this section also considers the importance of gaining inspiration from the theoretical discourses of Islamism. The first is Bobby S. Sayyid's perspective on the Islamist orientation in wrestling for Islam as "a master signifier," where sharia activism can be constructed as a deliberate attempt that

1 Quintan Wictorowicz, ed., *Islamic Activism: A Social Movement Theory Approach* (Indiana: Indiana University Press, 2004), p. 2.

2 Mazen Hashem, "Contemporary Islamic Activism: The Shades of Praxis," *Sociology of Religion* 67, no. 1 (March 2006): 23–41, p. 24.

3 Ibid.

4 Thomas Olesen, "Social Movement Theory and Radical Islamic Activism," in *Islamism as Social Movement*, ed. Thomas Olesen and Farhad Khosrochavar (Aarhus: Centre for Studies in Islamism and Radicalisation (CIR), 2009), p. 9.

 | DOI:10.1163/9789004534896_005

aims at establishing the supremacy of sharia in the legal and public spheres of Indonesia.[5] In doing so, the Islamist groups spread the "inter-discursive nature of Islam" an idea that integrates *dīn* (religion), *dunyā* (mundane life) and *dawla* (state) as vehicles for shariatisation. The second is Salwa Ismail's concept on the informal arena of the Islamist movement.[6] According to this concept, sharia activism functions as the social, legal and political activity of MUI to consolidate the ordinary potential for encouraging the process of shariatisation in Indonesia. This concept is also close to what is popularly referred to as politics of "the informal people," a way for ordinary people to strive for social changes in their everyday life.[7] Asef Bayat says, "every day practices are bound to shift into the realm of politics."[8] In the case of MUI, the sharia activism referred to here is the persistent and systematic efforts from supporters of MUI aimed at the inclusion and formalisation of sharia provisions into the legal and public spheres of Indonesia.

4.2 The Legal and Political Structure of Indonesia

A shariatisation movement cannot merely exist through its own ideological and organisational capacity. It needs the support of external factors. This section explains those external factors, namely the political and legal opportunities provided by the state that has enabled the Council to mobilise efforts to increase sharia acceptability in the legal and public spheres. Theoretically speaking, the success of such an effort or movement is affected by many factors, one of them being the political, legal, and social context. In the tradition of social movement theories, these are called external factors. Sidney Tarrow defines political opportunity as the "consistent—but not necessarily formal, permanent or national—dimensions of political environments that either encourage or discourage people from using collective action."[9] Jack Goldstone

5 Bobby S. Sayyid, *A Fundamental Fear: Eurocentrim and the Emergence of Islamism* (London & New York: Zed Books, 1997), pp. 47–48.

6 Salwa Ismail, *Rethinking Islamic Politics: Culture, the State and Islamism* (London & New York: I.B. Tauris, 2006), p. 23.

7 Asef Bayat, "Un-Civil Society: The Politics of 'the Informal People,'" *Third World Quarterly* 18, no. 1 (1997): 53–74, pp. 55–7; Asef Bayat, *Life as Politics: How Ordinary People Change the Middle East* (Amsterdam: Amsterdam University Press, 2010).

8 Bayat, "Un-Civil Society: The Politics of 'the Informal People'", p. 58.

9 Sidney Tarrow, *The New Transnational Activism* (Cambridge: Cambridge University Press, 2005), p. 23; Sasha Costanza-Chock, "Transmedia Mobilization in the Popular Association of the Oaxacan People, Los Angeles," in *Power in Movement: Social Movements and Contentious Politics* (Bristol: Intellect Books, 1998), 271, 98.

and Charles Tilly broadly refer to political opportunity as "the probability that social protest actions will lead to success in achieving a desired outcome."[10] Both authors also include a discursive opportunity within the notion of political opportunity.[11] McAdam outlines political opportunity as "a set of formal and informal political conditions that encourage, discourage, channel and otherwise affect movement activity."[12]

The concept of the political structure opportunity is useful as a means of explaining MUI's role in facilitating the process of shariatisation. As the ulama council that serves as a *tenda besar* (large tent) for Indonesian Islamic organisations, MUI is not just an ordinary organisation but a collective of individual activists and Muslim scholars with similar interests and aspirations to implement sharia in Indonesia. It is important to see how this organisation creates the process of crafting appeals,[13] benefitting from the favourable political opportunity shaped by the post-reform era. There are three reasons why MUI has become an effective vehicle for sharia mobilisation. Firstly, it has more experience in dealing with state matters, including such legislation-related processes as lobbying, proposing counter legal drafts, and making recommendations to Indonesian lawmakers. MUI also knows more about the strategy and methods for introducing sharia into the body of Indonesian law. Secondly, MUI is also more widely accepted by various Islamic organisations, due to its accommodation of their interests and ideological inclinations. Thirdly, MUI has successfully tailored the shariatisation project to convince Islamic organisations to join its greater shariatisation movement.

The analytical framework of political opportunity structure used here relies on Doug McAdam's four-point concept: first, the openness of the political

10 Jack A. Goldstone and Charles Tilly, "Threat (and Opportunity) Popular Action and State Response in the Dynamics of Contentious Action," in *Silence and Voice in Contentious Politics*, ed. Ronald R. Aminzade et al. (Cambridge: Cambridge University Press, 2001), p. 337.

11 William A. Gamson, "Bystanders, Public Opinion, and the Media," in *The Blackwell Companion to Social Movements*, ed. David A Snow, Sarah A Soule, and Hanspeter Kriesi (Malden: Blackwell Publishing, 2004), 242–61 p. 249; Marco Giugni, "Political Opportunity: Still a Useful Concept?," in *Contention and Trust in Cities and States*, ed. Charles Tilly and Michael Hanagan (Dordrecht, Heidelberg, London & New York: Springer, 2011), 271–86, p. 274; Myra Marx Ferree et al., *Shaping Abortion Discourse: Democracy and the Public Sphere in Germany and the United States* (Cambridge: Cambridge University Press, 2002), pp. 61–85.

12 John L. Campbell, "Where Do We Stand? Common Mechanisms in Organizations and Social Movements Research," in *Social Movements and Organization Theory*, ed. F. Davis Gerald, Doug McAdam, and Richard Scott William (Cambridge: Cambridge University Press, 2005), 41–68, p. 44.

13 Meyer, "Opportunities and Identities: Bridge Building in the Social Movements", p. 8.

system; second, the national elite alignment; third, the presence of elite allies, and fourth, state capacity.[14] In the Indonesian context, openness of the political system refers to the birth of the *reformasi* period at the end of the Suharto era. The national elite alignment refers to the polarisation of the national elites of Indonesia that followed the collapse of the ruling regime. The presence of elite allies refers to the networks and allies of MUI's shariatisation. Finally, state capacity is analysed through the framework employed in this section, to examine the state's weakness in governing Indonesia. These four elements represent the four dynamic components of the political opportunity structure that has allowed MUI to forge its shariatisation project.

4.2.1 Reformasi *as an Open Stage*

The dawn of *reformasi*[15] in 1998 created a great opportunity for all Muslim groups, including MUI, to present their Islamic identity in the public sphere. Some Islamic groups that had struggled in hiding during the Suharto era (1966–1998) rose and sought the re-establishment of their banned organisations.[16] Those that set up new Islamic parties believed that the tremendous political change in 1998 would give them the chance to gain electoral support from Muslim voters.[17] For MUI, *reformasi* is an era in which the pressure of the ruling regime no longer exists and a greater freedom to articulate aspirations and

14 Doug McAdam, "Conceptual Origins, Current Problems, Future Direction," in *Comparative Perspective on Social Movements*, ed. John D. McCharty and Mayer N. Zald (Cambridge: Cambridge University Press, 1996), 23–41, pp. 26–29. Nella Van Dyke and Holly J. McCammon, eds, *Strategic Alliances: Coalition Building and Social Movements* (Minneapolis: University of Minnesota Press, 2010).

15 An Indonesian expression used to indicate the shift of power from an authoritarian regime to a more democratic one, referred to in English as the reform era.

16 Martin van Bruinessen, "Genealogies of Islamic Radicalism in Post-Suharto Indonesia," *South East Asian Research* 10, no. 2 (2002): 117–54, pp. 117–118; Elizabeth Fuller Collins, *Indonesia Betrayed: How Development Fails* (Hamspire & Burlington: University of Hawaii Press, 2007).

17 Andreas Ufen, "Mobilising Political Islam: Indonesia and Malaysia Compared," *Commonwealth & Comparative Politics* 47, no. 3 (2009): 308–33, p. 318. The movements of the Islamic parties are relatively observable and measurable because they are public about their programmes. The parties needed to obey state regulations regarding general elections and political parties. The sharia element of these Islamic parties is evident through their use of Islam as their basic ideological foundation and also through the integration of sharia into their programmes, both implicitly and explicitly. From the perspective of procedural democracy, the presence of these Islamic parties was tolerable, despite their obvious commitment to sharia in their platforms and agenda, because they adhered to the procedural steps required to be accepted as part of a modern democracy. As part of the camp of Islamic groups that ardently adopted Islam as "the country's moral and ethical guide," MUI gained great benefit from the downfall of the Suharto regime and the new

criticise the state, including its existing national legal system, has begun. In short, the reform era of Indonesia has enabled MUI to mobilise religious, financial and human resources to fulfil its aims.

The post-Suharto regimes have tried to strengthen Indonesia's openness through state policies. Indonesian presidents Baharuddin Jusuf Habibie (1998–1999), Wahid (1999–2001), Megawati Sukarno Putri (2002–2004), and Yudoyono (2004–2014) have all shown their commitment for democratisation, freedom and respect for human rights. One of the hallmarks of *reformasi* was the relatively transparent and fair process of the 1999 general elections. The 1999 general elections not only met the technical definitions of fairness and openness, but also attracted many political parties of different ideological backgrounds to participate in the electoral process, including seventeen Islamic parties.[18] As a democratic space, Indonesia's *reformasi* has generated a favourable condition for all actors, including Islamic parties and organisations, to play their role in propagating religion in the legal and public spheres. Hefner states that *reformasi* is not only a blessing for democratisation, but also a vehicle for the emergence of sharia politics.[19] Studies on democratisation always indicate the early process of a newly democratic country, like Indonesia, is rarely smooth given the unstable circumstances of the political system on the road towards a consolidated democracy. Democracy is not only an arena for its proponents but also for its opponents, since both sides have equal rights to define what it means. This is precisely the dilemma of democracy. On the one hand, it promotes democratic values such as openness, transparency, tolerance, and respect for human rights—including civil and political rights—but, on the other hand, a consolidated and mature model of democracy cannot ban and reject the values of opposition groups which are procedurally clothed in accordance with democratic mechanisms, even if applying these values is in practice in opposition to the substance of democracy. This is what must be considered within the process of *reformasi* in Indonesia with respect to

openness of the political structure. See Adam Schwarz, "Indonesia After Suharto," *Foreign Affairs* 76, no. 4 (1997): 119–34, p. 131.

18 Aris Ananta, Evi Nurvidya Arifin, and Leo Suryadinata, *Emerging Democracy in Indonesia* (Singapore: Institute of Southeast Asian Studies, 2005), pp. 9–15; Syamsuddin Haris, ed., *Pemilu Langsung Di Tengah Oligarki Partai: Proses Nominasi Dan Seleksi Calon Legislatif Pemilu 2004* (Jakarta: Gramedia Pustaka Utama, 2005), p. 3.

19 Robert W. Hefner, "Indonesia: Shariʿa Politics and Democratic Transition," in *Shariʿa Politics: Islamic Law and Society in the Modern World* (Indiana University Press, 2011), 280–303, pp. 281–2.

the sharia aspirations of bodies like MUI and other Islamic organisations and parties.[20]

The uncertain situation of this first phase of Indonesia's democratic consolidation is a political opportunity for MUI. Amin indicates that MUI is benefitting from this situation,[21] asserting that "this stage has paved the way for MUI to synergise its potential in ensuring the formalisation of sharia."[22] There are several concrete examples of how *reformasi* has resulted in a strong repositioning of MUI, as discussed below.

The annulment of Act No. 8/1985 on Organisasi Kemasyarakatan (Ormas, mass organisations) was a clear political opportunity produced by the *reformasi* era.[23] This law was anti-democratic in nature, Article 1 obliging all organisations to embrace Pancasila as their sole ideology.[24] On the basis of this law, the establishment of any organisations not based on Pancasila during the Suharto era was regarded as unconstitutional because it could threaten the unity of the state and also conflicted with the basic value of Indonesia, *bhinneka tunggal ika* (unity in diversity). After Habibie took his oath as the third president of Indonesia, on 21 May 1998, one of his important decisions that eventually underpinned the resurgence of religion-based movements in Indonesia was the revocation of this law. Habibie approved this change due to strong demands from civil society organisations, including Islamic groups. If Indonesia was to become a democratic state, then civil and political liberties should be protected and legal rulings forbidding the expression of freedom and liberties should also be amended.

Indonesia's new political openness also became apparent through the deregulation of the party system. In the 1970s, under the Suharto regime, the former multi-party system was fused into only two political parties, the PPP and the Partai Demokrasi Indonesia (PDI, Indonesia's Democracy Party), in addition to the one functional group, Golkar. In the reform era, Indonesia has

20 Robin Bush, "Regional Sharia Regulations in Indonesia: Anomaly or Symptom?," in *Expressing Islam: Religious Life and Politics*, ed. Greg Fealy and Sally White (Singapore: ISEAS, 2008); Hefner, "Indonesia: Shari'a Politics and Democratic Transition;" Marcus Mietzner, *Military Politics, Islam and the State in Indonesia: From Turbulent Transition to Democratic Consolidation* (Singapore: ISEAS, 2009).

21 Interview with Ma'ruf Amin, Jakarta, 2010.

22 Ibid.

23 T. Lindsey and S. Butt, Indonesian Law (OUP Oxford, 2018), pp. 37–50.

24 Article 1 states: "An organisation which is voluntarily set up by Indonesian citizens on the basis of common activity, profession, function, religion, belief in God, as a means to engage in the development process to achieve national objectives within the framework of the Unitary state of the Indonesian Republic which is based on Pancasila."

reverted to a multi-party system, enabling all people and groups to establish political parties on the basis of their beliefs and religions. Islamic political parties, ideologically based on Islam and striving for the implementation of sharia in Indonesia, included the PPP, PBB, PK and other smaller parties. These parties successfully pushed for MPR Decree No. X/1999 to replace MPR Decree No. II/1983 that had obliged all political parties and organisations in Indonesia to adhere to Pancasila as their sole ideology. MPR Decree No. X/1999 transformed Indonesia's political system from a secular to religious-friendly one in which many Islamic parties may now flourish.

At the normative and practical level, two legal products directly encouraged the implementation of MPR's Decree No. X/1999: firstly Act No. 2/1999 on Political Parties and secondly Act No. 3/1999 on General Elections.[25] Act No. 2/1999 outlines the number of permissible political parties, thus kickstarting the multi-party system. As a result of this political liberalisation, Dewi Fortuna Anwar has noted, there were around 200 new political parties registered at the Ministry of Justice, but only forty-eight passed legal verification in order to participate in the 1999 general elections. It should be understood that none of these laws enforce Pancasila as the ideology of the Indonesian people, but it remains the ideology of the state. This means that the Indonesian people—including organisations, political parties and associations—can have a different ideological affiliation to the state ideology. The law assures freedom for all political parties as well the freedom to adopt any other ideologies, including Islam, with the exception of communism (which is still banned). On this basis many Islamic political parties began to desert Pancasila and embrace Islam.

Another related law revoked from Indonesia's national legal system during the Habibie era was the anti-subversion law/1963. Political analyst Dewi Fortuna Anwar has described this law as a draconian one.[26] It was manipulated by Suharto as a means to shut down Islamic organisations and Islamic political parties or all those defined as his political and ideological opponents. Other supporting legislation for shariatisation during the Habibie administration can be seen in the issuance of Act No. 9/1998 on Freedom of Speech in the Public Sphere and the ratification of ILO (International Labour Organisation) Convention No. 87 concerning freedom of association as well as Presidential

25 Dewi Fortuna Anwar, "The Habibie Presidency: Catapulting Towards Reform," in *Soeharto's New Order and Its Legacy: Essays in Honour of Harold Crouch*, ed. Edward Aspinall and Greg Fealy (Canberra: ANU E Press, 2010).

26 Ibid.

Decree No. 83/1998.[27] The latter laws mainly regulate the freedom of labour groups to organise and establish unions or labour associations. These laws can provide legal standing and arguments for MUI to strategically employ in the general environment of national freedom and reform.

At the regional level, shariatisation has gained political and legal opportunities from the increased autonomy of provincial and district governments granted by the central government through the issuance of Act No. 22/1999 on Regional Autonomy or Decentralisation.[28] Although it had been passed as state law, Indonesian lawmakers—at both the executive and legislative levels—subsequently viewed it as inadequate for accommodating the dynamic and rapid transition of the political system towards a consolidated democracy.[29] In order to adjust to the needs of Indonesia's post reform era, Act No. 22/1999 had to be revised. Thus Act No. 22/1999 was amended by Act No. 32/2004 in an endeavour to refine and improve the former. The primary objective of this law was to share the central government's authority and power with the regional governments at the provincial and district levels: thirty-three provincial governments and more than 450 district administrations. Within this legal framework, the regional governments have full authority to govern their own regions, with the exception of five strategic fields: defence, finance, foreign affairs, law, and religion.

However, despite these five limitations imposed on the authority of regional governments, sharia-based bylaws (*peraturan daerah*, abbreviated as *perda*, also referred to as regional regulations) have been issued by many regional governments. Yet in the vast number of cases of sharia bylaws legislated at the regional level, such as in Aceh, Bulukumba, and Cianjur, lawmakers never refer to their legal products as sharia or Islamic regional regulations, most likely to avoid controversy. Should these regulations be referred to as sharia regulations they may firstly invite criticism from the general public for conflicting with the fundamental characteristics of Indonesia's legal system, which is neutral and respects pluralism, and secondly be suspected as part of an attempt to establish an Islamic state within the Unitary State of the Republic of Indonesia or NKRI. "The politics of un-naming" in the case of sharia bylaws is a method that appears to be employed by sharia propagators at the provincial and district levels to ensure the smooth process of shariatisation under regional autonomy.[30]

27 Ibid.

28 Bush, "Regional Sharia Regulations in Indonesia: Anomaly or Symptom?"

29 Lili Romli, "Cakupan Usulan Penyempurnaan Kebijakan Otonomi Daerah," in *Membangun Format Otonomi Daerah*, ed. Syamsuddin Haris (Jakarta: LIPI Press, 2006), 159–75, p. 159.

30 This is the impression I obtained from interviews conducted with local actors who promote the application of sharia law in their regions.

What is important is not the sharia label but rather substance; no matter what the law is called, its contents must be aligned with sharia or Islamic principles.

MUI's interest in sharia legislation at the regional level could be seen as early as 2006. Through its recommendations during the Ijtima' Ulama (Ulama Meeting Forum), MUI endorsed the regional sharia bylaws issued by regional governments such as Aceh, Bulukumba, and Cianjur. This endorsement is based on an assumption that the enactment of Islam-inspired regional regulations is a necessary means to increase the piety of Indonesians.[31] The 2011 MUI recommendation clearly supports the sharia bylaws movement in two ways. Firstly, MUI encourages provincial and district governments throughout the country that have not yet produced sharia bylaws to think about drafting and issuing these laws in their own regions. Secondly, MUI central, provincial and district boards are called on to demonstrate their real support to boost and continue efforts to draft sharia regional regulations to enable the implementation of sharia at the village level. These two recommendations clearly indicate MUI's support for the shariatisation process at the regional government level.

All the above-mentioned legal, formal, and institutional changes of Indonesia's political system provide more chances for MUI to introduce sharia into the legal and public spheres of Indonesia. The democratisation of the legal and political system has created two possibilities: the promotion of democratisation by opening up the political and legal system and/or the emergence of movements which are contrary to democracy. MUI is in a position to benefit greatly from both of these possibilities. In the first scenario it can create a political opportunity structure to enshrine sharia through democratic mechanisms such as general elections, and in the second it can create a political opportunity structure for shariatisation through encouraging non-democratic substantive mechanisms, such as Islamic rebellions against the legal ruling regime. However, the former possibility is the more likely one. The following sections outline political opportunity structures related to this first possibility.

4.2.2 *Divided National Elites*

One external factor contributing to the rapid expansion of shariatisation is the reality of divided national elites within Indonesia. What is meant here by national elites are those with social, political, and cultural leadership capacity, ability, and position, at the national, regional or district levels. Included in this category are leaders of mass organisations, political parties, parliament members, bureaucrats, and most importantly Muslim leaders. Wright Mills depicts the characteristics of national elites in the context of Southeast Asia as figures

31 MUI, *Himpunan Fatwa MUI Sejak 1975*, p. 863.

who often hold positions in governmental offices, bureaucratic agencies, and military centres.[32] In a country with a strong hierarchical system like Indonesia, the national elites have considerable position in influencing the construction of societal and political cohesion as well as changes in society. National elites with moral and political credentials are powerful groups who can lead public opinion. Their recommendations, what they say and do, have an impact on society and can help directly bring about social change. Following Suharto's resignation in 1998, the national elites of Indonesia were free to express and articulate their ideas. This included the pro-sharia national elites, who had been in hiding during the New Order era and were now free to promote their aspirations regarding the implementation of sharia.

This section examines the divisions among the national Muslim elites of Indonesia regarding the use of the political opportunity structure to promote shariatisation. There are those who agree and disagree with putting sharia in the public sphere. The discourse of divided national elites is widely discussed in social movement theory. McAdam describes the divided elites as "the stability or instability of that broad set of elite alignments that typically undergird polity."[33] The division in the national elite has great potential to offer new political actors of such movements the opportunity to become "allies among the political elite" within the state.[34] Andras Bozóki argues that divided elites are more of a phenomenon of authoritarian regimes than of consolidated democracy.[35] However, the actual configuration of national elites in the context of Indonesia's post-Suharto era is rather different. Here, the divided national elites are more apparent due to the lack of control the ruling regime has over them. Theoretically speaking, the reform era has created a space for the creation of a larger coalition of national elites for the facilitation of profound democratisation, but at the practical level, what was anticipated has not always been realised in the way that was expected. The experience of Indonesia tells us that the national elites became divided soon after the birth

32 Case William, "Interlocking Elite in Southeast Asia," in *Elite Configuration at the Apex of Power*, ed. Mattei Dogan (Leiden: Brill, 2003).

33 "Conceptual Origins, Current Problems, Future Direction," in *Comparative Perspective on Social Movements*, ed. John D. McCharty and Mayer N. Zald (Cambridge: Cambridge University Press, 1996), 23–41, p. 27.

34 Mattei Dogan, "Introduction: Diversity of Elite Configurations and Clusters of Power," in *Elite Configuration at the Apex of Power*, ed. Mattei Dogan (Leiden: Brill, 2003), 1–16, p. 11; Doug McAdam, John D. McCarthy, and Mayer Zald, eds., *Comparative Perspectives on Social Movements: Political Opportunities, Mobilizing Structures, and Cultural Framings* (Cambridge: Cambridge University Press, 1996).

35 Andras Bozóki, "Theoretical Interpretations of Elite Change in East Central Europe," in *Elite Configuration at the Apex of Power*, ed. Mattei Dogan (Leiden: Brill, 2003), 215–48.

of the democratic state. This situation of divided national elites is a kind of political opportunity that has the potential to stimulate shariatisation.

In the reform era, the pro-sharia national elite, who had no role to play during the Suharto era, have begun to reinvent their ideals of sharia enactment to be included into the current agenda of Islamisation. Abu Bakar Ba'asyir (b. 1938) is a very interesting case of one such member of the pro-sharia elite. From 1985 to 1999, he lived in political asylum in Malaysia due to his rejection of the Suharto regime's attempts to enforce Pancasila as the sole ideology of Indonesia.[36] It seems that Ba'asyir thought that the resignation of Suharto in May 1998 would create a more favourable situation to forge the shariatisation that he had always imagined. On this basis, since his return to Indonesia, although he has had to deal with allegations that he is the commander (*amīr*) of the terrorist network *Jama'ah Islamiyah* (JI) and has received a fifteen-year prison sentence for supporting for a terrorist shariatisation campaign in Aceh province, Ba'asyir remains a vocal proponent of sharia.[37] Although his ideas are more radical[38] than those of MUI, both Ba'asyir and MUI share some similarities. Ba'asyir, for instance, wants to dismantle the existing secular legal system and replace it with Islamic divine law, including the enforcement of Islamic criminal law,[39] while MUI wants to shariatise the entirety of Indonesians' lives through a sharia economy and halal certification and labelling programme. In this case, MUI has been fortunate to benefit from a similar trajectory of the shariatisation agenda to that promoted by Ba'asyir's, especially regarding his arguments for sharia's applicability in everyday life. MUI also has a similar inspiration to Ba'asyir for his unrelenting desire to replace Kitab Undang-Undang Hukum Pidana (KUHP, Indonesia's Penal Code) with sharia, a spirit that can be seen from the published recommendations of the Kongres Umat Islam Indonesia

36 1985 was the year in which State Law No. 8/1985 on Mass-Organisation was passed prohibiting all community organisations from using any ideology other Pancasila, including Islam, as a founding principle.

37 Noorhaidi Hasan, "September 11 and Islamic Militancy in Post-New Order Indonesia," in *Islam in Southeast Asia: Political, Social, and Strategic Challenges for the 21st Century* (Singapore: Institute of Southeast Asian Studies, 2005), 301–24, pp. 309–10; Jacques Bertrand, "Political Islam and Democracy in the Majority of Muslim Country of Indonesia," in *Islam and Politics in Southeast Asia*, ed. Johan Saravanamuttu (Singapore: ISEAS, 2010), 45–64, p. 58.

38 "Capres Syariah: Muqaddimah dari Revolusi! Siapa Mau Ikut?!!" *Voa Islam*, 13 March 2012, http://www.voa-islam.com/news/indonesiana/2012/03/13/18149/capres-syariah-muqaddimah-dari-revolusi-siapa-mau-ikut/, viewed on 21 July 2022.

39 "Ustadz Abu Bakar Ba'asyir: Pancasila Itu Syirik, Allahu Akbar!" *Mimbar al-Qalam*, 8 May 2013, http://mimbaralqalam.wordpress.com/2013/05/08/ustadz-abu-bakar-baasyir-pancasila-itu-syirik-allahu-akbar/, viewed on 21 July 2022.

(KUII, Indonesian Congress for Muslim Community) held in 1999. In short, both Ba'asyir and MUI share a belief in the importance of incorporating sharia as part of the state law of Indonesia.

Another national figure who has politically and culturally contributed to MUI's attempts to shariatise Indonesia's state law is Habibie, president of Indonesia (1998–1999) and also the former general chairman of ICMI. Habibie was a politically determined actor, because his leadership helped Indonesia to survive the turbulence of the transition era; he was also involved in creating the political opportunity structures that established MUI as a prominent shariatisation actor. At the time he held the position of Minister of Research and Technology and general chairman of ICMI, Habibie gave significant support for the establishment of LPPOM and the BMI (Muamalat Islam Bank). Both institutions are clear examples of the success of MUI in realising ideas of sharia in the economy. MUI itself managed to organise the first KUII in the reform era, and through this congress it was able to bring its agenda to consolidate and solidify the support of Indonesian Muslims for Habibie as president in the short term and shariatisation in the long term.[40] In addition, KUII 1998 also published a controversial recommendation that banned women from being heads of state.

Habibie did not act alone. He was supported by members of national elites aligned within ICMI, such as leading Muhammadiyyah figures (Rais, Malik Fadjar, and Watik Pratikno), some representatives of other Islamic organisations, and also Islamic political parties such as the Golkar, PPP, PAN, and PBB. Alongside Habibie, a new *santri*[41] elite group was emerging within Angkatan Bersenjata Republik Indonesia (ABRI, the Armed Force of Indonesia). Those following Habibie were called the ABRI Hijau or green ABRI (green being identified with Islam) and those in opposition to him were called ABRI *merah putih* or Pancasilais (*merah putih* meaning red-white, the colours of the national flag, symbolising Indonesian nationalism, and Pancasilais meaning supporting the national ideology).[42] The ABRI Hijau elite members were those who had supported the establishment of ICMI in the 1990s.[43] Key members included

40 This issue will be further explained in the next section.

41 *Santri* is a word adopted from Sanskrit, meaning a student of a traditional Islamic boarding school (*pesantren*). See Z. Dhofier, *Tradisi Pesantren: Studi Tentang Pandangan Hidup Kyai* (Jakarta: Lembaga Penelitian, Pendidikan, dan Penerangan Ekonomi dan Sosial, 1980).

42 Rinakit Sukardi, *The Indonesian Military after the New Order* (Copenhagen: NIAS Press, 2005), p. 83.

43 Schulte Nico G. Nordholt, "Kekerasan Dan Anarki Negara Indonesia Modern," in *Orde Zonder Order: Kekerasan Dan Dendam Di Indonesia 1965–1998*, ed. Huub de Jonge and

Faisal Tanjung, R. Hartono, Syarwan Hamid and Z.A. Maulani (d. 2005).[44] The ABRI Hijau had been promoting Islamic identity within the armed forces of Indonesia by showing their support for Islamic groups. Maulani was also actively engaged in MUI, involved in a special taskforce set up by MUI responsible for countering allegations that Indonesia was a hive of Islamic terrorism. He investigated and proposed the counter-argument that all terrorist attacks taking place in Indonesia were backed and engineered by America and other Western countries to protect their political, economic and religious interests. Maulani argued that Western groups always use these concerns to promote "Islamophobia."[45]

When Habibie took his oath to replace Suharto in 1998, there were other national Muslim groups who stood opposed to Habibie. Muslim scholars who voiced different sentiments from the pro-Habibie elite were led by the late Wahid, Rakhmat and M.H. Ainun Nadjib (an Indonesian artist and poet). Wahid and his alliance were often called the *kelompok kultural* (cultural group) and Habibie and his alliance were called the *kelompok struktural* (structural group). The "cultural group" tended to focus on the cultivation of Islam as a cultural symbol, the application of the substance of Islam, and an escape from political Islam. The "structural group" tended towards the cultivation of Islam in the political realm. The main criticism of Wahid and his friends of the Habibie group, who were sourced mostly from ICMI members, was that this organisation could give rise to political and Islamic sectarianism.[46] The elite factionalism became more apparent when Wahid moved to establish an alliance with other groups such as military factions, non-Muslim minority groups and nationalist politicians. In this situation, Abdurrahman Wahid and Megawati's closer ties can be seen as example of a traditional Islam-nationalist alliance, although Wahid publicly stated that his close relationship with Megawati was based on long familial bonds between his grandfather (Hasyim Asy'ari, founder of Nahdlatul Ulama) and his father (Wahid Hasyim, the first Minister of Religious Affairs under Sukarno) and her family, Megawati being the

Frans Hüsken (PT LKiS Pelangi Aksara, 2003), 83–107, p. 101; Sukardi, *The Indonesian Military after the New Order*.

44 A. Pambudi, *Kalau Prabowo Jadi Presiden* (Yogyakarta: Penerbit Narasi, 2009), pp. 42–6; Sukardi, *The Indonesian Military after the New Order*, p. 83.

45 The interview was conducted in Jakarta. My informant did not want to be mentioned by name.

46 Mietzner, *Military Politics, Islam and the State in Indonesia: From Turbulent Transition to Democratic Consolidation*, 2009, p. 84.

oldest daughter of first president Sukarno.[47] Wahid's alliance with Megawati placed him in a more secure political position because it also gave him the support of the largest nationalist groups of Indonesia. Megawati's position as General Chairperson of the PDIP, the largest nationalist party of Indonesia in the 1999 general elections, made her a trusted person for sustaining the legacy of Sukarno.[48] In a similar fashion, in order to seek Islamic legitimacy, the Habibie faction approached large Islamic organisations with a different outlook from Wahid's NU to gain their support. MUI was a great ally of Habibie for three reasons. Firstly, MUI was Suharto's corporatist Islamic organisation and the Habibie group established ICMI under the auspices of Suharto, so they both had similar backgrounds. Secondly, almost all the key positions within MUI were dominated by elite members of modernist Islamic groups who were also ICMI loyalists. Thirdly, MUI had also been active in supporting the establishment of ICMI.

Although the polarisation of the national elites can be seen as a sign of disunity in Indonesian Muslim politics, it has created a great deal of social and political capital that has allowed MUI to promote its ideas on the incorporation of sharia within the public and legal spheres. One positive aspect of divided elites is that it allows more than one path for a particular group to choose and align with to achieve their goals. Under these circumstances MUI could choose between becoming an alternative group to two national elites or joining one of them. At this time, MUI showed a greater tendency to align with the ICMI elite.

4.2.3 *Friends of Shariatisation*

As previously mentioned, MUI is not a single actor but has friends and allies supporting its programmes. Friends or allies here are not necessarily those organisations that have organisational closeness, but may also be those with ideas and aspirations similar to MUI. In this regard, the institutions categorised as friends of MUI are what William Caroll and Ratner[49] call those who share common viewpoints and also a sense of collective identity with the Council in promoting sharia. As the large tent (*tenda besar*) of Indonesian

47 Greg Barton, *Gus Dur: The Authorized Biography of Abdurrahman Wahid* (Jakarta: Equinox Publishing, 2002), p. 45.

48 However, a key factor in Wahid's opposition to the Habibie group was due to Habibie's client-patron relationship with the former President Suharto, under whom NU branches had been increasingly marginalised from accessing finances. See Marcus Mietzner, *Military Politics, Islam and the State in Indonesia: From Turbulent Transition to Democratic Consolidation* (Singapore: ISEAS, 2009), p. 84.

49 William K. Caroll and R.S. Ratner, "Master Framing and Cross-Movement Networking in Contemporary Social Movement," *Sociological Quarterly* 37, no. 4 (1996): 601–25, 604.

Muslim organisations,[50] MUI has never pretended to be a single institutional actor. As a socio-culturally and politically constructed forum for Indonesian Muslim organisations, unifying many of their representatives, MUI has networks and allies that align with its goals. The Council can be seen as a central, indispensable actor because of its bargaining power with the state, especially since the reform era,[51] and its diverse experience working on and dealing with issues of the national legislation process, its leadership and authorship of the sharia discourse.

The well-established networks and allies of MUI are a real force. One example was an event organised by a number of Islamic organisations and political parties on 5 August 2005. After the Friday prayer session at the al-Azhar mosque,[52] representatives of thirty-one Muslim organisations gathered on the occasion of a *tabligh akbar* (religious public outreach) regarding their appeal to defend eleven fatwas issued by MUI at the National Congress in 2005. The participant organisations at that forum included the Komite Islam untuk Solidaritas Dunia Islam (KISDI, Islamic Committee for International Solidarity), the DDII, Badan Kerja Sama Pondok Pesantren Indonesia (BKSPPI, Collaboration Body for Indonesian Islamic Boarding School), HTI, Syarikat Islam (Islamic Union), Al-Irsyad (a non-*sayyid*[53] Arab community organisation), the ICMI, FPI, Ikatan Dai Indonesia (IKADI, the Indonesian Association of Muslim Preachers), Tim Pembela Muslim (TPM, the Muslim Lawyer Team), al-Ittihad, and the MMI. Support was also to be found from political parties such as PPP, PBB, PKS, and Partai Bintang Reformasi (PBR, the Reform-Star Party). Mashadi (the chair of Forum Umat Islam) stated that "we wanted to express our concern regarding the disgraceful actions of some religious figures and their tendency to distort the facts, as if to imply that MUI's fatwas do not recognise the importance of religious tolerance and to suggest that the fatwas are ridiculous."[54]

MUI's allies can, therefore, be divided into two main groups: firstly, Muslim organisations, and secondly, Islamic political parties. One example of the first

50 Interview with anonymous respondent, Jakarta, 2011.

51 Interview with Ismail Yusanto, Jakarta, 2011.

52 The Al-Azhar mosque is an important symbol of Islamic urban activity in Jakarta and is identified with the Muslim struggle in Indonesia and as a centre of Islamic propagation, dominated by Indonesian Islamist groups. The construction of the mosque was completed in 1958.

53 *Sayyid* is a title for the descendants of Prophet Muḥammad from the male lines of Hasan and Husayn. R. Khanam, *Encyclopaedic Ethnography Of Middle-East And Central Asia* (*3 vols.*) (New Delhi: Global Vision Publishing House, 2005), p. 724.

54 Gatra, "Dukungan Fatwa MUI Forum Umat Islam Tabligh Akbar Usai Sholat Jumat," *Gatra* (Jakarta, August 2005).

group is ICMI (the Indonesian Association of Muslim Intellectuals), which was established in 1990 as a non-state agency for the Muslim middle class to obtain positions within the state administration.[55] Although MUI is older than ICMI, the presence of the latter has contributed to strengthening the position of the former. MUI, for instance, enjoyed privileges offered by ICMI in the latter period of Suharto's reign, as indicated by the establishment of the BMI, LPPOM and many other bodies in which MUI has positioned itself as part of Islamic groups that are keen to promote Islam as "the country's moral and ethical guide."[56]

HTI (Hizbut Tahrir Indonesia) can also be said to be a strategic ally of MUI. Besides having its representatives within the board-member structure of MUI, this transnational Islamic organisation shares many of the Council's ideas, for example regarding the place of Islam in the legal system. Ismail Yusanto (spokesperson of HTI and board member of MUI since 2005) admits that his transnational organisation does not always get involved in all aspects of MUI's agenda, but shares common goals in the form of sharia banks, halal certification and the ban of "heretical" Islamic groups such as Ahmadiyah and Shīʿa, as well as the prohibition of liberalism, secularism and pluralism.[57] In this regard, Yusanto affirms that HTI will contribute to the agenda of sharia formalisation with the help of MUI's position as a credible *dīniyya* (religious) and *siyāsiyya* (political) organisation.[58] Yusanto argues that HTI still believes MUI's agenda is of great benefit to the *umma*. As a *ṭarīqa* (method), Yusanto adds, HTI shares the vision and mission of MUI,[59] and the two are clearly allies. Another pertinent example of HTI's tendency to associate itself with MUI can be seen through the circular, *Pernyataan Hizbut Tahrir Indonesia, Dukungan Terhadap Fatwa-fatwa MUI* ("The Statement of HTI in Support of MUI's Fatwa") which was published by the organisation on 2 August 2005. This statement was issued in support of MUI's fatwa published in the 2005 National Congress, which had been criticised by "progressive liberal Muslim and secular groups" such as JIL,

55 Greg Fealy, "Indonesian Politics 1995–1996: The Making of Crisis," in *Indonesia Assessment: Population and Human Resources*, ed. Gavin W. John and Terence H. Hull (Singapore: Institute of Southeast Asian, 1997), 19–38, p. 25; Hefner, "Islam, State, and Civil Society: ICMI and the Struggle for the Indonesian Middle Class"; Hefner, *Civil Islam: Muslims and Democratization in Indonesia*, 2011.

56 Adam Schwarz, "Indonesia After Suharto," *Foreign Affairs* 76, no. 4 (1997): 119–134, p. 131.

57 Interview with Ismail Yusanto, Jakarta, 2011. Ismail Yusanto began to be active within MUI from the 2005–2010 period, and was vice deputy of the Research Commission. This is a strategic commission with a mission to discuss and study deviant groups. I conducted the interview with them on the occasion of MUI MUNAS in Pondok Gede, 2011.

58 Interview with Ismail Yusanto.

59 Ibid.

the International Centre for Islam and Pluralism (ICIP),[60] the International Conference on Religion and Peace (ICRP), the Lembaga Bantuan Hukum (LBH, pro bono Legal Aid Institute) and some others. The statement made five important points. Firstly, it proclaimed that MUI fatwas were correct because they had been decided by competent experts, based on valid arguments and reflecting the role of ulama as heirs of the Prophet. Secondly, the fatwas rejected an inclusive theology that admits all religions, considering them equal. Thus the MUI fatwas are legitimate, as in the field of faith Muslims should be "exclusive" (this term is often used by Indonesian activists and also scholars to denote the rejection of the righteousness of other religions). Thirdly, HTI endorsed the MUI fatwa banning pluralism because such "isms" can lead Muslims to commit other major sins such as interreligious marriage, attending events of interfaith religious prayers and many others. Fourthly, HTI supported the MUI fatwa declaring the Ahmadiyah to be a deviant sect. Fifthly, it appealed to all Indonesian Muslims to follow and obey the MUI fatwas.

Although HTI has frequently claimed that it is a peaceful Islamist organisation, it has shown sympathy towards the violence waged by some Muslim groups and organisations against the Ahmadiyah in particular. Another significant role played by HTI was to criticise the hegemony of the pro-market and free trade neo-liberal notions embraced by such Muslim groups as JIL and to suggest sharia as the alternate system. HTI has been actively engaged in campaigning for anti-secularism, liberalism, and pluralism in many events. Speaking on behalf of the MUI board members and as a HTI spokesperson, Yusanto proposed to MUI that it issue fatwas on such crucial issues within society as economic policies and regulations which did not support efforts to strengthen the economic potential of the *umma*.[61]

DDII (Dewan Dakwah Islamiyah Indonesia, the Council of Islamic Propagation of Indonesia) is a longstanding ally of MUI, established in 1967 in response to the quality of Islamic propagation in Indonesia.[62] According to them, Indonesian people needed a process of profound Islamisation.[63] Many people associate this *daʿwa* organisation with the Masyumi party.[64] Traditionally

60 The ICIP, established in 2003, is an Indonesian NGO that works on issues of pluralism, Indonesian Islam, and democracy.

61 Ibid.

62 "Dewan Da'wah Islamiyah Indonesia," 2022, https://dewandakwah.com, viewed on 21 July 2022.

63 R. Michael Feener and M.E. Cammack, *Islamic Law in Contemporary Indonesia: Ideas and Institutions* (Harvard: Harvard University Press, 2007), p. 103.

64 Hefner, *Civil Islam: Muslims and Democratization in Indonesia*, 2011, pp. 109–13; Robert W. Hefner, "Islam and Nation in the Post-Suharto Era," in *The Politics of Post-Suharto*

speaking, the DDII has had a rather close connection to MUI because of the similar concerns and orientations of these two organisations regarding the application of sharia law in Indonesia. Beside their similar missions, Anwar Haryono[65] had specific expectations that MUI should present Muslim aspirations to the government.[66] Haryono asserts that MUI and the Forum Ukhuwah Islamiyah (Forum of Islamic Brotherhood, currently a MUI organ) can be an effective medium to lead Islamic politics in Indonesia because of their strategic position as an umbrella for Islamic organisations.[67] As MUI's ally of longest standing, the DDII has contributed to creating sharia discourse within both MUI and broader society. In addition, until recently, some DDII senior officials remain accommodated in the MUI board membership and their presence, along with the "hardliner wing of MUI", forms the pro-sharia group within the organisation.

Ridwan, a leading DDII figure and the Chairman of MUI for the Arts and Culture division, for instance, argues that sharia must be first implemented from within MUI. He is insistent that MUI officials and staff have to perform the *salat jama'ah* (collective daily prayer) on time. He also promotes the usage of the *dinar* as the national currency of Indonesia though, historically speaking, this coin is not unique to the Islamic tradition[68] but was adopted by the Umayyad from the Sassanian tradition that used silver coins in Iran and Iraq whilst the Byzantine tradition used gold and copper in Syria and Egypt.[69]

MUI also receives ample support from the FUI (Forum Ukhuwah Islamiyyah, Islamic Brotherhood Forum), which was highly visible in its mobilisation of crowds of supporters for demonstrations and rallies to pressure Indonesian lawmakers to pass the Pornography Law, in accordance with MUI's own views on the issue. These mass demonstrations were held together with other Islamic organisations on 21 May 2006 as a show of force in favour of the anti-pornography

---

Indonesia, ed. Adam Schwarz and Jonathan Paris (New South Wales: Council on Foreign Relations, 1999), 40–72, p. 48; R. Michael Feener, *Muslim Legal Thought in Modern Indonesia* (Cambridge: Cambridge University Press, 2011), pp. 102–6; Luth, *M. Natsir, Dakwah Dan Pemikirannya*.

65 A. Harjono, *Indonesia Kita: Pemikiran Berwawasan Iman-Islam* (Jakarta: Gema Insani Press, 1995).

66 Bernhard Platzdasch, *Islamism in Indonesia: Politics in the Emerging Democracy* (Singapore: Institute of Southeast Asian Studies, 2009), p. 121; R. Michael Feener, *Muslim Legal Thought in Modern Indonesia* (Cambridge, MA: Cambridge University Press, 2007), p. 111.

67 Platzdasch, *Islamism in Indonesia*.

68 Interview with Cholil Ridwan, Jakarta, 2011.

69 Wijdan Ali, *The Arab Contribution to Islamic Art: From the Seventh to the Fifteenth Centuries* (Cairo: American Univ in Cairo Press, 1999), p. 47.

bill and to pressure lawmakers to pass the bill.[70] These efforts reaped success when Indonesian lawmakers passed the bill on 30 October 2008. The most striking achievement was when President Yudoyono issued Presidential Order No 25/2012 as a concrete follow-up to the Pornography Act in 2008.[71] This can be considered another victory for MUI in promoting sharia-based national law, as the organisation had long been demanding this step from President Yudoyono.[72]

The FPI is undeniably a close ally of MUI. This Islamic "vigilante" organisation views itself as a guardian responsible for guarding the implementation of MUI fatwas in society, for instance in relation to the ban on deviant Islamic groups such as the Ahmadiyah and on the prohibition of secularism, liberalism and pluralism. The FPI's strong emphasis on the implementation of sharia is evident from the statement of Habib Rizieq Shihab (the general chairman of FPI, known as HRS) that Muslims should uphold sharia and apply it as the law of Indonesia.[73] As evidence of FPI support for MUI fatwa, on 1 June 2008, for instance, this organisation attacked Aliansi Kebangsaan dan Kebebasan Beragama dan Berkeyakinan (AKKBB, the Alliance for Nationhood, Faith and Religious Freedom), which had held a massive rally to promote faith and religious freedom. The AKKBB was rallying at the Monumen National (MONAS, the National Monument, a historical site of Indonesia) in Jakarta on the anniversary of the proclamation of Pancasila, using it as momentum to appeal for public support in promoting and respecting the diversity of Indonesia's cultures and beliefs, including the Ahmadiyah and other groups judged deviant by MUI. AKKBB's demonstration was also a response to incidents and assaults conducted by radical Islamic groups against so-called deviant and liberal Islamic groups.

From the perspective of FPI and its *lasykar* (paramilitary forces), the AKKBB rally created social anxiety and intentionally provoked Muslim groups such as MUI. The FPI felt obliged to respond to the rally by attacking the crowd at the demonstration. Many people from the AKKBB group were injured and hospitalised due to the attack. The FPI elite defended the attack as part of their

70 Rachmadi Raden, "Ribuan Orang Demo Tuntut Berlakukan Undang-Undang Anti Pornografi," *Tempo*, 21 May 2006, https://metro.tempo.co/read/77781/ribuan-orang-demo-tuntut-berlakukan-undang-undang-anti-pornografi, viewed on 21 July 2022.

71 "SBY Bentuk Tim Khusus Anti-Pornografi," *Detik News*, 13 March 2012, https://news.detik.com/berita/d-1865370/sby-bentuk-tim-khusus-anti-pornografi, viewed on 21 July 2022.

72 Interview with Ma'ruf Amin, Jakarta, 2010.

73 M.B. Hooker, *Indonesian Syariah, Defining a National School of Islamic Law* (Singapore: ISEAS, 2008), p. 47; Fealy, *Voices of Islam in Southeast Asia: A Contemporary Sourcebook*.

efforts to guard the MUI fatwa banning the Ahmadiyah, secularism, liberalism and pluralism, and declared that any group that rejected this MUI fatwa was an opponent of Islam.[74] In response to the MONAS tragedy, instead of issuing a warning to the FPI, MUI blamed the government of Indonesia for not publishing a Surat Keputusan Bersama (SKB, Joint Decree) of three ministries—the Ministry of Religious Affairs, the Ministry of Home Affairs and the Attorney General—banning the Ahmadiyah. MUI secretary Anwar Abbas stated during a press conference, initiated by the Forum Ukhuwah Islamiyah, that the delay in publication of the SKB had created uncertainty which had been used by "certain groups" to defend the presence of Ahmadis in Indonesia. The "certain parties" here referred to groups under the AKKBB alliance, comprising the WI (Wahid Institute), JIL, ICIP, and all those who individually signed the alliance's petition.[75] Importantly, MUI did not condemn the FPI aggression against the AKKBB group, which gave rise to the public assumption that MUI supported the FPI. The Council reminded all groups that its fatwa on the ban of Ahmadis should not be enforced through violence, however,[76] although MUI and FPI have both argued that violence is legally permissible in response to provocation by anti-Islamic groups.[77] Ridwan added that the MONAS tragedy was only 'smoke', and to eliminate the problem the 'fire', which was its source, had to be extinguished. What he meant by the 'fire' were efforts to defame Islam by certain groups.[78] Islamic vigilante groups also believed in the conspiracy theory that the AKKBB demonstration was supported by Western and international Judeo-Christian organisations that had long sought the decline of Islam in Indonesia.

In Central Java, the strategic ally of MUI is the MMI (Majelis Mujahidin Indonesia, the Indonesian Mujahidin Council). The MMI can be categorised as a national organisation because its branches are spread across Indonesia,

74 Information on the involvement of the FPI in the attack on AKKBB can be seen in International Crisis Group's briefing on "Implikasi SKB (Surat Keputusan Bersama) tentang Ahmadiyah," Crisis Group Asia Briefing No. 78, 7 July 2008.

75 "Kubu Liberal Versus Islam, Pasca Monas", Era Muslim, 9 June 2008, http://www.eramuslim.com/berita/tahukah-anda/kubu-liberal-versus-islam-pasca-monas.htm, viewed on 21 July 2022. The Era Muslim website covers news on the activities of the Islamist groups of Indonesia.

76 MUI, *Fatwa Munas VII Majelis Ulama Indonesia* (Jakarta: Majelis Ulama Indonesia, 2005), p. 137.

77 This issue will be discussed in more detail in the section on "Policing Faith and Belief."

78 "KH. Cholil: Insiden Monas Cuma Asap Saja," *Hidayatullah*, 2008, https://hidayatullah.com/berita/nasional/read/2008/06/07/41314/kh-cholil-insiden-monas-cuma-asap-saja.html, viewed on 21 July 2022.

but its headquarters are located in Yogyakarta. As mentioned on the MMI official website, this organisation was established as the result of the First Mujahidin Congress in Yogyakarta on 5–7 August 2000, attended by 1800 participants from twenty-four provinces of Indonesia. The main objective of this group is to implement sharia as the solution for the multi-faceted crises faced by Muslim society and humanity.[79] The MMI views its presence as motivated by the phenomena of *pengingkaran sharia* (sharia denial) by the Indonesian people, which requires its presence to counter this problem. In this regard MMI has been very active in promoting sharia by demanding Indonesian lawmakers amend Article 29 of the 1945 Constitution on religious freedom with the Jakarta Charter or the Medina Charter.[80] During the General Session of the MPR on 15 August 2000, MMI lobbied lawmakers from PPP, Golkar and PBB to convey its aspirations outlined in the *Shahifah Yogyakarta* (Charter of Yogyakarta).[81] MMI is close to MUI because both organisations share the same view on the enactment of sharia law in Indonesia. To some extent, MMI's strategy for the establishment of sharia law might differ from MUI's, but at the substantive level both organisations share the same belief that it is necessary to incorporate sharia into national law.

The support of MMI for MUI fatwa was reflected in the statements of its spokesperson, Fauzan al-Anshari, during a public discussion on "*Menyikapi Perbedaan Fatwa MUI*" (Addressing the Difference of MUI Fatwas) organised

79 For further official MMI statements, visit http://majelismujahidin.com/about/mengenal-majelis-mujahidin/, viewed on 13 May 2012. The website is regularly updated and has become an effective platform for this organisation to campaign and communicate its ideas and thoughts not only with its members but also with its opponents.

80 Salim, *Challenging the Secular State: The Islamization of Law in Modern Indonesia*, 2008, p. 84; Hosen, *Shari'a & Constitutional Reform in Indonesia*.

81 The *Yogyakarta Shahifah* is the declaration of a charter resulting from the Kongres Mujahidin I and is called the *Yogyakarta Shahifah*. The points of the charter are as follows: (1) The unity and integrity of independent and sovereign Indonesia is our expectation. (2) The thesis that Indonesia will disintegrate if the sharia is upheld is unjustifiable. (3) As sharia is *fitrah* (Indonesian-Arabic expression for natural) for all human beings, its absence will lead to the disintegration of the state together with multifaceted crises in Indonesia. (4) The application of sharia for the *umma* and the application of norms of other religions—Christianity, Buddhism, and Hinduism—for their believers are the solution to this fragmentation of the state. (5) Part of human rights is to implement sharia for Muslims, which is also assured by the Article 29 of the 1945 Constitution. (6) Sharia contains universal values which are also recognised by other religions, therefore, when implemented, it will be provide protection not only for Muslims but for all citizens of Indonesia regardless of their religion. (7) Muslims who reject sharia can be categorised as *munāfiq* (hypocrites) and against human rights. This charter can be viewed on MMI's official website.

by Radio 68H[82] on 5 August 2005 at the Oriental Bar of the Mandarin Hotel, Jakarta. Al-Anshari expressed his organisation's willingness to advocate MUI fatwas. Present in the talk-show discussion were Amin, Dawam Rahardjo, Syafi'i Anwar (Executive Director of ICIP), and Musdah Mulia.[83] In response to questions regarding rumours that MMI was prepared to take a frontline position in securing MUI fatwas, either through debate or *jihad* (religious war), al-Anshari stated that MMI was the first institution ready to defend the implementation of eleven fatwas issued by MUI at the 2005 National Congress. He blamed the lack of sharia courts in Indonesia for the inability to protect the purity of the Islamic creed, even though the General Attorney of Indonesia, through its institutional organ, Badan Koordinasi Pengawas Aliran Kepercayaan (BAKORPAKEM, Body of Coordination and Supervision of Mystical Beliefs) has included the Ahmadiyah on the long list of *aliran sesat* (deviant sects).[84] MMI's main concern here is not to question the legality of MUI fatwa, which is based on sharia, but rather that the state itself possess a legal mechanism to outlaw deviant sects through a judiciary process. According to al-Anshari, MMI is more than ready to challenge any liberal groups in public debate. In addition the group is also ready to wage a *jihad* if this is only way to respond to liberal Islamic groups.

In Solo, central Java, MUI shariatisation gained public attention through the auspices of Majelis Tafsir Al-Qur'ān (MTA, Qur'ān Exegesis Council) that disseminated the ideas of MUI through both its radio-broadcasting of *ta'līm* (religious learning) and other activities. The MTA was established by Abdullah Thufail Saputra on 19 September 1972 in Solo with the goal of bringing Muslims back to the Qur'ān as the primary source of Islamic teachings.[85] As a trader who has had the opportunity to travel across Indonesia, he observed that many Indonesian Muslims did not understand the content of the Qur'ān. He referred to Prophet Muḥammad's saying that the Muslim community will not become an excellent *umma* if they do not start from the earliest thing that improved the community, namely the Qur'ān. After the era of Abdullah Thufail's leadership, the MTA now is led by Muhammad Sukino, a Javanese animist convert. Under his leadership, the organisation has

82 Radio 68 H is a private radio station. Its broadcasts are relayed to more than sixty radio stations throughout Indonesia.

83 A transcript of this debate is available at http://www.mail-archive.com/is-lam@milis.isnet.org/msg00852.html, viewed on 12 May 2012.

84 A broader account of *aliran sesat* can be seen in Chapter 6.

85 Muhammad Asif and Muhammad Muafi Himam, "Propagating Puritan Islam in Surakarta: Reading the Biography of Abdullah Thufail Saputra," *Indonesian Journal of Islamic Literature and Muslim Society* 4, no. 2 (2019): 109–34.

expanded, establishing branches in other regions outside Solo and even regions outside Java. On its website, the MTA uploads MUI fatwas to justify their arguments.[86] Furthermore, the MTA has good relations with MUI elite members such as Ridwan. As a form of support for the MTA, Ridwan attended the opening of a new MTA office building and told the audience that their leader, Ahmad Sukino, was qualified to be nominated as president of Indonesia. The general chairman of MUI's regional branch of Solo is an active adherent of MTA. Establishing a good connection with MUI is very important for the MTA, because this organisation—with its literal and puritan method of understanding and disseminating Islam—is being targeted by mainstream groups of Islam as a deviant sect.[87]

Islamic political parties supporting MUI's ideas of shariatisation include the PPP, PBB, and PK (now PKS) in their attempts to amend Article 29 of the Indonesian Constitution with the Jakarta charter or *Piagam Madinah* (Medina Charter). The PPP and PBB are two Islamic parties that have not only supported but also initiated moves to amend Article 29.[88] Some Islamist organisations also ideologically linked to MUI, such as the HTI, FPI, DDII and others, banded together to pressure and support the PPP and PBB to work towards the inclusion of the Jakarta Charter in Article 29.[89] Because of the ideological militancy of PPP and PBB, Abdul Munir Mulkhan, a Muhammadiyah scholar, has categorised these two parties as ideologist-traditionalist.[90] The PPP clearly promotes the implementation of sharia. Enthusiasm for adopting sharia was evident when in 1998 the PPP reemployed the *kaʿba* and Islam as the symbol and ideology of the party. However, the most tangible support for sharia offered by the party is not only apparent from its position in attempting to amend Article 29 of the 1945 Constitution with the Jakarta Charter, but

86 Information from Sunarwoto, who is doing research on the MTA, from a personal conversation in Istanbul on 27 April 2012. See also his article: Sunarwoto, "Dakwah Radio in Surakarta: An Contest for Islamic Identity," in *Islam in Indonesia: Contrasting Images and Interpretations*, ed. Jajat Burhanudin and Kees van Dijk (Amsterdam: Amsterdam University Press, 2013), 195–214.

87 Syaifudin Zuhri, "Majelis Tafsir Al-Qur'an Amd Its Stuggle for Islamic Reformism," in *Islam in Indonesia: Contrasting Images and Interpretations*, ed. Jajat Burhanudin and Kees van Dijk (Amsterdam: Amsterdam University Press, 2013), 227–41; Sunarwoto, "Dakwah Radio in Surakarta."

88 Platzdasch, *Islamism in Indonesia*, p. 189; Hefner, "Indonesia: Shariʿa Politics and Democratic Transition," p. 294.

89 Akbar Tanjung, *The Golkar Way: Survival Partai Golkar Di Tengah Turbulensi Politik Era Transisi* (Jakarta: Gramedia Pustaka Utama, 2007), p. 203.

90 Abdul Munir Mulkhan, *Politik Santri: Cara Menang Merebut Hati Rakyat* (Yogyakarta: Kanisius, 2009), pp. 219–20.

also from other examples, for instance the party's backing of MUI's ban of the Ahmadiyah and other deviant groups. Suryadharma Ali, PPP General Chair and Minister of Religious Affairs (2009–2014), has stated that the PPP stands unreservedly behind MUI with regards to the ban on the Ahmadiyah.[91] The PPP is also ideologically aligned with MUI and inclined towards sharia.[92] The PBB, claiming to be a new Masyumi party,[93] has agreed that the Indonesian state should be responsible for promoting Islam through the distillation of sharia as the legal system of the country.[94] The party believes in the idea that Muslims should live under the rule of sharia. The PBB was one of the parties supporting MUI fatwa at the *tabligh akbar* (public preaching) organised by the Forum Umat Islam in al-Azhar Mosque[95] on 5 August 2005.

The PKS stands beside other Islamic parties promoting sharia in Indonesia. Hidayat Nurwahid, the former president of PKS's predecessor, the PK (Justice Party),[96] stated that this party[97] agreed to the Medina Charter as an alternative to replace Article 29 of 1945 Constitution. He prefers to refer to the Medina Charter rather than the Jakarta Charter, a reference to the first Islamic charter from the first century AH that guaranteed equality in religious and cultural entitlement, no compulsion to follow a religion (Arabic: *lā ikrāha fī al-dīn*), respect for diversity and plurality of beliefs, and most importantly a promise that all believers could freely practice their faiths and religions.[98] The Medina Charter is viewed as an answer to the challenges emerging from the

91 "Pemerintah Isyaratkan Larang Ahmadiyah," 2011, https://kemenag.go.id/read/pemerintah-isyaratkan-larang-ahmadiyah-z3nk.

92 Ibn Hamad, *Konstruksi Realitas Politik Dalam Media Massa, Sebuah Studi Critical Discourse Analysis Terhadap Berita-Berita Politik* (Jakarta: Granit, 2004), p. 97; Platzdasch, *Islamism in Indonesia.*

93 Masyumi was originally established in 1943 as an umbrella of various Islamic organisations consisting of traditionalist and modernist groups. The Masyumi party was abolished by Sukarno in the 1960s. The most prominent Masyumi figure was Muhammad Natsir (d. 1993) who led this party from 1949 to 1958. Natsir strongly opposed Pancasila as the official ideology of Indonesia, and wished to replace it with sharia. Luth, *M. Natsir, Dakwah Dan Pemikirannya.*

94 Platzdasch, *Islamism in Indonesia*, p. 188.

95 The initiative to build the al-Azhar mosque came from fourteen leading Masyumi figures under the supervision of Syamsuddin, the Ministry of Social Affairs. The mosque was completed in 1958.

96 The Justice Party (*Partai Keadlian* or PK) is the forerunner to the PKS.

97 PK failed to meet the electoral threshold in 1999 that it needed to contest the 2004 general elections.

98 See interview with Nurwahid at "PKS Solusi Permasalahan Bangsa," *Tokoh*, 13 September 2003, https://tokoh.id/publikasi/wawancara/pks-solusi-permasalahan-bangsa/, viewed on 21 July 2022.

diversity and plurality of Indonesia's religions, ethnicities and cultures. The PKS, through the participation of Mashadi, a key PKS activist, strove for real support to secure the implementation of eleven MUI fatwas during al-Azhar's 2005 *tabligh akbar*. Tifatul Sembiring, former PKS President and Minister of Information and Communication (2009–2014), states that the PKS urges all Islamic organisations to follow the MUI fatwa banning the Ahmadiyah.[99]

It can thus be seen that the shariatisation of Indonesia promoted by MUI is supported by numerous allies. MUI has the most prominent role in this movement due its greater experience and its richer ideas and material resources with regard to shariatisation.

4.2.4 *A Weak State*

State weakness is the fourth analytical category of the political structure opportunity theory, and sheds light on how the struggle for shariatisation benefits from the weakness of the state. At least three examples of the weak Indonesian state that potentially create chances for MUI to promote sharia in the public and legal spheres can be identified: the first is the weakness of the state's apparatus in enforcing the law; the second is the minimal efforts of the state in providing prosperity to the people; and the third is the inability of the state to implement the principles of good governance. With no improvements in these areas, openings are provided for MUI to introduce sharia into national legislation. The weakness of the state in enforcing the law can be seen by the noncommittal attitude of the state apparatus and Indonesian lawmakers towards consistency in activities such as drafting bills, legislating state law, and implementing it under the agreed hierarchy of the national legal system. One example is the initiative of Indonesia's lawmakers to invite MUI to participate in drafting state law through public hearings. The hearing mechanism is indeed an important tool for a democratic system like Indonesia that requires a legal means to listen to the aspirations of its citizens, but it becomes constitutionally complicated when the aspirations of MUI are accommodated over the religious and cultural pluralism of Indonesia into the content of state law, including some bills not related to Islam. This is a fine political opportunity for MUI, but not for others. Amidhan Shaberah,[100] MUI chairman in the field of halal certification until 2015, indicates that since the reform era, Indonesian lawmakers have been culturally obliged to involve MUI in the process of

99 "PKS: Fatwa MUI Tentang Ahmadiyah Permanen," *Hukum Online*, 25 July 2005, https://www.hukumonline.com/berita/a/pks-fatwa-mui-tentang-ahmadiyah-permanen-hol13250?page=2.

100 For more information on Amidhan, see: https://tirto.id/m/kh-amidhan-shaberah-km.

national legislation through public hearing mechanisms.[101] The new tradition of inviting MUI to all bill hearings appeals to the MUI logic that all national laws will inevitably intersect with sharia as the vast majority of stakeholders in Indonesian law are Muslims.

Another lack of consistency is apparent in the enforcement of law and order; misunderstandings and inconsistencies in the implementation of the law become fertile soil for those seeking the institutionalisation of sharia into Indonesia's legal system. Since the reform era, this has become a contested issue. Many forms of legal activism promoted by MUI and other Islamist organisations that take place in the provinces and districts of Indonesia occur because of this lack of legal consistency.

Under the 1945 Constitution, all citizens of Indonesia are guaranteed equal rights to believe in and practice their religions, yet political pressure from majority groups often undermines this equality before the law. Examples of this are the attacks perpetrated by Islamic vigilante groups against the Ahmadiyah in the island of Lombok (in the Nusa Tenggara Barat province), Bogor and Kuningan (both districts in West Java), and many other places where the police have done nothing to prevent death and destruction in Ahmadiyah camps. The police are tasked with maintaining national stability by providing full protection to adherents of all religions. However, they are often trapped in the same way of thinking as MUI, permitting radical Islamic groups to destroy the Ahmadiyah and accusing it of provoking the attacks as a deviant sect which threatens Indonesia's unity in diversity. On many occasions the police have failed to protect Ahmadis from attacks by Islamist groups. On 15 July 2005, the police were unable to secure the annual Ahmadiyah meeting in Bogor from brutal, bloody aggression by the Gerakan Umat Islam (GUI, Islamic Community Movement).[102] They also completely failed to anticipate the violent attacks incited by the FPI and its networks against the peaceful rally organised by the AKKBB on 1 June 2008.[103] The most recent and murderous attack suffered by the Ahmadis, which took place unhindered by the police, was in Cikeusik, Banten province, on 2 February 2011.[104]

---

101 Interview with Amidhan, Jakarta, 2010.

102 John Olle, "The Majelis Ulama Indonesia Vesus 'Heresy': The Resurgence of Authoritarian Islam," in *State of Authority: The State in Society in Indonesia*, ed. Geert Arend van Klinken and Barker Joshua (Ithaca: Cornell South East Asia Publication, 2009), 95–116, p. 101; Julie Chernov-Hwang, *Peaceful Islamist Mobilization in the Muslim World: What Went Right* (New York: Palgrave Macmillan, 2009), p. 98.

103 Chernov-Hwang, *Peaceful Islamist Mobilization in the Muslim World: What Went Right*, p. 101.

104 Human Rights Watch, "World Report 2012: Events of 2011" (Seven Stories Press, 2012).

In this regard, the state ceded moral ground to MUI, with the result that it has maximised its efforts to promote shariatisation. MUI's success in demanding the Minister of Religious Affairs, Ministry of Home Affairs and General Attorney publish a Joint Decree limiting Ahmadiyah preaching activities in the public domain is evident. At this crucial moment in the general public discourse, MUI pressured the government to issue the joint decree by declaring that it supported all groups which were in favour. MUI knew that the ruling regime was confused as to whether to publish the decree or not, and so it confidently assured the government that this would serve as a solution to end horizontal conflict in society. Finally, the joint decree was officially published by the government in 2008.

The second weakness of the state is its slow economic recovery from the financial crisis of 1998. The post-reform era administrations of Habibie, Wahid, Megawati, Yudoyono and even Jokowi have not yet shown significant progress in this field. Although since the Yudhoyono administration Indonesia has moved toward more stable economic development, as indicated by praise from global economic institutions such as the International Monetary Fund (IMF) and World Bank, it has not had a real effect on the everyday lives of Indonesians. The Indonesian state remains unable to deliver services to increase the prosperity of its citizens, while the state itself proclaims in the 1945 constitution that it is a welfare state, which theoretically has to prioritise services for its people. If the state remains like this, it will suffer a loss of credibility and also motivate people to consider alternative state systems.

For MUI, this situation is a political and legal opportunity to pursue the establishment of a sharia-based economic system as an alternative. MUI is consciously using this opportunity to delegitimise the state's position in the eyes of the people, based on its failure to accomplish its chief responsibility to provide a better quality of life. MUI believes shariatisation can offer a solution to overcome the problems faced by the country, and is demanding the institutionalisation of the sharia economy within the framework of the Indonesian legal system. According to the Constitution, Indonesia follows *sistem ekonomi pancasila* (the Pancasila economic system), but MUI believes that in practice the country has adopted a more liberal or capitalist system. Through its fatwas, recommendations and public appeals, MUI and its allies often accuse the government of excessive practices of liberalism and capitalism and praise sharia as a far better alternative solution.

MUI economists have tried to offer a new interpretation of the *ekonomi Pancasila* concept from a sharia viewpoint, for instance as formulated by Adiwarman A. Karim, a MUI activist and proponent of sharia banking. Karim argues that the Pancasila economic system has actually accommodated the *maqāṣid al-sharīʿa* (objectives of Islamic law) which can be seen in the five principles of Pancasila: protecting belief (*ḥifẓ al-dīn*) being the same as *ketuhanan yang maha esa* (belief in one God); a life (*ḥayā*) is the same as *perikemanusiaan yang adil dan beradab* (the notion of a just and civilised humanity); the integrity of family (*nasl*) is similar to *persatuan Indonesia* (the unity of Indonesia); protecting reason (*al-ʿaql*) is equivalent to *kerakyatan yang dipimpin oleh hikmat kebijaksanaan dalam permusyawaratan perwakilan* (protecting democracy guided by wise and consultative leadership); and the security of property (*māl*) is similar to *keadilan bagi seluruh rakyat Indonesia* (implementing social justice).

As a result, the legal recognition of sharia economy—especially sharia banks—can be seen in Act No. 21/2008[105] and Act No. 23/1999.[106] Within this law, the establishment of the sharia bank targets not only Muslim customers, but also non-Muslim customers. This means that this law is intended to become public law, and not part of personal law. Since its establishment, MUI has felt confident that the implementation of a sharia economy would contribute to the prosperity of Indonesian people, viewing it as the only economic system that is able to deliver real prosperity for the *umma* because it relies on justice and fairness.[107] However, as indicated by Timur Kuran, in many Islamic countries where the growth of sharia banks has mushroomed, religious rationales have been given greater priority than "economic justification."[108] Kuran's opinion is valid for the Islamic banking industry in Indonesia too because MUI aims to apply the principles of sharia in the economy first, and then worry about creating profit as a consequence. This business attitude has been popularised by the expression *bisnis di jalan Allah* (making business in the path of Allah). In Kuran's perspective this is the crucial point of the Islamic banking system.[109] For the proponents of sharia banking, "the overriding objectives of the sharia banking are reassertion of Muslim identity, the reaffirmation of Islam's relevance to the modern world, and the restoration of Islamic authority."[110] Kuran indicates that the emergence of sharia banks in the era of globalisation is an

105 MUI, *Himpunan Fatwa MUI Sejak 1975*, p. 922.

106 Ediana Dian Rae, "Arah Perkembangan Hukum Perbankan Syariah," *Buletin Hukum Perbankan Dan Kebanksentralan* 6, no. 1 (2008): 7–13, p. 10.

107 Interview with Ma'ruf Amin, Jakarta, 2010.

108 Timur Kuran, "Islamism and Economics, Policy Prescriptions for a Free Society," in *Islam and the Everyday World Public Policy Dilemmas*, ed. Sahrab Behdad and Nomani Farhad (London & New York: Routledge, 2006), 38–65, p. 40.

109 Ibid.

110 Interview with Ma'ruf Amin, Jakarta, 2010.

Islamist agenda.[111] However, whatever the reason advanced by the propagators of the sharia banking system and sharia finance industry, the position of the state—especially in the legal context of Indonesia—must remain neutral. To ensure sharia banking is legal in Indonesia, the state has the right to issue a legal umbrella for the operation, but in doing so the banking law should be legislated not in the domain of public law but more appropriately in the domain of personal law, taking into consideration of the whole philosophy and hierarchy of the Indonesian legal system.

The third weakness of the state is in managing the public affairs of citizens on the foundation of good governance. The principles of good governance are still only weakly enforced and so the people of Indonesia, including Muslims, willingly seek to embrace an alternative system. The state's failure to overcome high-level corruption and improve poor bureaucratic performance has led MUI and others to seek their own solution. MUI argues that the secular system of state administration has not successfully empowered the *umma*. The organisation often cites unresolved issues of corruption, the lack of transparency and morality in governance, the increased poverty of the Indonesian people, the free market national economy, and many other issues. Those who have perpetrated corruption both in the New Order era as well as the post-reform era must be punished in accordance with the law, but this has yet to come to pass.[112] MUI sees this as a weakness of the post-reform era administration, as the downfall of Suharto did not result in a new tradition of governing the state of Indonesia. Richard Robison and Vedi R. Hadiz state that some elements of the Suharto government did not disappear with the advent of reform, but on the contrary, they were able to adjust themselves to survive within the new system of the democratic reform era.[113] MUI's position in this case is to play an "intermediary role:" to criticise the inability of the new reformist regime to eliminate the vestiges of Suharto's power on one hand, and to take advantage of the inability of the state to deal with this issue on the other. This latter presents itself as a political structure opportunity for MUI.

MUI and its networks have paid particular attention to the state's weakness in maintaining and implementing good governance. This means that besides playing its basic role as the *khādim al-umma* (the guardian of the Muslim community), MUI has obtained extensive knowledge on the workings of the state,

111 Kuran, "Islamism and Economics", p. 38.

112 Dick Howard, "Good Governance and the Indonesian Economy," in *Gus Dur and the Indonesian Economy*, ed. Anthony L Smith (Singapore: ISEAS, 2001), 83–92, p. 85.

113 Vedi Hadiz and Richard Robison, *Reorganising Power in Indonesia: The Politics of Oligarchy in an Age of Markets* (London: Routledge, 2012), p. 223.

which can eventually open up the space both to criticise the state's weaknesses and encourage sharia. In 2000, the fourth National Congress issued a fatwa on "*rishwa* (*suap*), *ghulūl* (*korupsi*) and gifts to officials" proclaiming that corruption and gift-giving to state officials with ulterior motives, for instance for the purpose of obtaining "kickbacks", are unlawful under sharia. There are many other fatwas on the importance of embracing religious or sharia morality in managing public affairs. MUI not only issues fatwas, but also offers an Islamic prescription for overcoming the state's lack of courage in combatting social issues. Most MUI leading activists and adherents believe in the coherency of sharia law, and when something has been set in a fatwa this opens a doorway for it to become a law. Indonesian lawmakers often 'window shop' various sources and groups when drafting laws. One of the sources and groups they often consult is MUI. Despite its obvious support for radical Islamic groups since the collapse of the New Order,[114] Indonesian lawmakers continue to consider MUI as an important institution with regard to fatwa and religious advice. What differentiates MUI's role between the Suharto and post-reform eras is that the organisation is no longer dependent on the state. In fact, MUI's role is often critical and it can take a strong stance against state policy, such as its opposition to the draft law on Halal Product Assurance.

From the examples mentioned above, it is clear that shariatisation does not only rely on the presence of internal factors, but also external ones. The weak performance of the state is one of these factors, providing a fertile political ground for sharia proponents seeking to justify the importance of a new order of Indonesia. However, this political structure opportunity alone is not sufficient to explain the full context of MUI shariatisation. Further theoretical analysis is needed, and will be elaborated in the next section.

4.3 Framing Shariatisation

This section seeks to illuminate how MUI has transformed the idea of shariatisation from the level of discourse to that of practice (a movement). First, the space between MUI's idea and the collective action to foster shariatisation needs a conceptual bridge. This bridge is called the "frame", and the activity of making the frame is called "framing." This theoretical framework, taken from the discourse of social movement theories, seeks to shed light on how MUI has framed the fashioning of sharia in the legal and public spheres of Indonesia.

114 Robert Pringle, *Understanding Islam in Indonesia: Politics and Diversity* (Singapore: Editions Didier Millet, 2010), p. 139.

The notion of frame used here is actually motivated by the limits of the analytical framework of political structure opportunity in taking into account the complicated phenomenon of shariatisation that not only involves the structure of politics, but also the structure of ideas and cultures. Cathy Schneider, in her study on political opportunities and framing in the case of Puerto Rican identity in New York, has demonstrated the relationship of framing and political structure opportunity. Schneider states that the concept of framing is useful in order to link the macro-level concept of political opportunity structure and the micro-level of mobilisation.[115] This is why a complementary theoretical approach is required to analyse the actions of MUI not merely influenced by the political structure, but also by the social and cultural contexts.

Framing analysis was first introduced in 1954 by Gregory Bateson.[116] Todd Gitlin then adopted this framework into the list of theoretical approaches of social movements in the 1980s through his study on negative frame conducted by the *New York Times* to describe the Students for a Democratic Society (SDS) movement.[117] Since then, many sociologists such as William Gamson, Bruce Fireman, Steven Rytina,[118] and David Snow have tried to develop the usage of this concept as one of the central approaches in the study of social movement organisations. Sidney Tarrow, for instance, states that this analysis became famous because David Snow and his collaborators introduced this framing into the discourse of social movements in the 1980s.[119] Snow is the first person who underscored the importance of constructing "a special frame of frames" which can be used by the activists of such an organisation to draw on the support of followers, reflect their goals and attract media to cover their activities.[120]

Inspired by the work of Erving Goffman that denotes frames as "schemata of interpretation" that enable individuals "to locate, perceive, identity, and label" occurrences within their life space and the world at large, Snow and Benford came to produce a definition of framing. Both state that the collective action

115 Cathy Schneider, "Political Opportunities and Framing Puerto Rican Identity in New York City," in *Frames of Protest: Social Movements and the Framing Perspective*, ed. Hank Johnston and John A. Noakes (Maryland: Rowman & Littlefield, 2005), 141–62, p. 164.

116 John A. Noakes and Hank Johnston, "Frames Of Protest: A Road Map To A Perspective," in *Frames Of Protest: Social Movements And The Framing Perspective*, ed. Hank Johnston and John A Noakes (Maryland: Rowman & Littlefield, 2005), 1–33, p. 3.

117 Ibid.

118 These three sociologists developed frame in their collaborative work, *Encounters with Unjust Authority* (1982), where they demonstrate how interpretive processes influence the rise of collective action. See Noakes and Johnston, "Frames of Protest," p. 3.

119 Sidney Tarrow, *The New Transnational Activism* (Cambridge: Cambridge University Press, 2005), p. 61.

120 Ibid.

frame is constructed with the intention to "mobilize potential adherents and constituents, to garner bystander support, and to demobilize antagonists."[121] The collective action frames are strategically established to generate a particular result such as to attract new members, to mobilise committed followers, to acquire resources, and so forth.[122] Snow and others conceptualise framing as "the process through which movement actors engage in interpretive work to produce and maintain meaning for movement participants and potential supporters, as well as antagonists."[123] However, it is important to mention here that the frames of movement are actually very dynamic, changeable, contestable and reproducible during a process of the movement. As a consequence of this, the frames are very much influenced by the socio-cultural aspects where they are constructed.[124] In short, Snow points out "interpretative schema that simplifies and condenses 'the world out there' by selectively punctuating and encoding objects, situations, events, experiences, and sequences of action."[125] The framing or frame is the best aspect of the cultural approach, as Tom Salman and Assies state, that pertinently functions as "socio-cultural perceptions and the construction of shared understanding that justify, dignify and motivate collective action."[126] Both remind us that the framing processes as an intermediary tool is important in order to "bring the element of meaning and definition"[127] to the case of MUI, especially because the organisation is a body of clerics which primarily works on providing religious meaning in the cultural domain.

With regard to the role of MUI, some conceptual resemblances to framing have definitely been built on materials taken from sharia. Sharia, which from the perspective of social movement organisations theory can be called

---

121 Doug McAdam, "The Framing Function of Movement Tactics: Strategic Dramaturgy in the American Civil Rights Movement," in *Comparative Perspectives on Social Movements: Political Opportunities, Mobilising Structures and Cultural Framings*, ed. Doug McAdam, John D. McCarthy, and Mayer Zald (Cambridge: Cambridge University Press, 1996), 338–56.

122 Ibid.

123 Lyndi Hewitt and Holly J McCammon, "Explaining Suffrage Mobilization: Balance, Neutralization and Range in Collective Action Frames," in *Frames of Protest: Social Movements And The Framing Perspective*, ed. Hank Johnston and John A Noakes (Maryland: Rowman & Littlefield, 2005), 33–53, p. 37.

124 Robert D Benford and David A Snow, "Framing Processes and Social Movements: An Overview and Assessment," *Annual Review of Sociology* 26 (2000): 611–39, p. 628.

125 Noakes and Johnston, "Frames of Protest," p. 3.

126 Tom Salman and Willem Assies, "Anthropology and the Study of Social Movements," in *Handbook of Social Movements Across Disciplines*, ed. Bert Klandermans and Conny Roggeband (New York: Springer, 2009), 205–66, p. 228.

127 Ibid, p. 227.

"cultural stock", here means the material source Islamic activists employ to seek out "meanings, beliefs, ideologies, practices, values, myths, narratives and the like."[128] This understanding is strengthened by Wictorowicz, who adds that the processes of framing, in the context of Islamic activism, are usually formed in analytical accounts that mirror fundamental cultural issues such justice and injustice.[129] Here, the sharia frame is appropriate given that justice and injustice are two prevailing issues in sharia. In short, the sharia frame is actually used to assemble connectedness between faith and belief (the content of sharia) by MUI, as the frame maker, and its supporters, as frame receivers. From the results of my interviews and written sources, there are several obvious frames that MUI employs to clothe the agenda of shariatisation.

4.3.1 *Al-Amr bi al-Maʿrūf wa al-Nahy ʿan al-Munkar*

One of MUI's main responsibilities is to command right and forbid wrong, in Arabic *al-amr bi al-maʿrūf wa al-nahy ʿan al-munkar*, or in Indonesian commonly shortened to *amar makruf nahi munkar*. MUI believes that this command not only applies to Muslims, but also to non-Muslims as demanded by the Qurʾān. In Islam, *amar makruf nahi munkar* is not only an individual duty (*farḍ al-ʿayn*), but also a collective one (*farḍ al-kifāya*) and as a consequence, this command not only binds every individual but the entire Muslim community. It demands that all Muslim works and deeds should be framed with the intent of following this doctrine. Theologically speaking, commanding right and forbidding wrong explicitly refers to the Qurʾān and the tradition of the Prophet Muḥammad.[130] Many Indonesian Muslim activists such as the FPI, MMI, HTI, NU, and Muhammadiyah agree that commanding right and forbidding wrong is the highest religious model of moral behaviour in Islam (*ḥisba*).[131] In the context of shariatisation, the tenet of *amar makruf nahi munkar* connects the discourse of sharia and its implementation. This slogan

128 Benford and Snow, "Framing Processes and Social Movements," p. 629.

129 Quintan Wictorowicz, ed., *Islamic Activism: A Social Movement Theory Approach* (Indiana: Indiana University Press, 2004), p. 15.

130 Michael Cook, *Commanding Right and Forbidding Wrong in Islamic Thought* (Cambridge: Cambridge University Press, 2004); Ahmed Abdelsalam, "The Practice of Violence in the Ḥisba Theories," *Iranian Studies* 38, no. 4 (2005): 547–554.

131 All these organisations prioritise their policy of acting as *muḥtasib* (moral inspector). The FPI, for instance, adopts this principle within the mission of its organisation. Ibn Taymiyya's book, *al-Amr bi al-Maʿrūf wa al-Nahy an al-Munkar*, has been translated to Indonesian by Akhmad Hasan with title *Amar Maʾruf Nahi Munkar* (*Perintah Kepada Kebaikan, Larangan dari Kemungkaran*). This book was published under the sponsorship of *Wizāra al-Shuʾūn al-Islāmiyyah* (Department of Islamic Affairs) of Saudi Arabia.

is therefore useful as a frame because it outlines a religious duty for Muslims to engage in and implement sharia norms in their daily life.

Historically speaking, the concept of commanding right and forbidding wrong has evolved over time since the inception of MUI. This notion was first adopted and mentioned in its founding charter by the Council in 1975.[132] However, during the Suharto regime the application of commanding right and forbidding wrong was too state-oriented. MUI used it to justify the project of the ruling regime by including dedication and devotion to the state agenda as part of this Islamic tenet. MUI associated this justification with its interpretation of the concept of *ūlū al-amr* as the political entity that all Muslims should be devoted to. This is in line with the mainstream opinion of Sunnī sources saying that Muslims should not rebel against their political leaders.[133] Within this framework, each Muslim who actively engages in the development programme of the state can be judged as applying the tenet of commanding right and forbidding wrong.[134] As a consequence of this interpretation, the tenet of *al-amr bi al-maʿrūf wa al-nahy ʿan al-munkar* tends to be used a frame to legitimise the role of the ruling regime. In short, from 1975 to 1998 MUI framed the notion of commanding right and forbidding wrong as active participation and engagement in the process of *pembangunan nasional* (the national development of Indonesia).

Since the fall of Suharto, this tenet has been utilised by MUI in a different manner. It has been mostly used to support making Indonesia more shariatised even though this attempt can be regarded as being against the principles of a non-theocratic state. In 2000 MUI began to underscore its responsibility as the special envoy for *amar makruf nahi munkar* by explaining what is right (*kebenaran*) and what is wrong (*kebatilan*) with consistency (*istikomah*) and wisdom (*hikmah*).[135] In 2005, it was pointed out that MUI was a space for those who wanted to dedicate themselves as defenders of *daʿwa* (the call to Islam). In this last context, *amar makruf* indicates the active engagement of a Muslim

---

132 MUI, *15 Tahun Majelis Ulama Indonesia*, p. 53.

133 Barbara Z.E. Zollner, *The Muslim Brotherhood: Hasan al-Hudaybi and Ideology* (London & New York: Routledge, 2009), p. 122; Asma Asfaruddin, "Obedience to Political Authority: An Evolutionary Concept," in *Islamic Democratic Discourse: Theory, Debates, and Philosophical Perspectives*, ed. Muqtedar Khan (Oxford: Lexington Books, 2006), 37–62, p. 50. In the tradition of Shīʿa, *ūlū al-amr* is understood to mean Shiʿī *imāms* (spiritual leaders). See Hussein Abdul-Raof, *Theological Approaches to Qurʾanic Exegesis: A Practical Comparative-Contrastive Analysis* (London & New York: Routledge, 2012), p. 44.

134 MUI, *15 Tahun Majelis Ulama Indonesia*, p. 54.

135 MUI, *Buku Materi Kongres Umat Islam Indonesia V, "Kepemimpinan Umat Untuk Kesejahteraan Bangsa* (Jakarta: Panitia Pengarah Kongres Umat Islam Indonesia V, 2010), p. 11.

in changing and refining the situation of the community and state to bring them into accordance with sharia. This is what MUI refers to as *khayr al-umma* (the chosen community).[136]

MUI explicitly mentions three verses of the Qur'ān that emphasise the importance of enforcing *amar makruf nahi munkar* in its organisation's vision, *Wawasan Majelis Ulama Indonesia* (Vision of MUI). In this document, MUI refers to a verse in the chapter of Āl ʿImrān (3:104) that invites Muslims to enjoin what is right and forbid what is wrong. Those who do this will be included among the *mufliḥūn* (successful persons). The next verse is from the chapter of al-Tawba (9:71), stating that male and female Muslim believers who love each other are those who command right and forbid wrong, performing prayers, paying religious alms and obeying God and His Messengers. The last verse is also from Āl ʿImrān (3:110) and contains *akhbār* (information) that the best community is that which performs *amar makruf nahi munkar* and this can be applied or the *ahl al-kitāb* (the community of the Book) who are believers.[137]

Amar makruf nahi munkar has been a central MUI tenet since the early history of its establishment, being used properly as a frame to outline sharia norms implementing activities in the legal discourse and practice of Indonesia since 1998. Since then MUI has developed a set of moral premises, not only based on the orthodoxy of Islam, the Qur'ān and the tradition of the Prophet Muḥammad, but also on the wishes of contemporary Islam such as combatting the excessive globalisation that has resulted in permissiveness and liberalism. MUI does not address the criteria of commanding right because it has been clearly mentioned in Islam, therefore there is no need to explain it again. In the "Recommendation and Propagation Agenda" session of the 2005 KUII, the chairperson Muhammad al-Khathath[138] (former leader of HTI and now main leader of FUI) states that a new form of *munkar* which is supported by globalisation through information and communication technology is the most serious challenge faced by Indonesian Muslims.[139] Ismail Yusanto, who spoke at the session, argued that Islamic liberalism is part of *munkar* and therefore is a serious challenge to the *daʿwa* strategy of Indonesian Muslims.[140]

136 MUI, *Dokumentasi Kongres Umat Islam Indonesia IV, Ukhuwah Islamiyah Untuk Indonesia Yang Bermartabat*, 2005, p. 25.

137 Karni et al., *35 Tahun Majelis Ulama Indonesia*, pp. 272–4.

138 His original Javanese name was Gatot, but when he became the leader of an Islamic organisation he changed it to the Arabic sounding Khathath.

139 MUI, *Kongres Umat Islam Indonesaia IV: Proses Dan Dinamika Permusyawaratan*, p. 275.

140 Ibid, 272–3.

The effective use of the frame commanding right and forbidding wrong was evident in MUI's ability to mobilise the hundred thousand people march in support of the bill on pornography and to demand the government ban on Ahmadiyah and other sects considered heretical.[141] Commanding right and forbidding wrong can be understood as the chief frame of MUI in attempting to ground sharia in everyday life. More importantly, enforcing this normative prescription is not only of great concern for MUI, but also for its network and allies such as FPI, FUI, HTI and MMI. Sociologically speaking, as a frame, commanding right and forbidding wrong is more interesting because it also stimulates and provides a new role for its adherents within their social and political environments, for instance, to become the organ of *ḥisba* (moral or sharia police).[142] As one illustration of this, some MUI fatwas related to the ban of *munkarāt* (wrongs) is instrumentalised by radical Islamic groups as a theological justification for being *muḥtasib* (a moral inspector). This rationalisation is employed by such Islamist organisations as the FPI and FUI in undertaking "raids" against stores selling drugs and alcohol, and prostitution dens that they believe to be centres of *munkarāt* (wrongs). They mobilise because they feel obliged by the doctrine of their religion to embrace commanding right and forbidding wrong in their practical lives. The position of MUI fatwa in this context is to provide sharia legitimacy for MUI followers and allies so that they can play the role of moral police by closely monitoring the religiosity of their Muslim brothers and sisters. In a democratic system such as Indonesia this can potentially generate tensions within the Muslim community, because religion in the tradition of the nation-state is perceived as part of the private domain—no one can legally interfere in the religiosity of others. However, in the particular context of Indonesian politics, the position of religion is ambiguous due to the philosophical foundation of the state which treads a middle-contested area between secularism and theocracy. MUI as a tent of ulama organisations in Indonesia has the greater flexibility to enhance sharia norms by applying *amar makruf nahi munkar*. This seems to be occurring because the battle to insert sharia into the positive law of Indonesia is increasingly prevalent compared to previous decades. Commanding right and forbidding wrong has become an

141 On Islamic mass mobilisation to support the bill on pornography, see "Pengawal RUU APP Demo DPR", *Detik News*, 18 May 2006, http://news.detik.com/read/2006/05/18/125252/597666/10/pengawal-ruu-app-demo-dpr?nd771108bcj, viewed on 22 July 2022.

142 The term *Polisi Moral* and *Polisi Syariah* are popularly used in some regional governments of Indonesia that have passed sharia bylaws such as Aceh, Makassar, and Cianjur. In Aceh, the term used is *wilayat al-hisbah*. Alyasa Abubakar, *Bunga Rampai Pelaksanaan Syariat Islam* (*Pendukung Qanun Pelaksanaan Syariat Islam*) (Banda Aceh: Dinas Syariat Islam Aceh, 2009).

effective battle cry which goes beyond the private sphere into the public. The shariatisation of Indonesia will not be discernible without establishing a control or *ḥisba*, which can be found in the doctrine of commanding right and forbidding wrong.

4.3.2 *Ukhuwwa Islāmiyya*

Ukhūwwa Islāmiyya (Islamic brotherhood) is another vibrant aspect of MUI that is important to consider here. MUI often employs this concept to describe the idea of *waḥdat al-umma* (the unity of the Islamic community), and wants to integrate all Muslims in Indonesia under the spirit of Islamic brotherhood. The Council refers to the spirit of *waḥdat al-umma* as mentioned in the Qur'ān, Sūrat al-Anbiyā' verse 92, "Messengers, this community of yours is one single community and I am your Lord, so serve Me,"[143] in the preamble of *Pedoman Dasar MUI* (The Basic Statutes of MUI). This verse demonstrates that the unity of the Muslim community is a fundamental condition of implementing God's law. At the practical level, *ukhuwwa Islāmiyya* is expected by MUI to stimulate a sense of integration for Indonesian Muslims, which can also finally create a unity of Muslim aspirations. Islamic brotherhood is a vehicle to promote solidarity between Indonesian Muslims and the desire to have their own law adopted or based on sharia.

One of the historical motives for the establishment of MUI was the willingness of Indonesian ulama and the ruling regime to cooperate in improving harmony and unity of all Indonesian people.[144] Islamic brotherhood is a concrete prescription that promotes the unity of Muslims. MUI categorises the brotherhood in three forms. First is *ukhuwwa waṭaniyya* (national brotherhood) meaning brotherhood tied to citizenship in the unitary state of the Indonesian republic. It means Indonesian Muslims as the citizens of Indonesia can interact and share responsibility with others of different religious (or non-religious) affiliations. Although conceptually well-formulated, it is practically very difficult to apply it considering the diverse political and ideological interests of Islamic groups. Second is *ukhuwwa bashariyya* (brotherhood of humanity), which relates to our reality as human beings. In this concept, all people are brothers or sisters, and all are God's creatures.[145] Third is *ukhuwwa Islāmiyya* meaning that all Muslims are one family because of their commonality in faith. To this end, through the 2005 KUII, MUI formulated seven

143 Arabic text: "*inna hādhihi ummatukum ummatun wāḥidatun wa anā rabbukum fa'budūn.*"

144 MUI, *15 Tahun Majelis Ulama Indonesia*, p. 46.

145 MUI, *Dokumentasi Kongres Umat Islam Indonesia IV, Ukhuwah Islamiyah Untuk Indonesia Yang Bermartabat* (Jakarta: Majelis Ulama Indonesia, 2005), pp. 97–98.

ethical principles as the foundation for applying these normative guidelines in the practical lives of Indonesian Muslims. These principles are *tasāmuḥ* (tolerance), *tawassuṭ* (moderation), *taʿāwun* (cooperation), *musāwā* (equality), *al-takāful al-ijtimāʿī* (social solidarity), *istiqāma* (consistency) and *maḥabba* (love).[146] Conceptually speaking, the three forms of brotherhood and the ethical principles mentioned above should be equally practised by all Muslims; practically speaking both the *ukhuwwa waṭaniyya* and *ukhuwwa bashariyya* submit to the implementation of *ukhuwwa Islāmiyya*.

The principle of *tasāmuḥ* advocates that all citizens of Indonesia with their various ideological, racial and religious backgrounds show respect and tolerance for one another. This principle is envisioned to accommodate the diverse, plural and heterogeneous social and cultural realms of the people of Indonesia. In this way MUI also states that all Muslims should avoid the practice of *takfīr* (accusing one another of being infidels). However, the interpretation of this tenet is limited by MUI's adherence to the Sunnī creed, in which any expressions of the Muslim faith regarded as heretical must be brought back to the Sunna. The practice of *tasāmuḥ* should not violate the integrity of belief as a Muslim. Thus, MUI rejects the notion of pluralism which is understood by its fatwa commission as being similar to religious syncretism.[147] The practice of *tawassuṭ* (moderation), *musāwā* (equality), and *maḥabba* (love) should also be based on a strict understanding of Sunnī theology. Moderation means that MUI should take a middle path between Islamic streams, both liberal and radical Islam, and the adherents of these streams should be brought back into the right path of Islam as mentioned in the 2005 fatwa. Regarding *musāwā*, MUI states that the principle of equality should be applied proportionally by Muslims, with the majority being privileged over the minority and no absolute equality. *Maḥabba* means that love between Muslims has greater priority than love between fellow human beings. MUI's network of Islamic organisations such as FPI, MMI and HTI usually refer to the Qurʾānic verse, "*ashshiddāʾ ʿalā al-kuffār ruḥamāʾ baynahum*" (hatred for non-believers and love for fellow Muslims). They also enforce the notion *al-walāʾ wa al-barāʾ*, love and enmity for God's sake, in dealing with non-Muslims. This notion is also implemented as the main framework of Salafi organisations.[148]

---

146 Ibid, pp. 106–109.

147 This term was used by Clifford Geertz in his book *The Religion of Java, 1976*. Geertz denotes three types of Javanese: first is the *abangan* (syncretistic Muslim), second is *santri* (purist Muslim) and third is *priyayi* (aristocratic Muslim). Despite some criticism, this analytical categorisation remains much relied on by social scientists who analyse Indonesian issues.

148 Devin R. Springer, *Islamic Radicalism and Global Jihad* (Washington: Georgetown University Press, 2009), p. 50; Jaos Wagemakers, "The Transformation of a Radical Concept:

With particular regard to Indonesia's shariatisation, it can be concluded that the Islamic brotherhood has been framed as a means to solidify togetherness among Indonesian Muslims, promoting the view that the formalisation of sharia is a pre-condition for establishing an Islamic legal order and unifying the *umma*. This is supported by the statement of Ichwan Sam, Secretary General of MUI, that the unity of the *umma* has become the organisation's priority. He argues that the Muslim community should avoid *ikhtilāf* (juristic disagreement) and if the *umma* have different opinions, these should not become a trigger to break up society.[149] In solidifying the frame, MUI holds the principle of Islamic legal maxims: "avoiding dissent is recommended" (*al-khurūj min al-ikhtilāf sunnatun*). However, as a frame, the Islamic brotherhood of MUI contains two binary positions between exclusion and inclusion, which are vulnerable to the threat of conflict. Despite the inclusive and exclusive application of this frame, only Sunnīs are accommodated within it. While MUI has an ambiguous attitude with regard to the theological status of the Shīʿa, the Ahmadiyah are definitely viewed as outside the Islamic brotherhood agenda, unless they return to mainstream Sunnī beliefs. The exclusive interpretation of *ukhuwwa Islāmiyya* is necessary because through this frame MUI can target its followers to support the socialisation of sharia.

4.3.3 *Sharia Is the Solution*

The sharia frame is backgrounded by the belief of MUI that sharia not only regulates matters of religion (*al-dīn*), but also deals with the affairs of daily life (*al-dunyā*). As sharia encompasses both *al-dīn wa al-dunyā*, shariatisation is stated as a necessity.[150] Although MUI is not an Islamic party, its way of thinking, using Bobby Sayid's perspective, is in broad accord with Islamist parties in other countries such as the Muslim Brotherhood (Egypt), Hamas (Palestine), El-Nahdah (Tunisia) and many others with regards to the supremacy of sharia and the gradual integration of *dīn wa dawla*, religion and state.[151] Although MUI has a different framework regarding the form in which sharia should be implemented, it still sees the supremacy of sharia and also the unity of religion and politics as the ideal state form for Indonesian Muslim citizens and other Muslims as well. For those Muslim countries unable to enforce the totality of

---

Al-Wala' Wa al-Bara' in the Ideology of Abu Muhammad al-Maqdisi," in *Global Salafism: Islam's New Religious Movement*, ed. Roel Meijer (New York: Columbia University Press, 2011), 81–106, p. 86.

149 Interview with Ichwan Sam, Jakarta, 2010.

150 Interview with Asrorun Niam, Jakarta, 2010, with Ma'ruf Amin, Jakarta, 2010, and with Sahal Mahfudh, Jakarta, 2011.

151 Sayyid, *A Fundamental Fear: Eurocentrim and the Emergence of Islamism*, p. 7.

Islam in the form of Islamic governance, influence over state law is seen as the best alternative and this is what MUI has struggled for. Those who hold that the supremacy of God's law is the principle part of their Islamic belief are highly motivated to apply sharia in positive law, in no matter what type of state they live, being confident that the incorporation of sharia will contribute to ending the hegemony of the radical secular political system that has sidelined the aspirations of political Islam groups. Since the reform era, MUI has become involved in promoting sharia by presenting such solutions as the establishment of sharia banks, sharia-based finance industry, and the halal assurance system to overcome the complexity of problems generated by the secular system. In other words, MUI believes in "*syariah adalah solusi*"—or in Arabic, *al-sharīʿa huwa al-ḥall*—meaning that sharia is the solution.

MUI consistently approaches the lawmakers of Indonesia to consider the adoption of sharia into the state law by arguing that it can become a solution for the economic, political and more importantly legal malaise of Indonesia. MUI does not hesitate to often take a critical stance against the state's dependence on secular ideology rather than sharia precepts. In this regard, MUI has agreed to support Islamist movements calling for the replacement of the Indonesian Penal and Legal Code with an Islamic justice system because the Code contains many legal provisions that contradict sharia. MUI also proposes real solutions to economic crises through the establishment of sharia banks and the sharia finance industry. The MUI ulama also lobby Indonesian lawmakers to produce laws that allow the organisation to take over all responsibility related to halal certification and labelling to ensure safer, healthier consumption of pure products (*ḥalāl wa ṭayyib*). In this regard, the Council wants the state to appoint it as the sole legal agency to control and supervise the flow of food and commodities produced by domestic and international companies. Although LPPOM issues halal certificates, it does so without strong legal support from the state. While the debate on state halal product assurance continues, MUI is seeking to extend LPPOM's functions through parliamentary process.

Like other frames, most of the discourse on the idea that "the sharia is the solution" has intensified in public debate following MUI's ideological shift from Pancasila to Islam in 2000. Since then, MUI has consistently drawn on all of its activities within the frame that sharia is a real solution for all problems facing human beings. Amin indicates that the political openness of the reform era has had a positive aspect, "to express our Indonesian Muslims' need to apply sharia law as the national legal system of Indonesia."[152] The slogan

152 Interview with Ma'ruf Amin, Jakarta, 2010.

mensyariahkan masyarakat dan memasyarakatkan syariah (shariatisasing society and socialising sharia) has become increasingly popular and disseminated among MUI's allies. HTI, in its official website, for instance, states that the slogan "sharia is the solution" was crystallised in 2005, which was an important year for MUI in its shift towards a more conservative path. For instance, one of the fourteen recommendations of the 2005 KUII was to declare that sharia is a way to overcome the delicate issues created by the formulation of the nation state in Indonesia since its independence. More recent protests held by MUI and its associate organisations on pornography and "pornographic activities" are actually examples of their rejection of the secular system of life that demarcates religion and the public domain in Indonesia.

The current model of shariatisation is, of course, rather different in scope and orientation from the general characteristics of Islamisation that took place in the pre-reform era. Instead of shariaitisasing Indonesia, Islamisation in the pre-reform era took the form of merging Islam with local traditions.[153] However, now there is a strong tendency in MUI's shariatisation to uproot the local aspects of Indonesian Islam and replace them with the characteristics of the international purist expression of the relition based on the Middle East Islam of Saudi Arabia, Yemen, Egypt and Palestine. The adoption of "sharia is the solution" as a frame of shariatisation can therefore be viewed as reasonable because this term has a historical and conceptual connection with international Islamist movements in other Islamic countries. This frame is an adoption of the Islamist battle cry for "*al-Islām huwa al-ḥall*" (Islam is the solution) which was first introduced by the Muslim Brotherhood. This slogan began to be popularly used to frame the struggle by pro-sharia propagators not only in the context of the Islamist movement in the Middle East, but also in Southeast Asian countries, especially Malaysia and Indonesia since the beginning of the second millennium. In Indonesia, the national economic crisis which accompanied the fall of the Suharto regime also created significant distrust of the secular economic and political system of Indonesia. The mushrooming of the sharia-based economy and sharia-based financial institutions since that period is evidence of people's distrust of the conventional banking system and the finance industry, as their operations are mostly based on the notion of liberal and secular economy.

153 Georg Stauth, *Politics and Cultures of Islamization in Southeast Asia, Indonesia and Malaysia in the Naneteen-Nineties* (Bielefeld: Trancript Verlag, 2002), p. 268.

4.4 The Mobilisation of Sharia

Although Muslims are the majority in Indonesia, including sharia in the legal and public spheres is not taken for granted. In order to have sharia incorporated as an integral part of positive law, Indonesian Muslims have to struggle. Thus far the mobilisation of sharia in Indonesia has been fostered by Islamic political parties through several legislations directed to accommodate sharia within the state law, as well as Islamic organisations through cultural and informal approaches such as influencing, lobbying and also applying pressure on lawmakers to take sharia into consideration in drafting the law. Sharia mobilisation here means all the activities attempted to consolidate a space to prepare sharia to become part of the legal and public sphere in Indonesia. Using Jayanti Barua's concept of mobilisation,[154] sharia mobilisation is a kind of process by which the implicit energy is made available for collective sharia movement.

Effective mobilisation always needs an effective strategy, which means the success of sharia mobilisation depends much on how the main actor of this movement strategically articulates its enterprises to gain support from its supporters and networks. MUI, indeed, does not always create an entirely new strategy, but rather seeks to maximise the usage of existing activities. Among the wide array of MUI activities, there are four that can be identified as the strategy of sharia mobilisation: The National Congress, the Meeting of Ulama, the Congress of the Indonesian Islamic Community, and media and publications. These four activities were selected as strategies for sharia mobilisation as they have widespread range and influence in reaching out to the Muslim public in support of the discourse of shariatisation. This is what in social movement organisations theory is often called "mesomobilisation."[155] It means that MUI uses the existing structure of the organisation, its activities and programmes, to organise the social and ideological integration of its diverse supporters and networks to achieve its goals.

4.4.1 *National Congress*

The National Congress of MUI (Musyawarah Nasional, MUNAS) is an organisational hallmark of MUI due to its authority as the highest forum for deciding

154 Jayanti Barua, *Social Mobilisation and Modern Society* (New Delhi: Mittal Publications, 2001), p. 1.

155 David S. Meyer and Suzanne Staggenborg, "Thinking About Strategy," in *Strategies for Social Change*, ed. Gregory M Maney et al. (Minneapolis: U of Minnesota Press, 2012), 3–23, p. 14; Jürgen Gerhards et al., *Mesomobilization Context: Organizing and Framing in Two Protest Campaigns in West Germany* (Berlin: Wissenschaftszentrum Berlin, 1991).

what is and is not important for this ulama confederation. The basic statutes of the organisation, election of board members, and determination of policies and programme are all discussed in this forum.[156] The National Congress is also an arena for MUI members to communicate with and reach out to the Muslim public. From 1975 to 2010, MUI has successfully held eight national congresses. The first Congress took place in 1975 and discussed three important issues: religion and national security, religion and national development, and the Islamic mission and interfaith issues. All of the issues raised in the first National Congress were in accordance with the broad agenda of national development in Indonesia in that era. The second congress, held in Jakarta in 1980, discussed national development, stability, and defence, as well as international issues. Development issues focused on the side effects of national development such as the increased gap between the rich and the poor, corruption, increased crime, moral decadence, and so on. The 1980 National Congress also recommended the intensification of Pancasila and P4 (the mandatory indoctrination of Pancasila values), which MUI helped promote, the equal distribution of national development outcomes, and the improvement of national discipline and morality enforcement.[157]

Some issues discussed in the second National Congress were reiterated in 1985. At the third National Congress, for instance, MUI recommended the expansion of worship practices such as daily and Friday prayers as a priority for the sake of human development in Indonesia. MUI persuaded state and non-state organisations to provide a place of worship at work.[158] This was MUI's starting point for the de-privatisation of Islam.[159] Performing Islamic rites was no longer understood as merely a private but rather a public matter because it needed intervention from other outside individuals. MUI also recommended to the government of Indonesia that it broadcast television programmes on how to recite the Qur'ān.[160] Interestingly, many employees who did not practise the compulsory five daily prayers and Friday prayer in their own homes nonetheless performed prayers in their office out of fear of being judged to be bad Muslims. Through this third congress, MUI also called for ulama, Muslim leaders, intellectuals, women and young people to affiliate with

156 MUI, *20 Tahun Majelis Ulama Indonesia*, p. 48.

157 Ibid; MUI, *15 Tahun Majelis Ulama Indonesia*; Karni et al., *35 Tahun Majelis Ulama Indonesia*.

158 In Indonesia, this place of worship is generally called *musholla*, adopted from Arabic *muṣallā* (place of performing worship).

159 MUI, *20 Tahun Majelis Ulama Indonesia*, p. 95.

160 At this time the Indonesian television station was owned by the state. There were no private television stations until after 1985.

Islamic organisations. MUI promoted the ulama in particular as motivators of national development, understood as Indonesian developmentalism. Besides this, other controversial topics were debated such as pornography, *kelompok sesat* (Islamic deviant groups),[161] sadism and the national lottery.[162] On international affairs, MUI called on the United Nations to take concrete action to end the war in Lebanon, Iraq-Iran, and Afghanistan, and also to protect the al-Aqsa Mosque in Jerusalem from Israeli occupation forces and to express solidarity for the sovereignty of Palestine as a nation-state.[163] MUI also called on the Kingdom of Saudi Arabia to improve security assurances for Indonesian migrant workers employed there.[164] However, they also supported the Suharto regime's efforts to increase cooperation not only with Muslims, but also with other ASEAN countries in the fields of religion, culture, economy and transfer of technology and science.

The fourth National Congress organised in 1990 was used by MUI to express its appreciation for the success of Suharto in improving the country. In this way MUI helped repay Suharto for his contribution to the development of the organisation. The fifth National Congress was held at around the same time as the latest stage of Suharto's national development agenda, referred to as the take-off era. The 1994–1999 sixth five-year plan[165] was focused on the advancement of science, national technology, and industry. Recognising the importance of the take-off era for Suharto, MUI used this moment to display its support for him and his national development agenda, rejecting some Islamisation projects proposed at the National Congress because they did not fit with the regime's ideological and development priorities.

The sixth National Congress was held in 2000 at the transition between the Old Order and the New Order. MUI therefore needed to state its position towards the reform era and clarify its connection with the former Suharto regime. This was a challenge for MUI because many elements of Indonesian society remained unconvinced that the Council would support the *reformasi* agenda, especially given its close relationship with the Suharto regime. Many mass organisations declared their alignment with the vision of a new Indonesia free of corruption and respectful of democratic and human rights,

161 In this period, the Bahai faith was an issue.

162 MUI, *20 Tahun Majelis Ulama Indonesia*, pp. 95–96.

163 Ibid, p. 97.

164 Ibid, p. 98.

165 In 1993 Suharto announced his second 25-year plan for the national development of Indonesia which, like the first, was divided into five-year blocks called *Rencana Pembangunan Lima Tahun* (*Repelita*, Five Year Development Plan). The Take-Off era began with Repelita VI (1994–1999) which was the first era of the second long-term plan.

but in fact they remained committed to the worldview of Suharto. The 2000 National Congress was an opportunity for MUI to demonstrate its independence from Suharto on the one hand and to display its new identity as an ulama organisation working for the interest of the *umma* on the other. The 2000 National Congress also produced guidelines condemning thirteen instances of *kemungkaran* (wrong-doing), the most heinous being *aliran sesat* (deviant sects).[166] Amin stated that *aliran sesat* is the most obvious wrong that Indonesian Muslims should combat.[167]

The 2000 National Congress proved quite effective for MUI in establishing the Council's pathway to promote its *umma*-oriented agenda. MUI's success was evident from its reception from the Muslim public and the state. In his speech at the opening session of the seventh National Congress in 2005, President Yudhoyono affirmed that his government had a similar mission to MUI, namely to crack down on all kinds of *kemungkaran*, crime, pornography and so forth to secure the future of the nation. Yudhoyono sought MUI's support for his government, explicitly recognising MUI as the sole authoritative religious institution whose fatwa and recommendations could be used a reference for the production of state policy. He stated that not all matters related to state affairs could be resolved through formal legal channels and that this was where MUI could play a role, asking MUI to focus its central role on shaping and defining the concept of Islamic *ʿaqīda* for all Muslims throughout the country.[168] This statement indicates the increased status of MUI in the Yudhoyono regime. MUI had not achieved this special recognition under the previous presidents Wahid and Megawati. In fact, Wahid had attempted to balance MUI's authority as just one of several fatwa institutions. Even under Suharto, MUI was not the sole institution tasked with policing the faith of Muslim society. Despite the fact that MUI had long issued fatwas banning heretical Islamic movements, it was the legitimacy conferred on MUI by President Yudhoyono at the 2005 Congress that gave MUI more confidence to voice its strict views on Islamic belief.[169] The issuance of the eleven fatwas at the Congress, which generated heated public debate, was evidence of the

166 MUI, *Mengawal Aqidah Umat: Fatwa MUI Tentang Aliran-Aliran Sesat Di Indonesia* (Jakarta: Sekretariat Majelis Ulama Indonesia, n.d.).

167 Interview with Ma'ruf Amin, Jakarta, 2010.

168 "Presiden SBY Harap MUI Lebih Aktif Memberi Saran," *Detik News*, 26 July 2005, https://news.detik.com/berita/d-410467/presiden-sby-harap-mui-lebih-aktif-memberi-saran, viewed on 22 July 2022.

169 The role of MUI in policing Islamic beliefs is elaborated in Chapter 6.

significant increase in MUI's role.[170] All these were issued to protect the purity of Muslim society's beliefs from the destructive influence of heresy, in keeping with MUI's mission and public function.

The eighth National Congress was held on 25–28 July 2010 in Jakarta. In this forum, MUI gained more influence in staging its organisational and public function. President Yudhoyono and Vice-President Boediono opened and closed the National Congress and both, again, praised the strengthened role of MUI in restoring Indonesian morality, especially considering that it was held at a time of a pornography scandal involving Ariel, a prominent pop singer from the band Peterpan. President Yudhoyono also stated that business and political conduct in Indonesia was exceeding the boundaries of religious law in pursuit of their goals. Implicit in his speech was the government of Indonesia's endorsement of MUI's halal certification and sharia-based finance and banking industries. The 2010 Congress formulation of the shariatisation agenda was presented in a more constructive and strategic way.

In short, MUI uses the occasion of the National Congress as a powerful strategy to strengthen its position before the state and also other Islamic organisations. This event, held every five years, is an opportunity for MUI to promote its products and communicate and articulate its activities to the Indonesian public. Some MUI shariatisation products are not only of interest for Muslims but also for non-Muslims, such as sharia banks and halal certification. MUI also uses the National Congress as a means to increase its bargaining position *vis a vis* the state, non-Muslims and other Islamic organisations such as NU and Muhammadiyah. While these latter two Muslim organisations provide most of the members of MUI's board, in some cases their views and goals, for instance on fatwas and political stance, may differ.

4.4.2 *The Meeting of Ulama*

The establishment of a broad consensus among the ulama is an important strategy for MUI to consolidate the idea of shariatisation at the level of discourse and also at the Muslim grassroots level. In doing so, MUI has run an ulama forum for conducting a collective *ijtihād* called the Ijtima Ulama (Meeting of Ulama) every three years since 2003, which is usually attended by around 1000–1500 ulama from the Fatwa Commissions of all the MUI branches in Indonesia. This Meeting of Ulama is the most genuine MUI product of the reform era. Other Islamic organisations such as NU, Muhammadiyah

170 MUI, *Himpunan Keputusan Musyawarah Nasional VII Majelis Ulama Indonesia 2005* (Jakarta: Sekretariat Majelis Ulama Indonesia, 2005); MUI, *Himpunan Fatwa MUI Sejak 1975*.

and Persatuan Islam (Persis) organise similar meetings for their ulama, but only MUI officially uses the term Ijtima Ulama. The term indicates that what is decided and achieved at the forum is viewed as an *ijmāʿ* (consensus) of Indonesian ulama.[171] In fact, the Meeting of Ulama produces a broad Indonesian consensus on the idea and meaning of sharia implementation in the legal and public sphere of Indonesia. The first Ijtima Ulama was held in Jakarta on 14–16 December 2003 and produced some decisions on the prohibition of bank interest and terrorism, as well as the method for determining the starting date for the months of Ramaḍān, Shawwāl, and Dhū al-Ḥijja.[172] A consensus on pornography was also achieved to pressure lawmakers to turn the anti-pornography and pornographic activities bill into law.

In 2006 the second Meeting of Ulama was held at the famous Muslim boarding school Pesantren Gontor, Ponorogo, East Java. This was an attempt by MUI to obtain support from this modern *pesantren*, considered a leading institution by other modern *pesantren* in Indonesia. *Pesantren* tend to be sociologically and theologically categorised as either modern and associated with Muhammadiyah, or traditional and associated with the NU. Pesantren Gontor is unique in not being associated with either. Its students (*santri*) use English in their daily communication alongside modern Arabic. As the earliest Islamic boarding school in Indonesia using a bilingual learning process, this *pesantren* attracts many students not only from Indonesia but also from abroad, and a number of its alumni have gone on to take up important roles in the national leadership of Indonesia.[173] Many Muslim leaders in Indonesia are graduates of this *pesantren*, such as Muzadi and Din Syamsuddin (former general chairman of Muhammadiyah). This *pesantren* has also produced alumni like Ba'asyir, Amrozi and many other suspected terrorists. The choice of holding the 2006 Meeting of Ulama there was to stress that MUI is not only rooted in the traditionalist community but also in modern *pesantren*.[174]

---

171 MUI, *Ijma' Ulama: Keputusan Ijma' Ulama Komisi Fatwa Se-Indonesia III* (Jakarta: Majelis Ulama Indonesia, 2009).

172 MUI, *Himpunan Fatwa MUI Sejak 1975*, p. 807.

173 Presentation by Fahmy Hamid Zarkasyi on "the *Pondok Pesantren* Islamic Education System in Indonesia (maintaining tradition and responding modernity)" at Deutscher Orientalistentag, Muenster University, Germany, on 24 September 2013.

174 Although the total number of modern *pesantren* in Indonesia is still less than that of traditional *pesantren*, their contribution to the development of Indonesian Islam is quite significant. Tasirun Sulaiman, *Wisdom of Gontor*, vol. 19 (Bandung: PT Mizan Publika, 2009); Arief Subhan, "The Indonesian Madrasah: Islamic Reform and Modernization of Indonesian Islam in Twentieth Century," in *Varieties of Religious Authority: Changes and Challenges in Twentieth-Century Indonesian Islam*, ed. Azyumardi Azra, Kees Van Dijk, and Nico J.G. Kaptein (Singapore: Institute of Southeast Asian Studies, 2010), 126–36, p. 126.

The Gontor Ijtima Ulama broke new ground due to MUI's success in systematically formulating three important themes in its consensus: firstly, *Masā'il Asāsiyya Waṭaniyya* (nation state issues), secondly, *Masā'il Wāqiʿiyya Muʿāṣira* (contemporary problematics); and thirdly, *Masā'il Qānūniyya* (legal issues).[175] These three themes reflect the urgent discourse of Indonesians. Under the first topic, a final consensus was achieved supporting the NKRI form of state, but without limiting the role of religion because the NKRI was established as an *ikhtiyār* (free choice) to sustain the benevolent role of religion and to achieve Indonesian prosperity. The consensus obliged Indonesian Muslims as a majority to secure the unity of the NKRI from separatist threats with the warning that any separatists would be judged as *bughāt* (rebels), which in Islamic law means being subject to sharia sanctions. This statement was intentionally issued in response to separatist movements such as the Free Aceh Movement in Aceh, the Free Papua Movement in Papua, and groups in Bali reacting to shariatisation efforts in other parts of the country.[176] The Ijtima Ulama also declared religion to be a source of inspiration and guidance for the NKRI to help avoid conflict between the framework of religion and the framework of nationhood.[177] Under the topic of *Masā'il Wāqiʿiyya Muʿāṣira*, some issues for which a consensus was reached included banning *SMS berhadiah* (SMS lotteries), *nikah di bawah tangan* (unregistered marriage)[178] and the use of foreign loans and debt to fund the national development programme, which is not in line with sharia. This meant that the 2006 Ulama Consensus rejected interest-based foreign loans and debts.[179] The final consensus for the second topic was on the need for effective management of Indonesia's natural resources, concluding that the exploration of natural resources should be balanced with similar efforts to protect the environment.[180]

Ministry of Religious Affairs estimates that the whole number of *pesantren*—traditional and modern—in Indonesia is more than fourteen thousand.

175 "Bahas RUU APP, MUI Akan Kumpulkan 1.000 Ulama di Gontor," *Detik News*, 22 May 2006, https://news.detik.com/berita/d-600008/bahas-ruu-app-mui-akan-kumpulkan-1000-ulama-di-gontor, viewed on 22 July 2022.

176 MUI, *Himpunan Fatwa MUI Sejak 1975*, p. 836.

177 MUI, *Himpunan Fatwa MUI Sejak 1975*.

178 There is a lack of official numbers, but it is assumed that there are a high number of unregistered marriages. Usually they occur in rural areas, as do second marriages in polygamous relationships.

179 MUI, *Himpunan Fatwa MUI Sejak 1975*, pp. 847–51.

180 Islamic arguments, especially from the Qur'an, Sunna (tradition of Prophet Muhammad) and opinion of classical ulama, were also included. See MUI, *Himpunan Fatwa MUI Sejak 1975*, pp. 853–855.

Aspiration for the shariatisation of state law within the 2006 Ijtima Ulama can be discovered on the third topic of *Masā'il Qānūniyya*. Some of the consensuses achieved in this forum were four bills, two proposed revisions to existing laws, and one on MUI support for sharia regional regulations in districts such as Bulukumba, Cianjur, Cilegon on Java, Padang in West Sumatera, and many other places. MUI, for the second time since 2003, issued an official statement addressed to lawmakers calling for the bill on pornography to be passed as state law by June 2006. This reminder was understandable due to the strong debate and controversy the bill had generated in the Indonesian public, MUI wanting to demonstrate its support to the Indonesian Muslim majority. The forum also demanded that revisions to the content of the pornography draft law should only be made following consultations with MUI. The Meeting of Ulama in 2006 also agreed to reject the bill on *Penghapusan Diskriminasi Ras dan Etnis* (the elimination of race and ethnicity) due to concerns that religious defamation would not be criminalised and but instead be considered a human right in the draft bill.[181] Three things were demanded concerning the state law on sharia banking: first, the bill on sharia banking should be passed; second, the authority to publish fatwas should continue to be granted to the National Sharia Council of MUI; third, the presence of sharia advisory boards in each sharia bank should be maintained.

The 2006 Meeting of Ulama also agreed to respond to the draft law on *Hukum Terapan Peradilan Agama Bidang Perkawinan* (applied law on marriage in religious or Islamic courts) by indicating first that this law was essential for the Muslim community in Indonesia, and second that all issues on marriage in the Muslim community should refer to MUI fatwas.[182] The draft was composed in 2003 and intended as a legal umbrella to justify the use of Kompilasi Hukum Islam (KHI, Compilation of Islamic Laws) which had not bound religious courts when dealing with family law issues since its publication as a Presidential Decree No. 01/1991. When the bill is enacted, sharia family law can be implemented in its totality within the Indonesian legal system. Some Muslim scholars and activists have criticised this law because it can lead to envy from the minority. Furthermore the bill reflects a conservative point of view, adopting a literal interpretation of the classical schools of Islamic law, in contradiction to the spirit of the Indonesian legal realm. Some items in the bill that have been criticised by NGO activists and Muslim scholars are, for instance, Article 33 (a prohibition on interfaith marriage), Article 19 (on marriage guardianship, where the *wālī al-nikāḥ* or marriage guardian is stipulated

181 Ibid, p. 861.
182 Ibid.

as being a male Muslim, females and non-Muslims not being allowed), Article 20 (a ban on female witnesses), and Article 111 (stating that only men are allowed to initiate divorce), in addition to the fact that polygamy remains tolerated. Whatever the criticism, MUI insisted on fighting for this law because it provides the opportunity for religious courts to implement sharia law in the Indonesian legal system.

Particular attention was also paid to the draft revision of Act No. 32/1992 on *kesehatan* (health). MUI desired the revision of some articles of this law, as it did not explicitly mention legal marriage as an obligatory aspect for the process of reproduction.[183] The 2006 Ijtima Ulama arrived at the consensus that articles on reproductive rights within this law must always be related to legal marriage. The consensus also stated that medicine and herbs must not only be safe and effective but also lawful. Regarding abortion, the 2006 Ijtima Ulama demanded that the Act must refer to MUI fatwa No. 4/2005.[184] MUI's will to establish the supremacy of fatwa over state law is obvious here and thus, by implication, a will to shariatise national laws that do not accord with sharia.

The 2006 Meeting of Ulama also evaluated the prevalent but sensitive phenomena of sharia bylaws in various provinces and districts of Indonesia, as related to the aspiration of Muslims as the majority population. The consensus made two important recommendations. The first was that MUI should motivate other regions that had not yet drafted *peraturan daerah syariah* (local sharia regulations) to do so. The second was that all levels of MUI should support the legislation and application of sharia and other Islam-related regulations in provinces, districts, sub-districts, and villages.[185] It is obvious from this consensus that MUI's support for the NKRI does not preclude it from also supporting sharia. In fact, MUI regards the enactment of sharia law as legal in the context of the NKRI. MUI does not view the implementation of sharia law within a non-theocratic state like Indonesia as a rejection of the modern democratic state, but restates that the two can be fully compatible.

More vocal mobilisation for the implementation of sharia law was evident in the *Ijtima Ulama* 2009. Being held in January, nine months before the presidential elections in October 2009, it added to the national political debate. The 2009 Meeting of Ulama was held in Padang Panjang, West Sumatera, a place geographically far from the centre of Indonesian politics, yet still politically influential in that the fatwa and recommendations produced were extensively reported by the media. Due to the vast number of the Ijtima's participants, the

183 Ibid, p. 826.
184 This issue will be explained in more depth in Chapter 6.
185 MUI, *Himpunan Fatwa MUI Sejak 1975*, p. 863.

event was held at four locations: the gatehouse of Padang Panjang municipality, Pondok Pesantren Diniyyah Puteri (Islamic boarding school for female students), Pondok Pesantren Serambi Mekah (Islamic boarding school of Veranda of Mecca) and Pondok Pesantren Tawalib (Islamic boarding school for knowledge seekers).

The points of consensus in the 2009 Ijtima Ulama were also categorised under three topics, as previously. Under the nation-state or *Masāʾil Asāsiyya Waṭaniyya* section, consensus was achieved regarding the relationship between the nation state and religion in the context of the NKRI, the role of religion in promoting morality within the state, the implementation of Islam as a blessing for the universe (*raḥmatan li al-ʿālamīn*) and electoral rights in the 2009 elections. All these issues highlight the undeniable role of religion in the context of the Indonesian nation state. Some points of the consensus on the finality of the NKRI form of state were reiterated in this forum because of the importance of this issue. Despite MUI's declaration that the issue of the NKRI had been settled, it does not reject legal attempts to formalise sharia into the state law of Indonesia. This framework was well-received by Islamic organisations such as FPI, HTI, and MMI which had long fought for the implementation of sharia law in Indonesia.[186]

Under the topic of contemporary issues or *Masāʾil Fiqhiyya Muʿāṣira*, there were many points of consensus, for instance endorsing Islamic endowments, religious alms, the Islamic legal validity of smoking, vasectomy, yoga, and organ banks, including those for eyes. Two fatwas of the Consensus generated controversy: the first was the ban of smoking, and the second on the unlawful status of yoga.[187] Yoga itself became a controversy in Indonesia after Malaysia's National Fatwa Council issued a fatwa that prohibited its practice on the grounds of syncretism.[188] With regard to smoking, the forum agreed that the Islamic legal status on smoking in general is *al-khilāf mā bayna al-makrūh wa al-haram* (there are different opinions declaring it to be either disapproved or prohibited) and that smoking becomes unlawful when it is done in public places, and in front of children and pregnant women. On the basis of this decision, the 2009 Meeting of Ulama agreed to ask first that Indonesian lawmakers draft a state law that outlaws smoking in public areas; second, that central and regional governments draft regulations banning smoking in public areas,

---

186 MUI, *Ijmaʾ Ulama: Keputusan Ijmaʾ Ulama Komisi Fatwa Se-Indonesia III* (Jakarta: Majelis Ulama Indonesia, 2009), pp. 1–42.

187 Ibid, pp. 43–90.

188 "Malaysian Islamic Body Bans Yoga for Muslims," *NBC News*, November 23, 2008, https://www.nbcnews.com/id/wbna27857578, viewed on 22 July 2022.

and in front of children and pregnant women; third, that strict punishment should be executed on those who break the regulation; fourth, that direct and indirect cigarette advertisements should be banned; and fifth, that scientists should conduct research on the benefits of tobacco as an ingredient for goods other than cigarettes.[189] Some groups of ulama rejected the MUI fatwa banning smoking, believing it had been influenced by the *fiqh* of Wahhabism and foreign agencies (Bloomberg Foundation). NU ulama rejected the consensus because of its negative impact on tobacco plantations which are mostly cultivated by NU communities in Central Java, East Java and Madura. In fact, they demonstrated their rejection by insisting on smoking cigarettes at their meetings such as the NU Congress in South Sulawesi in 2010.[190] Some NU board members of MUI also still smoked at headquarters after the fatwa.[191] Thus it would appear the fatwa on smoking has yet to gain full acceptance, even among the MUI ulama. However, the ban on smoking in public has been officially passed as a provincial law in Jakarta.

The 2009 Ijtima Ulama reached consensus on the topic of legal issues or *Masāʾil Qānūniyya* for some bylaws and regulations. The forum reconsidered the bill on halal product assurance. The participants of the forum agreed to demand the Indonesian lawmakers state in their bill that halal product assurance is compulsory. This means that all commodity producers need to obtain halal certification from MUI. They also decided that fatwas on the halal status of commodities should be issued by an authoritative and legitimate fatwa institution, which, the 2009 Ijtima Ulama explicitly stated, could only be MUI.[192] The legislation of Act No. 21/2008 on sharia banking was also given special attention, the forum demanding the government of Indonesia publish the implementing regulation (*peraturan pemerintah*) of this act, which is required to implement the practice of sharia banking into state law. Within the Indonesian legal system, all legislated acts should be accompanied by an implementing regulation.[193] The 2009 Ijtima Ulama also asked the government of Indonesia to facilitate the development of sharia economy by providing infrastructure and supporting regulations.

---

189 MUI, *Ijma' Ulama: Keputusan Ijma' Ulama Komisi Fatwa Se-Indonesia III*, pp. 85–6.

190 I observed this phenomenon when participating in the Muktamar Nahdlatul Ulama (Congress of Nahdlatul Ulama), in Makassar in 2010, and also when visiting the headquarters of this organisation in Jakarta, where many ulama and activists were still smoking cigarettes.

191 After the fatwa was passed, I did not observe any change in behaviour among ulama at the MUI headquarters in Jakarta. Smokers usually leave the MUI building and smoke outside.

192 MUI, *Ijma' Ulama: Keputusan Ijma' Ulama Komisi Fatwa Se-Indonesia III*, p. 91.

193 Ibid, p. 93.

Similarly, a *peraturan pemerintah* was also demanded by the forum for Act No. 44/2008 on Pornography. Many groups supporting this law criticised the government, saying it had not taken the law seriously because the implementing regulation was not published after the act was issued.[194] Thus the 2009 Ijtima Ulama asked the government to draft the implementing regulation with the help of MUI. Consensus on the draft law on Hukum Materiil Peradilan Agama Bidang Perkawinan (Material Law on the Religious Judicature of Marriage) was invoked again in this forum as a way to include the Kompilasi Hukum Islam (KHI, Compilation of Islamic Law). As mentioned earlier, the KHI, which is regulated under Presidential Decree No. 1/1991 within the state law, did not have a strong position within the framework of the Indonesian legal system,[195] meaning that a legal umbrella from a higher level of law was needed in this regard.

The Ijtima Ulama events show that MUI has the ability to consolidate the views of ulama from various regions and organisational backgrounds throughout Indonesia to agree on sharia issues. The Ijtima Ulama has an important social meaning because of its success in offering a religious reference point and inspiration for sharia propagators to mobilise their resources in the interests of shariatisation. It can further be claimed to be a form of Islamic mobilisation because it is not just a formal ulama gathering, but also a meeting to discuss solutions to national problems. Therefore, topics listed for discussion in this ulama forum are always based on real social issues affecting Indonesian Muslims and offer some recommendations which provide practical guidance to overcoming the problems.

4.4.3 *Congress of the Indonesian Islamic Community*

The Congress of the Indonesian Islamic Community or Kongres Umat Islam Indonesia, initiated by the organ of MUI known as Forum Ukhuwah Islamiyah (FUI, Islamic Brotherhood Forum), is a means to consolidate the strength of the *umma*. This is the largest MUI gathering bringing together not only ulama, activists, Islamic organisations, Muslim scientists, and experts and professionals, but also the Muslim public. This is a meeting among the "communities of discourse" of MUI, to use Robert Wuthnow's term from the contexts of the reformation, European enlightenment, and socialism.[196] Each congress,

194 Interview with Ma'ruf Amin, Jakarta, 2010.

195 MUI, *Ijma' Ulama: Keputusan Ijma' Ulama Komisi Fatwa Se-Indonesia III*, p. 97.

196 Robert Wuthnow, *Communities of Discourse: Ideology and Social Structure in the Reformation, the Enlightenment, and European Socialism* (Cambridge, MA: Harvard University Press, 2009).

especially since 1998 has been attended by thousands of participants and the budget for this event is two billion Indonesian Rupiah (approximately USD $200,000).[197] This money is used to pay for accommodation, transportation, payments to organising committees, speakers and panellists, and other costs.

The KUII was first established in the pre-independence era of Indonesia. The first, second, third and fourth KUII were held in Cirebon (1922), Garut (1924), Surabaya (1924), and Yogyakarta (1925).[198] Azyumardi Azra states that the establishment of the KUII was actually motivated by the increase of religious polarisation among Indonesian Muslim communities, especially related to the emergence of a new social-religious Muslim group called *kaum muda* (progressive young Muslim scholars) influenced by the ideology of Pan-Islamism and the desire to consolidate the unity of the *umma*. This phenomenon generated a response from the *kaum tua* (traditional Muslim scholars) and influenced the birth of the Nahdlatul Ulama (NU) organisation in 1926.[199] From 1975 to 1998, no KUII were held as the Suharto regime was afraid that it could be used as a means to consolidate the power of the Muslim community and thus threaten the power of Suharto. In the New Order, Islamic civil society organisations and the Muslim middle class were not as strong and there were no groups capable of supporting such a gathering.

The KUII was reorganised and reinstated by MUI after Suharto stepped down in 1998 as an effective forum to rebuild and reconnect the scattered spirit of Islamic brotherhood in Indonesia. The first KUII after Suharto's resignation was held in Jakarta on 3–7 November 1998. Azra asserts that the 1998 KUII responded to the political euphoria of Muslim society in the post-reform era. Many political parties were established, including Islamic parties,[200] and there was clear political friction among Muslim communities both ideologically and politically. The reorganisation of KUII was employed by MUI as an important initiative to provide a public forum to integrate the potential strengths of Muslim communities, political parties and organisations. From the perspective of MUI, the Islamic brotherhood needed to be strengthened to attain what

197 Interview with Ichwan Sam. A Muhammadiyah activist, Fauzan, mentioned this sum at the KUII forum in 2005 in a special session of the group that discussed and drafted the *Ukhuwah Islamiyah* agenda. He criticised the effectiveness of the KUII, stating that many of the items discussed and recommended were not sufficiently concrete. Given the huge budget of the KUII, he asserted that a more concrete agenda should have been produced.

198 Azyumardi Azra, "Kongres Umat Islam: Sebuah Pengantar," in *Kumpulan Hasil-Hasil Kongres Umat Islam Indonesia: Umat Islam Menyongsong Era Indonesia Baru* (Jakarta: Dewan Pimpinan Majelis Ulama Indonesia, 1999), iii–xiv, p. viii.

199 Ibid.

200 Ibid, p. iv.

Indonesian Muslims had dreamt for the post-reform era, the KUII being the proper vehicle to implement this. MUI's success in holding the 1998 KUII can be measured from two parameters: firstly, the several thousand participants attending the congress, and secondly, the wide-ranging topics and themes discussed there, from Islam to the economy, politics and education. The 1998 KUII was proof of MUI's commitment to finding solutions to all the delicate problems that the state of Indonesia faced in the post-reform era.[201]

The re-emergence of the 1998 KUII occurred at a time of particular political turmoil. The legitimacy of Habibie's rise to presidency from vice-president was contested among Indonesian groups approaching the Sidang Istimewa MPR (SI MPR, a special session of the People's Consultative Assembly) on 10–13 November 1998). The anti-Habibie faction wanted the main agenda of the MPR 1998 Special Session to be the annulment of Habibie's presidency, which they considered unconstitutional. To put pressure on Habibie, demonstrations were held in major cities of Indonesia, from Jakarta to Manado, with, it is claimed, over 24,000 people participating. In Jakarta itself, 11,000 students and pro-democracy activists surrounded the MPR-DPR building in Senayan. The groups demanded that Habibie be replaced by a transitional presidium government, that the general elections be speeded up, and that Suharto be brought to court. The pro-Habibie groups were not silent but tried to respond to this agitation by employing the argument of brotherhood, namely that all Muslims should support the Habibie presidency because he is a Muslim. The pro-Habibie groups, as stated by Ahmad Tirto Sudiro, acting General Chairman of ICMI, were ready to face any political movement that rejected what had been constitutionally determined. The groups organised *apel siaga umat Islam* (Muslim community mobilisation meetings) in mosques in fifty sub-districts around Greater Jakarta (Jabodetabek, an acronym for Jakarta, Bogor, Depok, Tangerang and Bekasi). The 1998 KUII was viewed as inseparable from this drama, the congress being seen as a "*gong*" or final episode of the mass-mobilisation in support of Habibie's presidency. Faisal Biki,[202] the leader of the Forum Umat Islam Penegak Keadilan dan Konstitusi (FURKON, the Muslim Society Forum for Justice and Constitution Enforcement) indicated that mass mobilisation was needed to secure Senayan (the district in Central Jakarta where Indonesia's parliament is located), in other words Habibie's presidency. He claimed that one hundred thousand people were ready. Eggi

201 Ibid.

202 Faisal Biki is the younger brother of Amir Biki, an Islamist protester who died in a clash between civilians and Indonesian military in Tanjung Priok, North Jakarta, in 1984. This tragedy is popularly called *peristiwa Tanjung Periok* (the tragedy of Tanjung Priok).

Sudjana (b. 1959), an ICMI member and also chairperson of Persaudaraan Pekerja Muslim Indonesia (PPMI, Union of Indonesian Muslim Labour), stated that the Habibie regime had promoted the interests of the Muslim public. The Islamist groups anticipated that Pancasila would be removed from its position as the state ideology in return for their support for Habibie. Although they did not succeed in their aims, the experience taught them that demanding the state change its ideology is a demand that might succeed in a different context. The KUII congress itself showed MUI's tendency to pave the way for the success of the Habibie groups' agenda.

Despite the political turmoil, the 1998 KUII demanded the assurance of sharia implementation in the 1945 Constitution, the removal of Pancasila as the sole ideology for social and religious organisations, the ban on women running for president, the elimination of indigenous beliefs, and the prohibition of religious groups that pollute the purity of Muslim society's belief. The KUII stipulated the legislation of three state laws pertaining to pilgrimage, religious almsgiving and Islamic endowment. In the domain of ethics, the KUII demanded the appointment and promotion of public officials based on considerations of morality; the application of Islamic ethics in leadership; the implementation of Muslim society as an *umma wasaṭiyya* (moderate society); adherence to Islamic ethics in everyday life, as an example to other societies; the establishment of networks and cooperation with other Islamic organisations to prevent Muslim youths from moral decadence; the issuance of strict policy and regulations on the distribution of alcohol; and the increased quality of worship for the *umma*.[203] The 1998 KUII also demanded that the state-owned and privately-owned TV stations selectively broadcast programmes in compliance with religious norms, and supported the establishment of Islam-based TV stations, the maximisation of function of mosques for the good of Muslim society, the extension of hours for teaching Islamic subjects at elementary school through to higher education institutions, and greater emphasis on issues surrounding worship and ethics.[204] The congress also supported the Indonesian government's policy of allowing foreign Islamic universities to establish branches in Indonesia, which allowed Islamic states like Saudi Arabia and Iran to have a greater institutional reach; Saudi Arabia, for instance, has a branch of al-Imam Muḥammad Ibn Saʿūd Islamic University

203 MUI, *Kumpulan Hasil-Hasil Kongres Umat Islam Indonesia, Umat Islam Menyongsong Era Indonesia Baru* (Jakarta: Dewan Pimpinan Majelis Ulama Indonesia, 1999).

204 This aspiration has been accommodated within a new curriculum of national education, formulated in 2013, that extends to the teaching of religion. See "Jam Mapel Pendidikan Agama Ditambah," *JPNN*, 27 January 2013, https://www.jpnn.com/news/jam-mapel-pendidikan-agama-ditambah, viewed on 21 July 2022.

in Jakarta.[205] The Iran connection also established ICAS, the Islamic College for Advanced Studies, in Jakarta.[206] The KUII also advised that all Islamic educational organisations and institutions should establish a Konsorsium Pendidikan Islam (Consortium for Islamic Education). This suggestion was intended to unite efforts to improve the quality and quantity of Islam education. The KUII 1998 also proposed the month of Ramaḍān (the fasting month) be declared a national holiday for schools and encouraged the government and Muslim society as a whole to give religious endowments (*waqf*) as a funding resource for the development of Islamic education institutions.

The last thing that the KUII demanded was the establishment of a brotherhood forum for Islamic organisations and political Islam. Islamic groups should prioritise consensus over all problems and refer to the Qur'ān and Sunna, the Islamic community should provide *tabāyun* (clarification) in solving national problems, all Indonesian believers and the people of Indonesia in general should reject all issues that could lead to the disintegration of the state, and the Muslim community throughout the world should increase cooperation in all aspects of life and use consensus as a means to resolve conflict, with the aim of realising Islamic brotherhood.[207]

The KUII is not only an arena for establishing Islamic brotherhood, but also for consolidating certain ideas of Islamic solidarity. The strong presence of a radical Islamic agenda and personnel was evident within the organisation of the KUII 2005. Although Islamist groups were not officially part of the 2005 KUII organising committee, these activists were very active in making their voices and aspirations heard in discussions, panels and forums within the congress.[208] In addition, some of them led plenary sessions and discussions within the KUII. Ridwan,[209] for instance, chaired the team responsible

205 On the role of LIPIA in Indonesia, see "Rektor Universitas Imam Berharap, LIPIA Jadi Teladan Di Indonesia," *Hidayatullah*, 10 April 2017, https://hidayatullah.com/berita/nasional/read/2017/04/10/114666/rektor-universitas-imam-berharap-lipia-jadi-teladan-di-indonesia.html, viewed on 21 July 2022.

206 The main branch of ICAS is in London, UK. See https://www.islamic-college.ac.uk, viewed on 25 September 2020.

207 MUI, *Kumpulan Hasil-Hasil Kongres Umat Islam Indonesia, Umat Islam Menyongsong Era Indonesia Baru*, p. 4.

208 MUI, *Kongres Umat Islam Indonesaia IV: Proses Dan Dinamika Permusyawaratan*, pp. 11–7. The Surat Keputusan (Decision Letter) published by MUI in 2004 names prominent activists of Islamist organisations such as Ismail Yusanto, spokesperson of HTI, and Husein Umar, chairman of DDII.

209 Cholil Ridwan declares himself to be the representative of the fundamentalist wings of MUI. The rest of the team were Abdurrahman Suparno (Secretary), Tulus Musthofa

for formulating the KUII agenda on Islamic brotherhood.[210] The team issued recommendations regarding the importance of establishing a spirit of Islamic brotherhood among Muslim organisations. The KUII recommendations also stated that Islamic brotherhood should be implemented not only at the national level, but also at the regional and international levels. Solidarity in support of the independence of Palestine was an important recommendation. Ismail Yusanto, HTI spokesperson, chaired the session that specifically discussed education and media.[211] Some education and media issues discussed during the session included the Act on Education and the role of media in society. Yusanto claimed that Indonesia's media did not care about their mission to educate. He criticised the prevalent tendency of Indonesian media to maximise its function as a *tontonan* (exhibition) and minimise its function of guiding society.[212] Fauzan al-Anshari (the MMI chairman) led the session on politics and law, which enabled him to promote the agenda of his organisation. Apart from that, the topics discussed in this forum were closely related to real issues in Indonesia.[213] The Islamist groups in the 2005 KUII were not only active in chairing sessions, but were also very vocal in expressing their aspirations in other important sessions. The 2005 KUII also issued the *Deklarasi Jakarta* (Jakarta Declaration), a title hinting at the *Piagam Jakarta* (Jakarta Charter). The declaration stated that Indonesian Muslims should take responsibility for improving the country by enforcing the doctrine of *al-amr bi al-maʿrūf wa al-nahy ʿan al-munkar*. Indonesian Muslims should also engage in promoting belief, piety, ethics, and progress, promoting sharia as a solution to resolving "various national problems." The declaration called on the central government to accelerate the application of sharia law in Aceh by supporting the sharia economic system alongside the conventional system, and demanding Indonesian

(IKADI, Yogyakarta), Muhammad Rahmat Kurnia (Hizbut Tahrir Indonesia), Rahma (PP. Wanita al-Irsyad al-Islamiyah) and Djauhari Syamsuddin (PP. Sarikat Islam).

210 MUI, *Dokumentasi Kongres Umat Islam Indonesia IV, Ukhuwah Islamiyah Untuk Indonesia Yang Bermartabat*, p. 385.

211 MUI, *Kumpulan Hasil-Hasil Kongres Umat Islam Indonesia, Umat Islam Menyongsong Era Indonesia Baru*, p. 426. The complete members of the team were Mustanir (IKADI), Abu Muhammad Jibril (MMI), Ohan Sudjana (Syarikat Islam Indonesia), Ulil Amri Safri (Sekolah Tinggi Islam Muh Natsir), Faisal Ilahi Fikrin (PII, Pelajar Islam Indonesia), Imam Mawardi, Masyitoh Umar, Z.S. Nainggolan (Pondok Pesantren al-Ittihadiyah), Agussalim Sitompul (KAHMI), Amiruddin A. Fikri (HTI) and Djaja Jauhari (MUI of West Java).

212 MUI, *Kumpulan Hasil-Hasil Kongres Umat Islam Indonesia, Umat Islam Menyongsong Era Indonesia Baru*, p. 438.

213 The complete team of this session were Muhammad Rahmat Kurnia (Secretary of HTI), Abd. Rahim Yunus (MUI of South Sulawesi), Farid Wajdi (HTI), Abdurrahman (Perstuan Islam), Ferry Nur (KISPA) and Ubaidilah Salman.

lawmakers amend several chapters and articles of the Indonesian Penal Code (KUHP) in accordance with the provisions of sharia law.[214] Altogether the 2005 KUII 2005 can be seen as an important moment for Islamist groups within MUI.

The KUII is also a strategic event for strengthening *umma* leadership. The 2010 KUII formulated concrete actions that focused on three topics: leadership, strengthening the capacity building of Islamic (sharia) institutions, and establishing networks with other organisations and institutions.[215] On the issue of Islamic leadership, the 2010 KUII stated it should be based on the principle of *ḥirāsa al-dīn wa siyāsa al-dunyā* (applying religion and managing daily life), as well as being *mutadayyin* (religious) and *mutamaddin* (civilised), and *raḥma li al-ʿālamīn* (a blessing for all God's creatures). On the issue of Islamic capacity-building, the 2010 KUII claimed the importance of proliferating Muslim community movements. In implementing this idea, MUI stated that Islamic institutions and organisations should refer to good intent, integrated plans, valid Islamic *manhaj* (method), and the promotion of *ukhuwwa Islāmiyya* (Islamic brotherhood), *tawassuṭ* (moderation) and *tawāzun* (balance). The most effective movement outlined in the 2010 KUII was *iṣlāḥiyya* (reformism), promoting *ʿaqīda* (Islamic faith), sharia, education, economic development and social and cultural advancement.[216] In this context, collective awareness requires the presence of an institution responsible for coordinating the potentials of Islamic communities, and this is a space where MUI can play a role.[217] With regards to the issue of Islamic networking, the 2010 KUII considered it important to establish social ties, communication and institutional networking among Islamic organisations based on a unified Muslim society (*umma wāḥida*) and moderate community (*ummatan wasaṭa*). They recommended that it could be done in many ways, such as through mailing lists, Facebook, and many other methods of networking.[218] On the issue of *umma* leadership and shariatisation, the KUII ordered that national law should consider the aspirations of Muslims in the field of goods and products. The 2010 KUII encouraged Indonesian Muslims to increase their sense of belonging and commitment to advancing the sharia economy and sharia

214 MUI, *Deklarasi Jakarta* (Jakarta: Badan Pekerja Kongres Umat Islam Indonesia IV, 2005), pp. 1–5.

215 MUI, *Buku Materi Kongres Umat Islam Indonesia V, "Kepemimpinan Umat Untuk Kesejahteraan Bangsa* (Jakarta: Panitia Pengarah Kongres Umat Islam Indonesia V, 2010).

216 Ibid, p. 14.

217 Ibid.

218 Ibid, pp. 18–21.

finance industry. The congress also asked the state to bestow consistent political support for further development of the sharia economy.[219]

4.4.4 *Media and Publications*

MUI knows that media and publications are important tools in promoting the Islamic cause. As a result, it has included media and publications as a significant part of its programme in mobilising people for the cause of promoting sharia in the legal and public spheres of Indonesia. MUI has, for instance, created its own media such as *Mimbar Ulama* and *Jurnal Halal* and also published compilations of fatwa, reports, and proceeding of meetings, congresses and many other activities in the form of printed books. The media and publication programme is intended as a means for MUI to disseminate its main ideas to Indonesian Muslims and the broader population. Since the reform era, MUI has intensified its usage of media and publications to promote its work. This can be seen from the increasing number of items they have independently published over this period of time. In the globalised world, media and publications are a key vehicle to reach the Muslim audience.

This section describes the two types of media and publications that underpin MUI's shariatisation project. The discussion in the first section is focused on MUI-produced magazines, websites, booklets, books and so forth, while the second describes the national media and publications that cover MUI's shariatisation activities. External media and publications can further be categorised according to their source, coming from supporting or opposing groups. Pro-MUI media and publications are usually published by institutions or organisations with the same ideological perspective, while anti-MUI media and publications originate from Islamic NGOs and non-Islamic groups that are critical of MUI's role. Besides these two categories, there are also public and professional media and publications which are neutral in character. MUI thus benefits not only from its own media and publications, but also from newspapers, magazines, and books published by other institutions that support their general orientation.

Theoretically speaking, access to the public through mediatisation and publications is highly valued by organisations. MUI, using the analytical framework of Bert Klandermans and Sjoerd Goslinga which is borrowed from Kielbowicz and Scherer (1986), takes mediatisation and also the use of publications into serious consideration,[220] firstly to reach out to the Muslim

219 Ibid, p. 63.

220 B. Klandermans and S. Goslinga, "Media Discourse, Movement Publicity, and the Generation of Collective Action Frames: Theoretical and Empirical Exercises in Meaning

public. Through this medium, it is not only able to transmit its ideas but can also initiate and lead Islamic mobilisation through the inspiration of articles, opinions, news, and fatwas published in its magazines, booklets, books and other kinds of printed and online materials. Secondly, media and publications are an important bridging vehicle for MUI with other groups, both Islamic political groups and radical Islamic organisations. Many shariatisation movements in Indonesia are inspired by articles and opinions accessed either from MUI's media and publications or those in the public domain. When the fatwa banning the Ahmadiyah was issued to the general public by MUI and then reported by internal MUI and external media in 2005, Islamic organisations banded together in support. Third, media and publications can be used by MUI to gain the trust of its members. In particular, information and knowledge published by MUI's media has the impact of sustaining and maintaining an intellectual and ideological connection between the organisation and its followers.

MUI has had its own media and publications since the beginning of the organisation's existence. The oldest MUI magazine is *Mimbar Ulama* (The Ulama Podium) which first appeared under Hamka's leadership (1975–1981) and continues to be published today. *Mimbar Ulama* is chiefly aimed at disseminating information and knowledge related to Islam in general and also MUI policies, fatwas and recommendations in particular. The readership of *Mimbar Ulama* during the early days was confined to MUI members, from the village and sub-district level through to the centre and the senior state officials in ministerial departments, because it was funded by the state budget through the Ministry of Religious Affairs. In order to attract the interest of international readers, an English edition has also been published.[221] The need for an English version of *Mimbar Ulama* is understandable, as MUI actively interacts with international Islamic organisations such as the Organization of Islamic Conferences, Jabatan Kemajuan Islam Malaysia (JAKIM, Department of Islamic Development Malaysia), Jabatan Mufti Kerajaan Brunei (JMI, State Mufti's Office of Brunei), Majelis Ugama Islam Singapore, (MUIS, Islamic Religious Council of Singapore) and many others.

In the early stages of Indonesian reform, and due to the national financial crisis, efforts were made to publish *Mimbar Ulama* on the MUI website only.

Construction," in *Comparative Perspectives on Social …* (Cambridge: Cambridge University Press, 1996), 312–37.

221 This information was given to me by Yusuf (usually called Ucup), MUI staff member and librarian, who has worked for MUI since its establishment. I did not see any examples of the English edition because MUI did not keep them in its library, although Yusuf said they would be kept somewhere. Interview with Muhammad Yusuf, Jakarta, 2010.

This took place under Chief Editor Said Budairi, a former senior journalist of *Duta Masyarakat*.[222] This occurred simultaneously with the digitalisation of MUI programmes through the building of an official website, and was expected to help overcome an essential challenge related to limited MUI finances, namely the the need for paper, ink and various other associated printing costs associated with publishing the magazine, which was intended to be widely read by the Muslim community in various locations.[223] However, this was ultimately only partially successful as MUI subsequently decided to reprint *Mimbar Ulama*, although the electronic edition can still be read on the MUI website.

The content of *Mimbar Ulama* has changed over time, adjusting to the socio-political climate of Indonesia. However, in general it can be said that the *Mimbar Ulama* content during the pre-reform era was supportive of the national programme of the ruling regime. To some extent, the magazine did not show an interest in political and Islamic militancy issues, mostly to avoid conflict with the state. Some articles on religious issues were quite stimulating and polemical at the time, but they did not extend to religion-related political topics such as the enactment of sharia law or Islamic militancy. Under the strict state control of national media and information at that time, *Mimbar Ulama* was prevented from discussing sensitive and critical issues which were not in line with the grand narratives of the state's politics.

After the resignation of Suharto, *Mimbar Ulama* began publishing more sensitive articles and writings. The October 1999 (No. 254) edition of the magazine bore the headline *Menuju Indonesia Baru* (Towards a New Indonesia) with a photo of the 1999 People's Consultative Assembly meeting on its front cover. From its tagline, it was evident that MUI was signposting its willingness to move forward from the old authoritarianism to the new era of Indonesian openness and democracy. In doing so, the organisation needed to decouple itself from all forms of Suharto's legacy, and was relatively successful in this regard; this is evident from the institutional and organisation reforms which have been internally conducted since 2000. MUI now also uses *Mimbar Ulama* as a rigorous means to promote its shariatisation project. This can be seen from the magazine's articles, news and information which tend to indirectly promote a spirit of Islamic revivalism that critically challenges the state ideology of Indonesia. One example is the article published in the 2011 January edition

222 *Duta Masyarakat* was a NU-owned newspaper. This newspaper has been published again since the beginning of the reform era in the 2000s with a mostly East Javanese readership.

223 Interview with Asrori S. Karni, Jakarta, 2010.

of *Mimbar Ulama* entitled *Agenda Konsolidasi Regulasi Negara: Pertarungan Nilai dan Ideologi Belum Selesai*, ("The Agenda of State Regulation Consolidation: An Unfinished Contestation over Values and Ideology") written by Asrorun Ni'am Sholeh, a MUI activist and the Secretary of the Fatwa Commission. In this article, he underlined the need for MUI to optimise its role in influencing the drafting process of state law.[224] Sholeh offered some ways of increasing shariatisation, first by including MUI fatwa into draft laws and other regulations; second, developing the understanding that religion is an important variable for the development of the nation and state-building of Indonesia; and third, increasing MUI active advocacy for the drafting of sharia bylaws.[225] In the future, Sholeh indicated, MUI should ensure that that all laws are influenced by religion.[226] Articles written by MUI activists like this are common in *Mimbar Ulama*.

The second magazine produced by MUI is *Jurnal Halal* which is published by LPPOM. This magazine is devoted to covering issues on lawful goods according to Islam. The magazine releases regular reports listing companies that have certified their products with LPPOM. The *Jurnal Halal* also provides a column on religious consultation which emphasises halal issues. This consultation column is edited by two experts; a *fiqh* scholar and a scientist representing MUI. The former specialises in answering questions related to issues of Islamic law and the latter is responsible for replying to matters that deal with non-sharia issues. One example of the former's responses is, for instance, in answer to a question sent by Kharisma B from Bekasi, West Java, asking about the legal status of attending a banquet held by non-Muslims:

> [A]ssalamu'alaikum Warahmatullah, I would like to ask you, Ustadz, for an explanation regarding the Islamic legal status of attending a banquet organised by non-Muslims because in the company where I work the board directors are mostly non-Muslims and they always invite us (staff) to celebrate and eat together during their religious festivals which usually take place at individual residences, restaurants or even in a meeting hall.

Maulana Hasanuddin, Vice-Chairman of the Fatwa Commission, who is the fiqh scholar responsible for this column, answered the question with the

224 "Agenda Konsolidasi Regulasi Negara: Pertarungan Nilai Dan Ideologi Belum Selesai," *Mimbar Ulama Indonesia* (Jakarta, January 2011), p. 32.

225 Sholeh, "Agenda Konsolidasi Regulasi Negara: Pertarungan Nilai Dan Ideologi Belum Selesai," January 2011.

226 Ibid.

following points.[227] He stated that firstly, according to Islam, Muslims are not restricted from interacting with other members of society regardless of their religion, provided no exchange of faith or syncretism occurs. Secondly, he stated that in general it is permitted to attend a meal with non-Muslims, provided the food and drink served is lawful, and if there is any suspicion (*shubha*) as to whether the food or drink is lawful, it should not be consumed. Thirdly, if the invitation is related to a specific religious ritual, Muslims are not allowed to attend as they are not allowed to syncretise their belief with other beliefs.[228] Hasanuddin took the example of Christmas where bread and drink related to worship are served; these cannot be consumed by Muslims as it can be categorised as a form of religious syncretism. To strengthen his answer, Hasanuddin quoted the MUI fatwas of 1981 and 2005 banning Muslims from attending Christmas celebrations.

In addition to magazines, MUI also publishes books, flyers and booklets. MUI has published many books, most of them records of the organisation's activities. There has been a long tradition within MUI in which all its activities as well as its fatwas are documented in the form of printed volumes. In 1980, MUI published *Keputusan-Keputusan Musyawarah Nasional II Majelis Ulama Indonesia* (Decisions of the Second Majelis Ulama Indonesia Congress) containing fatwas and recommendations. At the time, fatwas and recommendations resulting from the National Congress and Fatwa Commissions as well as other meetings were integrated into volumes. More comprehensive and systematic publications have only begun since the reform era, with the *Himpunan Fatwa Majelis Ulama Indonesia* (Compilation of Majelis Ulama Indonesia Fatwa), published by the Directorate General for Muslim Affairs and Pilgrimage of the Ministry of Religious Affairs as one example. This volume, printed in 2003, might be the first complete edition of MUI's fatwas.

Compilation of fatwas and recommendations have also been issued surrounding events such as the 2005 National Congress and Ijtima Ulama. This can be seen, for instance, in the publication of *Fatwa MUNAS VII Majelis Ulama Indonesia* (Fatwa of MUI National Congress VII) which was based on the 2005 National Congress, and *Keputusan Ijtima Ulama Komisi Fatwa SeIndonesia III* (Decisions of National Meeting of Indonesian Ulama III), based on the 2009 Ijtima Ulama. The former volume compiles eleven fatwas agreed upon in the

227 Interview with Maulana Hasanuddin, Jakarta, 2018.

228 Maulana Hasanuddin, "Hukum Mengikuti Jamuan Makan Pemeluk Agama Lain," *Jurnal Halal*, 2011, 26–7, p. 26.

National Congress[229] and the latter contains twenty fatwas and recommendations regarding matters of the nation state, contemporary *fiqh*, law and legislation. In 2011, MUI also released *Himpunan Fatwa MUI Sejak 1975* (Fatwa Compilation of MUI from 1975 to 2011), the most complete compilation of MUI fatwas and recommendations to date, codifying all the MUI fatwas and recommendations which had been published since 1975. In keeping with MUI's role as the authoritative fatwa giver on the sharia economy and the sharia banking and finance industry through the National Sharia Board, a compilation of fatwas regarding sharia banking and the finance industry, *Himpunan Fatwa Dewan Syariah Nasional MUI* (Fatwa Compilation of the Sharia National Board of MUI) was also published in 2006. This volume has become a reference point for national sharia banks and sharia finance institutions in creating their products and commodities.

MUI is also concerned to document its history since its inception and activities. In 1982, for instance, MUI published *Majelis Ulama, Umat dan Pembangunan* ("The Ulama Council, the Umma and Development") which was a record of the minutes and agenda of the MUI National Working Meeting on 7–10 March 1982. MUI also published *15 Tahun Majelis Ulama* Indonesia ("Fifteen Years of MUI") in the 1990s, while the most contemporary history of MUI's journey is *35 Tahun Majelis Ulama Indonesia* ("Thirty-Five Years of MUI"), released in 2010. Another important book is the *Indonesian Halal Directory 2011*. This attractive directory, which is printed in bilingual form (English and Indonesian), is intended to update the list of companies and halal commodities either from Indonesia or other countries that have registered their products and commodities and obtained halal certificates from LPPOM.[230]

Through all the above-mentioned MUI publications, MUI displays its presence in the public sphere. MUI also holds strong significance for the Muslim community, as can be seen from how Muslim people refer to and use MUI media and publications either as sources of information and knowledge or as justification for their actions. MUI itself needs them as a way to publicise its shariatisation project.

Apart from its own media, MUI also benefits from coverage in national media and publications. So far, in general, the activities of MUI have received moderately positive coverage from both printed and electronic media in Indonesia.

229 The 11 fatwas were on (1) Intellectual copyrights, (2) Shamanism (*perdukunan*) and divination (*peramalan*), (3) Interfaith prayer, (4) Interreligious marriage, (5) Interreligious inheritance, (6) Criteria of public interest, (7) Pluralism, liberalism and religious secularism, (8) Revocation of individual property for public interest, (9) Women leading prayers, (10) The death sentence for specific crimes, and (11) the Ahmadi sect.

230 LPPOM, *Indonesia Halal Directory 2001*.

Some national printed and online media have paid particular attention to nationwide events such as the National Congress, Ulama Consensus, KUII and also new fatwas that are controversial in nature. This coverage by the national media is an acknowledgement of the important role of MUI for Indonesian Muslim readers in particular, where lack of coverage of MUI activities might cost them their Muslim readership. Generally speaking, in publishing reports and articles on MUI, most of the national media have tried to be fair and balanced. However, some newspapers, such as *Republika* especially, and *Pelita*, tend to be more positive and sympathetic to MUI, reporting on its role not just for the sake of the readers but also for religious reasons. This is because these two newspapers have historical and ideological connections with the Muslim political struggle. *Republika*, for instance, was founded by ICMI and although the newspaper now belongs to a different owner, the spirit of being the voice of the Muslim community remains unchanged. This can be seen from the newspaper's articles and reports, which are inclined to support Muslim interests and agendas, including the shariatisation of Indonesia. This editorial decision is a strategic choice for *Republika*, enabling it to fill the gap in the national media where there is no major national newspaper that represents the interests of the Indonesian Muslim majority. It provides a special column called *Info Halal* (Halal Information), for example, which reports on many issues of Islamic lawfulness. In 2009, the newspaper reported on the strict position of MUI towards the Minister of Religious Affairs, who wanted to withdraw the authority to issue halal certification from MUI. *Republika* also provided more coverage of MUI's demands on Indonesian lawmakers to grant the organisation the authority to issue fatwas on the legal status of products and commodities. Its support of MUI is also apparent in its opinion column, usually on page six of the newspaper, which tends to provide articles and opinions on Islam that support MUI's role.

The regional magazine *Suara Hidayatullah*, published in Balikpapan, Kalimantan, tends towards a similar pro-MUI coverage. This magazine is available online as well as in print.[231] In reporting the clarification of Health Minister Siti Fadilah Supari on her slip of the tongue delivered on 13 July 2009 at the Tanwir II Aisyiyah Muhammadiyyah, stating that MUI had no right to decide the lawfulness of the meningitis vaccine, for example, *Hidayatullah* clearly sided with MUI, arguing that she should seek their forgiveness for her statement. In this matter, *Suara Hidayatullah* clearly chose MUI over the Minister as having the highest authority over matters of national health. *Hidayatullah* also defends MUI from any allegations from business groups

231 The online version can be seen at http://www.hidayatullah.com, viewed on 21 July 2022.

regarding the high cost of obtaining halal certificates from LPPOM. In its article on this issue, *Hidayatullah* only reported from the MUI perspective and did not try to write a balanced report. In addition, *Hidayatullah* has an info-halal rubric.[232] Other online media sympathetic to MUI are www.nahimunkar.com,[233] and www.eramuslim.com. Despite some differences, these online media provide news, articles, features and so forth that are mostly in support of MUI's positions. They usually pick up MUI's ideas—either in the form of fatwas, recommendations, or individual statements from MUI's board members—as reference for their work in responding to actual issues such as the pervasiveness of *aliran sesat*, secularism, liberalism, pluralism and many other matters.

Some books have also made quite a contribution to supporting the promoting MUI shariatisation ideas and programmes. This can be seen from the provocative titles of books published, which include, for instance, *Islam Liberal: Sejarah, Konsepsi, Penyimpangan dan Jawabannya* ("Liberal Islam: History, Concept, Deviance and Answer"),[234] *Bahaya Islam Liberal* ("The Dangers of Liberal Islam"),[235] *Ahmadiyah dan Pembajakan al-Qurʾān* ("The Ahmadiyah and the Hijack of the Qurʾān"),[236] and a number of other titles. Publishing houses producing books like these include Pustaka al-Kautsar and Gema Insani. Both these publishers are specialists in publishing books on Islam but also publish polemical books on Wahhabism. Despite the relatively small number of such publishing houses, their captive market is quite specific, gaining strong popularity for example among Islamist activists of the *tarbiyya* movement.

4.5 Conclusion

Sharia activism, consisting of many different layers of movement, determines the success of MUI in shifting sharia from the private sphere to the legal and public spheres of Indonesia. The MUI struggle for the shariatisation of Indonesia indicates that this movement is a kind of multifaceted activism that aligns not only with sharia aspirations, but also with the interests of the legal

232 Info Halal, *Hidayatullah*, https://hidayatullah.com/berita/nasional/info-halal, viewed on 21 July 2022.

233 This online magazine was founded by Hartono Ahmad Jaiz, former senior journalist of *Pelita* and prolific pamphlet writer for the Wahhabi movement in Indonesia.

234 By Adian Husaini and Nuim Hidayat, published by Gema Insani.

235 By Hartono Ahmad Jaiz, published by Pustaka al-Kautsar.

236 By M. Amin Jamaluddin, published by Lembaga Penelitian dan Pengkajian Islam (LPPI, Institute for Research and Islamic Studies).

and political circumstances of Indonesia. Although MUI sharia activism in substance contains a challenge to the legal and political system of Indonesia, procedurally it still follows the principles of the Pancasila state. On this basis, MUI sharia activism directs the shariatisation of Indonesia by using existing political and legal opportunities, strategies and frames within which shariatisation is planned and conducted, leading to a formal incorporation of sharia into the existing state system of Indonesia. This is MUI's preferred means of preventing opposition to its sharia activism from those who do not support its shariatisation agenda. It remains silent, however, about its allies and groups that employ stronger tactics to impose sharia on the legal and public spheres of Indonesia. MUI's shariatisation agenda for Indonesia occupies the middle ground, anticipating maximum result with minimum risk, indicating that sharia activism, like any other, contains the elements of politics and pragmatism combined with religiosity.

CHAPTER 5

Regional Shariatisation: The Presence of MUI in Aceh, Bulukumba and Cianjur

5.1 Introduction

Although perhaps hopes of establishing a national Islamic state in Indonesia died out in 2002 when the MPR decided to reject the amendment of Article 29 of the 1945 Constitution proposed by Islamic political parties,[1] this has not meant the end for opportunities to incorporate parts of sharia into the legal and public spheres of Indonesia. The failure of shariatisation to secure a national Islamic state meant that this struggle turned its orientation to the regional level of Indonesia, and regional sharia-inspired bylaws have rapidly increased at the district and provincial levels. This phenomenon is referred to in this book as regional shariatisation. Komisi Nasional Perempuan (KOMNAS Perempuan, The National Commission for Elimination of Violence Against Women) reports that the number of regencies that have implemented sharia-inspired bylaws or discriminative *perda* (laws) in any category since 2008 stands at 282 overall.[2] Sharia bylaws have continued to be passed until recently. The KOMNAS Perempuan states that there are 421 local regulations that contain discriminatory content;[3] this discrimination happens because the *perda* follow sharia. There were 491 regencies/municipalities in 2013, which may increase to 545 by 2025, whereas the number of provinces wasa 33 in 2013 and may increase to 44 by 2025. Hefner states that the prevalence of these bylaws at the regional government level are used by sharia propagators, such as MUI, FPI, HTI and

1 Luthfi Assyaukanie, *Islam and the Secular State in Indonesia* (Singapore: ISEAS, 2009); Bernhard Platzdasch, *Islamism in Indonesia: Politics in the Emerging Democracy* (Singapore: Institute of Southeast Asian Studies, 2009); Nadirsyah Hosen, "Religion and the Indonesian Constitution: A Recent Debate," *Journal of Southeast Asian Studies* 36, no. 3 (2005): 419–40.

2 This number was obtained from the observation of *Komnas Perempuan* on the tendency towards sharia inclusion in regional regulations: "Komnas Perempuan Temukan 282 Perda Diskriminatif," *Kompas*, 23 November 2012 http://nasional.kompas.com/read/2012/11/23/05393810/Komnas.Perempuan.Temukan.282.Perda.Diskriminatif, viewed on 21 July 2022.

3 "Perda-perda yang 'diskriminatif' menurut Komnas Perempuan," BBC News, 20 November 2018, https://www.bbc.com/indonesia/indonesia-46261681, viewed on 21 July 2022.

 | DOI:10.1163/9789004534896_006

many others, as evidence from the field to convince Indonesian lawmakers at the national level that there is a real demand for sharia-based regulations.[4]

The main question here is: "How does MUI contribute to regional shariatisation?" This is examined by focusing on the role of MUI in three regions that are currently imposing various forms of shariatisation: Aceh (North Sumatra), Bulukumba (South Sulawesi) and Cianjur (West Java). Aceh has legal rights for the implementation of sharia in its positive law, but both Bulukumba and Cianjur do not. Geographically speaking, Aceh is located in Sumatra Island, Bulukumba in Makassar, and Cianjur in West Java, representing different interactions and experiences in regard to the efforts of implementing the sharia. Locally speaking, the religious expression of people living there differs with their locality, and this research aims to see how such differences play a role in the agenda of shariatisation. Since the reform era began in 1998, MUI's influence has been apparent in almost all of the public spheres in Indonesia. The organisation is represented in all the provinces and districts of Indonesia, using its strong authority to influence the national policy-making process, and in this regard receiving greater state recognition than other Muslim organisations. MUI fatwas have been adopted as the inspiration and reference point for composing draft concepts of law initiated by both the executive and legislative bodies in Indonesia at the national and also regional level. This section will examine the increased role of MUI—either directly from its headquarters or through its local branches—in guiding shariatisation at the regional level. In the twenty-first century the prevalent use of Facebook, Twitter and other social media enables an easy flow of information from the national to the regional level, helping to underpin the direct influence of MUI on the outskirts of Indonesia. The Muslims of Aceh, South Sulawesi or West Java can easily enjoy fatwas or discourses issued by the national office of MUI in Jakarta in real time.

One strong indicator that MUI is involved in the trajectory of shariatisation at the regional level is evident in the statement made by Amin:

> [I]f there is a local regulation whose substance is based on sharia that has to be abrogated, of course, there are also a lot of local regulations that need to be revised. Local regulations that are anti-alcohol or anti-prostitution are examples of local regulations that regulate social

---

4 Robert W. Hefner, "Shari'a Politics and Indonesian Democracy," *The Review of Faith & International Affairs* 10, no. 04 (2012): 61–9, p. 66.

order. MUI will endorse and recommend that local governments draft their local laws on social order.[5]

This statement was issued by Amin to respond to those who opposed the sharia bylaws. The support of MUI in Jakarta of *perda syariah* is clear in this statement, with its stated goal being the establishment of social order but nothing opposed to the goals of Indonesian law in general. Thus MUI endorses the involvement of its branches in the provinces and districts to boost the legislation of sharia-inspired local regulations. MUI mechanisms for influencing regional shariatisation operate in two ways: firstly, disseminating discourse regarding the importance of *perda syariah* through the legal opportunity provided by State Law No. 32/2004 on Regional Autonomy,[6] and secondly through the endorsement of what Edward Aspinall calls "societal Islamisation from below."[7] Here, MUI mobilises and collaborates with Islamic mass organisations at the national and provincial levels to endorse more drafting of sharia bylaws at the regional level. Hefner identifies others campaigning for regional shariatisation such as the FPI, MMI and HTI and KPPSI,[8] which are on a similar trajectory to MUI.

What has happened in Aceh, South Sulawesi (Bulukumba) and also West Java (Cianjur) reflects the ability of the actors of regional shariatisation in using what social movement theory calls, "political, legal and cultural structure opportunity."[9] In the case of Aceh, the special autonomy it has been granted is the main vehicle for the region's implementation of sharia law. For Bulukumba and Cianjur, regional autonomy made it possible to pass sharia bylaws. A cultural opportunity was provided in the form of religious discourse by MUI and other Islamic organisations framing the implementation of sharia bylaws as nothing problematic for the new Indonesia. In fact, what has happened in

5 "MUI: Indonesia Hanya Punya Perda Ketertiban Umum, Bukan Perda Syariah," *Voa Islam*, 18 June 2012, http://m.voa-islam.com/news/indonesiana/2012/06/18/19552/tidak-ada-perda-syariahyang-ada-perda-ketertiban-umum/, viewed on 21 July 2022.

6 The regionalisation of sharia obtains its legitimacy from the publication of State Law No. 22/1999, which was then revised with State Law No. 32/2004 on regional autonomy.

7 See Edward Aspinall, "Politics of Islamic Law in Aceh," presented at the Association of Asian Studies Annual Meeting 2007, 22–23 March.

8 Robert W. Hefner, "Shariʿa Politics and Indonesian Democracy," *The Review of Faith & International Affairs* 10, no. 04 (2012): 61–69, p. 66.

9 D. McAdam, J.D. McCarthy, and M.N. Zald, *Comparative Perspectives on Social Movements: Political Opportunities, Mobilizing Structures, and Cultural Framings* (Cambridge: Cambridge University Press, 1996); Giugni, "Political Opportunity: Still a Useful Concept?"; Jan Michiel Otto, *Sharia and National Law in Muslim Countries: Tensions and Opportunities for Dutch and EU Foreign Policy* (Amsterdam: Amsterdam University Press, 2008).

Bulukumba, Cianjur and other places implementing *perda syariah* also reflects an amalgamation between the politicisation and commodification of Islam. Its politicisation is evident in how sharia is used to legitimise and sustain power.[10] Here, the religion of Islam is instrumentalised in the pursuit of political goals which, according to Mohammed Ayoob, can be categorised within the definition of "Islamism."[11] Commodification is evident in the way religion is exchanged for the collection of resources and capital.[12] In this regard, some sharia bylaws on the obligation to wear the *jilbāb* (Indonesian expression for veil) and pay *zakāt* to state officials are clear examples that boost the accumulation of capital for Muslims. The regional shariatisation is also used to further convince Indonesian Muslims at the provincial and district level that sharia law and the mainstream model of Islam are the purest form of religion. Some *perda* on the limitation of *aliran sesat* (deviant sects), for instance, are strong indications of a narrowing of space for non-mainstream Islam.

This section is concerned with shariatisation in three regions. The first region is Aceh, which was granted the special privilege by the central government to apply sharia as its positive law. The case of Aceh is an exceptional one, but nevertheless some propagators of shariatisation have tried to use it as a precedent for demanding that a similar decision be taken for their own districts and provinces. The second region is West Java, and the district of Cianjur in particular. The sharia movement in West Java does not draw much on the successful experience of Aceh in enacting sharia as part of the positive law of the region, as this resulted from the very specific history and needs of Aceh and its relationship with the national government. The issuing of sharia-inspired bylaws in West Java emerged as a kind of political euphoria stemming from the reform era. The third region is South Sulawesi, where sharia propagators sought to benefit both from the success of Aceh in struggling for the application of sharia and the glorious past of Islam in the region. The sharia-based

10 Shahram Akbarzadeh and Abdullah Saeed, eds., *Islam and Political Legitimacy* (London & New York: Routledge, 2013), p. 10; Bryan Turner, *Islam: Islam, State and Politics* (London & New York: Routledge, 2003).

11 Mohammed Ayoob, *The Many Faces of Political Islam, Religion and Politics in the Muslim World*, 2008, p. 2.

12 Vineeta Sinha, *Religion and Commodification: "Merchandizing" Diasporic Hinduism* (New York: Routledge, 2010); Pattana Kitiarsa, ed., *Religious Commodifications in Asia: Marketing Gods* (London & New York: Routledge, 2008); Greg Fealy, "Consuming Islam: Commodified Religion and Aspirational Pietism in Contemporary Indonesia," in *Expressing Islam: Religious Life and Politics in Indonesia*, ed. Greg Fealy and Sally White (Singapore: ISEAS, 2008), 15–39.

regulations implemented in these three provinces have been taken as examples for other regions to follow.[13]

There are three issues to be highlighted regarding the role of MUI in the three regions. First, is the support—discourse and action—provided by both the central and regional offices of MUI in the production of sharia-inspired bylaws. The second issue is the MUI actors involved in these movements. The third is the examples of the sharia-inspired bylaws resulting from MUI's influence. This section is based on my fieldwork in these three regions, meeting with senior members of regional MUI branches and members of different Islamic organisations and also carrying out some interviews with regional government officials, together with written sources gathered during fieldwork.

5.2 Aceh

Aceh is the most interesting focus of regional shariatisation in Indonesia. Since 1999, Aceh has been given special autonomy by the state of Indonesia to employ sharia as its local political and legal system, and is the only province in Indonesia with the right to incorporate sharia into its system of politics and law. However, according to the local narrative, the enactment of sharia law in this province was not a mere gift from the central government in Jakarta but is related to a long historical struggle, in particular to the role of ulama in this province.[14] Aceh was the first place where Islam arrived in the archipelago and established strong Islamic kingdoms.[15] The tradition of living closely with sharia is a long one, and is still continued by ulama through traditional *dayah*

13 Robertus Robet, "Perda, Fatwa and the Challenge to Secular Citizenship in Indonesia," in *State and Securalism: Perspective from Asia*, ed. Michael Heng Siam-Heng and Ten Chin Liew (Singapore: World Scientific Publishing Co. Pte. Ltd., 2010), 263–78; Nicholas Parsons and Marcus Mietzner, "Sharia By-Laws in Indonesia: Legal and Political Analysis," *Australian Journal of Asian Law* 11, no. 2 (2009): 190–217; Robin Bush, "Regional Sharia Regulations in Indonesia: Anomaly or Symptom?" in *Expressing Islam: Religious Life and Politics*, ed. Greg Fealy and Sally White (Singapore: Iseas, 2008).

14 Edward Aspinall, *Islam and Nation: Separatist Rebellion in Aceh, Indonesia* (Redwood City, CA: Stanford University Press, 2009); Iskhak Fatonie, "Decentralization and Local Governance in Post Conflict Societies: Sustainable Peace and Development, the Case of Aceh, Indonesia" (University of Wien, 2011).

15 M.C. Ricklefs, *A History of Modern Indonesia since c.1200* (Redwood City, CA: Stanford University Press, 2009); Hadi, *Islam and State in Sumatra: A Study of Seventeenth Century Aceh*, 2004; Anthony Reid, "Aceh and the Turkish Connection," in *Aceh: History, Politics and Culture* (Singapore: Institute of Southeast Asian, 2010), 26–38; Fatonie, "Decentralization and Local Governance in Post Conflict Societies", pp. 44–7.

(Acehnese: traditional Islamic boarding school) education and also through the institutionalisation of the ulama as an organisation. What has been granted for Aceh cannot therefore be easily duplicated elsewhere.

MUI was established in Aceh under the name of MPU (Majelis Permusyawaratan Ulama Aceh, the Acehnese Ulama Advisory Council), which reflects the different social and political history of ulama institutionalisation in this region. Prior to MUI's establishment in Jakarta in 1975, Aceh already had its own ulama organisation, a council that existed during the sultanate era of Aceh. *Qānūn al-Ashī*[16] (the Law of Aceh) mentions that the highest body of the Acehnese sultanate, led by the Qāḍi Malik al-ʿAdil (the title used by ʿAbd al-Raʾūf al-Singkilī), had four *shaykh al-islām* (grand scholars of Islam) with backgrounds in the four schools of Islamic law in a era when the Acehnese four queens (*sultanah*) ruled Aceh from 1641 to 1699.[17] This body is similar to the Fatwa Council in the modern Indonesian era. The ulama council did not exist in the colonial period of Aceh (1873–1947), and the issuing of fatwas was handled by an individual *muftī* from the Acehnese ulama.

Six years before Indonesian independence, Persatuan Ulama Seluruh Aceh (PUSA, the All Acehnese Ulama Association) was established on 5 May 1939 by ulama of the younger generation (*kaum mudo*), such as Daud Beureueh (its first chairman, b. 1899) and Teungku Hasbalah Indrapuri (b. 1888).[18] One of its tasks was to provide answers for religious questions posed by Acehnese Muslims. Eric Morisson states that PUSA was intended as a means to a "glorious future, where all Muslims should be united through religious law."[19] In 1953, PUSA's position became quite precarious due to Daud Beureueh's support for the Acehnese.[20] On 1 September 1953, Beureuh proclaimed the entire region

16 Al-Ashi is the popular name for Aceh in Arabic literature.

17 Majelis Permusyawaratan Ulama, *Kumpulan Fatwa-Fatwa Majelis Ulama Daerah Istimewa Aceh* (Aceh: MPU Provinsi Nangroe Aceh Darussalam, 2005), p. 1; Ali Hasjmy, *Apa Sebab Rakyat Aceh Sanggup Berperang Puluhan Tahun Melawan Agresi Belanda?* (Jakarta: Bulan Bintang, 1977), pp. 32–40.

18 Aspinall, *Islam and Nation: Separatist Rebellion in Aceh, Indonesia*, p. 28; Nazaruddin Sjamsuddin, *The Republican Revolt: A Study of the Acehnese Rebellion* (Singapore: Institute of Southeast Asian Studies, 1985), p. 5; Alfian, "The Ulama of the Acehnese Society," in *Readings on Islam in Southeast Asia*, ed. Ahmad Ibrahim, Sharon Siddique, and Yasmin Hussain (Singapore: Institute of Southeast Asian Studies, n.d.), 82–86, p. 84.

19 Eric Morris, "Aceh: Social Revolution and the Islamic Vision," in *Regional Dynamics of the Indonesian Revolution: Unity from Diversity*, ed. Audrey R. Kahin (Honolulu: University of Hawaii Press, 1985), 82–110, p. 84; Aspinall, *Islam and Nation: Separatist Rebellion in Aceh, Indonesia*, p. 29.

20 M. Isa Sulaiman, "From Autonomy to Periphery: A Critical Evaluation of the Acehnese Nationalist Movement," in *Verandah of Violence: The Background to the Aceh Problem*, ed. Anthony Reid (Singapore: NUS Press, 2006), 122–49, p. 128.

of Aceh to be an independent territory: *Negara Islam Indonesia* (Indonesian Islamic State).[21] This declaration could be viewed as a support of a similar declaration by Kartosuwiryo's Darul Islam on 8 August 1949 in West Java.[22] This delegitimised PUSA from the perspective of the Indonesian state. Hence the responsibility for issuing fatwas was taken over by national mass-based Islamic organisations with representatives in Aceh such as Nahdlatul Ulama, Persatuan Islam (Perti, West Sumatera, 1930), al-Wasliyah (North Sumatera, 1930), and Muhammadiyah. The consultative meeting of the Acehnese ulama held on 17–18 December 1965 in Banda Aceh announced the establishment of a new ulama organisation called the Majelis Permusyawaratan Ulama Aceh (MPUA, Acehnese Ulama Advisory Council), which included a body responsible for issuing fatwas.[23]

The meeting also produced a blueprint for the role of the ulama in the local Acehnese context as well within the framework of the Indonesian nation-state. There were two groups of recommendations issued at this meeting. The first recommendations concerned the tasks of Acehnese ulama in the domain of statecraft: to examine and manage sharia; to issue fatwas and serve as judges in religious courts; to advise the government and state apparatus; to respond to issues on sharia and contemporary problems of nation and society; to engage in efforts to defend the state ideology, Pancasila, and guide the United Republic of Indonesia towards a socialist society blessed by God (Indonesian: *masyarakat sosialis*); and to integrate the potential of Islam in support of the Indonesian Revolution.[24] The second set of recommendations concerned the tasks of the ulama in society, such as to become a treasury of knowledge and counsellor to the people; manage mosques, *meunasah* (small mosques) and other places of Islamic worship; guide and lead Muslims in implementing the Jakarta Charter and the application of sharia law in Aceh; and to command right and forbid wrong.[25]

In 1967, based on the Policy Letter of the Aceh Governor, No. 26/Kpts/II/1967, the MPUA changed its name to Majelis Ulama Propinsi Daerah Istimewa Aceh (MUPDIA, the Ulama Council of Special Aceh Province).[26] Eight years later, in 1975, Majelis Ulama Indonesia (MUI) was established in Jakarta, and many Acehnese claim that its organisational structure was an imitation of

21 Ibid, p. 130.

22 Ibid.

23 Majelis Permusyawaratan Ulama, *Kumpulan Fatwa-Fatwa Majelis Ulama Daerah Istimewa Aceh* (Aceh: MPU Provinsi Nangroe Aceh Darussalam, 2005), p. 2.

24 Ibid, p. 3.

25 Ibid.

26 Ibid, p. 5.

MUPDIA.[27] In the MUI National Congress held in Jakarta on July 1982, it was agreed that all MUI regional branches should use the name Majelis Ulama Indonesia, so MUPDIA's name was changed to Majelis Ulama Indonesia Propinsi Daerah Istimewa Aceh (MUIPDIA, the Council of Indonesian Ulama of Special Aceh Province). Although the MPU (Majelis Permusyawaratan Ulama) had been mentioned in State Law No. 44/1999, it was officially chosen in June 2001 as the name for the Acehnese ulama in recognition of its historical association as the name of the first ulama association in the 1960s.[28] MPU is still currently used as the name of this ulama organisation.

It can be seen that the historical development of the ulama council in Aceh was a dynamic process, no doubt influenced by the climate of local politics. Although the MPU role cannot be isolated from the legal and political position of the national MUI in Jakarta, which is not a state body due to the real implementation of Aceh's privileged rights, the MPU now plays an advisory role to the local Aceh government. However, it is not located as part of the local government because formation and membership of MPU is determined by consensus among ulama and its members from the level of *gampong* (Acehnese: village), subdistrict, district and province.[29] This election process is very dynamic and less subject to intervention from the Aceh government.[30] The election results are then submitted to the provincial Acehnese government for formal recognition.

MPU's position is stronger than it was under the Suharto regime. It actively demanded special autonomy for this region to implement sharia law, despite the dilemma this posed for the central government in possibly influencing the emergence of similar aspirations from other provincial governments, and most importantly its contradiction of the Indonesian Constitution. Although the MPU was not the only actor demanding the Islamisation of state law in Aceh, as the highest Islamic authority it had a stronger role within the state apparatus and society due to its history and the respect that the Acehnese have for ulama.

27 Interview with Muslim Ibrahim, Banda Aceh, 2010.

28 Arskal Salim, *Challenging the Secular State: The Islamization of Law in Modern Indonesia* (Honolulu: University of Hawaii Press, 2008), p. 154.

29 Markku Suksi, *Sub-State Governance through Territorial Autonomy: A Comparative Study in Constitutional Law of Powers, Procedures and Institutions* (Heidelberg, Dordrecht, London & New York: Springer, 2011), p. 430; M.B. Hooker, *Indonesian Syariah, Defining a National School of Islamic Law* (Singapore: ISEAS, 2008).

30 Interview with Muslim Ibrahim, Banda Aceh, 2011.

5.2.1 *The Ulama Advisory Council (MPU) as Public Sharia Body*

There were at least three strong reasons behind the early adoption of shariatisation in Aceh. The first is Aceh's long history and culture as an Islamic region. Islamic sultanates existed in Aceh for many centuries, and the Acehnese claim this as evidence of its historical uniqueness, recognised in the special status of the province. Thus, even though it is part of the modern Indonesian state, Aceh still demands privileges on the basis of its historical and cultural legacy. The second reason is political in nature; the establishment of sharia law was offered by the central government to the local government of Aceh as part of the mechanism to resolve the conflict and violence between the Indonesian military and the Free Aceh Movement. The first initiative for special autonomy for Aceh was formulated by Act No. 44/1999 on *Penyelenggaraan Keistimewaan Pemerintahan Daerah Istimewa Aceh* (the Implementation of the Privileged Status of Aceh). The third is the strong desire of the Acehnese, especially their Islamic civil society organisations, to enact sharia law in their region. When Act No 44/1999 allowed the enforcement of sharia as positive law, the general response of the Acehnese was very enthusiastic. Most Acehnese seemed to support the decision, because the implementation of sharia law was one of the main goals that had been fought for in the province.

In the elucidation of Act No. 44/1999, there were four important points mentioned relating to the role of MPU. The first mentioned was the long historical struggle of the Acehnese indicating an endurance inspired by religious life, strong *adat* law and Islamic culture in facing colonialism. The second referred to the religious life of the Acehnese, underpinning an unending struggle and nationalist spirit in fighting against imperialism, with their defence of independence having greatly contributed to the strengthening of the Indonesian state. The third described the strong religious life of the Acehnese, respectful of customary law, cherishing the position of ulama in prestigious positions in society, state and life. Fourthly, with regard to all the above-mentioned points and for the purposes of Acehnese local government administration requiring the certainty of legal rule, a ruling on *keistimewaan Aceh* (the privileged status of Aceh) needed to be granted.[31] The term *keistimewaan* in this law refers to the recognition by the central government in Jakarta of the Acehnese struggle as being inspired by the values of spirituality, morality and humanism. The privilege granted to Aceh covered four domains: religious life, *hukum adat* (customary law), education, and the involvement of ulama in the policy-making process of the Aceh local government.

31 Abubakar, *Bunga Rampai Pelaksanaan Syariat Islam (Pendukung Qanun Pelaksanaan Syariat Islam)*, pp. 1–2.

Despite many observers stating that Act No. 44/1999 was a political trick of the Jakarta central government to ensure Aceh remained part of the territory of Indonesia,[32] this law was an important step in strengthening the official role of MPU due to the strong position it gave ulama in their communities. Before this law was promulgated MPU's role was quite weak, as were its sharia responsibilities, and it would only comment on cultural and theological matters of Muslim society. The MPU had no official position in the structure of the local government body of Aceh. The role of the Acehnese ulama council was mostly apparent from its Fatwa Commission, historically the dominant part of the organisation. The Fatwa Commission supported the local government of Aceh by publishing fatwas, recommendations and advice. With the enactment of Act No. 44/1999, the MPU's role and responsibilities moved beyond the cultural and theological domains and it became a public body in Aceh. Article 9, Paragraphs 1 and 2 of the Act state that Aceh has the right to have an ulama council called the Majelis Permusyawaratan Ulama (MPU), with the status of an independent institution, charged with advising the policy-making of local government on matters of governance, development, society and the Islamic economy.[33] A more detailed explanation of the MPU can be seen in the *Qanun* (from the Arabic *qānūn* meaning law, this term is commonly used to refer to regional regulations produced in Aceh from 2002 onwards) on this ulama institution.[34]

When the peace agreement was signed between the central government and the Gerakan Aceh Merdeka (GAM, the Free Aceh Movement) under the facilitation of Martti Ahtisaari (the President of Finland 1994–2000) in 2005, there was great concern among the Acehnese ulama, especially those who supported integration with Indonesia, regarding the future position of sharia implementation in the region and also the role of MPU in LoGA (Law on the Governing of Aceh). This concern was visible in my interviews with Muslim Ibrahim, the MPU General Chairman, and also other Acehnese Muslim scholars and activists. The Acehnese ulama feared the peace agreement negotiators

32 Moch Nur Ichwan, "Offcial Ulema and the Politics of Re-Islamization: The Majelis Permusyawaratan Ulama, Sharīʿatization and Contested Authority in Post-New Order Aceh," *Journal of Islamic Studies* 22, no. 2 (2011): 183–214, p. 189.

33 Suksi, *Sub-State Governance through Territorial Autonomy: A Comparative Study in Constitutional Law of Powers, Procedures and Institutions*, 2011.

34 More elaboration on Qanun of Aceh see M.B. Hooker, *Indonesian Syariah, Defining a National School of Islamic Law* (Sin: ISEAS, 2008); Dinas Syari'a Islam Aceh Dinas Syari'at Islam, *Himpunan Undang-Undang Keputusan Presiden Peraturan Daerah/Qanun Instruksi Gubernur Edaran Gubernur Berkaitan Pelaksanaan Syari'at Aceh* (Banda Aceh: Dinas Syari'at Islam Aceh, 2009).

from GAM would not agree to implement sharia law in Aceh as one of agendas for discussion in the peace negotiation forum.[35] Their fear was understandable considering the ideological foundation of GAM was not Islam but secular values (ethnicity).[36] Furthermore, the presence of MPU as a public body of Aceh according to Act No. 44/1999 was not given great consideration in the peace negotiation process. MPU worked hard to convince all elements of the Acehnese groups involved in the negotiation process in Helsinki, including both the government of Indonesia and GAM, to preserve the existence of the ulama council. Finally, the presence of sharia law and MPU were accommodated in the Helsinki peace agreement document.

Further explanation of the role of MPU can be seen in Act No. 11/2006 on Law on the Governing of Aceh (LoGA),[37] which further strengthened MPU's position in Aceh. Article 1, Paragraph 16 of this act states that "Aceh Ulama's Consultative Assembly is an assembly whose members consist of Muslim scholars and intellectuals as the partners of the Aceh government and local parliament." A more detailed description of the MPU is provided in Chapter XIX, consisting of three articles (138 to 140) and eight paragraphs. Article 138 states firstly that the MPU is established in the districts and municipalities of Aceh and that its members consist of Muslim scholars and intellectuals who are knowledgeable in the sciences of Islam, also mentioning women's representation, and secondly that the MPU is independent in nature and its members are elected in a consultative meeting of Acehnese ulama. Thirdly, the status of MPU is described as a partner of the Aceh government and local parliaments at the provincial and district levels, and fourthly that other provisions related to the organisational structure, tasks and status of MPU are regulated in the *Qanun* of Aceh (*perda*). Specific tasks of the MPU are mentioned in Articles 139 and 140. The first is that MPU has the right to issue fatwas that can be taken into consideration by the Aceh government in making decisions concerning governance as well as regional, societal and economic development. The second is that MPU may issue fatwas, whether requested or not, regarding the affairs of governance, regional, societal and economic development, and thirdly that advice may be given to the public pertaining to dissenting opinions on Islamic issues. Further details of MPU's status are elaborated in the *Qanun* of

35 Interview with Muslim Ibrahim, Banda Aceh 2011.

36 Tim Kell and Cornell University Modern Indonesia Project, *The Roots of Acehnese Rebellion, 1989–1992* (Ithaca: Cornell Modern Indonesia Project, Southeast Asia Program, Cornell University, 1989), p. 65.

37 A comprehensive study on the LoGA and Aceh decentralization can be seen in Fatonie, "Decentralization and Local Governance in Post Conflict Societies: Sustainable Peace and Development, the Case of Aceh, Indonesia."

Aceh No. 2/2009. In this *Qanun*, the MPU is given the following tasks: first, giving advice, considerations and suggestions to the Aceh government and parliament on the basis of sharia law; second, monitoring the administration of the Aceh government from the perspective of sharia law; third, conducting research, institutional development, translations, publications, and archiving of documents related to sharia law; and fourth, providing education for ulama.[38]

On the basis of this authority, MPU's role in fostering the process of the shariatisation of Aceh, especially in making public discourse and influencing the legislation process and sharia implementing offices such as Dinas Syariah (sharia office) and Mahkamah Syariah (sharia court) of Aceh, is quite extensive. Muslim Ibrahim, the MPU General Chairman, states that there are two possible ways for MPU to influence the shariatisation process in Aceh. The first is through the issuance of fatwas and recommendations, and the second is through direct involvement in the process of legal policy-making.[39] Marrku Suksi states that the MPU fatwa is one of very important points of departures for the local Aceh government in producing its rulings.[40] According to Lucinda Peach, this is the means by which religion influences the process of law-making.[41] Some sections of Aceh *Qanun*, for instance, have adopted MPU fatwas or the MPU may even draft the law before it is discussed in Aceh parliamentary session. Another important MPU role is to monitor the implementation of *Qanun* so that sharia law is not distorted. In this case, MPU can issue a warning letter to the Governor of Aceh should a policy be issued which is outside the corridor of sharia or if there are *Qanun* which are not well-implemented. MPU also can publish fatwas for the public about what they can and cannot do in relation to their religion. The concern of MPU here is how sharia law can operate effectively and publicly. If required, thhey can also arrange hearings and consultation sessions with the Governor and local parliament of Aceh.[42] As an example, one of MPU's important bodies is the Division of Law and Legislation. Its main task is to analyse, and to review advice and suggestions for the process of drafting new *qanun*. This commission can

38 Dinas Syari'at Islam, *Himpunan Undang-Undang Keputusan Presiden Peraturan Daerah/ Qanun Instruksi Gubernur Edaran Gubernur Berkaitan Pelaksanaan Syari'at Aceh*, p. 628.

39 Interview with Muslim Ibrahim, Banda Aceh, 2011.

40 Markku Suksi, *Sub-State Governance through Territorial Autonomy: A Comparative Study in Constitutional Law of Powers, Procedures and Institutions* (Heidelberg, Dordrecht, London & New York: Springer, 2011), p. 430.

41 Lucinda J. Peach, *Legislating Morality: Pluralism and Religious Identity in Lawmaking* (Oxford & New York: Oxford University Press, 2002).

42 Interview with Muslim Ibrahim, Banda Aceh, 2011.

undertake studies and research on sharia and other related aspects, and its results are submitted to the MPU Chairman. This division is MPU's backbone in the field of sharia legal drafting.

5.2.2 *Belief and Public Morality*

MPU's strong presence in the Aceh legal and public spheres is evident through its regulation of the belief system that Acehnese Muslims must embrace. The MPU and Aceh local government are the two authorities designated with the responsibility of securing *keagungan* (dignity) and *kesucian agama Islam* (sanctity of Islam). The dignity and sanctity of Islam here refer to the pure implementation of Islam and protection from the pollution of deviant ideas from mainstream practice and Islamic thought. Since 2000, MPU has been given the authority to formulate integrated steps to prevent the dignity of Islam from being denigrated, reduced and weakened.[43] This responsibility is implemented by the Aceh MPU through its role in controlling the religious belief of the Acehnese. In other provinces religious belief may be a private matter, but in Aceh it is part of the state's domain. Aceh's MPU also aims to have the state decree that the official sharia law applied in Aceh follows the Sunnī Islam tradition.

To control religious belief, the Aceh MPU issued a fatwa titled "*Pedoman Identifikasi Aliran Sesat*" (Guidance in Identifying Deviant Groups) in 2007. This guidance is mostly adopted from the central MUI concept on a similar topic. MPU states that this fatwa is a form of implementation of Qanun No. 11/2002, especially Chapter 3, Article 6 which states that MPU is responsible for issuing fatwa to respond to beliefs which are regarded deviant either by the people of Aceh or by the local government. Like its mother organisation MUI in Jakarta, MPU feels obliged to protect the *ʿaqīda* of Acehnese Muslims from any threats of *aliran sesat*. All the definitions, criteria and methods for determining any such group as deviant closely follow those of MUI in Jakarta.[44] After issuing the 2007 fatwa on Guidance in Identifying Deviant Groups, MPU issued at least two fatwas that are closely related to it. The first was a fatwa on *bidʿa* (religious innovation, often with a negative connotation)[45]

43 Dinas Syari'at Islam, *Himpunan Undang-Undang Keputusan Presiden Peraturan Daerah/ Qanun Instruksi Gubernur Edaran Gubernur Berkaitan Pelaksanaan Syari'at Aceh*, p. 264; Hooker, *Indonesian Syariah, Defining a National School of Islamic Law*, 2008, p. 246. See Qanun No. 05/2000.

44 Fatwa MPU Nanggroe Aceh Darussalam No. 04/2007.

45 On *bidʿa*, see *Reconfiguring Islamic Tradition: Reform, Rationality, and Modernity* Samira Haj, *Reconfiguring Islamic Tradition: Reform, Rationality, and Modernity* (Redwood City, CA: Stanford University Press, 2008), p. 56.

and *shubha* (doubt) in 2009.[46] In this fatwa, the MPU prohibited the use of utterances popularly pronounced among Ṣūfīs such as "*wujūduka dhanbun*" (your existence is sin), the assertion that the ascension of the Prophet Muḥammad was not physical but spiritual only, the belief that *al-ṣirāṭ al-mustaqīm* (a straight bridge in Islamic eschatology) does not exist in the hereafter, and numerous others.[47] This fatwa was then strengthened by MPU fatwa No. 08/2012 that regulated "*Pemahaman Pemikiran dan Pengalaman yang Menyimpang dari Islam*" (Understanding Thoughts and Experiences That Deviate from Islam). All three of these fatwas have become MPU's solid foundation in determining what should be considered *aliran sesat* in Aceh, and are well-founded on similar fatwa issued by the MUI headquarters in Jakarta.

The local state authority of Aceh itself has asked its ulama to seriously pay attention to the growing number of deviant sects in the region.[48] In the period of 2009/2010, it was reported that eleven deviant sects had been identified in Aceh, and ten had been officially condemned as deviant by the MPU.[49] Among them, for instance, was Lembaga Dakwah Islam Indonesia (LDII, the Institute for Indonesian Islamic Propagation), which has also been banned by MUI in Jakarta, as well as Millah Abraham and other *aliran sempalan* (breakaway ideologies) in the region of Idra Makmoe, East Aceh, and other places. Millah Abraham (from the Qur'ānic term *millata ibrahīma*) or belief of Abraham, has gained currency in Banda Aceh but is suspected of mixing the teaching of the Qur'ān and the Bible. The Aceh MPU is closely monitoring this group. In 2010, the MPU district of Biruen, in Aceh province, opened a *sidang istimewa* (public trial) of five members of Millah Abraham, and forced them to publicly recant their misinterpretation of the pure *ʿaqīda*. The process began with the General Session of the Bireuen MPU, and then the adherents of the Millah Abraham proclaimed their return to the true Islam; the MPU required that the recitation of *shahāda* (proclamation of Islam) be witnessed by the local police and also the public.[50] This model has now become the standard model of repentance for deviant groups throughout Aceh. In 2013, MUI issued a fatwa on the

46 Fatwa No. 06/2009.

47 In this fatwa MPU lists seventeen utterances categorised as *bidʿa*. See Fatwa No. 06/2009.

48 "Ulama Aceh Minta Perkembangan Aliran Sesat Diwaspadai," *Merdeka*, 1 September 2013, https://www.merdeka.com/peristiwa/ulama-aceh-minta-perkembangan-aliran-sesat-diwaspadai.html, viewed on 21 July 2022.

49 "11 Aliran Sesat Ditemukan Di Aceh," *Anterokini*, 26 October 2010, https://anterokini.com/2010/10/26/11-aliran-sesat-ditemukan-di-aceh/, viewed on 21 July 2022.

50 "Ratusan Jemaat Sekte Murtad Millah Abraham Bersyahadat Masuk Islam," *Voa Islam*, 23 April 2011, https://www.voa-islam.com/read/indonesiana/2011/04/23/14304/ratusan-jemaat-sekte-murtad-millah-abraham-bersyahadat-masuk-islam/, viewed on 21 July 2022.

deviant thought of Ahmad Barmawi, the leader of the al-Mujahadah Islamic Boarding School, located in South Aceh.[51] The MPU asked Ahmad Barmawi and his pupils to repent their theological errors. Ahmad Barmawi, however, disagrees with the fatwa, claiming that MPU has discredited him. He wants to sue MPU for its fatwa because he states it is not based in reality, claiming: "That is really scurrilous slander. I have never committed idolatry. This is an extraordinary slander. What MUI has uncovered is not correct."[52] The Aceh Judicial Monitoring Institute (AJMI) also criticised the MPU fatwa against Ahmad Barmawi, stating that MPU does not have the right to determine the issue of deviant belief; that right belongs to the sharia court.[53] MPU did not revoke its fatwa, however.

Not only do they control the question of deviant beliefs, but MPU is also working to oversee and control "*Kristenisasi*" (Christianisation) and "*Pemurtadan*" (apostasisation). The Aceh MPU views both these matters as great threats to the belief of Acehnese Muslims. The issue of Christianisation began to attract MPU's attention during Aceh's recovery from the tsunami disaster in 2004. To alert Acehnese Muslims of the dangers of *Kristenisasi* and *Pemurtadan*, MPU published a fatwa titled "*Pendangkalan Aqidah dan Pemurtadan*" (the Trivialisation of Belief and Apostasy) in 2010. Politically speaking, the fatwa was issued to protect the Acehnese from the torrential flow of foreigners to Aceh, who offered not only humanitarian aid but also beliefs and ideologies that could change the belief and ideology of Acehnese Muslims. Thus, MPU issued that the fatwa that all Muslims were obliged to protect their belief and that of their Muslim brothers from the dangers of belief trivialisation and apostasy. Muslims who went astray were to be brought back to the straight path of Islam.

During this era, MPU interrogated some foreign NGOs suspected as being actors of *pemurtadan*. During the tsunami, according to local rumour, seventeen foreign NGOs were identified as undertaking Christianisation under the cover of humanitarian aid. Muslim Ibrahim, MPU General Chairman, indicated that *aksi pemurtadan* really happened in Aceh packaged as humanitarian aid.[54] The discourse on "apostasisation" was not only prolific in the

51 Fatwa No. 01/2013.

52 "MPU Fatwakan Ajaran Ahmad Barmawi Sesat," *Aceh Tribun News*, 1 March 2013, https://aceh.tribunnews.com/2013/03/01/mpu-fatwakan-ajaran-ahmad-barmawi-sesat, viewed on 21 July 2022.

53 Kurniawan, "Aspek Hukum Fatwa Majelis Permusyawaratan Ulama (MPU) Tentang Aliran Sesat," *Jurnal Dinamika Hukum* 14, no. 2 (2014): 310–23, p. 322.

54 Interview with Muslim Ibrahim, Banda Aceh, 2011.

capital city of Banda Aceh, but also in peripheral districts such as Aceh Jaya. Here, to overcome the *pemurtadan* mission by Christian and deviant groups, the regional office of the Ministry of Religious Affairs placed a special staff member responsible for monitoring the movement of Christianisation and apostasisation in each village (Acehnese: *gampong*). The rumours of both Christianisation and apostasisation did not in fact stop with the end of the rehabilitation and reconstruction of Aceh in 2009, but continue to the present day. On 23 September 2010, at the Friday sermon in the Lamgugup Mosque, Syiah Kuala, Banda Aceh, Muhammad Nazar, the Vice Governor of Aceh, astounded listeners with his controversial statement that an estimated 20,000 Acehnese Muslims had been converted to different religions. However, such a rumour is difficult to prove concretely. Rumours of *pemurtadan* and *Kristenisasi* are popularly discussed and debated in the public space, but there are no clear figures for how many Acehnese Muslims have converted to different religions or beliefs. Numbers are mentioned, but are not based on real data. The issues of apostasisation and Christianisation are politically used and sustained by both local religious and state authorities, namely MPU and the regional office of the Ministry of Religious Affairs, to sustain and increase their status in the eyes of the Acehnese.

Other issues are also raised. Since sharia was officially proclaimed as positive law in Aceh, besides *ʿaqīda*, there are other important issues regulated in *qanun* on the application of sharia that involve the role of MPU. The first concerns worship, as regulated by *qanun* No. 11/2002. In this *qanun*, MPU is the place where sharia public implementing agencies such as the Aceh government and Dinas Syariah (Sharia Office) that operate the Wilayatul Hisbah (Moral Police) can inquire about the proper practice of worship among Acehnese society. MPU is responsible for announcing Islamic festivities such as ʿĪd al-Fiṭr and ʿĪd al-Aḍḥā, and also other issues related to the Muslim community. Every Christmas, the MPU publishes a circular reminding Acehnese Muslims not to express Christmas greetings or attend Christmas celebrations.[55] When a band from Jakarta wishes to stage a concert in Aceh, MPU has the right to issue the recommendation on whether or not the band should be allowed to perform there. Some bands from Jakarta have been rejected because they could lead to *maʿṣiya* (sin), the uncontrolled mixing between men and women in the audience, as happened at a concert by Nidji in 2003. In 2007, a band called Ungu from Jakarta was rejected by MPU and the Banda Aceh district

55 This recommendation refers to the MUI fatwa in Jakarta.

government for a similar reason. The Acehnese government insists that MPU should never give up its promotion of sharia.[56]

5.2.3 *Qanun Jinayat*

Although sharia has officially been enacted in Aceh, it does not yet cover the implementation of *jinayat* (Indonesian expression for *jināya*: Islamic offense). MPU's role in endorsing the implementation of Islamic criminal law has been visible since 2009. The visible expression of the demand for the implementation of Islamic criminal law in Aceh began with the drafting of *qanun* No. 11/2002. The *qanun* stated the implementation of criminal law in Aceh would be instigated by MPU as the responsible organ. The Dewan Perwakilan Rakyat Aceh (DPRA, Aceh Parliament) approved Qanun Jinayat and its implementing regulation in 2009.[57] However, when former GAM spokesperson Irwandi was elected as the Governor of Aceh (2007–2012) he refused to sign the Qanun Jinayat agreed by the old DPRA, and thus the Qanun Jinayat could not be gazetted. Yusuf Irwandi (b. 1960) stated that the *qanun* had been unilaterally decided by the DPRA, without GAM involvement.[58] He also stated that the existing three *qanuns* were sufficient to handle violations to sharia. Therefore, the implementation of Qanun Jinayat and its implementing regulation was not a pressing need. Irwandi did not agree with the provision of stoning to death (*rajm*) within this *qanun* as the punishment for adultery.[59]

MPU approached the local government to resolve this deadlock. Although Irwandi's rejection was based on human rights, it invited much speculation. Some groups linked the rejection with Free Aceh Movement's secular ideology, but some believed that Governor Irwandi would sign it at the right moment, and when it suited his personal political interests. For MPU, Irwandi's reluctance to approve the Qanun Jinayat was an obstacle for the implementation of sharia law in Aceh. MPU regarded it as a serious matter and sent a team, comprised of senior Aceh ulama Abu Tumin (b. 1932),[60] Abu Kuta

---

56 A.G. Berutu, *Formalisasi Syariat Islam Aceh Dalam Tatanan Politik Nasional*, Cet. 1 (Yogyakarta: Pena Persada, 2020), pp. 73–80.

57 Interview with Syahrizal and and Muslim Ibrahim, Jakarta, 2010.

58 "Qanun Jinayat Tidak Sah: Gubernur", *Acehkita*, 30 September 2009, http://www.acehkita.com/berita/qanun-jinayat-tidak-sah-gubernur/, viewed on 03 August 2013.

59 The provision of *'uqūbā al-rajm* for adultery is regulated in Chapter 24, Article 1.

60 Abu Tu Min is a nickname of Muhammad Amin. He was born around 1932 in Gampong Kuala Jeumpa, Aceh and founded a *dayah* (Islamic Boarding School) called Dayah Almadinatuddiniyyah Alinatudiniyyah Babussalam, Blang Bladeh, Bireuen. He said that the intention of his *dayah* is to educate Acehnese ulama in sharia not only at the discursive but also at the practical level.

Krueng,[61] Shaykh Adnan Mahmud of Bakongan,[62] and Walid Nuh to persuade Irwandi to sign the *qanun*. They expected that by sending the senior ulama, Irwandi would change his mind about the Qanun Jinayat. Until the end of Irwandi's administration, however, the MPU campaign was unsuccessful. The fate of the Islamic criminal law depended both on the efforts of MPU and local Aceh lawmakers, and also the pressure of Muslims who were demanding the promulgation of this law. In 2012 MPU again demanded the caretaker governor of Aceh, Tarmizi A. Karim, to sign Qanun Jinayat, stating that the enactment of Islamic criminal law would be the key to peace in Aceh.[63] But, until Irwandi ended his service as Aceh governor in 2012, MPU efforts were unsuccessful.

As a result of the Aceh governor elections on 25 June 2012, Zaini Abdullah (b. 1940) and Muzakir Manaf (b. 1963) were elected as new governor and vice-governor of Aceh. The new governor and vice-governor, like Irwandi, also come from the GAM faction. When the new governor was elected, the demand to implement the *Jinayat* was re-echoed by 35 Islamic organisations in Aceh, such as the FPI, DDII, and many others.[64] According to statements from members of the DPRA, the Qanun Jinayat will be prioritised for legislation during this new era. Governor Zaini Abdullah in the DPRA parliamentary session on 4 March 2013 stated that the implementation of complete sharia is important in Aceh. He has also consulted with the President of Indonesia, Yudoyono, about the demands of Acehnese people to legislate the Qanun Jinayat. The political nuances of the debate surrounding the Qanun Jinayat among political actors in Aceh are clear. The local government of Aceh is using this issue to bargain with the central government in Jakarta, reserving it as a weapon should there be a problem related to Jakarta's support of the implementation of special autonomy in Aceh.

61 Abu Kuta Krueng is nickname of Usman b. Ali. He was born in 1937, in Pidie Jaya, Aceh, and runs a *dayah* called Darul Munawarah. Abu Kuta Krueng is not only popular among Acehnese, but also among Sumatran Muslims.

62 Haji Adnan Mahmud was born in 1905. He was a very charismatic ulama of Southern Aceh who ran Dayah Ashabul Yamin. See "Profil Abu Kuta Krueng (Tgk H. Usman Ali Pimpinan Dayah Darul Munawarah)," http://www.suaradarussalam.id/2021/11/profil-abu-kuta-krueng-tgk-h-usman-ali.html, viewed on 21 July 2022.

63 "MPU Desak Gubernur Teken Qanun Jinayah," *Aceh Tribun News*, 30 March 2012 http://aceh.tribunnews.com/2012/03/30/mpu-desak-gubernur-teken-qanun-jinayah, viewed on 21 July 2022.

64 "Ormas Islam Tagih Janji Gubernur", *Aceh Tribun News*, 7 May 2013, http://aceh.tribunnews.com/2013/05/07/ormas-islam-tagih-janji-gubernur, viewed on 21 July 2022.

5.3 Bulukumba, South Sulawesi

The focus of this section is on MUI's role in the implementation of sharia-inspired bylaws in South Sulawesi by considering the case of the Bulukumba district, located on the south-east tip of South Sulawesi. The district of about 400,000 people was selected as a research area due to its swift adoption of sharia bylaws in comparison to other districts in the province. The question to be addressed here is: "What is the role of MUI and what were its actions in support of the drafting of sharia bylaws in Bulukumba?"

Some experts claim that demands to implement sharia-inspired bylaws in the province of South Sulawesi as a whole cannot be separated from the historical background of South Sulawesi's Islamic kingdoms.[65] This claim may be true, but media information and interviews conducted by the researcher indicate that demands for sharia law in this region intensified once the implementation of sharia law was granted to Aceh in 1999, indicating that this has a higher impact than Sulawesi's past or local dynamics. Michael Buehler states that the greatest number of districts of the South Sulawesi province adopted sharia bylaws just after Aceh was granted special status under Act No. 44/1999 to apply sharia law.[66] South Sulawesi has introduced the largest number of sharia bylaws in Indonesia after Aceh.

The domino effect of sharia enforcement in Aceh on the discourse and practice of shariatisation in South Sulawesi was first apparent from the holding of the Konggres Umat Islam Se-Sulawesi Selatan Pertama (First Congress of South Sulawesi's Islamic Community) held on 19–21 October 2001. The Congress, which was held over three days, was dedicated to discussing special autonomy for the application of sharia law in South Sulawesi.[67] This Islamic

65 Dik Roth, "Many Governors, No Provinces: The Struggle for a Province in the Luwu-Tanah Toraja Area in South Sulawesi," in *Renegotiating Boundaries: Local Politics in Post-Suharto Indonesia*, ed. Henk Schulte Nordholt and Gerry van Klinken (Leiden: KITLV Press, 2007), 121–50, p. 142; Anne Booth, "Splitting, Splitting, Splitting Again: Brief History of the Development of Regional in Indonesia since Independence," *Bijdragen Tot de Taal-, Land -En Volkenkunde* 167, no. 1 (2011): 31–59; Ricklefs, *A Historty of Modern Indonesia since C, 1200*; I.K. Khan, *Islam in Modern Asia* (New Delhi: M.D. Publications Pvt. Ltd., 2006), p. 131.

66 Michael Buehler, "The Rise of Sharia Bylaws in Indonesian Districts: An Indication for Changing Patterns of Power Accumulation and Political Corruption," *South East Asia Research* 16, no. 22 (2008): 255–85, p. 256; Cf. Hamdan Juhannis, "The Struggle for Formalist Islam in South Sulawesi from Darul Islam to Komite Persiapan Penegakan Syariah Islam (KPPSI)" (Australian National University, 2006).

67 "Who is calling for Islamic Law?" *Inside Indonesia*, 29 July 2007, http://www.insideindonesia.org/feature-editions/who-is-calling-for-islamic-law, viewed on 21 July 2022.

event in Makassar, the capital city of South Sulawesi, was in itself an indication of the role played by MUI through the Forum Ukhuwah Islamiyah (FUI, Forum of Islamic Brotherhood), which is the organ of the South Sulawesi MUI branch and was the main organiser of the Congress.[68] According to informant Siradjuddin Idris, Deputy Secretary of the Komite Persiapan Penerapan Syariah Islam (KPPSI, Committee for the Preparation of Islamic Sharia), MUI's involvement in the congress was evident in two instances. Firstly, MUI's endorsement of the sharia movement in South Sulawesi was indicated by the attendance of Sanusi Baco (Chairman of MUI South Sulawesi Branch) at the ceremony to launch KPPSI in 2000.[69] Baco signed the KPPSI charter, thus indicating his support for the sharia movement. Some MUI board members also became KPSSI board members.[70] Idris stated that the KPPSI was an organisation whose main agenda was to prepare the impl“mentation o” sharia law in South Sulawesi through attaining special autonomy, like Aceh.[71] The most important item on the agenda for the KPPSI was therefore to win the hearts of the lawmakers in particular and the people of South Sulawesi in general to successfully attain this goal.

As a very important KPPSI figure, Siradjuddin Idris explained that often a person of his influence in South Sulawesi has a dual or triple role; sometimes he speaks as a Muhammadiyah member, and on other occasions as a member of the NU. This is because affiliation and devotion to such Islamic organisations in South Sulawesi is not as rigid as in Java. In other words, a Muslim activist or politician sometimes acts through multiple identities. On this basis, Idris states, the involvement of MUI board members in the KPPSI structure was a matter of their multiple identity roles as Muslims. Sanusi Baco was the General Chairman of South Sulawesi MUI who signed, together with Achmad Ali and Abdurrachman Bassalamah, the declaration to establish the KPPSI.[72] When questioned, Baco did not deny his involvement with the KPPSI but said this does not mean he is in total agreement with their agenda. He claims he can understand the desire to promote shariatisation in South Sulawesi but does not agree with the complete implementation of sharia law as promoted

68 Heriyansah Anugrah and Ridho Alhamdi, "Kebajikan Syariah Di Akar Rumput: Menelusuri Motif Politik Terbitnya Peraturan Desa Tentang Hukuman Cambu Di Kabupaten Bulukumba," *POLITEA: Jurnal Politik Islam* 3, no. 2 (2020).

69 Zainal M. Anwar, "Formalisasi Syari'at Islam Di Indonesia, Pendekatan Pluralisme Politik Dalam Kebijakan Publik," *Millah* X, no. 2 (2011): 191–212, p. 201.

70 Interview with Siradjuddin Idris, Makassar, 2011.

71 Ibid.

72 Interview with Siradjuddin Idris, Makassar, 2011. See also "Who is calling for Islamic Law?" *Inside Indonesia*, 29 July 2007.

by the KPPSI.[73] Baco fully supports the model in which sharia law is adopted into the local South Sulawesi regulations in the form *perda syariah* without turning it into a province that employs sharia as its positive law, as is the case of Aceh. The South Sulawesi MUI agrees with the model of shariatisation that has been implemented in Bulukumba because it is not aimed at changing the existing law.[74] Baco states he believes in the eternal values enshrined in sharia but does not judge those who do not support this agenda as less committed to Islam.[75] This is what Asep Bayat describes as the phenomenon of sharia without an Islamic state;[76] the state here is no longer a determinant factor in the implementation of sharia. South Sulawesi or Bulukumba can remain part of the Indonesia Pancasila state while also employing laws based on sharia. This codification of sharia in the local regulation can also be understood as an expression of increased Islamic piety of the people in the regions, or what Saba Mahmood would term the politics of piety.[77]

There are two layers that can be used to look at the role of the MUI branch of Bulukumba. The first is from the perspective of the organisational role of MUI, and the second is from the perspective of the role of MUI individual actors such as its board members. The organisational role of the Bulukumba MUI district branch can be seen from the main tasks it implements. Like all MUI branches across Indonesia, the Bulukumba MUI branch is a fatwa giver and advisor on affairs of religion and morality to society and also the local government. The Bulukumba MUI branch can issue fatwas, responses, suggestions and recommendations to the people and the local government of Bulukumba. As the Bulukumba MUI does not have an official position as part of the local government, it is limited to providing advice. The vice chairman of this MUI branch, Tjamiruddin, states that Patabai Pabokori, when he was district head, always consulted with the branch to get ideas and concepts in order to draft *perda syariah*. MUI also often offered solutions for overcoming problems faced by the people of Bulukumba (1995–2005), for instance regarding the *zakāt* and Qurʾānic literacy.[78] Pabokori was very thankful for the support provided

73 Interview with Sanusi Baco, Makassar, 2011.

74 Ibid.

75 Sukron Kamil and Chaeder S. Bamualim, eds., *Syariah Islam Dan HAM, Dampak Perda Syariah Terhadap Kebebasan Sipil, Hak-Hak Perempuan, Dan Non-Muslim* (Jakarta: CSRC & Konrad Adenauer Stiftung, 2007), p. 134.

76 Asef Bayat, *Making Islam Democratic: Social Movements and the Post-Islamist Turn,* (Redwood City, CA: Stanford Univrsity Press, 2007).

77 Saba Mahmood, *Politics of Piety: The Islamic Revival and the Feminist Subject* (New Bruncswick, NJ: Princeton University Press, 2011).

78 Interview with Tjamiruddin, Bulukumba, 2011.

by MUI and therefore funded its activities, programmes and daily operational costs. Another MUI role was to consolidate the support of Muslim organisations such as NU and Muhammadiyah behind the local lawmakers of Bulukumba in legalising sharia bylaws.[79]

The role of MUI actors can be seen from the case of Tjamiruddin, General Chairman of the Bulukumba MUI branch, an important figure behind the implementation of *perda syariah* in this district. Like Pabokori, he stated that sharia law was needed to deal with the problems faced by the Bulukumba district. As a key MUI figure, Tjamiruddin was also asked by Pabokori to prepare the drafts of some *perda syariah*; in fact, Tjamiruddin admitted, he was directly involved in drafting four *perda syariah* legislated in Bulukumba. According to Tjamiruddin, the implementation of these *perda syariah* did not conflict with the national laws of Indonesia because the sharia bylaws are not legally binding. He states that there is no enforcement to obey the sharia bylaws, even for Muslims; they are only morally binding. Tjamiruddin gave the example of Perda No. 02/2003 (Management of Professional Zakat, Donation and Alms) whose subjects are Muslim civil servants and those able to donate, such as limited numbers of wealthy Muslims. Should they refuse to obey this regulation, a punishment is stipulated in theory. Yet in reality sharia bylaws are implemented in an ethical and moral sense, not in a legal one.

Although the Bulukumba MUI branch supports the adoption and implementation of sharia-inspired bylaws, it challenges excessive legalisation of sharia regulations. For instance, it rejected the idea promoted by KPPSI to apply Islamic criminal law. As the main Islamic organisation striving for total implementation of sharia law in South Sulawesi, the KPPSI is very influential in local government circles in Bulukumba. When governing this district, Pabokori was very close to the KPPSI and indeed the second Kongres Umat Islam (KUI/Islamic Community Congress)[80] was held in Bulukumba on 25 March 2005 following a personal guarantee from Pabokori. However, in the case of *ḥudūd* (fixed punishment for offence which has been determined in the Qur'ān and Sunna), MUI's position differed from that of KPPSI, an example of MUI's different stance from other such bodies that is sometimes overlooked by observers studying this institution. It is important to note that Pabokori followed the stance of MUI.

The role of MUI in the context of the Bulukumba sharia movement appears to be one of educating and advising on a model of sharia implementation compatible with national Indonesian law. The core concern of MUI is to balance

79 Interview with Patabai Pabokori, Makassar, 2011.

80 This Congress is different from the KUII organised by MUI.

between the implementation of sharia on the one hand and the values of *keindonesiaan* (being Indonesian) on the other. In this case, the Bulukumba MUI branch did not agree with those striving for the total adoption of sharia law in this district.[81] It tried to explain to the people of Bulukumba that the implementation of sharia bylaws did not mean that the district was becoming an Islamic state. After having legislated Perda No. 05/2003 on *berpakaian Muslim dan Muslimah* (appropriate Muslim clothing), for instance, some groups in Bulukumba said that Muslim women who did not wear *jilbāb* should be prevented from participating in the public sphere. On this matter, the Bulukumba MUI responded that the obligation to follow Muslim dress codes was not compulsory for Muslims because they did not live in an Islamic state. The Bulukumba MUI branch regards what has happened in society as a politicisation of *perda syariah*, mostly by those who promote the total implementation of sharia law in Bulukumba.

5.3.1 Perda Syariah *as Public Morality*

Many people claim that the establishment of sharia law in South Sulawesi was closely related to the founding of the KPPSI in Makassar, the capital. Yet this assumption does not totally hold true for Bulukumba, as the sharia movement here had begun long before KPPSI's establishment. The establishment of sharia law is mostly related to Bulukumba local politics, such as the strong ambition of local district leader Patabai Pabokori, the support of MUI and Muslim organisations such as NU and Muhammadiyah, and society in general. The legislation of sharia bylaws in Bulukumba began to proliferate from 1995 under Pabokori.

There are many interconnected social, cultural and political factors in this region that have led to the issuance of the *perda syariah*. However, the strongest argument used by the people of Bulukumba to enforce sharia bylaws was a decline in morality leading to an emergence of criminal elements. Pabokori said that Bulukumba at the time was backward, especially with regards to security, a high rate of criminality, many gambling houses, and various other matters destructive towards Bulukumba society. Pabokori mentioned that the root cause of all these social problems was the tradition of uncontrolled drunken behaviour in this district, with many cafes selling alcoholic drinks throughout the area.[82]

Another factor was the low level of Islamic education in that area. Bulukumba MUI Vice Chairman Tjamiruddin spoke of the high illiteracy

---

81 Interview with Sanusi Baco in Makassar and Tjamiruddin in Bulukumba, both 2011.

82 Interview with Patabai Pabokori, Makassar, 2011.

rate among Bulukumba Muslims with regard to recitation of the Qur'ān. This statement was supported by Pabokari who discovered from his own survey of local governmental offices and schools that around 20–30% of the local population was unable to recite the Qur'ān. Pabokori was also disappointed that pilgrims traveling to Mecca and Medina, from South Sulawesi in general and from Bulukumba in particular, were unable to recite the Qur'ān properly. As a Muslim, Pabokori was keen to ensure his people could live guided by Islamic morality and doctrine such as wearing the *ḥijāb* for female Muslims, studying the Qur'ān, paying religious alms and gifts, and so on. He thus felt obliged to revitalise the Islamic religiosity of the people of Bulukumba by supporting Islamic activities, such as the rehabilitation of the Remaja Masjid (Adolescent Mosque), TK (Taman Kanak-Kanak)/TPA (Taman Pendidikan Al-Qur'ān, Muslim Kindergarten/Childcare) and so on, allocating a specific budget to fund these programmes. Pabokori claimed that the primary intention of enacting sharia-inspired bylaws in Bulukumba was not to build an Islamic state but to decrease the high rate of criminality, robbery and juvenile delinquency. Another objective was to increase the piety of Bulukumba Muslim society. When asked by foreigners and journalists about his ambition to establish an Islamic state, Pabokori answered that he "had no thoughts about the Islamic state issue, but just wanted to implement the teachings of Islam."[83] As a Muslim leader, he felt obliged to do something because some of his people in Bulukumba were unable to recite the Qur'ān, female Muslims were not wearing the *ḥijāb* and most were not following their religion correctly. Pabokori invited Bulukumba community leaders to discuss the problems and, most of those attending the meeting agreed that one of the many possible solutions to these problems was to adopt sharia law.

In response, the Bulukumba district began to issue *perda syariah*, beginning with regulating morality through issuing sharia bylaws on public morality, with the argument that the Bulukumba community, whose population was almost 100% Muslim, would run well if they followed sharia. Although the solution proposed by district head Pabokori invited controversy, especially from local businessmen who felt their cafes and restaurants would be bankrupt, eventually the local regulations were issued. The discourse created by Pabokari, with the full support of Bulukumba MUI and other Muslim groups such NU, Muhammadiyah and KPPSI, was the dominant narrative. Those who rejected local regulations on public morality were afraid of being assumed to be against Islam and so kept silent because they did not want to be judged as enemies of religion. This was particularly due to the nature of the social

83 Ibid.

discourse developed by sharia propagators which tended to judge those critical of *perda syariah* or reluctant to implement them as liberal and secular.

What was done by district head Pabokori did not reflect a proper understanding of the state law on decentralisation (regional autonomy) because it is clear that under this law religion is a domain that should be handled by the central government in Jakarta. Pabokori positioned himself as the representative of the (Muslim) majority in Bulukumba desiring sharia. In addition, a claim that non-Muslims also supported the implementation of *perda syariah* was also circulated. When asked, "How can a district head have a different legal opinion from the state law?" Pabokori replied that while it was true that the state laws on regional autonomy (1999 and 2004) prohibit regional governments—provincial and district—from regulating religious matters, he did not consider his enacted *perda* to be religious. The MUI and local legislators agreed because they saw that this is what the people of Bulukumba desired.

There were four sharia-inspired bylaws issued. The first was Perda No. 03/2002 on Larangan, Pengawasan, Penertiban dan Penjualan Minuman Beralkohol (Banning, Supervision, Control and Sale of Alcoholic Drinks). The second was Perda No. 02/2003 on Pengelolaan Zakat, Profesi, Infak dan Sedekah (Management of Professional *Zakāt*, Alms and Donations). The third was Perda No.05/2003 on Berpakaian Muslim dan Muslimah (Male and Female Muslim Dress Codes) and the fourth was Perda No. 06/2003 on Pandai Baca al-Qur'ān Bagi Siswa dan Calon Pengantin (Mandatory Qur'ān Reading Skills for Students and Prospective Married Couples). In order not to conflict with Act No. 32/2004, these four local regulations, even though they were focused on religion, were not called *perda syariah*, but "*Perda* Crash Programme". Pabokori termed them *Perda Amar Maʿruf* (commanding right and forbidding wrong) (local regulation on commanding right).[84] The naming convention was to circumvent Act No. 32/2004, which prohibits *perda* that govern religion. Although the *perda* were not issued at the same time, they aimed to respond to the multi-dimensional crisis of the Bulukumba district.

Perda No. 03/2002 on Banning, Supervision, Control and Sale Alcoholic Drinks was issued first because the most urgent problem facing this region was uncontrolled alcohol consumption. The root cause of the social crisis that had led to many conflicts, crimes, and deaths was too much alcohol. Alcoholic drinks were easily found in cafés and restaurants. The District Head of Bulukumba thought that to eliminate various crimes the best start was to remove their source, i.e. alcoholic drinks,[85] and claimed that the

84 Interview with Patabai Pabokori, Makassar, 2011.

85 Ibid.

implementation of the *perda* was a success, dramatically reducing the crime rate by 80%. Sharia propagators in other regions tried to capitalise on this success as a role model for sharia implementation in their own regions, and tried to persuade their communities with the example of Bulukumba. One reader of Hidayatullah, for example, wrote to the news platform about the success of *perda syariah* in Bulukumba:

> Some regions that have adopted *Perda Syariah* show evidence of significant change, creating public good (*maslaha*) in society. This *maslaha* has an impact on both Muslims and non-Muslims in Bulukumba. The rise of *Perda Syariah* indicates the need for sharia as a means of social order. There is increasing awareness in Muslim society that sharia is the remedy for all problems that they face in everyday life. Implementing sharia is an obligation for all Muslims. The true Muslim will not deny the law of the Qur'an.[86]

There are many who agree with this perspective. Pabokori himself has received compliments from many people about his sharia initiative. In addition, he admits that during his administration in Bulukumba he had many guests from different districts asking for his prescription in successfully implementing the sharia drafting process into local regulations.

Perda No. 02/2003 on "Management of Profession Zakat, Donation and Alms" was issued as a legal umbrella for fund-raising to support Islamic projects that became prioritised programmes of the Bulukumba local government. Tjamiruddin claims that he had been consulted over the draft *perda* before the legislation was approved.[87] The local government claimed that the number of those paying Islamic alms, gift and donations significantly increased as a result of the perda. Twelve villages in Bulukumba were set up under the pilot project of this programme. Contributions collected from the fund-raising were allocated to pay for the operational costs of Islamic kindergartens, BKPRMI (local mosque organisations) and many other projects. The *perda* further benefitted from a decree issued by the Director General of Tax in Jakarta that allows the deduction of up to 2.5% of a person's gross income for *zakāt* payment. With this new ruling, the Bulukumba local government could subtract 2.5% from

---

86 "Ada Masalah Apa dengan Perda Syariah, Hingga Banyak yang Paranoid?", *Hidayatullah*, 18 June 2012, https://hidayatullah.com/redaksi/surat-pembaca/read/2012/06/18/1439/ada-masalah-apa-dengan-perda-syariah-hingga-banyak-yang-paranoid.html, viewed on 26 July 2022.

87 Interview with Patabai Pabokori, Makassar, 2011.

the wages of its staff as *zakāt* to be given to the Badan Amal Zakat (BAZ, Local *Zakāt* Administrator).[88] The money collected for *zakāt*, alms to be distributed for the poor, was also distributed to fund Lasykar Jundullah (literally "soldiers of God") many of whom were recruited from local petty criminals and thugs. The money was an incentive for them to move from crime to supporting the district of Bulukumba in promoting sharia bylaws.

Perda No. 05/2003 was on Male and Female Muslim Dress Codes. This *perda* regulates the wearing of a *jilbāb* (the veil or *ḥijāb*) by female local bureaucrats and the people of Bulukumba in general. Pabokori stated in an interview that he had no preference about the style of veil or concern about the various fashionable and trendy models of veils, provided that it covered that part of the body that should be covered (Indonesian: *aurat*).[89] The implementation of this local sharia bylaw was spearheaded by Pabokori's relatives, especially his wife and then, senior officials in the Bulukumba district. Pabokori said:

> [Y]ou imagine, when the wife of the District Head wears a *sanggul* (Javanese-style bun), all the wives of the sub-district leaders and high officials will want to do the same as the as the wife of their leader. Wearing a *sanggul* is very costly because the wives must go to the beauty salon to get prepared. The husbands' salaries will run out because their wives are always at the beauty salon. When their money runs out, it causes tension. In promoting the wearing of *jilbāb*, I always keep *jilbāb* in my car. When I visit some regions where I find many women do not wear *jilbāb*, I give them one, or 25 thousand Indonesian rupiah to purchase one. This is my way of promoting the idea of wearing *jilbāb*.[90]

Pabokori then went on to promote the wearing of *jilbāb* in state schools and also the private sector and the Bulukumba bureaucracy. Pabokori's actions in this regard indicate that his understanding of Islam is very formalistic and scriptural. He is unaware that the Islamic discourse on wearing the veil is rich and varies from one school of Islamic thought to another. Pabokori, apparently, has not followed the national discourse on *jilbāb* in Indonesia, as introduced by Quraish Shihab (a leading Indonesian Muslim scholar on Qur'ānic exegesis) and Madjid, that wearing the veil is not compulsory in Islam.[91] Pabokori's view

88 Buehler, "The Rise of Sharia Bylaws in Indonesian Districts: An Indication for Changing Patterns of Power Accumulation and Political Corruption", p. 265.

89 Interview with Patabai Pabokori, Makassar, 2011.

90 Ibid.

91 Ahmad Gaus, *Api Islam Nurcholish Madjid: Jalan Hidup Seorang Visioner* (Jakarta: Penerbit Buku Kompas, 2010), p. 191; Moh. Quraish Shihab, *Jilbab, Pakaian Wanita Muslimah: Pandangan Ulama Masa Lalu & Cendekiawan Kontemporer* (Jakarta: Lentera Hati, 2004).

is closer to what the Salafi group believes, as he considers wearing *jilbāb* to be an Islamic obligation. He claimed the success in implementing the *perda* was due to two grounds: first, it reduced the cost of living for men and women, and second, it was good for health because women's skin and hair were covered from direct sunlight.[92] This policy enjoyed a greater reception in Bulukumba because of the support given by local Islamic organisations such as MUI, NU and Muhammadiyah.

The last local regulation successfully legislated in Pabokori's era was Perda No. 06/2003 on Mandatory Qur'ān Reading Skills. This *perda* was intended to raise awareness among Bulukumba Muslims on the importance of being able to recite, understand and then practise the teachings of the Qur'ān. It was estimated that those unable to recite the Qur'ān in this district numbered around 20% (72,252) of the total population (360,126). Apart from the relatively low level of Qur'ān literacy among Bulukumba residents, the *perda* was inspired by the personal experience of Pabokori on the pilgrimage to Mecca and Medina. He saw many people from his district remaining silent in *ḥaramān* (Mecca and Medina) because they could not recite the Qur'ān. This situation was distressing for him because the *ḥajj* or pilgrimage should be the best moment to worship God, and the best worship is to recite the Qur'ān.[93] This *perda* covers more activities than the three previous *perda syariah*; hundreds of Islamic kindergartens were built by the local government at the district and sub-district level, with full support from the annual regional budget (APBD) of Bulukumba. The Bulukumba district claimed that this programme successfully reduced Qur'ānic illiteracy to 5.5%.

However, in response to many public speculations regarding the rapid approval of sharia bylaws in the regency of Bulukumba that extended beyond public morality, Patabai Pabokori stated that he would never apply the provision of the Islamic *ḥudūd* law of cutting off the hands of thieves. Tjamiruddin, Vice Deputy of the Bulukumba MUI, also did not agree with the application of the *ḥudūd* law, saying that their goal was simply to cut crime and create social order and peace.

In the post-Pabokori era, the shariatisation of Bulukumba has become more intensive with a more extensive resonance both inside and outside the province. The village of Padang, for example, tried to enact the *ḥudūd* law for their community.[94] When I tried to confirm this case with the Bulukumba

92 Interview with Patabai Pabokori, Makassar, 2011.

93 Ibid.

94 "Gelora Syariah Mengepung Kota," Gatra, 1 May 2006, http://arsip.gatra.com//artikel.php?id=94078, viewed on 21 July 2022.

government bureaucracy, they did not deny the case but said that the application of *ḥudūd* law in that village was not done seriously. In addition, they said it was illegal because it was an extra-legal jurisdiction; the *kepala kampong* (village head) did not have the legal authority to implement the law.[95] Tjamiruddin said that MUI agreed with the application of sharia law, but disagreed with the application of *ḥudūd* law in that village. Application of the Islamic law of *ḥudūd* is, firstly, not simple, and secondly, sharia bylaws should be framed within the construction of nation-state law.[96]

In short, it suffices to say that the implementation of sharia bylaws in Bulukumba will remain contested among different groups in the future of this region. Sharia bylaws are coloured by the nuance of local politics, such as the local elections, parliamentary elections and so on. Sharia bylaws are often used for political commodification. This was evident in how candidates for the positions of Bulukumba major used the issue of sharia bylaws as the main issue in their campaigns. Here, the Bulukumba MUI will still play an important role because sharia bylaws activity needs Islamic legitimacy and the MUI branch is delivering that promise. It seems that entanglement between local elite politics and religious institution is an important issue in the sharia bylaws of Bulukumba.

5.4 Cianjur, West Java

West Java is an Indonesian province with a long history of Islamic rebellions.[97] The establishment of the West Java provincial MUI cannot be separated from this history of Islamic separatist movements initiated by Darul Islam/Tentara Islam Indonesia (DI, Abode of Islam/TII, Indonesia's Islamic Armed Forces) in the region.[98] Some ulama in the province had been concerned about the impact of the rebel Islamic movements on the unity of the ulama, and the

95 Interview with Muhammad Ali Saleng (Head of Legal Bureau of Bulukumba district), Bulukumba, 2011.

96 Interview with Patabai Pabokori, Makassar, 2011.

97 Islamic rebellions also occurred in Aceh, Makassar, Maluku and other places.

98 For more details on DI/TII in West Java see Chiara Formichi, *Islam and the Making of the Nation: Kartosuwiryo and Political Islam in Twentieth-Century Indonesia* (Leiden: KITLV Press, 2012); Amelia Fauzi, "Darul Islam Movement (DI), Struggling for an Islamic State of Indonesia," in *Southeast Asia Historical Encyclopedia, From Angkor Wat to East Timor*. ABC-CLIO; C. Van Dijk, *Rebellion Under the Banner of Islam: The Darul Islam in Indonesia* (The Hague: Martinus Nijhoff, 1981).

ulama in West Java were experiencing difficulties in undertaking *daʿwa* activities because they were facing intimidation at the hands of the state as well as rebel groups. Thus in 1956 the ulama of West Java began to communicate with the Indonesian military about overcoming this problem. In 1957, they organised a meeting in Tasikmalaya, a district of West Java, with the Indonesian military's second regiment, based in West Java. The meeting resulted in an agreement to set up the Badan Musyawarah Alim Ulama (BMAU, Ulama Advisory Body). Local informant Hafidz Ustman claimed that the West Javanese institution could be understood as a local embryo of the national MUI that was established around twenty years later, in 1975.[99] A similar claim was also made by Acehnese ulama, who have stated that MUI was modelled on their own ulama organisation.

This section focuses on the MUI branch of Cianjur, a very important district in West Java that played a role in the implementation of sharia-inspired bylaws. Although the Cianjur MUI branch is not the sole actor promoting the adoption of sharia law in this region, as an Islamic fatwa council at the district level it has played an important role in influencing the process of local policy. Historically speaking, Muslim people in this district claim that the application of sharia law in Cianjur began in the fifteenth century CE.[100]

Based on my observations, the public discourse on the emergence of sharia-based regulation in West Java as a province over the last decade is more related to the local history of this region, a fertile soil for shariatisation. H. Chep Hermawan, who claims to be a representative of Cianjur MUI and coordinator of local Islamic organisation GARIS (Gerakan Reformis Islam, Islamic Reformist Movement) states that by supporting the implementation of sharia in West Java he is striving to ensure the continuation of the legacy of Kartosuwiryo, the leader of the Darul Islam rebellion in West Java.[101] The late Hafidz Ustman, former chairman of the West Javanese provincial MUI, states:

99 The historical influences on the establishment of the national MUI are still being contested. Acehnese ulama say that the establishment of the national MUI was influenced by the Aceh ulama organisation, while the ulama of West Java claim that their region was the main influence. Interview with Muslim Ibrahim, Banda Aceh, 2011, and interview with Hafidz Utsman, Jakarta, 2011.

100 Rohmat Suprapto, *Syariat "Kacapi Suling" & Syariat Progresif* (*Pergulatan Politik Dan Hukum Di Era Otonomi Daerah*) (Yogyakarta: Samudera Biru, 2001), p. 69.

101 Formichi, *Islam and the Making of the Nation: Kartosuwiryo and Political Islam in Twentieth-Century Indonesia*, 2012.

> [I]n general, the Muslim community in West Java is very religious in comparison to the Muslim community in Central Java. Since the reform era, their awareness of the application of sharia law has significantly increased. Their involvement in efforts to adapt state laws to religion is also increasing. The most striking issue is the increased control of the distribution of alcoholic drinks, and also controls on gambling in society.[102]

Although shariatisation tensions in West Java are relatively high, the West Java MUI claims that its Muslim community in general is very tolerant and open-minded towards other religious groups. This statement was issued by the West Javanese provincial MUI in response to the criticisms of several NGOs that Muslim tolerance in the region had dramatically decreased since some regencies drafted sharia bylaws. The Setara Institute for Democracy and Peace, an NGO working on the issue of religious pluralism, announced that there were thirty-three violations of religious freedom in 2007, seventy-three in 2008, fifty-seven in 2009, ninety-one in 2010, fifty-seven in 2011, and seventy-six in 2012. The Setara Institute of West Java thus ranked the local government as the most intolerant of all the provinces of Indonesia in the period 2008 to 2012.[103] In response, the West Java MUI stated that non-Muslims are also breaking regulations in establishing places of worship in West Java without a proper permit.[104] In relation to religious freedom in this province, the West Java MUI has always positioned itself as the guardian of Muslim society and the provincial government of West Java, especially since the appointment of a governor from the PKS in 2008, who is also very supportive of the implementation of sharia bylaws. The popularity of Governor Ahmad Heryawan among Islamic groups is high due to his commitment to fighting "non-sharia attitudes" in West Java. He clearly agrees with the Ahmadiyah being pronounced a deviant sect, stating that "the principal teaching of Ahmadiyah is against the teaching of Islam."[105] This was an inappropriate statement to make in his

102 Interview with Hafidz Utsman, Jakarta, 2011.

103 "Jawa Barat 'Juara' Kasus Intoleransi Di Indonesia," *Detik News*, 16 November 2012, https://news.detik.com/berita-jawa-barat/d-2092833/jawa-barat-juara-kasus-intoleransi-di-indonesia, viewed on 22 July 2022.

104 "MUI Jabar: Umat Islam Di Jawa Barat Sangat Toleran Dalam Beragama," Arrahmah, 24 December 2010, https://www.arrahmah.id/2010/12/24/mui-jabar-umat-islam-di-jawa-barat-sangat-toleran-dalam-beragama/, viewed on 22 July 2022.

105 "Aher: Ajaran Ahmadiyah Itu Melanggar Dan Timbulkan Perselisihan," *Era Muslim*, 7 May 2013, https://www.eramuslim.com/berita/nasional/aher-ajaran-ahmadiyah-itu-melanggar-dan-timbulkan-perselisihan.htm, viewed on 22 July 2022.

official position as Governor of West Java. His comment is against the neutral principle of Indonesian law, and contradicts the religious freedom stipulated by the Constitution, since it encourages the average Muslim in West Java to see his contentious views as normal.

The role of the West Java provincial MUI is somewhat different from that of Aceh. Unlike MUI's official connection with the local government in Aceh, their position in West Java is as an informal advisor on Muslim affairs and morality, both for the local government and society. Nevertheless, politically and socially the West Java MUI is considered important by both the provincial government and its people. It is a place to seek consultation on Islamic issues, for example those who want to open sharia banks must obtain permission from the MUI National Sharia Board.[106]

The West Java MUI has many branches that are spread throughout the twenty-six districts of this region. Of this total, the branches that support the implementation of sharia-inspired bylaws are the MUI branches of Cianjur, Tasikmalaya, and Garut. It is not easy to establish the connection between the support for shariatisation in these three districts, but historically speaking they were the Darul Islam/Tentara Islam Indonesia movement's heartlands.[107] However, the DI/TII and the more recent sharia bylaws are two very different means of struggling for sharia in society. Shariatisation takes advantage of the weakness of state regulations on decentralisation, while the DI/TII used violence to fight against the legitimate government of Indonesia. It would nevertheless appear that the sharia bylaw movement has been inspired by past Islamic rebel movements in West Java, although this needs further research.

The MUI Cianjur branch's active engagement in the implementation of sharia-inspired bylaws in Cianjur can be seen from its role in the initial process of the sharia movement. Under the leadership of Abdul Halim, the MUI branch of Cianjur has tried to become a representative for many other local Muslim organisations. Abdul Halim states that the Cianjur MUI has a very clear role: to support the needs of the Muslim community in drafting sharia bylaws. He says:

> Considering the recent situation in Indonesia, what we want to struggle for are the rights of Muslims in applying their sharia law. In doing so, Indonesian Muslims can propose the inclusion of sharia into state law at the national level and draft sharia bylaws at the district level.

106 Interview with Hafidz Utsman, Jakarta, 2011.

107 van Dijk, *Rebellion Under the Banner of Islam*; Formichi, *Islam and the Making of the Nation*.

> At the national level, we (MUI) have been successful in mobilising one million people to demand the lawmakers of Indonesia pass the [anti-]pornography law.[108]

A more concrete role of the Cianjur MUI is to compile and accommodate the aspirations of ulama groups who have struggled for the issuance of sharia-inspired bylaws. For this purpose, the MUI branch of Cianjur organised a large-scale gathering together with other local Muslim organisations at the Masjid Agung Cianjur (the Grand Mosque of Cianjur) on 1 Muḥarram 2000 (the first month of the Islamic calendar) to discuss sharia problems faced by Muslims in the region. There were forty Cianjur Islamic organisations that participated in a successful public campaign on the implementation of sharia bylaws in this district, led by MUI. The results of the meeting were read before the head of the Cianjur district. This gathering can be understood as an early step towards enforcing sharia-inspired bylaws in this region. As a result of this meeting, mainstream Muslim groups demanded the district of Cianjur include the implementation of Islamic sharia into the official programme of the local government as almost 99% of the Cianjur population are Muslims. Halim argued this majority was significant for the implementation of the programme of sharia law.[109] One year later, MUI—together with another thirty-five Muslim organisations and NGOs in Cianjur—took the initiative to declare the implementation of sharia law on 26 March 2001, or 1 Muharram 1422 AH,[110] using the occasion of the Islamic New Year to symbolise the rebirth of Islam. A joint pledge (Indonesian: *ikrar bersama*) was declared at that time, organised by MUI and the Muslim community of Cianjur. The pledge declared that:

> First, sharia is the way of life for human beings to achieve prosperity, security, justice and peace here on earth and in the hereafter as well as ensuring Cianjur becomes a healthy region, blessed by God; second, the implementation of sharia law is needed in society and the state in a gradual, constitutional, and harmonious manner, in accordance with the legacy of the prophet Muḥammad in the framework of NKRI; third, the policy makers of the Cianjur local government, especially the parliament,

108 Interview with Abdul Halim, Cianjur, 2010.

109 MUI Kabupaten Cianjur, *30 Tahun MUI Cianjur: Selayang Pandang Perjalanan Panjang MUI Cianjur* (Cianjur: Majelis Ulama Indonesia (MUI) Kabupaten Cianjur, 2009), p. 38.

110 Ibid, p.39.

> must accept, study, develop, receive and implement societal and state life based on Islamic norms in order to establish Cianjur as "*Sugih Mukti Tur Islam*" (rich, respected, and Islamic).[111]

Local actors who were expected to act on the *Ikrar Bersama* were the local *umarā'* (governing body at the district level of Cianjur), MUI, and the Muslim community of Cianjur. The government was recommended to increase the annual regional budget allocated for Islamic religious affairs. MUI, particularly Abdul Halim, the Cianjur MUI Chairman and his staff were asked to increase *daʿwa* activities. While the Muslim community was asked to establish the Majelis Ukhuwah Umat Islam (MUUI, Council of Muslim Community Solidarity) and Silaturahmi dan Musyawarah Umat Islam (SILMUI, Solidarity Meeting for Muslim Community), it is important to add that the joint pledge was signed by Halim, indicating the strong role played the Cianjur MUI branch in influencing the emergence of sharia-inspired bylaws.

5.4.1 Perda Akhlakul Karimah[112]

One of the concrete actions taken in response to the recommendations above was the publication of District Head Decree No. 36/2001. Wasidi Swastomo, the District Head of Cianjur from 2001–2006, signed this decree after having consulted with the Cianjur MUI branch. The decree orders the establishment of Lembaga Pengkajian dan Pengembangan Islam (LPPI, Institute for the Study and Development of Islam). Many people claim that the decree can be considered as the first legal source of drafting sharia bylaws in Cianjur.

The main tasks of the LPPI are to produce the basic format of sharia law implementation in the district of Cianjur, to prepare a strategic plan on the empowerment of the Islamic education system and economy, to intensify *daʿwa* activities, to compile data and research on the understanding and implementation of sharia law, and to produce publications and promote LPPI activities.[113] What is meant by the basic format of sharia implementation here is the general profile of what should be achieved in the first decade from 2001–2011. The LPPI successfully produced a concept for applying

111 Suprapto, *Syariat "Kacapi Suling" & Syariat Progresif (Pergulatan Politik Dan Hukum Di Era Otonomi Daerah)*, pp. 69–70.

112 *Akhlakul Karimah* is an Indonesian term adopted from the Arabic, *al-akhlāq al-karīma* meaning Islamic ethics or morality.

113 MUI Kabupaten Cianjur, *30 Tahun MUI Cianjur: Selayang Pandang Perjalanan Panjang MUI Cianjur*, p. 40.

sharia-inspired bylaws, referred to as the *Gerbang Marhamah*, an acronym from "*Gerakan Pembangunan Masyarakat Berakhlakul Karimah*" (Movement for the Development of a Moral Society). The *Gerbang Marhamah* is a strategic plan targeting the establishment of sharia-inspired bylaws over a ten-year period (2001–2011).

In order to more effectively promote the unity of Muslim society in support of the implementation of *Gerbang Marhamah*, it was finally decided to establish the MUUI (Majelis Ukhuwah Umat Islam, the Council of Muslim Community Solidarity) on the occasion of the SILMUI on 26 March 2003. In 2005, the second SILMUI was organised which produced several recommendations addressed to the following groups. Firstly, all Muslim communities in Cianjur were advised to start implementing sharia law in their daily life. Secondly, the local government of Cianjur was asked to respond to, support, facilitate and follow up the recommendations published on the importance of the Cianjur government issuing *perda* on the *Programme Pelaksanaan Akhlakul Karimah* (Programme to Implement Morality). In order to speed up this process, it was recommended that the local government set up a Badan Penggerak Akhlakul Karimah (Body for Moral Motivation) or change and improve the task of the LPPI. The recommendations also mentioned that the Cianjur district head and local parliament should serve as the locomotive for this movement. Thirdly, Muslim organisations in Cianjur were asked to remain solidly united in fostering the implementation of sharia law.[114]

In 2006, the district of Cianjur issued Perda No. 04/2006 on Islamic Ethics (Indonesian-Arabic: *akhlakul karimah*), aimed at the inclusion of Islamic ethics into the local daily laws of this regency. The process of issuing the *perda syariah* took five years after the celebration of *Gerbang Marhamah*, under the constant influence of MUI and other Muslim groups. This local regulation represents an adoption of the strategic plan of *Gerbang Marhamah*. In response to the launch of this regulation, the people of Cianjur were divided into two groups. MUI and its allies enthusiastically supported the *perda*, while secular and nationalist groups argued that it contradicted Indonesian's mainstream ideology. The latter group argued that the publication of Perda No. 03/2006 contained a hidden agenda for shariatising Indonesia at the regional level. From the MUI perspective, the *perda syariah* should be understood as guidance for the local government of Cianjur in developing rulings and policies. Halim stated that the programmes of the district should be aimed at

114 MUI Kabupaten Cianjur, *30 Tahun MUI Cianjur: Selayang Pandang Perjalanan Panjang MUI Cianjur*, p. 42.

preventing anything opposed to or challenging the content of the *perda*.[115] He intended the *perda* on morality to become an umbrella for other regional laws of Cianjur, and saw it as an ideal model for implementing sharia in the local context of Cianjur.[116] He views Islamic governance as enabling the morality of individual Muslims to contribute to the formation of social and political order. Thus, if the Cianjur local government were able to enforce this regulation, he believed that sharia would be automatically implemented. Furthermore, as a local regulation, Perda No. 03/2006 legally binds all citizens of Cianjur, including non-Muslims, to comply with the content of the law. This can be seen in Chapter III, Article 3, which states that all those living in Cianjur are obliged to adhere to this law in their daily lives.

Although the *perda* was successfully enacted, this did not mean that it was well implemented. This can be seen by the lack of activities following its issuance; there have been almost no meaningful movements to support the enforcement of public morality. The local Cianjur government, for instance, has not developed any clear policies and programmes to ensure its implementation. Furthermore Tjetjep, the new Cianjur District Head, has renamed Swastomo's legacy, *Gerbang Marhamah,* as *Cerdik Marhamah*, with an emphasis towards increasing the quality and quantity of education.[117] Although proponents of sharia bylaw movements in this regency criticised the change, the *Perda Cerdik Marhamah* seems to be more realistic and promising. Under this programme, staff with a good understanding of the delicate aspects of sharia implementation can be better prepared.

Furthermore, it seems that the application of this bylaw in Cianjur has not improved law and order in the district, although there have been many sharia operations such as raids on alcohol vendors and areas of prostitution. Action against the Ahmadiyah group in this district usually refers to the fatwa from MUI headquarters, not to the *perda*.

5.4.2 Jilbabisasi, Aliran Sesat *and* Gerakan Pemurtadan

As happened in the district of Bulukumba, the visibility of sharia bylaws in Cianjur began to intensify after the publication of Circular Decree No. 551/2717/ASSDA.1/9/2001 on "*Gerakan Aparatur Berakhlakul Karimah dan Masyarakat Marhamah*" (Movement for Good State Bureaucracy and Blessed Society). This decree was followed by the publication of Circular Decree No. 061/2896/Org

115 Ibid, p. 50.

116 Interview with Abdul Halim (Chairman of Cianjur MUI), Cianjur, 2010.

117 Suprapto, *Syariat "Kacapi Suling" & Syariat Progresif (Pergulatan Politik Dan Hukum Di Era Otonomi Daerah)*, p. 144.

regulating the weekday uniforms for female and male Cianjur regional government staff,[118] which obliged Muslim bureaucrats to follow a Muslim dress code. Women were obliged to wear the *jilbāb* and men a *baju koko* (a collarless shirt adopted from China).[119] Although the circular decree applied to both men and women, it was more noticeably applied to women's attire and was thus referred to by the term *jilbabisasi* (Indonesian expression for the *jilbāb* movement). The theological reasoning behind the operation of this decree is based on the strong belief among ordinary Muslims that the bodies of women can easily incite social immorality. On this basis, schoolgirls are obliged to wear *jilbāb* even if they are non-Muslims.

The enforcement of *jilbāb*-wearing in Cianjur has sparked criticism from women activists who reject the policy for its increasing marginalisation of women as independent human beings in the public sphere.[120] Another issue raised is that *jilbabisasi* has been used by local political actors as a bargaining tool. If local politicians want to succeed in electorate politics, either as district head or local legislator, *jilbabisasi* is a very good platform for Muslim voters. However, for those female Muslims who support this policy, *jilbabisasi* is a sharia obligation that protects the Muslim public from the danger of immorality. This latter viewpoint is held by MUI and many local Islamic organisations in Cianjur.

Abdul Halim, the Cianjur MUI Chairman, also reveals that *aliran sesat sesat* (deviant Islamic groups) is the issue that most concerns the Cianjur MUI. This follows the fatwa from MUI Jakarta on the activities of deviant groups in the regency.[121] Cianjur was a fertile soil for the development of Jamaah Ahmadiyah Indonesia (JAI, Indonesian Ahmadiyah Congregation). In 2011, as a result of MUI pressure, the Cianjur local government closed down the operation of the Ahmadiyah mosque. Abdul Halim and Cecep Hermawan, a coordinator of

---

118 Sri Wiyanti Eddyono, "Politicization of Islam During the Democratic Transition: New Challenges for the Indonesian Women's Movement," Jakarta: SCN-CREST, 2010.

119 Euis Nurlaelawati, "Sharia Bylaws: The Legal Position of Women in Children and Women in Banten and West Java," in *Regime Change, Democracy and Islam: The Case of Indonesia*, ed. C. Van Dijk (Leiden, 2013), 11–81, pp. 48–9; Dewi Candraningrum, "Unquestioned Gender Lens in Contemporary Indonesian Sharīʿa Ordinances (Perda Syari'ah)," *Al-Jāmiʿah* 45, no. 2 (2007): 290–320.

120 "'Aku Ingin Lari Jauh' Ketidakadilan Aturan Berpakaian Bagi Perempuan Di Indonesia," Human Rights Watch, 2021, https://www.hrw.org/sites/default/files/media_2021/03/indonesia0321_bahasa_0.pdf, viewed on 22 July 2022.

121 "MUI Cianjur Minta Ahmadiyah Keluar Dari Islam," *Antara News*, 21 February 2011, https://www.antaranews.com/berita/246914/mui-cianjur-minta-ahmadiyah-keluar-dari-islam, viewed on 22 July 2022.

GARIS, witnessed the closing of the mosque by the Cianjur local government.[122] In 2012, two hundred people from the Sunnī majority of Cianjur burnt down the Ahmadiyah mosque, Nur Hidayah, located in the sub-district of Cisaat, Cianjur, claiming that the Ahmadiyah had not kept their promise not to use it as a place of worship.[123] The Sunnī group were angry that the Ahmadiyah were still using the mosque to perform Friday prayers. This was perceived as a violation of the Joint Decree of Three Ministries—the Ministry of Home Affairs, Ministry of Religious Affairs and General Attorney—in June 2008 ordering the Ahmadiyah to stop their activities.[124] However, Firmanysah, the head of the Ahmadiyah youth organisation, claimed the closure of the mosque was not official as it lacked a letter of authority from the Cianjur local government.

In 2013, two Ahmadiyah Cianjur Islamic schools or *madrasa* and three mosques were closed down, with arguments based on the content of the Joint Decree on Ahmadiyah; such arguments had also been used by MUI and allied groups in previous years at the national level to stop the activities of the Ahmadis. The three mosques closed were al-Ghafur (the Ahmadiyah mosque of Ciparay), Baitun Nasir (the Ahmadiyah mosque of Neglasari) and al-Mahmud, the Ahmadiyah mosque of Cicakra). The central role of the Cianjur MUI in closing the Ahmadiyah can be seen from observing the actions of H. Cepi, a representative of MUI in Cipanas, a sub-district of Cianjur. It was reported by local media that H. Cepi led the anti-Ahmadiyah group:

> At 18.00, around 300 people arrived at al-Mahmud, Cicakra, slightly fewer than the crowd that had originally gathered, some having left. Dedi Supriyadi, from the local Campaka Police Station, Rudi, an intelligence officer from the Campaka Police Station, H. Chep from Cipanas MUI and 20 FPI members stepped into the yard of the mosque. H. Cepi was seen opening the door of the mosque and one of the FPI members turned off the lights. One of them had brought a board to be nailed across the mosque doors. The Ahmadiyah tried to ask the FPI for a letter of authority

122 "Muspida Cianjur Tutup Tempat Ibadah Ahmadiyah," *Hidayatullah*, 2 March 2011, https://hidayatullah.com/berita/nasional/read/2011/03/02/46788/muspida-cianjur-tutup-tempat-ibadah-ahmadiyah.html, viewed on 22 July 2022.

123 "Massa Rusak Tempat Ibadah Ahmadiyah Di Cianjur," *Republika*, 17 February 2012, https://www.republika.co.id/berita/lzizfl/massa-rusak-tempat-ibadah-ahmadiyah-di-cianjur, viewed on 22 July 2022.

124 "Serangan Masjid Ahmadiyah Di Cianjur," *BBC News*, 17 February 2012, https://www.bbc.com/indonesia/berita_indonesia/2012/02/120217_ahmadiyah, viewed on 22 July 2022.

> but they responded "Don't ask us for a letter of authority. Your question will stimulate the crowd's anger. This is a mandate from Allah." Finally, the FPI members sealed the two mosques and one Islamic school shut.[125]

H. Chep's involvement signals the strong role played by MUI in regulating deviant groups in the regency. Besides Ahmadiyah, other local so-called *aliran sesat* causing concern to the Cianjur MUI were some local Ṣūfī orders in the district. MUI so far has categorised eighteen local Ṣūfī orders and groups as *sesat*. One such group is called Islam Bai'at. The heresy of this group is a doctrine that obliges all followers to proclaim their *shahāda* before the leader of the group, a practice which according to the Cianjur MUI is not valid in Islam.[126] Besides Islam Bai'at, the Cianjur MUI banned Di Bawah Naungan Wahyu (In the Shadow of God's Revelation), a group led by Fianes Eddy Wongso Dimejo who has proclaimed himself to be the next prophet after Muḥammad. In addition to these two examples, the Cianjur MUI also opposes the presence of those *aliran sesat* already denounced by the MUI fatwa in Jakarta as the LDII, Lea Eden, and many others.

As can be seen in the above description of the closing down of the Ahmadiyah mosques and the banning of other deviant sects, the local bureaucracy and police are also involved, besides MUI and Islamic organisations. Furthermore, based on the attacks and raids of the Ahmadiyah in Cianjur, it would appear that the state bureaucracy and law enforcement are always on the side of those against the Ahmadiyah. The Joint Decree on Ahmadiyah never recommended the destruction of Ahmadiyah property, merely limiting the propagandising activities of this group in the public sphere. The Joint Decree still entitles the Ahmadiyah to perform their rituals in their own mosques. Yet anti-Ahmadiyah sentiments in Cianjur and elsewhere are often articulated by MUI and FPI in the form of closing down or even destroying Ahmadiyah property whilst the state bureaucracy and police remain silent. A similar treatment also applies to other *aliran sesat*. Their right to religious freedom is protected by the Indonesian Constitution, but in reality the law enforcement agencies do not act to protect this right. Thus it is clear that the religious authority that rests in the hands of MUI and other local Islamic organisations has a stronger

125 A full account of the closing down of the three mosques can be found at "Inilah Kronologis Pemasangan Palang Kayu Di Tiga Masjid Ahmadiyah Di Cianjur," *KBR*, 21 July 2013, https://kbr.id/nusantara/07-2013/inilah_kronologis_pemasangan_palang_kayu_di_tiga_masjid_ahmadiyah_di_cianjur/55131.html, viewed on 22 July 2022.

126 "Aliran Islam Bai'at Muncul Di Cianjur," *Tempo*, 15 September 2012, https://nasional.tempo.co/read/429647/aliran-islam-baiat-muncul-di-cianjur, viewed on 22 July 2022.

power to maintain social order than the police or other local state bureaucracy. This also indicates the strong power of sharia bylaws in the region.

Besides their occupation with *jilbabisasi* and *aliran sesat*, the Cianjur MUI and other Islamic organisations in the district are involved in a deep struggle for denouncing "*gerakan pemurtadan*" (apostasy) in the district.[127] The Vatican and American Evangelists are accused by MUI and Islamic groups as the main actors behind *gerakan pemurtadan*, particularly in Cianjur and in West Java in general. Lembah Karmel (Karmel Valley), a 600-hectare centre located in Cianjur, is suspected by MUI and other radical Islamic groups in Cianjur as being a centre for converting West Javanese Muslims to Christianity through the guise of medical assistance. To counter Lembah Karmel, MUI and other Islamic authorities in Cianjur have established the Pesantren al-Barkah, funded mainly by the Internationales Zentrum Für Islamische Wissenchaften in Germany. Despite efforts by MUI and Islamic groups to staunch the flow of *pemurtadan* movements, it is still a challenge and, as in many other places, a highly political one. MUI and allied Muslim groups in Cianjur will maintain a high focus on this issue to also retain the support of their local Muslim community in a form of politicisation of religion.

5.5 Conclusion

Three conclusions can be drawn on the role of MUI in the implementation of sharia-inspired bylaws in Aceh, Bulukumba and Cianjur. Firstly, those promoting the implementation of regional sharia-inspired bylaws have made use of the decentralisation law to achieve their aims. This can be seen, for instance, by considering the sharia bylaws produced in Cianjur, Aceh and Bulukumba. All the drafts of these bylaws refer to the hierarchy of Indonesian state law, and National Law No. 32/2004 on decentralisation as the legal references for their authority. Although National Law No. 32/2004 clearly states that authority over religious matters are not to be devolved to the regions, the local governments of Aceh, Cianjur and Bulukumba have employed this law to underpin their bylaws. Although the sharia-based local regulations are not called *perda syariah*, the historical processes and content of these laws reflect the substance of sharia or, more precisely, of Islamic morality. Therefore, it is understandable that many people simply refer to them as sharia-inspired bylaws.

127 "Ribuan Orang Dimurtadkan, AGAP Tutup 23 Gereja," *Detik News*, 24 August 2005, https://news.detik.com/berita/d-428505/ribuan-orang-dimurtadkan-agap-tutup-23-gereja, viewed on 22 July 2022.

Secondly, the mixed political interests of two parties, local MUI ulama and the local district heads, lie behind the issuance of these *perda*. This was evident in the initiative of the Cianjur MUI branch to organise sharia events to mobilise support for a political leader on their side, one promoting the implementation of *Gerbang Marhamah*. Cianjur District Head Swastomo obtained a strong endorsement from the Cianjur MUI because of his active promotion of the application of sharia-inspired bylaws in this region. He issued the decree on the establishment of LPPI in 2001 and also the Surat Bupati No. 451/2712/ASSDA.I (Letter of Regent, No. 451/2712/ASSDA.I) on 6 September 2001 obliging local government employees to participate in communal prayers and wear Islamic attire. The same pattern of a mutual interest-based relationship can be seen in the district of Bulukumba, in the province of South Sulawesi, where the local MUI ulama endorse the local political leaders. The district heads all clearly understood that the implementation of sharia bylaws was not permitted under the decentralisation law. Nevertheless, Pabokori, for example, still issued the *perda syariah*, but without referring to Islam or sharia. Hence the sharia-inspired bylaws in South Sulawesi are called *perda pendidikan* (education ordinances) and in Bulukumba are referred to as a Crash Programme. The implementation of regional sharia-inspired bylaws is thus a kind of intermingling of sharia with local politics, which can be described as the politicisation of religion. MUI's role is as the legitimising actor for the ruler or political leader proposing the bylaws.

Third, MUI plays a role institutionally and through individuals at the central, provincial and district levels in imposing its influence on the drafting and implementation of sharia bylaws. The institutional case is demonstrated by the role of the MPU in Aceh, while in the case of individuals it can be seen in the role of MUI in Bulukumba and Cianjur. It is also important to note that MUI can play a role in softening sharia bylaws movements, directing them from a fundamentalist, militant tone towards a more moderate one. There are many examples of this, such as the role played by the MUI branch of Bulukumba in preventing the district from implementing the Islamic criminal law promoted by KPPSI. A similar example can be seen in Aceh, where the MPU rejected the implementation of the *Qanun Jināya*, which was aimed at adopting penal punishments applied in some Middle Eastern Islamic countries. If MUI is able to play this kind of moderate role, then Indonesia's future as a nation-state is more secure.

CHAPTER 6

MUI's Discourse and Its Relevance for Shariatisation: Case Studies of Fatwa

6.1 Introduction

Fatwa and *tawṣiyya* are two important instruments for MUI in promoting its authority over the regulation of sharia norms in the legal and public spheres of Indonesia. In previous chapters these were referred to as part of MUI's discourse. The question to be answered here is: How does this MUI discourse, fatwa and *tawṣiyya*, impact on the absorption of sharia norms in the legal and public spheres of Indonesia? This question is stimulated by the increased appeal of MUI products referred to by the state and society in regulating and implementing sharia precepts since the beginning of the reform era in 1998. In the legal sphere, MUI fatwas are influential in both supporting and opposing state rulings. In the public sphere, MUI's discourse is discernible through the way fatwas are negotiated and contested in social discourse and practice. There are two possibilities: on one hand, it may be that the prevailing MUI shariatisation might indicate a form of compatibility between democracy and sharia, as these religious guidelines are seemingly easily incorporated into the legal system and order of Indonesia, which is not a sharia-based state. On the other hand, however, the use of religious terminology in Indonesian legal discourse and practice may be seen as disrupting the political concept of the Pancasila state, which by definition is religiously neutral.[1] The proliferation of MUI fatwa and Islamic legal advice is a form of favouritism privileging a particular interpretation of sharia or a particular religion in a democratic state like Indonesia. It can also be said to be a kind of sharia-based discrimination, as the legal discourse of non-Muslim citizens is not considered here. The inclusion of sharia rulings into Indonesia's legal discourse and practice can create a quandary between accommodating sharia as a way of respecting religious freedom on the one hand and minimising Indonesia's legal discourse and practice from the intervention of religion as a way of maintaining the neutrality of the state on the other. It seems the dialogue between these two trends will remain

1 The term secular state for Indonesia here means that the state does not use religion as a political system.

 | DOI:10.1163/9789004534896_007

critical in the near future of Indonesia, although religion and the state may possibly be reconciled.

Some studies reveal that the intersection of fatwa and national law is not a new phenomenon.[2] There has been a long overlapping between the sacred and the secular, but the concept has been a political taboo since the idea of the nation-state was adopted in Muslim countries such as Indonesia and Malaysia. In a fact, a close relationship between Islam and secular law continues to various degrees.[3] A coexistence and inter-influence between sharia and non-sharia legal discourse and practice can take place when both evolve and experience a similar trajectory. In the case of Indonesia, the incorporation of MUI fatwa into Indonesian legal orders and norms presents an interesting case. These fatwas are perceived differently among different religious groups and even among Islamic groups themselves. Those who deny the possibility of a harmonious co-existence between secular laws and sharia assume that the presence of sharia in the legal sphere and the public sphere is problematic because it will threaten the religious neutrality of the state. For those who accept that secular law and sharia can co-exist, however, the espousal of sharia has no impact on the form of state because the possibility of implementing it lies within the framework of the modern nation-state. This diversity of perceptions of the impact of shariatisation can be viewed through its coverage in the legal and public spheres, which the discourse of MUI has attempted to order and regulate. In general, it can be categorised into three major themes: firstly, how the MUI discourse affects belief and worship, secondly how it regulates public morality, and thirdly how it prescribes Islamic norms. This study attempts to present a different approach compared to general studies on fatwa. Rather than employing the lens of a single discipline, this chapter relies on the use of a cross-cutting approach combining different theoretical perspectives from various disciplines from Islamic legal theory and jurisprudence to theology and religious studies to anthropology. The increased observance of MUI

2 Abdullahi Ahmed An-Na'im, *Islam and the Secular State: Negotiating the Future of Shari'a* (Cambridge: Harvard University Press, 2009); Jan Michiel Otto, ed., *Sharia Incorporated: A Comparative Overview of the Legal Systems of Twelve Muslim Countries in Past and Present* (Amsterdam: Amsterdam University Press, 2010).

3 Birgit Krawietz, "Justice as a Pervasive Principle in Islamic Law," in *Islam and the Rule of Law, Between Sharia and Secularization*, ed. Birgit Krawietz and Helmut Reifeld (Berlin: Konrad Adenauer Stiftung, 2008), 35–48, p. 9; William Safran, ed., *The Secular and the Sacred: Nation, Religion and Politics* (London & New York: Routledge, 2002); M.K. Masud, B.M. Messick, and D.S. Powers, *Islamic Legal Interpretation* (Cambridge, Massachusetts, London: Harvard University Press, 1996).

fatwa and advice in the legal and public sphere is not uniform, but a complex phenomenon that requires the focus of various disciplines to understand.

6.2 Deviant Groups and Islamic Worship

6.2.1 Takfīr

The discourse on deviant groups indicates that the MUI fatwas on *ʿaqīda* (belief) have a privileged place in the public sphere. This accords with the Islamic tenet that positions *ʿaqīda* as the key foundation of Islam (*uṣūl al-dīn*). MUI is keen to protect the authenticity of *ʿaqīda* from factors that can dilute its purity. As the most authoritative fatwa body, MUI sets up fatwa and general rulings on pure *ʿaqīda*. These fatwa function to police the thoughts and beliefs expressed and adhered to by Indonesian Muslim society. The word "police" here refers to MUI's attempt to ensure all Indonesian Muslims adhere to Sunnī Islam. Thus, according to MUI, the Ahmadiyah, Shīʿa and other groups viewed as being outside the Sunnī belief system have to be regulated, restricted and/or banned, being considered as the subjects of *ḥisba* (inspection).[4] Borrowing the perspective of "denomination theory" in the context of Western Christian countries,[5] the mainstream groups of any religious community, including the Sunnī Islam of Indonesia, often regard the other smaller denominations, whose theological stance differs, as a problem. Both Köstenberger and Kruger state that those who uphold orthodoxy often view the presence of deviant groups as parasites to their religion.[6] Talal Asad states that orthodoxy always creates power relations in which Muslims who follow an Islamic orthodoxy will control, condemn and replace other Muslims who are considered heterodox and incorrect.[7]

---

4 Michael Cook, *Forbidding Wrong in Islam: An Introduction* (Cambridge: Cambridge University Press, 2003); Michael Cook, *Commanding Right and Forbidding Wrong in Islamic Thought* (Cambridge: Cambridge University Press, 2004).

5 Mark Sedgwick, "Establishments and Sects in the Islamic World," in *New Religious Movements in the Twenty-First Century*, ed. Philip Charles Lucas and Thomas Robbins (New York: Routledge, 2004), 231–56, p. 239.

6 Andreas Köstenberger and Michael Kruger, *The Heresy of Orthodoxy: How Contemporary Culture's Fascination with Diversity Has Reshaped Our Understanding of Early Christianity* (Wheaton, IL: Crossway, 2010), p. 58; Talal Asad, *The Idea of an Anthropology of Islam* (Washington, DC: Center for Contemporary Arab Studies, Georgetown University, 1986).

7 Asad, *The Idea of an Anthropology of Islam*; Kambiz Ghaneabassiri, "Religious Normativity and Praxis Among American Muslims," in *The Cambridge Companion to American Islam* (Cambridge: Cambridge University Press, 2013), 208–27.

Before the MUI fatwas on belief-related issues are elaborated below, it is relevant to explain what is meant by *aliran sesat* and the MUI process for declaring a person to be an unbeliever (*takfīr*). The term *kāfir* is ascribed to those who, in the tradition of Western scholars, are referred to as heretics. MUI employs two terms to distinguish between the actions of such "heretics": *kesalahan* (mistake) and *kesesatan* (deviance). Those who have a mistaken understanding and practice related to an aspect of Islamic jurisprudence are deemed sinful, whilst those have a deviant understanding or practice related to the principle of *ʿaqīda* are described as adherents of a false belief. Those who practice the wrong *ʿaqīda* are seen by MUI to be committing apostasy. Thus the Indonesian term *aliran sesat* is used to condemn those viewed by MUI to be *kāfir*. Dutch anthropologist Martin van Bruinessen wrote an Indonesian language article on "*gerakan sempalan*" (break-away movements) in which he correctly defines *aliran sesat* or *gerakan sempalan* as a movement or religious stream which is regarded as deviating from the belief, rites and position of the *umma* majority.[8]

In order to provide a strong conceptualisation of *aliran sesat,* MUI has developed two interconnected approaches so that the state and the Indonesian Muslim community can easily comprehend this issue. First, the MUI criteria on *aliaran sesat* is expected to become a point of reference for the state, Islamic organisations and lawmakers when it comes to defining these groups. Second, MUI wants the method used to categorise *aliran sesat* to be based on a clear methodology. It has therefore produced a set of ten criteria defining "heresy." The first is rejection of one of the six foundations of Islamic belief (*rukn al-imān*) or one of the five foundations of Islam (*rukn al-Islām*). The second is believing and obeying a faith that is not in line with the teaching of the Qurʾān and Sunna. The third is believing in divine revelation after the Qurʾān. The fourth is denying the authenticity of the content of the Quran. The fifth is making interpretations of the Qurʾān without considering and the science of Qurʾānic exegesis. The sixth is rejecting the Sunna as the second legitimate source of Islam after the Qurʾān. The seventh is humiliating, underestimating, or denigrating the dignity of the Prophet Muḥammad. The eighth is refusing to accept that Muḥammad is the last Prophet of Islam. The ninth is changing any fundamental religious activity, for example claiming that *hajj* can be performed in places other than Mecca. The tenth is pronouncing other Muslims

8 Martin van Bruinessen, "Gerakan Sempalan Di Kalangan Ummat Islam Indonesia: Latar Belakang Sosial-Budaya," *Ulumul Qurʾan* III, no. 1 (1992): 16–27.

unbelievers without presenting a strong argument from sharia.[9] These ten criteria are considered if a group is judged to be *aliran sesat.*

The second approach is a set of procedural steps to determine the *ʿaqīda* status of a group and whether or not it should be understood as *sesat*, led by the Commission of Study and Research. The Commission performs the following steps. The first process is to gather information, evidence, information, news, and all related data that can reflect the thoughts of such individual or groups who are under research and investigation. To gather more information, the Commission conducts a series of dialogues with the individuals and groups who are suspected of being heretical. Through these dialogues, MUI hopes that these individuals and groups will come to understand their mistakes and return to religious orthodoxy. Yet MUI's experience indicates that efforts to return such groups to the proper sharia through dialogue are mostly unsuccessful, perhaps because the dialogue process is dominated and directed by MUI and the supposedly heretical individuals or groups have no right to defend their faith.[10] It would therefore be preferable to include a third party to act as a mediator. In a democratic country like Indonesia, the position of MUI and the heteretical individuals and groups are equal, meaning that MUI should not act as referee in this process of dialogue. Many progressive Muslim scholars like Mas'udi from the Nahdlatul Ulama have criticised MUI's stance as *wakil Tuhan* (representative of God) in determining the belief of Muslim individuals and groups and judging them to be *sesat* (heretical).[11]

The second part of the investigation is to invite Islamic experts with a deep understanding of the thoughts and activities of the deviant groups in order to carry out a legal examination. Since the theological framework used here is Sunnī, experts who take a different approach are not qualified to testify in this process. As this process is a form of Islamic mission to change the belief of heretical individuals and groups to what MUI considers the proper path of *ʿaqīda*, it is not open to philosophical debate and functions as a form of indoctrination. During the third part of the process, MUI's Commission of Study and Research invites the heretical individuals and group (especially group leaders) to enter a discussion with Islamic experts to verify information related to their ideas and activities. If the Commission and experts find evidence for

9 MUI, *Mengawal Aqidah Umat: Fatwa MUI Tentang Aliran-Aliran Sesat Di Indonesia* (Jakarta: Sekretariat Majelis Ulama Indonesia, n.d.), pp. 7–8; Syafiq Hasyim, "The Council of Indonesian Ulama (Majelis Ulama Indonesia, MUI) and Religious Freedom" (Irasec's Discussion Papers 12, 2011), p. 10.

10 Hasyim, "The Council of Indonesian Ulama (Majelis Ulama Indonesia, MUI) and Religious Freedom."

11 Interview with Masdar F. Mas'udi, Jakarta, 2010.

theological deviance at this stage, they issue a strong recommendation to bring them back from their false *ʿaqīda*. The fourth step in the process is to conclude and present the research findings to a meeting of MUI board members. Finally, based on the research findings prepared by the Commission, the MUI board instructs the Fatwa Commission to discuss the Islamic legal and theological aspects of the findings, to be followed up with the issuance of a fatwa.

All these steps can be seen in the table below.

TABLE 1 MUI procedure for defining deviant sects[a]

Step 1 **Initiation**	**Step 2** **Research & Investigation**	**Step 3** **Discussion & Further Investigation**	**Step 4** **Decision**	**Step 5** **Public announcement of judgment**
Islamic community, MUI branches & Islamic organisations	Delegating research and investigation =>			
		Handing in result of research and investigation		
Proposing =>	Commission of Research and Investigation		=>	
Central Board of MUI in Jakarta	Recommendation or further investigation	Central Board of MUI	No fatwa is recommended	=>
			or	
			A fatwa is recommended	*Tawṣiya* (religious advice)
				Fatwa

a This table is adopted from the MUI fatwa compilation on deviant groups, *Mengawal Aqidah Umat, Fatwa MUI tentang Aliran-Aliran Sesat di Indonesia* MUI, *Mengawal Aqidah Umat: Fatwa MUI Tentang Aliran-Aliran Sesat Di Indonesia*, n.d., p. 11.

It should be noted here that the increasing rise of heretical groups in Indonesia's public sphere can be understood in two ways. From a positive perspective, religious groups in Indonesia have become more courageous in claiming their basic rights due to the increase in civil liberties and political openness since the reform era, and the Indonesian media has more freedom in making news accessible to the public. In addition, the scrutiny of international institutions and media has contributed to the appearance of this issue at the global and transnational level.[12]

The perspective espoused by MUI, however, is that the rise of heretical groups should be stopped, as it could threaten the correct implementation of Islam. MUI and its ally groups judge these heretical groups to be violating the religious rights of the mainstream believers. By claiming an Islamic obligation to protect the belief system of the mainstream group, MUI refuses to tolerate their rise in the public sphere as it may cause social unrest. In this regard, MUI feels obliged to make concerted efforts to challenge them in its capacity as fatwa-maker, with the purpose of protecting others from heresy. Because most of discourse on heretical groups starts from the issue of their belief system, MUI has introduced many fatwas on *aliran sesat* that can be seen in statements banning Islam Jama'ah, Ahmadiyah, Darul Arqam, Jama'ah Muslimin Hizbullah, and many others—including, to some degree, Shīʿa. In this regard, MUI uses the protection of Sunnī *ʿaqīda* as the main theological argument. It means that all groups of Indonesian Muslims that adhere to theological notions that oppose the *ʿaqīda* of the Sunnī can be judged as heretical. It is thus clear that the belief system of Sunnī Islam is understood by MUI to be the only proper theological system in Indonesian Islam. This is a claim associated with the prediction of the Prophet Muḥammad, as reported in various versions of the *ḥadīth*, that Islam will deviate into seventy-three sects (*firqa*), the only "safe" sect being Sunnī (*ahl al-sunna wa al-jamāʿa*).[13]

12 "Indonesia: Rights Record Under Scrutiny at UN", Human Rights Watch, 15 May 2012, http://www.hrw.org/news/2012/05/15/indonesia-rights-record-under-scrutiny-un, viewed on 22 July 2022. See also the US government's executive summary on religious freedom in 2015: http://www.state.gov/j/drl/rls/irf/religiousfreedom/index.htm#wrapper, viewed on 22 July 2022.

13 Ibn Taymiyya, *Sharḥ Al-ʿAqīda al-Wāsaṭiyya* (Riyadh: Dār al-Salām li al-Nashr, 1989), p. 219. Debates on "who" should be included within the groups of Ahl al-Sunna wa al-Jamāʿa in Indonesia can be seen in Fauzan Saleh, *Modern Trends in Islamic Theological Discourse in Twentieth Century Indonesia* (Leiden: Brill, 2001), pp. 75–85; Siradjuddin Abbas, *I'itiqad Ahlussunnah Wal-Jama'ah* (Kelantan: Pustaka Aman, 1999), Djohan Effendi, *Pembaruan Tanpa Membongkar Tradisi: Wacana Keagamaan Di Kalangan Generasi Muda NU Masa Kepemimpinan Gus Dur* (Jakarta: Penerbit Buku Kompas, 2010), pp. 36–7.

Among the earliest Islamic groups of Indonesian Islam declared as heretical are Islam Jam'ah and Jama'ah Muslim Hizbullah. Islam Jama'ah was founded by Madigol Nurhasan Ubaidah Lubis in 1915. In 1971, because of the controversy surrounding it, the Suharto regime outlawed the group. Instead of accepting Suharto's decision, however, Islam Jama'ah simply continued to carry out its activities using different names, including Darul Hadits in 1952, Lembaga Karyawan Islam (Lemkari, Islam's Working-Class Institution) in 1972, and Lembaga Dakwah Islam Indonesia (LDII, Indonesian Islamic Propagation Institute in 1990.[14] Islam Jama'ah[15] was then banned by MUI for introducing new several concepts, for instance giving more obedience to the *amīr al-mu'minīn* (general leader of the believers)[16] than to parents, claiming that Islam Jama'ah is the most correct path of Islam, and separating from non-members of the Jama'ah.[17]

On 28 August 1978, through its fatwa, MUI declared the Jama'ah Muslimin Hizbullah to be a heretical group in response to a request from the Attorney General of Indonesia, specifically related for four key issues.[18] The first concerned the group's practice of doing *bayʿa* (pledging allegiance) to their leader. The second issue related to the basic Islamic concepts of *jamāʿa* (community), *imāma* (leadership), *khilāfa* (caliphate) and *bayʿa*, which are understood differently by this group. The third was Jama'ah Muslimin Hizbullah's insistence on continuing their activities, even though MUI had banned them. The fourth was to get deeper information on the group.[19] In response to the request of the Attorney General, MUI noted that Jama'ah Muslimin Hizbullah

14 Sutiyono and Ahmad Dzulfikar, *Benturan Budaya Islam: Puritan & Sinkretis* (Jakarta: Penerbit Buku Kompas, 2010), p. 124; Bambang Irawa Hafiludin, Derby Murti Nasution, and Zainal Arifin Aly, *Bahaya Islam Jama'ah, Lemkari, LDII: Pengakuan Mantan Gembong-Gembong LDII, Ust. Bambang Irawan Hafiluddin, Ust. Debby Murti Nasution, Ust. Zaenal Arifin Aly, Ust. Hasyim Rifa'in, Fatwa-Fatwa Ulama Dan Aneka Kasus LDII.* (Jakarta: Gema Insani, 1998), pp. 1–2; Sutiyono and Dzulfikar, *Benturan Budaya Islam: Puritan & Sinkretis*, 2010.

15 Islam Jama'ah has many other names such as *Darul Hadits*, *Lembaga Karyawan Islam* (Lemkari, Islam's Working Class Institution) and *Lembaga Dakwah Islam Indonesia* (LDII, Indonesian Islamic Propagation Institute). See Sutiyono and Dzulfikar, *Benturan Budaya Islam*, p. 184; Hafiludin, Nasution and Aly, *Bahaya Islam Jama'ah, Lemkari, LDII*, pp. 1–2.

16 MUI, *Himpunan Fatwa MUI Sejak 1975*, p. 38.

17 MUI, *Himpunan Fatwa Majelis Ulama Indonesia* (Jakarta: Departemen Agama, 2003), p. 98.

18 MUI, *Himpunan Fatwa MUI Sejak 1975*, p. 35.

19 Hasyim, *The Council of Indonesian Ulama (Majelis Ulama Indonesia, MUI) and Religious Freedom*, pp. 11–12; MUI, *Mengawal Aqidah Umat: Fatwa MUI Tentang Aliran-Aliran Sesat Di Indonesia*, n.d., p. 80; MUI, *Himpunan Fatwa MUI Sejak 1975*, p. 35.

embraced theological teaching that was different from the mainstream Islam of Indonesia, and judged them to be deviant from Islam.

The next deviant group defined by MUI is the Ahmadiyah of Qadian. The Ahmadiyah sect is divided into the Ahmadiyah of Qadian and the Ahmadiyah of Lahore; the Qadian branch in particular is judged as *kafir* due their belief that Mirza Ghulam Ahmad continued a line of prophethood from the Prophet Muḥammad,[20] while the Ahmadiyah of Lahore views Mirza Ghulam Ahmad as a *mujtahid* (renewer of the age).[21] However, MUI considers both factions to be dangerous sects for the purity of Islamic belief. MUI also denounced the Inkar Sunnah as heretical because of their rejection of the Sunna on 27 June 1994.[22] The MUI fatwa related to this group has two main points, first that this group rejects Sunna as the second important source of Islam after the Qur'ān and second that they could pose a threat to the Muslim community as well as the national security of Indonesia.[23]

Some groups are judged *takfīr* or deviant by MUI on the basis of mysticism, meaning that Ṣūfī orders that differ from mainstream groups are rejected (*ghayr al-muʿtabar*: not a well-considered position). This applies in the case of the Darul Arqam, a Malaysian group rejected by MUI in 1994 because they believe that Aurad Muhammadiyah[24] was revealed by God through the Prophet Muḥammad to Shaykh Suhaymi (b. 1925, founder of the group) at the Kaʿba when he was in a conscious state.[25] MUI declares that Islam as a religion has been complete since the death of Muḥammad, meaning that there can be no new religion or doctrine and no new prophet after Muḥammad. MUI therefore states that the teaching of Darul Arqam is false and needs correction. A similar case is the Messianist group led by Lia Aminuddin (d. 2021) that was banned by MUI due to its claim that Aminuddin was accompanied by and received revelation from the Angel Gabriel. This belief elicited various negative responses from Indonesian Muslims who cannot accept anyone other than the Prophet Muḥammad meeting Gabriel.

20 MUI, *Himpunan Fatwa MUI Sejak 1975*, p. 40.

21 Iqbal Singh Sevea, "The Ahmadiyya Print Jihad in South and Southeast Asia," in *Islamic Connections: Muslim Societies in South and Southeast Asia*, ed. R. Michael Feener and Iqbal Singh Sevea (Singapore: Institute of Southeast Asian Studies, 2009), 134–48, p. 137.

22 This name is taken from its rejection of the tradition of the Prophet Muhammad (*Sunna*), which is regarded as the second primary source of Islam after the Qur'ān.

23 MUI, *Himpunan Fatwa MUI Sejak 1975*, pp. 52–53.

24 *Aurād Muhammadiyah* is a guidance for the followers of this group to perform *dhikr* (silently recite the names of God in prayer).

25 Judith Nagata, "Religious Ideology and Social Change: The Islamic Revival in Malaysia," *Pacific Affairs* 53, no. 3 (1980): 405–39, p. 418.

MUI considers that the presence of deviant groups is not only a theological challenge to the belief of Indonesian Muslim mainstream organisations but also poses a political threat to the state. It therefore calls for political and legal state intervention. MUI believes that if there are legal and political restrictions to the *aliran sesat* in the public space, a harsh reaction from mainstream groups is bound to follow. This reflects MUI's drive for the distribution of power between the state and religious authorities in managing the issue of deviant groups. In the era of Suharto's government, the Coordinating Agency for Monitoring Mystical Beliefs in Society—commonly known as Badan Koordinasi Pengawas Aliran Kepercayaan Masyarakat (BAKORPAKEM) under Indonesia's Office of the Attorney General—was the government authority responsible for monitoring and observing the activities of deviant groups.[26] Religious authority was distributed among main Islamic organisations such as Nahdlatul Ulama, Muhammadiyah, and MUI.[27] During that era, many fatwas on deviant groups issued by Islamic authorities were triggered by requests from state authorities such as the Attorney General, which the state authorities then followed up. Not much has changed in the current reform era except for the increasingly dominant role of MUI as a fatwa body for *ʿaqīda*-related issues. Prominent figures from both NU and Muhammadiyah revealed in interviews that MUI's authority in regulating beliefs has significantly increased since these two organisations allowed MUI to take the lead in handling *ʿaqīda*-related fatwas. Muhammadiyyah and NU decided to take a smaller role to promote unity of belief in the *umma*. The late Ahmad Fatah Wibisono, chairman of the Majlis Tarjih of Muhammadiyah, clarified that the unity of the *umma* would be ensured through the centralisation of fatwa on *ʿaqīda* in the one body. Wibisono argued that Islamic organisations could have different stances on *fiqh*-related issues, but not on the issue of *ʿaqīda*.[28] Several important NU figures also chose not to issue belief-related fatwas. Although members of the NU community demanded their own fatwas on the Ahmadiyah and Shīʿa, after long discussion among the NU elite the organisation failed to reach an independent position. When I asked Siradj and Deputy Chairman As'ad Ali about

26 Human Rights Watch, "In Religion's Name, Abuses against Religious Minorities in Indonesia," 2013, p. 42; Uli Parulian Sihombing, *Menggugat Bakor Pakem: Kajian Hukum Terhadap Pengawasan Agama Dan Kepercayaan Di Indonesia* (Jakarta: Indonesian Legal Resource Center, 2008).

27 Martin van Bruinessen, "Gerakan Sempalan Di Kalangan Ummat Islam Indonesia: Latar Belakang Sosial-Budaya," *Ulumul Qur'an* III, no. 1 (1992): 16–27; Hasyim, *The Council of Indonesian Ulama (Majelis Ulama Indonesia, MUI) and Religious Freedom.*

28 Interview with Ahmad Fatah Wibisono, Jakarta, 2011, and interview with anonymous Muhammadiyah member, Jakarta, 2011.

this issue, both simply answered, "*urusan akidah adalah urusan MUI*": the matter of *ʿaqīda* is MUI business.[29]

To increase the legal status of its fatwas on deviant groups, MUI has been attempting to persuade the state and lawmakers to accommodate them, or at least the ideas and spirit, into the legal rulings of Indonesia. In this way the fatwas would gain legal and political influence and could eventually be used to control and regulate deviant groups.[30] MUI supports the implementation of State Law No. 01/PNPS/1965 on blasphemy, as its content is very close to the spirit of MUI fatwas on deviant groups. The Council categorises deviant groups as those who insult and denigrate Islam. Normally blasphemy laws are employed to convict acts which insult religion, but in Indonesia the blasphemy law is used to charge deviant groups which have strayed from mainstream religion, as when MUI declared its opposition to the Ahmadiyah, Shīʿa, and other deviant groups on the grounds that their beliefs are blasphemous or defame Islam. On many occasions, MUI have supported the prosecution of the Ahmadi, Shīʿa and other so-called heretical groups under this law. It would seem that encouraging the implementation of this law is a fundamental method for MUI to maintain the supremacy of the true faith.

The blasphemy law was first promulgated in Indonesia in response to what was perceived by mainstream religions as an emergency situation. This law was registered in the Sukarno era, under pressure from religious groups—particularly Islamic political groups—to protect mainstream religions from the challenge of *aliran kebatinan* (indigenous belief). Niels Mulder stated that the legislation of Act No. 01/PNPS/1965 was related to the formulation of the official definition of religion in 1961. As a consequence of this definition, the indigenous beliefs that had challenged the mainstream religions of Indonesia since the 1950s were excluded from the definition of religion. The Ministry of Religious Affairs (MORA) listed 360 *aliran kebatinan* in Java alone in 1953.[31] The *kelompok kebatinan* held a strong position, and because of their influence Islamic parties were defeated in the 1955 general elections. In order to control

---

29 Interview with Said Aqil Siradj, Jakarta, 2010, and interview with As'ad Ali, Jakarta, 2011.

30 John Olle, "The Majelis Ulama Indonesia Versus 'Heresy': The Resurgence of Authoritarian Islam," in *State of Authority: The State in Society in Indonesia*, ed. Geert Arend van Klinken and Barker Joshua (Ithaca: Cornell South East Asia Publication, 2009), 95–116.

31 Ihsan Ali-Fauzi, Samsu Rizal Panggabean, and Trisno S. Sutanto, "Membela Kekebasan Beragama: Catatan Pengantar," in *Membela Kebebasan Beragama: Percakapan Tentang Sekularisme, Liberalisme, Dan Pluralisme, (Buku 2)* (Jakarta: Lembaga Studi Agama dan Filsafat, 2010), p. xviii; Niels Mulder, *Mysticism in Java: Ideology in Indonesia* (Yogyakarta: Kanisius, 2005); Sairin Weinata, ed., *Himpunan Peraturan Di Bidang Keagamaan* (Jakarta: BPK Gunung Mulia, 1994), p. 263.

the increase of *aliran kebatinan*, the Ministry of Religious Affairs established the Pengawas Aliran Kepercayaan Masyarakat (PAKEM, Monitoring Agency for Belief in Society) in 1954, and then passed Act No. 01/PNPS/1965 in 1965.

Over four decades later, on 1 December 2009, a number of religious groups and NGOs joined together to file a judicial review of Act No. 01/PNPS/1965 with the Constitutional Court (Mahkamah Konstitusi, MK).[32] One argument used to support the review was that mainstream religious groups, both Muslim and non-Muslim, had misused the law as a source of legitimacy to ban other groups deemed to be deviant. The Constitutional Court rejected the judicial review, however, and Act No. 01/PNPS/1965 remains law in Indonesia. The court based its decision on the argument that the law was needed to sustain religious harmony.[33] Despite the fact that the Constitutional Court stated that its decision was to accommodate between the two groups—mainstream and non-mainstream—that contested the case, the legal material indicated that the verdict relied more on evidence presented by mainstream groups. This was also evident in a similar case in which testimony was given by Muzadi, representing Nahdlatul Ulama, and Din Syamsuddin, representing Muhammadiyah, during hearing sessions of the Constitutional Court.[34] Suryadharma Ali, the Minister of Religious Affairs (2009–2014), argued that if the law were jettisoned, the state of Indonesia could face serious danger because religion-based conflicts could be triggered. As an opponent of the judicial review, MUI's position was evident in the statements made by Amin, who stated that the judicial review would lead to freedom without limits in Indonesia. If the Constitutional Court accepted the judicial review, the ban on religious heresy and blasphemy would have no legal support. Amin insisted that it should therefore be rejected, and that the status of the law should instead be strengthened. He further argued that Indonesia needed stricter regulations to overcome the problems of heretical groups.[35]

After the resignation of Suharto in 1998, the issue of the Ahmadiyah worsened. As the holder of *ʿaqīda* authority in Indonesian fatwa, MUI has identified

32 Abdurrahman Wahid, Dawam Rahardjo, Musdah Mulia, Maman Imanul Haq and some NGOs were among those who filed the judicial review of State Law No. 1/PNPS/1965 at the Constitutional Court Mahkamah Konstitusi, "PUTUSAN Nomor 140/PUU-VII/2009" (2009), pp. 1–3.

33 The council of Protestant churches (PGI, Persekutuan Gereja Indonesia) is now also facing an increasing number of deviant sects.

34 Mahkamah Konstitusi, PUTUSAN Nomor 140/PUU-VII/2009.

35 "KH Ma'ruf Amin: Ada UU PNPS Saja Aliran Sesat Menjamur, Apalagi Tidak Ada!," *Hidayatullah*, 30 November 2014, https://hidayatullah.com/berita/nasional/read/2014/11/30/34168/kh-maruf-amin-ada-uu-pnps-saja-aliran-sesat-menjamur-apalagi-tidak-ada.html, viewed on 22 July 2022.

the Ahmadiyah as their main target. The first fatwa against the Ahmadiyah was issued in the 1980s, and the issue reemerged in 2005. The re-issuance of this Islamic edict was the result of various reasons, including a growing demand among mainstream Muslim groups to stop their spread in Indonesia. Unlike the situation in the Suharto era, when public discourse on the Ahmadiyah was manageable and did not involve violence or public hatred, during the reform era this was not the case: three Ahmadiyah followers were killed in mob violence at Cikeusik, for example.[36] Perhaps this is partly due to the fact that almost all mainstream Muslim organisations—such as Nahdlatul Ulama, Muhammadiyah and Persatuan Islam—gave their support to the MUI fatwa denouncing the Ahmadiyah as deviants from the proper path of Islam.[37] Muzadi, for instance, recommend that Ahmadi followers in Indonesia should form a new religion, since the Ahmadiyah cannot be part of Islam due to their belief that Mirza Ghulam Ahmad is a prophet after Muḥammad.[38] Din Syamsuddin also rejected the Ahmadiyah for the same reason, and for claiming that they are the only true Muslims.[39] Persatuan Islam clearly accuses Mirza Ghulam Ahmad of plagiarism of the Qur'ān.[40]

The government perspective on the Ahmadiyah was not so different from the perspective of mainstream Muslim organisations. Suryadharma Ali, the Minister of Religious Affairs (2009–2014), made a statement in a parliamentary inquiry organised in response to the tragedy of Cikeusik that strengthened MUI's fatwa condemning the Ahmadiyah.[41] All these indicate that the position of MUI is still influential among representatives of the state and the Muslim community. Despite the fact that the heresy of Ahmadiyah belief is very clear for Nahdlatul Ulama and Muhammadiyah, however, neither organisation agreed with the bloodshed against Ahmadis perpetrated by Islamist and vigilante groups such as FPI. Komnas Perempuan (the National Commission

36 On 6 February 2011, three Ahmadis were killed by a militant Islamic group in Cekeusik, Banten.

37 Hasyim, *The Council of Indonesian Ulama (Majelis Ulama Indonesia, MUI) and Religious Freedom*, p. 13.

38 "Hasyim Muzadi: Mau Aman Ahmadiyah Agama Baru", Republika, 23 February 2011, https://www.republika.co.id/berita/breaking-news/nasional/11/02/23/165633-hasyim-muzadi-mau-aman-ahmadiyah-agama-baru, viewed on 22 July 2022.

39 "Din Syamsuddin: Ahmadiyah Anggap Pemeluk Keyakinan Lain Kafir", Tribun News, 5 March 2011, https://www.tribunnews.com/nasional/2011/03/05/din-ahmadiyah-anggap-pemeluk-islam-orang-kafir, viewed on 22 July 2022.

40 Maman Abdurrahman, *Mirza Ghulam Ahmad Plagiator Al-Qur'an: Studi Banding Antara Ayat-Ayat Tadzkirah Dan Ayat-Ayat al-Qur'an* (Bandung: Rahman Press, 2011).

41 "Menag: Ahmadiyah Qadiyan Yang Sesat," Kemenag, 9 February 2011, https://kemenag.go.id/read/menag-ahmadiyah-qadiyan-yang-sesat-lnx6, viewed on 22 July 2022.

on Violence Against Women) stated that there have been 342 attacks on this group in the five years since the MUI fatwa on the Ahmadiyah was issued in 2005.[42] Attacks on Ahmadis continue to happen today, during Jokowi's presidency.

MUI's second target after the Ahmadiyah is the Shīʿa. The Shīʿa community is significant, forming the second largest Muslim group in Indonesia after the Sunnī. In the calculation of the Ikatan Jama'ah Ahlul Bayt Indonesia (IJABI, Association of Ahlul Bayt Congregation), there are 2.5 million Shīʿa followers in Indonesia.[43] The Shīʿa community first received MUI's attention in 1984, when the organisation published a recommendation (*tawṣiyya*) on Shīʿa thought. The *tawṣiyya* was fairly mild, and only indicated some of the main differences between Sunnī and Shīʿa without describing them as *kāfirūn* (unbelievers),[44] even though the intention was to target Shīʿa as part of *aliran sesat*. In 2011, however, the Shīʿa community was declared to be part of *aliran sesat*. Shortly after, in 2013, an Islamic boarding school (Yayasan Pesantren Islam, YAPI) managed by the Shīʿa community in Bangil—an area in the Pasuran regency in East Java where a large number of the Shīʿa community have lived since the colonial period—became the target of attacks and intimidation. Human Rights Watch reports that 200 protesters entered the YAPI buildings and destroyed property and the buildings of a kindergarten, primary school, middle school and two high schools in February 2013.[45] In addition to physical destruction, the Shīʿa community in this region have also suffered spiritual attacks: it was reported that a Sunnī cleric from the Sunnī al-Bayyinat Foundation (Indonesian: *Yayasan Sunnī al-Bayyinat*), Surabaya, delivered a hate speech calling on the local Sunnī to purify the area of Bangil from the presence of the Shīʿa community in 2007.[46] The local state apparatus has passive throughout, and made no arrests even though the attacks could be categorised as human rights violations. This signifies the reluctance of the authorities to curb violations related to religious issues and authorities that involved mainstream Muslim groups.

42 "Penyerangan Kepada Ahmadiyah Sudah 342 Kali," Oke News, 7 February 2011, https://nasional.okezone.com/read/2011/02/07/337/422265/penyerangan-kepada-ahmadiyah-sudah-342-kali, viewed on 22 July 2022.

43 Human Rights Watch, "In Religion's Name, Abuses against Religious Minorities in Indonesia," 2013, p. 21.

44 MUI, *Himpunan Fatwa MUI Sejak 1975*, p. 46.

45 Human Rights Watch, "In Religion's Name, Abuses against Religious Minorities in Indonesia," 2013.

46 Ibid.

Anti-Shīʿa violence rapidly escalated. On December 2011, there was a shocking attack on the Shīʿa community in Sampang, Madura.[47] This event, known as the *peristiwa Sampang* (the Sampang incident) was triggered by a local Sunnī group that accused Tajul Muluk, a local Madurese Shīʿa cleric, of preaching Shīʿa thought in Sampang, a regency where the majority is Sunnī.[48] The local Sunnī propagators held several public protests that ended with physical assaults and violence against the Shīʿa group. As a result of the attacks, the land and property (thirty-seven houses) of the tiny Shīʿa community (around 200 people) in Sampang was destroyed.[49] The Sampang tragedy denotes the seriousness of hatred among the Indonesian Sunnī against the Shīʿa, which exists not only at the discursive level of the elites in Jakarta or other major cities but also at concrete level among the grassroots community. Such incidents have taken place not only in Sampang and Bangil, but also in other places such as Bandung, West Java and Solo, Central Java.[50]

Following the Sampang Incident, there was a difference of opinion between the central board of MUI in Jakarta and the provincial chapter in East Java. This centred around MUI's recommendation (*tawṣiyya*) on the Shīʿa in 1984, which did not clearly mention heresy; if the denunciation of the Shīʿa communities in Sampang and Bangil as heretical relied on this *tawṣiyya*, it was misguided.[51] The central board members of MUI in Jakarta were not united in their understanding of the Shīʿa. Umar Shihab (a senior member of the MUI ulama) and Din Syamsuddin included the Shīʿa in the family of Islam, while Ridwan and his supporters stated that the sect was heretical and that Shīʿa believers had no place in the organisation.[52] He called for reconsidering the board membership of Khalid al-Walid, a graduate from Qum in Iran, for example, because he

47 Madura is a small island to the north of Surabaya, East Java, that consists of four regencies: Bangkalan, Sampang, Pamekasan and Sumenep.

48 The population of this town is estimated to be 876,950. Almost all are Sunni adherents and members of the NU community.

49 Rachmah Ida and Laurentius Dyson, "Konflik Sunni-Syiah Dan Dampaknya Terhadap Komunikasi Intra- Religius Pada Komunitas Di Sampang-Madura," *Masyarakat, Kebudayaan Dan Politik* 28, no. 1 (2015): 33–49, p. 35.

50 "Ribuan Umat Islam Saksikan Deklarasi ANNAS Solo Raya," Annas Indonesia, 2 January 2017, https://www.annasindonesia.com/read/698-ribuan-umat-islam-saksikan-deklarasi-annas-solo-raya, viewed on 22 July 2022.

51 It is also important to note that in the hierarchy of MUI's legal output, the position of *tawsiyya* is lower than that of fatwa.

52 "MUI Pusat Sulit Keluarkan Fatwa Syiah Sesat Karena Ada Penyusupan," Hidayatullah, 12 December 2012, https://hidayatullah.com/berita/nasional/read/2012/12/12/64776/mui-pusat-sulit-keluarkan-fatwa-syiah-sesat-karena-ada-penyusupan.html, viewed on 22 July 2022.

was a member of the Shīʿa.[53] Ridwan's shouting, however, was unsuccessful in getting attention from the elite of MUI, and Sahal Mahfudh, the General Chairman, did not comment on this controversy, refusing to welcome a group of Sunnī Madurese ulama who came to meet him as his house in Pati, Central Java, to consult him about a fatwa about the heresy of the Shīʿa community in Sampang.[54]

The situation worsened when the provincial branch of MUI in East Java issued its own fatwa on the heresy of Shīʿa on 21 January 2012,[55] without any consultation with the central board of MUI[56] and only three weeks after the MUI branch of the Sampang regency had passed a fatwa on the same issue. Although this fatwa aimed to specifically address the heresy of the Shīʿa in Sampang, as the product of fatwa it could be generalised, at least, as a denunciation of the entire Shīʿa community in East Java. This fatwa came to the attention of the central board of MUI, because regulations state that the central board must authorise the issuance of any fatwa with national resonance. The provincial and regency chapters of MUI should at the very least consult the central board if they wish to issue a fatwa that relates to national issues, such as the issue of Shīʿa heresy.[57]

The Sampang incident was a national tragedy for Indonesia. Around 200 families became refugees, staying in the Sampang Sports Complex, because their homes had been displaced.[58] The local government of Sampang asked the Sampang Shīʿa to move from their temporary refugee camp in Sampang to Sidoarjo, Rumah Susun Puspo Agro, 113km from Sampang, on 20 June 2013. The deputy mayor of Sampang, Fadhilah Budiono, stated that this decision was taken by the local authority to provide a safer place for the Sampang Shīʿa

53 MUI's head office did not abolish the fatwa of the provincial branch of East Java. See "MUI Pusat Bantah Akan Batalkan Fatwa MUI Jatim Soal Syiah," *Hidayatullah*, 6 September 2012, https://hidayatullah.com/berita/nasional/read/2012/09/06/62183/mui-pusat-bantah-akan-batalkan-fatwa-mui-jatim-soal-syiah.html, viewed on 22 July 2022.

54 I obtained this information from Masykuri Abdillah, a Muslim scholar who is also active in MUI, when he visited Berlin on 19 June 2013.

55 See Keputusan Fatwa Majelis Ulama Indonesia (MUI), Prop. Jawa Timur No. Kep-01/SKF-MUI/JTM/2012.

56 Human Rights Watch, "In Religion's Name, Abuses against Religious Minorities in Indonesia," p. 60. Then, A-035/MUI/Spg/1/2012 was signed by Mahmud Huzaini (head of the Fatwa Commission), Mahrus Zamroni (secretary of the Fatwa Commission), and Moh. Sjuaib (secretary general).

57 MUI, *Himpunan Fatwa MUI Sejak 1975*, p. 939.

58 "Sunnis Stick to Demands for Shiite Conversion," *Jakarta Post*, https://www.thejakartapost.com/news/2013/11/08/sunnis-stick-demands-shiite-conversion.html, 8 November 2013, viewed on 6 July 2021.

community.[59] However, this relocation was differently perceived by mainstream Muslim organisations. Siradj (former general chairman of NU) stated that the relocation of the Sampang Shīʿa was evidence of the weakness of government policy-making, and said the relocation was a temporary rather than a permanent solution. However, he remained hopeful that the local government's treatment of the Sampang Shīʿa in the camp would meet humanitarian standards.[60] Muhammadiayah General Chairman Din Syamsuddin asked for the government of Indonesia to build a bridge to reconcile the local Sunnī and Sampang Shīʿa communities.[61] Yet Suryadharma Ali, the representative of the Indonesian government, made a statement in support of the fatwa of the East Java MUI that blamed the Shīʿa community itself for the Sampang Incident. He also declared the Shīʿa to be heretical,[62] and asked them to repent and return to Sunnī teachings.[63] This request was of course rejected by the Sampang Shīʿa on the grounds that it was baseless. Iklil Almilal responded to Suryadharma's request by saying that both the Shīʿa Sampang and Madurese Sunnī were Muslims, followers of Islam. Ali's position indicated that the government of Indonesia was not neutral as regards the Sunnī-Shīʿa conflict of Sampang.

Once again, this incident indicates that MUI fatwas on deviant groups in the post-reform era of Indonesia have a tremendous impact on the public sphere. In the legal realm, the power of MUI fatwas is evident through the revitalisation of the blasphemy law as a legal provision against deviant groups. Donald L. Horowitz, for instance, reports that the blasphemy law was used much more sparingly in the Suharto era.[64] Since 1998, however, around

---

59 "The Sampang Shīʿa was Relocated from Sampang to Sidoarjo", BBC News, https://www.bbc.com/indonesia/berita_indonesia/2013/06/130620_syiah_sampang_dipindah_sidoarjo, 20 June 2013, viewed on 12 July 2022.

60 "PBNU menilai relokasi warga Syiah bukan langkah tepat", *Antara News*, 21 June 2013, https://www.antaranews.com/berita/381240/pbnu-menilai-relokasi-warga-syiah-bukan-langkah-tepat, viewed on 22 July 2022.

61 "Muhammadiyah minta pemerintah rekonsiliasi konflik Syiah", *Antara News*, 24 June 2013, https://www.antaranews.com/berita/381724/muhammadiyah-minta-pemerintah-rekonsiliasi-konflik-syiah, viewed on 22 July 2022.

62 "Sebut Syiah Sesat, Ikatan Jamaah Ahlul Bait Sesalkan Komentar Menteri Agama", *Rep ublika*, 27 January 2012, https://www.republika.co.id/berita/dunia-islam/islam-nusantara/12/01/27/lyfnwj-sebut-syiah-sesat-ikatan-jamaah-ahlul-bait-sesalkan-komentar-menteri-agama, viewed on 22 July 2022.

63 "Warga Islam Syiah Sampang menolak 'bertobat'", *BBC News*, 26 July 2013, https://www.bbc.com/indonesia/berita_indonesia/2013/07/130726_syiah_sampang_tolak_sda, viewed on 22 July 2022.

64 Donald L. Horowitz, *Constitutional Change and Democracy in Indonesia* (Cambridge: Cambridge University Press, 2013), p. 251.

180 people have been convicted under this law. Most of them are Christians and members of deviant groups.[65] Tajul Muluk, the Shīʿa leader of Sampang, for instance, was sentenced to two years' imprisonment on the basis of the blasphemy law. Five years earlier, in 2008, a joint decree on the limitation of Ahmadiyah activities was signed by the Minister of Home Affairs, the Minister of Religious Affairs and the Attorney General. The Constitutional Court also rejected the judicial review of Act 01/PNPS/1965 on blasphemy due to the prevalent public opinions of mainstream groups opposed to this judicial process. All these cases demonstrate that MUI fatwas have a strong influence on legal discourse and practice in Indonesia.

It is also interesting to look at how transnational perspectives are used as a framework when it comes to dealing with deviant groups. It seems that local deviant groups such as Islam Jama'ah, Lia Eden, Inkar Sunnah and many more have no international resonance and are less politically significant than transnational Islamic sects such as the Ahmadiyah and Shīʿa. International agencies and NGOs are concerned about the oppression faced by these groups, but the state and mainstream Muslims organisations such as MUI, Muhammadiyah, NU and many others have ignored pressure from these agencies. Mainstream Muslim groups seem to know that there will be no effective response to concerns raised by international groups on the implementation of religious freedom and human rights in Indonesia, even when raised by multilateral and bilateral organisations such the UN, the European Commission and ASEAN. In fact, Indonesia is often viewed by the international community as the most tolerant Muslim country in the world, as evidenced by the granting of the Appeal of Conscience Foundation's World Statesman Award to President Yudoyono in 2013 for his success in managing religious harmony and tolerance, despite criticism from many Indonesian local and international NGOs for this recognition, citing ongoing intolerance and violence against religious minorities taking place in Indonesia. MUI furthermore released a public statement welcoming Yudoyono's acceptance of the award,[66] indicating the closeness of MUI and Yudoyono's administration.

Unfortunately, MUI's rejection of both the Ahmadiyah and Shīʿa had wide support from the ordinary Muslim public of Indonesia. In the case of the Ahmadiyah, for instance, the Setara Institute's opinion poll found that 52.6% of 3000 respondents did not agree that Ahmadis were "brothers in belief" (*saudara seiman*) for other Indonesian Muslims. In addition, 38.8% of respondents

65 Ibid.

66 "Heboh Penghargaan Toleransi, MUI Dukung SBY," *Tempo*, 28 May 2013, https://nasional.tempo.co/read/483869/heboh-penghargaan-toleransi-mui-dukung-sby, viewed on 22 July 2022.

wanted the government of Indonesia to ban the Ahmadiyah.[67] A survey by Lingkaran Survei Indonesia (LSI) stated that 46.6% of the Indonesian public felt uncomfortable about having Ahmadi neighbours, and 41.8% did not want Shīʿa neighbours.[68] On this basis, MUI and its alliance were very confident in demanding the government of Indonesia to mimic the model of Pakistan in managing the Ahmadiyah, where Pakistani authorities had categorised it not as an Islamic sect, but a religious minority.[69] In moving in this direction, MUI and its alliance put high pressures on the Indonesian Ahmadis to publicly pronounce their religious status to be non-Muslim. While MUI and its alliance attempted this several times, however, the Ahmadis have rejected it.[70] MUI did not stop there, but also tried to convince the government of Indonesia—especially MORA—to disallow Indonesian Ahmadis from performing *hajj* in Mecca and Medina. This demand was based on the policy of the Saudi government—which has already declared that the Ahmadiyyah is not part of Islam—that bans Ahmadis from coming to Mecca and Medina, as well as arresting and detaining all those who are categorised as Ahmadis living in the country.[71] Amin—General Chairman of MUI from 2015 to 2020—stated that the government of Indonesia should forbid Ahmadis from undertaking *hajj* because of their "heretical" beliefs,[72] and in response MORA took steps to ensure that they would not be granted permission to go to Mecca and Medina.

The public support of ordinary Muslims for MUI's attitudes to the Shīʿa was also evident in the actions of the provincial branch of MUI in East Java. The Sampang Shīʿa was denounced by the East Java provincial branch of MUI,

67 "Survei Setara: Masyarakat Anggap Ahmadiyah 'Saudara Sebangsa,'" *Investor*, 8 September 2011, https://investor.id/national/survei-setara-masyarakat-anggap-ahmadiyah-saudara-sebangsa, viewed on 22 July 2022.

68 This survey was carried out in October 2012. There were 1200 respondents, with a margin error of 2.9%. See "Survei LSI: Orang RI Tidak Nyaman Bertetangga Dengan Orang Beda Identitas," *Detik News*, 21 October 2012, https://news.detik.com/berita/d-2068342/survei-lsi-orang-ri-tidak-nyaman-bertetangga-dengan-orang-beda-identitas, viewed on 22 July 2022.

69 Ishtiaq Ahmed, "Religious Nationalism and Minorities in Pakistan," in *The Politics of Religion in South and Southeast Asia*, ed. Ishtiaq Ahmed (New York: Taylor & Francis, 2011), 81–101, p. 88.

70 "MUI Kembali Tegaskan Ahmadiyah Bukan Islam," Republika, 13 November 2014, https://republika.co.id/berita/nasional/umum/14/11/13/neyzfo-mui-kembali-tegaskan-ahmadiyah-bukan-islam, viewed on 22 July 2022.

71 "Saudi Arabia: Stop Religious Persecution of Ahmadis", *Human Rights Watch*, 23 January 2007, https://www.hrw.org/news/2007/01/23/saudi-arabia-stop-religious-persecution-ahmadis, viewed on 22 July 2022.

72 "MUI Minta Depag Larang Ahmadiyah Berhaji," *Republika*, 8 September 2009, https://republika.co.id/berita/dunia-islam/islam-nusantara/09/09/08/74715-mui-minta-depag-larang-ahmadiyah-berhaji, viewed on 22 July 2022.

which stated that they have no right to live on the island of Madura. It was evident in the statement of Abdussomad Buchori (chairman of the East Java provincial branch of MUI) supporting the policy of Sampang government to relocate the Shīʿa community from Sampang.[73]

In relation to the position of Shīʿa in general, the position of MUI runs contrary to the Amman Message (2004),[74] which declares the Shīʿa to be part of Islam. It seems that MUI and other mainstream Muslim organisations in Indonesia such as NU, Muhammadiyah and Persatuan Islam are too political in their perspective on Shīʿa, and their judgment on the deviance of this sect is not based on careful study; it is merely based on the ideology of the supremacy of Sunnī teaching. Jaʿfariyya and Zaydiyya are two important and prominent Shīʿa groups that are theologically close to the Sunnī. In this case, the position of MUI is not defensible. In addition, MUI follows Indonesian Salafi groups that misrepresent the true teaching of these two gropus. This is ironic, because the Indonesian government[75] and representatives of mainstream Muslim groups in Indonesian[76] have all signed this declaration. See Table 2 below:

TABLE 2 Comparative table of *Aliran Sesat*[a] by MUI and Agreed Islamic Sects according to the *Amman Message*

Deviant Islamic groups banned by the MUI fatwa	**Recognised sects according to the *Amman Message***
Shīʿa[b]	Ḥanafī (Sunnī)
Ahmadiyah	Mālikī (Sunnī)
Islam Jama'ah	Shāfiʿī (Sunnī)

a MUI, *Mengawal Aqidah Umat: Fatwa MUI Tentang Aliran-Aliran Sesat Di Indonesia*, n.d., pp. 44–51.

b According to the fatwa issued by the central branch of MUI, extreme (*rāfiḍa*) Shīʿa beliefs are considered dangerous. The East Java MUI, however, judge Shīʿa to be deviant from Islam.

73 "Tragedi Karbala di tanah Madura", Merdeka, 18 March 2013, https://www.merdeka.com/khas/tragedi-di-karbala-di-tanah-madura-tragedi-syiah-sampang-4.html, viewed on 22 July 2022.

74 The Amman Declaration consisted of three points: the recognition of eight legal schools of thought (*madhāhib*) including Shīʿa; a ban on pronouncing disbelief (*takfīr*) upon others recognised as Muslims; and clarification on the issuing of religious edicts.

75 Alwi Shihab (Minister of Foreign Affairs), Maftuh Basyuni (Minister of Religious Affairs), and Rabhan Abd al-Wahhab (Ambassador of the Republic of Indonesia to Hashemite Kingdom of Jordan.)

76 Hasyim Muzadi, Rozy Munir, Masyhuri Naim, Muhammad Iqbal Sullam (NU), Tutty Alawiyyah (Islamic women's organisation), and Din Syamsuddin (Muhammadiyah).

TABLE 2 Comparative table of *Aliran Sesat* by MUI and Agreed Islamic Sects (*cont.*)

Deviant Islamic groups banned by the MUI fatwa	Recognised sects according to the *Amman Message*
Darul Arqam	Ḥanbalī (Sunnī)
Sunna Rejectionist (Inkar Sunnah)	a-Ibāḍīyya
Jama'ah Muslimin Hizbullah	Ash'ari
Lia Eden	Ja'farī (Shī'a)
Al-Qiyadah al-Islamiyah	Zaydī (Shī'a)
Wahidiyah (Ṣūfī order)	Ẓāhirī
Babur Ridha	Sufi
Lembaga Soul Training	Wahhābī
Thariqat Tajul Khalwatiyah wa Samaniyah	Deobandi
Pengajian al-Haq	

The fatwa on *aliran sesat* began to attract greater public attention when it targeted not only heresy in religious beliefs but also *aliran pemikiran* (deviant thinking), with MUI extending its stance on the danger of heresy to include secular groups. MUI categorises secular approaches such as pluralism and liberalism as a threat to religious life in Indonesia, and have particularly targeted JIL and other groups with a secular approach as "heretical." In 2005, they issued Fatwa No.7/MUNAS VII/MUI/11/2005 banning pluralism, secularism and liberalism. There are three reasons behind the issuance of this fatwa. First, the increasing openness of the Muslim community in Indonesia to these three concepts, which can be said to challenge the purity of Islam. Second, MUI believes that pluralism, secularism and liberalism have polarised Muslim communities and led to increasing levels of hardship. Third, MUI felt that the Muslim community needed a compass to act as guidance, in the form of a fatwa.[77] On the basis of this assessment, MUI stated four main points in its fatwa. First, that liberalism, secularism, and pluralism are against the doctrine of Islam. Second, that Muslim societies of Indonesia are not allowed to embrace these three concepts. Third, that in the domain of faith and worship Muslim societies should be exclusive, meaning that they are prohibited from mixing and combining their faith and rituals with others. Fourth, that in the domain of social and cultural life Muslim societies should be inclusive,

77 MUI, *Himpunan Keputusan Musyawarah Nasional VII Majelis Ulama Indonesia 2005* (Jakarta: Sekretariat Majelis Ulama Indonesia, 2005); Adian Husaini, *Pluralisme Agama: Haram: Fatwa MUI Yang Tegas & Tidak Kontroversial* (Jakarta: Pustaka Al-Kautsar, 2005).

meaning that they should live peacefully with non-believers. Overall, all Indonesian Muslims should resist embracing liberalism, secularism, and pluralism in their daily life.[78]

Fundamentally speaking, MUI has its own conception of pluralism, secularism and liberalism, which does not rest on any academic discussions. It states that pluralism is a notion that conveys the idea that all religions are the same, and hence the correctness of all beliefs and faiths in the world is relative. No believer should claim that his or her religion is the only true one and that others are wrong. MUI believes that pluralism means that believers of different religions will all go and live together in heaven; it therefore seems that MUI equates pluralism with religious relativism. Secondly, MUI states the plurality of religions is a social fact in many countries and places. MUI agrees with the concept of plurality rather than pluralism, because the latter notion resides the domain of belief, which should be kept pure. Thirdly, MUI considers religious liberalism to involve allowing interpretations of verses of the Qur'ān and tradition of the Prophet Muḥammad on the basis of an absolute freedom of thought, and asserts that religious liberalism can only accept religious teaching that complies with rational thinking. Fourthly, secularism is an ideology that creates a division between secular and non-secular life. For MUI, religion in secular domain exists only to regulate the connection between God and human beings, while relationships between people are part of the social contract.[79]

This fatwa has elicited various responses from progressive and moderate Muslim groups who did not agree with it, as it contradicts the religious freedom which is part of the Indonesian Constitution and universal human rights. Those who rejected this fatwa argued that the concepts of secularism, liberalism and pluralism have not been well-studied by MUI, and that the organisation did not consider the rich academic and scientific discussion on the subject. Instead, MUI seems to interpret these three concepts on the basis of their own ideology and political inclinations. Even some prominent figures from within MUI, such as Din Syamsuddin and Slamet Effendy Yusuf, have expressed their disagreement with the content of this fatwa.[80]

---

78 MUI, *Mengawal Aqidah Umat: Fatwa MUI Tentang Aliran-Aliran Sesat Di Indonesia* (Jakarta: Sekretariat Majelis Ulama Indonesia, n.d.); Syafiq Hasyim, "The Council of Indonesian Ulama (MUI) and Aqidah-Based Intolerance: A Critical Analysis of Its Fatwa on Ahmadiyya and 'Sepilis,'" in *Religion, Law and Intolerance in Indonesia*, ed. Tim Lindsey and Helen Pausacker (New York & London: Routledge, 2016), 211–33.

79 MUI, *Mengawal Aqidah Umat: Fatwa MUI Tentang Aliran-Aliran Sesat Di Indonesia*, n.d., pp. 91–95.

80 Interview with Slamet Effendy Yusuf, Jakarta, 2010.

Despite MUI's claims that this fatwa is non-political, at the practical level it provides an open stage that benefits radical and Islamist Muslim groups. Such groups instrumentalise this fatwa as means to attack all Muslim groups that have a different conception on the role of Islam in Indonesia as liberal, pluralist and secular. Prominent Muslim scholars and intellectuals—such as Wahid, Harun Nasution, Madjid, Syafi'i Ma'arif, Siradj, Shihab and many others—have been attacked as a result. These scholars, the radical groups claim, are agents promoting Western values who pose a threat to the development of Islam in Indonesia because they are liberal.[81] They have accused liberal Islamic groups of being influenced by Christianity and Orientalism.[82] Television programmes, newspapers, Facebook and Twitter often become a public space for radical and Islamist groups to promote hatred and hate speech targetting those who oppose the MUI fatwa. MUI has remained silent on this matter, even though some Muslim important figures who are associated with the organisation have been stigmatised.

6.2.2 *Worship*

As can be seen from the categorisation of MUI's fatwa, the organisation regards the domain of worship (Islamic rites) as the second most important issue after the domain of belief (*ʿaqīda*). This view reflects the importance of *ʿaqīda* in the hierarchy of Islamic teaching: the first duty of each Muslim is belief, and the second is worship. In Islam worship is a private matter for each individual Muslim. However, it is argued here that although worship belongs to the private sphere, the MUI fatwa on worship has shifted this religious practice from private to public. Further, the popular view of nationalist secular groups interprets the bringing of Islamic rites into the public sphere as equivalent to attempting to enshrine the religion in the state, since worship is one of the most visible aspects of any religion.[83] For this group, the growing observance of worship in the public sphere is viewed as a clear drive towards shariatisation. In response, MUI and its supporters nevertheless assert that creating a framework around their worship is part of their rights as citizens of Indonesia. MUI relies on the argument of religious freedom guaranteed by the Constitution of Indonesia that all believers are guaranteed the right to perform their religious practices. An observation on internal discussions among MUI activists shows

81 Hartono Ahmad Jaiz and Agus Hasan Bashori, *Menangkal Bahaya JIL Dan FLA* (Jakarta: Pustaka Al-Kautsar, 2004); Husaini, *Pluralisme Agama: Haram : Fatwa MUI Yang Tegas & Tidak Kontroversial.*

82 Adnin Armas, *Pengaruh Kristen-Orientalis Terhadap Islam Liberal: Dialog Interaktif Dengan Jaringan Islam Liberal* (Jakarta: Gema Insani Press, 2003).

83 Robet, "Perda, Fatwa and the Challenge to Secular Citizenship in Indonesia", p. 263.

that fashioning worship in the public sphere is intended both to promote and propagate Islam and to challenge the secular tendency of Indonesian Muslims. MUI adheres to the vision of Islam as not only discourse but also practice, as not only private but also public.[84] This is, in effect, the spirit of MUI's shariatisation. Rejecting the promotion of worship in the public sphere is deemed to be part of the secular and liberal agenda that confines worship to a private and individual domain. MUI is very critical of Muslim scholars and activists who advocate the personalisation or privatisation of Islamic rites, accusing them of having a hidden agenda to secularise and liberalise Indonesia.

Despite granting freedom of religion, the law never explicitly refers to any form of public worship, so it could be inferred that worship is perceived by the state to be a private matter. The state can facilitate but not promote worship. It can, for instance, provide transportation for pilgrims and build religious affairs offices for the six recognised religions.[85] In doing so, the Constitution declares the state shall be equal and fair in maintaining its distance from involvement in the ritual aspect of religion and belief. According to the Indonesian Constitution, the state cannot dictate that believers follow a specific religious interpretation or precept, even if it is followed by the majority. Indonesia follows the principle of separating the realm of religion and worship from politics.

Generally speaking, concerns regulated in the MUI fatwa on worship are closely related to three issues: implementing public piety, administrating Islamic rites in the public sphere, and purifying Islamic rites. These three matters are of great interest due to their intermingling with Islamic conceptions on worship, which—in the most traditional sources of Islamic jurisprudence—is a private issue between God and each believer. This means that neither the state nor societal groups can enforce or interfere with a specific style or act of worship. This is realised in the Indonesian Constitution by a formal guarantee of religious freedom for all citizens regardless of their beliefs, religions, ethics or gender. When MUI seeks ways to regulate Islamic rites in the public sphere, it means that the organisation has a different understanding of the position of worship from that either conventionally discussed in Islamic jurisprudence or in the Indonesian Constitution.

---

84 Interview with Ichwan Sam, Jakarta 2010; interview with Zainut Tauhid, Jakarta, 2010; interview with Asrorun Niam Sholeh 2011.

85 All these tasks are the responsibility of Ministry of Religious Affairs (MORA). However, the fact that MORA only facilitates the six religions recognised by the state has been criticised as an act of discrimination, particularly against adherents of indigenous religions and other minorities.

A widespread suspicion in Indonesia is that the proliferation of Islamic worship in the public sphere is a sign of the return of Islam to the arena of Indonesian politics. At the domestic level there is an understandable fear, given the country's experience with Islamic rebellions in the early formation of this state,[86] and at the international discursive level it is connected with sociological arguments on secularism, which separates religion from politics and generally assumes the presence of religious symbols in the public sphere as a threat to the nation-state.[87] This latter view reflects the long American sociological debate that designates secularism as an absolute divide between the Church and state.[88] However, this notion cannot be applied entirely to the context of contemporary Indonesia. In Islam there is little distinction between the religious and the political. Following Tagore's argument, the religious in Islam cannot always be always equated with the religious from the perspective of Western secularism, with its historical and discursive links with Christendom.[89] In fact, the political can also be a way of expressing Islamic piety.[90]

This section argues that the leitmotif behind the promotion of worship in the public sphere is MUI's will to shape and reconfigure the piety of Indonesian Muslims. In doing so, the domain of worship has shifted from the private to the public sphere. A subsequent argument is that by presenting the issue of worship as a public one, the act of worship can be controlled both by society and the state. When the worship of Indonesian Muslims can be controlled, then public welfare and prosperity can also be achieved. In defining public welfare,

86 Amelia, "Darul Islam Movement (DI), Struggling for an Islamic State of Indonesia"; Formichi, *Islam and the Making of the Nation: Kartosuwiryo and Political Islam in Twentieth-Century Indonesia*, 2012.

87 Indonesia has faced many Islamic rebellions such as the DI/TII in West Java, Aceh, and Sulawesi, as well as other religion-based separatist movements. Karl D. Jackson, *Traditional Authority, Islam, and Rebellion: A Study of Indonesian Political Behavior* (California: University of California Press, 1980); Edward Aspinall, *Islam and Nation: Separatist Rebellion in Aceh, Indonesia* (Redwood City, CA: Stanford University Press, 2009); C. van Dijk, *Rebellion Under the Banner of Islam: The Darul Islam in Indonesia* (The Hague: Martinus Nijhoff, 1981).

88 Saranindranath Tagore, "Rawlsian Liberalism, Secularism, and the Call for Cosmopolitanism," in *State and Securalism: Perspective from Asia*, ed. Michael Heng Siam-Heng and Ten Chin Liew (Singapore: World Scientific Publishing Co. Pte. Ltd., 2010), 37–59, p. 37.

89 Tagore is referring to Charles Taylor's idea of *saeculum*. See Charles Taylor, "Modes of Secularism," in *Secularism And Its Critics*, ed. Rajeev Bhargava, vol. 2 (Oxford University Press, Incorporated, 2005).

90 Saba Mahmood, *Politics of Piety: The Islamic Revival and the Feminist Subject* (New Brunswick, NJ: Princeton University Press, 2011).

MUI refers to spiritual and physical welfare and prosperity (Indonesian: *kesejahteraan lahir dan batin*), which can be attained through standardised religious worship.

Various strategies to impose Islamic worship rites in the public sphere have been attempted by MUI. In the Suharto era, it used the strategy of involving high state officials to act as role models of piety, and published an Islamic advice document titled *Kepeloporan Pejabat Dalam Melaksanakan Ibadah* ("State Officials as Role Models in the Practice of Worship") in 1976. This recommendation could be seen as MUI's first attempt to inject the discourse of worship into the public sphere. The path chosen by MUI could be explained through the patron-client relationship of Weberian thought,[91] in which political leaders are effective social and cultural role models for their families and communities in all fields, including worship. MUI therefore believed that leaders' social and political behaviour and attitudes in managing the country were the key to success for the national development programme, and this could be achieved through their obedience in worship. The best leaders for this purpose were those who combined a key role in both the political and religious spheres. This is what MUI meant when it said that the success of Indonesia's national development should combine material and spiritual aspects,[92] and the promotion of worship in the public sphere is part of this effort.

The strategy of involving public officials as role models showed signs of success when Suharto established many places of worship through his Yayasan Amalbakti Muslim Pancasila (Pancasila Muslim Charity Foundation), set up in 1982. The foundation was established to support Indonesian Muslims by providing Muslim places of worship. Despite this being a private initiative of Suharto, it had a public impact, and through it the president showed his enthusiastic response to the emergence of the Indonesian Muslim middle class, whose commitment to religion had become increasingly apparent in the public sphere. Although, as Ira Lapidus mentioned, the Suharto regime's focus remained at the level of endorsing personal piety,[93] nevertheless it was an apt response to the general paradigm of Islamic modernism, which was more inclined towards the refinement of the individual and personal rather

91 S.N. Eisenstadt and Luis Roniger, *Patrons, Clients and Friends: Interpersonal Relations and the Structure of Trust in Society*, vol. 3 (Cambridge: Cambridge University Press, 1984); S.N. Eisenstadt, *Power, Trust, and Meaning: Essays in Sociological Theory and Analysis* (Chicago: University of Chicago Press, 1995), pp. 202–38; Toby E. Huff and Wolfgang Schluchter, eds., *Max Weber and Islam* (Transaction Publishers, 1999), p. 32.

92 MUI, *Himpunan Fatwa MUI Sejak 1975*, p. 123.

93 Ira M. Lapidus, *A History of Islamic Societies* (Cambridge: Cambridge University Press, 2002), p. 674.

than the public piety of each Muslim. Following Suharto's establishment of the foundation, a policy was issued by Korp Pegawai Negeri Republik Indonesia (KORPRI, the Indonesian Civil Servant Corp, Decree No: Kep-04/Raker/1982) on 27 November 1982, obliging Muslim civil servants to donate a small amount of their salary ranging from 50 to 100 Indonesian Rupiah (equivalent to 10–20 US cents) as a monthly compulsory contribution for the Foundation. In 1983, the Commander in Chief of the Indonesian Army, Benny Moerdani (d. 2004), a Catholic and a Suharto loyalist, published Decree 8/381/P/07/11/02/Set which instructed all members of the Indonesian Armed Forces—which at that time included the police—to donate a certain amount of their salary ranging from 50 to 2000 Indonesian Rupiah (10 cents to 1 USD)[94] as a compulsory monthly donation to the Foundation.[95] From the funds collected from 1982 to 2011, the Foundation successfully built 999 mosques across Indonesia, mostly called Masjid Pancasila (Pancasila mosques, after the Foundation) and two mosques abroad: the Masjid al-Hikmah in New York, and a second in Port Moresby, the capital of Papua New Guinea. MUI regarded the establishment of Pancasila mosques as an important initiative and symbol of Islam in the public sphere. The response of Muslim communities was quite positive, as indicated by mushrooming places of worship/prayer rooms in public offices. Muslim employees had more opportunities not only to worship but also learn about aspects of their religion, such as the Qur'ān, *fiqh* and so on. It also contributed to providing job opportunities for graduates of Islamic higher institutions like *pesantren*, state Islamic universities and so on. In the post-Suharto era, the Minister of Home Affairs signed Ministerial Regulation No. 50/2011 that made the provision of places of worship in both private and public offices obligatory.

However, implementing Islamic piety is not only associated with increasing the number of places of worship, but also persuading Indonesian Muslims to improve themselves through fatwas on how to worship properly in Islam. It would seem that MUI fatwas on worship—such as *Puasa Bagi Penerbang* ("Fasting for Flight Crew"), *Kiblat* ("The Direction of the *Ka'aba*"), *Pil Anti Haid* ("Anti-Menstruation Medication"), *Shalat Jumat Bagi Musafir* ("Friday Prayers for Travellers") and many others—can be understood as an attempt to equate individual piety with public piety. All these fatwas were provided by MUI to guide Muslims towards correct forms of worship, which they see as an important step towards piety.

94 1 USD in the Suharto era was equivalent to 2000 IDR.

95 Yayasan Amalbakti Muslim Pancasila, *999 Masjid: Yayasan Amalbakti Muslim Pancasila 1982–2009* (Jakarta: Yayasan Amalbakti Muslim Pancasila, 2009).

A further implication of the extension of Islamic rites into the public sphere is the established need to administer religion. Clifford Geertz indicated in his *Religion of Java* that a similar phenomenon of religious administration took place in the 1960s.[96] Overseeing and managing worship are effective ways of increasing the benefit of worship for the broader public; this is what sociologists refer to as the bureaucratisation of religion. Using Michele Dillon's argument, the administration of religion is behind MUI's aspiration to rationalise certain worship practices.[97] This MUI preference for involvement in the administration of religion is visible in such practices as the payment of *zakāt*, determining the beginning of the fasting month, and some other issues.

The administration of *zakāt* payment (Islamic almsgiving) is one clear example. In Indonesia, this practice was traditionally carried out without following any particular prescription or guidance from either the state or Islamic organisations. Those paying *zakāt* had the freedom to distribute their alms to one of eight social groups of deserving recipients (*al-aṣnāf al-thamāniyya*). However, MUI believes that this tradition of paying *zakāt* has had a relatively low impact on the interests of the broader community as it has not been collectively organised. Islamic almsgiving has the potential to boost the economy of the Muslim community, so MUI sought a method of transforming it from being a private matter for each individual Muslim to a public matter of the *umma* by proposing a bill on its administration. Since 1982, MUI has therefore been addressing the observance of Islamic almsgiving.[98]

MUI published a fatwa called *Mentasharufkan Dana Zakāt untuk Kegiatan Produktif dan Kemaslahatan Umum* ("Distributing Islamic Almsgiving for Productive Activity and Public Interest") in 1982 that prescribes the way Indonesian *muzakki*s (almsgivers) pay their alms in the interests of productivity. MUI orders that almsgiving for the needy (*faqīr*, Indonesian: *fakir*) and the poor (Arabic: *miskīn*, Indonesian: *miskin*) or other *zakāt* recipients can be distributed to finance, business, or entrepreneurship activities and the portion of *sabīl li-Allāhi* (the path of God) can be used to fund public interest projects. From the perspective of *maṣlaḥa*, this fatwa was quite progressive, but controversial because it was against the discourse of Islamic jurisprudence commonly adhered to by Indonesian Muslims. Following the Shāfiʿī school of

96 Clifford Geertz, *The Religion of Java* (Chicago: University of Chicago Press, 1976), p. 207.

97 Michele Dillon, *Handbook of the Sociology of Religion* (Cambridge: Cambridge University Press, 2003), 127; Wolfgang Schluchter, *Rationalism, Religion, and Domination: A Weberian Perspective* (Berkeley, Los Angeles & Oxford: University of California Press, 1989).

98 MUI's recommendation regarding the intensification of Islamic alms payment (*Intensifikasi Pelaksanaan Zakat*) was published on 26 January 1982. MUI, *Himpunan Fatwa MUI Sejak 1975*, pp. 153–8.

Islamic law, most Indonesian Muslims do not agree with distributing alms as MUI suggested, and traditionalist ulama of Indonesia, especially Nahdlatul Ulama, criticised this decision. This group believes that *zakāt* has to be used for food and drink, and not as capital for business. Despite such criticism, MUI continued to promote its fatwa. In 1996, MUI issued another fatwa that allows the use of alms for funding education, education here being interpreted by MUI as the path of God (*sabīl li-Allāh*). The issuance of this latter fatwa seemed to have a political link with the ICMI scholarship programme, since it could be used as a theological justification for fundraising targeting the Indonesian *muzakkī*.

At the level of state legal discourse, the MUI fatwa on almsgiving was strengthened by State Law No. 38/1999 on the Management of Almsgiving. This law was promulgated at the time of burgeoning Islamic charity movements in Indonesia. Among these charity initiatives were, for instance, the Lembaga Amil Zakat, Infaq dan Shadaqoh (LAZIZ, the Institute for Charity, Islamic Alms, Donation and Gifts), Dompet Du'afa (the Community Wallet for Marginalised People),[99] and many other related institutions. The Badan Amil Zakat Nasional (BAZNAS, National Almsgiving Collector Agency) was established following this law, and was the first national agency that it officially promoted.[100] Later, Act No. 23/2011 on almsgiving amended Act No. 38/1999, strengthening the process of managing *zakāt* in the public sphere through the centralisation of alms-collection through a state-sponsored almsgiving agency. The new law does not allow the charitable foundations of traditional Islamic boarding schools, social organisations, mosques and others to collect and distribute alms from and for Muslim societies. Most alarming is the five-year prison sentence or fine of 500 million Indonesian Rupiah (USD 50,000) that can be imposed on those collecting and distributing alms without permission from BAZNAS. Arguing for religious freedom, some social activists complain that the new law on almsgiving will kill democracy because the state has narrowed the scope of civil society organisations to participate in organising its collection.

In 2003, *zakāt* administrators began to target professionals and civil servants through the MUI fatwa on *zakāt profesi* (profession-based almsgiving). Two Muslim scholars, Amin Rais and Jalaludin Rakhmat, had proposed this

99 Dompet Dua'afa is an institution established by *Republika* (a national newspaper) to collect donations from readers.

100 Salim, "Zakat Administration in Politics of Indonesian New Order", p. 353.

idea in the 1990s.[101] Rais states that the percentage of *zakāt profesi* can be as high as 20% of the salary.[102] The thinking of these Muslim scholars is similar to that of Yūsuf al-Qaraḍāwī and his two Egyptian senior ulama, Abū Zahra (1898–1974) and ʿAbd al-Wahhāb Khallāf (1989–1974).

In 2011, the management of *zakāt* payment was further defined by the MUI fatwa on *amil zakāt* (an Indonesian expression for the Islamic Almsgiving Administration). Through this fatwa, MUI provides space for state intervention for issuing certification for *zakāt* administration. In March 2011, MUI granted authority to the *amil zakāt* to approach and persuade prospective almsgivers. This means that the *amil zakāt* has greater prominence in the public sphere. Thus, despite following the principle of state neutrality towards religion, Indonesian lawmakers seem to approve attempts by Islamic groups to promote the state regulation of almsgiving through the establishment of regulators such as BASNAZ, LAZIZ and many others.

Religious administration is also evident in MUI's role in dominating the process for determining the dates of Islamic rites such as the beginning of Ramaḍān (the fasting month), the celebration of ʿEid al-Fiṭr, and many other important religious days. Since 2004, MUI has played a powerful role in the Sidang Isbat,[103] the meeting of Islamic organisations held by the Ministry of Religious Affairs (MORA) and legitimised by MUI to determine the first day

101 Jalaluddin Rakhmat, *Islam Aktual: Refleksi-Sosial Seorang Cendekiawan Muslim* (Penerbit Mizan, 1991), pp. 184–5; M. Amien Rais, *Cakrawala Islam: Antara Cita Dan Fakta* (Bandung: Mizan, 1987), p. 61.

102 Abd. Rahim Ghazali, ed., *M. Amien Rais Dalam Sorotan Generasi Muda Muhammadiyah* (Bandung: Mizan, 1998); Muhammad Najib, *Melawan Arus: Pemikiran Dan Langkah Politik Amien Rais* (Jakarta: Serambi, 1999), p. 67; Rais, *Cakrawala Islam: Antara Cita Dan Fakta,* p. 61.

103 *Isbat* is a Indonesian word taken from Arabic, *ithbāt,* meaning fixedness. See Rohi Balbaaki, *Al-Mawrid* (Beirut: Dar El-Elm LilMalayin, 1995), p. 398. This meeting is organised by the Ministry of Religious Affairs and is supported by MUI to seek agreement on the first day of Ramaḍān, ʿEid al-Fiṭr and Eid al-Aḍhā. The meeting usually begins with an opening ceremony by MORA staff to welcome the delegates of Muslim organisations and also foreign embassies of Islamic countries who have their representatives in Jakarta. The recitation of the Qurʾān follows. The Minister of Religious Affairs leads the session, accompanied by the MUI General Chairman, the General Director of Binmas Islam sitting in front of the U-shaped meeting room. The Minister reports on the sighting of the moon, which is performed by MORA staff in regional offices. Then the Minister invites participants to respond from their own findings, because other Islamic organisations also conduct their own moon-sighting. On the basis of all responses and certain agreed-upon parameters, the first date of Ramaḍān or ʿEid al-Fiṭr or Eid al-Aḍhā is decided. In the last five years, the Sidang Isbat has been criticised by many anti-corruption and human rights activists as unhelpful because it costs a lot of money and does not support the unity of Islam.

of Ramaḍān. Supported by an MUI fatwa of 2004, the authority of the Sidang Isbat was legislated in Act No. 3/2006 on Religious Courts.[104] MUI believes that Indonesian Muslims are vulnerable to social and theological tensions because of their differing religious opinions, a prominent example being the different stance of Islamic organisations in determining the beginning of religious festivities, especially ʿEid al-Fiṭr and ʿEid al-Aḍḥā. MUI believes its guiding influence is needed here to achieve a common approach for the sake of the unity of the Islamic community (*waḥdat al-umma*). For many years, Indonesian Muslims have been divided between those who determine the start of Ramaḍān, Shawwāl, and Dhū al-Ḥijja by means of astronomical calculations (*ḥisāb*) and those who wait to sight the new crescent moon (*ru'ya bi al-hilāl*).[105] Muhammadiyah tends to follow the first method and MUI, NU, Persatuan Tarbiyah Islamiyah, al-Wasliyah and many others the second. Muhammadiyah believes that the use of pure astronomical calculations are the best and most accurate method for determining the start of the new month, while MUI and NU argue that sighting the new moon is a sharia obligation. Both MUI and NU contend the matter is not one for contention and dispute because it is clearly covered by sharia. MUI concedes that astronomical calculations may be used, but not as the sole method to determine the advent of a new month. In the Suharto era such vigorous debates were not so visible in the public sphere due to the strong control of the ruling regime. In fact, up to the present day, Muhammadiyah still believes that the *ḥisāb* method is a credible and valid way to predict the coming of a new month, although its opinion is different from the other largest Indonesian Islamic organisations. In fact, the leaders of Muhammadiyah have long expressed their criticism of the Sidang Isbat's method that tended to accommodate *ru'ya bi al-hilāl* as a means of deciding the arrival of both Ramaḍān and ʿEid al-Fiṭr, and often refused to send a representative to the Sidang Isbat. Thus Indonesian Muslims are always divided into two distinct groups in celebrating Ramaḍān and ʿEid al-Fiṭr; first, those who follow the practice of *ru'ya bi al-hilāl*—the NU (40 million members), MUI, Perti, Persis and many others—and second, the Muhammadiyah community (approximately 30 million members) who follow the method of *ḥisāb*.

MUI and its supporters have put pressure on MORA to exclude those with different views, thus favouring the *ru'ya* method. In this regard, the harmony

104 See Article 52A: "Religious Court gives determination on moon-sighting witness for deciding first day of the month according to lunar calendar."

105 Iik Arifin Mansurnoor, "Islam in Brunei Darussalam and Global Islam: An Analysis of Their Interaction," in *Islam in the Era of Globalization: Muslim Attitudes towards Modernity and Identity*, ed. Johan H Mueleman (London & New York: Routledge, 2002), 71–98, p. 91.

of the *umma* has been narrowly defined by MUI as a common approach that accords with MUI's preference for determining the advent of Islamic festival dates. This simplistic interpretation of *waḥdat al-umma* is misleading and ignores many other pressing issues that could be used as a common platform for consolidating the unity of the Indonesian Muslim community, such as eradicating poverty, combatting corruption, and stopping religious-based violence, all of which have contributed to the establishment of schisms. It would appear that enforcing uniformity in determining the first day of important Islamic dates leads to more harm (*mafsada*) than public beneficence (*maṣlaḥa*), since instead of seeking consensus among the *umma* the fatwa rails against social disunity and disintegration. Some experts suggest that the government should distance itself from being involved in holding the Sidang Isbat because all citizens are equally protected by state law in practising their belief. The rational path for the government would be to determine the range of national holidays and allow Muslim groups the freedom to determine for themselves the start of the fasting month and celebration of ʿEid al-Fiṭr and ʿEid al-Aḍḥā.

The next trend in MUI's management of religious practice in the public sphere is their desire to purify religious practices such as worship and female circumcision. The purification of religious practice is intended to cleanse Islam from the intrusion of non-Islamic elements and to correct Islamic practices. Both these intentions are visible in the MUI fatwa on *doa bersama* (interfaith prayer), female circumcision and others. It is well known that Indonesian Muslims have some religious traditions that are mixed with local practices.[106] However, MUI has begun to campaign against some local traditions that are not always congruent with what Ernest Gellner describes as "high Islam." Following Gellner's typology, many religious practices in Indonesia can be categorised as the expression of "low Islam", being inauthentic, localised and full of religious innovation.[107] Borrowing Nasim A. Jawed's depiction of the Pakistan case, MUI plays its role as the representative of High Islam, which is puritan and literalist, and hopes to convert practices of Low Islam to High Islam by promoting a proper and pure form of religion.[108] From Gellner's perspective, MUI is part of the triumph of High Islam in the global Islamic

106 M.C. Ricklefs, *A History of Modern Indonesia since c.1200* (Redwood City, CA: Stanford University Press, 2009), p. 3.

107 Nasim A. Jawed, *Islam's Political Culture: Religion and Politics in Predivided Pakistan* (Austin: University of Texas Press, 1999), p. 162; Ernest Gellner, *Postmodernism, Reason and Religion* (London & New York: Routledge, 1992), p. 9.

108 Jawed, *Islam's Political Culture: Religion and Politics in Predivided Pakistan*.

resurgence.[109] The argument behind this religious practice fatwa is that, as part of the global *umma*, Indonesian Muslims should practice their religion properly, according to the tradition of High Islam.

MUI has introduced several other fatwas regulating the religious practice of Indonesian Muslims. In 2005, it shocked Indonesian Muslims with its fatwa banning *doa bersama* (interfaith collective prayer), issued on the grounds that interfaith prayer endangered the purity of Muslims' faith. Although MUI was fully aware that this was a sensitive issue, interfaith prayer having long roots as a genuine part of Indonesian tradition, nevertheless it issued a strong fatwa in response to perceived public concern. MUI concluded that interfaith prayer is *bid'a* (a forbidden religious innovation) as it was not practised in the era of the Prophet Muḥammad, and also *haram* (banned) when it is performed by participants of different religions reading prayers together, led by non-Muslims. This fatwa clearly demonstrates MUI's opposition, despite the support for interfaith prayer from a number of authors who compiled a book titled *Fiqh Lintas Agama* ("Interfaith in Islamic legal jurisprudence").[110] The authors argued that the practice of interfaith prayer is valid in Islam because the inner belief (*īmān*) of each person will not decrease as a result of actions such as participating in interfaith prayers. The group stated that *tawḥīd* (the unity of God) is deeply rooted in the hearts of the faithful and, further, that by appreciating others' prayers they increase their belief in God. The authors thus follow the logic that what determines one's faith is not external actions but internal belief (*niyya*).[111]

From a political perspective, this fatwa weakens the principle of mutual respect and tolerance among diverse religions, which is the cornerstone of the Pancasila Indonesian state ideology. Through this fatwa, MUI completely rejected the tradition of collective prayer that has long been practised by the Indonesian state and diverse religious communities. In the Suharto era, interfaith collective prayer was conducted to express the collective identity of Indonesia as a tolerant religious country. This fatwa has produced social anxiety among Indonesian Muslims regarding their perception of themselves as

109 Ernest Gellner, *Postmodernism, Reason and Religion.*

110 This book was published by the Paramadina Foundation (Indonesian: Yayasan Paramadina) and Gramedia. The Paramadina Foundation was established by Muslim scholar Nurcholsih Madjid who was famous for his ideas on the need for Indonesian Muslims to undertake Islamic reform (Indonesian: *pembaharuan*, Arabic: *tajdīd*) and secularisation.

111 Paul R. Powers, *Intent in Islamic Law: Motive and Meaning in Medieval Sunnī Fiqh* (Leiden: Brill, 2006), p. 43; Bernard G. Weiss, *The Spirit of Islamic Law* (Georgia: University of Georgia Press, 2006), p. 186.

being part of a pluralist and tolerant *umma*. Yet, incredibly, public calls for collective prayer to be rejected have gained more support of late.

Another aspect of MUI's concern to correct Islamic religious practices in accordance with pure Islam is evident in its support for the legal validity of female circumcision. In 2008, MUI issued a fatwa that banned Islamic legal opinions, recommendations or regulations that criticised the practice of female circumcision. The social and cultural background of this fatwa is complex and has a discursive link with the attitudes towards feminism and gender equality prevalent in Indonesia since 1994's International Conference on Population and Development. Indonesia was one of the first Islamic countries to ratify international instruments for women's rights and gender equality. Indonesia ratified CEDAW (the Convention on the Elimination of all Forms of Discrimination against Women) in 1984, and in 2000, President Wahid issued Presidential Decree No. 9/2000 on *pengarusutamaan gender* (gender mainstreaming). At the civil society level, many projects and activities aimed at improving gender equality and women's empowerment have been implemented, all of which make it easier for Indonesian Muslims to accommodate the ideas of Islamic feminism. One of the critical issues that Indonesian Muslim feminists discuss is the practice of female circumcision, and their campaign to ban it was well-received by society and the state. As a result, the 2006 Circular Decree of the Department of National Health—via the Director General of Social Health for Community Health Building, No. HK. 00.1.3.1047a–recommended the prohibition of medicalised female circumcision. This decree led to the state's clinics and hospitals denying medical assistance to those who wanted to circumcise their daughters.

In response to the controversy that followed, MUI stated that the ban on female circumcision was against true Islam and that female circumcision was a part of Islamic observance, even though its legal status remains contested among Muslim jurists. In its fatwa, MUI concluded that female circumcision is human nature—*fitrah* in Indonesian, from the Arabic term *fitrī*—that positive legal discourses banning female circumcision conflict with the norms of sharia, and that female circumcision is permissible only by severing the clitoral column (praeputium). The *fitrah* MUI refers to here is that women should be circumcised because of their sexuality. In many sources of local Islam in Southeast Asia and Africa it is often mentioned that circumcision for women can reduce and control their sexual desires and pleasures.[112] If they are not

112 Nurul Ilmi Idrus, "Islam, Marriage and Gender Relations in Bugis Lontara': A Critical Analysis of the Lontara' Daramatasia," in *Gender and Islam in Southeast Asia: Women's Rights Movements, Religious Resurgence and Local Traditions*, ed. Susanne Schroeter

controlled, they can lead men and themselves to commit sin. This is the logic behind the concept of *fitrah*. In defence of its fatwa, MUI referred to Aḥmad b. Ḥanbal, who stated that male circumcision is recommended and for females it is honourable;[113] al-Shawkāni, in his *Nayl al-Awṭār*, who reported that the Prophet Muḥammad ordered women of the *Anṣār*[114] to dye their nails and be circumcised, but fairly;[115] and Abū Dawūd, who quoted reminders of the Prophet Muḥammad's call for those conducting circumcision to ensure that not too much pain is inflicted on the female.[116] MUI refers to ulama consensus that female circumcision is part of sharia and regards female circumcision as a place closed to *ijtihād* because Islamic texts are very clear on this issue: "no *ijtihād* when there is a text."[117] The Ḥanbali school of Islamic law put forward by Ibn Qudāma (1147–1187) in *al-Mughnī* indicates that circumcision is compulsory for men and valid for women. Abū Bakr Shaṭṭā in *I'ānat al-Ṭālibīn* argues that cutting off part of the clitoris is obligatory in female circumcision, stating the "lesser cut off is more esteem" (*wa taqlīluhu afḍal*). Two opinions of contemporary Muslim jurists referred to are those of Wahba al-Zuḥaylī in *al-Fiqh al-Islāmī wa Adillatuhu* and Jadd al-Ḥaq in *Buḥūth wa Fatāwā Islāmiyya fī Qaḍāyā Mu'āṣira*. Al-Zuḥaylī agrees to a minor form of female circumcision, whereas the latter supports all previous opinions arguing that female circumcision is part of the nature of Islam (*anna al-khitān li al-rijāl wa al-nisā' min fiṭra al-Islām wa sha'ā'irihi*), adding that no ulama disallows the practice of female circumcision or views it as harmful. In its support of female circumcision, however, MUI stands in opposition to the International Organisation of the Islamic Conference that has banned female circumcision as un-Islamic and a violation of human rights.

The fatwa can be criticised from various perspectives. Daniel Njoroge Karanja states that the discourse of this fatwa does not refer to the numerous forms of female circumcision that were not only practised within the tradition of the Semitic religions (Islam, Christianity and Judaism) and also within tribal

---

(Leiden: Brill, 2013), 95–110, pp. 106–107; Ellen Gruenbaum, *The Female Circumcision Controversy: An Anthropological Perspective* (Pennsylvania: University of Pennsylvania Press, 2001), pp. 156–157.

113 Arabic: *al-khitān sunna li al-rijāl, makrama li al-nisā'*.

114 Women who gave help to the Muslims who emigrated from Mecca in Year 1 AH.

115 A complete Arabic version of the *ḥadīth* is *yā nisā' al-anṣār ikhtadibna ghamsan wā akhtafidna wa lā tunhikna wa iyyākum wa kufrāna al-na'ami.*

116 A complete Arabic version of the ḥadīth: *anna amratan kānat takhtinu bi al-madīnati faqāla lahā al-nabiyyu ṣallā llāhu 'alayhi wa sallam la tunhuk fa inna dhālika aḥẓā ila al-mar'a wa aḥabbu ilā al-ba'li.*

117 Arabic version: *lā ijtihād ma'a al-naṣṣ*.

societies,[118] but is rather a kind of idealisation of female circumcision that should be performed. So far it is estimated that 80 million women have been subject to this practice, and 5000 are vulnerable to being violently circumcised each day.[119] Studies have shown that in many cases infibulation—also known as Type III female genital mutilation—can result in trauma.[120] Because female circumcision has a harmful impact on the body and emotional state of women, some modern Muslim scholars such as Jamal Badawi, a modern Muslim jurist of Egypt, have called for a ban when its practice violates and threatens the sexual pleasure of women, adding that it has no theological basis in the Qurʾān and *ḥadīth*.[121] The fatwa further incites division between those who support the fatwa and those who do not, leading to social and emotive mobilisation. Supporters claimed that the issuance of this edict is indicative of the state's backing for the inclusion of sharia into the legal system of Indonesia, as it was issued in response to a question by the Ministry of Women's Empowerment and intended to counter the Ministry of Health's circular decree that forbade female circumcision.

6.2.3 *Public Morality*

The issue of public morality is one of the main reasons behind the importance of MUI in Indonesia. This can be seen in its institutional aim to command right and forbid wrong (*al-amr bi al-maʿrūf wa al-nahy ʿan al-munkar*) for Indonesian society. To borrow Michael Cook's perspective, MUI has a duty to "right wrong" (*taghyīr al-munkar*),[122] which includes anything the organisation considers to be deviant from the agreed moral standard of sharia norms. It is therefore understandable that MUI has a very ambitious agenda in promoting sharia as public morality in Indonesia. The organisation believes that over the last decade the public morality of Indonesians has declined, and the promotion of sharia offers an answer to this problem. Beyond the theological argument, guiding public morality can contribute to social and public order. As a non-state entity, MUI can support lawmakers and the state to adopt sharia as the primary

118 Daniel Njoroge Karanja, *Female Genital Mutilation in Africa* (Michigan: Xulon Press, 2003).

119 H.A. Jawad, *The Rights of Women in Islam: An Authentic Approach* (Oxford: Palgrave Macmillan, 1998), p. 52.

120 Ibid.

121 Mustafa Rogaia Abusharaf, "Female Circumcision: Multicultural Perspectives," in *Female Circumcision: Multicultural Perspectives*, ed. Rogaia Mustafa Abusharaf (Pennsylvania: University of Pennsylvania Press, 2007), 1–26, pp. 2–3; Jamal A. Badawi, *Gender Equity in Islam: Basic Principles* (American Trust Publications, 1995).

122 Cook, *Forbidding Wrong in Islam: An Introduction*, p. 4; Cook, *Commanding Right and Forbidding Wrong in Islamic Thought*.

grounds for regulating and implementing public morality. Borrowing Samuli Schielke's argument in his study on *mūlids* (saints-day festivals) in Egypt,[123] enacting sharia as public morality is part of MUI's effort to realise an Islamic moral geography of public space. Employing religion for public morality means grappling with the question of what is good for society.[124]

The problem is that the notions of public morality held by Indonesians, even Muslims, are not solely based on sharia. Indonesia is tied to *adat* law, social consensus, international and transnational conventions and many other matters that should also be considered as sources of public morality. This is a consequence of Indonesia being a state with the principle of legal pluralism. On the basis of John Rawls' concept of institutional neutrality, the state cannot promote, enforce or favour a set of rules for its citizens which are based on particular religious values.[125] Issuing Islamic edicts as a key source of public morality in Indonesia thus becomes a problematic issue. Sharia prescriptions have their own standards on what should be done to promote public morality, while non-sharia prescriptions offer different prescriptions for the same purpose. Some issues can be reconciled but, as Indonesia is a non-sharia-based state, tensions persist. Nevertheless, MUI tends to promote sharia as the primary marker of public morality, as can be seen from its willingness to regulate public immorality through its fatwa and advice, focused on regulating and limiting the body and mind and normalising sharia in the public sphere.

MUI has concluded that one of the most crucial issues facing Indonesia is declining public morality due to an inability to anticipate and control the proliferation of immoral behaviour and practices of Indonesians, including Muslims. The organisation has therefore determined that a set of edicts is needed to limit the flow of immorality by controlling the bodies and minds of Muslims, particularly women. In her study on the *zinā* (adultery) ordinance in Pakistan, Shahnaz Khan reveals that public morality is always related to regulating the morality of women,[126] and regulating the morality of women is a matter of controlling women's bodies. This understanding is closely related

123 Samuli Schielke, "Policing Ambiguity: Muslim Saints-Day Festivals and the Moral Geography of Public Space in Egypt," *American Ethnologist* 33, no. 4 (2008): 539–52.

124 Robert Kunzman, *Grappling with the Good: Talking about Religion and Morality in Public Schools* (Albany: State University of New York Press, 2006).

125 Tagore, "Rawlsian Liberalism, Secularism, and the Call for Cosmopolitanism", p. 39; Klosko and Wall, *Perfectionism and Neutrality: Essays in Liberal Theory*, ed. Steven Wall and George Klosko (Oxford: Rowman & Littlefield Publishers, 2004), p. 5; John Rawls, *Political Liberalism: Expanded Edition* (New York: Columbia University Press, 2011).

126 Shahnaz Khan, *Zina, Transnational Feminism, and the Moral Regulation of Pakistani Women* (Vancouver: UBC Press, 2011), p. 56.

to a general assumption in Muslim communities, particularly Indonesia, that still perceives women to be a source of *fitna* (immorality).[127] If the community requires good public morality, there should be regulations to prevent women from displaying parts of the body considered to be seductive. Nawal el Saadawi shows that all negative perceptions of women's bodies in Islam is due to the inherited concept that Eve was a follower of the Devil and the bodies of women are therefore the abode of Satan.[128] Saadawi relates this common belief to two popular sayings of the Prophet Muḥammad: "Whenever a man and a woman meet together the third party is always Satan," and "After I have gone, there will be no greater menace to my nation and more liable to create anarchy and trouble than women."[129] This depiction of women is widespread in the popular discourse of Indonesian Muslims.[130]

The function of public morality here is to control women's bodies. Some examples of the "uncontrolled body and mind" of women that MUI perceives as morally challenging are issues such as abortion, pornography, wearing un-Islamic clothing, interfaith marriage and so forth. MUI fatwa's on abortion does not stop at the practice of abortion but targets the prevalence of sexual promiscuity as the root cause. The HTI and other radical Islamic groups state that a weak law on abortion can lead Muslims towards sexual promiscuity, and many Indonesian groups criticised the shortage of clear legal provisions banning abortion as it was considered crucial for maintaining public morality. To fill this vacuum, MUI formulated a fatwa in 2000 which stated that abortion which takes place before the *nafkha al-rūḥ* (when the soul is believed to enter the foetus at forty days) is permitted without need for medical justification, and abortion after this is prohibited unless medical reasons can justify it.[131] To gain more attention from the public and policy makers, MUI published a second fatwa in 2005 in response to reported increasing cases of abortion. It is estimated that induced and/or unsafe abortions in Indonesia may number 2–3 million per year, roughly translating to twenty-nine abortions for every thousand women of reproductive age (from fifteen to forty-nine years old).[132]

---

127 Nawal El Saadawi, *The Hidden Face of Eve: Women in the Arab World* (London & New York: Zed Books, 2007), p. 203.

128 Ibid, p. 204.

129 Ibid.

130 See, for example, Badawi Mahmud, *100 Pesan Nabi Untuk Wanita Salihah* (Bandung: Mizan Pustaka, 2008).

131 MUI, *Himpunan Fatwa MUI Sejak 1975*, p. 399.

132 "MUI: Kami Yang Lebih Dulu Izinkan Aborsi," *Tempo*, 16 November 2014, https://nasional.tempo.co/read/622297/mui-kami-yang-lebih-dulu-izinkan-aborsi, viewed on 22 July 2022.

The 2005 fatwa provide more exceptions to the rule, with rape victims being allowed abortions, and in cases of women who become pregnant outside marriage. The granting of abortion for rape victims is a response to the local, national and international Islamic legal discourses on Muslim rape victims in religiously motivated conflicts in areas such as Ambon (Indonesia), Bosnia (Europe) and many other places. In the case of extra-marital pregnancies, the fatwa can contribute to resolving the social shame of unmarried women who fall pregnant. This fatwa is quite progressive. By allowing such women to terminate their pregnancy, MUI prioritises the interests of the mother. In this issue MUI relies on the Islamic legal opinion of ʿAṭiyya Ṣaqr in his book *Aḥsan al-Kalām fī al-Fatāwā wa al-Aḥkām*. Ṣaqr refers to the Shāfiʿī school of Islamic law that allows the termination of pregnancy for women who have committed adultery. However, social and cultural circumstances must also be considered: if the woman lives in a society with a more permissive attitude towards extra-marital sex, she is not permitted to have an abortion because this could encourage further cultural promiscuity. With exception of the last issue, all the Islamic legal arguments used in the second fatwa are similar to those of the first.[133] Although some conditions of the legal provisions on abortion in Act No. 36/2009 on Health are similar to those of the MUI fatwa,[134] Amin states that upper limit for abortion of six weeks (or forty-two days), as stipulated under the act, is equivalent to killing the baby. MUI allows abortion up to forty days' gestation. The organisation received strong support from HTI, which was an active anti-abortion campaigner in 2005 with around 700 HTI members staging a street march protesting against the legalisation of abortion. On 16 September 2005, a similar protest attended by one hundred HTI members took place before the regional parliamentary building of East Java.[135] This Islamic transnational organisation used this narrative to publicise its stance on abortion and its solution of returning to the principles of sharia. However, finally Act No. 36/2009 was introduced in 2009.

133 MUI, *Himpunan Fatwa MUI Sejak 1975*, p. 456.

134 In addition, Act No. 36/2009 promotes and strengthens the content of MUI fatwa on abortion, which is evident, for instance, in Chapter 75 of the Law, which states that abortion is forbidden unless there is a medical emergency detected in the first stage of pregnancy. An emergency is defined as a condition that would cause maternal death or genetic deficiencies that may adversely affect the infant in later stages of their life. Importantly, Act No. 36/2009 also allows abortion for women who are victims of rape. This point is similar to the MUI fatwa. One point of difference between the MUI fatwa and Act No. 36/2009 is the upper age limit of the foetus for which abortion is allowed.

135 "HTI Tolak Legalisasi Aborsi," *Surabaya Post*, 16 September 2005 (not available online.)

The second moral case on control of the body and mind is reflected in the MUI fatwa on pornography. The fatwa on pornography and pornographic activities was issued in 2001 and is based on several moral considerations such as the prevalence of pornographic materials and pornographic actions—otherwise known as *pornoaksi*, a phrase combining the word *porno* (porn) and *aksi* (action)—in society in both the print and electronic media and day-to-day behaviour. It was stated that pornography and pornographic activities have resulted in negative consequences for Indonesians, especially in the behaviour of the younger generation and also in the destruction of Indonesian family values through sexual promiscuity, unwanted pregnancy, abortion, the spread of STDs (sexual transmitted diseases) and other sexual orientations considered abnormal, such as homosexuality. For MUI, ignoring pornography and pornographic activities will lead to the perpetuation of harm. Concerted efforts to stop pornography and pornographic activities should therefore be taken, such as a new legal stance with harsh sentences for those who are found guilty of pornography and pornographic activities. Another important consideration for MUI was that it believed that many Muslims and the state were not paying full attention to Islamic teachings on pornography and pornographic activities.[136]

However, the real target of the fatwa was actually women, as could be seen from some of the terms used such as as "direct and indirect viewing"; eroticism in painting, drawing, writing, and the voice; "wild desire"; *ʿawra* (the part of the body that should not be uncovered); uncovered, transparent and/or body-shaping garments; seclusion (*khalwa*); and women's guardians (*maḥram*), all of which are closely associated with women's bodies.[137] Following the arrest of some gay men in Aceh in 2009, the focus expanded to include same-sex couples. MUI demanded that producers and publishers of pornographic materials such as Playboy and editors of national media, both print and electronic, stop any activity forbidden in the fatwa. MUI also demanded the government of Indonesia issue a state law accommodating the content of the fatwa and also hard sanctions to act as a deterrent (*ẓawājir*) to those committing such actions and to strike fear (*mawāniʿ*) into those that might in future consider any involvement in pornography or pornographic activities.[138] The argument used

136 MUI, *Himpunan Fatwa MUI Sejak 1975*, pp. 410–1.
137 Ibid, p. 416–417.
138 Ibid, p. 417.

by MUI to justify its fatwa was the Islamic legal theory of blocking the means. According to Wahba al-Zuḥaylī, for instance, protecting the eyes from looking is blocking the means by which a person can be led into harmful and sinful action.[139] What is meant by "the means" here are all pornographic materials.

Another example of a MUI fatwa regulating women's bodies is *Pakaian Kerja Bagi Tenaga Medis Perempuan* ("Dress Code for Female Medical Personnel"), issued in 2009. There are three aspects to this MUI fatwa. Firstly, all the woman's body should be covered except for her hands and face. Secondly, female medical attendants may have their hands visible up to their elbows, but only in the case of emergencies. Thirdly, when in medical environments uniforms should be made from materials which are not transparent or show the body shape. In this matter MUI refers to the Islamic legal opinions of Muslim jurists such al-Shīrazi's (d. 1083) *Muhadhdhab,* and al-Nawawī's (d. 1277) *Majmūʿ Sharḥ al-Muhadhdhab* and *al-Mabsūṭ*.[140] Al-Shīrazi states that anyone can uncover the *ʿawra* for the purpose of medical treatment and circumcision. Al-Nawawī, in correction of al-Shīrazi, states that it is the state of emergency, not the need itself, that makes it permissible for people to expose their *ʿawra*.[141] Arms may be shown in an emergency, although what is meant by "emergency" is not fully defined. This issue should be properly resolved by referring to the concept of public interest rather than emergency, since it is not a rare occurrence but the daily experience of medical workers. Borrowing al-Ṭūfī's concept, eliminating harm, which in this context means the transmission of diseases, is a fundamental part of protecting the public and individual interest.[142]

A central aspect of the fatwa examples above is related to the concept of women's *ʿawra* in Islamic legal debates. In the modern discourse of Islamic jurisprudence on *ʿawra*, the Qur'ānic verses used by MUI as the Islamic legal foundation defining ʿawra can be understood differently. In the opinion of Qāsim Amīn, "facial veiling and seclusion" are mentioned in Sūrat al-Nūr [24]:

139 Wahba Al-Zuḥaylī, *Al-Tafsīr al-Munīr Fī al-ʿAqīda Wa al-Sharīʿa Wa al-Manhaj, Vol.* IX (Damascus: Dār al-Fikr, 2003), p. 549.

140 MUI is not clear about the author of the last source, although there is more than one al-Mabsūṭ, including al-Mabsūṭ of Sharakhsī (d. 1096), who followed the Ḥanafī school of Islamic law, al-Mabsūṭ of al-Bayhaqī (d. 1066), who followed the Shāfiʿī school, and others.

141 MUI, *Himpunan Fatwa MUI Sejak 1975*, pp. 536–9.

142 Najm al-Dīn Al-Ṭūfī, *Risāla Fi Riʿāyat al-Maṣlaḥa* (Cairo: Dār al-Miṣriyya al-Lubnāniyya, 1993), p. 23.

30–31[143] and Sūrat al-Aḥzāb [33]: 59[144] as ways the wives of the Prophet were protected as the mothers of believers (*umm al-muʾminīn*).[145] As such, their public appearance must be guarded by a specific dress code, as hinted in the verses of the Qurʾān above, to distinguish them from other women and wives. In Amīn's opinion, two types of *ʿawra* that must be covered can be assumed. The first is a ritual *ʿawra*, where almost the whole body of women is covered except the face and hands. This model should be followed in prayer. The second is the social *ʿawra*, referring to the concept of *maʿrūf* (from the Arabic word *ʿurf*, custom), namely a dress code that commonly applies in certain social and local traditions of the Muslim community. The former is applied in the daily prayers and the latter is applied in daily interactions and business. Leading Indonesian Muslim scholars of a similar opinion to Amīn, such as Madjid and Shihab, argue that veiling the whole body like an Arab woman is not prescribed by sharia but is a cultural norm. Similar to Qāsim Amīn, Fadwa El Guindi defines *ʿawra* as the "notion of privacy or private space and time rather than a woman's body."[146] El Guindi states that the best definition of *ʿawra,* on the basis of direct investigation from the Qurʾān, is "inviolate vulnerability."[147] El Guindi argues that the concept of *ʿawra* in the Qurʾān and *ḥadīth* is close to the notion of "men's immodesty" during their worship and concludes that *ʿawra* is a kind of "immodest exposure of men's genitals" and not "a blemish on women's bodies" as suggested by many Islamic interpretations.[148]

---

143 "(30) [Prophet], tell believing men to lower their glances and guard their private parts: that is purer for them. God is well aware of everything they do. (31) And tell believing women that they should lower their glances, guard their private parts, and not display their charms beyond what [it is acceptable] to reveal; they should let their headscarves fall to cover their necklines and not reveal their charms except to their husbands, their fathers, their husbands' fathers, their sons, their husbands' sons, their brothers, their brothers' sons, their sisters' sons, their womenfolk, their slaves, such men as attend them who have no sexual desire, or children who are not yet aware of women's nakedness; they should not stamp their feet so as to draw attention to any hidden charms. Believers, all of you, turn to God so that you may prosper." M.A.S. Abdel Haleem, *The Qur'an* (New York: Oxford University Press, 2005), p. 222.

144 Prophet, tell your wives, your daughters, and women believers to make their outer garments hang low over them[a] so as to be recognized and not insulted: God is most forgiving, most merciful. M.A.S. Abdel Haleem, *The Qur'an* (New York: Oxford University Press, 2005), p. 271.

145 Nikki R. Keddie, *Women in the Middle East: Past and Present* (New Jersey: Princeton University Press, 2012), p. 71; Charles Kurzman, *Modernist Islam, 1840–1940: A Sourcebook: A Sourcebook* (Oxford & New York: Oxford University Press, 2002), pp. 61–69.

146 Fadwa El Guindi, *Veil: Modesty, Privacy and Resistance* (New York: Berg, 1999), p. 141.

147 Ibid, p. 142.

148 Ibid.

Normalising sharia is the other main MUI concern, with the aim of preventing Indonesia from being overtaken by immorality in a society ruled by secular culture and lacking religious values. In MUI's struggle against what it considers to be immoral, it promotes the normalisation of sharia in an attempt to spread religious normativity; normativity, in this context, refers to Shelly Tremain's concept of "the power of social and legal norms that are imposed upon people."[149] In the context of the Muslim community, sharia is the source of normativity, as it contains regulations for Muslims and any disobedience and deviation will result in punishment. Tremain calls this a normative norm or *point norm*.[150] There are two aspects of normalisation, one that produces stability (no social unrest) and the other that generates conformity or compatibility. These two prominent features of normalisation can be seen in a number of MUI fatwas.

The first case of a MUI fatwa that can be described as related to sharia normalisation, particularly with regards to stability, is the 2005 law on interfaith marriage. MUI believes that the number of interfaith marriages is increasing, and that this has stimulated controversy and social instability. It is particularly worried about the support for interfaith marriage as a matter of human rights and public interest (*maṣlaḥa*) as stated by some Muslim activists and scholars from organisations such as the State Islamic University of Jakarta, the Paramadina Foundation, the Liberal Islam Network, the Wahid Institute, the International Conference on Religion and Peace (ICRP), and other institutions that support the practice of interfaith marriage. Any attempts to legalise interfaith marriage in Indonesia are perceived by MUI to be un-Islamic. The 2005 fatwa states that interfaith marriage is illegal, even for male Muslims who marry non-Muslims among the *ahl al-kitāb* (people of the Book, i.e. followers of monotheistic faiths). In 1984, MUI unequivocally stated that interfaith marriage between a Muslim male and non-Muslim female was a topic of differing opinions among the different schools of Islamic law, yet in 2005 it definitively stated that such an interfaith marriage is not valid, as it causes greater harm than good. MUI refers to Sūrat al-Baqara [2]: 221[151] and Sūrat

149 Shelley Lynn Tremain, *Foucault and the Government of Disability* (Michigan: University of Michigan Press, 2005), p. 93; Kambiz Ghaneabassiri, "Religious Normativity and Praxis Among American Muslims," in *The Cambridge Companion to American Islam* (Cambridge: Cambridge University Press, 2013), 208–27, p. 22.

150 Tremain, *Foucault and the Government of Disability*, 2005.

151 "Do not marry idolatresses until they believe: a believing slave woman is certainly better than an idolatress, even though she may please you. And do not give your women in marriage to idolaters until they believe: a believing slave is certainly better than an idolater, even though he may please you. Such people call [you] to the Fire, while God calls [you] to the Garden and forgiveness by His leave. He makes His messages clear to people,

al-Mumtaḥana [60]:10[152] that clearly forbid religious mixed marriage. The fatwa also quotes the report of Abū Hurayra regarding the Prophet Muḥammad's recommendation to marry women for their property, genealogy, beauty and most importantly religion. The Islamic legal precept (*al-qawāʾid al-uṣūliyya*) used by MUI is that which states "rejecting the harm is more important than taking benefit,"[153] meaning that interfaith marriage causes more harm than good. The fatwa also refers to the concept of eliminating any pretexts to illegal ends (*sadd al-dharāʾiʿ*), and forbids interfaith marriage on the grounds that marriage with a non-Muslim woman may lead Muslim men to become sinful. If we borrow Felicitas Opwis's concept, *sadd al-dharāʾiʿ* is MUI's rationale that the fatwa is in the interests of Muslims.[154] In forbidding interfaith marriage, MUI considers that it is protecting the religiosity of Muslim women and men. To support their judgment, MUI and its supporters popularised the idea that Christianity and Judaism had changed their teachings. They also use the *ikhtiyāṭ* (caution) argument here to prevent the post-marriage conversion of spouses to the religion of the other. This argument is particularly employed to prevent Muslim women from being converted by their Jewish or Christian husbands. The general assumption behind this idea is that the faith of Muslim women is weaker and more vulnerable than that of men.

The MUI view described above is against the common discourse of Islamic exegetical traditions, which respects the *ahl al-kitāb*. Ibn ʿAbbās states with regards to the lawfulness of chaste women among the *ahl al-kitāb* marrying Muslim men: "*tazwīj al-ḥarāʾir al-ʿafāʾif min ahl al-kitāb ḥalāl lakum.*"[155] Ibn Kathīr records different views among ulama regarding this issue. He stated that the *ahl al-kitāb* meant in this verse in the Shāfiʿī school of Islamic law is *al-isrāʾil* (the people of Israel). Some others state it is *al-dhimmiyyāt dūn*

so that they may bear them in mind." See M.A.S. Abdel Haleem, *The Qurʾan* (New York: Oxford University Press, 2005), p. 25.

152 "You who believe, test the believing women when they come to you as emigrants—God knows best about their faith—and if you are sure of their belief, do not send them back to the disbelievers: they are not lawful wives for them, nor are the disbelievers their lawful husbands. Give the disbelievers whatever bride-gifts they have paid—if you choose to marry them, there is no blame on you once you have paid their bride-gifts—and do not yourselves hold on to marriage ties with disbelieving women. Ask for repayment of the bride-gifts you have paid, and let the disbelievers do the same. This is God's judgment: He judges between you, God is all knowing and wise." See Haleem, *The Qurʾan*, p. 369.

153 Arabic tekst: *dar al-mafāsid muqaddam ʿalā al-jalb al-maṣāliḥ.*

154 Felicitas Opwis, "Maslaha in Contemporary Islamic Legal Theory," *Islamic Law and Society* 12, no. 2 (2005): 82–223, p. 104.

155 Ibn ʿAbbās, *Tanwīr Al-Miqbās* (Beirut: Dār al-Kutb al-ʿIlmiyya, 1992), p. 116.

al-ḥarbiyyāt (non-Muslim citizens of an Islamic state). Ibn Kathīr refers to the exegesis of Ibn 'Umar on the unlawfulness of marrying *al-naṣrāniyya* (Christians). Ibn Umar, reported by al-Bukhārī, stated "*lā a'lamu shirkan a'ẓam min an taqūl inna rabbahā 'Īsā*" (I recognise no form of polytheism greater than declaring that Jesus is God).[156] However, Ibn Kathīr does not deny that many of the Prophet Muḥammad's companions married Christian women and that they did not view this as dangerous.[157] With regard to the opinions mentioned above, *mushrik* (idolaters) and *kuffār* (unbelievers) are considered different from *ahl al-kitāb* (the people of the Book). Muslim men are not allowed to marry the former, while it is lawful for them to marry women from the latter. Al-Zuḥaylī stated that few ulama disagree with the lawfulness of Muslim men marrying *al-mukhṣanāt al-kitābiyyāt* (chaste women of people of the Book).[158] On this basis, al-Zuḥaylī's position is more moderate than MUI because he does not question that Christians and Jews should be considered *ahl al-kitāb*.

Despite the different interpretations that exist, MUI wants this fatwa to become the social norm among Indonesian Muslims. It seems that it has been successful, as the practice of interfaith marriage that existed in the 1970s and the 1980s under the facilitation of the Civil Registry is now disappearing. Simon Butt indicates that permissiveness towards mixed marriages ended when Suharto issued a Presidential Decree instructing the Civil Registry not to allow Muslims to register mixed marriages.[159] Socially and politically speaking, the Civil Registry does not register mixed marriages because they could be construed as being against the mainstream opinion of Indonesian Muslims. Indonesian citizens who wish to marry a partner from a different religion usually do so abroad, in places like Singapore or Australia; state law still recognises the legality of marriages performed overseas. In the last decade, MUI's narrative on the invalidity of interfaith marriage has gained tremendous support, particularly from radical Islamic groups who accuse those practising and facilitating interfaith marriage as followers of *Sepilis* (Indonesian acronym of secularism, liberalism and pluralism), ideologies that have been outlawed by MUI since 2005.

156 Ibn Kathīr, *Tafsīr Al-Qur'an al-'Aẓīm, Vol. 1*, ed. Sāmī b. Muhammad Al-Salāma (Dār al-Tayyiba li al-Nashr wa al-Tawzī', 1999), p. 583.

157 Ibid, pp. 582–584.

158 Wahba Al-Zuḥaylī, *Al-Tafsīr al-Munīr Fī al-'Aqīda Wa al-Sharī'a Wa al-Manhaj, Vol. III* (Damascus: Dār al-Fikr, 2003), p. 448.

159 Simon Butt, "Polygamy and Mixed Marriage in Indonesia: Islam and the Marriage Law in Courts," in *Indonesia: Law and Society*, ed. Tim Lindsey (New South Wales: Federation Press, 2008), p. 278.

Besides producing stability, the normalisation of sharia is also aimed at generating conformity or compatibility. As MUI sees it, this mainly applies to Western concepts that should be normalised to conform to the standards of sharia. One example is evident in the MUI fatwa on human rights, in which the international declaration of universal human rights is only considered acceptable in so far as it is compatible with the norms of Islam. MUI states that human rights are not a concept built in a vacuum that each country interprets according to its cultural, social and legal ability. The organisation's criticism of the concept of human rights is aimed at re-igniting the long-running debate between the particularistic and universal camps. MUI itself supports the former camp where human rights are considered to be based on Indonesia's dominant cultural and social values, which are derived from Islam. This perspective can be seen in its criticism of the articles of the Universal Declaration of Human Rights, interpreted within the framework of individualism, which MUI interprets to mean excessive and extreme freedom that lead to free sex, alcoholism, and so forth. Aside from the matter of individualism, MUI has also identified several articles of the Universal Declaration of Human Rights as being against the norms of Islam: Article 16, paragraphs 1 and 2 on the freedom to choose a life-partner, and on marriage and divorce; Article 18 on religious freedom or religious conversion; and Article 23 on vocational matters.[160] In short, MUI states that the concept of human rights must refer to a balance between an individual's rights and duties, between individual rights and society's rights, and between freedom and responsibility—and that all these are to be found in Islam. MUI therefore claims that the concept of human rights must be based on Islamic norms.

How are other discourses of human rights prevailing? The Islamic discourse on human rights such as women's rights, the abolition of slavery, and religious freedom is variously and differently understood from one Muslim scholar to another. Abdullahi an-Naʿim states that the content of Qur'ān and Sunna are conclusively regarded as the fixed basic texts of Islam, but many people obstruct the full implementation of their truths.[161] In an-Naʿim's opinion, what is needed is a rereading of the Islamic texts related to human rights. The issue of human rights in Islam requires a newly crafted consensus among Muslim scholars adjusted to the empirical needs of contemporary Muslim society. In its fatwa on human rights, MUI is not explicit because the Qur'ānic verses cited are neutral and open to different interpretations. However, the tendency to employ the interpretations of Muslim scholars over secular ones is

160 MUI, *Himpunan Fatwa MUI Sejak 1975*, pp. 400–401.
161 An-Naʿim, *Islam and the Secular State*, p. 12

clear from arguments employed in the fatwa, for instance the criticism of the right to the freedom to choose one's spouse, freedom of religion, and others covered in the Universal Declaration of Human Rights. Abdulaziz Sachedina suggests that tensions should not be created between Islam and human rights because the basic idea of human rights was derived from the traditions of the Abrahamic religions, including Islam, in which the human rights of all human beings are regarded as inviolable (*dhū ḥurma*).[162] Thus should a disagreement in interpretation arise between Islam and the Universal Declaration of Human Rights, according to al-Naʿim there should be a return to the principle of consensus-seeking, while Sachedina asserts the inviolability of human rights. It is clear from this that a new interpretation of the texts of Islam is urgently needed. When reference is made, for instance, to the notion of protecting religion based on Islamic respect for religion, what is intended is protection for Islam *an sich*; religions other than Islam are not included as protected beliefs. The discourse on Islamic jurisprudence states that non-Muslims can ensure their security in Muslim lands in certain ways, such as through paying a tax. Apostates and heretical groups are excluded from the domain of the *ḥifẓ al-dīn* (religious protection). Sachedina, for instance, argues that apostasy and heresy are "at odds with human rights articles"[163] as their endorsement of freedom of religion includes the freedom to change religion (religious conversion), which is rejected by most ulama. To overcome the conflict between Islamic theology and the Universal Declaration of Human Rights, Sachedina suggests an open dialogue is needed between traditionalist Muslim scholars and human rights advocates. Aside from this practical advice, the new conceptualisation of *maqāṣid* is very helpful for this purpose. The five necessities (*al-ḍarūriyyāt al-khamsa*) of sharia should be redefined by considering contemporary circumstances so that the meaning of religious protection should be expanded to cover all believers regardless of their religion and gender, not just Muslims. It is interesting to note here that Felicitas Opwis states that the concept of *ḥifẓ al-ʿaql* (thought protection) is interpreted not just as protection for Islamic groups but also a broader freedom of thought.[164]

There are further examples of MUI edicts that function to confirm the normativity of Islam such as a fatwa titled *Bias Gender* (Gender Bias) issued in 2000 that orders adjustment or compatibility between gender-based equal

162 Abdulaziz Sachedina, *The Islamic Roots of Democratic Pluralism* (Oxford & New York: Oxford University Press, 2000), p. 116.

163 Ibid, p. 189.

164 Felicitas Opwis, "Maslaha in Contemporary Islamic Legal Theory," *Islamic Law and Society* 12, no. 2 (2005): 82–223, p. 188.

rights and the teaching of Islam,[165] and a fatwa on the death penalty for criminal acts, which tries to refute the international discourse that this model of punishment is against human rights. MUI recommends that Indonesia maintain the death penalty for serious criminal acts.[166] However, this does present the organisation with a dilemma. Radical Islamic groups such as the FPI reject the death penalty in terrorism cases. The FPI reacted strongly to the 9 November 2008 execution of three so-called Bali bombers Amrozi, Mukhlas and Imam Samudra, perpetrators of the 2002 Bali bombing, condemning it as the Indonesian state submitting to the demands of a non-Islamic "foreign power." MUI's fatwa states that the death penalty is still needed as a means for sharia to regulate the lives of citizens.

6.2.4 *Proper Islam: Halal Lifestyle and Sharia Economy*

Proper Islam means that all Muslims are obliged to follow Islam as it is prescribed by sharia. This is related to doing acts which are permitted (*ḥalāl*) and avoiding those which are not permitted (*haram*), adhering to purity and abandoning impurity, and enjoining good and forbidding wrong.[167] Each Muslim is obliged to act in this manner at all times—in belief, religious practice, consumption and business relations (*muʿāmala*). Talal Asad calls this the orthodoxy of Islam. Asad says, "whenever Muslims have the power to regulate, uphold, require or adjust correct practice, and to condemn, exclude, undermine, or replace incorrect ones, there is the domain of orthodoxy."[168] Preserving purity is a central precept in sharia. There are two important fields of MUI fatwa in which Indonesian Muslims can implement proper Islam: halal

165 MUI, *Himpunan Fatwa MUI Sejak 1975*, pp. 393–394.

166 Ibid, p. 496. MUI refers to Wahba al-Zuḥaylī in his book, *al-Fiqh al-Islām wa Adillatuhu*, which states that criminals whose offences cannot be otherwise stopped should be punished by death. He uses the term *al-mufarriq*, a person who divides the unity of the Muslim community, and those who encourage new innovations in worship as examples of such criminals. What al-Zuḥaylī wants to say is that sharia permits the death sentence for *muʿtādī al-iḥrām* (bastards), *mudminī al-khamr* (drug sellers), *duʿāt al-fasād* (intruders), *muḥrimī amni al-dawla* (enemies of the state), and the like (MUI, *Himpunan Fatwa MUI Sejak 1975*, p. 501.) MUI also states that the death sentence is compatible with the Indonesian legal code and laws such as the Penal Code of Indonesia, State Law No. 1/2002 on terrorism, and some others. Finally, the content of the fatwa recognises two things: that Islam recognises the existence of the death penalty according to Islamic criminal laws, and that the state has the right to punish criminals.

167 Fischer, *The Halal Frontier: Muslim Consumers in a Globalized Market*, p. 6; Cook, *Forbidding Wrong in Islam: An Introduction*; Cook, *Commanding Right and Forbidding Wrong in Islamic Thought*; Fischer, *Proper Islamic Consumption: Shopping Among the Malays in Modern Malaysia*.

168 Asad, *The Idea of an Anthropology of Islam*, p. 15.

lifestyle and sharia economy. However, proper Islam can also interact with religious commodification as these fields can be related to trade.[169] The following section explains how the MUI fatwa tackle the two fields through fatwa and their impact on the social and legal spheres of Indonesia.[170]

6.2.4.1 *Halal* Lifestyle

Based on interviews with several MUI board members—Amin, Ichwan Sam, Amidhan, and Nazratuzzaman[171]—and reading of the Indonesia media, it is clear that MUI considers a halal lifestyle to be a very serious matter. They argue that sharia prescriptions on halal lifestyle are binding for all Muslims,[172] being convinced that good (pure) consumption determines the quality of worship. Mary Douglas states that "holiness and impurity are at opposite poles."[173] Our bodies must be clean from impurity when we want to perform acts of devotion; this means that what is consumed by Muslims, such as food, drink, cosmetics and medicines, must be lawful in the sight of God. In anthropological studies of the world's religions, impurity is a hindrance and purity is the medium for worshippers to reach out to the divine. Douglas Davies states the concept of purity has a close association with holiness and supernatural presence (God).[174] The notion of purity here relates to human beings as the agents of worship who must be clean and free from pollution. Therefore, in Islam, the dichotomy between purity and impurity is a very important one, and to ensure a clear distinction between pure and impure goods for Indonesian Muslims, some form of strong authority is required. MUI argues that the ulama and the state are the two sides of the same coin, both responsible for regulating halal issues, the former representing Islamic authority and the latter representing political authority. Johan Fischer calls this interactive process "halalisation."[175]

---

169 Fealy, "Consuming Islam: Commodified Religion and Aspirational Pietism in Contemporary Indonesia"; Sinha, *Religion and Commodification: "Merchandizing" Diasporic Hinduism*; Kitiarsa, *Religious Commodifications in Asia: Marketing Gods*.

170 When this book was written, the bill regulating this aspect of *halal* lifestyle was still being debated in the legislative body.

171 Interviews with: Ma'ruf Amin, Jakarta, 2010; Ichwan Sam, Jakarta, 2010; Amidhan, Jakarta, 2010; Nazratuzzaman, Jakarta, 2010.

172 LPPOM, *Indonesia Halal Directory 2001*, p. 22.

173 Mary Douglas, *Purity and Danger: An Analysis of Concepts of Pollution and Taboo* (London & New York: Routledge, 2003), p. 7.

174 Douglas Davies, *Anthropology and Theology* (Oxford & New York: Berg, 2002), p. 97; Carolyn Rouse and Janet Hoskins, "Purity, Soul Food, and Sunni Islam: Explorations at the Intersection of Consumption and Resistance," *Cultural Anthropology* 19, no. 2 (2004): 226–49.

175 Fischer, *Proper Islamic Consumption: Shopping Among the Malays in Modern Malaysia*.

However, the halal lifestyle requires not only the issuing of fatwa and halal certificates but also involves social, legal, political and economic commodification. How is the halal lifestyle regulated by MUI fatwa and how does it impact on the social, legal, and economic lives of Indonesian Muslims?

The halal lifestyle is ordered by MUI under LPPOM, as detailed in Chapter 3 of this book. The halal fatwa is drawn up by MUI and LPPOM is the implementing agency that issues the halal certificates.[176] Aspects of the halal lifestyle regulated by MUI are classified into three categories: firstly, standardisation; secondly, method or process; and thirdly, some fatwa on goods which are permitted and not permitted in sharia. They cover the regulation of food, drink, medicine and cosmetics.

Standardisation means that MUI produces a set of rules that forms a general code of conduct for determining the lawfulness and unlawfulness of food, drink, medicine and cosmetics. MUI regulates this through its fatwa *Standardisasi Fatwa Halal* ("The Standardisation of Halal Fatwa") issued in 2003.[177] This fatwa regulates basic issues such as the standardisation of alcoholic content, mechanical slaughtering, growth media,[178] expiry dates of certification, especially for international certifiers,[179] and some other issues concerning what is permitted for consumption by Indonesian Muslims and what is not. All alcoholic products are categorised as unlawful if the alcohol content is above 1%. MUI regulates the standardised procedure for mechanical slaughtering covering the basic requirements, such as the capability of the slaughtermen and the process used. It also bans food labelling that uses a brand or symbol for

176 LPPOM, *Indonesia Halal Directory 2001*, p. 20.

177 Fatwa No. 4/MUI/2003.

178 MUI states that microbes raised and derived from lawful and pure (*ṭāhir*) enrichment are acceptable. The consumption of products derived from microbes that use unlawful and impure compounds in their enrichment medium, either in their first or final stage of development, is forbidden. MUI reminds people who use products derived from microbes to trace their lawfulness up to the stage of microbe refreshment. From a social and political perspective, these issues legitimatise MUI to conduct laboratory investigations to determine the halalness of such products and commodities.

179 In general, the expiry limit of halal certificates for imported meat is based on shipments, and for local meat has a limit of six months. For flavour products, the certificate is valid for one year. For general goods, local and imported, there is a six-month expiry date. MUI will carefully scrutinise the standard operational procedures and fatwas relied on by international certifiers. If their validity is doubtful, MUI will review their halal certification. MUI has its own standard of halalisation and international certifiers are obliged to adjust to this. Should there be contamination from the lick of a dog or pig, for example, MUI adopts the Shāfiʿī school of Islamic law, which obliges a person to wash seven times using soil, mud or other materials that can eradicate the saliva. MUI, *Himpunan Fatwa MUI Sejak 1975*, pp. 698–701.

food and drink that is considered idolatrous or relates to unlawful animals or products, such as pigs, dogs or alcohol. Some Chinese labels for foods that have deep cultural roots in Indonesia and are guaranteed not to contain any illicit ingredients—such as *bakso* (meat balls), *bakmi* (noodles), *bakwan* (fried vegetable patties), *bakpia* (small sweet pastries), and *bakpao* (steamed buns)—are excluded from this ban, even though the names are adopted from Chinese and they might otherwise have been suspected of containing pork or other unlawful products.[180]

The standardisation fatwa is helpful in reminding Indonesian Muslims what products they can legitimately consume. For instance, many people are not concerned about the alcoholic content in traditional foods and drinks. Some traditional foods, such as *tape* (fermented cassava), *legēn* (traditional wine extracted from the palm tree) and durian fruit have a high alcohol content, but many people still consume them. The government tolerates a much higher alcoholic content level than MUI. Presidential Decree No. 3/1997 allows the sale of drinks with an alcohol content ranging from 1% to 20% in limited places. MUI's limit of 1% alcohol content is therefore a counter-discourse to the state's regulation that far exceeds the norms of sharia.

It is important to explain why MUI desires to regulate the method of process of halalness. In the discourse of Islamic jurisprudence, permitted foodstuffs are not only determined by their intrinsic essence (*halāl lidhātihi*), but equally importantly by their extrinsic essence (*halāl lighayri dhātihi*). The Islamic legality of such products depends on the method or process used to produce them. For instance, beef is lawful for consumption as long as it is produced through a slaughtering process permitted by sharia. This fatwa is very important as the means to inform producers and consumers which products are permissible under sharia. One example of how MUI regulates this can be seen in the fatwa titled *Penyembelihan Hewan Secara Mekanis* ("Mechanical Slaughtering of Animals") of 1976.[181] The fatwa spells out general guidelines on how the animal-slaughtering process should be properly conducted in accordance with sharia. MUI concludes that using a technological process for slaughtering is permissible under sharia based on the concept of *iḥsān* (closely

180 MUI points out that Muslim are not allowed to consume products prohibited under sharia, such as bacon. MUI also stresses the illegality of consuming food or drink that uses the name of haram products, such as whisky, brandy, beer and so on. This latter stance does not have a strong legal standing in Islam. Although any products derived from pigs and dogs are haram, Islam never states that using their names is also prohibited. This aspect of the fatwa seems to reflect an irrational argument, as all these animals are the creatures of God.

181 Issued on 18 October 1976, without a number.

related to *istiḥsān*: juristic preference).[182] Some examples of MUI's advice that relates to the issue of halal methods or processes can be seen in the fatwa *Cara Penyucian Ekstrak Ragi dari Sisa Pengolahan Bir* ("How Yeast Extraction of Beer Should Be Performed"),[183] *Penyucian Alat Produksi yang Terkena Najis Mutawassiṭa* ("Cleansing Production Tools from Middle Impurity")[184] and *Air Daur Ulang* ("Water Recycling")[185] and so forth.

The MUI standardisation and methods or processes of halalisation referred to when issuing halal certificates are based on its fatwa titled *Penetapan Produk Halal* ("Certification of Halal Products"),[186] which functions as the basis for determining the lawfulness of products.[187] MUI's role in this matter has generated a degree of public controversy. The Wahid Foundation, for instance, has stated that MUI's fatwa on halal lifestyle is part of its agenda of Islamic commodification. Ahmad Suaedy, former director of the Wahid Foundation, asserted that halal certification is big business and that MUI earns considerable sums of money by monopolising it.[188] Sociologically speaking, this activity can be called a form of Islamic commodification because it involves the collection of capital and economic interest, using the legitimacy of religion.[189] MUI has rejected these claims, saying that the fees paid to obtain halal certificates are insignificant and are expended on auditing and laboratory investigations as part of the process. Furthermore, it claims the process is transparent and that people can read how much they should pay for halal certification, as the service fees are openly published.[190] However, the fact that MUI can fund 20% of its activities from the halal service alone shows that an element of commodification does exist.[191]

In general, there are not many examples of food, drink, medicines or cosmetics that are individually regulated by the MUI fatwa. The few exceptions

182 Wael B. Hallaq, *The Origins and Evolution of Islamic Law* (Cambridge: Cambridge University Press, 2005), p. 208.
183 Fatwa No. 10/MUI/2011.
184 Fatwa No. 09/MUI/2011.
185 Fatwa No. 02/MUI/2010.
186 Fatwa No. 01/MUI/2011.
187 MUI, *Himpunan Fatwa MUI Sejak 1975*, pp. 669–76.
188 Interview with Ahmad Suaedy, Jakarta, 2010.
189 Sinha, *Religion and Commodification: "Merchandizing" Diasporic Hinduism*; Fealy, "Consuming Islam: Commodified Religion and Aspirational Pietism in Contemporary Indonesia"; Kitiarsa, *Religious Commodifications in Asia: Marketing Gods*; Muhammad ʿĀbid Al-Jābirī, *Al-ʿAql al-ʿArabī al-Siyāsī: Muḥaddātuhu Wa Tajalliyātuhu* (Beirut: Markāz Dirāsāt al-Waḥda al-ʿArabiyya, 2007).
190 Interview with Nazratuzzaman, Jakarta, 2010.
191 Interview with Zainut Tauhid, Jakarta, 2010.

include the prohibition on cicada, narcotics and crab; individual fatwa have been issued on these items due to the high levels of controversy and anxiety they generate in society. The MUI regulation of the lawfulness of foodstuffs is most clearly determined under the MUI fatwa "*Makanan dan Minuman Yang Bercampur Dengan Najis*" (Foods and Drinks Mixing with Impurity), published in the 1980s. This fatwa stated that all foods and drinks tainted by impurity are prohibited and should be avoided. The fatwa also states that all foods and drinks polluted by impurities should be submitted to a laboratory investigation to determine their Islamic legal validity.[192] This fatwa is brief and quite old, but it remains in use as a basic reference to judge other products such as medicines and cosmetics. Despite being short, this fatwa is also the first MUI statement to press for a laboratory investigation on the Islamic permissibility of such products.

Given the above explanation on standards and methods, and also examples of fatwas, it would seem that the determination of halal status is quite clear and simple. The *ijtihād* process is also uncomplicated because fatwa-makers have been provided with general guidelines, and the question of lawfulness is clearer when also based on laboratory research. Problems usually arise from the social, political and legal implications of the fatwas. One MUI fatwa that generated strong public debate was *Penggunaan Vaksin Meningitis Bagi Jamaah Haji Atau Umrah* ("Use of Meningitis Vaccine for Pilgrims") in 2009–2010. The Saudi Government had demanded that all Indonesian pilgrims be vaccinated against meningitis before departing for Mecca and Medina. The Ministry of Health, as the responsible state agency, used a meningitis vaccine produced by Glaxo Smith Kline (GSK), which stated that the vaccine was free from pig fat, and on 4 May 2009 The Ministry of Health also stated that the vaccine-making process did not use pig fat as a growth medium.[193] However, MUI discovered that this claim was not true, and the meningitis vaccine was found to be contaminated. MUI came to this conclusion after hearing evidence from its auditor, Anna P. Roswien, through cross-reference with GSK information, that contamination with pig enzymes had occurred in the vaccine production process. This issue was raised in the MUI board meeting on 6 June 2009. The MUI internal discussion about the legal status of the vaccine invited debate from various sectors of the Indonesian Muslim public, since the vaccination was a requirement for all pilgrims.

192 MUI, *Himpunan Fatwa MUI Sejak 1975*, p. 607.

193 "Menkes Ragu Vaksin Meningitis Mengandung Enzim Babi," *Republika*, 28 April 2009, https://www.republika.co.id/berita/46689/menkes-ragu-vaksin-meningitis-mengandung-enzim-babi, viewed on 22 July 2022.

Fadhilah Supari, the Minister of Health (2004–2009), said that MUI did not have the authority to determine the Islamic legal status of the meningitis vaccine, in a statement on 13 June 2010.[194] This statement elicited a strong reaction from MUI Chairman Amidhan who responded that MUI did have the authority to issue this fatwa as mandated by Act No. 7/2006 on *pangan* (food). The Chairman of the MUI Fatwa Commission, Anwar Ibrahim, claimed that MUI was the correct institution for issuing this legal status because of its scholarship and Islamic competency. This controversy finally ended when the Minister of Health visited the office of MUI in mid-July 2009 and reached a compromise, which resulted in a new fatwa being published on 16 July 2010 to amend the 2009 fatwa that legalised the use of the meningitis vaccine (Mencevax™ ACV135Y) produced by Glaxo Smith Kline Beecham Pharmaceutical. In the 2010 fatwa, MUI ordered the use of a halal vaccine, Meningococcal, produced by Zheijiang Tianyuan Bio Pharmaceutical, Co. Ltd.[195] After the fatwa was issued, the Ministry of Health, along with the Ministry of Religious Affairs, made the use of this vaccine obligatory. This did not signal that the issue had been finalised, as criticism emerged from Salafi organisations. The Majelis Mujahidin Indonesia (Indonesian Mujahidin Council) considered the MUI fatwa on meningitis and polio to be part of an international Zionist conspiracy to destroy the young generation of Muslims and MUI had been trapped into becoming part of it. MMI criticised statements by Ma'ruf Amin, in which he said that MUI's fatwa permitting the use of the polio vaccine could be changed when a new halal vaccine was invented. According to MMI, Amin should have consulted experts before voicing his opinion in public, as it was general knowledge that the almost all vaccines produced in the modern world utilise pig enzymes. MMI proposes the replacement of the vaccine by adopting what they call the "Islamic medicinal prescription" introduced by the Prophet Muḥammad (*al-ṭibb al-nabawī*).[196]

But what about those cases where the product is *haram* (unlawful)—or its halalness is debatable—but there appear to be no adverse effects on society? One such case was that of the MUI fatwa on MSG (Monosodium Glutamate) produced by PT. Ajinomoto in 2000–2001. This fatwa resulted in a public debate involving President Abdurrahman Wahid (1999–2001). The company had already obtained a halal certificate for its product, but based on laboratory

194 "MUI: Menkes Resahkan Masyarakat," *Republika*, 15 June 2009, https://www.republika.co.id/berita/56282/mui-menkes-resahkan-masyarakat, viewed on 22 July 2022.

195 MUI, *Himpunan Fatwa MUI Sejak 1975*, p. 792.

196 "Konspirasi Di Balik Fatwa Halal Vaksin Haji & Imunisasi," Arrahmah, 15 January 2011, https://www.arrahmah.id/2011/01/25/konspirasi-di-balik-fatwa-halal-vaksin-haji-imunisasi/, viewed on 22 July 2022.

investigations MUI determined that PT. Ajinomoto was using pig enzymes in its product (MSG). Investigations from June 1999 to November 2000 indicated that Ajinomoto had changed the MSG ingredients, allegedly mixing it with bacto soytone—an enzymatic digest of soy—containing pork enzymes.[197] PT. Ajinomoto applied to MUI for an extension of the halal certificate, but LPPOM investigation results indicated that the product was contaminated by the pork enzyme; as a result, MUI banned MSG production by PT. Ajinomoto on 16 December 2001. Thanks to a sophisticated technological process the MSG itself did not contain pork enzymes, but MUI argued that its Islamic legal judgment was not made on the basis of the final product but on the original ingredients, which were allegedly generated from pig derivatives. Therefore, in MUI's view, the final Islamic legal status of the product was unlawful. MUI deferred to the Islamic legal maxim "when the lawful and the unlawful meet, the lawful is defeated," *idhā ijtamaʿa al-ḥalāl wa al-haram ghuliba al-ḥalāl*.[198] Although the fatwa was correct in legal terms, however, socially and economically it could cause more harm than benefit. President Wahid rejected the fatwa, insisting that the government's position was different from that of MUI. Using the concept of *istiḥāla* (understanding the process of physical and chemical transformation or conversion of materials which affect the status of lawfulness or unlawfulness)[199] and social argument (*maṣlaḥa*), President Wahid argued that when no pork enzyme was found in the final product, the legal status returns to its (lawful) origin,[200] and therefore it must be judged halal.[201] In his socio-economic argument, Wahid stated that MUI's prohibition of the Ajinomoto product should consider the social reality: the fatwa would result in hardship for thousands of Indonesian workers, who would be sacked by the company following the ban.[202]

This controversy demonstrates that MUI also needs to employ a social and political analysis in determining halal issues. Much criticism, including from lawmakers, was levelled at MUI over its position as the sole fatwa-issuer. This can be seen from MUI's vulnerable role in regulating halal lifestyle under State

---

197 MUI, *Himpunan Fatwa MUI Sejak 1975*, p. 663.

198 Karni et al., *35 Tahun Majelis Ulama Indonesia*; MUI, *Himpunan Fatwa MUI Sejak 1975*, pp. 662–8.

199 Mohammad Hashim Kamali, *The Parameters of Halal and Haram in Shariʿah and the Halal Industry*, 23 (Herndon, VA: IIIT, 2013), p. 20.

200 "Gus Dur: Semuanya Sama-Sama Membela Umat," Liputan, 10 January 2001, https://www.liputan6.com/news/read/6199/gus-dur-semuanya-sama-sama-membela-umat, viewed on 22 July 2022.

201 Ibid.

202 Karni et al., *35 Tahun Majelis Ulama Indonesia*, p. 122.

Law on Act No. 7/2006 on *pangan* (food). Indonesian lawmakers proposed a draft law on halal product assurance that threatened the authority of MUI as the sole authority on halal issues since 2014, and it was rumoured that the Ministry of Religious Affairs wanted halal certification to be regulated by an independent state agency.[203] Despite some tensions and controversies, sufficient appreciation has been given to MUI for its halal work, Indonesia being identified as one of three countries—together with Saudi Arabia and Singapore—with the best halal activity system. Indonesia has a well-organised monitoring of halal food processing, supported by the community, and requires halal certificates for all imported goods.[204] MUI believes it is successful in regulating halal lifestyles in the legal and public spheres of Indonesia, and as a result its position as the sole authority on fatwa and halal certification should be defended. Finally, in 2014, the responsibility of issuing halal certificates shifted from LPPOM to BPJPH, with MUI remaining as the halal fatwa issuer within the BPJPH structure.

6.2.4.2 Sharia Economy

This section examines how the sharia economy has evolved its potential to support its success in Indonesia, in what form non-*ribā* products are invented, and how they have become an alternative in the Indonesian economy. MUI argues that the low level of economic prosperity of Indonesians in general and Muslims in particular is because the economic systems and lifestyle rely on *ribā* (interest/profit). They claim this needs to be altered through a new system that can raise the economic wellbeing of Indonesia. MUI. through its role in the DSN (Dewan Syariah National, or Sharia National Board, elaborated in Chapter 3), believes that Indonesian Muslims can achieve prosperity through the introduction of a sharia economy.[205] There are two main reasons that MUI believes support the promotion of sharia economy. The first is that the *ribā*-based economy has not delivered its promise of prosperity for society as a whole. The effectiveness of the interest-based Indonesian economy was exhausted by the financial crisis of 1998. The second is that the introduction

203 The debate in the legislative body on the *Jaminan Produk Halal* law draft is still in process, and the position of MUI as the only halal certifier has not yet been decided. State Law No. 33/2014 on Halal Product Assurance states that the body responsible for halal certification has now changed from LPPOM to BPJPH.

204 Mian N. Riaz and Muhammad M. Chaudry, *Halal Food Production* (London & New York: CRC Press, 2004).

205 Amin, "Pointers Pidato Ketua DSN-MUI Dalam Acara Pembukaan Ijtima Sanawi (Annual Meeting) DPS Tahun 2010."

of sharia economy not only frees Indonesia from the injustices of an interest-based economy but also functions to increase the piety of Indonesian Muslims. By rejecting the use of interest, MUI is sure that a sharia-based economy will create justice and welfare, not only for Muslims but for all human beings. Beside domestic issues, the establishment of sharia economy is able to respond to the global development of the Muslim world. Some Islamic countries established sharia banks in the 1970s and the 1990s. Egypt and Kuwait built sharia banks in 1977, Iran in 1978, Saudi Arabia in 1988, Turkey in 1985 and Malaysia in 1983.[206] The International Development Bank (IDB), of which Indonesia is an important member, was set up in 1972. However, all the above concerns are inspired by the one fundamental argument that the spirit of applying this economic lifestyle is purely based on Islam. In Ibrahim Warde's terms, what MUI is trying is to obtain is "pure" finance,[207] pure finance being money earned from a system free from *ribā*. Warde, however, states that commerce has been a central tradition of Islam, although gaining profit from pure finance (*ribā*) is debatable.[208]

MUI projects that Indonesia, with its population of 240 million, has great potential as a market for the sharia economy. In the mid-1990s, MUI began its public critiques of the *ribā* system of capitalist and socialist economy and promoting sharia economy in the legal and public spheres. American anthropologist Hefner recognises MUI's significant contribution in initiating the implementation of sharia economy through providing a conceptual framework for a non-*ribā* economy.[209] The role of MUI in regulating the sharia banking and finance industry, including the insurance and stock exchange market, has become increasingly important, as indicated through elements of Indonesian state law that provide it with a decisive role through the establishment of the DSN, for controlling aspects related to sharia within the operation of the Lembaga Keuangan Syariah (LKS, Sharia Financial Institutions). In addition, MUI is now the sole fatwa-issuer regarding matters of sharia economy. Other

206 Clement M. Henry and Rodney Wilson, "Introduction," in *The Politics of Islamic Finance*, ed. Clement M Henry and Rodney Wilson (Edinburgh: Edinburgh University Press, 2004), 1–16, p. 7.

207 Ibrahim Warde, "Global Politics, Islamic Finance and Islamic Politics Before and After 11 September 2001," in *The Politics of Islamic Finance*, ed. Clement M. Henry and Rodney Wilson (Edinburgh: Edinburgh University Press, 2004), 37–62, p. 40.

208 Ibid.

209 Robert W. Hefner, "Islamizing Capitalism: On the Founding of Firts Islamic Bank," in *Shari'a and Politics in Modern Indonesia*, ed. Arskal Salim and Azyumardi Azra (Singapore: Institute of Southeast Asian Studies, 2003), 148–67.

major Islamic organisations in Indonesia such as NU and Muhammadiyah also accept MUI's role in this sphere.[210]

In 2000, to defend the non-interest system, the DSN published a fatwa calling for the prohibition of *ribā*.[211] In addition to clarifying MUI's stance on *ribā*, this fatwa was timely in unifying the different opinions of Indonesian Muslims regarding the legal status of interest-charging banks. From the era of Wahid's leadership, NU had established People's Lending Banks (Bank Perkreditan Rakyat, BPR) known as Nusuma that operated on a conventional interest system. Likewise, some Muhammadiyah banks remain unclear as to whether their system can be said to follow the norms of sharia. MUI's position on banning *ribā* was clarified in 2003 when the organisation strengthened its 2000 fatwa. The content of the 2003 fatwa is not very different from that of the 2000 fatwa, but indicates a stricter MUI position in confronting the operation of the *ribā* system. Through this fatwa, MUI judges that the practice of profit-taking, as currently applied in conventional financial institutions such as banks, insurance (*takāful*), the stock market, and so on, can be categorised as *ribā*.[212] Politically speaking, this stance can now be held by MUI because of the openness of reform era. Some policies have begun to be listed by lawmakers to support the operation of a non interest-based economy. MUI's fatwa outlines that, where sharia financial institutions are not found, Muslims are not allowed to make any transactions and contracts under the usury system. MUI can only tolerate the use of a non-sharia system of contracts in an emergency. Arguments for this are based on the opinions of classical and modern Islamic legal jurists such as al-Nawawī (d. 1277) in *al-Majmūʿ*, Ibn al-ʿArabī (d. 1148) in *Aḥkām al-Qur'ān*, Sharakhsī (d. 1096) in *al-Mabsūṭ*, Muhammad Abū Zahra in *Buḥūth fi al-Ribā*, Yūsuf al-Qaradāwī (b. 1926) in *Fawā'id al-Bunūk*, and Wahba al-Zuḥaylī (b. 1932) in his *al-Fiqh al-Islāmī wa Adillatuhu*. MUI also refers to fatwas issued by international and national Islamic institutions such as the Majmaʿ Buḥūth al-Islāmiyya of al-Azhar University, Cairo, in 1965, Majmaʿ al-Fiqh al-Islāmī of OIC in 1985, Lajnah Tarjih Muhammadiyah in 1968, and Munas Alim Ulama and Konbes NU in 1992.[213]

In its support of sharia economy, MUI issued several fatwas related to sharia economic products through the DSN. The characteristics of DSN fatwas are different from other MUI fatwas in that they are mostly issued proactively, to seek

210 Interviews with: As'ad Ali, Jakarta, 2010; Fatah Wibisono, Jakarta, 2010; Bachtiar Effendy, Jakarta, 2010.

211 *Himpunan Fatwa Dewan Syariah Nasional MUI*, 2006, p. 423.

212 Ibid.

213 MUI, *Himpunan Fatwa MUI Sejak 1975*, pp. 807–10.

customers and create a new sharia market, and are not dependent on requests from society. Only four models of sharia economy products released by MUI will be discussed here. The first is a product called *muḍāraba* (profit-sharing contract). The launch of this product was not a particularly innovative step, as Islamic countries commonly employ it in the first stage of developing their sharia economy. Gafoor simply defines *muḍāraba* by explaining that "two parties, one with capital and the other with know-how, get together to carry out a project."[214] MUI's confidence in the product is due to its economic potential to safeguard the Indonesian economy. As generally assumed by practitioners of sharia economy elsewhere, this model is close to economic justice and fairness. MUI's choice is also reasonable, as the *muḍāraba* contract is the core of other sharia products because of its flexibility as the umbrella of other products, which are familiar to Indonesian Muslims. Some products that MUI issued under the *muḍāraba* contract, for instance, are cheque, savings and deposit account facilities.[215] MUI allows all these banking products provided they are used within the scheme of profit-loss sharing and non-predetermined or fixed return.[216] In the view of Muslim jurists, *muḍāraba* is lawful because it is based on an ulama consensus, a number of the Prophet Muḥammad's companions having practised this model.[217] The Islamic legal maxim stating that "contracts are generally permissible exempting a legal argument that indicates its prohibition" (*al-aṣl fī al-muʿāmala al-ibāḥa illā an yadulla dalīl ʿalā*

214 A.L.M. Abdul Gafoor, "Mudaraba-Based Investment and Finance," 2001, http://users.bart.nl/~abdul/article2.html, viewed on 22 July 2022.

215 Dewan Syariah Nasional, *Himpunan Fatwa Dewan Syariah Nasional MUI*, pp. 1–75.

216 Ibid, pp. 1–6. According to the concept of *muḍāraba*, the requirements are as follows: (1) The bank customer plays the role of *ṣāhib al-māl* (investor) and the bank plays the role of *muḍārib* (fund manager). (2) As the *muḍārib*, the bank has full rights to manage the invested funds and make use of them for business and economic enterprises. (3) The capital value must be clearly stated and paid in the form of cash. (4) Profit sharing must be proclaimed in the form of *niṣba* (a share) when opening a new account. (5) The bank, as *muḍārib*, covers the operational giro costs from its profit-share. (6) The bank is now allowed to deduct the customer's *niṣba*. The concept of *waḍīʿa* means that: (1) *Waḍīʿa* is a deposit (*titipan*). (2) It can be recalled any time. (3) There is no fee to be paid except in the form of gift (*ʿaṭāya*) from the side of bank. Dewan Syariah Nasional MUI-Bank Indonesia, *Himpunan Fatwa Dewan Syariah Nasional MUI*, p. 6.

217 The DSN cites this opinion from al-Zuḥaylī's *al-Fiqh al-Islāmī wa Adillātuhu*, vol. 4, p. 838 (1989). It defines *muḍāraba* as a contract of cooperation between two individuals or groups in which the first individual or group acts as *mālik* (owner) and *ṣāḥib al-māl* (investor) that provides all the capital, while the second individual or group as *ʿāmil* (implementing individual or group), *muḍārib* (participant borrower) or customer acts as the fund (capital) manager. Earned profit will be fairly shared between the two participating individuals and groups based on a pre-arranged contract agreement. Dewan Syariah Nasional MUI-Bank Indonesia, *Himpunan Fatwa Dewan Syariah Nasional MUI*, p. 39.

taḥrīmihā) is also used to support the fatwa. Through its fatwa, the DSN regulates all aspects of *muḍāraba*, from which a few key issues can be teased out. The first concerns the capital; a hundred percent of transactions are backed by the Lembaga Keuangan Syariah (LKS, Sharia Financial Institutions),[218] and the *muḍārib* (client) is allowed to use the money but must follow a pre-arranged contract and sharia-based business principle. The DSN states that the LKS may incur a loss if there is no evidence of the customer committing a deliberate mistake, being careless, or breaking the agreed contract.[219] The latter becomes a crucial issue for customers, because at the practical level the LKS will never want to incur any losses. On this basis, the customers may file many complaints about the difference between sharia and conventional financing if they also suffer a loss by returning a certain percentage of the capital they borrow from LKS. This should not take place, but it often occurs in practice. Second is the necessity of providing collateral. Interestingly, DSN requires collateral from the *muḍārib* (client), which is not demanded in sharia law despite the fact that the entrepreneur can get their money back if they are not charged for committing blatant mistakes. The fund manager cannot withdraw their invested capital if they cannot offer evidence to absolve them of fraud. As a result, this Islamic legal opinion would be difficult to carry out as a means to increase the competitiveness of this product, because in this case there is no fundamental difference between *muḍāraba* and non-sharia models of financing. As for the political and economic consequences, the product cannot be effectively used as a vehicle to help Muslim entrepreneurs improve their businesses.

The second contract model is *murābaḥa,* which Muhammad Akram Khan, a former deputy-general auditor of Pakistan, briefly defines as "sale of goods with an agreed-upon profit mark-up on the cost."[220] This means that the buyer knows the price and agrees to pay additional charges.[221] To avoid the Islamic legal prohibition on selling and buying money, it is said that the *murābaḥa* contract is not a financing agreement but a sale agreement.[222] According to

218 The sharia institutions included in LKS are, for example, sharia banks, sharia insurance companies, the sharia stock exchange, and some others.

219 This illustration can be seen in the "Fatwa Tentang Pembiayaan Mudharabah (qiradh), on Ketentuan Biaya," point 6 (Dewan Syariah Nasional MUI-Bank Indonesia, *Himpunan Fatwa Dewan Syariah Nasional MUI*, p. 43).

220 Muhammad Akram Khan, *Islamic Economics and Finance: A Glossary* (London & New York: Routledge, 2012), p. 26.

221 Said M. Elfkahani, M. Kabir Hassan, and Yusuf M. Sidani, "Islamic Mutual Funds," in *The Handbook of Islamic Banking*, ed. M. Kabir Hassan and K. Mervyn Lewis (Massachusetts: Edward Elgar Publishing, 2007), 256–276, p. 259.

222 Ibid.

the *murābaḥa* model, as laid down by MUI, a seller sells an item to a buyer with an explicitly specified price that incorporates a degree of profit margin for the seller. This transaction requires the seller to declare their costs accurately, and on the basis of this the amount of the profit margin can be agreed between the seller and the buyer.[223] The discourse on *murābaḥa* transactions has been broadly elaborated by traditional Muslim jurists such as Ibn Rushd, al-Kasāni and many others. MUI needs to produce this fatwa because of its significance for the commercial practices of sharia banks, and especially to attract investment. Socially and economically speaking, the rational argument behind the fatwa is that Muslim businessmen and entrepreneurs need capital and financial assistance to run their businesses and enterprises from banks, and this must be based on sharia norms. Despite MUI's efforts to situate *murābaḥa* as a vital element of Indonesia's sharia banks, some criticisms of this practice must be considered. There is the potential for misuse of this product, as has been the case with many international sharia banks. Misuse of *murabāḥa* can potentially ruin the industry. At the practical business or banking level, Islamic banks may offer a "commodity *murabāḥa* agreement" even when no actual exchange of commodities takes place; cash transactions are more common. For businesspeople, this circumstance is embarrassing and poses a threat for the industry.[224] This financing model lacks the potential for trust-building, which is the core of business tradition.

The third model is *mushāraka*, a system of financing based on a partnership contract among two, three or more parties or individuals on a joint enterprise, in which all the involved groups participate equally in the apportioning of profits and risks. The DSN views this system as better than the conventional system of financing followed by non-sharia banks in its potential to create a concrete financial share. Within the system, LKS—namely banks or insurance companies—hold an equal position to other shareholders in theory, but in practice they usually act as primary funders.

There are some crucial issues with the models of sharia corporation business contracts that the DSN regulates. Firstly, the DSN states that capital sharing must exist in a concrete form such as cash, gold, silver or other properties

223 Dewan Syariah Nasional MUI-Bank Indonesia, *Himpunan Fatwa Dewan Syariah Nasional MUI*, pp. 23–4. See also "Murabahah," *Islamic Finance*, http://www.islamic-finance.com/item_murabaha_f.htm, viewed on 22 July 2022.

224 "Misused Murabaha Hurts Industry Islamic Banks Warned against Commodity Murabaha," Arabian Business, 1 February 2008, https://www.arabianbusiness.com/gcc/uae/misused-murabaha-hurts-industry-122008, viewed on 22 July 2022.

of similar value.[225] Additionally, the DSN also grants the right for LKS to ask other shareholders to provide collateral, which is specifically required by sharia. In this regard, the DSN justifies an extra-sharia mechanism to secure the LKS capital as the primary shareholder.[226] This is an inconsistent feature of this system, where the rights of sharing partners (clients) are inferior to those of LKS. Secondly, DSN does not require an equal distribution of tasks among shareholders but those who assume a larger responsibility will obtain a greater share of the profits as long as all these issues have been agreed to in a pre-arranged contract. The second discussion pertains to the legal status of down payment, indemnification, and the mechanism of dispute resolution and distribution of revenue. These issues are important due to their influence on the image of the sharia-based economy in general. DSN has issued a particular fatwa on the legal validity of the down payment. This issue is interesting because the Islamic jurisprudence texts never clearly mention the permissibility of charging a down payment to the client or the borrower. However, DSN has decided that the mechanism of requiring a down payment is needed in order to gauge the seriousness of the clients in obtaining a financial injection from LKS.[227] However, this also indicates that the financier must be protected from risks. This can be seen in the fatwa's legal considerations, which elaborate that the matter of down payment is a mechanism of the *murābaḥa* contract to secure against losses. Because this fatwa is not deeply rooted in the tradition of Islamic jurisprudence on contracts (*fiqh al-muʿāmala*), Islamic legal arguments used by DSN-MUI are quite general and do not refer to the specific opinions of Muslim jurists. In two verses of the Qur'ān, Sūrat al-Baqara [2]: 282 and Sūrat al-Mā'ida [5]: 1, there are mentions of contracts but not down payments. One *ḥadīth* regarding a peace-mechanism (*ṣulḥ*) is also mentioned as an argument. DSN-MUI also cites three legal maxims: there should be neither harm nor reciprocating harm (*lā ḍarār wa lā ḍirar*), the origin of the contract is lawful unless an argument forbidding the transaction is found (*al-aṣl fī al-muʿāmala al-ibāḥa illā an yadulla dalīl ʿalā taḥrīmihā*), and harm must be eliminated (*al-ḍarār yuzālu*).[228] With regard to these opinions, MUI has determined that charging a down payment is permitted, but it must rely on a mutual contract between the parties or individuals. The criticism here is that charging a down payment to the client follows the logic of non-sharia-based

225 Dewan Syariah Nasional MUI-Bank Indonesia, *Himpunan Fatwa Dewan Syariah Nasional MUI*, p. 52.
226 Ibid.
227 Ibid, p. 79.
228 Ibid, pp. 23–24.

banks, in which protection is prioritised for the owner of capital, not for the borrower. This is the general paradigm of capitalism, in which the capital of the lender should be protected from losses.

Besides the down payment, MUI has also produced an Islamic legal clause that regulates the payment of indemnification for clients who renege on the conditions stipulated in the predetermined agreement. This is applied in the concept of *muḍāraba*. In this regard, the crucial issue is not about the verdict, but concerns who decides this agreement. In most cases, the LKS has a stronger position in formulating the contract agreement content, and what they determine to be careless or intentional fault and fraud are more representative of LKS's views than those of the clients. In this regard, the position of the customer is not well protected. As a consequence, the interests of the client defer to those of the financier. Like the legal status of the down payment, the concept of indemnification due to the mistake of the client has, in fact, no conceptual root in the discourse of *muḍāraba*. Originally speaking, the notion of *muḍāraba* is based on trust (*yad al-amāna*).[229] Given these two issues, it seems that this economic system's objective of empowering the welfare of Indonesian people cannot yet be achieved, because the sharia economy remains dependent on the interests of the capital providers, which are very few in number.

The fourth example of a sharia economic contract is insurance (*takāful*). Now, as the number of middle-class Indonesian Muslims has increased, sharia insurance has become one of the most prominent sharia financing modes in Indonesia. MUI is aware that many more Indonesian Muslims are insuring themselves against future risks. This fatwa contains quite detailed rulings on sharia insurance. The DSN defines sharia insurance (*takāful*)[230] as a contract which is established as a means for mutual help in hedging future risks through the mechanism of investment based on sharia norms.[231] The definition used by DSN is similar to Mohd Ma'sum Billah's definition that sharia insurance is to be operated on "the basis of shared responsibility, brotherhood, solidarity and mutual cooperation or assistance, which provides for mutual financial security and assistance to safeguard participants against a defined

229 Dewan Syariah Nasional MUI-Bank Indonesia, *Himpunan Fatwa Dewan Syariah Nasional MUI*, p. 46.

230 This is derived from the Arabic root *ka-fa-la*, meaning "to help or to take care of one's needs."

231 Dewan Syariah Nasional MUI-Bank Indonesia, *Himpunan Fatwa Dewan Syariah Nasional MUI*, p. 133.

risk."[232] Furthermore, DSN states that sharia insurance is to be implemented through two modes of sharia financing: the first is through commercial contracts (*tijāra*), which involves loss and profit sharing (*muḍāraba*); and the second is non-commercial contracts (*tabarru'*) which often entails gift-giving mechanisms. In the former model, the sharia insurance client is regarded as an investor (*ṣāhib al-māl*) and the insurance company as the manager of the fund. In the latter model, a customer gives their money to another client as a gift and the insurance company acts as the manager of the gift-giving fund. Based on this agreed contract, DSN also points out that a customer should pay a premium, which allows them the right to claim on the basis of the predetermined contract among the parties.

The important problem that should be addressed here is how all products of the so-called sharia economy are evolving in the legal and public spheres. One prominent issue that was evident at the Annual Meeting of the Sharia Supervisory Board in 2010 was the complaint mechanism for the misconduct of sharia contracts. MUI talked about sharia arbitration as a space for one of the two parties to comply with their tasks and duties in the agreed contract. Provisions for arbitration are found in all fatwa on sharia contracts, but as a justice system to provide resolution for both the financier and the customer, with sharia arbitration receiving greater emphasis. So far, few sharia-related economy cases have been brought to the National Agency of Sharia Arbitration for resolution, and those that have lack clear results.[233] In addition, the DSN does not have data on this issue. In short, the lack of attention to the function of arbitration will influence the process of developing sharia economy as a method for empowering the welfare of the Muslim community.

Another possible formidable barrier for the sharia economy is related to the distribution system of revenue applied in the above-mentioned contacts. MUI has outlined a mechanism to deal with this issue: the first is the principle of revenue distribution that is focused more on the accountancy and bookkeeping used by the sharia financial institutions; the second concerns the system of revenue distribution that regulates profit-sharing based on sharia principles. In the second, the sharing model can use net-revenue-sharing and profit-sharing. The former aims to share income from business and the latter aims to share the gains.[234] MUI decided that the best method was

232 M.M. Billah, *Applied Takaful and Modern Insurance: Law and Practice* (Sweet & Maxwell Asia, 2007), p. 405.

233 Interview with Asrori M. Karni, Jakarta, 2010.

234 Dewan Syariah Nasional MUI-Bank Indonesia, *Himpunan Fatwa Dewan Syariah Nasional MUI*, p. 87.

net-revenue-sharing, to be based on a predetermined agreement between the financier and the borrower. The critical point of this mechanism was not the content, but its application and implication at the practical level in how far it can create fairness and justice for the financial institutions and customers. The real problem of sharia banks and sharia financial institutions when it comes to sharing revenue is its image. Since net-revenue-sharing, which is applied in sharia financial institutions, seems to be similar to what is practiced in conventional banks, many Muslims feel reluctant to use sharia banks or sharia finance institutions, even when some studies have indicated bright prospects for net-revenue-sharing in the future.

Related to sharia insurance is the issue of how sharia insurance companies manage the money of the clients, and whether this follows the concept of pure money. DSN points out that trusted insurance companies should invest the collected funds from the client's premium and that it is lawful for insurance companies to reinsure the money with other, larger insurance companies, remaining in the framework of sharia norms. The trusted insurance company will gain a share of the profit if it uses the model of commercial contract-based insurance, and if it uses the model of non-commercial contract-based insurance it will gain a fee based on the agreement.[235] This means that a different mode of sharia financing will create different opportunities for sharia insurance companies to gain income.

From a conceptual perspective, the authenticity of the sharia insurance paradigm remains questionable, at least from the view of traditional Islamic jurisprudence. But the crucial issue here is its implementation at the practical level. The market of sharia insurance in Indonesia has grown exponentially over the years. Over the period of 2007–2011, the sharia insurance industry posted an increase of 67.33%, much higher than the growth in the non-sharia insurance industry, which was only 15.93%.[236] This phenomenon should be accompanied by good service for the clients, but in fact a lot of sharia insurance undertakings lacked good sharia-compliant mechanisms. Sharia insurance companies should therefore be able to create an image that the products of sharia insurance are not only different from those offered by conventional insurance companies, but also come with added benefits and safety. It is important to think in terms of the social and economic data on the habits of Indonesian customers. By preferring the sharia-financing model, they are not only attracted by

235 Dewan Syariah Nasional MUI-Bank Indonesia, *Himpunan Fatwa Dewan Syariah Nasional MUI*, p. 134.

236 "Butuh Akselerasi Perkembangan Industri Asuransi Syariah," *Sindo Weekly Magazine*, 2012 (not available online.)

the Islamic legal aspect of the sharia insurance but also by its benefits. They prefer sharia insurance if they receive good service, return on investment, and competitiveness. Another crucial problem is related to the issue of reinsurance, considering the limited number of large sharia companies operating in Indonesia. This is important to consider because the stock of sharia insurance should be reinsured in a sharia company. This attempt must go along with the basic principle of sharia insurance: that it should be free of hazards, corruption, interest, speculation and violation. This is a major challenge for sharia insurance companies in Indonesia.

Finally, having studied the financial products and transactions of different sharia economic products, one should conclude on some critical notes. Historically speaking, the concept of sharia economy is not a system of theory and practice that is purely developed from and within Islam. This is visible in the concept of *muḍāraba* and other models of sharia transactions that were practised long before the coming of Islam. Another weakness of the sharia economy is related to its numerous products, which were not developed in response to the internal needs of Muslim people but in response to the global capitalist economy. This is not a phenomenon exclusive to Indonesia, but it also affects the worldwide sharia economy. This can be seen by looking at the various brands of sharia economy, which are actually parallel with or imitate the products of the conventional capitalist economy. This is because the conceptualisation of the sharia economy is built on the basis of reaction to the economic construction of the West. In addition, to further simplify the matter, the theorisation of the sharia economy is adopted from the discourse of *al-fiqh al-muʿāmala*. In this regard, the sharia economy can be seen as the politicisation of traditional Islamic jurisprudence. Sharia insurance is one of the visible examples of how the discourse of traditional Islamic jurisprudence is being instrumentalised to respond to the global economic market. It is not unusual that the prevalent phenomena of sharia banks in Indonesia are regarded as the shariatisation of capitalism.[237]

Last but not least, the common assumption of general Indonesian customers and also the holders of sharia financial products is that the sharia economy will not die. This matter was answered in the Annual Meeting of the Sharia Supervisory Board in 2010, which stated that sharia economy is like any other economy.[238] It can collapse if the market does not come up with a good

---

237 Syafiq Hasyim, "The Political Economy of Sharia and the Future Trajectory of Democracy in Indonesia," *Perspective*, 26 December 2019, https://www.iseas.edu.sg/images/pdf/ISEAS_Perspective_2019_108.pdf, viewed on 22 July 2022.

238 This is the conclusion I drew from my observation of the meeting, which took place on 10–13 December 2010.

response. Inherently, the sharia economy also brings complicated risks that are difficult to deal with. Being realistic about the weaknesses and strengths of the sharia economy is a good way to sustain and maintain a brighter future for this economic model. It is also realistic to see the sharia economy as of one of MUI's shariatisation efforts, one that can flexibly respond to democratisation.

6.3 Compliance and Social Resistance

The increasing religious authority of MUI in general and the prevalent use of MUI fatwa and Islamic advice in the legal and public spheres of Indonesia in particular has led to two different camps of compliance and resistance within Indonesian society. The former argues that MUI should have a greater role in the legal and public spheres, while the lattter believes that the organisation's role should be limited to the non-legal and political spheres, stating that its discourse can be applied to law but should not be compulsory. This section seeks to examine the positions of these two groups, particularly the issues they focus on and the arguments they use to support their positions. The array of issues includes questioning the increasing religious authority of MUI in the context of the nation-state of Indonesia, the monopolisation of fatwa-making, and the expansion of MUI in controlling the public sphere.

The increasing religious authority of MUI in the legal and public spheres is understood by some groups as an attempt by MUI to re-inject religion into politics. The MUI fatwas that order and influence public policy and state rulings are a form of incursion of religion into the regulation of the state.[239] However, MUI argues that it has remained within the domain of its responsibilities and follows agreed democratic procedures, claiming the authority to integrate *al-dīn* (religion) and *al-dawla* (the state) through its fatwas and advice. Legally speaking, MUI's argument in striving for religious authority is similar to that used by Islamist groups who want Indonesia to implement sharia, citing the Pancasila principle of "*Ketuhanan Yang Maha Esa*", belief in one God, and articles of religion in the Indonesian Constitution. Mahfudh (MUI-NU), Amin (MUI-NU), Muzadi (NU), and Din Syamsuddin (Muhammadiyah) support the idea of incorporating sharia elements into Indonesian law without transforming the state into an Islamic state. FPI shares this position, but MMI and HTI

239 Suhadi Cholil et al., "Annual Report on Religious Life in Indonesia 2009" (Yogyakarta, 2009), p. 20.

are very clear in their rejection of it.[240] For MMI and HTI, MUI's efforts are just a preliminary step towards the real shariatisation of Indonesia.[241] HTI is striving for a caliphate system and MMI calls for a total sharia state with the enforcement of sharia criminal law as its main hallmark. For the opposing camp, the burgeoning reception of MUI fatwa in legal discourse and practice is a real challenge for the neutral position of the state, and its adherents believe the state should not tolerate the inclusion of sharia prescriptions within the law, rulings, or any other binding regulations. Tensions were evident, for instance, when the draft law on anti-pornography and pornographic activities was prepared by lawmakers. MUI and the Ministry of Religious Affairs had prepared the draft, known as RUU-APP.[242] MUI viewed the state law on pornography as a kind of moral policing for Indonesia and, together with pro-sharia Islamic organisations such as Forum Ukhuwah Islamiyyah, Forum Umat Islam, FPI, HTI and many others, mobilised a huge rally called the "One Million Man Demonstration" in Jakarta on 21 May 2006 to pressure lawmakers into passing the draft law.[243] Within the two largest Muslim organisations, NU and Muhammadiyah, members were divided about the RUU-APP legislation. Those supporting the legislation were mostly mainstream members, while a few opposed the draft law. Thanks to the backing of the MUI, NU and Muhammadiyah elites, the legislation of the RUU-APP gained a broader reception from Muslim communities in general. The NU Sharia-Advisory Board (Indonesian-Arabic: *Syuriah NU*) for instance, released a public statement[244] that supported the draft law.[245] Eventually, the Act on Pornography was passed in 2008.[246]

240 Fealy, "Islamic Radicalism in Indonesia: The Faltering Revival?"; M.B. Hooker, *Indonesian Syariah, Defining a National School of Islamic Law* (Singapore: ISEAS, 2008), pp. 47–8.

241 Interview with Ismail Yusanto, Jakarta, 2010.

242 "KH Sahal: MUI Konsisten Kawal RUU Pornografi," *NU Online*, 27 October 2008, https://www.nu.or.id/warta/kh-sahal-mui-konsisten-kawal-ruu-pornografi-EFyvA, viewed on 22 July 2022.

243 "Aksi Sejuta Umat Dukung RUU APP Akan Digelar 21 Mei," Detik News, 15 May 2006, https://news.detik.com/berita/d-595008/aksi-sejuta-umat-dukung-ruu-app-akan-digelar-21-mei?nd771108bcj=, viewed on 22 July 2022.

244 This statement was approved by Sahal Mahfudl General Chairman of NU Sharia-advisory body), Nasaruddin Umar (NU General Secretary), Hasyim Muzadi (NU General Chairman of Executive Body) and Endang Turmudzi (General Secretary).

245 "Pernyataan Pengurus Besar Nahdlatul Ulama (PBNU) Tentang RUU Anti Pornografi Dan Pornoaksi RUU APP," NU Online, 20 March 2006, https://nu.or.id/taushiyah/pernyataan-pengurus-besar-nahdlatul-ulama-pbnu-tentang-ruu-anti-pornografi-dan-pornoaksi-ruu-app-YHpfL, viewed on 22 July 2022.

246 In Indonesian the draft law is called RUU APP (*Rancangan Undang-Undang Anti Pornografi dan Pornoaksi*).

The growing religious authority of MUI also strengthens its position as the most reliable fatwa-giver in Indonesia. MUI supporters approve this position, arguing that Indonesian Muslims need a single voice to unite them and represent them in applying sharia prescriptions. The other camp disapproves of this position, arguing that allowing MUI to be the only authoritative fatwa-giver will endanger democracy and multiculturalism in Indonesia, a country that is a non-Islamic theocratic state, and that it is important to maintain the diversity of Islam. NU and Muhammadiyah are agreed in promoting MUI as the sole fatwa-issuer on issues pertaining to belief, halalisation and sharia economy. Din Syamsuddin and Ahmad Fatah Wibisono of Muhammadiyah have stated that their organisation will not issue fatwas on these three issues.[247] Nahdlatul Ulama (NU) also concurs that a greater responsibility for issuing fatwas on belief has been granted to MUI and has therefore only issued a few such fatwas themselves, demonstrating their support for MUI's growing authority in this matter. When MUI issued the fatwa banning the Ahmadiyah, it received full support from both NU and Muhammadiyah. Both of these organisations agreed that Ahmadiyah was a deviant form of Islam. Muzadi has often stated that Ahmadiyah is no longer part of Islam and Din Syamsuddin suggests that the Ahmadis should use a name other than Islam to refer to their religion. When civil society organisations from Islamic and secular backgroundss filed a judicial review of Act No. 01/PNPS/1965 at the Constitutional Court, all Islamic organisations such as NU, Muhammadiyah, MUI, and elements of Islamist organisations such as FPI, HTI, MMI, and FUI defended the act.

Opposing groups argue that granting more authority to MUI in the issuance of fatwas gives the organisation the chance to monopolise Islamic thought and thus damage freedom of expression in democratic Indonesia. Besides MUI, other Islamic organisations have their own fatwa-issuing bodies: NU has Bahsul Masa'il Forum; Muhammadiyah has Lembaga Tarjih Forum; and Persatuan Islam (the third-largest Islamic organisation) has Lembaga Hisbah. The undemocratic impact of MUI's domination of fatwa can be seen in the cases of sharia economy and halal lifestyle issues. Sharia banks and sharia-financial institutions in Indonesia are now required to obtain certificates from and have their operations overseen by MUI's DSN. In the field of halal food certification, Zaim Saidi, an NGO activist and proponent of Islamic economics, states that MUI monopolisation is packaged in the name of expertise and laboratory research. This is despite the fact that this process is simpler and easier in other

247 Interview with Ahmad Fatah Wibisono, Jakarta, 2011.

countries—such as Malaysia, Singapore, Australia, and America.[248] Three relevant issues are raised here by the opposing group. Firstly, the monopolisation of fatwas tends to result in MUI adopting an authoritarian stance, as no differing opinions from other fatwa bodies are recognised.[249] Secondly, there is a concern that a non-representative organisation or non-elected body has the power to regulate and control the religious freedom and religious liberties of Indonesians. Thirdly, the monopolisation of fatwa authority leads to the possibility of Islamic commodification. However, this criticism is made by independent Muslim scholars, Islamic NGOs and activists, and not by MUI-member Islamic organisations. Although NU, for instance, tried to issue halal certificates in its National Congress of 2010, they also officially suggested that all halal-related issues should be submitted to MUI.[250] This position is shared by Muhammadiyah. In the case of belief issues, the monopolisation of MUI has led this organisation to becoming the *ʿaqīda* police. This is clearly visible in how MUI controls the categorisation of various belief groups. Those who follow Sunnī beliefs are defined as mainstream, while those who are different are defined as *sesat* (deviant). MUI has very clearly banned the Ahmadiyah, Shīʿa, and other local "deviant" groups. In this regard, different beliefs are used by MUI as an argument for labelling such groups as "others". MUI's approach to this matter constitutes a great problem for religious tolerance in Indonesia.

The expansion of religion in regulating and controlling private matters has created significant concern among Indonesians, especially secularist groups. From the MUI perspective, Islam does not clearly differentiate between the public and private spheres. Many MUI activists believe that a clear distinction between the private and public is a Western construction,[251] and that this distinction reflects how strongly Western paradigms influence the thought of Indonesian Muslims. According to Asrorun Niam Sholeh, the separation of the private and public spheres is dangerous because it could impede shariatisation in Indonesia. Many groups such as JIL, the International Conference on Religion and Peace, the Wahid Institute, and secularists, consider religion to be

248 "Zaim Saidi: Di luar Negeri Prosedur Halal Lebih Sederhana," Republika, 4 December 2008, https://www.republika.co.id/berita/dunia-islam/islam-nusantara/08/12/04/18424-zaim-saidi-di-luar-negeri-prosedur-halal-lebih-sederhana, viewed on 22 July 2022.

249 M. Mukshin Jamil and Rusmadi, *Membendung Despotisme Wacana Agama: Kritik Atas Otoritarianisme Fatwa MUI Tentang Pluralisme, Liberalisme, Dan Sekulerisme* (Semarang: Walisongo Press, 2010).

250 This is based on my observation of the NU National Congress held in March 2010 in Makassar, South Sulawesi.

251 Interviews with Ma'ruf Amin, Jakarta, 2010; Asrorun Niam Sholeh, Jakarta, 2010; Ichwan Sam, Jakarta, 2010; Slamet Effendy Yusuf, Jakarta, 2010.

a private matter. Yet pure Islam recognises no distinction between the public and private sphere. All aspects of human life are regulated in Islam, so Islamic purists believe that beliefs, dress code, marriages, consumption and commerce should be overseen by sharia.

Regulating such private matters under the supervision of sharia will provide a complex role for MUI in a new authoritarian social-Islamic regime in Indonesia. MUI's desire to manage all aspects of human life, mundane and sacred, private and public, is criticised as being against democracy and human rights by those who argue that the Constitution of Indonesia clearly separates the public and private realms. Debates on public versus private spheres can be seen in the issues of pornography, abortion, and so forth. MUI tried to convince lawmakers that Islamic norms on these issues could be introduced as part of public law and has ultimately been successful.

CHAPTER 7

The Dilemma of Electoral Politics and the Politics of the *Umma*: MUI's Trajectory of Shariatisation in the Era of Joko Widodo's Presidency

7.1 Introduction

When Jokowi was elected as Indonesian President in 2014, some Muslim organisations, inclduing MUI, were concerned over his commitment to the interests of Islam and the Muslim community (*umma*). MUI was very critical of Jokowi's leadership, esepcially in his first term (2014–2019), in relation to the agenda of shariatisation. This is understandable, as it was clear that shariatisation—MUI's main priority—would not continue as expected. The organisation's historical trajectory reflects various programmes and a broader agenda, yet it has been consistent in pursuing shariatisation in the legal and political spheres throughout.

President Jokowi was first elected in 2014 as Yudoyono's successor, and then reelected to serve a second term from 2019–2024. As mentioned in previous chapters, during Yudoyono's presidency (the SBY period) the role of MUI was strong and influential. Many assumed that the organisation would face serious challenges in promoting shariatisation during the Jokowi era due to his very different social, political and cultural background. Jokowi inclines to the nationalist-secular ideology, which is frequently at odds with MUI's ideology of normative Islam, and his supporters expect him to restrict the growth of any form of identity politics. Yet Jokowi and MUI have surprised expectations by working together; rather than minimising the organisation's role, this collaboration has strengthened MUI's agenda of shariatisation in Indonesia.

This chapter is devoted to analysing MUI's agenda of shariatisation in the presidential era of Jokowi, specifically how the organisation pursued its agenda of shariatisation in certain key issues. Three of these issues are examined in depth: first, MUI's efforts to influence Indonesian electoral politics. At both national and local levels, the organisation has attempted to increase its influence in elections and promote political leaders who share its vision. Second, MUI has tried to reorient itself with regard to the notion of the *umma* (the Muslim community.) From 1975 onwards, MUI focused on the interests

DOI:10.1163/9789004534896_008

of the government rather than that of the *umma*.[1] Since the reform era, however, the organisation has become increasingly concerned with the interests of the *umma*, a trend that has become particularly visible during the Jokowi period as evidenced by MUI's involvement in political events such as general elections, Islamist mobilisation such as the Aksi Bela Islam movement (ABI, Action to Defend Islam), and other cases. Third, MUI's increasing involvement in state political leadership, particularly during Jokowi's second term, focusing on the transition of Amin—the leader of MUI, who had long been critical of government—to becoming vice-president of Indonesia. There are two key points relating to this development: first is the declaration of MUI's role as the close "friend of government" (*ṣadīq al-ḥukūma*), meaning that the organisation functions to support and justify the Jokowi administration. The second is its change in stance from conservative to moderate, with the effect of introducing more moderate principles to guide the lives of Indonesian Muslims. Discussions on how the concept of *wasaṭiyya* (moderation) is implemented at the practical level also forms part of the analysis.

7.2 MUI and Electoral Politics

Although there were many protests and disappointments regarding the result of 2014 general elections, especially from the side of Prabowo-Hatta's supporters, the transition of power from SBY to Jokowi took place without any violence. When the official result of the elections was announced by the Komisi Pemilihan Umum (KPU, National Commission of General Elections), Prabowo-Hatta rejected the outcome and withdrew from the electoral process, claiming that it had been fraudulent.[2] Following this accusation, mass demonstrations were mobi the refusal of Prabowo-Hatta, mass-demonstrations were mobilised around the country, especially in Jakarta, to delegitimise the election results.[3] This turbulence did not destabilise the generally peaceful political climate of Indonesia, however, and the situation remained under

1 Syafiq Hasyim, "The Council of Indonesian Ulama (Majelis Ulama Indonesia, MUI) and Religious Freedom" (Irasec's Discussion Papers, 12, 2011).

2 Prabowo-Hatta stated that the 2014 presidential elections were corrupt. See "Klaim Pemilu Curang, Prabowo Merasa Tersakiti", *Tempo*, 6 August 2014, https://nasional.tempo.co/read/597679/klaim-pemilu-curang-prabowo-merasa-tersakiti, viewed on 22 July 2022.

3 "Prabowo Subianto Tarik Diri dan Tolak Hasil Pilpres 2014", *VOA*, 22 July 2014, https://www.voaindonesia.com/a/prabowo-subianto-tarik-diri-dan-tolak-hasil-pilpres-2014/1962515.html, viewed on 22 July 2022.

control. Jokowi was finally sworn as president with Jusuf Kalla (JK) as vice-president after the Constitutional Court took the decision to reject Prabowo-Hatta's appeal of on 20 October 2014.[4] After some negotiatian, Prabowo-Hatta finally came to accept Jokowi's presidency, easing the political tension, and it became clear that Indonesia had successfully navigated the most crucial general elections in its history.

Although MUI did not clearly indicate its political support for Jokowi-JK, it recognised the outcome of the elctions.[5] The organisation, through the political attitudes of its elites, was divided into two groups: those who supported Jokowi-JK, even if not clearly articulating this position, and those on the side of Probowo-Hatta, who were vocal in their support. Ridwan, for example, was a strong backer of Prabowo-Hatta, and publicly stated that there was "a difference in *madhhab* (school of Islamic law), but we are as one in politics for the victory of the *umma*," (Indonesian: *berbeda dalam madhhab, satu dalam politik untuk kemenangan umat*). Ridwan clearly stated that he was on the side of Prabowo-Hatta because he wanted to prevent future generations of young Indonesian Muslims from the dangers of secularism, liberalism and pluralism that would be promoted by Jokowi-JK, and because he believed that Prabowo-Hatta would bring about the victory of the *umma*.[6] The MUI elites who supported Jokowi-JK, however, did not publicly defend their position. Many remained silent.

As a Muslim organisation, MUI thrived during the SBY years, and had a strong and well-established institutional capacity at the time of Jokowi's election in 2014. As discussed in previous chapters, MUI produced a considerable number of fatwas and Islamic recommendations during the SBY period that were generally accommodated by the government. In addition, SBY had issued Presidential Regulation No. 151/2014 that legalised the funding if MUI from the state budget.[7] SBY was the only Indonesian President who provided this privilege for MUI, and it was not issued to any other Muslim organisations. The influence of MUI in the legal and public spheres was also evident in the

4 "Ini Penjabaran Lengkap Putusan MK Tolak Gugatan Prabowo-Hatta", *Kompas*, 22 August 2014, https://nasional.kompas.com/read/2014/08/22/11025921/Ini.Penjabaran.Lengkap.Putusan.MK.Tolak.Gugatan.Prabowo-Hatta?page=all, viewed on 22 July 2022.

5 "Indonesia Resmi Dipimpin Jokowi, MUI: Bersyukurlah Kepada Allah", *Republika*, 22 October 2014, https://www.republika.co.id/berita/nasional/politik/14/10/22/ndt6v7-indonesia-resmi-dipimpin-jokowi-mui-bersyukurlah-kepada-allah, viewed on 22 July 2022.

6 "Beda Mazhab tapi Satu dalam Politik", RMOL, 27 May 2014, https://politik.rmol.id/read/2014/05/27/156963/Beda-Mazhab-tapi-Satu-dalam-Politik-, viewed on 22 July 2022.

7 "Bantuan Pendanaan Kegiatan Majelis Ulama Indonesia", Database Peraturan, 17 October 2014, https://peraturan.bpk.go.id/Home/Details/41666/perpres-no-151-tahun-2014, viewed on 22 July 2022.

State Law on Pornography, the Joint Ministerial Decree on the Ahmadiyah, and many others.[8]

Despite its good organisational capacity, MUI played the role of a pressure and interest group during the first half-term of Jokowi's presidency. This was firstly because the organisation had not yet come to understand Jokowi's leadership style. Secondly, it had not made any clear contribution to the new president's success in the 2014 elections. Thirdly, it was aware that many of Jokowi's supporters were not in favour of MUI. None of these challenges caused the organisation to give up, however, and it was confident in its position as the most respected ulama organisation in negotiating with Jokowi.

The following sections address how MUI has used electoral politics at various levels from 2012 onwards to promote its own agenda. Electoral politics are, of course, not the core business of MUI. Unlike political parties, officially speaking, MUI has no direct connection with the general elections. It can, however, influence voters—even though it is characterised as an Islamic civil society organisation, and electoral politics are the domain of political society organisations.[9] Functioning as a pressure or interest group, it nevertheless has an impact on both the state and Muslim communities.[10] As a pressure group, it examines the political landscape to see if its agenda can be promoted, while as an interest group it assesses whether or not the current situation can further the interests of Muslims. As a result, there is evidence that MUI is relevant in electoral politics.

Exerting its influence on electoral politics has therefore become one of MUI's methods of furthering its agenda of shariatisation. Through this means, MUI can win followers from among ordinary people, politicians, and community leaders, and it grants its support to candidates who can potentially benefit the organisation in the future. This can be seen in the case of the 2017 Jakarta gubernatorial election. During the Suharto period, general elections were not based on the system of direct election and therefore had no relevance for MUI. Since the reform era and the adoption of the system of direct election—one man, one vote—the organisation has had more opportunity to promote shariatisation through playing a role in this process.

---

8 Syafiq Hasyim, "The Council of Indonesian Ulama (MUI) and Aqidah-Based Intolerance: A Critical Analysis of Its Fatwa on Ahmadiyah and 'Sepilis,'" in *Religion, Law and Intolerance in Indonesia*, ed. Tim Lindsey and Helen Pausacker (New York: Routledge, 2016), 211–33.

9 Jean L. Cohen and Andrew Arato, *Civil Society and Political Theory* (Massachusetts: MIT Press, 1994).

10 On Islamic civil society as pressure group see Patricia Sloane-White, *Corporate Islam: Sharia and the Modern Workplace* (Cambridge: Cambridge University Press, 2017) p. 21.

It is essential for MUI to put its fingerprint on important national events connected with the agenda of the *umma*. Electoral politics are undeniably one of the most important political occasions for both the *umma* and the state. In terms of Bayat's perspective on life as politics,[11] the general elections can be seen as a strategic field where the lives of ordinary people (*umma*) or their agenda can be implemented as part of the affairs of state. For MUI, bringing sharia into the legal and political spheres of Indonesia is a priority for all Indonesian Muslims, meaning that it becomes a form of populist agenda. MUI understands that general elections at various levels—regional and national elections, and presidential and parliamentary elections—can be used as an opportunity to formalise sharia. As an ulama organisation, MUI therefore cannot allow an important political event such as a general election to take place without becoming involved and attemtping to use its influence with Muslim voters. The organisation has an interest in placing general elections as an issue not only for political parties, but also for Muslim organisations.

The general elections are an arena where MUI can attract public attention towards its own agenda. It exerts it influence in two ways: first through the change of leadership, meaning that it can endorse candidates with similar aspirations and directly influence voters and politicians to elect leaders who will promote shariatisation. The second is through its ability to publicise its own agenda during the campaign session, and to promote it to candidates. Both these forms of influence can take the form of the issuance of fatwa and Islamic recommendations.

7.2.1 *The MUI Fatwa on General Elections*

Although the political atmosphere of Indonesia is dynamic, the role of MUI in general elections is a perplexing issue. In the Suharto era, MUI consistently supported the president's reelection.[12] During this period, the organisation naturally took a different approach to political parties, aiming to create Islamic an argument for Indonesian Muslims about the importance of supporting Suharto as president. MUI's championing of Suharto was understandable, since it relied heavily on his continued good will.[13] The mutual support

11 Asef Bayat, *Life as Politics: How Ordinary People Change the Middle East* (Amsterdam: Amsterdam University Press, 2010).

12 Muhammad As'ad, "Religion and Politics in Indonesia: Attitudes and Influences of the Indonesian Council of Ulama on the General Elections" (Leiden, Leiden University, 2010).

13 Ibid, p. 34; Donald J Porter, *Managing Politics and Islam in Indonesia* (London & New York: Routledge Curzon, 2004).

between Suharto and MUI on many issues was the historical and political consequence of their intimate relationship.[14]

The stance of MUI on general elections has shifted from a dependent to a more independent one due to the demand for social and political change in the post-Suharto era. MUI is no longer reliant on the ruling regime, and can choose which political party to support based on its own agenda. In addition, the organisation may have a different political standpoint from the ruling government of Indonesia. Again, despite MUI is not a political party and has no official ties with any political party, but since the introduction of the direct system of elections in 1999 it is understood to have an influence on voters, with the ability to endorse candidates and issue recommendations in their favour. Indonesian Muslim voters often wait for MUI's electoral recommedation before deciding how to vote, meaning that the Islamic identity of candidates can become the most important factor in presidential campaigns. Since the beginning of the reform era, MUI has taken the meritocratic approach into consideration when delivering political support, but identity politics still takes precedence, being based on theology, while merit is situated in social and political factors. MUI's support of Anies Baswedan rather than Ahok in the 2017 Jakarta gubernatorial election, despite the fact that Ahok had already shown himself a successful leader, is an obvious example. During the Suharto ero such prioritisation of identity politics had not been possible, and it was not considered important. Since then, MUI has justified its preference for identity politics through the theological argument that religion is the most important quality in a leader. Yet this keeps the organisation trapped in a narrow political corridor limited to Muslim groups, when Jakarta is a diverse city with a substantial non-Muslim population.

In the 2009 presidential elections, although all presidential candidates were Muslims,[15] MUI still maintained certain criteria for the election of Muslim leaders through its fatwas and recommendations. These fatwas and recommendation were intentionally issued to provide guidance for Indonesian

14 Muhammad Atho Mudzhar, *Fatwa of the Council of Indonesian Ulama: A Study of Islamic Legal Thought in Indonesia 1975–1988* (Jakarta: INIS, 1993); Moch Nur Ichwan, "Towards A Puritanical Moderate Islam: The Majlis Ulama Indonesia and the Politics of Religious Orthodoxy," in *Contemporary Developments in Indonesian Islam: Explaining the "Conservative Turn,"* ed. Martin van Bruinessen (Singapore: ISEAS, 2013), 60–104.

15 The presidential candidates in 2009 were Susilo Bambang Yudoyono-Budiono, Megawati Sukarno-Putri, Prabowo Subianto, and Jusuf Kalla-Wiranto.

Muslims in choosing their leaders, particularly national leaders. As a fatwa-giver, MUI was confident that issuing such guidance was part of its responsibility because, according to the Sunnī teaching,[16] the issue of leadership (Arabic: *imāma*) falls under the domain of Islam. A leader is essential to any Muslim society. On this basis, MUI understands providing guidance on elections to be an Islamic obligation in the same way as leadership itself; failing to do so could be judged as sinful. Indonesian Muslims should also seek guidance and direction from authoritative bodies when choosing their leader. MUI defines itself as the only authority of Indonesian Islam able to offer this direction through its fatwas and Islamic recommendations.

In 2009, MUI held its annual *Ijtima' Ulama* in Padang,[17] West Sumatera, known to be one of the most strongly Muslim regions in Indonesia. On this occasion, the organisation produced a directive and comprehensive fatwa on electing leaders and the importance of general elections for the Indonesian *umma*. The fatwa was divided in two sections, the first concerning voting rights and consisting of four items as follows: (1) According to Islam, general elections are the method of choosing Muslim leaders or parliamentary representatives who fulfil requirements based on the aspirations of Muslim people and the interests of the state. (2) Electing a leader is mandatory in order to reconcile leadership (*imāma*) and government (*'imāra*). (3) Leadership and government in Islam require certain prescribed conditions as way of implementing public welfare. (4) Leaders should be selected who share the prescribed personal characteristics of Prophet Muḥammad. They should be faithful and pious, honest, trustworthy, active, idealistic, capable, and dedicated to the struggle for Muslim interests.[18]

The second part of the fatwa consists of two recommendations: (1) Muslims are advised to elect leaders who can enjoin right and forbid wrong (*al-'amr bi al-ma'rūf wa al-nahy 'an al-munkar*). (2) The government and the Elections Committee need to intensify socialisation regarding the implementation of

16 Abu al-Hasan al-Mawardi, *Al-Ahkam al-Sultaniyyah*, ed. Ahmad Jad (Cairo: Dar al-hadith, 2006).

17 This Ijtima' Ulama was attended by seven hundred MUI ulama representatives of from all over Indonesia. "MUI Selenggarakan Ijtima Ulama Komisi Fatwa III di Padang Panjang, Sumbar", Republika, 23 January 2009, https://www.republika.co.id/berita/breaking-news/nasional/09/01/23/27618-mui-selenggarakan-ijtima-ulama-komisi-fatwa-iii-di-padang-panjang-sumbar, viewed on 22 July 2022.

18 MUI, *Himpunan Fatwa MUI Sejak 1975* (Jakarta: Erlangga, 2011); Syafiq Hasyim, "MUI and Its Discursive Relevance for 'Aksi Bela Islam': A Growing Trend of Islamic Conservatism in Indonesia," in *Rising Islamic Conservatism in Indonesia: Islamic Groups and Identity Politics*, ed. Leonard C. Sebastian, Syafiq Hasyim, and Alexander R. Arifianto (London & New York: Routledge, 2021), 116–32.

elections in order to increase the participation of the community, since this is part of the community's rights. This fatwa was issued in Padang Panjang, West Sumatera, on 26 January 2009. As the chairman of MUI, Amin put his signature on this fatwa.[19]

Politically speaking, two issues related to the fatwa are important to consider here. The first regards when the fatwa was issued, namely when Amin was a member of Yudoyono's Presidential Advisory Council as well as the chairman of MUI who led the Fatwa Commission. In terms of timeframe, the fatwa was issued approximately five months before the presidential elections on 08 July 2009. These two things show that the MUI fatwa cannot be separated from the political agenda, and that this was recognised by MUI itself. Although this fatwa was issued in the framework of general elections at the national level, it also applies to regional elections at the provincial and district level.

7.2.2 *The 2012 Jakarta Gubernatorial Election: MUI and a Muslim Leader as a Must*

The 2009 MUI fatwa on general elections indicates that the Council not only understands the importance of national elections but also provincial, district and mayoral leadership in Indonesia. As the largest Muslim democratic country, Indonesia holds 514 general elections at district and administrative-city level and thirty-four elections at provincial level. The largest general elections are the presidential and parliamentary elections.[20] Successfully influencing political leadership from regional to national level is not only recommended but compelled by MUI's form of political Islam that MUI. Besides the fact that the existence of leadership is an obligation in the Sunnī tradition, it is also part of the politics of *al-ʿamr bi al maʿrūf wa nahy ʿan al-munkar* (commanding right and forbidding wrong). This also means commanding Muslim leadership and forbidding non-Muslim leadership, and is therefore one of the reasons behind the special attention MUI have given to the leadership of the Special City of Jakarta, and consider the gubernatorial election to be the second most important after the presidential election, Jakarta being the capital city and the barometer of social and political life in Indonesia. The country's economy and business is also centred on the capital. As non-political party, MUI can only

19 MUI, *Himpunan Fatwa MUI Sejak 1975*; Hasyim, "MUI and Its Discursive Relevance for 'Aksi Bela Islam': A Growing Trend of Islamic Conservatism in Indonesia."

20 Topo Santoso and Ida Budhiati, *Pemilu Di Indonesia: Kelembagaan, Pelaksanaan Dan Pengawasan* (Jakarta: Sinar Grafika, 2019); Ni'matul Huda and Imam Nasef, *Penataan Demokrasi Dan Pemilu Di Indonesia Pasca Reformasi* (Jakarta: Kencana, 2017).

exert its influence through its endorsement of a candidate with similar ideas on sharia, and by recommending this candidate to voters. This form of politics has been practised by MUI in gubernatorial elections since the inception of the post-reform era, and Islamic sentiments surrounding the Jakarta gubernatorial election remains very high.[21] When the organisation selects an appropriate candidate, it offers support through fatwa and recommendations (*tawṣiyya*), as demonstrated when it backed Baswedan in the Jakarta gubernatorial election of 2017. It also issues Islamic statements to express disagreement with a particular candidate, as was the case with Ahok in the same election campaign.

There have been two gubernatorial elections in Jakarta so far that have been foci for MUI to exercise its discourse and influence, in 2012 and 2017. This section is devoted to scrutinising the 2012 Jakarta gubernatorial election, which put forward two strong pairs of candidates in the second round: firstly, the pair of Jokowi and Basuki Tjahaja Purnama (known as Ahok), and secondly, the pair of Fauzi Bowo (governor of Jakarta from 2008–2012) and Nachrowi. Jokowi-Ahok was nominated by two secular-nationalist parties, Gerindra (Prabowo's party) and PDIP, while Fauzi Bowo and Nachrowi were nominated by Partai Demokrat (SBY's political party) and its coalition parties such as PKS, PPP and PKB. The elections followed soon after the issuance of 2009 MUI fatwa that clearly stated that a political leader must have strong personal characteristics as a pious and practising Muslim. In this regard, the pair of Jokowi-Ahok did not meet the criteria of the MUI fatwa. Jokowi himself does not come from a family with a strong Islamic background, while Ahok is Chinese and Christian. However, in the context of the 2012 Jakarta gubernatorial election, the position of MUI was somewhat complex, firstly because many MUI elites had an intimate connection to Prabowo Subianto as the leader of Gerindra party, meaning that MUI was reluctant to publicly criticise Jokowi-Ahok, and secondly because Jokowi as a governor candidate was an *abangan* Muslim, according to Geertz's categorisation in his famous book *The Religion of Java*.[22]

However, MUI signalled its support for Fauzi Bowo and Nachrowi because both had more credentials as Muslim leaders than Jokowi-Ahok. Fauzi Bowo was the incumbent and had a pious family background, while his vice-governor, Nachrowi, was also a retired general and a respected Muslim figure among the Betawi (Jakarta) community. MUI's inclination to encourage Fauzi Bowo and Nachrowi was evident in the statement of Amidhan, chairman of

---

21 "Kuatnya Sentimen Agama di Pilgub Jakarta," Tirto, 14 February 2017, https://tirto.id/kuatnya-sentimen-agama-di-pilgub-jakarta-ciZn, viewed on 22 July 2022.

22 Clifford Geertz, *The Religion of Java* (Chicago: University of Chicago Press, 1976).

MUI, who asserted that Muslims could elect non-Muslim leaders when the leaders have proven their competency. The argument was based on his interpretation of the opinion of Ibn Taymiyyah (a classical Muslim jurist and activist, 1263–1328) that Muslims can elect non-Muslim leaders when just Muslim leaders cannot be found. This was a way of saying that there were non-Muslims capable of leadership, but in this case there were also Muslims in Jakarta who, according to Amidhan, had the characteristics of justice.[23] Muslim leaders should therefore priority for Jakarta Muslim voters. MUI's support was thus clearly pronounced by Amin, the acting leader of MUI at that time. Fauzi Bowo had been a successful leader in Jakarta (2007–2012), according to Amin, and MUI issued the recommendation for Jakarta Muslim voters to elect him.[24] Despite the involvement of MUI in supporting Fauzi Bowo and Nachrowi in the 2012 Jakarta elections, however, they were unsuccessful; Jokowi and Ahok were elected. Jakarta Muslim voters were clearly able to accept Jokowi and Ahok as their governor and vice-governor.

The political tensions ignited by identity politics in Jakarta were then further stoked when Ahok replaced Jokowi as governor of Jakarta in 2014, following Jokowi's election to the presidency. Although this replacement was a normal constitutional procedure, Ahok's new position as governor of Jakarta was unacceptable to some groups of Muslims, as seen in the protest movement organised by FPI and other local elements in Jakarta.[25] In addition, those who rejected the governorship of Ahok appointed a pseudo-Muslim governor, Fahrurrozi from the FPI, as a sign of their protest.[26] In their view, Ahok was not considered appropriate even to become the leader of a small community such as a *rukun tetangga* (RT, the smallest unit of the village). Since then, many protest movements motivated by identity politics have been organised to delegitimise the governorship of Ahok in Jakarta. Despite increasing challenges to his leadership, however, Ahok was able to continue his role as governor up to the

23 "MUI: Umat Islam Boleh Pilih Pemimpin Nonmuslim", Berita Satu, 7 August 2012, https://www.beritasatu.com/archive/64726/mui-umat-islam-boleh-pilih-pemimpin-nonmuslim, viewed on 22 July 2022.

24 "MUI Akui Dukung Foke-Nara dalam Pemilukada DKI", Era Muslim, 19 September 2012, https://www.eramuslim.com/berita/nasional/mui-akui-dukung-foke-nara-dalam-pemilukada-dki.htm#.W4PVB_ZuKUk, viewed on 22 July 2022.

25 Agung Wicaksono, "Gubernur DKI Jakarta Dipilih Presiden: Sebuah Wacana Yang Patut Dipertimbangkan," *Jurnal PolGov* 1, no. 1 (2019): 35–56.

26 "Akademisi: Gubernur Tandingan Bentuk Perlawanan Terhadap Negara", Wartakota, 5 December 2014, https://wartakota.tribunnews.com/2014/12/05/akademisi-gubernur-tandingan-bentuk-perlawanan-terhadap-negara, viewed on 22 July 2022.

2017 Jakarta gubernatorial election. Many people felt that Ahok was successful in making very significant improvements during the period of his leadership.[27]

7.2.3 *The 2014 Presidential Elections: MUI and the Polarisation of Indonesian Muslims*

The 2014 presidential elections was crucial, and it ended up becoming the starting point of MUI's deeper immersion in political contestations in Indonesia. To provide a positive contribution to public order in the run-up to the election, MUI issued two important messages: first, to persuade all Muslims to use their right to vote, and second, to avoid money politics. These two normative public messages were unremarkable. In relation to the first, MUI stated that abstaining from voting in the elections (*golput*, literally meaning the white group, those who do not use their voting rights) was prohibited in Islam.[28] *Golput* indicates negligence in fulfilling one's duties as a decent and responsible citizen of Indonesia. As decent and responsible Muslim citizens, MUI asked Muslims to use their voting rights to elect the figure of their choice. On this level, MUI still retained a neutral political position, and it can be understood as a progressive response to the function of elections in the context of Indonesian democracy and modern citizenship. For MUI, elections are the gateway to change and determine the future of the *umma* in the context of political, social, and legal life, since this is how citizens select their leaders and representatives in the executive and legislative chambers to run the affairs of state and society. This mechanism can bring either favourable or unfavourable results for the Indonesian *umma*, and a responsible citizen should therefore use their right to vote as part of their contribution to creating a better Indonesia for the *umma*.

Although the fatwa did not explicitly endorse a particular presidential candidate, MUI eventually outlined their criteria for a Muslim leader. For MUI, a presidential candidate is a determinant actor for the future of Indonesia, and should therefore be a great focus of attention for all Indonesian Muslims. To this end, MUI recommended that all Indonesian Muslims vote for a presidential candidate whose religion is Islam, and who is trustworthy, equipped with good morality, able to deliver the public mandate, commanding right and forbidding wrong, promoting reformism (*iṣlāḥ*), and implementing public

27 Michael Hatherell, *Political Representation in Indonesia: The Emergence of the Innovative Technocrats* (London: Routledge, 2019).

28 "MUI Keluarkan Fatwa Haram Golput, Partisipasi Pemilih Meningkat," VOA, 22 March 2014, https://www.voaindonesia.com/a/mui-keluarkan-fatwa-haram-golput-partisipasi-pemilih-meningkat/1876637.html, viewed on 22 July 2022.

welfare and justice. According to MUI, the national leadership of Indonesia should remain under the control of Muslim groups, and Jokowi—who had won the Jakarta gubernatorial election in 2012—was nominated by his party, the PDIP, to run for president. At that time, Jokowi was paired with Jusuf Kalla (JK) as his running mate. JK is a prominent Muslim figure from Makassar, Eastern Indonesia, representing the nationalist Golkar party;[29] the PDIP was considering the importance of identity politics as a means of winning the hearts of Muslim voters by pairing him with Jokowi. Yet this did not eliminate the prejudice some Muslims felt towards the PDIP as a secular party, if we apply Clifford Geerzt's *aliran* (deviant) theory to *abangan* (Javanese syncretic) parties.[30] The PDIP continued to be depicted as anti-Islam, with pro-communist and pro-China views.

One group within MUI believed that it was important to support Jokowi-JK because there was real certainty about their support for shariatisation, for example in the promotion of the sharia economy and halal lifestyle. However, the Council was not solidly behind a single presidential candidate in the 2014 presidential elections. At the institutional level, MUI tried to be neutral, but its tendency to support Jokowi-JK is traceable from the closeness of Din Syamsuddin, as the general chairman of MUI at the time, to JK.[31] In addition, the internal situation of MUI approaching the elections was infused with sorrow, following the death of its charismatic leader, Mahfudh. From 2005 to 2014, Mahfudh occupied the highest leadership position of two prestigious Muslim organisations, as MUI general chairman and also as the general chairman of Nadhlatul Ulama's sharia body (Syuriah PBNU). As leader of MUI, he was recognised as very careful regarding politics. He often issued reminders for all members of MUI about the importance of taking a neutral stance in practical politics, saying that if the organisation wished to play a political role, then it should focus on high politics. However, Mahfudh's strict leadership model did not exert much influence on other elite members of MUI who were relatively eager to take part in the realm of practical politics. In January 2014, at

29 William R. Liddle and Saiful Muzani, "Indonesian Democracy from Transition to Consolidation," in *Democracy, Islam and Indonesia*, ed. Mirjam Kuenkler and Alfred Stephan (New York: Columbia University Press, 2013), 23–52, p. 33; Merle Calvin Ricklefs, *Islamisation and Its Opponents in Java: A Political, Social, Cultural and Religious History, C. 1930 to the Present* (Honolulu: Hawai'i University Press, 2012), p. 276.

30 Clifford Geertz, *The Religion of Java* (Chicago: University of Chicago Press, 1976).

31 "Indonesia Resmi Dipimpin Jokowi, MUI: Bersyukurlah Kepada Allah", Republika, 22 October 2014, https://www.republika.co.id/berita/nasional/politik/14/10/22/ndt6v7-indonesia-resmi-dipimpin-jokowi-mui-bersyukurlah-kepada-allah, viewed on 22 July 2022.

the death of Mahfudh, MUI leadership was given to his deputy chairman, Din Syamsuddin. Din Syamsuddin was the general chairman of Muhammadiyah and had been deputy chairman of MUI since 2010. He is a professor at the State Islamic University Syarif Hidayatullah Jakarta, with a PhD degree from UCLA in the United States, and also was an active politician in Golkar during the Suharto era. Din Syamsuddin led Muhammadiyah from 2005–2010 and 2010–2015. During his chairmanship of MUI, the organisation had an institutional tendency to support Jokowi-JK, based on the argument that national leadership was not only determined by the president, but also by the vice-president. JK was a key reason for some MUI elites to support Jokowi, being recognised as the model of a successful Muslim businessman, a member of NU's leadership and the Himpunan Mahasiswa Islam (HMI, Student Islamic Association), and also having good relations with Muhammadiyah. JK is also very close to MUI because many MUI leaders are also former HMI activists.

However, ordinary members of central MUI in Jakarta leaned more towards the Prabowo-Hatta alliance. This pair was seen as more promising with regards to the agenda of shariatisation, particularly in the case of Prabowo, who was closely connected to MUI elites when he was still an active military general before his dismissal in 1998. After he was discharged, Prabowo fled overseas to Jordan, seeking political asylum from the Jordanian royal family. After some years in political exile, Prabowo returned to Indonesia and built a political party, Gerakan Indonesia Raya (Gerindra, the Great Indonesia Movement). Prabowo found his political moment when in the general elections in 2004 he was nominated as the running mate of Megawati Sukarnoputri through a political coalition between PDIP and the Gerindra party. Although Megawati and Prabowo did not win, it served as a political platform for Prabowo so that he could once again begin to build his political profile.[32]

Other MUI elites supported a different Islamic figure in the 2014 presidential elections. Ridwan, for instance, wanted Rizieq Shihab[33] nominated for president, although this stance was criticised. Political parties argued that presidential nominations should take place through political mechanisms, while Rizieq Shihab and his supporters were not members of any party. Ridwan's standpoint, however, gained support from other Islamist activists such as the secretary general of FUI (Front Umat Islam, the Muslim Community Front),

32 Femi Adi Soempeno, *Prabowo: Dari Cijantung Bergerak Ke Istana* (Yogyakarta: Galangpress, 2009); S.K. Mahtani and J.M. Tesoro, *Prabowo: Saya Tak Pernah Berkhianat* (Michigan: Milestone Pub. House, 2009).

33 FPI has been officially banned by the government of Indonesia since 23 December 2020.

al-Khattath.[34] The reluctance of MUI's board members to support Jokowi-JK was also evident in Natsir's[35] movement that nominated Muslim figures such as Rais, Anis Matta, and Mahfud MD (all non-partisan alumni of HMI) as presidential candidates. Natsir argued that these nominations were the aspiration of an *umma* coalition that consisted of many Muslim organisations. The MUI initiative to consolidate the Muslim coalition was protested by Baitul Muslimin (PDIP's Muslim wing) as a form of partisanship.[36] Hamka Haq criticised MUI's partisan stance, although there was another group within MUI which sided with Jokowi-JK, stating that MUI's political ambition had become greater than that of political parties.

Ultimately, the 2014 presidential elections saw Jokowi-JK was elected as the president and vice-president of Indonesia (2014–2019). The results of the elections—legislative and executive—produced a degree of polarisation among Indonesian Muslims, to which MUI contributed but ironically had no power to reverse. Furthermore, from 2014 to 2019 MUI played an important role in exacerbating this polarisation, using its authority to offer a more intensive shariatisation agenda. In addition to increasing polarisation, the 2014 presidential elections showed an early focus on issues of populism, identity politics and Islam.

7.2.4 *The 2017 Jakarta Gubernatorial Election as a Stage of Islamist Mobilisation*

The 2017 Jakarta gubernatorial election brought out the tensions among Jakarta voters that had been building for years, with MUI taking centre stage. The election was contested by Ahok, Baswedan and Agus Harimurti Yudoyono. Although the nomination of Ahok as the gubernatorial candidate for Jakarta was predictable, it nonetheless generated public controversy due to his religious and ethnic identity (Christian Chinese). There is no legal impediment to a Chinese or Christian person holding office, but the majority of Jakarta Muslims and leaders still have reservations about it. In the history of Jakarta, no governors have held different beliefs from the mainstream Muslim population, and the nomination of Ahok was understood as a serious challenge to

34 "Rizieq Syihab Calon Presiden 2014", *Tempo*, 23 August 2013, https://nasional.tempo.co/read/506798/rizieq-syihab-calon-presiden-2014, viewed on 22 July 2022.

35 Bachtiar Natsir is an MUI board member and was the leading figure behind Gerakan Nasional Pembela Fatwa-Ulama (GNPF-Ulama, National Movement to Defend the Fatwa of Ulama) and the 212 movement.

36 "Baitul Muslimin PDI-P Kecam Sikap MUI Soal Koalisi", *Kompas*, 24 April 2014, https://nasional.kompas.com/read/2014/04/24/0710537/Baitul.Muslimin.PDI-P.Kecam.Sikap.MUI.Soal.Koalisi.Partai.Politik, viewed on 22 July 2022.

Islam by mainstream Muslim groups. These groups, including MUI, expected Ahok to decline the gubernatorial candidacy due to his religious and ethnic identity,[37] but he insisted on running alongside Djarot Saiful Hidayat from the PDIP.

The Muslim community in Jakarta has some unique characteristics: they are traditionalist in their religious outlook, like NU, and are also keenly conservative and militant in their political outlook, for example in rejecting non-Muslim leaders. This attitude seems to be on the rise across Indonesia. From 2016 to 2018, for instance, the number of those rejecting the leadership of non-Muslims increased from 39% to 52%.[38] In this regard, MUI contributed to strengthening the position of the Jakarta mainstream Muslim groups by disallowing the nomination of Ahok as the governor of Jakarta, even though he had made great strides in developing the city. Jakarta Muslims did not admit the success of Ahok's leadership in transforming Jakarta as an example of ideal leadership, and many argued that moral and religious development is much more important than material development. In this regard, they prioritised religion as the ultimate goal of gubernatorial leadership in Jakarta, which Ahok could not, in their view, implement. They regarded the Ahok leadership as being detrimental to Islam.

In order to strengthen its role in the 2017 Jakarta gubernatorial election, MUI issued a special opinion outlining that Muslims were forbidden to vote for Ahok because of his religion and ethnicity. In this case, MUI and its allied Islamist groups displayed their ability to shape views and aspirations regarding non-Muslim leadership among Jakarta Muslims. This section examines the MUI initiative in challenging the nomination of Ahok and its impact on democracy in Jakarta in particular, and democracy in Indonesia more generally given that Jakarta is the capital. The discussion focuses on the alliance of MUI and the so-called GNPF-Fatwa MUI (MUI's National Safeguard Movement for Fatwa) to promote populist shariatisation and identity politics and how it has impacted on the quality of democracy, as well as the tensions and contestation between Islamist alliance groups and moderate Islamic organisations such as NU.

Based on the case of Ahok, it is enough to say that Indonesia is heading towards a new wave of populist shariatisation that can be seen in the

37 "Ini rapor merah ala FPI untuk Ahok hingga tak pantas jadi gubernur", *Merdeka*, 1 June 2015, https://www.merdeka.com/jakarta/ini-rapor-merah-ala-fpi-untuk-ahok-hingga-tak-pantas-jadi-gubernur.html, viewed on 22 July 2022.

38 "Anti-Pemimpin Nonmuslim Meningkat Usai Kasus Ahok", *CNN Indonesia*, 25 September 2018, https://www.cnnindonesia.com/nasional/20180924195859-32-332825/anti-pemimpin-nonmuslim-meningkat-usai-kasus-ahok, viewed on 22 July 2022.

emergence of various mass-protest mobilisations, mainly established by the urban conservative Muslim community. The city of Jakarta, in this regard, can be seen as the main site of populist shariatisation. A populist orientation to governing and administrating the state is not a new phenomenon in Indonesia; former leaders such as Sukarno, Suharto, Habibie, Wahid, Megawati and Yudoyono have all applied a degree of populism in at least maintaining economic subsidies for citizens. MUI and its alliance, especially the GNPF-MUI or Ulama and the Gerakan 212 (the 212 Movement), have used populist orientation under the legitimacy of sharia. The GNPF-MUI or Ulama is an organisation that initiated the Islam-based national protest movement known as the 212 Movement. This was born as a response to a particular political event in Jakarta. On 27 September 2016, Ahok visited the island of Pramuka, part of Kepulauan Seribu, Jakarta, to meet with *kerapu* fish farmers in a routine public meeting between the governor of Jakarta and its people. At this stage, MUI had an uneasy alliance with Ahok. During the meeting, however, there was a small mistake in Ahok's speech which could be construed as blasphemy. After the speech, an Islamist media activist called Buni Yani[39] posted a very short version of this speech on Facebook that created the impression that Ahok had insulted the Qur'ān and the ulama, sparking a public backlash.

Benefitting from this controversy, MUI issued *Pendapat dan Sikap Keagamaan Majelis Ulama Indonesia* ("The Religious Opinion and Standpoint of the Council of Indonesian Ulama") on 16 October 2016. MUI claimed that a "religious opinion" had a higher status than fatwa, even though it was only published in this particular case. In its *Pedoman Dasar* (Foundational Guidance), MUI only published two kinds of products: fatwa and *tawṣiyya* (Islamic recommendations). As mentioned in the previous chapters, a fatwa is issued as a legal opinion for those who seek it and *tawṣiyya* is published to provide reminders and recommendations for the government. Until the Ahok case, the nomenclature "religious opinion" was not recognised in the hierarchy of MUI decisions. The emergence of the *Opinion* also indicated a strange decision-making method. According to some sources, it was not drafted and agreed in a meeting of members of the Fatwa Commission.[40] It also did not include a process of *tabāyun* (clarification or fact-checking) with Ahok. In many cases of issuing fatwas, including on deviant sects, MUI has used the mechanism of *tabāyun* as method to gather more information from those directly involved. In the case

39 Buni Yani has a Western educational background. He gained his Master's degree from Ohio State University and a PhD scholarship at Leiden University from KITLV, the Netherlands.

40 This information came from an anonymous source in Jakarta, 2018.

of Ahok, MUI never invited him to provide clarification on the content of his speech, even though he had issued a public apology.

The case of Ahok's speech stimulated the establishment of GNPF-MUI, founded by Bachtiar Natsir. It also led to the creation of Aksi Bela Islam (ABI, Action to Defend Islam). It appears that MUI agreed to the establishment of GNPF-MUI, as it never gave a clear clarification about the usage of the term "MUI" in the organisation's name, although it clarified that GNPF-MUI was not an official part of MUI, despite a widespread belief to the contrary. In fact, by attaching the name of MUI to this organisation or movement, GNPF-MUI was very successful in mobilising those who were anti-Ahok. In addition, GNPF-MUI, through ABI, was able to pressure to National Police of Indonesia to raise Ahok's case from the level of *penyelidikan* (research) to that of *penyidikan* (investigation). This meant that Ahok had to be brought to trial. The National Police had initially said that Ahok's case would be dealt with after the 2014 elections, but they were forced to back down due to strong pressure from GNPF-MUI and other Islamist groups in the form of protests involving hundreds of thousands of people. In the face of this pressure, Jokowi also relented, sacrificing his erstwhile ally, Ahok, and allowing the police investigation to proceed. Ahok received some support from NU senior members, including Siradj, who said that Ahok's speech could not be categorised as blasphemy, but was also strongly opposed by others such as Amin, the leader of NU's sharia advisory body.[41] The NU elites were thus divided into those who believed that Ahok was guilty of blasphemy and those who did not. Despite this division of opinions within Muslim organisations, GNPF-MUI continued putting pressure on the government even after Ahok was declared a blasphemy suspect.[42] Their reasoning was that they wanted to monitor the legal process. During the trial MUI's position was of key importance, as Amin became witness for the prosecution. Ahok was ultimately sentenced to two years in prison without appeal.[43]

The two-year sentence for Ahok did not end GNPF-MUI's political machinations. The group used the Ahok case as a political stage to criticise the policy of Jokowi's ruling regime, particularly their alleged neglect of the interests of

41 "GP Ansor Akan Perangi Ahok, Ketua Umum PBNU: Don't Worry", *KBR*, 1 February 2017, https://kbr.id/nasional/02-2017/gp_ansor_akan_perangi_ahok__ketua_umum_pbnu__don_t_worry/88479.html, viewed on 22 July 2022.

42 "GNPF-MUI: Diperkirakan 3 Juta Umat Islam Ikut Aksi 2 Desember", *Detik News*, 29 November 2016, https://news.detik.com/berita/d-3357813/gnpf-mui-diperkirakan-3-juta-umat-islam-ikut-aksi-2-desember, viewed on 22 July 2022.

43 "'Ahok': Police name Jakarta governor as blasphemy suspect", *BBC News*, 16 November 2016, https://www.bbc.co.uk/news/world-asia-37996350, viewed on 22 July 2022.

ulama. In order to expand their role, the name of GNPF-MUI was changed to GNPF-Ulama.[44] With this new name, their focus was not only on defending (Indonesian: *bela*) MUI fatwas but fatwas of ulama more broadly. Interestingly, they introduced a new definition of ulama which is based on a group's self-definition and has a more political than academic dimension, unlike the traditional criteria for ulama prescribed in the Islamic tradition. Those who have limited knowledge of Islam but lend their support to this movement are declared to be ulama. This could be seen in some activities organised by the group, where some speakers were declared to be ulama despite lacking the knowledge and traditional criteria required. Despite being fully aware of this, GNPF-Ulama continued to present these figures as ulama for electoral purposes. In other words, they created their own concept of ulama in the hopes of gaining wider support from the *umma*. This was a way of reaching out for more recognition and legitimacy from the Muslim grassroots, since most ulama in the traditional sense did not share their political stance. Amin himself, after his success in acting as a witness for the prosecution against Ahok, moved closer to Jokowi, while under their new name, GNPF-Ulama began to criticise MUI and Amin for their closeness to Jokowi. But they were not able to directly confront Amin over this issue due to his continuing strong role in MUI. Still, their move to establish some distance between themselves and Amin reflects the fact that they were being driven by political interests more than by MUI fatwas.

To maintain and sustain their movement, particularly in the run-up to the 2019 general elections, the Islamist groups established an alumni organisation. This organisation was dispersed and divided into many groups, each of which claimed to be the true successors of the ABI 212 Movement. This indicates that it lacked unity, giving of a sense of being a large crowd rather than an organised movement. As indicated in many experiences of social movements around the world, conflict often arises among the first initiators and elites of the movement. Since the exile of Rizieq Shihab to Mecca, Saudi Arabia, because of several alleged cases in Indonesia,[45] the movement has lost a key orchestrator, and has remained organised but lacked unity. Attempts to find a new leader have so far been unsuccessful. Ustadz Abdus Somad (known as UAS) from Riau, Sumatera, was one such possibility, but had previously shown little interest in being part of political movements. While it is true that his public views

44 "Agenda Politik di Balik GNPF Ulama & Alumni 212", *Tirto*, 2 May 2018, https://tirto.id/agenda-politik-di-balik-gnpf-ulama-alumni-212-cJKe, viewed on 22 July 2022.

45 "Rizieq Shihab, antara Kabur atau Diasingkan," *Tirto*, 3 December 2019, https://tirto.id/rizieq-shihab-antara-kabur-atau-diasingkan-emJD, viewed on 22 July 2022.

are not far removed from those of the 212 Movement, he also has ties with NU, having been educated in al-Wasliyah, a closely affiliated traditional Muslim organisation in Sumatera. His ritual practices are also similar to those of NU. He had struggled to make a name for himself within this organisation, so was very willing to join and support the 212 Movement, where he could become a major figure.

The 2017 Jakarta gubernatorial election resulted in the victory of Baswedan-Sandiaga Uno, with the strong support of Islamist mobilisation, while Ahok was given a two-year sentence for blasphemy. This election can therefore be seen as the most blatant example of the use of identity politics in the quest for victory in Indonesian gubernatorial elections.

7.2.5 *The 2019 Presidential Elections: Jokowi's Reconciliation with MUI through Ma'ruf Amin*

The 2019 presidential elections brought the relationship between Jokowi and MUI closer. The president and the Ulama Council had not been intimate before the emergence of the ABI 212 Movement in 2016–17. Jokowi took the initiative to approach MUI, through Amin as the general chairman, to ask for support in face of ABI's attacks on the government. Jokowi wanted to MUI to break from ABI, and offered the Council the opportunity to get involved in a national project on asset redistribution. In response to Jokowi's offer, Amin visited the Presidential Palace for negotiations.[46] Jokowi planned to distribute around 12.7 million-hectares of sleeping land to Islamic organisations such as MUI, NU, Muhammadiyyah and others.[47] The redistribution of these assets became an entry point for Jokowi and MUI to develop a closer relationship.

Collaboration between Jokowi and Amin, representing MUI, have since extended beyond the asset redistribution project. Jokowi demonstrated his support for some of MUI's other projects, for example the sharia economy, while Amin was invited to back Jokowi's agenda. However, the position of MUI, as an organisation, remained unclear regarding the second half of Jokowi's presidential term. One group within the organisation—mainly composed of Muhammadiyah and some small organisations—remained very critical of the president. Yet this division within MUI did not disrupt the rapprochement process between Jokowi and Amin. Jokowi's closer relationship with Amin

46 "MUI Ambil Peran Redistribusi Aset", Republika, 30 March 2017, https://nasional.republika.co.id/berita/nasional/umum/17/03/30/onmad2365-mui-ambil-peran-redistribusi-aset, viewed on 22 July 2022.

47 "MUI Sambut Baik Rencana Jokowi Bagikan Tanah Untuk Pesantren," RMOL, 26 April 2017, https://politik.rmol.id/read/2017/04/26/289051/mui-sambut-baik-rencana-jokowi-bagikan-tanah-untuk-pesantren, viewed on 22 July 2022.

resulted in the decision to make Amin his running mate in the 2019 presidential elections.

There were two strong candidates for this role: Mahfud MD and Amin. Mahfud MD is a senior politician who had a modernist as well as traditionalist background of Islamic activism. While studying, Mahfud was active in the modernist Islamic student organisation HMI, despite his NU family background in Madura. He was appointed as chairman of the Korps Alumni Himpunan Mahasiswa Islam (KAHMI, Corps of Islamic Student Association Alumni) as well as being an important figure in NU. It is true that HMI is not a NU student association, although many of its members, like Mahfud himself, also have NU affiliations. President Wahid reinvented Mahfud MD as a prominent political figure and asked him to become a member of his cabinet, as Minister of Defence, during his term in office (1999–2001), also trusting him as the vice-chairman of the PKB. When Wahid was impeached by the Indonesian parliament in 2001, it was the end of Mahfud's role as Minister of Defence, and he later became more visible as a NU political figure.

Amin is a senior member of the NU ulama as well as MUI, with political experience as a PPP politician during the Suharto era and the founder of the PKB, together with Wahid, in the post-reform period. Despite his long experience as a politician, the Indonesian public see him primarily as one of the ulama as a result of of his prominent position in both NU and MUI, which makes him one of the best-known ulama in the country. His high leverage is evident in his position as both general chairman of MUI and general head of NU's Sharia Advisory Board, the highest position within the largest Muslim organisation in Indonesia. He is therefore a very influential figure, not only among NU and MUI groups but also among other Muslim organisations, including radical and conservative groups such as FPI, because of his leanings towards Islamic conservativism and statism. Amin was one of the architects behind the MUI fatwa banning the Ahmadiyah as well as many other controversial MUI fatwas.

In the context of the 2019 presidential elections, the Indonesian public expected Mahfud MD to be Jokowi's preference for running mate. Mahfud was recognised as being more capable than Amin in the context of political administration. The public expectation, however, did not fit in with Jokowi's plan. Amin was promoted by a coalition of political parties—PDIP, Golkar, Nasdem, PKB and PPP—in addition to NU, and Jokowi also hoped to win the support of MUI; as a result, he chose Amin rather than Mahfud.[48] Shortly before this decision was announced, a public statement cast doubt on Mahfud's position in

48 "Jalan Buntu Mahfud MD, Dua Kali Gagal Jadi Cawapres", *Tirto*, 10 August 2018, https://tirto.id/jalan-buntu-mahfud-md-dua-kali-gagal-jadi-cawapres-cRsj, viewed on 22 July 2022.

the NU as part of a plot by NU elites. Siradj demonstrated his support for Amin by stating that Mahfud's position in NU was questionable, as full members are required to be active in NU-affiliated organisations such as IPNU, PMII and others. He still recognised Mahfud as part of NU, however, because his family in Madura were members.[49] This statement was supported by two leaders of NU's affiliated political parties, Muhaimin Iskandar from PKB and Romahurmiziy from PPP.[50] While Siradj claimed that his statement was not aimed at delegitimising the nomination of Mahfud, the public could easily understand that NU did not endorse Mahfud as Jokowi's running mate. NU itself is not a political party, but as Indonesia's largest Islamic organisation it has great influence and its position cannot be disregarded by those in power. Within MUI, mainstream groups also agreed to back Amin's nomination. MUI members have various organisational background, with most coming from NU, Muhammadiyah, and other Muslim organisations such as Persis, Perti and al-Wasliyah. Because NU had already decided to endorse Amin, its members within MUI followed, as did members of Muhammadiyah.

In the face of much controversy and political drama, Jokowi finally chose Amin as his vice-presidential candidate in the last minutes of 9 August 2018.[51] This decision came as a surprise to Jokowi's followers, since Amin had a record of opposing many of Jokowi's policies, especially in the first term of his presidency.[52] In 2016, for instance, under Amin's leadership, MUI issued a fatwa to provide a theological argument supporting allegations against Ahok, the governor of Jakarta, when he was accused of blasphemy in his speech in the islands of Seribu.[53] The target was not only a shot at Ahok, but also at Jokowi. This is evident from MUI's statement, through Muhyiddin Junaidi, warning Jokowi to respond to the huge demonstration against Ahok organised by the

49 "Said Aqil: Mahfud MD Bukan Kader NU," *CNN Indonesia*, 8 August 2018, https://www.cnnindonesia.com/nasional/20180808192555-32-320668/said-aqil-mahfud-md-bukan-kader-nu, viewed on 22 July 2022.

50 "Usulan Ma'ruf Amin Cawapres dan Manuver PPP di Internal NU", *Tirto*, 15 July 2018, https://tirto.id/usulan-maruf-amin-cawapres-dan-manuver-ppp-di-internal-nu-cN7Y, viewed on 22 July 2022.

51 "Jokowi Resmi Tunjuk Ma'ruf Amin sebagai Cawapres", *Kompas*, 9 August 2018, https://nasional.kompas.com/read/2018/08/09/18260341/jokowi-resmi-tunjuk-maruf-amin-sebagai-cawapres, viewed on 22 July 2022.

52 "Jokowi Tunjuk Ma'ruf Amin Jadi Cawapres di Pilpres 2019", *DW*, 9 August 2018, https://www.dw.com/id/jokowi-tunjuk-maruf-amin-sebagai-calon-wakil-presiden-di-pilpres-2019/a-45018121, viewed on 22 July 2022.

53 Daniel Peterson, *Islam, Blasphemy, and Human Rights in Indonesia: The Trial of Ahok* (New York: Routledge, 2020); Hasyim, "MUI and Its Discursive Relevance for 'Aksi Bela Islam': A Growing Trend of Islamic Conservatism in Indonesia."

ABI 212 Movement, issued because the organisation doubted the president's commitment to take Ahok's case to trial.[54] On 1 November 2016, Amin met Jokowi in the Presidential Palace and directly afterwards stated that the president had agreed to speed up the process of Ahok's trial.[55] Many of Jokowi's followers were disappointed by this turn of events, and consequently decided not to support Jokowi in the 2019 presidential elections.

The politics of MUI, represented by Amin, can be said to have been quite successful in the last quarter of Jokowi's first term. MUI had clearly won its battle with the president. In this, Amin's role was crucial. His nomination was supported by Jokowi's political coalition, but Jokowi seems to have been more influenced by social and religious considerations in his choice of Amin over Mahfud MD as running mate in the 2019 general elections—a choice which ensured he would not face any challenge from the so-called pseudo-Islamic authority. In this regard, Jokowi followed political pragmatism. The position of Amin as the vice-president of Indonesia, however, can be understood, paradoxically, as both the success of MUI's politics and also the Council's submission to the ruling power.

7.3 The *Umma* and Islamic Discourse in Indonesian Conceptualisation

Since 2012, the populist orientation of Indonesian Muslim groups has grown more prominent, and social and political movements have become consolidated under the banner of defending the interests of the *umma*. In the 2014 presidential elections, Muslim groups were mobilised to vote Prabowo-Hatta in the name of the *umma*. In the 2017 Jakarta gubernatorial elections, ABI mobilised the *umma* to defeat Ahok. Since then, the term *umma* has become a political magnet. This section is devoted to the politics of the *umma* in the Jokowi era, and examines how MUI deploys it to further its own agenda, highlighting how the concept of the *umma* is discussed and debated in Islamic tradition.

In Islamic discourse, the term *umma* has been differently understood over time, and its meaning shifts depending on the context. In the early history of Islam, the *umma* did not always take the form of an Islamic state. According

54 "MUI Peringatkan Jokowi Agar Merespons Demonstran", *Republika*, 4 November 2016, https://nasional.republika.co.id/berita/nasional/politik/0g42ji377/mui-peringatkan-jokowi-agar-merespons-demonstran, viewed on 22 July 2022.

55 "MUI: Jokowi Perintahkan Polisi Proses Hukum Ahok", Tempo, 26 July 2016, https://nasional.tempo.co/read/816651/mui-jokowi-perintahkan-polisi-proses-hukum-ahok, viewed on 26 July 2022.

to Nasr Hamid Abu Zayd, who discusses the concepts of *muntij al-thaqāfī* and *muntaj al-thaqāfī*, the *umma* can be understood as the producer of human civilisation (*muntij al-thaqāfī*) as well as its product (*muntaj al-thaqāfī*).[56] As the producer of human civilisation, the concept of the *umma* should be seen as immutable, like the word of God, and should be transformed into practice. This means that if the concept of the *umma* is understood as the Islamic political system, it must also be implemented in everyday political life. Islamist groups such as the Muslim Brotherhood, al-Qaeda, Islamic State and many others embrace this understanding. Of course, when Abu Zayd discusses the *umma* and the word of God as *muntij al-thaqāfī*, this is not intended to strengthen the argument of Islamist groups but to suggest that the source of Islamic civilisation is also the source of inspiration and spirit. At the same time, the *umma* as the product of Islamic civilisation means that the concept is the result of human thought rather than a sacred construct. In this sense, the notion of *umma* is subject to change and transformation. At the practical level, the concept of *umma* is open to being implemented in any political, social and legal form.

Employing Abu Zayd's concept, however, the concept of *umma* must be located in a dynamic dialogue between the *umma* as *muntij al-thaqāfī* and as *muntaj al-thaqāfī*. Taking Abdolkarim Soroush's perspective on the difference between religion and religious knowledge, the concept of *umma* is a branch of religious knowledge, not religion itself.[57] Locating the concept of *umma* in the category of religious knowledge means that its implementation at the practical, social, political and legal levels should be guided by human wisdom, which is adaptive and temporal in nature.[58] Najih Ayubi states that Islamic jurists add an ideological dimension to the concept of *umma*, using the term to describe those living under the banner of theological belief. In short, the *umma* refers to an Islamic political entity, whether an Islamic state or government, but may also manifest in various other forms.[59]

In the context of Indonesia, the term *umma* has long been deployed as a cultural rather than political expression to denote the Indonesian Muslim community. This is due to the fact that, politically speaking, the country has embraced the concept of a nation-state, which is different from the concept of

56 Nasr Hamid Abu Zayd, *Mafhūm Al-Naṣ: Dirāsa Fī 'Ulūm al-Qur'ān* (Cairo, 1990).

57 Abdolkarim Soroush, *Reason, Freedom, and Democracy in Islam: Essential Writings of Abdolkarim Soroush* (Oxford: Oxford University Press, Incorporated, 2002), p. 32.

58 Ibid.

59 N.N. Ayubi, *Political Islam: Religion and Politics in the Arab World*, (London: Routledge, 1991).

umma defined by Islamist groups. The term *umma* is translated into colloquial Indonesian as *umat* (group of people, community), which linguistically speaking does not specifically refer to the Muslim community. In the historical and political narrative of Indonesia, the notion of *umma* has been used to illustrate the deep commitment of Muslim communities to the struggle and defence of their religion and their nation-state.[60]

The Suharto era preserved the meaning of *umma* as the Muslim community who politically and legally dwell within the framework of the nation-state of Indonesia. Indonesia follows the principle of single citizenship, as do many Muslim countries, meaning that an individual cannot become a citizen of another state. The emergence of new Muslim nation-states in the post-colonial era with a similar approach to citizenship contributed to the decline of the concept of the *umma*. In addition, under the Suharto regime all Muslim organisations in Indonesia were prohibited from having political or legal ties with foreign or international groups; they were ordered to embrace Pancasila as their basic ideology. This was the Suharto regime's means of domesticating and de-sacralising the concept of *umma*. For Suharto, all Indonesian citizens could be defined as members of the *umma* which, in Indonesian, is referred to as "*umat manusia Indonesia*" (the Indonesian community). The Suharto regime wanted the term *umma* to refer to all citizens of Indonesia, where the Muslim community was a key group but other religious communities also existed. The Indonesian expression "*umat manusia*" was often used in the official speeches of senior state officials. The word *umma* was often also used with *beragama*—*umat beragama*—meaning the community of believers.

To conclude, public discussions on the *umma* in Indonesia must therefore be situated and framed in the context of the nation-state, not in the political and historical context of Islam. Michael Laffan uses the term "ecumene"—a local *umma*—to describe the establishment of Indonesian nationhood.[61] The impact of Western ideas regarding the discourse of state formation can thus be traced to the colonial period in Indonesia. Since this time, Indonesia has not used the term *umma* in its political and ideological form, as used in classical Islamic literature. In the post-colonial era, the notion of the *umma* refers to the community of Indonesian Muslims residing under the Pancasila nation-state.

---

60 MUI, *Buku Materi Kongres Umat Islam Indonesia V, "Kepemimpinan Umat Untuk Kesejahteraan Bangsa* (Jakarta: Panitia Pengarah Kongres Umat Islam Indonesia V, 2010); MUI, *Kongres Umat Islam Indonesaia IV: Proses Dan Dinamika Permusyawaratan* (Jakarta: BPKUII IV, 2005).

61 Michael Laffan, *Islamic Nationhood and Colonial Indonesia: The Ummah below the Winds* (London & New York: Routledge Curzon, 2003).

7.3.1 *The Politics of the* Umma *and* MUI

Although MUI is not a political party, this does not mean that politics have no place in its discourse and practice. The Council believes that politics in the broader sense is not restricted to political parties, and that it can implement its agenda through political action. MUI does not have a clear definition of politics, however, and simply wishes to use it as a tool to promote its interests. The organisation defines the *umma* as the Indonesian Muslim community, excluding non-Muslims.[62] As a civil society organisation, the role of MUI in the politics of the *umma* is different from that of Islamic political parties. The politics of the *umma* is not merely electoral politics, but also political awareness surrounding the collective agenda of the Muslim community. It involves influencing, persuading, and winning the hearts of political actors to support the community's interests, and depends not on victory in the election ballot but on the ability to strategise to promote the agenda of the *umma*. MUI, for instance, has played a significant role in promoting the inclusion of sharia in state legislation, despite not being a political party, and constructs discourse—in the form of fatwas and religious recommendations—that furthers the *umma*'s struggle. In this section, "the politics of the *umma*" refers to the use of politics in the interests of the Muslim community; for MUI, this means spreading its agenda to the government representatives who can implement it. In studies of Islam, the notion of the *umma* represents a holistic vision of the Muslim community ranging from social, cultural, political, economic, ideological to theological issues. It is not only related to particular issues of formal politics, but also to the politics of everyday life of the Muslim community.[63]

Sociologically speaking, MUI's interest in politics is motivated by its desire for influence in everyday Indonesian political life, as demonstrated in its request for formal representation in parliament.[64] The political majority rejected this request, however, since MUI is not a political party. Although representatives of non-political organisations were allowed a place in parliament during the Suharto period, this has not been permitted since the beginning of the post-reform era. Nevertheless, MUI can still influence parliamentary decision-making through politicians who are favourable to the organisation's aspirations. Since the time of SBY, these aspirations are routinely taken into

62 MUI, *Buku Materi Kongres Umat Islam Indonesia V, "Kepemimpinan Umat Untuk Kesejahteraan Bangsa*, 2010; MUI, *Mengawal Aqidah Umat: Fatwa MUI Tentang Aliran-Aliran Sesat Di Indonesia* (Jakarta: Sekretariat Majelis Ulama Indonesia, n.d.).

63 Bayat, *Life as Politics: How Ordinary People Change the Middle East*, 2010.

64 "MUI Minta Fraksi, Pimpinan DPR: Aspirasi Bisa Dititipkan ke Parpol," *Detik News*, 27 April 2017, https://news.detik.com/berita/d-3485203/mui-minta-fraksi-pimpinan-dpr-aspirasi-bisa-dititipkan-ke-parpol, 22 July 2022.

consideration in the context of many legal and political issues. In addition, the influence of MUI as fatwa-giver is very clear in the everyday life of Indonesia. The significant influence of its fatwas and recommendations in national legislation is evident in the state laws, policies and regulations that accommodate the organisation's agenda, such as legislation on sharia banking, halal issues, and public morality. On this basis, MUI should be confident in its influence on policy-makers as means to further the interests of the *umma*. The Council see shariatisation as the highest priority for the *umma*, both in daily life and in the legal and political spheres, and the struggle for the implementation of sharia has been at the core of its ideological agenda since the beginning of the post-reform era. Yet it understands the challenges and limits when it comes to shariatisation; establishing an Islamic state, for example, would be almost impossible, being against the national consensus that Pancasila is the only state form for Indonesia, and most Islamic organisations—including MUI, NU, and Muhammadiyah—have accepted this. MUI has unambiguously stated that it is committed to Indonesia as a Pancasila state,[65] and has formulated strategies to propagate sharia within this framework by shariatising the content of the Pancasila state and the content of the Indonesian *umma*. Shariatising the content of the Pancasila state is conducted through the fields of politics, economy, law, culture and wider issues of state. Shariatising the content of the *umma* is implemented through the lifestyle, culture and tradition of Muslim communities. This strategy has been used since the post-reform era, and continues today under Jokowi.

The discourse on the politics of the *umma* is not new to MUI, but it has only begun intensively implementing it since the first term of Jokowi's presidency. This was a crucial moment for the organisation, which had not yet established a working relationship with the new president. Using the discourse of the *umma* therefore became very important; the choice to align with the Muslim community was not only a strategic move, but also suited to the political context of the time. MUI's alignment with the interests of the *umma* frequently manifests in its support for populist movements, such as the the series of Islamic mobilisation movements in 2016 and 2017.

The struggle to retain an important role in the Jokowi administration prompted MUI to adapt through revitalising the politics of *umma*, which provides the organisation with legitimacy. During the era of SBY, Jokowi's predecessor, MUI held a prominent status through its dual role policing morality and *'aqīda* (belief), but could not be sure of retaining this authority under the new president, who was relatively new on the political scene and had no previous

65 MUI, *Himpunan Fatwa MUI Sejak 1975*.

connections with the organisation. Shariatisation remained a non-negotiable and unchanging goal. Simply put, shariatisation is the Council's central ideology, regardless of any change in the political landscape of Indonesia. In case of challenges from Jokowi, MUI would find a way to respond without sidelining the agenda of shariatisation. Aligning itself with the *umma* was therefore a clever strategy to prepare for such challenges and to increase its bargaining power: if Jokowi rejects its agenda, MUI can claim that the *umma* supports it. In this regard, MUI is better prepared to deal with Jokowi than vice versa; it has experience of working with various regimes, not all of which shared its vision, and has learned to adapt.

Globally speaking, the use of the *umma* in support of the argument for bringing sharia into the legal and political spheres is not only found in Indonesia. Shariatisation as an expression of identity politics is a trans-regional as well as global phenomena across the Muslim world, according to scholars such as Robert Hefner, Tamir Moustafa and Patricia Sloane-White. Hefner refers to it as reflecting the increase in Islamic piety and observance in the Muslim world.[66] For many years, for instance, Malaysia has promoted shariatisation in all aspects of public life. Sloane-White refers to this as "corporate Islam," depicting Malaysia as if it were a big Islamic corporation.[67] Singapore, a non-Islamic country, has also tried to develop a sharia-friendly public life for Muslim citizens by accommodating halal lifestyles,[68] and many Islamist activists in countries as varied as Pakistan, Egypt and Malaysia have endorsed the increasing role of religion in the legal and public spheres.[69] In the context of Indonesia, MUI has been a pioneer in the struggle for shariatisation. In the Jokowi era, it has taken the politics of *umma* as its approach, using the agenda of the ordinary Muslim community as an approach to dealing with the government.[70]

---

66 Robert W. Hefner, "Introduction: Shari'a Politics: Law and Society in the Modern Muslim World," in *Shari'a Politics: Law and Society in the Modern Muslim World*, ed. Robert W. Hefner (Bloomington and Indianapolis: Indiana University Press, 1–54); Tamir Moustafa, *Constituting Religion: Islam, Liberal Rights, and the Malaysian State* (Cambridge & New York: Cambridge University Press, 2018); Sloane-White, *Corporate Islam: Sharia and the Modern Workplace.*

67 Ibid.

68 Norshahril Saat, ed., *Fulfilling the Trust: 50 Years of Shaping Muslim Religious Life in Singapore* (Singapore: World Scientific Publishing Co. Pte. Ltd., 2018).

69 Moustafa, *Constituting Religion*, p. 2.

70 Moch Nur Ichwan, "Towards A Puritanical Moderate Islam: The Majlis Ulama Indonesia and the Politics of Religious Orthodoxy," in *Contemporary Developments in Indonesian Islam: Explaining the "Conservative Turn,"* ed. Martin van Bruinessen (Singapore: ISEAS, 2013), 60–104; Tim Lindsey, "Monopolising Islam? The Indonesian Ulama Council and

Prioritising the concerns of the *umma*, however, was new for MUI. During the Suharto era, it main goal was to serve the government.[71] Although Suharto had supported the creation of the Council, he did not extend it much freedom in dealing directly with the interests of the *umma*, and wanted to ensure that it was fully supportive of the ruling regime.[72] As a result, the organisation was largely unable to focus on grassroots issues or engage in political activities. Much has changed over the two decades since the end of the New Order administration, and MUI has developed strong links with the Indonesian people as well as with the state.[73] The election of Jokowi in 2014, however, brought unexpected changes, and in the early years it proved difficult for MUI to situate its role in the context of Indonesian politics. Jokowi was a new figure on the political scene, and the absence of clear information on his personal background was challenging for the organisation. When he first came to power, his priorities were seen as being far removed from those of MUI. Through his responses to the issues it raised, however, the Council came to understand him better, and the two gradually formed a close alliance. In its bid for support, the strength of the *umma* was of vital importance.

7.3.2 *The Jokowi Administration*

Since MUI's transformation from the position of guardian of government to guardian of the *umma* in the post-Suharto era, it has developed its role to include the facilitation of a number of Islamic groups, enabling them to pursue shariatisation by capitalising on the issues of the *umma*. Due to the political system of Indonesia, the *umma* cannot be represented by the state. Instead, its representatives are Islamic groups and organisations, and MUI is the umbrella organisation that brings all of these together. As *tenda besar*, MUI can enable "homogenising political identities," to use Vedi R. Hadiz's words, among the divergent Indonesian Muslim organisations.[74] However, its focus seems to be consistent: namely, to extend the realisation of sharia in the legal and public

State Regulation of the 'Islamic Economy,'" *Bulletin of Indonesian Economic Studies* 48, no. 2 (2012): 253–74; Nadirsyah Hosen, "Behind the Scenes: Fatwas of Majelis Ulama Indonesia," *Journal of Islamic Studies* 2, no. 15 (2004): 147–79.

71 Syafiq Hasyim, "Fatwas and Democracy: Majelis Ulama Indonesia (MUI, Indonesian Ulema Council) and Rising Conservatism in Indonesian Islam," *TRaNS: Trans-Regional and -National Studies of Southeast Asia* 8, no. 1 (2020): 21–35.

72 Donald J. Porter, *Managing Politics and Islam in Indonesia* (London & New York: Routledge Curzon, 2004), pp. 82–83.

73 Syafiq Hasyim, "Fatwas and Democracy: Majelis Ulama Indonesia (MUI, Indonesian Ulema Council) and Rising Conservatism in Indonesian Islam," 2020.

74 Vedi R. Hadiz, *Islamic Populism in Indonesia and the Middle East* (Cambridge: Cambridge University Press, 2016), p. 5.

spheres of Indonesia without changing the political system. As a result, it supports any social movement that shares this unchanging goal. Anything beyond the agenda of shariatisation is categorised as a flexible issue. In its organisational framework, matters related to doctrine and shariatisation are considered unchangeable, while the tactics employed to achieve its goals are changeable. In order to implement the unchangeable agenda, MUI can collaborate with Islamic organisations that are not necessarily in the same ideological camp. MUI's relationship with HTI (Hizbut Tahrir Indonesia) is one example. The two were able to work together towards shariatisation, but it became clear that HTI's vision of shariatisation, unlike MUI's, involved changing the form of the Indonesian nation-state. MUI could no longer collaborate with the group, and supported a law to ban HTI in Indonesia.[75]

MUI did not relent in its project to promote shariatisation in the public sphere after the formulation of the new Jokowi-JK government (2014–2019), and it hoped to persuade the new leadership to turn its attention to the interests of the *umma*. The organisation was generally understood as having supported the opposing candidates, Prabowo-Hatta, in the election campaign, even though some of its elite had backed Jokowi-JK, and the first two years of the new administration saw a tense relationship between the political and religious leadership. MUI receives an annual government grant, delivered through the Ministry of Religious Affairs, but in 2015 it was delayed. Many speculated that the delay was intentional on the part of the government in retaliation for MUI's lack of support in the elections; the most strongly anti-Jokowi members of MUI were particularly keen to circulate this rumour. In reality, there was another explanation. The Ministry of Finance had changed the system of distributing funds, and the MUI administration was slow to adjust to the new system. As a result, they did not receive their usual funding in the first year of Jokowi's presidency. In 2016 they received double the usual budget in compensation, so the problem was resolved and Amin expressed optimism about working with the new government. Nevertheless, the issue had created uneasiness and become the source of unnecessary tension that lasted for the first two years of Jokowi's presidency, with some leading MUI members assumed that the issue of the delayed budget was part of Jokowi's strategy to attack MUI and marginalise the interests of the *umma*.

It is particularly interesting to note MUI's willingness to use any perceived weaknesses of the new administration to win favour with the *umma*.

75 "Ketua Umum MUI Dukung Langkah Pemerintah Bubarkan HTI," *Kompas*, 19 July 2017, https://nasional.kompas.com/read/2017/07/19/14304671/ketua-umum-mui-dukung-langkah-pemerintah-bubarkan-hti, viewed on 22 July 2022.

The Council attempted to gain public sympathy on the issue of the delayed payment of its government grant in 2015, for example. Amirsyah Tambunan (Deputy Secretary General of MUI) claimed that MUI was prepared to continue its activities, despite no longer being supported by the state budget.[76] His statement failed to mention that the funding had only been delayed, not cut off completely. Others who opposed the new president promoted this misinformation, with Salafi online media portraying Jokowi as anti-Islam, accusing him of spending thirty billion rupiah on Christmas celebrations in Papua while denying MUI its annual funding of a mere three billion rupiah.[77] Thus MUI exploited the adverse political landscape to increase its standing with the *umma*.

The relationship between MUI and Jokowi did not become immediately close after the issue of the delayed budget had been resolved. Jokowi remained reluctant to approach MUI for a number of reasons. First, he had no experience in dealing with the organisation. He had begun his political career at the local level, while MUI operates mainly in the national arena. Jokowi had been mayor of the city of Solo, then governor of Jakarta from 2012 to 2014, meaning that he had had limited interaction with the elites of central MUI. When he became president, he had only limited knowledge of MUI and other Islamic organisations. Second, many of Jokowi's supporters noted the political role played by MUI with regards to the shariatisation of Indonesia. Many assumed that MUI has intentionally produced fatwas contradicting the principles of the Pancasila state, such as the fatwa against pluralism, secularism and liberalism.[78] In 2005, particularly, MUI had issued a number of fatwas that seemed to challenge the more inclusive and progressive appraoch to religion in everyday life, and instead fuelled identity politics and populist Islam.[79] In addition, MUI was criticised for using religion as a tool for political ends, and believe that its shariatisation policy sought to change the political structure

---

76 "Pemerintah Hentikan Bantuan Dana untuk MUI", Republika, 12 March 2015, https://www.republika.co.id/berita/nasional/umum/15/03/12/nl3ova-pemerintah-hentikan-bantuan-dana-untuk-mui, viewed on 22 July 2022.

77 "Ironi Pemerintahan Jokowi: Hapus Dana untuk MUI, tapi DirencanakanRp1 triliun untuk partai politik," Nahimunkar, 17 March 2015, https://www.nahimunkar.org/ironi-pemerintahan-jokowi-hapus-dana-untuk-mui-tapi-direncanakanrp1-triliun-untuk-partai-politik/, viewed on 22 July 2022.

78 Syafiq Haysim, "ISEAS Perspective 2021/3 "Indonesia's MUI Today: Truly Moderate or Merely Pragmatic?," https://www.iseas.edu.sg/articles-commentaries/iseas-perspective/iseas-perspective-2020-3-indonesias-mui-today-truly-moderate-or-merely-pragmatic-by-syafiq-hasyim/, viewed on 22 July 2022.

79 MUI, *Himpunan Fatwa MUI Sejak 1975* (Jakarta: Erlangga, 2011); MUI, *Mengawal Aqidah Umat: Fatwa MUI Tentang Aliran-Aliran Sesat Di Indonesia*, n.d.

of Indonesia. As a result, some of Jokowi's supporters urged him to curb MUI's influence.

The 2016 case against Ahok, governor of Jakarta, however, marked the beginning of Jokowi's change of position regarding MUI. As discussed earlier in this chapter, part of Ahok's speech during a visit to a fishing village sparked accusations of blasphemy after it was posted on social media.[80] MUI responded strategically. Its fatwa against Ahok became the theological reason for the establishment of GNPF-MUI,[81] which was behind the demonstrations of the ABI movement.[82] ABI succeeded in pressuring Jokowi to bring Ahok's case to trial. Throughout this tumultuous period, Jokowi and Amin, as leader of MUI, were in close communication. As a result, MUI made the decision to distance itself from GNPF-MUI, asking the group to change its name, and Amin stated GNPF-MUI had no connection with MUI, despite the fact that in earlier statements he had claimed to have inspired its creation.[83]

The protest movements that developed around the Ahok case provided MUI with an opportuntiy to push a model of shariatisation that aligned itself with the concerns of the people and challenged Jokowi. Through negotiations with Amin, the president and the ulama Council eventually established a working relationship, leading to Amin becoming vice-president of Indonesia in addition to the head of MUI. Amin himself became the principal agent for the rapprochement of Jokowi and MUI, to the benefit of both parties. With this new relationship, going forward, the president can count on MUI's support in the field of politics, while MUI has free reign to pursue its agenda of shariatisation.

7.3.3 *Localising the Identity Politics of the* Umma

MUI's shariatisation project has never sought to establish a sharia state in Indonesia, and has always localised the identity politics of the *umma* in the context of Pancasila. This section highlights the significance of the *umma* in the cultural and social landscape of Indonesia, and illustrates how the Pancasila state can contain it. This can be done through connecting *īmān* (faith) and

80 Daniel Peterson, "The Majelis Ulama Indonesia and Its Role in the Ahok Conviction," *Australian Journal of Asian Law* 21, no. 1 (2020): 1–18.

81 "Ma'ruf Amin Sang Inspirator GNPF-MUI Penggerak Aksi 212", *Viva*, 10 August 2018, https://www.viva.co.id/berita/politik/1063437-ma-ruf-amin-sang-inspirator-gnpf-mui-penggerak-aksi-212?page=3&utm_medium=page-3, viewed on 22 July 2022.

82 Hasyim, "MUI and Its Discursive Relevance for 'Aksi Bela Islam': A Growing Trend of Islamic Conservatism in Indonesia." Peterson, *Islam, Blasphemy, and Human Rights in Indonesia: The Trial of Ahok*.

83 "Ma'ruf Amin: GNPF Bukan Bagian MUI", *Detik News*, 31 January 2017, https://news.detik.com/berita/d-3409988/maruf-amin-gnpf-bukan-bagian-mui, viewed on 22 July 2022.

nationalism. *Īmān* is understood by Indonesian Muslims as a fundamental principle of Islam, and supports and strengthens national brotherhood. The Arabic expression,"*ḥubb al-waṭn min al-īmān*," means that loving the nation is part of the Muslim faith. This slogan was introduced by an Indonesian Muslim NU scholar, Wahhab Hasbullah,[84] who argued that Islam is compatible with the concept of nationalism in the context of the modern nation-state. This concept is particular to Indonesia; similar expressions are not found in the tradition of other Muslim countries. The ability of Indonesian Muslims to associate *imān* with the presence of the nation-state shifts the idea of the *umma* to a national context, but not a theocratic one: Indonesia becomes *dār al-muʿāhada* or *dār al-ʿahd wa al-shahāda* (the state of consensus) rather than *dār al-islām* (the state of Islam).[85] Theoretically speaking, the concept of Indonesia as *dār al-muʿāhada* or *dār al-ʿahd wa al-shahāda* is currently being developed by the Muslim scholars of MUI, NU and Muhammadiyah, providing a theological underpinning to support the existence of Indonesia as a Pancasila state. This comes not only as a response to the efforts of HTI, MMI and other Islamist organisations to undermine Pancasila, but also to create stronger compatibility between Islam and the nation-state.

Localising the notion of the *umma* into the context of the nation-state of Indonesia can be understood as the country's success in reconciling Islamic tenets and local wisdom regarding Islam as a political entity—an achievement that differentiates Indonesia from other Muslim countries.

Abdel Ḥamid al-Ghazālī, who studied the thinking of Ḥasan al-Bannā, for instance, clearly states that the meaning of the *umma* is gradually constructed, but inclined to the establishment of a political Islamic state.[86] However, at the practical level, in the contemporary political discourse of Middle East the *umma* is no longer considered as the global Muslim community, but rather as the national Islamic community. Vedi R. Hadiz agrees that the definition of *umma* is increasingly changing from the supranational to the national.[87] On the basis of Hadiz's study, covering Indonesia, Turkey and Egypt, it appears that Indonesia is part of a wider phenomenon across the Muslim world. Most

84 I heard this from many members of the NU elite, who often glorify their commitment to the NKRI by quoting Hasbullah. Muslims often believe that *ḥubb al-waṭan min al-īmān* is a hadīth.

85 Syamsul Hidayat, "Negara Pancasila Sebagai Darul 'Adhi Wa Al-Syahadah Wawasan Dan Kontribusi Muhammadiyah Bagi NKRI," *Tajdida* 14, no. 1 (2016): 12–17.

86 Abdel Hamid El-Ghazali, *The Way to Revival the Muslim Ummah: A Study of the Thinking of Imam Al-Bana* (Cairo: Al-Falah Foundation, 2001).

87 Vedi R. Hadiz, *Islamic Populism in Indonesia and the Middle East* (Cambridge: Cambridge University Press, 2016), p. 2.

Muslims reject any project aimed at the establishment of a global *umma*, such as that aggressively promoted by Hizbut Tahrir, which advocates the idea of a global *umma* through the concept of *khilāfa*. The majority of Muslim countries in the Middle East have denounced Hizbut Tahrir, and Indonesia has followed, with Hizbut Tahrir Indonesia's (HTI) activists seen as lacking credibility and unable to provide any clear formulation of the political concept of the global *umma*.

MUI, following the issuance of State Law No. 16/2017 on Mass Social Organisation, has taken a very critical stance on the position of HTI, judging that this organisation is opposed to the Pancasila state system.[88] In addition, Amin endorses a government ban on similar organisations. Still, although MUI has accused HTI of breaking the national law of Indonesia, it has not yet categorised as heretical, and Amin has stated that it remains within the broad spectrum of legitimate Islamic groups. Its theological position does not does not make it one of the deviant sects (*aliran sesat*) like the Ahmadiyah, and to some extent the Shiʿa.[89] MUI's decision to include HTI in the Islamic camp is understandable, because many HTI members also served on MUI's executive board during the 2005–2020 period. Ismail Yusanto and Muhammad al-Khattath—both of whom had backgrounds in HTI—served as MUI board members in that period. Theologically speaking, MUI categorises the beliefs of HTI as part of Sunnī Islam. This decision is debatable, as from the perspective of Sunnī classical Islamic jurisprudence HTI could be categorised as a rebellious group (*bughāt*) against the state.

In the context of Indonesia, the term *umma* takes on a different meaning. It is no longer understood as a global political or national political entity, but as the Indonesian Muslim community. The "affairs of the *umma*" means the affairs of the Indonesian Muslim community. This meaning is interesting when it comes to the historical development of MUI, since the notion of the *umma* is similar to the notion of populism.[90] In its early days, MUI was not deeply concerned with the *umma*'s interests, largely because it was established as an intermediary to facilitate communications between the government and Islamic organisations such as NU and Muhammadiyah—but representing

88 "Menurut MUI, Ideologi dan Aktivitas HTI Bertentangan dengan Pancasila", *Kompas*, 21 July 2017, https://nasional.kompas.com/read/2017/07/21/05100001/menurut-mui-ideologi-dan-aktivitas-hti-bertentangan-dengan-pancasila, viewed on 22 July 2022.

89 "MUI Tegaskan, Ormas Islam HTI Tidak Sesat atau Menyimpang", *Hidayatullah*, 9 May 2017, https://hidayatullah.com/berita/nasional/read/2017/05/09/116341/mui-tegaskan-ormas-islam-hti-tidak-sesat-atau-menyimpang.html, viewed on 22 July 2022.

90 Federico Finchelstein, *From Fascism to Populism in History* (California: University of California Press, 2017), p. 238.

the interests of the state rather than the Muslim community. Its programmes were determined by the ruling regime, and Suharto did not want to disturb the harmony between religion and the state by granting it a mandate to develop projects directly impacting the *umma* such as schools, mosques, and *pesantren*. In addition, in its role as fatwa-giver MUI was expected to provide Islamic legal opinions for the state rather than for the Muslim community.[91] Thus, in its early years, MUI was consistent in representing the interests of the government in the dialogue between the state and Islamic organisations rather than representing the *umma*. The paradigm shift took place after the resignation of Suharto in 1998, reflecting a political change within in MUI elite.[92] MUI was becoming a more independent organisation, in need of a new patron.[93]

MUI's move from acting as guardian of the state to guardian of the Muslim community can also be understood as the result of internal organisational reflection. The Council came to understand that its alienation from the *umma* had been a mistake. The coming of the reform era in 1998 provided a moment for MUI to rethink its role and prioritise the concerns of the *umma*. From that moment, the organisation began designing programmemes and activities to narrow the gap between itself and the interests of the Muslim community, describing them as *demi umat* (on the behalf of Muslim community). Its project of shariatisation is understood as being in line with the aspirations of *umat Islam* (the Muslim community). MUI also uses the term *umat Islam* as a political tool, arguing that agenda of various Muslim groups should be reconciled and consolidated into a single agenda of the *umma*. Amin has stated that the *umma* is large in number, but its political weight is insufficient; as a result, Indonesian Muslim communities are falling behind other groups in the country. Using an Arabic proverb, Amin describes the Muslim community as "*kathīr fī-l-jumla qalīl fī-l-dawra*": many in number but small in its role. This is, in fact, a common phenomenon across the Muslim world. The Muslim-majority communities of Malaysia, Egypt, Pakistan and many other countries suffer from minority syndrome, especially when facing America, Europe, Israel, and

91 MUI, *15 Tahun Majelis Ulama Indonesia*, ed. H.S. Prodjokusumo (Jakarta: Sekretariat Majelis Ulama Indonesia, 1990); MUI, *20 Tahun Majelis Ulama Indonesia*, ed. H.S. Prodjokusumo (Jakarta: Sekretariat Majelis Ulama Indonesia, 1995); Karni et al., *35 Tahun Majelis Ulama Indonesia*.

92 The discussion around this issue has been elaborated in the previous chapters. See also Ichwan, "Towards A Puritanical Moderate Islam: The Majlis Ulama Indonesia and the Politics of Religious Orthodoxy."

93 Syafiq Hasyim, "The Council of Indonesian Ulama (Majelis Ulama Indonesia, MUI) and Religious Freedom" (2011); Ichwan, "Towards A Puritanical Moderate Islam: The Majlis Ulama Indonesia and the Politics of Religious Orthodoxy."

Christian communities in the West. In recent years, Indonesian Muslims have also developed a heightened sense of danger regarding China and its influence on the country's economic and political situation, and the increasing flow of direct investment from China revives old memories about the role of the Chinese government in support of the Communist Party of Indonesia. In short, in the face of these challenges, Indonesian Muslims need to consolidate the potential of the *umma*.[94]

In recent decades, the understanding of the term "the *umma*" has become increasingly exclusive, and is now predominantly used by Indonesian Muslims to refer to their own community. MUI has played a part in this evolution; its fatwas dealing with the affairs of the *umma* refer only to those who embrace Sunnī Islam. The fatwa on heresy, for example, states that follows of the Ahmadiyah and Shīʿa are not "true Muslims." Only "true Muslims" can become members of MUI; adherants to deviant sects (*aliran sesat*) are not considered part of the *umma*. The meaning of the *umma* has thus become political—in the popular imagination it increasingly linked to the concept of political Islam—rather than cultural.

A further change in the notion of the *umma* has taken place since the emergence of a more populist expression of shariatisation following the 2014 presidential elections. MUI and some other Muslim groups found themselves facing a clear enemy in the figure of Ahok, a Chinese Christian, who had replaced Jokowi as governor of Jakarta. In response, the organisation took on some of the qualities of a popular movement, mobilising supporters and organising demonstrations and protests, to oppose him. This movement became a central element in defining the contemporary understanding of the *umma* in Indonesia.

MUI's politics of the *umma* did not emerge from nowhere, but were developed over time. According to MUI's notion of *perlindungan umat* (*ḥimāyat al-umma* in Arabic, protection of the Muslim community), the *umma* should be protected from three "social ills": deviant beliefs (*al-aqīda al-fāsida*), false thoughts (*al-afkār al-bāṭila*) and ruthless behaviour (*al-akhlāq al-sayyiʾa*). The organisation had begun organising annual meetings (*Ijtimaʾ Ulama*) in 2006, with the aim to consolidate the movement (*tansīq al-ḥaraka*). Unifying the diverse interests of so many Muslim groups was almost impossible, and MUI was aware that the most realistic method of achieving greater cooperation was to allocate tasks and responsibilities in pursuit of a common goal, namely to glorify the religion of Islam and its communities (the *umma*). In this

94 Ma'ruf Amin, *Harmoni Dalam Keberagaman, Dinamika Relasi Agama-Negara* (Jakarta: Dewan Pertimbangan Presiden, 2011).

regard, the function of MUI in the constellation of the *umma* movement is as *wadah*—literally a vessel. As a *wadah*, MUI should be able to provide a favourable environment for all organisations.

After the 2016 *Ijtima Ulama*, the consolidation of the *umma* spread not only among the MUI network organisations but also to other Muslim groups. MUI's influence was essential, since it is is understood to represent the interests of Indonesian Muslims and can serve the needs of smaller organisations. Many leading figures in government have joined MUI. FPI, HTI, and many others—the so-called regressive Muslim organisations—have also supported MUI because it often voices their aspirations. In addition, MUI helps the upward mobilisation of non-mainstream Islamic organisations, as in the case of the 2017 gubernatorial elections in Jakarta, when MUI issued its fatwa titled *Pendapat dan Sikap Keagamaan Majelis Ulama Indonesia*. This was used by some organisations, such as GNPF-MUI, FPI, and many others, to consolidate and mobilise a series of protests, leading to the criminalisation and eventual sentencing of Ahok for blasphemy. In this example, an MUI fatwa functioned as a framing institution to bring together those who share MUI's beliefs.

To conclude, while MUI is unable to localise the concept of the *umma*, it has still proved an effective part of the political agenda. Politics is a crucial issue for MUI and other Muslim gropus who still believe in some form of political Islam; one of the methods to achieve it is through the shariatisation of the *umma*. Islamist groups try to achieve this not through introducing sharia content but through disseminating false information on shariatisation, and through criticising the state government. Unfortunately, many MUI fatwas strengthen this kind of movement. In this regard, the politics of the *umma* is addressed to the shariatised rather than the general *umma*.

7.3.4 *Populist Shariatisation: Contesting Social and Economic Justice for the* Umma

On many occasions, has MUI proclaimed that the social and economic well-being of the Indonesian *umma* takes second place to that of other religious groups in the country. Its economic standing is certainly weak in the context of both national and global capitalism; Din Syamsuddin states the economic self-reliance of the Muslim community was at its peak during the struggle for independence, and argues that the weakening economic ethos of the Indonesian *umma* is the result of the hegemony of the modern economic global system of capitalism and liberalism.[95]

95 Din Syamsuddin was General Chairman of MUI at the time of making this statement. "Din Syamsudin: Umat Islam Tertinggal dalam Segala Bidang", *Republika*, 8 January 2022,

MUI also believes that the government's economic policies exacerbate this inequality. Anwar Abbas—the deputy general chairman of MUI and also an elite member of Muhammadiyah—states that the Indonesian *umma* is currently being marginalised as a result of bad state policies.[96] He believes that state policy is biased against the Indonesian *umma*, contributing to their economic backwardness. Only two out of Indonesia's ten richest people are Muslim, according to Abbas: Chairul Tanjung and Aburizal Bakrie. This data, in his opinion, indicates the weakness of the Muslim community, and he urges Muslims to take a greater role in the economic sector. The MUI elite generally shares this view, blaming the state policy of Indonesia, international and global influence—particularly America and China—and non-Muslim monopolies on national businesses. In consequence, MUI argues that part of its role is to help overcome this social and economic inequality.

Economic inequality is not a new phenomenon, but during the 1980s and 90s the national economy was dominated by those close to Suharto. As a result, MUI remained silent on the issue, and discussions on inequality only emerged when Suharto began to seek allies from Islamic groups. In 1991, Suharto supported the establishment of ICMI (the Indonesian Association of Muslim Intellectuals) in Malang, East Java.[97] The overall goal of this new organisation was to provide strategies to overcome the social and economic inequality faced by the Indonesian *umma*. However, the organisation was more focused on handling on political, rather than economic, issues of the *umma*, and thus had little impact on the existing inequality.

In the aftermath of the Ahok blasphemy case, one of the reasons behind MUI's backing of the Islamist ABI movement was at least partly driven by the narrative of the inequality faced by the *umma* in the national economy. In the general framing of both MUI and ABI, the Indonesian *umma* needs to take large-scale action to force the state to respond to their suffering. Huge mobilisations, in the form of public protests, were seen as the best method. They argue that the social and economic gap should be reduced by

---

https://www.republika.co.id/berita/dunia-islam/islam-nusantara/15/01/08/nhuwr3-din-syamsudin-umat-islam-tertinggal-dalam-segala-bidang, viewed on 22 July 2022.

96 "Kalau umat Islam anti kebhinekaan, Indonesia enggak akan pernah ada!", *Merdeka*, 3 February 2017, https://www.merdeka.com/peristiwa/kalau-umat-islam-anti-kebhinekaan-indonesia-enggak-akan-pernah-ada.html, viewed on 22 July 2022.

97 Robert W. Hefner, *Civil Islam: Muslims and Democratization in Indonesia* (New Jersey: Princeton University Press, 2011); Robert W. Hefner, "Islam, State, and Civil Society: ICMI and the Struggle for the Indonesian Middle Class," *Indonesia*, no. 56 (1993): 1–35; M.S. Anwar, *Pemikiran Dan Aksi Islam Indonesia: Sebuah Kajian Politik Tentang Cendekiawan Muslim Orde Baru* (Jakarta: Paramadina, 1995).

empowering the economic capacity of the *umma*, also known as *pemberdayaan umat* (community empowerment), a phrase MUI uses to mean access to national economic resources. The economy is a long-standing issue in the history of Indonesian Muslim politics. As the majority group of this largest Muslim country, Indonesian Muslims feel unjustly treated by the state in the distribution of national wealth given that Indonesian's economy has been dominated by Chinese and non-Muslim businessmen. The case of Ahok was a potential opportunity for the ABI elites of ABI to further their own agenda: for them, Ahok represented the state, Chinese, non-Muslim and elite economy. In short, Ahok was the symbol of the social and economic injustice faced by Indonesian Muslims.

MUI believes in the importance of social and economic injustice issues, which can be seen in its effort to propose an alternative system of social and economic justice based on sharia. The organisation has long tried to contribute to strengthening the social and economic system of the *umma* through the shariatisation of finance, lifestyle, consumption and production industries. As mentioned in the previous section, MUI has endorsed the formalisation of the sharia-based financial system into the state law of Indonesia. This has been quite successful, because now sharia-based finance enterprise has obtained legal recognition from the state through State Law No. 21/2008 on Sharia Banking. Data from the OJK (Otoritas Jasa Keuangan, the Finance Service Authority) states that there are twelve General Sharia Banks (Bank Syariah Umum) with 2121 offices, twenty-two Sharia Unit Enterprises (Unit Usaha Syariah) with 327 offices, and 164 Sharia Financing Banks (Bank Pembiayaan Syariah) with 433 offices.[98] However, the market share of sharia banks remained very low at 4.61% (273.494 billion IDR) in 2015 compared to conventional banks. If this continues, it means that sharia banks are failing to attract Muslim clients, and MUI's attempt to strengthen the *umma* through this means is unsuccessful.

MUI also aims to empower the economy of the *umma* through increasing awareness on the importance of a halal lifestyle in consumption and production, and established LPPOM to provide halal certification. This initiative can be considered successful, as it has brought sharia doctrine into the legal and public spheres and prompted lawmakers to create specific laws on halal certification, particularly State Law No. 33/2014 on Halal Product Assurance, making halal certification compulsory for goods produced and marketed in Indonesia.

98 On the role of OJK, see "Perbankan Syariah dan Kelembagaannya," Otoritas Jasa Keuangan, https://www.ojk.go.id/id/kanal/syariah/tentang-syariah/Pages/PBS-dan-Kelembagaan.aspx, viewed on 22 July 2022/.

This is a huge accomplishment for MUI in promoting a sharia-compliant lifestyle. But how influential is this law in contributing to the economy of the *umma*? Both the sharia-based economy and halal lifestyle that MUI has struggled to promote have not generated a substantial response from the *umma*, perhaps because neither offers sufficient economic incentives. The challenge of implementing the halal economy through halal certification is, for instance, the degree to which halal certification is affordable for small enterprises in Indonesia such as street food vendors. There is a perception that the halal certification is more focused on large enterprises than small traders. These large enterprises are already accustomed to preparing international certifications and can more easily adapt to halal certification. As a result, there has been only a tepid response from the *umma* to this development, particularly when compared to their response to political agendas such as ABI, the 212 Movement, and others.

Since 2017, there have been new opportunities for the resurgence of the *umma* economy as a result of social mobilisation and also the policies of Jakarta's governor-elect, Baswedan. Still, results have been slow in coming. Electoral promises to provide financial facilities such as microcredit and soft loans or even grants for lower and middle-class entrepreneurs through OK-OC—Sandiaga Uno's programme that operated during his election campaign—have faced bureaucratic difficulties. Besides these programmes needing a supporting budget, they also need businesses ready to take advantage of the scheme. Baswedan's deputy, Sandiaga Uno, was the driving force behind this programmeme, but in 2019 he left his position to serve as Prabowo Subianto's vice-presidential running mate. Since 2020, Uno has become the Minister of Tourism and Creative Economy.[99] Attempts to promote the economic empowerment of the *umma* that are not based on their real interests can do more harm than good, since the community itself will not feel any emotional involvement. In this regard, MUI's influence has been limited; while it helped provide a narrative which brought Baswedan to power in Jakarta, it has been unable to influence his leadership since then, including on economic issues.

The involvement of MUI in the Islamic protest movement from 2016 to 2017, however, has increased its bargaining power with the Jokowi regime. Since the Ahok saga, the government has begun approaching leaders of the protest movement, particularly drawing in MUI's leader Amin as a new ally

99 "Sandiaga: Pariwisata dan Ekonomi Kreatif Bangkit 2021", *CNN Indonesia*, 30 December 2020, https://www.cnnindonesia.com/gaya-hidup/20201230152749-275-587920/sandiaga-pariwisata-dan-ekonomi-kreatif-bangkit-2021, viewed on 22 July 2022.

for Jokowi. Jokowi involves MUI in government projects, many of which are centred around the redistribution of assets, and his interest in the organisation was evident from his meeting with Amin on 30 March 2017, when Amin visited the presidential palace to discuss the issue of asset redistribution. Amin has stated that they spoke about Jokowi's concern over the economic gap between the rich and poor, and the redistribution of assets as a means to solving this problem.[100] The closer ties between Jokowi and Amin could be seen even more clearly in Jokowi's presence at the Kongres Ekonomi Umat event (Congress of the *Umma* Economy, KEU), held by MUI in Jakarta in 2017. In Jokowi's speech at the Congresss, he clearly outlined his need for MUI's support in projects aimed at reducing economic inequality in society (*redistribusi aset*), saying said that MUI could play a key role.[101] Moreover, he authorised the *pesantren* to manage and develop abandoned lands or assets.[102]

However, despite the success that comes from being recognised by the ruling regime, MUI has made little progress in its programmeme of empowering the *umma* economy. Here, MUI and ABI appear to have different views: MUI wants to enlarge its "established business agenda" while ABI want to create its own economic agenda. MUI frequently states its great interest in the state project of asset redistribution, while ABI is more interested in establishing mini-markets—called Minimart 212—which it sees as having higher potential than convential sharia business. In this regard, ABI is less interested in discussing sharia economy. This division between the two groups has been discernible from the beginning, and is rooted in political factors. MUI has more flexible approach, especially in dealing with the interests of the Jokowi government, while ABI has been clearly and consistently allied with Prabowo and opposition groups. Programmemes aimed at promoting social and economic justice for the *umma* by both MUI and ABI are thus not purely about economics but also serve political agendas.

The relationship between Jokowi and Amin has also gradually changed from an economic to a political one. Jokowi asked Amin to be his running mate

100 The General Chairman of MUI visited Jokowi to discuss on asset redistribution. "Temui Jokowi, Ketua MUI Bahas Redistribusi Aset", *Oke Finance*, 30 March 2017, https://economy.okezone.com/read/2017/03/30/320/1654834/temui-jokowi-ketua-mui-bahas-redistribusi-aset, viewed on 22 July 2022.

101 "Atasi kesenjangan ekonomi RI, MUI gelar Kongres Ekonomi Umat," *Merdeka*, 22 April 2017, https://www.merdeka.com/uang/atasi-kesenjangan-ekonomi-ri-mui-gelar-kongres-ekonomi-umat.html, viewed on 22 July 2022.

102 "Jokowi minta MUI bantu pemerintah kurangi kesenjangan di daerah", *Merdeka*, 22 April 2017, https://www.merdeka.com/uang/jokowi-minta-mui-bantu-pemerintah-kurangi-kesenjangan-di-daerah.html, viewed on 22 July 2022.

in the 2019 presidential election, partly because of Amin's involvement in conservative Islamic politics; with his support, Jokowi was protected from negative campaigns portraying him as anti-Islam. Yet his choice also created the impression that Amin had used MUI as a vehicle for his own practical political advancement.

It can therefore be seen that social and economic justice for the *umma* is combination of various issues—including political ones. In many cases, the political element trumps matters of economic equality, and the focus on social justice is political rhetoric to attract support from the *umma* without actually empowering it.

7.4 MUI and Its Political Dilemma

Since Amin became Jokowi's running mate in the 2019 elections, MUI has faced a dilemma. This dilemma became even more serious when Amin was officially sworn in as vice-president of Indonesia. The announcement of Amin's candidacy was a special moment for MUI, being the first time that a senior member had run for vice-president.[103] In selecting Amin, Jokowi considered his capacity as a senior ulama; his position in both MUI and NU gave him an edge over Mahfud MD, a prominent national Muslim figure who until the evening of the announcement was the presumptive vice-presidential candidate. By choosing Amin, Jokowi wanted to present an ideal coalition representing Islamic and nationalist credentials for the leadership of Indonesia. This was a first for Jokowi, as he had distanced himself from identity politics until this point in his career. When he was the mayor of Solo, for example, he was paired with Catholic FX Hadi Rudyatmo, even though Islamist parties such as PKS were important supporters, and his running mate for the 2012 Jakarta gubernatorial election was Ahok. In the 2014 presidential elections, however, he was paired with Jusuf Kalla because of Kalla's position as a Muslim figure, a businessman, and also a representative of non-Javanese groups.

From 2014 to 2019, Jokowi was depicted by radical and conservative Muslim groups such as FPI, GNPF-Ulama, and Forum Umat Islam (FUI) as an anti-Islamic force. Prior to the appointment of Amin as Jokowi's running mate, MUI also formed part of this camp. According to these groups, many of Jokowi's policies are designed to marginalise the interests of Muslims in Indonesia, and

103 "Jokowi Resmi Tunjuk Ma'ruf Amin sebagai Cawapres," Kompas, 9 August 2018, https://nasional.kompas.com/read/2018/08/09/18260341/jokowi-resmi-tunjuk-maruf-amin-sebagai-cawapres, 22 July 2022.

they believe that Jokowi has criminalised ulama (*kriminalisasi ulama*). In their view, many ulama who are critical of Jokowi have faced court action—such as Rizieq Shihab, the spiritual leader of FPI—although the government claims that these are normal cases. In short, they see Jokowi as an enemy of Islam. This view has similarities with Thomas Power's idea that democracy in the Jokowi era is moving in the direction of authoritarianism.[104]

Although MUI's fatwas have often dealt with political issues, the position of Amin as vice-presidential candidate placed the organisation in a new predicament. Senior MUI leaders had spent years crafting an image of the organisation as a neutral umbrella group which would protect the *umma*, but now it appeared to be taking a clear position in support of the government. That said, Amin's position could also be seen as the necessity for an ulama to accompany the president and guide him.

A more difficult issue emerged when it was discovered that MUI has no internal code of conduct regulating its leader, elites and board members when they are active in practical politics. In fact, since its establishment in 1975, MUI was set up as a home for the all the ulama of Indonesia regardless of their organisational background, providing a shield of sorts from political intervention. But as the organisation has developed, its increasing interaction with political parties and government has brought the organisation influence but also exposed it to the influence of others. As a result, its neutrality has come under threat. Amin's position as general head of the NU Sharia Board is clearer because that organisation has strict regulations on its members' involvement in practical politics: namely, that they must resign from NU. As a result, Amin resigned from NU when he became a candidate for the vice presidency, and from MUI when he was elected.[105]

Despite Amin's position as Jokowi's running mate, not all MUI branches supported him in the polling booth. Some, such as the MUI branch in Bukit Tinggi and in Agam districts, both in West Sumatera, demanded Amin resign from his position.[106] This is not entirely surprising as MUI itself has no institutional political preference—it is made up of different members who have their own political outlooks. However, broadly speaking there were three camps

104 Thomas P. Power, "Jokowi's Authoritarian Turn and Indonesia's Democratic Decline," *Bulletin of Indonesian Economic Studies* 54, no. 3 (September 2, 2018): 307–38.

105 "Ma'ruf Amin: Saya Mundur dari Ketum MUI Jika Terpilih Sebagai Wapres," *Detik News*, 22 September 2018, https://news.detik.com/berita/d-4224205/maruf-amin-saya-mundur-dari-ketum-mui-jika-terpilih-sebagai-wapres, viewed on 22 July 2022.

106 "Pengurus Daerah MUI Desak Kiai Ma'ruf Amin Mundur, Ini Alasannya", *Jawapos*, 12 August 2018, https://www.jawapos.com/nasional/politik/12/08/2018/pengurus-daerah-mui-desak-kiai-maruf-amin-mundur-ini-alasannya/, viewed on 22 July 2022.

on the question of Amin's candidacy in MUI. The first group are those who supported Amin. Many of these had a NU background, such Zainut Tauhid (Vice-General Chairman of MUI, 2015–2020), Masduqi Baedlowi (Head of Communication Commission, 2015–2020), Asrorun Ni'am Sholeh (Secretary of Fatwa Commission, 2015–2020) and many others. The NU element in MUI are a dominant group, and Zainut Tauhid has stated that they generally supported Jokowi-Amin.[107] The second group are those who opposed Amin, such as Natsir (2015–2020) and Zaitun Rasmin (2015–2020). These groups were mostly the different groups within MUI. The third group were those who declared their neutrality. Most of this group were from Muhammadiyah backgrounds, such as Anwar Abbas and the late Yunahar Ilyas (the Vice General chairman of MUI).

The position of the MUI elites from the Muhammadiyah group was also not monolithic. Some of them demonstrated their neutrality, while others expressly indicated their support for Prabowo-Sandi, or for Amin, such as M. Azrul (the coordinator of MUI's Economy Commission and Garda Matahari, Jokowi's volunteer organisation). From my observations in Central and East Java, Sumatera and other locations, Amin appeared to have been a reason why some Muhammadiyah members did not support Jokowi. Din Syamsuddin claimed neutrality, but his statements generally indicated support for Prabowo-Sandi. This tendency was understandable, as he had hoped to be chosen as Jokowi's running mate himself thanks to his close relationship with the president through his role as Special Envoy on matters of religious dialogue and world civilisational advancement. In the run-up to the election campaign, he expressed his readiness to become Jokowi's running mate, saying: "I heard that my name has been mentioned and promoted by such groups and political parties several times."[108] Soon after Jokowi chose Amin, Din Syamsuddin resigned from his position as the Special Envoy to Jokowi's government.[109]

These three camps in MUI did not publicly express their political preferences as MUI officials but as part of their rights as individual citizens. When they wanted to express their standpoint, they did so outside MUI. Bachtiar Nasir, for instance, expressed support for Prabowo and campaigned for him,

---

107 Interview with Zainut Tauhid, March 2019.

108 "Tanpa Basa-basi, Din Syamsuddin Bersedia Jadi Cawapres bagi Jokowi," *Kompas*, 4 August 2018, https://regional.kompas.com/read/2018/08/04/09183271/tanpa-basa-basi-din-syamsuddin-bersedia-jadi-cawapres-bagi-jokowi, viewed on 22 July 2022.

109 "Din Syamsuddin Ungkap Alasan Mundur dari Utusan Khusus Jokowi," *CNN Indonesia*, 25 September 2018, https://www.cnnindonesia.com/nasional/20180925194108-20-333151/din-syamsuddin-ungkap-alasan-mundur-dari-utusan-khusus-jokowi, viewed on 22 July 2022.

but not in his capacity as a MUI member.[110] It appears that senior members of MUI shared the consensus that they did not discuss practical politics within the organisation; Amin, for example, never discussed his candidacy while attending MUI official meetings.

We can see from this that while MUI has a relatively united voice when it comes to the shariatisation agenda, members had divergent views on politics. MUI's mission of shariatisation remains important regardless of the ruling regime. As Jokowi and Amin emerged victorious from the presidential campaign, it became clear that Amin's position in the palace would present a new challenge for MUI's shariatisation agenda. Amin would no longer be able to play the role that he once did within MUI—as vice president he is expected to act as a protector for all Indonesian citizens, regardless of their religion, belief system, gender and ethnicity.

7.4.1 *Ma'ruf Amin's Vice Presidency and MUI Moderatism*

Many people believe that Amin, through his position as vice-president of Indonesia, will use his inflence to steer MUI in a more moderate and progressive direction. The organisation has long been known for its conservatism, especially since the beginning of the post-reform era. Its fatwas, recommendations, and support for conservative religious models in the legal and public spheres have given it a reputation for being the source of Islamic conservatism in Indonesia.[111] Fatwas on the heresy of the Shīʿa, Ahmadiyah and other so-called "deviant" religious behaviours lend particular weight to this reputation, even though the organisation considers itself to be moderate.

MUI first introduced the concept of *Islam Wasathiyyah* (moderate Islam) in 2015, with *Wasatiyyah untuk Indonesia Berkeadilan dan Berkeadaban* (Moderatism for a Just and Civilised Indonesia) as the title of its ninth National Congress (MUNAS IX). Din Syamsuddin (who became General Chairman of MUI following the death of Sahal Mahfud in 2014) stated that *Islam Wasathiyyah* is the orientation of human being as God's creatures to prefer a middle way. In his view, Pancasila is the crystallisation of Islam's middle way, opposed to extremism, liberalism and other forms of heterodox religious

110 "Bachtiar Nasir Dukung Prabowo, Ini Tanggapan TKN," *Tagar*, 4 April 2019, https://www.tagar.id/bachtiar-nasir-dukung-prabowo-ini-tanggapan-tkn, viewed on 22 July 2022.

111 Hasyim, "MUI and Its Discursive Relevance for 'Aksi Bela Islam'"; Hasyim, "Fatwas and Democracy: Majelis Ulama Indonesia (MUI, Indonesian Ulema Council) and Rising Conservatism in Indonesian Islam."

tendency.[112] Din Syamsuddin argues that *Islam Wasathiyyah* is the *sirāṭ al-mustaqīm* (straight path of Islam).[113]

Given its professed adherence to *Islam Wasathiyyah*, it is important to consider how MUI deals with non-Muslims and with Muslim minority groups. The organisation's position on non-Muslim groups is clear: their status is protected in Islam, and MUI endorses interfaith dialogue as well as upholding the importance of peaceful co-existence. Religious harmony and tolerance are also publicly encouraged. Even so, it could be argued that MUI's focus on shariatisation potentially discriminates against non-Muslims, bringing the formalisation of halal and the sharia economy into the legal and public domain. However, MUI takes a different stance when dealing with minority Muslim groups. As the representative of Sunnī theology in Indonesia, it is very critical of those who are not Sunnī. Its position towards its non-Sunnī followers is extremely strict, for instance judging them as *kelompok sesat* (deviant sects). In 2005, MUI issued fatwas that categorised around fourteen Islamic minority groups as deviant from the doctrinal teaching of Islam, meaning from the Sunnī theology—and, despite its statements on the importance of adopting *Islam Wasatiyyah* in 2015, it has not revised these fatwas.[114]

Many hope that Amin, as vice-president, will guide MUI towards a more moderate orientation. Since his election, MUI has been divided on certain public issues related to Islam, with some members speaking out in support of the government and others more critical. This internal polarisation may have some benefit, acting as a mechanism of checks and balances for the organisation's internal affairs; debates and discussions among these opposing groups are necessary before issuing a fatwa or recommendation, for example. On the other hand, polarisation may adversely affect MUI's reputation as a united ulama organisation.

The internal polarisation of MUI is evident in many cases, for instance in its response to the programmeme on the certification of Muslim preachers proposed by Ministry of Religious Affairs (MORA) with the aim of eradicating Islamic radicalism and extremism among Muslim preachers. Fachrul Razi,

---

112 "Ketua MUI: Islam Wasathiyah, Islam Jalan Tengah", *MUI Digital*, 21 February 2017, https://mui.or.id/berita/551/ketua-mui-islam-wasathiyah-islam-jalan-tengah/, 22 July 2022.

113 "Apa yang Dimaksud Islam Wasathiyah?", *MUI Digital*, 3 July 2020, https://mui.or.id/bimbingan-syariah/paradigma-islam/28522/apa-yang-dimaksud-islam-wasathiyah-2/, 22 July 2022.

114 MUI, *Mengawal Aqidah Umat: Fatwa MUI Tentang Aliran-Aliran Sesat Di Indonesia*, n.d.; Hasyim, "The Council of Indonesian Ulama (MUI) and Aqidah-Based Intolerance."

Minister of Religious Affairs from 2019 to2020, stated that this programmeme was aimed at teaching Muslim preachers the soft skills necessary for moderate and effective preaching. However, the proposal was rejected by Anwar Abbas and Muhyiddin Junaidi (former vice-general chairman of MUI, 2020). Abbas threatened to resign from his position as MUI's general secreatary if MUI agreed to the programmeme, and both he and Junaidi stated that it would victimise Indonesian preachers, giving the impression that they were all radical Islamists.[115] On the other side of the debate, Amin's supporters argued that this programmeme was actually very similar to an earlier step taken by MUI called the standardisation of Muslim preachers.

The case of the legislation of the Omnibus Law is another clear illustration of the increasing polarisation within MUI. The Omnibus Law was proposed by Jokowi's government to make Indonesia a friendlier country for markets and investment. Although it stimulated public controversy, Jokowi insisted on proposing this law to parliament, and it was passed on 5 October 2020. All Muslim organisations, such as Muhammadiyah and NU, rejected the new law, and Muhammadiyah asked parliament to delay its implementation. NU stated that the Omnibus Law was oriented to a neo-liberal economy, which was evident in its articles on education.[116] One faction of MUI, represented by Muyiddin Junaidi and Anwar Abbas, released their *Taklimat MUI* ("MUI Public Announcement") in response, opposing the law on the grounds that it fuelled large businesses and capitalism. The MUI faction that generally supported Amin remained silent on the issue, indicating that they accepted the decision of the state.

The two cases above sugges that the driving factor behind MUI's polarisation is political economy rather than theology. Personal attitudes towards political-economic issues influence the statements of MUI board members, even when speaking in the name of the organisation. The two groups—one pro-government and the other more critical—are in conflict, and use MUI as a vehicle for expressing their own convictions. As a result, the two largest Muslim organisations in MUI—NU and Muhammadiyah —have become more clearly divided.

115 "Tolak Sertifikasi Penceramah, Anwar Abbas Ancam Mundur dari Sekjen MUI," *Detik News*, 5 September 2020, https://news.detik.com/berita/d-5160685/tolak-sertifikasi-penceramah-anwar-abbas-ancam-mundur-dari-sekjen-mui, 22 July 2022.

116 Syafiq Hasyim, "Indonesian Muslim Groups Oppose Omnibus Law," ISEAS, 16 October 2020, https://www.iseas.edu.sg/media/commentaries/indonesian-muslim-groups-oppose-omnibus-law/, viewed on 22 July 2022.

7.4.2 *The 2020 MUNAS-MUI and Aligning with the Government*

Despite the pandemic, MUI organised its *Musyarawah National* or National Congress, MUNAS X, at the Sultan Hotel, Jakarta, as well as online on 25–27 November 2020. This was a long-awaited forum, being crucial in the context of MUI's role and its relation to the affairs of state. The question of Amin's leadership was central to the Congress. The second term of Jokowi's presidency had begun, with Amin as vice-president. This was the first time the the general chairman of MUI had also held a leading role in national politics. Amin would not be standing for another term as general chairman—MUI's regulations state that the general chaiman and secretary general of the organisation cannot hold another position while in office—and it was necessary to nominate a new leader for the period of 2020–2025.[117]

MUNAS 2020 therefore become a battlefield of two MUI factions: those who endorsed Amin as vice-president, and those who were critical of his position. The former wished to instrumentalise the Congress as an institutional mechanism to defend the organisation from conservative elements and those critical of the state. After the nomination of Amin as Jokowi's running mate, MUI popularised the term *ṣadīq al-ḥukūma* (friend of the government) to show their support, and it was expected that they would support government programmemes and policies. As a "friend" of the government, it suggested that MUI would also provide religious justification for these policies. Amin restated this slogan at the Congress, emphasising the organisation's new role as *ṣadīq al-ḥukūma* and thus indicating his awareness that its support was essential for him to successfully carry out his new role as vice-president.[118]

For the second group, who opposed Amin, the priority at MUNAS 2020 was to purify MUI of those who had used the organisation as a vehicle for political power. Most of these came from modernist Islamic organisations such as Muhammadiyah and many were also on MUI's Board of Trustees (BPMUI), such as Din Syamsuddin, Didin Hafiduddin and many others. Since the beginning of Indonesia's post-reform era, MUI has been divided in a bicameral system. The first house is an executive body led by the general chairman, while the second house is an advisory board led by the head of BPMUI. This faction

117 "MUI Gelar Munas pada November 2020, Siapa Kandidat Ketua Umum?" *Kompas*, 20 October 2020, https://www.kompas.com/tren/read/2020/10/20/163200565/mui-gelar-munas-pada-november-2020-siapa-kandidat-ketua-umum-?page=all, viewed on 22 July 2022.

118 "Wapres Ma'ruf Ingatkan Peran MUI Sebagai Pelayan Umat dan Mitra Pemerintah", *Merdeka*, 28 November 2020, https://www.merdeka.com/peristiwa/wapres-maruf-ingatkan-peran-mui-sebagai-pelayan-umat-dan-mitra-pemerintah.html, viewed on 26 July 2022.

had been critical of Amin ever since his nomination as Jokowi's running mate two years earlier, and understood his acceptance to mean the politicisation of MUI. This is indicated in BPMUI's statement asserting that political actors should remain civilised and follow political ethics (*etika politik*), while abstaining from showing anger or hatred that risked polarising the Indonesian state.[119] The term "political ethics" reflects the state of MUI's internal politics and was intended as a criticism of Amin's actions, even though Din Syamsuddin—who had followers in both MUI and Muhammadiyah—had also hoped to be nominated as Jokowi's running mate.[120] Din Syamsuddin was expected to be one of the stronger candidates to replace Amin as general chairman of MUI, but did not attend the Congress for personal reasons. He sent his apologies, expecting the event to run in line with the organisation's guidelines.[121] However, his absence could also be interpreted as a criticism of the ethos of the Congress, which seemed intended to support and strengthen the ruling political regime.

The victory of MUI's pro-government faction was predictable. Miftachul Achyar, the head of NU's Sharia Advisory Board, was appointed as a new general chairman, replacing Amin. Achyar is a well-known figure able to sustain MUI's support for Amin and the government, although there was some concern over his lack of experience within the MUI organisation. All previous MUI leaders had previous experience as board members and Achyar was the first exception to this rule, indicating a break from the informal consensus on the need for organisational experience. Furthermore, Amin was appointed as head of the BPMUI, a position that previously belonged to Din Syamsuddin. This position offered Amin a means of remaining involved with the organisational direction of MUI over the next five-year period, thus consolidating his political office; since his nomination he had made his ambition for the role clear.

MUI's obvious tendency to align with the government is evident from the composition of its board, which is dominated by Amin's supporters. The absence of Din Syamsuddin, the late Tenku Zulkarnain, Natsir and some others on the board shows that MUI wants moderates as board members. The late Zulkarnaen, for example, often defended radicalism and extremism in social media, and as a result some people associated MUI with these views. It was

---

119 "Ini Sikap MUI terhadap Pencalonan KH Maruf Amin sebagai Cawapres," *Sindo News*, 29 August 2018, https://daerah.sindonews.com/artikel/jatim/1003/ini-sikap-mui-terhadap-pencalonan-kh-maruf-amin-sebagai-cawapres, viewed on 22 July 2022.

120 "Tanpa Basa-basi, Din Syamsuddin Bersedia Jadi Cawapres bagi Jokowi," *Kompas*, 4 August 2018, https://regional.kompas.com/read/2018/08/04/09183271/tanpa-basa-basi-din-syamsuddin-bersedia-jadi-cawapres-bagi-jokowi?page=all, viewed on 22 July 2022.

121 https://news.detik.com/berita/d-5268488/din-syamsuddin-dengan-menyesal-saya-tak-bisa-hadiri-munas-mui-ke-10, viewed on 3 March 2021.

not in the interests of Amin's group to provide him with a platform. Natsir, too, has also been open about his involvement in both national and international networks of Islamic extremism.[122] In the case of Din Syamsuddin, however, the issue was his criticism of the Jokowi regime. Having been close to the president in his role as Special Envoy on religious harmony, his disappointment at not being chosen as Jokowi's right hand led him to resign his post.[123] Later, he joined the opposition groups and became extremely critical of government policy. The pro-government faction of MUI appears to find radicalism and anti-government attitudes equally dangerous, and has made sure that the board is free of both.

To conclude, MUNAS 2020 illustrates two key points: the victory of the pro-government faction of MUI, and the way this dominance is expressed in the structure of the board membership. MUI's new role as *ṣadīq al-ḥukūma* (friend of the government) is clear.

7.4.3 *Shariatisation in the Public Sphere under the Jokowi Administration*

Many people, especially those who declare themselves to be Jokowi's opponents, have developed the political narrative that Jokowi's administration is marginalising Islam and decreasing its influence in Indonesia. They particularly refer to Jokowi's policies that criminalise ulama such as to Rizieq Shihab, Bahar bin Smith (a preacher), Ahmad Dani (a singer) and some others. From this perspective, Jokowi is seen to be using "law as a weapon."[124] This perception, however, is clearly mistaken: other government policies have promoted Muslim interests, for example furthering the institutionalisation of sharia in the legal and political realms. Under Jokowi, Indonesia has strategically strengthened and deepened shariarisation within the state and society, starting from the field of finance and the halal industry and also Islamic lifestyles, with the enforcement of religious values in the public sphere. This section focuses on the increasing trajectory of shariatisation in the public sphere during the Jokowi era.

---

122 "Bachtiar Nasir Jadi Tersangka, Berawal dari Aliran Uang ke Suriah yang Diduga Terkait ISIS," Wartakota Live, 7 May 2019, https://wartakota.tribunnews.com/2019/05/07/bachtiar-nasir-jadi-tersangka-berawal-dari-aliran-uang-ke-suriah-yang-diduga-terkait-isis, viewed on 22 July 2022.

123 "Din Syamsuddin Ungkap Alasan Mundur dari Utusan Khusus Jokowi," CNN Indonesia, 25 September 2018, https://www.cnnindonesia.com/nasional/20180925194108-20-333151/din-syamsuddin-ungkap-alasan-mundur-dari-utusan-khusus-jokowi, viewed on 22 July 2022.

124 "Law as a weapon: the 'criminalisation of ulama'", The University of Melbourne, March 20 2019, https://indonesiaatmelbourne.unimelb.edu.au/law-as-a-weapon-the-criminalisation-of-ulama/, viewed on 22 July 2022.

It is true that Jokowi is depicted as the foe of Indonesian Islam due to his uneasy relationship with MUI in his first term, and with other conservative Islamic groups such as FPI, HTI and many others. However, since then Jokowi has taken up the agenda of shariatisation through formalising sharia on halal issues. In 2014, in the era of SBY, Indonesian lawmakers agreed to legislate State Law No. 33/2014 on Halal Product Assurance. This law was intended as a legal umbrella for the government of Indonesia to govern and regulate the shariatisation of goods, business, and also lifestyle.[125] Halal certification—meaning that products must be certified, halal restaurants are promoted, and various other steps—is therefore chosen as an entry point. Legally speaking, public freedom in the choice of what to eat and drink is no longer guaranteed as a result of this law. Prior to the legislation, issues of halal certifcation were mainly left to MUI, and LPPOM—an MUI special body—was established to regulate this. Since MUI is an Islamic civil society organisation, its halal certification was not obligatory, and while the public was encouraged to consider its importance the state did not interfere with personal choice. Shariatisation was imposed through MUI, but at the societal and cultural level. Today, under the Jokowi administration, the state regulates all matters related to halal products, and State Law No. 33/2014 can be taken as a example of structural shariatisation.

The implementation of sharia as public morality and order has become particularly effective. MUI fatwas remains the main reference for the state in dealing with religious issues, and the National Police and state apparatus still approach MUI on questions of the Ahmadiyah, LGBT issues, and many others. MUI's position on deviant and minority groups such as the Ahmadiyah, Shīʿa, local religions, and other non-mainstream religious groups has not decreased in intensity. Many Ahmadi mosques, for example, remain closed by the surrounding Muslim communities.[126] Ahmadis who were displaced from their village in 2006 remain in refugee areas in Transito in Lombok, and the current government has done nothing to change this.[127] The Ahmadi community suffered another serious attack at the hands of local mainstream Muslims in

125 Fahmi Ali Hidaefi and Irwandi Jaswir, "Halal Governance in Indonesia:Theory, Current Practices and Related Issues," *Journal of Islamic Monetary Economics and Finance* 5, no. 1 (2019): 89–116.

126 "Bupati Garut Rudy Gunawan Pasang Badan Hentikan Pembangunan Masjid Ahmadiyah," *Pikiran Rakyat*, 7 May 2021, https://www.pikiran-rakyat.com/jawa-barat/pr-011884460/bupati-garut-rudy-gunawan-pasang-badan-hentikan-pembangunan-masjid-ahmadiyah, viewed on 22 July 2022.

127 "5 Fakta Relokasi Warga Ahmadiyah di Lombok Timur, Dianggap Tak Mau Berbaur hingga Rindu Kampung Halaman," *Kompas*, 18 June 2019, https://regional.kompas.com/read/2019/06/18/17183491/5-fakta-relokasi-warga-ahmadiyah-di-lombok-timur-dianggap-tak-mau-berbaur?page=all, viewed on 22 July 2022.

Lombok Timur on 19 and 20 May 2018.[128] The role of the government in protecting the Shi'a community from marginalisation is also unclear, and intimidation of the Shi'a community continues in areas such as Solo.[129] Some local minority beliefs are also still the target of attacks. Sunda Wiwitan believers in Kuningan, West Java, for instance, are still denied their access to their basic rights as citizens, being denied identity cards, and are often intimidated both by mainstream Islamic organisations such as MUI and FPI and by Satpol PP (Satuan Polisi Polisi Pamong Praja, the Public Order Enforcement).[130] In this situation, the local government itself obstructs believers from performing their religious rights.

Several crucial issues relating to Christian minority groups have also persisted. Jokowi's government remains silent on the long-disputed issue of building churches, such as the case of Gereja Yasmin in Bogor, and nothing has been done to provide them with protection. Around thirty-two churches were closed in the first term of the Jokowi administration.[131]

Jokowi's policy on the sharia economy is a particuarly clear illustration of the new administration's contribution to shariatisation. Approaching his second term, on 14 May 2019, Jokowi inaugurated *The Indonesian Masterplan for the Sharia Economy 2019–2024*.[132] The Indonesian Ministry of National Development Planning prepared the *Masterplan* in the president's first term, with the objective of providing "a joint guidance in developing the Islamic economy in Indonesia in order to contribute more to the welfare of the Indonesian people."[133] The plan targets four key issues: "(1) Strengthening the Halal Value

128 "Mataram enggan menambah pengungsi Ahmadiyah," *Antara News*, 25 June 2019, https://www.antaranews.com/berita/926536/mataram-enggan-menambah-pengungsi-ahmadiyah, viewed on 22 July 2022.

129 "Merunut Penyerangan Kelompok Intoleran di Solo & Diskriminasi Syiah," *Tirto*, 11 August 2020, https://tirto.id/merunut-penyerangan-kelompok-intoleran-di-solo-diskriminasi-syiah-fWY2, viewed on 22 July 2022.

130 "Sunda Wiwitan: Pembangunan makam dilarang karena 'khawatir musyrik', masyarakat adat keluhkan 'diskriminasi di rumah sendiri,'" *BBC News*, 23 July 2020, https://www.bbc.com/indonesia/indonesia-53505078, viewed on 22 July 2022.

131 "Ada 32 Gereja Ditutup Sepanjang 5 tahun, Jokowi Ke Mana?" *Tirto*, 20 February 2019, https://tirto.id/ada-32-gereja-ditutup-sepanjang-5-tahun-jokowi-ke-mana-dhkD, viewed on 22 July 2022.

132 "Punya Penduduk Muslim Terbesar, Presiden Jokowi: Saatnya Bangkitkan Potensi Ekonomi Syariah," Sekretariat Kabinet Republik Indonesia, 14 May 2019, https://setkab.go.id/punya-penduduk-muslim-terbesar-presiden-jokowi-saatnya-bangkitkan-potensi-ekonomi-syariah/, viewed on 22 July 2022.

133 Indonesian Ministry of National Development Planning, *The Indonesia Masterplan of Sharia Economy 2019–2024* (Jakarta: Indonesian Ministry of National Development Planning, 2019), xv.

Chain, which consists of the halal food and beverage industry, halal tourism industry, Muslim fashion industry, halal media and recreation industry, halal pharmaceutical and cosmetics industry and renewable energy industry; (2) Strengthening Islamic Finance; (3) Strengthening Micro, Small and Medium Enterprises (MSMEs); and (4) Strengthening the Digital Economy."[134] This makes Jokowi's commitment to the development of shariatisation very clear. When launching the *Masterplan*, Jokowi stated that the potential of the sharia economy was US$23 billion in 2023, and BSI (Bank Syariah Indonesia, the Indonesian Sharia Bank) should strategise to become an important player in this economic development.[135] His support for the sharia economy is also visible in the formulation of the executive management known as the Komite Nasional Keuangan Syariah (KNKS, National Committee of Sharia Finance) whose main task is to oversee the implementation of the *Masterplan*. The president appears certain that, following the Masterplan, Indonesia can become the hub of the global sharia economy; as a result, it is hardly possible to doubt his commitment to the development of shariatisation.

Jokowi has also consolidated the permission of senior members of his staff in economic initiatives related to shariatisation: Erick Thohir, Indonesia's Minister of State Enterprises, for example, is also Chairman of Masyarakat Ekonomi Syariah (the Sharia Economic Society, MES). MES is part of the historical culmination of Indonesia's sharia economy, which includes the ideological dimension of an alternative economic system. Amin, as vice-president and also one of the leading figures behind the sharia economy, also endorses Thohir's leadership of MES, and has stated that his appointment was based on his own merits.[136] Other ministers and senior staff in the Jokowi administration are also involved in the shariatisation of the national economy, and a number of them are MES members.

Another clear example of Jokowi's commitment to the sharia economy is the establishment of Bank Syariah Indonesia (the Indonesian Sharia Bank, or BSI). BSI is a merger of various state-owned sharia banks, namely Bank Syariah Mandiri, (BSM, the Sharia Mandiri Bank), Bank BNI Syariah (BNIS, the Sharia Indonesian State Bank), and Bank BRI Syariah (BRIS, the Sharia Indonesian People's Bank). None of these sharia banks significantly increased the proportion of sharia banking compared to conventional banks, with only 4.61% of the

134 Indonesian Ministry of National Development Planning, xv.

135 "Punya Penduduk Muslim Terbesar, Presiden Jokowi," Sekretariat Kabinet Republik Indonesia, 14 May 2019.

136 "Congrats! Erick Thohir Jadi Ketum Masyarakat Ekonomi Syariah," Detik Finance, 23 January 2021, https://finance.detik.com/berita-ekonomi-bisnis/d-5346139/congrats-erick-thohir-jadi-ketum-masyarakat-ekonomi-syariah, viewed on 22 July 2022.

market share in banking overall.[137] Without Jokowi's intervention, BSI would never have opened; this is due to the failure of the national sharia bank, Bank Muamalah Indonesia (BMI, the Indonesia Muamalah Bank). The BMI was a pioneer of national sharia banking established in 1990s, but was declared bankrupt during Jokowi's presidency; it remains open to new investment, but at the time of writing its future is unclear. Jokowi's endorsement of BSI was therefore a courageous move, showing his belief that sharia banking can transform the stagnant economy. In his speech at the opening of BSI, he emphasised five points. First, BSI should become an inclusive and universal bank, open to all clients regardless of their background. Second, it should use digital technology in order to establish a broader client base. Third, it should be able to attract millenials, who form around a quarter of Indonesia's population. Fourth, it should develop competitive sharia financial products. Fifth, it should become a barometer for the development of the sharia industry in Indonesia.[138] The important remaining question, however, is how to combine the strict principles of sharia banking with the principles of the mainstream financial system.

7.4.4 *Halal Certification for Covid-19 Vaccines*

On 3 March 2020, Indonesia declared its first case of Covid-19. As the pandemic spread, MUI issued a number of related fatwas. Among its fatwas on Covid-19, the most influential concerns the Sinovac vaccine. The government initially planned to buy vaccines from China, particularly Sinovac, as well as from other countries, but MUI's fatwa stated that the vaccination programmeme could not go forward without a fatwa to certify the halal status of the vaccine. Both Amin and Jokowi supported this fatwa, and stated that the vaccination programmeme would wait for a fatwa from MUI as well as health clearance from BPOM (the National Agency of Drug and Food Control). Nadhlatul Ulama took a different position on the matter, however, and its general chairman, Siradj, stated that he disagreed with MUI and considered the vaccine to be lawful even without halal certification, given the emergency situation. Even so, Jokowi chose to wait for the MUI fatwa on the vaccine, recognising it as part of his policy—perhaps because he feared creating any form of controversy that could decrease his popularity.[139] Fortunately, after studying all the ingredients

137 "Sejarah Perbankan Syariah," Otoritas Jasa Keuangan, https://www.ojk.go.id/id/kanal/syariah/tentang-syariah/Pages/Sejarah-Perbankan-Syariah.aspx, viewed on 22 July 2022.

138 "Lima Pesan Jokowi untuk BSI yang Beroperasi Hari Ini," Republika, 24 July 2021, https://republika.co.id/berita/qnucyv370/lima-pesan-jokowi-untuk-bsi-yang-beroperasi-hari-ini, viewed on 22 July 2022.

139 "Presiden: Vaksinasi Menunggu Izin Penggunaan Darurat BPOM dan Fatwa MUI," Presiden Republik Indonesia, 8 January 2021, https://www.presidenri.go.id/siaran-pers

used for the development of the vaccine and finding them to be halal, MUI issued the fatwa permitting the use of Sinovac on 8 January 2021, stating that it was pure (*suci*) and permissible.[140] BPOM also authorised the vaccine, and President Jokowi became the first person to be vaccinated with Sinovac.

Problems regarding the halal nature of the Covid-19 vaccine arose in the case of the AstraZeneca variant, however. The Indonesian government agreed to buy fifty million doses of the AstraZeneca vaccine, produced in collaboration between AstraZeneca and the University of Oxford, in December 2020. MUI's researchers investigated the ingredients that had gone into the vaccine and found that it included trypsin, a pork enzyme; they were therefore confident that it was contained a non-halal element. The AstraZeneca company refuted this finding, asserting that no pork derivatives had been used in making the vaccine.[141] Nevertheless, on the basis of this investigation, MUI issued a fatwa banning AstraZeneca. Cholil Nafis (Chairman of MUI in the field of *dakwa,* or propagation, issues) clarified that the non-halal status of AstraZeneca does not mean that this vaccine cannot be used, and that it is permitted in an emergency situation.[142]

The fatwa against AstraZeneca was not universally accepted among Muslim organisations, and NU issued a critical response. Marzuki Mustamar (the chairman of the East Java provincial branch) stated that the vaccine was indeed halal, despite the possible use of a pork enzyme during its production.[143] The reasoning behind this statement was not that it was an emergency situation (*ḍarūra*), as mentioned in the MUI fatwa, but because the pork enzyme had been transformed during the process of making the vaccine and the final product was halal. The East Java provincial branch of MUI, interestingly, also had a different legal opinion on the issue: Ma'ruf Khozin, its chairman, argued that

/presiden-vaksinasi-menunggu-izin-penggunaan-darurat-bpom-dan-fatwa-mui/, viewed on 22 July 2022.

140 "Akhirnya, MUI Pastikan Vaksin Corona Sinovac Suci dan Halal," Detik Health, 9 January 2021, https://health.detik.com/berita-detikhealth/d-5326767/akhirnya-mui-pastikan-vaksin-corona-sinovac-suci-dan-halal, viewed on 22 July 2022.

141 "Kata Kemenkes Soal Tripsin Babi dalam Vaksin AstraZeneca," DW, 24 March 2021, https://www.dw.com/id/kata-pemerintah-soal-tripsin-babi-dalam-vaksin-astrazeneca/a-56966950, viewed on 22 July 2022.

142 "Polemik Halal Haram Vaksin Astra Zeneca, MUI: Tidak Bisa Dihalalkan, Boleh Dipakai karena Darurat," Tribun News, 25 March 2021, https://www.tribunnews.com/corona/2021/03/25/polemik-halal-haram-vaksin-astra-zeneca-mui-tidak-bisa-dihalalkan-boleh-dipakai-karena-darurat, viewed on 22 July 2022.

143 "PWNU Jatim Sebut Vaksin AstraZeneca Suci dan Halal, Ini Alasannya ..." Kompas, 22 March 2021, https://surabaya.kompas.com/read/2021/03/22/154519378/pwnu-jatim-sebut-vaksin-astrazeneca-suci-dan-halal-ini-alasannya?page=all, viewed on 22 July 2022.

the halalness of AstraZeneca was not due to ḍarūra (the emergency situation) but to *istaḥala*, which means that impure things can be changed to pure ones either by themselves or through an external process. This position was thus closer to that of East Java NU than to the central board of MUI.

Learning from the cases of the Sinovac and AstraZeneca vaccines, it becomes clear that legal opinions on halal can be divided. MUI has a stronger legal standing than other Muslim organisations, as its fatwa on halal standards has become part of State Law No. 33/2014 on Halal Product Assurance. Yet its standards are based on the Shāfiʿī school of Islamic law, which is by no means the only approach. It would therefore be recommended that the Indonesian government should provide space for alternative understandings of theology, rather than promoting the Shāfiʿī school alone. Muslim citizens, communities and organisations should have the right to decide for themselves which orientation to follow, rather than limiting understanding to a single path.

7.5 Conclusion

While MUI is not a political party, it considers electoral politics to be an important issue and has shown increasing influence during Jokowi's presidency. The organisation's alignment with politicians and parties who are committed to implementing sharia contributes to the increasing polarisation of Indonesian Muslims, many of whom take MUI as their main point of reference in religious, social, and political life. When the organisation becomes involved in the political battlefield of the general elections, it has a strong influence on these voters.

Electoral politics and identity politics have both become important factors in contributing to the Islamic agenda in Indonesia, including shariatisation. More Muslims have begun to support the idea of state that incorporates sharia into legislation and public life, imagining an NKRI *bersyariah* (the sharia implementation based on the Unitary State of Indonesian Republic) as the future model of the Indonesian state. This term has become a unifying force for the various and diverse Islamist movements in Indonesia. Even Salafi-Wahhabi groups, who are usually reticent to take part in practical politics, lent their direct support to the Prabowo-Sandi campaign in 2019. These Islamist groups all agree that the election provided them with an opportunity to push their agenda on the national stage.

The question of how to instrumentalise the concept of the *umma* will play a critical role in the future development of Indonesian Islam. MUI has an important voice on this issue, but is no longer the sole organisation claiming to represent the interests of the *umma*; other groups arising from identity politics and populist movements, such as the ABI 212 Movement, are attracting increasing support. MUI faces a choice: to draw closer to the ruling regime and provide it with political legitimacy, as it did during the Suharto period, or to focus on the *umma*—even when this means opposing the government.

The use of populist issues for the goal of shariatisation seems likely to become particularly effective in Indonesian politics going forward. For several years, MUI has attempted to use the narrative of social, political and economic injustice to attract sympathy from the *umma*. Interestingly, this new populism is not just focused on the lowest classes in society, but increasingly on middle-class Muslims. As this segment of the population grows and wields more influence, it will further strengthen the use of populist shariatisation in Indonesia.

Jokowi has become the only Indonesian president to make a significant contribution to the shariatisation of public life. Since Amin became vice-president, Jokowi's role in the shariatisation of the economy has grown particularly visible. This may be because the sharia economy can also be understood as a normal economic phenomenon, and a state project to be promoted for the sake of economic advancement. A second explanation is the president's new alignment with Muslim figures such as Amin. In either case, the continued development of the sharia economy remains highly dependent on the support of the ruling regime.

CHAPTER 8

Concluding Reflections

MUI's approach to activism and discourse, through its fatwa and other Islamic recommendations, is widely assumed to be aimed at supporting the process of shariatisation in Indonesia. How successful has the organisation been in achieving its goals in the context of current Indonesian state-society dynamics? The answer is based the discourse and practice of MUI surrounding the establishment of sharia in the legal and public spheres. The role of the Fatwa Commission, the Law and Legislation Commission, the DSN and LPPOM, all discussed in Chapter 3, are examples of MUI's soft stance in regard to the implementation of sharia law. Its systematic mobilisation to establish a space for sharia in Indonesia is also evident in the way the organisation consciously employs political, cultural, and legal means to help pave the way to a more Islamised Indonesia, as detailed in Chapter 4. The findings of this book reveal that MUI's role in propagating sharia still takes place within the boundaries of Indonesia as a Pancasila state. Although many people may disagree with this statement, MUI has never stated that its agenda is to transform Indonesia into an Islamic state. Yet the paramount question concerns whether the inclusion of sharia in the legal and public spheres of Indonesia would be positive for the future of the country as a Pancasila state.[1]

Shariatisation has long manifested itself in the historical trajectory of Indonesia. MUI has been a vital part of this process since its establishment in 1975, and certainly in the decade following the advent of the reform era in 1998. Its drive to have sharia included in legislation and public life has increasingly prevailed, and it has clearly had a significant influence on the country's Islamisation. It should, however, be noted that MUI shariatisation efforts are multifaceted, and not only shaped by ideological and theological reasoning, but also by social, cultural and political influences. The complicated motivations and factors involved mean that any simple judgement on the role of MUI is problematic.

1 Budhy Munawar Rachman and Moh Shofan, *Argumen Islam Untuk Sekularisme* (Jakarta: Grasindo, 2010), pp. 22–4; Setara Institute, *Negara Harus Bersikap, Tiga Tahun Laporan Kondisi Kebebasan Beragama/Berkeyakinan Di Indonesia 2007–2009* (Jakarta: Setara Institute, 2010), p. 19; Suhadi Cholil et al., *Annual Report on Religious Life in Indonesia 2000* (Yogyakarta: Center for Religious and Cross-cultural Studies (CRCS) Graduate School Gadjah Mada University, 2009).

DOI:10.1163/9789004534896_009

•••

Although it has been integrated to some extent through the procedural path of democracy—public hearings, consultations, election campaigns, and legislation—shariatisation, namely the incorporation of sharia into the legal norms and practices of Indonesia, is generally understood as a pre-condition for the formation of an Islamic state. Yet MUI's goal is no longer the high ambition of establishing an Islamic state in Indonesia but rather a shift of focus to embedding sharia in the legal and public sphere. This follows several unsuccessful efforts by the Islamic parties—PPP, PKS, PAN, PBB—in advocating for the incorporation of sharia into the Indonesian Constitution in 2002.[2] Since then, almost none of the Islamic political parties continue to strive for a sharia-based state, and the strategy of shariatisation has shifted from the political to the cultural sphere. Islamic organisations, like MUI, have decided not to get involved in the day-to-day politics of Indonesia. For MUI, the clear limits of its shariatisation agenda are found in the framework of the Pancasila state. However, it should be said here that wrestling with sharia as the source of inspiration for drafting state law is procedurally constitutional and legitimate in the context of Indonesia's legal system, as far as it is agreed by lawmakers. These circumstances strengthen MUI's influence in enhancing shariatisation as recognised through its role as fatwa-giver on issues of deviant sects, halal certification, sharia banking and many important other issues.

This book has outlined how the nuances of MUI shariatisation are interwoven with various aspects from the domains of theology and culture to those of politics and, more importantly, law. The intensity of shariatisation also varies according to the underpinning concepts, opportunities, and movement models. It can be concluded there are two models of shariatisation: first, pre-emptive shariatisation for building a sharia-adopting state through the incorporation of Islamic legal norms into the national legal system and second, responsive shariatisation that is designed to respond to external issues at the national, transnational and global level as a means of expressing Islamic identity, exemplified when MUI talks about international human rights and religious freedom. The former is more strategic, and the latter is more volatile and also short-term oriented.

MUI's brand of shariatisation combines and internalises several tendencies of sharia orders with the Indonesian local context: the legal system, politics,

2 Luthfi Assyaukanie, *Islam and the Secular State in Indonesia* (Singapore: ISEAS, 2009), p. 189; Robert Pringle, *Understanding Islam in Indonesia: Politics and Diversity* (Singapore: Editions Didier Millet, 2010), p. 70.

and cultural structure of Indonesian society. The lack of influence of transnational Islamic organisations is also evident in MUI's fatwa and recommendations that scarcely refer to sharia discourses promulgated by ideologues and thinkers of the Muslim Brotherhood, Salafi groups, or Hizb ut-Tahrir. To avoid complicated restraints, MUI favours the typical model of "Indonesian shariatisation" that affirms Bayat's assertion of "Islamisation without an Islamic state" or the situation of post-Islamism[3] that favours both the penetration of the norms of sharia and the piety of Indonesian Muslims. In this way MUI has transcended formal political Islam whilst maintaining the essence of sharia.

The deliberate shift of MUI, especially with regard to the concept of the nation-state through the change in its ideological basis from Pancasila to Islam in 2000, therefore has two important meanings: first, to re-interpret the meaning of the first Pancasila principle "Belief in One God" as the expression of sharia norms and second, to demonstrate its genuine institutional characteristics in contrast to previous struggles that had focused on the inclusion of sharia in the national law as a means to change the state political system. Public discourses, official documents, and other related MUI publications are clear that the Unitary State of the Indonesian Republic or NKRI is final and there is no room for discussing and accommodating the establishment of an Islamic state in Indonesia. However, MUI believes that the inclusion of sharia into the existing state law of Indonesia is still possible, provided it is completed through a democratic process and based on a national consensus not opposed to the NKRI concept. Although MUI's methods for instigating sharia norms into the legal system of Indonesia are procedurally tolerable, this does not mean that the consequences are not problematic. Crucial issues remain and are evident. This can be seen, for instance, in some forms of discrimination and violence towards minority groups and women caused by the enactment of fatwa-influenced legislation, such as the publication of the joint decree of three state agencies—the Ministry of Religious Affairs, the Ministry of Home Affairs and the Attorney General—that limit the role of Indonesian Ahmadis, the Health Minister's Decree supporting the practice of female circumcision, and many others. In the modern concept of a nation-state, the state is prohibited from discriminating against its citizens on the basis of faith and religious affiliation.

•••

3 Asef Bayat, *Making Islam Democratic: Social Movements and the Post-Islamist Turn* (Redwood City, CA: Stanford University Press, 2007), p. 147; Asef Bayat, *Life as Politics: How Ordinary People Change the Middle East* (Amsterdam: Amsterdam University Press, 2010).

MUI's vigour in targeting the legal discourse and practice of Indonesia as one of its priorities for shariatisation is compelled by the fact that within a democratic state polity the legal system is the key forum for changing the circumstances of the state. MUI is fully conscious of this and aware that infusing the legal system of Indonesia with sharia norms, either explicitly or implicitly, would effectively enhance and evoke the process of shariatisation of Indonesia, no matter what the country's state form. Using Clifford Geertz's analysis, MUI's inclination to insert sharia into the law of Indonesia affirms that the legal arena is the necessary space to be contested as the "fabric of cultural and symbols" of sharia.[4] Hence monopolising the legal arena with the codes and symbols of sharia is a stepping-stone towards a deeper shariatisation. This makes sense because the discourse and practice of Indonesia's legal system are not based on a single source but originate from various legal systems, and sharia, as the "law" of the majority, is one important element.

The importance of the legal sphere for MUI has been indicated by its attempts to influence the national legislation of Indonesia. For many years, MUI has prioritised legislation within its programme and agenda, in addition to also engaging in discussions to formulate systematic discourse and activism to respond to and influence the process of national legislation of specific issues related to MUI's interests. This focus has long been rooted in the tradition of MUI, but since the reform era, when MUI established the Commission of Law and Legislation, the intensity of proposing draft laws has increased. Another MUI commission that deals with the process of legislation is the Fatwa Commission. In previous years MUI has pressured Indonesian lawmakers to approve the draft law on Pornography, to revise Act No. 38/1999 on Islamic Almsgiving Management and Act No. 32/1992 on Health, and so forth.[5] Furthermore, MUI is also very active in supporting the legislation of regional governments on the implementation of shariatisation, called *perda syariah* (sharia-based local regulation).

MUI's agenda with regard to national legislation is illuminated by its five categories of fatwa and recommendations: belief (*ʿaqīda*), worship, social and cultural, halal, and sharia economic issues. As previously described here, the issue of belief has become the vehicle for MUI's attempts at shariatisation. MUI has used its Sunnī faith as a prism to police the beliefs of others, categorised as untrue and not in accordance with the fundamental underpinnings

4 Clifford Geertz, *Local Knowledge: Further Essays in Interpretive Anthropology* (New York: Basic Books, 1983); Cf. Gay Bechor, *The Sanhuri Code and the Emergence of Modern Arab Civil Law (1932–1949)* (Leiden & Boston: Brill, 2007), p. 6.

5 MUI, *Himpunan Fatwa MUI Sejak 1975*, 2011, pp. 861–2.

of Islam, by labelling them as deviant. For MUI, protecting the *ʿaqīda* of mainstream Muslim is non-negotiable because it is an immutable aspect of Islam. However, the struggle of groups against MUI fatwa that label them deviant will continue as long as these groups insist that their faith is part of Islam. The legal discourse of religious freedom will therefore continue to be an important contested arena.

The logic behind MUI's concept on belief is that the dominant Sunnī Islam tradition of Indonesia needs to be defended because the majority of Indonesian Muslims are Sunnī adherents. This argument is reminiscent of that used by medieval Christians in opposing pagan religions, when those with different beliefs who were denounced as deviant. MUI will never shift from its position that the religious rights of Sunnī Muslims are violated by the presence of Ahmadiyah, Shīʿa and other so-called heretical groups, and that they should therefore be banned from Indonesia. An alternative discourse on this matter has been proposed by some, such as Mahfud MD, the former chief judge of Indonesia's Constitutional Court, who said that only God has the right to judge whether a group is heretical or not. He also stated that Indonesia's Constitution does not allow one group to be excluded because their beliefs differ from mainstream beliefs.[6] Nevertheless it is the MUI discourse, favouring one kind of Islam for all Indonesian Muslims, that remains paramount in society. In the 1945 Constitution, there is no mention of MUI being an official part of Indonesian government institutions. The Attorney General may allow a fatwa request to MUI, but MUI's answer cannot be used as a rationale for policy-making.

To some extent the state apparatus has downgraded the Constitution to accommodate pressure from the MUI, as can be seen in the case of Ahmadiyah and other so-called deviant groups. MUI's pressure on the state apparatus is not wrong, but the Indonesian state should be fair and impartial.[7] There are two reasons why the MUI fatwa on deviant groups should not be referred to by the state: firstly, the use of the MUI fatwa as the basis for enacting a law could be deemed as a violation of constitutionally guaranteed freedom of faith and belief, and secondly, imposing the beliefs of one religious group upon other religious groups conflicts with the notion of state neutrality. Masʾudi, for instance has argued that all religions of Indonesia, regardless of their political

6 I have heard this statement several times in his lectures and media statements. The last that I had the chance to attend was on "Pluralism *vs* Intolerance: A Constitutional and Legal Review in Indonesia," held by the Centre for Democratic Institutions, Australian National University, Canberra, on 26 November 2012.

7 Masdar F. Mas'udi, *Syarah Konstitusi UUD 1945 Dalam Perspektif Islam* (Jakarta: Alvabet, 2010), pp. 156–7.

party or ethnicity, have to be treated equally before the law.[8] MUI responds that its mandate is to guard the purity of Islamic belief because this should be the most protected domain in Islam and part of commanding right and forbidding wrong (*al-amr bi al-maʿrūf wa al-nahy ʿan al-munkar*).

With regard to sharia economy, MUI has waited since 2009 for a more definite agenda following the enactment of Act No. 21/2008 on sharia banking. However, now that authorisation has been given to MUI, the DSN (Dewan Syariah Nasional, National Sharia Board) is now the most authoritative legal entity together with the Central Bank of Indonesia that regulates the operation of sharia banks and sharia financial institutions. Concerning halal certification, MUI's final position is contingent on State Law No 33/2014 Halal Product Assurance. MUI is also critical of the draft laws that they have judged as being against sharia.[9] Besides monitoring draft laws, MUI also attempts to influence the judicial reviews and revisions of some existing acts, which MUI considers to be against the spirit of sharia. In short, MUI activities in legal discourse and practice will continue for the foreseeable future.

•••

MUI is quite astute in narrating the importance of having a sharia-inspired state law at both the national and regional level of Indonesia through a depiction of sharia as the remedy to cure the national illness. What is meant by the "national illness" here is the multi-crises Indonesia experienced—especially moral, political and legal crises—leading up to and after the resignation of Suharto. Like other sharia propagators in many different Islamic countries, MUI also instrumentalises this discourse as an inspiring source for campaigning for the institutionalisation of God's law in Indonesia. In Egypt's experience, the codification of sharia law promoted by ʿAbd al-Razzāq al-Sanhūrī (d. 1971), for instance, also used the narrative of the sickness in Egyptian society.[10] Sharia was considered the remedy for Egypt, which had based its national legislation on the French legal code.[11] MUI and other Muslim groups perceive the economic and political decay of Indonesia as a form of social and ethical illness. According to this view, the deterioration in Indonesia's economy and politics during the early reform era was caused by the

8 Ibid.

9 This criticism was published by MUI in the Ulama Consensus Meeting on 1 July 2012.

10 Gay Bechor, *The Sanhuri Code and the Emergence of Modern Arab Civil Law (1932–1949)* (Leiden & Boston: Brill, 2007), p. 24. Bechor states that Ṭahā Husein wrote an article titled "Egypt is Sick."

11 Ibid, p. 32.

implementation of "different systems" borrowed from non-Islamic countries, especially the West. Hence the established economic and political apparatus should be revisited and revised through a new system, closer to the dominant moral and religious values of Indonesia, namely Islam. According to this diagnosis, injecting the norms of sharia into the state of Indonesia is understood by MUI as an apt remedy to cure the sickness. However, it should be noted here that this is merely MUI's starting point in its pragmatic approach in implementing sharia. In this situation, the motivation for shariatisation does not merely rely on the ideology of having a sharia-based state, but rather stems from finding a solution to the real problems of Indonesian society.[12]

MUI's pragmatic approach to implementing sharia is also evident from the way it differs from conventional methods of enforcing independent legislation of sharia. Since its establishment in 1975 until the present, MUI has never proposed an independent codification of Islamic criminal justice law, unlike the MMI and the HTI,[13] even when the fundamental MUI ideology shifted from Pancasila to Islam. What has been done by MUI to avoid a total confrontation between sharia and national non-religious based law is relevant to what Hashim Kamali portrays as the harmonisation of sharia with the existing legal system of the state.[14] The preference for pragmatic sharia shows that the shariatisation promoted by MUI is more compatible with democracy. This is also the case with the shariatisation approach on matters of the economy and the halalisation of products and commodities.

Besides the importance of domestic factors, the pragmatic argument for shariatisation is also strengthened by the flow of globalisation and transnational Islamism. In response to globalisation, the sharia-inspired legal order has emerged to establish a clear distinction—on the basis of their personal and collective identity and experience as Muslims—between sharia law and Western law. As a response to transnational Islamic movements, the intermingling of state law and sharia is the way that Indonesian Muslims can identify themselves as members of worldwide transnational Islamist movements that want to implement sharia, even it is based on Indonesian Islam. This is evident

12 Ramond William Baker, *Islam Without Fear, Egypt and the New Islamist* (Cambridge: Harvard University Press, 2003), p. 112.

13 Tim Lindsey and Jeremy Kingsley, "Talking in Code: Legal Islamisation in Indonesia and the MMI Shari'a Criminal Code," in *The Law Applied: Contextualizing the Islamic Shari'a: A Volume in Honor of Frank E. Vogel*, ed. Peri J. Bearman, Wolfhart Heinrichs, and Bernard G. Weiss (London & New York: I.B. Tauris, 2008), 295–320.

14 Mohammad Hashim Kamali, "Sharʿīah and Civil Law: Towards a Methodology of Harmonization," *Islamic Law and Society* (*Koninklijke Brill NV*) 14, no. 3 (2007): 391–420, p. 391.

from the MUI discourse in Indonesian legal debates when discussing draft legislation, a discourse that greatly resembled the discourse of Wahhabism[15] in particular and of the Salafi[16] movement in general. The Act on Pornography, the Joint Decree of the Three Ministers, the campaign for economic sharia, the Blasphemy Law, and the prohibition of cigarette smoking are some clear examples of this global and transnational trajectory.

MUI's pragmatic sharia approach not only indicates its stance on the various models of shariatisation, but also brings into question the Western theoretical assumption that implementation of sharia law is the prerequisite condition for the formation of a sharia political entity, and it is part of the medievalisation of Islam. Some dominant understandings of sharia in the West view it as a threat to democracy and the rule of the national state law. Jan Michiel Otto states that there are three reasons why sharia is perceived this way in the West: first, the immutability and binding nature of sharia norms for all Muslims; second, a prevalent shariatisation movement in many Islamic countries, which is indicated by the Islamisation of state law; and third, the norms of sharia are against democracy and human rights.[17]

To some degree, the findings of this book indicate a similar answer in the Indonesian context. Firstly, incorporating the norms of sharia into the state law of Indonesia can reduce the probability of the state becoming more radicalised. This is possible because sharia aspirations have been accommodated within the Indonesian legal system. Since 1998, the power of political Islam has increased, and sharia proponents aspire to replace the fundamental state ideology of Pancasila with sharia. MUI believes that the accommodation of sharia within the Pancasila-based nation-state cannot be rejected or refuted as it has a strong place within the historical and sociological context of Indonesia. Secondly, MUI's success in incorporating sharia into state law can be seen as a way of persuading sharia proponents not to force a change from a Pancasila state to sharia-based one. By accommodating sharia into the positive

15 Wahhabism is the Islamic ideology associated with the thoughts of Muḥammad b. ʿAbd al-Wahhāb, a puritan figure from Saudi Arabia. Natana DeLong-Bas, *Wahhabi Islam: From Revival and Reform to Global Jihad* (New York: I.B. Tauris, 2007).

16 Salafi is taken from the Arabic root *salaf*, meaning those who lived in the formative period of Islam, and now refers to a group who aim revitalise the values of the *salafi* generation as part of their political struggle. They aim to establish the sharia system precisely as it was implemented by the first generation of Muslims.

17 Jan Michiel Otto, *Sharia and National Law in Muslim Countries: Tensions and Opportunities for Dutch and EU Foreign Policy* (Amsterdam: Amsterdam University Press, 2008). pp. 5–6; Jan Michiel Otto, ed., *Sharia Incorporated: A Comparative Overview of the Legal Systems of Twelve Muslim Countries in Past and Present* (Amsterdam: Amsterdam University Press, 2010).

law of Indonesia, the issue of establishing a sharia-based state is no longer valid. Within the Pancasila state, sharia can be implemented without changing the form of state of Indonesia, as can be seen from state regulations on sharia banking, halal food certification, and others.

However, although some aspects of shariatisation at the practical level seem to run smoothly, problems emerge when shariatisation deals with Islamic belief that can result in democratic deficit. This is evident from some complex discourses on various state laws and the MUI fatwa on the position of Islamic deviant groups. There is a tendency for Indonesian legal rulings to consider sharia prescriptions more than the guarantees of religious freedom in the Indonesian Constitution. In fact, many Indonesian citizens, and minority groups in particular such as the Ahmadiyah, Shīʿa and also adherents of indigenous local beliefs and faiths, are treated unjustly and unfairly by the state's rulings. What they experience is legal and social discrimination because as the citizens of Indonesia their rights to practise their beliefs are guaranteed by the Constitution, yet these rights are restricted by laws of less standing than the Constitution. This reality confirms many studies that portray state law and sharia as products of two different and incompatible legal systems.[18] The state laws of most democratic countries grant full protection of religious freedom and remain neutral in the face of different co-existing religions and beliefs. However, sharia devalues the rights to freedom of religion, thought and conscience and tends to advocate the rule of God's law as the supreme legal order. However, the pragmatic nature of MUI shariatisation provides a different answer to that generalised in these studies.

•••

This book has also established that the most visible strength of MUI shariatisation since the beginning of the reform era is its capability to create an interplay between discourse and practice or between intent and action in the sharia that is propagated. Attempts to connect the discourse and practice of sharia had long been tried unsuccessfully during previous Indonesian shariatisation episodes, when the discourse and imagined practice of shariatisation was tied to a promise of total change of the state's system. Of course, this method was impossible to implement when the regime was politically and legally very strong in its commitment to the secular system of state ideology, as was Suharto's regime. MUI thus has taken the attitude that the sharia discourse suitable for implementation is one related to everyday life issues of Indonesian

18 Otto, *Sharia Incorporated*.

Muslims. The organisation has been relatively successful in integrating the theoretical aspect of sharia into implementation in the legal discourse and practice of Indonesia, such as respect for justice and human rights.

During the Suharto era, having issued fatwas and Islamic advice, MUI did not attempt to push them into the level of practice. Fatwa and recommendations were mostly addressed to those who were already interested, with no public campaign or persuasion. This strategy was chosen because the legal and political system of Indonesia in the Suharto era was very powerful and would therefore retaliate if MUI pushed for its discourse to be implemented. With a more open political situation and also relative MUI independence in the post-reform era, there has been a concerted effort to actualise fatwas and Islamic recommendations in the whole enterprise of shariatisation. In other words, post Suharto, MUI has been working not only at the discursive level, introducing fatwas and Islamic recommendations for the Muslim public, but also operating at the movement level, stipulating, persuading, and making dialogue and advocacy in Muslim communities to incorporate shariatisation into the practice of Indonesia. MUI engages in moving forward with people and Islamic organisations through discussion and looking for steps to implement its edicts through MUI's forums and general Muslim public forums. MUI is using this to open legal debates on the practice of shariatisation.

In a broader perspective, the intermingled discourse and practice within the process of MUI shariatisation transformed shared memory into the enduring Islamic political imagery of Muslim people connecting religion and the state (*al-dīn wa al-dawla*). Here, MUI has shown its ability to adapt this concept to the Indonesian context by framing and implementing the merger of sharia and the legal and political discourse of Indonesia through adjusting suitable fatwa and recommendations with suitable practice. MUI's ability to adjust its concepts on shariatisation on the one hand and the views of common Indonesian citizens, who disagree with the notion of total separation between religion and state, on the other has gained popular support for its project of shariatisation from the Muslim public. Nonetheless, there were also negative consequences from the implementation of sharia-inspired government rulings related to religious freedom, such as the MUI defence of the blasphemy law, which are very problematic. Generally speaking, following Madjid's popular statement, "Islam Yes, Islamic Parties No,"[19] the position of MUI has been "Sharia Yes, Sharia State No."

19 Azyumardi Azra, *Indonesia, Islam, and Democracy: Dynamics in a Global Context* (Jakarta: Equinox Publishing, 2006), p. 183; Ahmad Gaus, *Api Islam Nurcholish Madjid: Jalan Hidup Seorang Visioner* (Jakarta: Penerbit Buku Kompas, 2010), p. 94.

MUI's shariatisation integrates discourse and practice, while at the same time securing the position of the Indonesian state as a non-theocratic polity, as its answer to secular groups in Indonesia that doubt its commitment to the nation-state. However, to borrow the analysis of Craig Colhoun,[20] it is unavoidable that the shariatisation of Indonesia will end with a higher elevation of Islam in various issues, from private to public. Although shariatisation efforts remain under the aegis of the national state law, some MUI fatwa conflict with this, such as the current MUI's refutation of the Constitutional Court's decision that legalises the paternity identity of an out-of-wedlock child with MUI fatwa No. 10/2012 that only recognises the child's family ties with its mother.[21] In this case, from the perspective of social movement organisation theory, MUI's position is to situate the relevance of religion as an ideological language for the whole enterprise of shariatisation in Indonesia's formal law.[22] As the kernel of Islam, the discourse of sharia is an important instrument to win the hearts of the general Muslim population of Indonesia, but the advocacy of sharia as a replacement for the existing legal system of Indonesia is seen as a retrogressive movement.

•••

An interesting phenomenon regarding the process of shariatisation within the legal system and public sphere of Indonesia is MUI's dual direction in both forging the movement and also building the arguments to support it. The movement has been claimed to be a one-sided initiative, stemming from MUI and other Indonesian pro-sharia groups who put relentless pressure on the state. This is a common assumption among those who criticise MUI and its allies as ambitious actors behind the shariatisation of Indonesia. My findings indicate that this claim is not entirely valid, as a robust initiative towards shariatisation also arises from the state itself. It is true that MUI and its allies always exert a strong pressure on the state, but in some cases the state itself also seeks

20 Craig Coulhon, "Secularism, Citizenship and the Public Sphere," in *Rethinking Secularism*, ed. Craig Coulhon, Mark Juergensmeyer, and Jonathan VanAnwerpen (Oxford & New York: Oxford University Press, 2011), 75–92, p. 75.

21 "MUI Ajak Ormas Islam Tolak Putusan MK", Hidayatullah, 17 March 2012, https://hidayatullah.com/berita/nasional/read/2012/03/17/57632/mui-ajak-ormas-islam-tolak-putusan-mk.html, viewed on 22 July 2022.

22 Rhys H. Williams, "From the 'Beloved Community' to 'Family Values': Religious Language, Symbolic Repertoires, and Democratic Cultures," in *Social Movements, Identity, Culture, and the State*, ed. David S. Meyer, Nancy Whittier, and Belinda Robnet (Oxford & New York: Oxford University Press, 2002), 247–65, p. 249.

religious legitimacy from MUI for governing matters that involve the affairs of Muslims. In fact, the tradition of requesting a fatwa from MUI began in the Suharto era. Here, the MUI fatwa not only functioned as guidance, but also as a legal source for drafting regulatory rules. The Attorney General, in addition, requests many fatwas from MUI when it comes to policing beliefs that might need an imprimatur.

More vibrant shariatisation discourse in the public sphere in the last decade has indicated the increased confidence and bargaining position of MUI *vis-à-vis* the state apparatus. So much so that even President Yudoyono has often stated that MUI is the most credible fatwa body of Indonesia. In addition, concerning matters of Islamic belief, Yudoyono preferred to receive fatwa from MUI than the fatwa bodies of other Islamic organisations such as NU, Muhammadiyah or Persatuan Islam. The Ministry of Women's Empowerment also requested a fatwa on the legal validity of female circumcision in response to the circular issued by the Ministry of Health about the recommendation for national hospitals and medical doctors to end the practice. The endorsement of the state for MUI's role in Islamic matters is evident in the establishment of the DSN and LPPOM. The DSN gained significant authority from the act on granting halal certificates for the establishment of sharia banks and sharia financial institutions, which includes supervising the financial activity and products and recruiting board members for sharia banks and financial institutions in Indonesia. On Islamic economic issues, Indonesian banks and others must consider the DSN fatwas on issues related to sharia banking and financial issues. MUI is still responsible for drawing up halal fatwa certification for foods, drinks, medicines and cosmetics under State Law No 33/2014. The outreach of these two MUI organisational bodies indicates the real picture of sharia implementation. Here MUI and the state share a mutual need in the process of shariatisation. In this regard, MUI seems to have known how to play its role as an indispensible Islamic contact for the state.

The second matter is related to the way MUI composes its arguments for shariatisation. For the purposes of shariatisation MUI has developed two standards in developing its discourse: secular and religious arguments. Secular arguments are used to strengthen the sharia argument. This can be seen in MUI fatwas that borrow the arguments of international democracy—civil, political and human rights—not to affirm the implementation of those discourses, but to defend the sharia. When responding to the prevalent persecution of the Ahmadiyah and also other deviant Islamic groups, such as the Lia Eden, Shīʿa, and other religious minorities, MUI employs the narratives of human rights to state that the Ahmadiyah and other heretical groups do not respect the religious freedom of Islam because they have broken the established consensus of mainstream Muslim groups on belief. When MUI talks about halal certification, it says that Muslim people in Indonesia have the right to protect what they consume from the pollution of impurity. What they talk about heretical groups, MUI argues that the religious rights of the majority must be considered and therefore any religious notion that deviates from the belief system of the mainstream has to be subdued. It does not consider the rights of minority groups. In this context, the discourse of human rights is pragmatically used to protect their own rights, an interpretation of human rights that does not accord with the core values of the international declaration on human rights.

•••

The system of legal pluralism used in Indonesia provides a chance for MUI to deepen the shariatisation process. It paves the way for the emergence of conflicting ingredients of the national legal system that result in the need for an alternative legal system. MUI has instrumentalised this circumstance to come up with more ideas to promote sharia as part of Indonesian law, which is against the objective of having a legally pluralistic system that includes norms, regulations, and institutions built by the society to ensure the national stability of law.[23] The state of Indonesia, with many laws originating in Islamic, colonial, customary, and tribal systems, is an actual example of such pluralism. To some extent, the presence of MUI can be said to be an indicator of legal pluralism in the context of its support of sharia for enriching Indonesia's national legal system. However, as a nation-state, Indonesia is limited in the extent it can accommodate the absorption of such a religion-based system into the national legal system. Here, inclusive and fair negotiation among the actors of various legal orders must play a role while this process should refer to the national law of Indonesia and universal human rights. The existence and implementation of more than one legal system in a single country, with all its ramifications, hampers the state's ability to mediate the diversity of legal orders.

The spirit of the reform era has yet to provide Indonesian lawmakers with a framework of legal pluralism that can adopt, limit, manage and harmonise the infiltration of sharia or other legal systems into the state law of Indonesia. The state's political reform, which began in 1998, was not accompanied by a significant legal reform, and thus caused the state law of Indonesia to fall into disarray. The phenomenon of conflicting legal orders and systems from the higher to the lower or from the lower to the higher strata of state law is a

23 The International Council on Human Rights Policy, *When Legal Worlds Overlap: Human Rights, State and Non-State Law* (Switzerland: ICHRP, 2009), p. 3.

clear example of this issue. President Wahid (1999–2001), for example, estimated that more than 3000 Indonesian rulings conflicted with each other. For instance, the most prominent cases are the conflicts between regional regulations and the national state law. Indonesia issued Acts on Regional Autonomy (1999 and 2004) authorising regional governments at the provincial and district levels to draft their own laws, except for the five domains regulated by the central government: religion, defence, security, fiscal matters, and foreign affairs. Shariatisation comes into play when regional lawmakers produce regulations infused with sharia norms without mentioning religion or sharia in the name of the bylaws. The legal system of Indonesia does not have a clear solution for this. In general, the state law has no strong legal mechanism that is able to deal with excessive influence from the dominant legal discourse of the country's religious majority. MUI and the sharia propagators use this loophole as the chance to promote shariatisation. The inability of Indonesia, which is often called a state of legal pluralism, to handle legal problems and narrow the gap between regional and national laws, for instance, has helped to broaden the space for shariatisation.[24]

There must be a legal arrangement in the future to ensure MUI's role in promoting the implementation of sharia and also enabling the state to be neutral and fair in dealing with the infiltration of other legal orders. The inability to provide this legal mechanism and the presence of various legal orders can lead to turbulence and problems due to the rise of contestation among different legal systems and orders. Those striving for sharia, such as MUI, assert that Indonesia should be regulated under Islamic law, while those struggling for a secular nation-state argue that the country should follow secular law. Although Indonesia's founding fathers agreed on Pancasila and the 1945 Constitution as Indonesia's basic ideology and state philosophy, contestation between the religious and secular groups has continued until the present day.[25] MUI uses this opportunity to advocate its methods in the contestation of shariatisation in Indonesia.

MUI is also quite clever in exploiting the new configuration of Indonesia since the reform era by taking advantage of legal and political loopholes to strengthen the capacity-building of the MUI institution that it then uses to support the project of shariatisation. With more social, political and financial

24 Scientific School for Government Policy, *Dynamism in Islamic Activism: Reference Points for Democratisation and Human Rights* (Amsterdam: Amsterdam University Press, 2006).

25 Assyaukanie, *Islam and the Secular State in Indonesia*, 2009; Arskal Salim, *Challenging the Secular State: The Islamization of Law in Modern Indonesia* (Honolulu: University of Hawaii Press, 2008); An-Na'im, *Islam and the Secular State: Negotiating the Future of Shari'a*, 2009.

incentives from the state and society, MUI now has more influence in public sphere. Through this, MUI, which was portrayed as a regimist ulama organisation during the Suharto era, has now acquired its own stage. The current role of MUI is very different from what Suharto expected: a harmonious Islamic organisation acting as an intermediary. Instead of promoting national religious harmony, MUI currently issues some fatwas that tend to contribute to social tensions among Indonesian believers. This specific role places MUI as a destabiliser of Indonesian legal pluralism.

•••

A strong feature of MUI shariatisation involves both commodification and politicisation. The presence of both is evident in the MUI halal project. Commodification can be seen in State Law No 33/2014 on halal product assurance). The politicisation of this issue was evident in the debates among the lawmakers of Indonesia regarding a fixed institution authorised to publish the halal certification. What is meant by politicisation is the contestation among different groups over who had the authority to publish halal certificates, which not only employed religious arguments but also other arguments including the political interests of such a group. As previously mentioned, MUI through LPPOM started the process of halal labelling, which, although it lacked a strong legal basis in state law, had the support of the Muslim consensus from the community and the initiative from MUI. Therefore, MUI's position was queried and challenged when the draft law on Halal Product Assurance was brought into the legislature for discussion. MUI has demanded that what has so far been conducted by LPPOM, namely halal certification, should be guaranteed within the new law. MUI thus approached the initiator of the draft law, the Ministry of Religious Affairs. According to information gathered during interviews, the Ministry of Religious Affairs plans to minimise the role of LPPOM and recommend the establishment of a new independent state agency to conduct halal certification and labelling. MUI's board members demand a continuing central role for LPPOM based on the historical fact that the first initiative for conducting halal certification came from MUI, so not to include LPPOM in the new law as the only halal certifier in Indonesia would overlook MUI's historical role and contribution. MUI has invested much in recruiting human resources, institutional capacity-building development and networking to become a reliable halal certifier. MUI's activists believe it would be a travesty if the Ministry of Religious Affairs does not recognise the contribution of LPPOM.

Despite challenges from many groups, MUI continues to strive for authorisation from the state to remain the sole issuer of halal certificates, although it was not confident this role would continue. Internal resource persons at MUI affirmed that the Ministry of Religious Affairs planned to establish an independent institution responsible for halal certification, a policy of the Minister of Religious Affairs, Suryadharma Ali, which was highly disappointing to the MUI leaders. Halal certification is not only about issuing a statement of lawfulness, but also about economic and profit interests, which are the foundation for the sustainability of MUI. Without an official legal umbrella, MUI can cover 20% of its operational budget from LPPOM profits, which means that more profits could be projected should the legal umbrella be granted to MUI. With the support of this new law, MUI would have more authority to force companies and producers to certify their products.

Besides the legal issue, what also threatens MUI in relation to this draft law are the criticisms from various other Islamic groups questioning its semi-official authority in monopolising the issuance of halal certificates. Indonesian lawmakers have proposed that the draft law on Halal Product Assurance should also accommodate the role of other large Islamic organisations, such as NU and Muhammadiyah.[26] MUI, through LPPOM, was the only institution to manage the issuance of halal certificates because of the full political backing granted by Suharto and his allies. ICMI strongly facilitated the creation of LPPOM as the first halal certifier in Indonesia. Along with the increase of political Islam in the final years of Suharto's reign, MUI became more powerful in holding this authority. This authority now was being questioned by some Islamic organisations because MUI's role in this matter has not been based on legal foundations, but only based on its claim as the ulama representative council.

Halal certification was also a sensitive matter for financial reasons. Other Islamic organisations claimed that MUI accumulated capital through this business. Previously they allowed MUI, as the forum of Indonesian ulama, to take the initiative to conduct halal certification, showing no interest in offering the service themselves. However, once LPPOM began to aggressively hold onto its monopoly NU, for instance, publicly stated its willingness to conduct halal certification. NU started this attempt from East Java, its largest social, cultural and political base. However, at the headquarters of MUI, NU asked for certification to initiate this approach and has also collaborated with some universities for laboratory tests of products and commodities. MUI's response has been a measured one because it realised that NU is the largest Islamic organisation in Indonesia and many leading MUI figures actually come from NU. Sharing the

26 "DPR Diminta Akomodasi NU dan Muhammadiyah di RUU Halal," Republika, 16 February 2013, https://www.republika.co.id/berita/nasional/politik/13/02/16/mibjoi-dpr-diminta-akomodasi-nu-dan-muhammadiyah-di-ruu-halal, viewed on 22 July 2022.

issuance of halal fatwa with other Islamic organisations would be a popular move with those organisations.

• • •

Sharia economy and finance are the most tangible example of MUI success in the project of Indonesian shariatisation beside halal certification. This is in keeping with prognoses of quite striking positive developments in the sharia economy, not only in the context of Indonesia, but also in the economic development of the Southeast Asia region. Indonesia's poorly-resourced state, especially with its the low investment in infrastructure, is still a major hindrance to this country achieving the highest economic growth in Southeast Asia, and it needs fresh money to fund multi-billion infrastructure projects. Indonesia's sharia banks and financing institutions can use this as a chance to transform their role and presence, and participate in financing large infrastructure projects. An optimistic forecast for the role of Islamic financing, which is evidenced by its growth and deepening market, makes economic analysts feel optimistic that the sharia banks of Indonesia can fund projects, and to some extent, that the financial scheme provided by the sharia system is perhaps better than that of conventional banks.[27]

MUI has prioritised this issue, because sharia financial institutions need further rulings and regulations from Indonesian legislators. Despite the progress that has been achieved so far in relation to the matter of Islamic banking, MUI still aims to improve the role of sharia financing institutions. MUI and the practitioners of sharia financial institutions still focus their attempts on proposing that the state grant them more authority. Discussions among the National Sharia Board's members that I observed in 2011 concerned the role of the Sharia Supervisory Board, which was still in its infancy and formalistic. In addition, its presence in banks or other sharia financial institutions tended to be merely as an institutional accessory, which means MUI still has more work to do on this issue.

However, the sharia economy in Indonesia is already on the right track. The current establishment of Islamic financial institutions seems to be successful at the image level in representing the profile of sharia economy. At the practical level, the sharia economy has not yet been able to prove its performance especially for the betterment of society, which is the ultimate social role of the sharia banks. In a larger context, the sharia banks and financial companies

27 Standard & Poor's Rating Service, *Islamic Finance Outlook September 2012* (New York: McGraw-Hill Publishing, 2012), p. 52.

have not yet proven their visible contribution for the creation of social and economic justice for Indonesian Muslims. As far as their broadened market outreach was to counter or react to the products of conventional banks or the financial industry, they have had little effect on the configuration of Indonesia's economy, which is largely unregulated capitalism that empowers the rich and marginalises the poor. If the agenda of MUI in deepening the shariatisation of economy is not aimed at changing this paradigm, then the market has trapped the sharia economy.

•••

Although the shariatisation of Indonesia propagated by MUI has begun, it has not yet reached its final destination. Some of its results have been tangibly achieved while others are still in progress. All the processes will have a direct and indirect impact on the state and society of Indonesia. More importantly, MUI's shariatisation efforts do not stop at promoting legal proposals to be adopted into state laws, but, as the findings of this research indicate, the organisation also employs social and political pressures on the process of lawmaking. Shariatisation usually starts from attempts to create discourse and activism to support monitoring and evaluating once a policy has become law. However, the tenor of MUI's shariatisation in the public sphere depends much on the political and legal opportunities provided by the state and also Islamic society in general. In this regard, MUI is also conscious that political and legal opportunity is not something that is given but that is contested. MUI has demanded that the lawmakers of Indonesia allow it to be involved in the process of national legislation related to issues that concern the Islamic community.

However, MUI's shift from pragmatic sharia, focused on political and economic interests, to idealistic sharia, focused on the perfect implementation of sharia throughout the national legal system, depends on various internal and external variables. Once the current movement of shariatisation is regarded as successful, MUI will move forward to more idealistic implementation of the sharia. The position of the state, in this regard, will also influence the extent to which MUI will proceed to impose this. If the state stays neutral, then MUI will have more chance to advocate for idealistic sharia because the Council will still have popular support from the Muslim community. Admittedly, internal support from within MUI and its allies will also become significant for the success of MUI's shariatisation efforts. More members of pro-sharia activists and organisations have joined MUI and are vigorous in pushing the Council to implement idealistic sharia. So far, the criticism of radical Islamic organisations in response to the efforts of MUI for legal Islamisation is that it is too pragmatic, working on the basis of political and economic interests and not on the basis of sharia demands. In short, it suffices to say that all these issues have become important factors that MUI considers in the process of shariatisation in Indonesia.

One thing that has slowed the progress of shariatisation is the political structure of Indonesia. The country will not significantly change the direction of its political system over the next two decades. It will remain a non-theocratic state. However, the stability of the political structure does not always match the social and cultural formation of Indonesia, which may possibly shift to prefer a more formal adherence to sharia norms. The role played by MUI in the last decade and next two decades remains focused on two levels. First, it will establish more discourses on the importance of sharia in Indonesia. Here, the position of MUI can be seen as a "sounding board," using Habermas's concept on the public sphere, of sharia aspiration.[28] Second, it will consolidate Islamic legal activism to support the implementation of the discourse. MUI will use its human and financial resources by executing both old and new strategies, designated to recapitalise on some trends and issues that the organisation will have to deal with and the challenges its shariatisation efforts will face.

Regardless of the historical background of its establishment as a regime-sponsored ulama council, MUI is just like many other ordinary institutions in Indonesia. Since it is not an official part of the state, there is no compulsion to accept MUI's products. Indeed, for instance, some fatwa on heretical groups would have no legal power if they were not legalised or adopted by the state through regulations. At the time of the MUI's creation, the state of Indonesia needed to set up a single fatwa organisation in anticipation of the pluralism of Islamic strands in Indonesia. MUI's original function was to accommodate the diversity of Muslim organisations, and it was conceived as an inclusive forum. By adjusting to the demands of political and social shifts, this role has changed. Fair treatment for heretical Indonesian Muslim groups requires a return to inclusiveness on the part of the MUI, and also the neutrality of the state.

It seems that MUI has become more adept in understanding the political and social realm of Indonesia, which is different from other Islamic countries such as Saudi Arabia, Egypt, Sudan, Algeria and others, that to some degree have applied sharia-based state law (*taṭbīq al-sharīʿa*) although they are also

28 Hugh Baxter, *Habermas, the Discourse Theory of Law and Democracy* (Redwood City, CA: Stanford University Press, 2011), p. 235.

under the delicate influence of the secular discourse of the legal system. Since the beginning of Indonesia's independence, the system of law enacted by this country is mostly a clear, rational and balanced separation between religion and *adat* (customary law) on one side and the secular (or political) domain on the other side. Some aspirations of sharia law have been incorporated into the national statutory law, but, so far, only for family and private law (*aḥwāl shakhṣiyya*). However, now MUI appears to be working more deeply and forcefully to promote the agenda of sharia codification and its implementation in the public sphere. In order for its efforts to be accepted by the whole of Indonesia, MUI has tried to substantively enhance its Islamic discourse that shariatisation does not contradict the existence of NKRI. Legally speaking, shariatisation is far for being judged as a political right for Indonesian Muslims, but is seen as politically and historically necessary for them. MUI will continue to advocate for gradual shariatisation by providing alternative legal drafts and consolidating social and political cohesiveness with the state and other Islamic organisations. Successful programmes and agenda implemented by MUI will be used as evidence that the organisation is capable of implementing a flexible form of shariatisation. In the public sphere, MUI will create more images of its commitment to NKRI, but at the practical level, the concrete agenda for shariatisation will also be improved.

•••

The position of MUI as a fatwa-giver remains important, and has become even stronger in the era of Jokowi's national leadership, especially given the position of Amin as Indonesian vice-president after the 2019 presidential elections. At the beginning of Jokowi's presidential first term, from 2014–2016, the relationship between Jokowi and MUI was strained. With its different political stance, and based on information from social media and other sources, MUI believed that Jokowi's policy was not inclined to advocate for its agenda. This assumption was based on Jokowi's background in secular-nationalist politics, and the lack of adequate information on the president's personal character; before his election, he had been a local leader and had escaped the organisation's attention. On the other side, Jokowi himself had little knowledge about the role of MUI. The first test of their relationship took place in 2014–2015, when MUI's annual government was delayed because the new president had changed the system of state grants to non-state organisations. MUI speculated that this delay in the payment of its funding was part of Jokowi's strategy to delegitimise its role. The misunderstanding was solve, however, and since 2015 MUI's subsidy has been paid every year.

The position of MUI, after this issue, remained very critical of the Jokowi adminstration. The president had become increasingly aware of MUI's relevance, however, and its influence on the public discourse of Islam in society and the state. During the early period of his leadership, criticism from progressive scholars and human rights activists on MUI's leniency towards Islamic radicalism and other undemocratic elements did not undermine this understanding, and the administration continued to offer the organisation its strong support. In addition, Jokowi invited MUI to become involved in some important national projects such as National Asset Redistribution.[29] The relationship between MUI and the Ministry of Religious Affairs has remained harmonious during the Jokowi era, generally speaking, despite both competing for influence in the legislative body over the draft law on Halal Product Assurance. MUI is obliged to hand over its authority on halal issues to the government's BPJPH as a consequence of State Law No. 33/2014, but the organisation still has a strong position within this halal state agency. It retains an important role in the issuance of halal fatwas, while LPPOM-MUI continues to perform its role as Lembaga Pemeriksa Halal (LPH, the halal investigation institute), as stated in the law.

The development of an increasing level of identity politics has left MUI with a dilemma. On one hand, the Council would like to ride the wave of populist Islamism to defend its consituencies and its shariatisation agenda, but also feels the need to distance itself from the political Islam movement given its commitment to defending Indonesia from any attempts to change the form of the state. In 2017, MUI became an inspiration for the establishment of the ABI movement because of its fatwa issued in response to Ahok's supposedly blasphemous speech. Later, in the run-up to the 2019 general elections, the organisation returned to a more neutral position. Since then, with Amin as vice-president of Indonesia, shariatisation has begun to take a different form. The earlier MUI shariatisation agenda started from a position of opposition, while now it compromises and collaborates with the ruling regime.

The position of Amin as Jokowi's right hand has great influence to shape the shariatisation agenda of MUI. Having become established as *khādim al-ḥukūma* (custodian of the government), since Amin's election it has reoriented itself as *ṣadīq al-ḥukūma*, the friend of the ruling government. As such, MUI is not only expected to be a friend to the current administration, but also to justify its policies. This has created a degree of internal division within the organisation, since not all board members agree to this role. Those who

29 "MUI Ambil Peran Redistribusi Aset", *Republika*, 30 March 2017, https://nasional.republika.co.id/berita/onmad2365/mui-ambil-peran-redistribusi-aset, viewed on 22 July 2022.

supported Amin's vice-presidency—mainly from Nahdlatul Ulama—welcome it, while those who did not—mainly from Muhammadiyah and other small organisations—tend to be more critical. In consequence, in order to make MUI's role as *ṣadīq al-ḥukūma* a success, the Council did a great deal of organisational reshuffling at its 2020 Congress. Critical figures such as Din Syamsuddin, Bahtiar Natsir, and the late Tengku Zulkarnaen lost their positions on the board. However, such criticism has not disappeared, even though it is rarely voiced by leaders such as Anwar Abbas (vice general chairman of MUI).

One great opportunity resulting from MUI's role as *ṣadīq al-ḥukūma* is an increased influence on government policy. Three clear examples of its success in this domain are the abolition of the presidential regulation on investment in alcoholic drinks,[30] the cancellation of Indonesia's roadmap of education—which originally did not mention the role of religion[31]—and the determinant role of the MUI fatwa on Covid-19 vaccines.[32] MUI's agenda of shariatisation has also been adopted by the Jokowi administration in the field of sharia economy, which is now more prominent than under previous governments. With Jokowi's support, sharia finance and banking has grown, as has the halal-based economy. In short, Jokowi—once described by Islamist groups as anti-Islam—has become a key figure in the advance of shariatisation. The close relationship between the Jokowi administration and MUI means that this Islamic organisation has a real opportunity to further promote its shariatisation agenda in the near future.

---

30 "Perpres Investasi Miras Dicabut, PPP: Jokowi Dengarkan Ulama," *Republika*, 2 March 2021, https://www.republika.co.id/berita/qpc3sk354/perpres-investasi-miras-dicabut-ppp-jokowi-dengarkan-ulama.

31 "Wapres Minta Ada 'Agama' di Peta Jalan Pendidikan," *Republika*, 10 March 2021, https://www.republika.co.id/berita/qpq65q9825000/wapres-minta-ada-agama-di-peta-jalan-pendidikan, viewed on 22 July 2022.

32 "Tanpa Fatwa MUI, Vaksinasi Covid-19 Belum Bisa Dilaksanakan," *Kompas*, 6 January 2021, https://www.kompas.tv/article/135762/tanpa-fatwa-mui-vaksinasi-covid-19-belum-bisa-dilaksanakan, viewed on 22 July 2022.

References

Abbas, Siradjuddin. 1999. *I'tiqad Ahlussunnah Wal-Jama'ah*. Kelantan: Pustaka Aman.

Abdelsalam, Ahmed. 2005. "The Practice of Violence in the Ḥisba Theories." *Iranian Studies* 38 (4): 547–54.

Abdul-Raof, Hussein. 2012. *Theological Approaches to Qur'anic Exegesis: A Practical Comparative-Contrastive Analysis*. London & New York: Routledge.

Abdurrahman, Maman. *Mirza Ghulam Ahmad Plagiator Al-Qur'an: Studi Banding Antara Ayat-Ayat Tadzkirah Dan Ayat-Ayat al-Qur'an*. Bandung: Rahman Press, 2011.

Abu Khalil, As'ad. 2001. "Against the Taboos of Islam: Anti Conformist Tendencies in Comtemporary Arab/Islamic Thought." In *Between the State and Islam*, edited by Charles Butterworth and William Zartman, 110–34. Cambridge: Cambridge University Press.

Abubakar, Alyasa. 2009. *Bunga Rampai Pelaksanaan Syariat Islam (Pendukung Qanun Pelaksanaan Syariat Islam)*. Banda Aceh: Dinas Syariat Islam Aceh.

Abusharaf, Mustafa Rogaia. 2007. "Female Circumcision: Multicultural Perspectives." In *Female Circumcision: Multicultural Perspectives*, edited by Rogaia Mustafa Abusharaf, 1–26. Pennsylvania: University of Pennsylvania Press.

Adamec, Ludwig W. 2009. *Historical Dictionary of Islam*. Maryland: Scarecrow Press.

Adams, Wahiduddin. 2004. *Pola Penyerapan Fatwa Majelis Ulama Indonesia (MUI) Dalam Peraturan Perundang-Undangan 1975–1997*. Jakarta: Departemen Agama.

Adams, Wahiduddin. 2012. "Fatwa MUI Dalam Prespektif Hukum Dan Perundangundangan." In *Fatwa Majelis Ulama Dalam Perspektif Hukum Dan Perundang-Undangan*, edited by Nahar Nahrawi, Nuhrison M. Nuh, Asrorun Ni'am Sholeh, and Abidin Zainal, 3–17. Jakarta: Puslitbang Kehidupan Keagamaan Badan Litbang dan Diklat Kementerian Agama RI.

Adelkhah, Fariba. 2006. "Reislamization in the Public Sphere." In *Public Islam and the Common Good*, edited by Armando Salvatore and Dale Eickleman, 103–118. Leiden & Boston: Brill.

Ahmed, Ishtiaq. 2011. "Religious Nationalism and Minorities in Pakistan." In *The Politics of Religion in South and Southeast Asia*, edited by Ishtiaq Ahmed, 81–101. New York: Taylor & Francis.

Akbar, Cholis. 2012. "MUI Ajak Ormas Islam Tolak Putusan MK", March 17. http://hidayatullah.com/read/21744/17/03/2012/mui-ajak-ormas-islam-tolak-putusan-mk.html.

Akbarzadeh, Shahram, and Abdullah Saeed, ed. 2013. *Islam and Political Legitimacy*. London & New York: Routledge.

Alfian. "The Ulama of the Acehnese Society." In *Readings on Islam in Southeast Asia*, edited by Ahmad Ibrahim, Sharon Siddique, and Yasmin Hussain, pp. 82–6. Singapore: Institute of Southeast Asian Studies.

Ali, Wijdan. 1999. *The Arab Contribution to Islamic Art: From the Seventh to the Fifteenth Centuries*. Cairo: American University in Cairo Press.

Ali-Fauzi, Ihsan, Samsu Rizal Panggabean, Nathanael Gratias Sumaktoyo, Anick H.T., Husni Mubarak, Testriono, and Siti Nurhayati. 2011. *Kontroversi Gereja Di Jakarta*. Yogyakarta: CRCS.

Ali-Fauzi, Ihsan, Samsu Rizal Panggabean, and Trisno S. Sutanto. 2010. "Membela Kekebasan Beragama: Catatan Pengantar." In *Membela Kebebasan Beragama: Percakapan Tentang Sekularisme, Liberalisme, Dan Pluralisme,* (*Buku* 2). Jakarta: Lembaga Studi Agama dan Filsafat.

Amin, Ma'ruf. 2010. "Pointers Pidato Ketua DSN-MUI Dalam Acara Pembukaan Ijtima Sanawi (Annual Meeting) DPS Tahun 2010". Jakarta.

An-Naʿim, Abdullahi Ahmed. 2009. *Islam and the Secular State: Negotiating the Future of Shariʿa*. Cambridge: Harvard University Press.

Ananta, Aris, Evi Nurvidya Arifin, and Leo Suryadinata. 2005. *Emerging Democracy in Indonesia*. Singapore: Institute of Southeast Asian Studies.

Ansell, Christopher. 2003. "Community Embeddedness and Collaborative Governance in the San Francisco Bay Area Environmental Movement." In *Social Movements and Networks: Relational Approaches to Collective Action: Relational Approaches to Collective Action*, edited by Mario Diani and Doug McAdam, 123–146. Oxford: Oxford University Press.

Anshari, Endang Saifuddin. 1979. *Piagam Jakarta 22 Juni 1945*. Bandung: Pustaka Perpustakaan Salman ITB.

Anwar, Dewi Fortuna. 2010. "The Habibie Presidency: Catapulting Towards Reform." In *Soeharto's New Order and Its Legacy: Essays in Honour of Harold Crouch*, edited by Edward Aspinal and Greg Fealy. Canberra: ANU E Press.

Anwar, Zainal M. 2011. "Formalisasi Syari'at Islam di Indonesia, Pendekatan Pluralisme Politik dalam Kebijakan Publik." *Millah* X (2): 191–212.

Arslam, Emre. 2012. "Nation, Islam, and Purity: The World-View of Turkish Ultra-nationalists in Germany." In *How Purity Is Made*, edited by Petra Roesch and Udo Simon, 333–53. Wiesbaden: Harrossowitz Verlag.

Asad, Talal. 1986. *The Idea of an Anthropology of Islam*, Washington, DC: Center for Contemporary Arab Studies, Georgetown University.

Asad, Talal. 2009. "Reflections on Blasphemy and Secular Criticism." In *Religion: Beyond a Concept*, edited by Hent de Vries, 580–609. New York City: Fordham University Press.

Asfaruddin, Asma. 2006. "Obedience to Political Authority: An Evolutionary Concept." In *Islamic Democratic Discourse: Theory, Debates, and Philosophical Perspectives*, edited by Muqtedar Khan, 37–62. Oxford: Lexington Books.

Al-ʿAshmāwī, Muḥammad Saʿīd. 1998. "The Sharia: The Codification of Islamic Law." In *Liberal Islam: A Source Book*, edited by Charles Kurzman, 49–58. Oxford & New York: Oxford University Press.

Aspinall, Edward. 2009. *Islam and Nation: Separatist Rebellion in Aceh, Indonesia.* Redwood City, CA: Stanford University Press.

Assyaukanie, Luthfi. 2009. *Islam and the Secular State in Indonesia.* Singapore: ISEAS.

Atjeh, Aboebakar. 1971. *Masuknya Islam ke Indonesia.* Semarang: Ramadan.

Atjeh, Aboebakar. 1977. *Aliran Syi'ah di Nusantara.* Jakarta: Islamic Research Institute.

Ayish, Muhammad Ibrahim, and Muḥammad 'Iṣām 'Āyiš. 2008. *The New Arab Public Sphere.* Berlin: Frank & Timme GmbH.

Ayoob, Mohammed. 2008. *The Many Faces of Political Islam, Religion and Politics in the Muslim World.* Michigan: Michigan University Press.

Azra, Azyumardi. "A Hadhrami Religious Scholar in Indonesia: Sayyid 'Uthman." In *Hadhrami Traders, Scholars and Statesmen in the Indian Ocean, 1750s to 1960s*, edited by Ulrike Freitag and William Clarence-Smith, 249–64. Leiden: Brill.

Azra, Azyumardi. 1999. "Kongres Umat Islam: Sebuah Pengantar." In *Kumpulan Hasil-Hasil Kongres Umat Islam Indonesia: Umat Islam Menyongsong Era Indonesia Baru*, iii–xiv. Jakarta: Dewan Pimpinan Majelis Ulama Indonesia.

Azra, Azyumardi. 2006a. *Islam in the Indonesian World, an Account of Institutional Formation.* Bandung: Mizan.

Azra, Azyumardi. 2006b. *Indonesia, Islam, and Democracy: Dynamics in a Global Context.* Jakarta: Equinox Publishing.

Azra, Azyumardi. 2013. "Distinguishing Indonesian Islam: Some Lessons to Learn." In *Islam in Indonesia: Contrasting Images and Interpretations*, edited by Jajat Burhanudin and Kees van Dijk, 63–74. Amsterdam: Amsterdam University Press.

Badawi, Jamal A. 1995. *Gender Equity in Islam: Basic Principles.* American Trust Publications.

Baker, Ramond William. 2003. *Islam Without Fear, Egypt and the New Islamist.* Cambridge: Harvard University Press.

Balbaaki, Rohi. 1995. *Al-Mawrid.* Beirut: Dar El-Elm LilMalayin.

Barton, Greg. 2002. *Gus Dur: The Authorized Biography of Abdurrahman Wahid.* Jakarta: Equinox Publishing.

Barua, Jayanti. 2001. *Social Mobilisation And Modern Society.* New Delhi: Mittal Publications.

Bastaman, Hanna Djumhana. 1995. *Integrasi Psikologi Dengan Islam: Menuju Psikologi Islami.* Yogyakarta: Pustaka Pelajar & Yayasan Insan Kamil.

Baxter, Hugh. 2011. *Habermas, the Discourse Theory of Law and Democracy.* Redwood City, CA: Stanford University Press.

Bayat, Asef. 1997. "Un-Civil Society: The Politics of 'the Informal People'." *Third World Quarterly* 18 (1): 53–74.

Bayat, Asef. 2007. *Making Islam Democratic: Social Movements and the Post-Islamist Turn.* Redwood City, CA: Stanford University Press.

Bayat, Asef. 2010. *Life as Politics: How Ordinary People Change the Middle East.* Amsterdam: Amsterdam University Press.

Bechofer, Frank, and David McCrone. 2009. *National Identity, Nationalism and Constitutional Change*. London: Palgrave Macmillan.

Bechor, Gay. 2007. *The Sanhuri Code and the Emergence of Modern Arab Civil Law (1932–1949)*. Leiden & Boston: Brill.

Benford, Robert D, and David A. Snow. 2000. "Framing Processes and Social Movements: An Overview and Assessment." *Annual Review of Sociology* 26: 611–639.

Berman, Paul Schiff. 2012. *Legal Pluralism: A Jurisprudence of Law Beyond Borders*. Cambridge: Cambridge University Press.

Bertrand, Jacques. 2010. "Political Islam and Democracy in the Majority of Muslim Country of Indonesia." In *Islam and Politics in Southeast Asia*, edited by Johan Saravanamuttu, 45–64. Singapore: ISEAS.

Booth, Anne. 2011. "Splitting, Splitting, Splitting Again: Brief History of the Development of Regional in Indonesia Since Independence." *Bijdragen Tot de Taal-, Land -En Volkenkunde* 167 (1): 31–59.

Bozóki, Andras. 2003. "Theoretical Interpretations of Elite Change in East Central Europe." In *Elite Configuration at the Apex of Power*, edited by Mattei Dogan, 215–248. Leiden: Brill.

Brown, Colin. 2003. *A Short History of Indonesia: The Unlikely Nation?* New South Wales: Allen & Unwin.

Brugger, Winfried, and Michael Mousa Karayanni, ed. 2007. *Religion in the Public Sphere: A Comparative Analysis of German, Israeli, American and International Law*. New York: Springer.

Buehler, Michael. 2008. "The Rise of Sharia Bylaws in Indonesian Districts: An Indication for Changing Patterns of Power Accumulation and Political Corruption." *South East Asia Research* 16 (22): 255–85.

Bunzl, John. 2004. "Introduction in God's Name?" In *Islam, Judaism, and the Political Role of Religions in the Middle East*, edited by John Bunzl. Gainesvile: University Press of Florida: University Press of Florida.

Bush, Robin. 2008. "Regional Sharia Regulations in Indonesia: Anomaly or Symptom?" in *Expressing Islam: Religious Life and Politics*, edited by Greg Fealy and Sally White, 174–91. Singapore: ISEAS.

Butler, Chris. 2012. *Henri Lefebvre: Spatial Politics, Everyday Life and the Right to the City*. London & New York: Routledge.

Butt, Simon. 2008. "Polygamy and Mixed Marriage in Indonesia: Islam and the Marriage Law in Courts." In *Indonesia: Law and Society*, edited by Tim Lindsey. New South Wales: Federation Press.

Campbell, John L. 2005. "Where Do We Stand? Common Mechanism in Organizations and Social Movements Research." In *Social Movements and Organization Theory*, edited by F. Davis Gerald, Doug McAdam, and Richard Scott William, 41–68. Cambridge: Cambridge University Press.

Campo, Juan Eduardo. 2009. *Encyclopedia of Islam*. New York: Infobase Publishing.

Candraningrum, Dewi. 2007. "Unquestioned Gender Lens in Contemporary Indonesian Sharīʿa-Ordinances (Perda Syari'ah)." *Al-Jāmiʿah* 45 (2): 290–320.

Caroll, William K., and R.S. Ratner. 1996. "Master Framing and Cross-Movement Networking in Contemporary Social Movement." *Sociological Quarterly* 37 (4): 601–25.

Chernov-Hwang, Julie. 2009. *Peaceful Islamist Mobilization in the Muslim World: What Went Right*. New York: Palgrave Macmillan.

Chew, Daniel. 2000. "Oral History Methodology: The Life History Approach." In *Oral History in Southeast Asia Theory and Method*, edited by P. Lim Pui Huen, James H. Morrison, and Kwa Chong Guan, 47–54. Singapore: Institute of Southeast Asian Studies.

Cholil, Suhadi, Zainal Abidin Bagir, Mustaghfiroh Rahayu, and Budi Asyhari. 2009a. *Annual Report on Religious Life in Indonesia 2000*. Yogyakarta: Center for Religious and Cross-cultural Studies (CRCS) Graduate School Gadjah Mada University.

Cholil, Suhadi, Zainal Abidin Bagir, Mustaghfiroh Rahayu, and Budi Asyhari. 2009b. "Annual Report on Religious Life in Indonesia 2009". Yogyakarta.

Collins, Elizabeth Fuller. 2007. *Indonesia Betrayed: How Development Fails*. Honolulu: University of Hawaii Press.

Cook, Michael. 2003. *Forbidding Wrong in Islam: An Introduction*. Cambridge: Cambridge University Press.

Cook, Michael. 2004. *Commanding Right and Forbidding Wrong in Islamic Thought*. Cambridge: Cambridge University Press.

Costanza-Chock, Sasha. 1998. "Transmedia Mobilization in the Popular Association of the Oaxacan People, Los Angeles." In *Power in Movement: Social Movements and Contentious Politics*, 271. Bristol: Intellect Books.

Coulhon, Craig. 2011. "Secularism, Citizenship and the Public Sphere." In *Rethinking Secularism*, edited by Craig Coulhon, Mark Juergensmeyer, and Jonathan van Anwerpen, 75–92. Oxford & New York: Oxford University Press.

Cribb, Robert. 1990. *Indonesian Killing of 1965–1966*. Melbourne: Centre of Southeast Asian Studies Monash University.

Cribb, Robert, and Audrey Kahin. 2004. *Historical Dictionary of Indonesia*. Lanham & Maryland: Scarecrow Press.

Crouch, Harold. 2010. *Political Reform in Indonesia after Soeharto*. Singapore: ISEAS.

d'Anjou, Leo. 1996. *Social Movements and Cultural Change: The First Abolition Campaign Revisited*. New York: Transaction Publishers.

Darmaputera, Eka. 1988. *Pancasila and the Search for Identity and Modernity in Indonesian Society: A Cultural and Ethical Analysis*. Leiden & Boston: Brill.

Davies, Douglas. 2002. *Anthropology and Theology*. Oxford & New York: Berg.

Davies, Martin L. 2006. *Historics Why History Dominates Contemporary Society*. New York: Routledge.

Della Porta, Donatella, and Mario Diani. 2009. *Social Movements: An Introduction.* Oxford: Blackwell Publishing.

DeLong-Bas, Natana J. 2007. *Wahhabi Islam: From Revival and Reform to Global Jihad.* New York: I.B.Tauris.

Dewan Syariah Nasional MUI-Bank Indonesia. 2006. *Himpunan Fatwa Dewan Syariah Nasional MUI.* Jakarta: Dewan Syariah Nasional Majelis Ulama Indonesia.

Dhakidae, Daniel. 2003. *Cendekiawan Dan Kekuasaan Dalam Negara Orde Baru.* Jakarta: Gramedia.

Dijk, C. Van. 1981. *Rebellion Under the Banner of Islam: The Darul Islam in Indonesia.* The Hague: Martinus Nijhoff.

Dillon, Michele. 2003. *Handbook of the Sociology of Religion.* Cambridge: Cambridge University Press.

Dinas Syari'at Islam. 2009. *Himpunan Undang-Undang Keputusan Presiden Peraturan Daerah/Qanun Instruksi Gubernur Edaran Gubernur Berkaitan Pelaksanaan Syari'at Aceh.* Banda Aceh: Dinas Syari'at Islam Aceh.

Dogan, Mattei. 2003. "Introduction: Diversity of Elite Configurations and Clusters of Power." In *Elite Configuration at the Apex of Power*, edited by Mattei Dogan, 1–16. Leiden: Brill.

Douglas, Mary. 2003. *Purity and Danger: An Analysis of Concepts of Pollution and Taboo.* London & New York: Routledge.

Drakeley, Steven. 2005. *The History of Indonesia.* Westport: ABC-CLIO.

Drewes, G.W.J. 1985. "New Light on the Coming of Islam to Indonesia?" In *Readings on Islam in Southeast Asia*, edited by Ahmad Ibrahim, Siddique Sharon, and Yasmin Hussain. Singapore: ISEAS.

Dzulfikriddin, M. 2010. *Mohammad Natsir Dalam Sejarah Politik Indonesia.* Bandung: Mizan.

Eddyono, Sri Wiyanti. 2010. "Politicization of Islam During the Democratic Transition: New Challenges for the Indonesian Women's Movement." Jakarta. SCN-CREST.

Effendi, Djohan. 2010. *Pembaruan Tanpa Membongkar Tradisi: Wacana Keagamaan Di Kalangan Generasi Muda NU Masa Kepemimpinan Gus Dur.* Jakarta: Penerbit Buku Kompas.

Effendi, Usman. 2008. "Berbahaya Kalau Lembaga Pemeriksa Halal Terlepas Dari MUI." *Jurnal Halal*, October.

Eickelman, Dale F. 2013. "Clash of Cultures? Intellectuals, Their Public, and Islam." In *Intellectuals in the Modern Islamic World: Transmission, Transformation and Communication*, edited by Stephane A. Dudoignon, Komatsu Hisao, and Kosugi Yasushi, 289–304. Routledge.

Eickelman, Dale F, and John W. Anderson, ed. 2003. *New Media in the Muslim World: The Emerging Public Sphere.* Indiana: Indiana University Press.

Eisenstadt, S.N. 1995. *Power, Trust, and Meaning: Essays in Sociological Theory and Analysis.* Chicago: University of Chicago Press.

Eisenstadt, S.N., and Luis Roniger. 1984. *Patrons, Clients and Friends: Interpersonal Relations and the Structure of Trust in Society*. Vol. 3. Cambridge: Cambridge University Press.

Elfkahani, Said M., M. Kabir Hassan, and Yusuf M. Sidani. 2007. "Islamic Mutual Funds." In *The Handbook of Islamic Banking*, edited by M. Kabir Hassan and K. Mervyn Lewis, 256–. Massachusetts: Edward Elgar Publishing.

Enayat, Hamid. 2005. *Modern Islamic Political Thought*. New York: I.B. Tauris.

Esposito, John L. 1999. "Contemporary Islam: Reformation or Revolution?" In *The Oxford History of Islam*, 643–90. Oxford & New York: Oxford University Press.

Esposito, John L. 2003. "Introduction: Modernising Islam and Reislamisation in Global Perspective." In *Modernizing Islam: Religion and the Public Sphere in Europe and the Middle East*, edited by John L Esposito, 1–14. New Brunswick & New Jersey: Rutgers University Press.

Farid, Mahmud, Usman Effendi, and Nadia. 2011. "Produk Unik Bersertifikat Halal Apa Tujuannya?" *Jurnal Halal*.

Farzana, Shaikh. 2008. "From Islamisation to Shariatisation." *Third World Quarterly* 29 (3): 593–609.

Fatonie, Iskhak. 2011. "Decentralization and Local Governance in Post Conflict Societies: Sustainable Peace and Development, the Case of Aceh, Indonesia". University of Vienna.

Fauzi, Amelia. 2005. "Darul Islam Movement (DI), Struggling for an Islamic State of Indonesia." In *Southeast Asia, Historical Encyclopedia, From Angkor Wat to East Timor*. Santa Barbara, CA: ABC-CLIO.

Fealy, Greg. 1997. "Indonesian Politics 1995–1996: The Making of Crisis." In *Indonesia Assessment: Population and Human Resources*, edited by Gavin W. John and Terence H. Hull, 19–38. Singapore: ISEAS.

Fealy, Greg. 2003. "Divided Majority, Limit of Indonesian Political Islam." In *Islam and Political Legitimacy*, edited by Shahram Akbarzadeh and Abdullah Saeed, 150–168. London & New York: Routledge.

Fealy, Greg. 2004. "Islamic Radicalism in Indonesia: The Faltering Revival?" *Southeast Asian Affairs* (1): 104–121.

Fealy, Greg. 2005. "Islamisation and Politics in Southeast Asia: The Contrasting Case of Malaysia and Indonesia." In *Islam in World Politics*, edited by Nelly Lahoud and Anthony H. Johns, 152–169. London: Routledge.

Fealy, Greg. 2006. *Voices of Islam in Southeast Asia: a Contemporary Sourcebook*. Singapore: Institute of Southeast Asian Studies.

Fealy, Greg. 2008. "Consuming Islam: Commodified Religion and Aspirational Pietism in Contemporary Indonesia." In *Expressing Islam: Religious Life and Politics in Indonesia*, edited by Greg Fealy and Sally White, 15–39. Singapore: ISEAS.

Federspiel, Howard M. 1998. *Indonesia in Transition: Muslim Intellectuals and National Development*. New York: Nova Science Publishers.

Federspiel, Howard M. 2009. *Persatuan Islam: Islamic Reform in Twentieth Century Indonesia*. Singapore: Equinox Publishing.

Federico, Finchelstein. *From Fascism to Populism in History*. California: University of California Press, 2017.

Feener, R. Michael. 2011. *Muslim Legal Thought in Modern Indonesia*. Cambridge: Cambridge University Press.

Feener, R. Michael, and Mark Cammack. 2007. *Islamic Law in Contemporary Indonesia: Ideas and Institutions*. Harvard: Harvard University Press.

Feith, Herbert. 2006. *The Decline of Constitutional Democracy in Indonesia*. Jakarta: Equinox Publishing.

Feldman, Noah. 2008. *The Fall and Rise of the Islamic State*. New Jersey: Princeton University Press.

Ferree, Myra Marx, William Gamson, Jurgen Gerhards, and Dieter Rucht. 2002. *Shaping Abortion Discourse: Democracy and the Public Sphere in Germany and the United States*. Cambridge: Cambridge University Press.

Fischer, Johan. 2008. *Proper Islamic Consumption: Shopping among the Malays in Modern Malaysia*. Copenhagen: NIAS Press.

Fischer, Johan. 2011. *The Halal Frontier: Muslim Consumers in a Globalized Market*. New York: Palgrave Macmillan.

Formichi, Chiara. 2012. *Islam and the Making of the Nation: Kartosuwiryo and Political Islam in Twentieth-Century Indonesia*. Leiden: KITLV Press.

Gamson, William. 2004. "Bystanders, Public Opinion, and the Media." In *The Blackwell Companion to Social Movements*, edited by David A. Snow, Sarah A. Soule, and Hanspeter Kriesi, 242–261. Malden: Blackwell Publishing.

Gamson, William. Bruce Fireman, and Steven Rytina. 1982. *Encounters with Unjust Authority*. Chicago: Dorsey Press.

Gatra. 2005. "Dukungan Fatwa MUI Forum Umat Islam Tabligh Akbar Usai Sholat Jumat." *Gatra*, August. http://arsip.gatra.com/2005-08-08/artikel.php?id=87036, viewed on 22 April 2012.

Gaus, Ahmad. 2010. *Api Islam Nurcholish Madjid: Jalan Hidup Seorang Visioner*. Jakarta: Penerbit Buku Kompas.

Gauvain, Richard. 2012. "Pure Blood and the Martyr: Ritual Potential among Modern Cairene Salafis." In *How Purity Is Made*, edited by Petra Roesch and Udo Simon, 285–308. Wiesbaden: Harrossowitz Verlag.

Gay, Peter. 1985. *Freud for Historians*. New York & Oxford: Oxford University Press.

Geertz, Clifford. 1976. *The Religion of Java*. Chicago: University of Chicago Press.

Geertz, Clifford. 1983. *Local Knowledge: Further Essays in Interpretive Anthropology*. New York: Basic Books.

Gellner, Ernest. 1992. *Postmodernism, Reason and Religion*. London & New York: Routledge.

Gerhards, Jürgen, and Dieter Rucht. 1991. *Mesomobilization Context: Organizing and Framing in Two Protest Campaigns in West Germany*. Berlin: Wissenschaftszentrum Berlin.

Ghaneabassiri, Kambiz. 2013. "Religious Normativity and Praxis among American Muslims." In *The Cambridge Companion to American Islam*, 208–27. Cambridge: Cambridge University Press.

Ghazali, Abd. Rahim, ed. 1998. *M. Amien Rais Dalam Sorotan Generasi Muda Muhammadiyah*. Bandung: Mizan.

Ghazzal, Zouhir. 2005. "The 'Ulama': Status and Function." In *A Companion to the History of Middle East*, edited by Youssef M. Choueiri, 71–86. Victoria: Blackwell Publishing.

Gillespie, Piers. 2007. "Current Issues in Indonesian Islam: Analysing the 2005 Council of Indonesian Ulama Fatwa No. 7 Opposing Pluralism, Liberalism and Securalism." *Journal of Islamic Studies* 2 (18): 202–240.

Girindra, Aisjah. 2008. *Dari Sertifikasi Menuju Labelisasi Halal*. Jakarta: Pustaka Jurnal Halal.

Gitlin, Todd. 1980. *The Whole World Is Watching: Mass Media in the Making & Unmaking of the New Left*. California: University of California Press.

Giugni, Marco. 2011. "Political Opportunity: Still a Useful Concept?" In *Contention and Trust in Cities and States*, edited by Charles Tilly and Michael Hanagan, 271–286. Dordrecht, Heidelberg, London & New York: Springer.

Goldstone, Jack A., and Charles Tilly. 2001. "Threat (and Opportunity) Popular Action and State Response in the Dynamics of Contentious Action." In *Silence and Voice in Contentious Politics*, edited by Ronald R. Aminzade, Jack A. Goldstone, Elizabeth J. Perry, William H. Sewell Jr, Sidney Tarrow, and Charles Tilly. Cambridge: Cambridge University Press.

Gruenbaum, Ellen. 2001. *The Female Circumcision Controversy: An Anthropological Perspective*. Pennsylvania: University of Pennsylvania Press.

Guenther, Olaf. 2012. "Purity in Danger: Strategies of Purifiying Oneself in a Hostile Environment. The Case Study of Soviet Central Asia." In *How Purity Is Made*, edited by Petra Roesch and Udo Simon, 353–68. Wiesbaden: Harrossowitz Verlag.

Guidère, Mathieu. 2012. *Historical Dictionary of Islamic Fundamentalism*. Maryland: Scarecrow Press.

El Guindi, Fadwa. 1999. *Veil: Modesty, Privacy and Resistance*. New York: Berg.

Hadi, Amirul. 2004. *Islam and State in Sumatra: A Study of Seventeenth Century Aceh*. Leiden: Brill.

Hadiz, Vedi. 2016. *Islamic Populism in Indonesia and the Middle East*. Cambridge: Cambridge University Press.

Hadiz, Vedi, and Richard Robison. 2012. *Reorganising Power in Indonesia: The Politics of Oligarchy in an Age of Markets*. London: Routledge.

Hafiludin, Bambang Irawa, Derby Murti Nasution, and Zainal Arifin Aly. 1998. *Bahaya Islam Jama'ah, Lemkari, LDII: Pengakuan Mantan Gembong-Gembong LDII, Ust. Bambang Irawan Hafiluddin, Ust. Debby Murti Nasution, Ust. Zaenal Arifin Aly, Ust. Hasyim Rifa'in, Fatwa-Fatwa Ulama Dan Aneka Kasus LDII.* Jakarta: Gema Insani.

Haj, Samira. 2008. *Reconfiguring Islamic Tradition: Reform, Rationality, and Modernity*. Redwood City, CA: Stanford University Press.

Haleem, M.A.S. Abdel. 2005. *The Qur'an*. New York: Oxford University Press.

Hallaq, Wael B. 1984. "Was the Gate of Ijtihad Closed?" *International Journal of Middle East Studies* 16 (01): 3–41.

Hallaq, Wael B. 1999. *A History of Islamic Legal Theories: An Introduction to Sunni Usul al-Fiqh*. Cambridge: Cambridge University Press.

Hallaq, Wael B. 2001. *Authority, Continuity and Change in Islamic Law*. California: Cambridge University Press.

Hallaq, Wael B. 2005. *The Origins and Evolution of Islamic Law*. Cambridge University Press.

Hamad, Ibn. 2004. *Konstruksi Realitas Politik Dalam Media Massa, Sebuah Studi Critical Discourse Analysis Terhadap Berita-Berita Politik*. Jakarta: Granit.

Hamka, Rusydi. 1981. *Pribadi Dan Martabat Buya Prof. Dr. Hamka*. Jakarta: Pustaka Panjimas.

Haris, Syamsuddin, ed. 2005. *Pemilu Langsung Di Tengah Oligarki Partai: Proses Nominasi Dan Seleksi Calon Legislatif Pemilu 2004*. Jakarta: Gramedia Pustaka Utama.

Hasan, Noorhaidi. 2005. "September 11 and Islamic Militancy in Post-New Order Indonesia." In *Islam in Southeast Asia: Political, Social, and Strategic Challenges for the 21st Century*, 301–324. Singapore: Institute of Southeast Asian Studies.

Hasan, Noorhaidi. 2006. *Laskar Jihad*. Ithaca: SEAP Publications.

Hasani, Ismail, and Bonar Tigor Naipospos. 2011. *Wajah Para Pembela Islam*. Jakarta: Pustaka Masyarakat Setara.

Hasanuddin, Maulana. 2011. "Hukum Mengikuti Jamuan Makan Pemeluk Agama Lain." *Jurnal Halal*.

Hashem, M. 2006. "Contemporary Islamic Activism: The Shades of Praxis." *Sociology of Religion* 67 (1) (March 1): 23–41.

Hasyim, Syafiq. "Fatwas and Democracy: Majelis Ulama Indonesia (MUI, Indonesian Ulema Council) and Rising Conservatism in Indonesian Islam." *TRaNS: Trans-Regional and -National Studies of Southeast Asia* 8, no. 1 (2020): 21–35. https://doi.org/10.1017/trn.2019.13.

Hasyim, Syafiq. "MUI and Its Discursive Relevance for 'Aksi Bela Islam': A Growing Trend of Islamic Conservatism in Indonesia." In *Rising Islamic Conservatism in Indonesia: Islamic Groups and Identity Politics*, edited by Leonard C. Sebastian, Syafiq Hasyim, and Alexander R. Arifianto, 116–32. London & New York: Routledge, 2021.

Hasyim, Syafiq. "The Council of Indonesian Ulama (Majelis Ulama Indonesia, MUI) and Religious Freedom," Irasec's Discussion Papers, 12, 2011.

Hasyim, Syafiq. "The Council of Indonesian Ulama (MUI) and Aqidah-Based Intolerance: A Critical Analysis of Its Fatwa on Ahmadiyah and 'Sepilis.'" In *Religion, Law and Intolerance in Indonesia*, edited by Tim Lindsey and Helen Pausacker, 211–33. New York: Routledge, 2016.

Hatherell, Michael. *Political Representation in Indonesia: The Emergence of the Innovative Technocrats*. London: Routledge, 2019.

Hefner, Robert W. 1993. "Islam, State, and Civil Society: ICMI and the Struggle for the Indonesian Middle Class." *Indonesia* (56): 1–35.

Hefner, Robert W. 2003. "Islamizing Capitalism: On the Founding of First Islamic Bank." In *Shari'a and Politics in Modern Indonesia*, edited by Arskal Salim and Azyumardi Azra, 148–167. Singapore: Institute of Southeast Asian Studies.

Hefner, Robert W. 1999. "Islam and Nation in the Post-Suharto Era." In *The Politics of Post-Suharto Indonesia*, edited by Adam Schwarz and Jonathan Paris, 40–72. New South Wales: Council on Foreign Relations.

Hefner, Robert W. 2001. "Public Islam and the Problem of Democratization." *Sociology of Religion* 62 (4): 491–14.

Hefner, Robert W. 2011a. *Civil Islam: Muslims and Democratization in Indonesia*. New Jersey: Princeton University Press.

Hefner, Robert W. 2011b. "Indonesia: Shari'a Politics and Democratic Transition." In *Shari'a Politics: Islamic Law and Society in the Modern World*, 280–303. Indiana University Press.

Hefner, Robert W. 2012. "Shari'a Politics and Indonesian Democracy." *The Review of Faith & International Affairs* 10 (04): 61–69.

Henry, Clement M, and Rodney Wilson. 2004. "Introduction." In *The Politics of Islamic Finance*, edited by Clement M. Henry and Rodney Willson, 1–16. Edinburgh: Edinburgh University Press.

Hewitt, Lyndi, and Holly J. McCammon. 2005. "Explaining Suffrage Mobilization: Balance, Neutralization and Range in Collective Action Frames." In *Frames Of Protest: Social Movements and The Framing Perspective*, edited by Johnston Hank and John A. Noakes, 33–53. Maryland: Rowman & Littlefield.

Hilmy, Masdar. 2010. *Islamism and Democracy in Indonesia*. Singapore: ISEAS.

Hoexter, Miriam, Shmuel Noah Eisenstadt, and Nehemia Levtzion, ed. 2002. *The Public Sphere in Muslim Societies*. New York: SUNY Press.

Hooker, M.B. 2008. *Indonesian Syariah, Defining a National School of Islamic Law*. Singapore: ISEAS.

Horowitz, Donald L. 2013. *Constitutional Change and Democracy in Indonesia*. Cambridge: Cambridge University Press.

Hosen, Nadirsyah. 2004. "Behind the Scenes: Fatwas of Majelis Ulama Indonesia." *Journal of Islamic Studies* 2 (15): 147–179.

Hosen, Nadirsyah. 2005. "Religion and the Indonesian Constitution: A Recent Debate." *Journal of Southeast Asian Studies* 36 (3): 419–440.

Hosen, Nadirsyah. 2007. *Shari'a & Constitutional Reform in Indonesia.* Singapore: Institute of Southeast Asian Studies.

Houben, Vincent J. 2003. "Southeast Asia and Islam." *ANNALS, APPSS* (588): 149–170.

Hourani, Albert. 1998. *Arabic Thought in the Liberal Age 1798–1939*. Cambridge: Cambridge University Press.

Howard, Dick. 2001. "Good Governance and the Indonesian Economy." In *Gus Dur and the Indonesian Economy*, edited by Anthony L Smith, 83–92. Singapore: ISEAS.

Huda, Ni'matul, and Imam Nasef. *Penataan Demokrasi Dan Pemilu Di Indonesia Pasca Reformasi*. Jakarta: Kencana, 2017.

Huff, Toby E., and Wolfgang Schluchter, ed. 1999. *Max Weber and Islam.* Transaction Publishers.

Human Rights Watch. 2012. "World Report 2012: Events of 2011". Seven Stories Press.

Human Rights Watch. 2013. "In Religion's Name, Abuses Against Religious Minorities in Indonesia."

Ibn ʿAbbās. 1992. *Tanwīr al-Miqbās*. Beirut: Dār al-Kutub al-ʿIlmiyya.

Ibn Ṣalāh. 1986. *Fatāwā wa Masāʾil Ibn Ṣalāḥ fī al-Tafsīr wa al-Ḥadīth wa al-Uṣūl wa al-Fiqh wa maʿahu Adab al-Muftī wa al-Mustaftī*. Edited by ʿAbd al-Muʿṭī Amīn Qalʿajī. Beirut: Dār al-Maʿrifa.

Ibrahim, Ahmad, Sharon Siddique, and Yasmin Hussain, ed. 1985. *Readings on Islam in Southeast Asia*. Singapore: ISEAS.

Ichwan, Moch Nur. "Towards A Puritanical Moderate Islam: The Majlis Ulama Indonesia and the Politics of Religious Orthodoxy." In *Contemporary Developments in Indonesian Islam: Explaining the "Conservative Turn,"* edited by Martin van Bruinessen, 60–104. Singapore: ISEAS, 2013.

Ichwan, Moch Nur. 2011. "Offcial Ulema and the Politics of Re-Islamization: The Majelis Permusyawaratan Ulama, Sharīʿatization and Contested Authority in Post-New Order Aceh." *Journal of Islamic Studies* 22 (2): 183–214.

Idrus, Nurul Ilmi. 2013. "Islam, Marriage and Gender Relations in Bugis Lontara': A Critical Analysis of the Lontara' Daramatasia." In *Gender and Islam in Southeast Asia: Women's Rights Movements, Religious Resurgence and Local Traditions*, edited by Susanne Schroeter, 95–110. Leiden: BRILL.

Indonesian Ministry of National Development Planning. *The Indonesia Masterplan of Sharia Economy 2019–2024*. Jakarta: Indonesian Ministry of National Development Planning, 2019.

Intan, Benyamin Fleming. 2006. *Public Religion and the Pancasila-Based State of Indonesia: An Ethical and Sociological Analysis*. New York: Peter Lang.

Ismail, Salwa. 2006. *Rethinking Islamist Politics: Culture, the State and Islamism*. London & New York: I.B. Tauris.

Jackson, Karl D. 1980. *Traditional Authority, Islam, and Rebellion: A Study of Indonesian Political Behavior*. California: University of California Press.

Al-Jābirī, Muḥammad ʿĀbid. 2007. *Al-ʿAql al-ʿArabī al-Siyāsī: Muḥaddātuhu wa Tajalliyātuhu*. Beirut: Markaz Dirāsāt al-Waḥda al-ʿArabiyya.

Al-Jabri, Mohammed Abed. 2009. *Democracy, Human Rights and Law in Islamic Thought*. London & New York: I.B. Tauris.

Jahroni, Jajang. 2008. *Defending the Majesty of Islam: Indonesia's Front Pembela Islam, 1998–2003*. Bangkok: Asian Muslim Action Network.

Jamil, M. Mukshin, and Rusmadi. 2010. *Membendung Despotisme Wacana Agama: Kritik Atas Otoritarianisme Fatwa MUI Tentang Pluralisme, Liberalisme, Dan Sekulerisme*. Semarang: Walisongo Press.

Jawad, H.A. 1998. *The Rights of Women in Islam: An Authentic Approach*. Oxford: Palgrave Macmillan.

Jawed, Nasim A. 1999. *Islam's Political Culture: Religion and Politics in Predivided Pakistan*. Austin: University of Texas Press.

Jenkins, Craig J., and William Form. 2005. "Social Movements and Social Change." In *The Handbook of Political Sociology: States, Civil Societies, and Globalization*, 331–349. Cambridge: Cambridge University Press.

Johns, A.H. 1985. "Islam in Southeast Asia: Problems of Perspective." In *Readings on Islam in Southeast Asia*, edited by Ibrahim Ahmad, Sharon Siddique, and Yasmin Hussain, 20–24. Singapore: Institute of Southeast Asian Studies.

Juhannis, Hamdan. 2006. "The Struggle for Formalist Islam in South Sulawesi from Darul Islam to Komite Persiapan Penegakan Syariah Islam (KPPSI)". Australian National University.

Kahin, George McTurman. 2003. *Nationalism and Revolution in Indonesia*. Ithaca: SEAP Publications.

Kamali, Mohammad Hashim. 2007. "Sharʿīah and Civil Law: Towards a Methodlogy of Harmonization." *Islamic Law and Society* (*Koninklijke Brill NV*) 14 (3): 391–420.

Kamil, Sukron, and Chaeder S. Bamualim, ed. 2007. *Syariah Islam Dan HAM, Dampak Perda Syariah Terhadap Kebebasan Sipil, Hak-Hak Perempuan, Dan Non-Muslim*. Jakarta: CSRC & Konrad Adenauer Stiftung.

Karanja, Daniel Njoroge. 2003. *Female Genital Mutilation in Africa*. Michigan: Xulon Press.

Karni, Asrori S., Musthafa Helmy, and Ahmadie Thaha. 2010. *35 Tahun Majelis Ulama Indonesia*. Jakarta: Komisi Informasi dan Komunikasi Majelis Ulama Indonesia.

Kathīr, Ibn. 1999. *Tafsīr al-Qurʾān al-ʿAẓīm, Vol. 1*. Edited by Sāmī b. Muḥammad al-Salāma. Dār al-Tayyiba li al-Nashr wa al-Tawzīʿ.

Keddie, Nikki R. 1972. *Scholars, Saints, and Sufis: Muslim Religious Institutions in the Middle East Since 1500*. Berkley, Los Angeles & London: University of California Press.

Keddie, Nikki R. 2012. *Women in the Middle East: Past and Present*. New Jersey: Princeton University Press.

Kell, Tim, and Cornell University. Modern Indonesia Project. 1989. *The Roots of Acehnese Rebellion, 1989–1992*. Ithaca: Cornell Modern Indonesia Project, Southeast Asia Programme, Cornell University.

Kepel, Gilles. 1986. *Muslim Extremism in Egypt: the Prophet and Pharoah*. Berkeley & Los Angeles: University of California Press.

Khan, I.K. 2006. *Islam in Modern Asia*. New Delhi: M.D. Publications Pvt. Ltd.

Khan, Muhammad Akram. 2012. *Islamic Economics and Finance: A Glossary. The Handbook of Islamic Banking*. London & New York: Routledge.

Khan, Shahnaz. 2011. *Zina, Transnational Feminism, and the Moral Regulation of Pakistani Women*. Vancouver: UBC Press.

Khanam, R. 2005. *Encycl. Ethnography Of Middle-East And Central Asia*. New Delhi: Global Vision Publishing House.

King, Dwight Y. 2003. *Half-Hearted Reform: Electoral Institutions and the Struggle for Democracy in Indonesia* (*Google eBook*). Westport: Greenwood Publishing Group.

Kitiarsa, Pattana, ed. 2008. *Religious Commodifications in Asia: Marketing Gods*. London & New York: Routledge.

Klandermans, Bert, and Sicco van Goslinga. 1996. "Media Discourse, Movement Publicity, and the Generation of Collective Action Frames: Theoretical and Empirical Exercises in Meaning Construction." In *Comparative Perspectives on Social…*, 312–337. Cambridge: Cambridge University Press.

Klandermans, Bert and Conny Roggeband. 2009. *Handbook of Social Movements Across Disciplines*. New York, Dordrecht, Heidelberg, London: Springer.

Klosko, Wall. 2004. *Perfectionism and Neutrality: Essays in Liberal Theory*. Edited by Steven Wall and George Klosko. Oxford: Rowman & Littlefield Publishers.

Köstenberger, Andreas Johannes, and Michael J. Kruger. 2010. *The Heresy of Orthodoxy: How Contemporary Culture's Fascination with Diversity Has Reshaped Our Understanding of Early Christianity*. Wheaton, IL: Crossway.

Krawietz, Birgit. 2008. "Justice as a Pervasive Principle in Islamic Law." In *Islam and the Rule of Law, Between Sharia and Secularization*, edited by Birgit Krawietz and Helmut Reifeld, 35–48. Berlin: Konrad Adenauer Stiftung.

Kull, Ann. 2005. *Piety and Politics*. Lund: Department of History and Anthropology of Religion Lund University.

Kuntowijoyo, and A.E. Priyono. 2008. *Paradigma Islam: Interpretasi Untuk Aksi*. Bandung: PT Mizan Publika.

Kunzman, Robert. 2006. *Grappling with the Good : Talking About Religion and Morality in Public Schools*. Albany: State University of New York Press.

Kuran, Timur. 2006. "Islamism and Economics: Policy Prescriptions for a Free Society." In *Islam and the Everyday World Public Policy Dilemmas*, edited by Sohrab Behdad and Farhad Nomani, 38–65. New York: Routledge.

Kurzman, Charles. 2002. *Modernist Islam, 1840–1940: A Sourcebook*. Oxford & New York: Oxford University Press.

Laffan, Michael. 2003. *Islamic Nationhood and Colonial Indonesia: The Ummah Below the Winds*. London & New York: Routledge Curzon.

Lapidus, Ira M. 2002. *A History of Islamic Societies*. Cambridge: Cambridge University Press.

Latif, Yudi. 2008. *Indonesian Muslim*. Singapore: Institute of Southeast Asian Studies.

Layish, Aharon. 2002. "The Qādī's Role in the Islamization of Sedentary Tribal Society." In *The Public Sphere in Muslim Societies*, edited by Miriam Hoexter, Shmuel N. Eisenstadt, and Nehemia Levtzion, 83–108. New York: State University of New York Press.

Lefebvre, Henri. 1991. *The Production of Space*. Oxford & Cambridge MA: Blackwell Publishing.

Lessnoff, Michael. 2007. "Islam, Modernity and Science." In *Ernest Gellner and Contemporary Social Thought*, edited by Sinisa Malesevic and Mark Haugaard. Vol. 2007. Cambridge: Cambridge University Press.

Levy, J.S., and M. Froelich. 1985. "Causes of the Iran-Iraq War." In *Regionalization of Warfare*, 127–143. New Bruncswick, NJ: Transaction Books.

Liddle, William R., and Saiful Muzani. "Indonesian Democracy from Transition to Consolidation." In *Democracy, Islam and Indonesia*, edited by Mirjam Kuenkler and Alfred Stephan, 23–52. New York: Columbia University Press, 2013.

Lindsey, Tim. 2012. "Monopolising Islam? The Indonesian Ulama Council and State Regulation of the 'Islamic Economy'." *Bulletin of Indonesian Economic Studies* 48 (2): 253–74.

Lindsey, Tim, and Jeremy Kingsley. 2008. "Talking in Code: Legal Islamisation in Indonesia and the MMI Shari'a Criminal Code." In *The Law Applied: Contextualizing the Islamic Shari'a : a Volume in Honor of Frank E. Vogel*, edited by Peri J. Bearman, Wolfhart Heinrichs, and Bernard G. Weiss, 295–320. London & New York: I.B. Tauris.

Lombardi, Clark B. 2006. *State Law as Islamic Law in Modern Egypt: The Incorporation of the Sharīʿa into Egyptian Constitutional Law*. Leiden: Brill Academic Pub.

LPPOM. 2011. *Indonesia Halal Directory 2001*. Jakarta: LPPOM MUI.

LPPOM MUI, and AIFDC ICU. 2010. *General Guidelines of Halal Assurance System*. Jakarta: LPPOM MUI.

Luth, Thohir. 1999. *M. Natsir, Dakwah Dan Pemikirannya*. Jakarta: Gema Insani.

Machmudi, Yon. 2008. *The Rise of Jemaah Tarbiyah and the Prosperous Justice Party (PKS)*. Canberra: ANU E Press.

Maher, Michael T. 2001. "Framing: An Emerging Paradigm or A Phase of Agenda Setting?" In *Framing Public Life: Perspectives on Media and Our Understanding of the Social World*, edited by Stephen D. Reese, Oscar H. Gandy, and August E. Grant, 83–94. New Jersey: Routledge.

Mahkamah Konstitusi. 2009. *PUTUSAN Nomor 140/PUU-VII/2009*.

Mahmood, Saba. 2011. *Politics of Piety: The Islamic Revival and the Feminist Subject*. New Bruncswick, NJ: Princeton University Press.

Mahmud, Badawi. 2008. *100 Pesan Nabi Untuk Wanita Salihah*. Bandung: Mizan Pustaka.

Majalah Tokoh Indonesia. 2006. "BeritaTokoh, Aisyah Aminy." *Majalah Tokoh Indonesia*. http://www.tokohindonesia.com/pustaka/mti-22-aisyah-amini/index.html, viewed on 21 December 2011.

Majelis Permusyawaratan Ulama. 2005. *Kumpulan Fatwa-Fatwa Majelis Ulama Daerah Istimewa Aceh*. Aceh: MPU Provinsi Nangroe Aceh Darussalam.

Mandaville, Peter G. 2002. *Transnational Muslim Politics: Reimagining the Umma*. Vol. 2002. London & New York: Routledge.

Mansurnoor, Iik Arifin. 2002. "Islam in Brunei Darussalam and Global Islam: An Analysis of Their Interaction." In *Islam in the Era of Globalization: Muslim Attitudes Towards Modernity and Identity*, edited by Johan H. Mueleman, 71–98. London & New York: Routledge.

Mas'udi, Masdar F. 2010. *Syarah Konstitusi UUD 1945 Dalam Perspektif Islam*. Jakarta: Alvabet.

Mas'udi, Masdar F., and Syafiq Hasyim. 1998. "KH. Syukri Ghozali: Arsitek Majelis Ulama Indonesia." In *Tokoh Dan Pemimpin Agama: Biografi Sosial Intelektual*, edited by Saiful Umam and Azyumardi Azra. Jakarta: PPIM.

Masud, M.K., B.M. Messick, and D.S. Powers. 1996. *Islamic Legal Interpretation*. Cambridge, Massachusetts, London: Harvard University Press.

McAdam, Doug. 1996. "Conceptual Origins, Current Problems, Future Direction." In *Comparative Perspective on Social Movements*, edited by John D. McCharty and Mayer N. Zald, 23–41. Cambridge: Cambridge University Press.

McAdam, Doug. 1996. "The Framing Function of Movement Tactics: Strategic Dramaturgy in the American Civil Rights Movement." In *Comparative Perspectives on Social Movements: Political Opportunities, Mobilising Structures and Cultural Framings*, edited by Doug McAdam, John D. McCarthy, and Mayer Zald, 338–56. Cambridge: Cambridge University Press.

McAdam, Doug, John McCarthy, and Mayer Zald, ed. 1996. *Comparative Perspectives on Social Movements: Political Opportunities, Mobilizing Structures, and Cultural Framings*. Cambridge: Cambridge University Press.

McAdam, Doug, and Richard Scott William. 2005. "Organization and Movements." In *Social Movements and Organization Theory*, edited by F. Davis Gerald, Doug McAdam, and Richard Scott William, 4–40. Cambridge: Cambridge University Press.

Mehden, Fred R. Von Der. 1993. *Two Worlds of Islam: Interaction Between Southeast Asia and the Middle East*. Florida: University Press of Florida.

Meyer, David S., and Suzanne Staggenborg. 2012. "Thinking About Strategy." In *Strategies for Social Change*, edited by Gregory M. Maney, Rachel V. Kutz-Flamenbaum, Deana A. Rohlinger, and Jeff Goodwin, 3–23. Minneapolis: U of Minnesota Press.

Meyer, Davis S. 2002. "Opportunities and Identities: Bridge Building in the Social Movements." In *Social Movements, Identity, Culture and the State*, edited by David S. Meyer, Nancy Whittier, and Belinda Robnett. Oxford, New York: Oxford University Press.

Mietzner, Marcus. 2009. *Military Politics, Islam and the State in Indonesia: From Turbulent Transition to Democratic Consolidation*. Singapore: ISEAS.

Mobeni-Kasheh, Natalie. 2004. *The Hadrami Awakening: Community and Identity in the Netherlands East Indies, 1900–1942*. Cornell: Cornell South East Asia Publication.

Mohamad, Herry. 2006. *Tokoh-Tokoh Islam Yang Berpengaruh Abad 20*. Jakarta: Gema Insani Press.

Morris, Aldon D., and Suzanne Staggenborg. 2004. "Leadership in Social Movements." In *The Blackwell Companion to Social Movements*, edited by David A. Snow, Sarah A. Soule, and Hanspeter Kriesi, 172–196. Malden: Blackwell Publishing.

Morris, Eric. 1985. "Aceh: Social Revolution and the Islamic Vision." In *Regional Dynamics of the Indonesian Revolution: Unity from Diversity*, edited by Audrey R. Kahin, 82–110. Honolulu: University of Hawaii Press.

Morrison, James H. 1998. "A Global Perspective of Oral History in South in Southeast Asia Theory and Method." In *Oral History in Southeast Asia Theory and Method*, edited by P. Lim Pui Huen, James H. Morrison, and Chua Chong Guan, 1–16. Singapore: ISEAS.

Morton, W. Scott, and Charlton M. Lewis. 2004. *China: Its History and Culture*. Columbus: McGraw Hill Professional.

Moustafa, Tamir. *Constituting Religion: Islam, Liberal Rights, and the Malaysian State*. Cambridge & New York: Cambridge University Press, 2018.

Mudzhar, Muhammad Atho. 1993. *Fatwa of the Council of Indonesian Ulama: A Study of Islamic Legal Thought in Indonesia 1975–1988*. Jakarta: INIS.

Mudzhar, Muhammad Atho. 2012. "Prolog: Fatwa MUI Sebagai Obyek Kajian Hukum Islam Dan Sumber Sejarah Sosial." In *Fatwa Majelis Ulama Dalam Perspektif Hukum Dan Perundang-Undangan*, edited by Nahar Nahrawi, Nuhrison M. Nuh, Asrarun Niam Sholeh, and Zaenal Abidin, xxv–xxxix. Jakarta: Puslitbang Kehidupan Keagamaan Badan Litbang dan Diklat Kementerian Agama RI.

Mueleman, Johan H. 2005. "The History of Islam in Southeast Asia: Some Questions and Debates." In *Islam in Southeast Asia: Political, Social, and Strategic Challenges for the 21st Century*, edited by K.S. Nathan and Mohammad Hashim Kamali, 362. Singapore: Institute of Southeast Asian Studies.

MUI. *Mengawal Aqidah Umat: Fatwa MUI Tentang Aliran-Aliran Sesat Di Indonesia*. Jakarta: Sekretariat Majelis Ulama Indonesia.

MUI. 1982. *Majelis Ulama, Ummat Dan Pembangunan*. Jakarta: Sekretariat Majelis Ulama Indonesia.

MUI. 1990. *15 Tahun Majelis Ulama Indonesia*. Edited by H.S. Prodjokusumo. Jakarta: Sekretariat Majelis Ulama Indonesia.

MUI. 1995. *20 Tahun Majelis Ulama Indonesia*. Edited by H.S. Prodjokusumo. Jakarta: Sekretariat Majelis Ulama Indonesia.

MUI. 1999. *Kumpulan Hasil-Hasil Kongres Umat Islam Indonesia, Umat Islam Menyongsong Era Indonesia Baru*. Jakarta: Dewan Pimpinan Majelis Ulama Indonesia.

MUI. 2003. *Himpunan Fatwa Majelis Ulama Indonesia*. Jakarta: Departemen Agama.

MUI. 2005a. *Dokumentasi Kongres Umat Islam Indonesia IV, Ukhuwah Islamiyah Untuk Indonesia Yang Bermartabat*. Jakarta: Majelis Ulama Indonesia.

MUI. 2005b. *Kongres Umat Islam Indonesaia IV: Proses Dan Dinamika Permusyawaratan*. Jakarta: BPKUII IV.

MUI. 2005c. *Fatwa Munas VII Majelis Ulama Indonesia*. Jakarta: Majelis Ulama Indonesia.

MUI. 2005d. *Himpunan Keputusan Musyawarah Nasional VII Majelis Ulama Indonesia 2005*. Jakarta: Sekretariat Majelis Ulama Indonesia.

MUI. 2005e. *Deklarasi Jakarta*. Jakarta: Badan Pekerja Kongres Umat Islam Indonesia IV.

MUI. 2009. *Ijma' Ulama: Keputusan Ijma' Ulama Komisi Fatwa Se-Indonesia III*. Jakarta: Majelis Ulama Indonesia.

MUI. 2010a. *Pedoman Penyelenggaraan Organisasi Majelis Ulama Indonesia*. Jakarta: Sekretariat Majelis Ulama Indonesia.

MUI. 2010b. *Himpunan Keputusan Musyawarah Nasional VIII Majelis Ulama Indonesia*. Jakarta: Majelis Mujahidin Indonesia.

MUI. 2010c. *Buku Materi Kongres Umat Islam Indonesia V, "Kepemimpinan Umat Untuk Kesejahteraan Bangsa*. Jakarta: Panitia Pengarah Kongres Umat Islam Indonesia V.

MUI. 2011. *Himpunan Fatwa MUI Sejak 1975*. Jakarta: Erlangga.

MUI Kabupaten Cianjur. 2009. *30 Tahun MUI Cianjur: Selayang Pandang Perjalanan Panjang MUI Cianjur*. Cianjur: Majelis Ulama Indonesia (MUI) Kabupaten Cianjur.

Mujīburraḥmān. 2006. *Feeling Threatened: Muslim-Christian Relations in Indonesia's New Order*. Amsterdam: Amsterdam University Press.

Mulder, Niels. 2005. *Mysticism in Java: Ideology in Indonesia*. Yogyakarta: Kanisius.

Muljana, Slamet. 2005. *Hindu-Jawa dan Timbulnya Negara-Negara Islam di Nusantara*. Yogyakarta: PT LKiS Pelangi Aksara.

Mulkhan, Abdul Munir. 2009. *Politik Santri: Cara Menang Merebut Hati Rakyat*. Yogyakarta: Kanisius.

N.A. Baloch. 2008. "The Advent of Islam in Indonesia and Some Problems Related to the History of Early Muslim Period." */Jurnal/Al-Jamiah/Al-Jamiah No. 22 Th. XV-1980/*. Yogyakarta: Perpustakaan UIN Sunan Kalijaga Yogyakarta.

Nagata, Judith. 1980. "Religious Ideology and Social Change: The Islamic Revival in Malaysia." *Pacific Affairs* 53 (3): 405–39.

Nair, Shanti. 1997. *Islam in Malaysian Foreign Policy*. New York: Routledge.

Najib, Muhammad. 1999. *Melawan Arus: Pemikiran Dan Langkah Politik Amien Rais*. Jakarta: Serambi.

Nasr, Seyyed Vali Reza. 1994. *The Vanguard of the Islamic Revolution: The Jama'at-i Islami of Pakistan*. London: I.B.Tauris.

Nasr, Vali. 2002. "The Iranian Revolution and Changes in Islamism in Pakistan, India and Afghanistan." In *Iran and the Surrounding World: Interactions in Culture and Cultural Politics*. Seattle: University of Washington Press.

Noakes, John A., and Hank Johnston. 2005. "Frames of Protest: A Road Map to a Perspective." In *Frames of Protest: Social Movements and The Framing Perspective*, edited by Hank Johnston and John A. Noakes, 1–33. Maryland: Rowman & Littlefield.

Noer, Deliar. 1973. *The Modernist Muslim Movement in Indonesia, 1900–1942*. Oxford: Oxford University Press.

Noer, Deliar. 1998. *Administrasi Islam Di Indonesia*. Jakarta: Rajawali.

Nordholt, Schulte Nico G. 2003. "Kekerasan dan Anarki Negara Indonesia Modern." In *Orde Zonder Order: Kekerasan Dan Dendam Di Indonesia 1965–1998*, edited by Huub de Jonge and Frans Hüsken, 83–107. PT LKiS Pelangi Aksara.

Nurlaelawati, Euis. 2013. "Sharia Bylaws: The Legal Position of Women in Children and Women in Banten and West Java." In *Regime Change, Democracy and Islam: The Case of Indonesia*, edited by C. van Dijk, 11–81. Leiden.

Olesen, Thomas. 2009. "Social Movement Theory and Radical Islamic Activism." In *Islamism as Social Movement*, edited by Thomas Olesen and Farhad Khosrochavar. Aarhus: Centre for Studies in Islamism and Radicalisation.

Olle, John. 2009. "The Majelis Ulama Indonesia Versus 'Heresy': The Resurgence of Authoritarian Islam." In *State of Authority: The State in Society in Indonesia*, edited by Geert Arend van Klinken and Barker Joshua, 95–116. Ithaca: Cornell South East Asia Publication.

Opwis, Felicitas. 2005. "Maslaha in Contemporary Islamic Legal Theory." *Islamic Law and Society* 12 (2): 82–223.

Opwis, Felicitas. 2010. *Maṣlaḥah and the Purpose of the Law: Islamic Discourse on Legal Change from the 4th/10th to 8th/14th Century*. Leiden & Boston: Brill.

Otto, Jan Michiel. 2008. *Sharia and National Law in Muslim Countries: Tensions and Opportunities for Dutch and EU Foreign Policy*. Amsterdam: Amsterdam University Press.

Opwis, Felicitas, ed. 2010. *Sharia Incorporated: A Comparative Overview of the Legal Systems of Twelve Muslim Countries in Past and Present*. Amsterdam: Amsterdam University Press.

Pambudi, A. 2009. *Kalau Prabowo Jadi Presiden*. Yogyakarta: Penerbit Narasi.

Parsons, Nicholas, and Marcus Mietzner. 2009. "Sharia By-Laws in Indonesia: Legal and Political Analysis." *Australian Journal of Asian Law* 11 (2): 190–217.

Passy, Florence. 2003. "Social Networks Matter. But How?" In *Social Movements and Networks: Relational Approaches to Collective Action: Relational Approaches to Collective Action*, edited by Mario Diani and Doug McAdam, 21–48. Oxford: Oxford University Press.

Peach, Lucinda J. 2002. *Legislating Morality: Pluralism and Religious Identity in Lawmaking*. Oxford & New York: Oxford University Press.

Peterson, Daniel. *Islam, Blasphemy, and Human Rights in Indonesia: The Trial of Ahok*. New York: Routledge, 2020.

Peterson, Daniel. "The Majelis Ulama Indonesia and Its Role in the Ahok Conviction." *Australian Journal of Asian Law* 21, no. 1 (2020): 1–18.

Platzdasch, Bernhard. 2009. *Islamism in Indonesia: Politics in the Emerging Democracy*. Singapore: Institute of Southeast Asian Studies.

Poesponegoro, Marwati Djoened, and Nugroho Notosusanto. 1992. *Sejarah Nasional Indonesia III: Zaman Pertumbuhan Dan Perkembangan Kerajaan Islam Di Indonesia*. Jakarta: Balai Pustaka.

Porter, Donald J. 2004. *Managing Politics and Islam in Indonesia*. London & New York: Routledge Curzon.

Powers, Paul R. 2006. *Intent in Islamic Law: Motive and Meaning in Medieval Sunni Fiqh*. Leiden: Brill.

Power, Thomas P. "Jokowi's Authoritarian Turn and Indonesia's Democratic Decline." *Bulletin of Indonesian Economic Studies* 54, no. 3 (September 2, 2018): 307–38.

Pringle, Robert. 2010. *Understanding Islam in Indonesia: Politics and Diversity*. Singapore: Editions Didier Millet.

Rabi', Abu Ibrahim. 1996. *Intellectual Origins of Islamic Resurgence in the Modern Arab World*. Albany: State University of New York Press.

Rachman, Budhy Munawar, and Moh Shofan. 2010. *Argumen Islam Untuk Sekularisme*. Jakarta: Grasindo.

Rae, Ediana Dian. 2008. "Arah Perkembangan Hukum Perbankan Syariah." *Buletin Hukum Perbankan Dan Kebanksentralan* 6 (1): 7–13.

Rahardjo, M. 2002. *Islam Dan Transformasi Budaya*. Jakarta: LSAF.

Rahmat, M. Imdadun. 2005. *Arus Baru Islam Radikal, Transmisi Revivalisme Islam Timur Tengah Ke Indonesia*. Jakarta: Erlangga.

Rahmat, M. Imdadun. 2008. *Ideologi Politik PKS: Dari Masjid Kampus Ke Gedung Parlemen*. Yogyakarta: PT LKiS Pelangi Aksara.

Rais, M. Amien. 1987. *Cakrawala Islam: Antara Cita Dan Fakta*. Bandung: Mizan.

Rakhmat, Jalaluddin. 1991. *Islam Aktual: Refleksi-Sosial Seorang Cendekiawan Muslim*. Penerbit Mizan.

Ramage, Douglas. 2005. *Politics in Indonesia, Democracy, Islam and the Ideology of Tolerance*. London & New York: Routledge.

Rasmussen, Lissi. 2007. *Bridges Instead of Walls: Christian Muslim Interaction in Denmark, Indonesia and Nigeria*. Minneapolis: Lutheran University Press.

Rawls, John. 2011. *Political Liberalism: Expanded Edition*. New York: Columbia University Press.

Reid, Anthony. 2010. "Aceh and the Turkish Connection." In *Aceh: History, Politics and Culture*, 26–38. Singapore: Institute of Southeast Asian.

Renard, John. 2009. *Tales of God's Friends: Islamic Hagiography in Translation*. California: University of California Press.

Riaz, Mian N, and Muhammad M. Chaudry. 2004. *Halal Food Production*. London & New York: CRC Press.

Ricklefs, M.C. 2009. *A History of Modern Indonesia Since c.1200*. Redwood City, CA: Stanford University Press.

Riddell, Peter. 2001. *Islam and the Malay-Indonesian World: Transmission and Responses*. London: C. Hurst & Co. Publishers.

Robet, Robertus. 2010. "Perda, Fatwa and the Challenge to Secular Citizenship in Indonesia." In *State and Securalism: Perspective from Asia*, edited by Michael Heng Siam-Heng and Ten Chin Liew, 263–78. Singapore: World Scientific Publishing Co. Pte. Ltd.

Roff, William R. 1976. "The Institutionalisation of Islam in the Malay Peninsula: Some Problems for the Historian." In *Profiles of Malay Culture: Historiography, Religion and Politics*, 66–73. Jakarta: Ministry of Education and Culture.

Romli, Lili. 2006. "Cakupan Usulan Penyempurnaan Kebijakan Otonomi Daerah." In *Membangun Format Otonomi Daerah*, edited by Syamsuddin Haris, 159–75. Jakarta: LIPI Press.

Rosidin, Didin Nurul Didin. 2010. "The Role of Identity of Religious Authority in the Nation-state: Egypt, Indonesia and South Africa Compared." In *Varieties of Religious Authority: Changes and Challenges in Twentieth-Century Indonesian Islam*, edited by Azyumardi Azra, Kees van Dijk, and Nico J.G. Kapten, 93–113. Singapore: Institute of Southeast Asian Studies.

Roth, Dik. 2007. "Many Governors, No Provinces: The Struggle for a Province in the Luwu-Tanah Toraja Area in South Sulawesi." In *Renegotiating Boundaries: Local Politics in Post-Suharto Indonesia*, edited by Henk Schulte Nordholt and Gerry van Klinken, 121–50. Leiden: KITLV Press.

Rouse, Carolyn, and Hoskins Janet. 2004. "Purity, Soul Food, and Sunnī Islam: Explorations at the Intersection of Consumption and Resistance." *Cultural Anthropology* 19 (2): 226–49.

Roy, Olivier. 1996. *The Failure of Political Islam*. Cambridge, MA: Harvard University Press.

El Saadawi, Nawal. 2007. *The Hidden Face of Eve: Women in the Arab World*. London & New York: Zed Books.

Santoso, Topo, and Ida Budhiati. *Pemilu Di Indonesia: Kelembagaan, Pelaksanaan Dan Pengawasan*. Jakarta: Sinar Grafika, 2019.

Saat, Norshahril, ed. *Fulfilling the Trust: 50 Years of Shaping Muslim Religious Life in Singapore*. Singapore: World Scientific Publishing Co. Pte. Ltd., 2018.

Sachedina, Abdulaziz. 2000. *The Islamic Roots of Democratic Pluralism*. Oxford & New York: Oxford University Press.

Saefuddin, Ahmad, and Jujun Suparjan Suriasumantri. 1987. *Desekularisasi Pemikiran: Landasan Islamisasi*. Bandung: Mizan.

Safran, William, ed. 2002. *The Secular and the Sacred: Nation, Religion and Politics*. London & New York: Routledge.

Saleh, Fauzan. 2001. *Modern Trends in Islamic Theological Discourse in Twentieth Century Indonesia*. Leiden: Brill.

Salim, Arskal. 2003. "Zakat Administration in Politics of Indonesian New Order." In *Shari'a and Politics in Modern Indonesia*, edited by Arskal Salim and Azyumardi Azra, 181–192. Singapore: Institute of Southeast Asian Studies.

Salim, Arskal. 2008. *Challenging the Secular State: The Islamization of Law in Modern Indonesia*. Honolulu: University of Hawaii Press.

Salman, Tom, and Willem Assies. 2009. "Anthropology and the Study of Social Movements." In *Handbook of Social Movements Across Disciplines*, edited by Bert Klandermans and Conny Roggeband, 205–66. New York: Springer.

Salvatore, Armando. 2009. "The Reform Project in the Emerging Public Spheres." In *Islam and Modernity Key Issues and Debates*, edited by Muhammad Khalid Masud, Armando Salvatore, and Martin van Bruinessen, 185–205. Edinburgh: Edinburgh University Press.

Salvatore, Armando, and Dale F. Eickelman. 2006. "Public Islam and the Common Good." In *Public Islam and the Common Good*, edited by Armando Salvatore and Dale F. Eickelman, xi–xxv. Leiden & Boston: Brill.

Samson, Allan A. 1985. "Indonesian Islam Since the New Order." In *Readings on Islam in Southeast Asia*, edited by Ahmad Ibrahim, Sharon Siddique, and Hussain Yasmin, 165–70. Singapore: Institute of Southeast Asian Studies.

Sardar, Ziauddin. 2011. *Reading the Qur;an:The Contemporary Relevance of the Sacred Text of Islam*. Oxford & New York: Oxford University Press.

Sardar, Ziauddin, and A.E. Priyono. *Jihad Intelektual: Merumuskan Parameter-Parameter Sains Islam*. Jakarta: Risalah Gusti.

Sayyid, Bobby S. 1997. *A Fundamental Fear: Eurocentrim and the Emergence of Islamism*. London & New York: Zed Books.

Schielke, Samuli. 2008. "Policing Ambiguity: Muslim Saints-Day Festivals and the Moral Geography of Public Space in Egypt." *American Ethnologist* 33 (4): 539–52.

Schluchter, Wolfgang. 1989. *Rationalism, Religion, and Domination: a Weberian Perspective*. Berkeley, Los Angeles & Oxford: University of California Press.

Schneider, Cathy. 2005. "Political Opportunities and Framing Puerto Rican Identity in New York City." In *Frames of Protest: Social Movements and the Framing Perspective*, edited by Hank Johnston and John A. Noakes, 141–62. Maryland: Rowman & Littlefield.

Schrode, Paula. 2012. "Practices and Meanings of Purity and Worship among Young Sunni Muslims in Germany." In *How Purity Is Made*, edited by Petra Roesch and Udo Simon, 309–332. Wiesbaden: Harrossowitz Verlag.

Schwarz, Adam. 1997. "Indonesia After Suharto." *Foreign Affairs* 76 (4): 119–134.

Scientific School for Government Policy. 2006. *Dynamism in Islamic Activism: Reference Points for Democratisation and Human Rights*. Amsterdam: Amsterdam University Press.

Sedgwick, Mark. 2004. "Establishments and Sects in the Islamic World." In *New Religious Movements in the Twenty-First Century*, edited by Philip Charles Lucas and Thomas Robbins, 231–56. New York: Routledge.

Seng, Lim How. 2000. "Interviewing the Business and Political Elite of Singapore." In *Oral History in Southeast Asia Theory and Method*, edited by P. Lim Pui Huen, James H Morrison, and Kwa Chong Guan, 55–65. Singapore: Institute of Southeast Asian Studies.

Setara Institute. 2010. *Negara Harus Bersikap, Tiga Tahun Laporan Kondisi Kebebasan Beragama/Berkeyakinan Di Indonesia 2007–2009*. Jakarta: Setara Institute.

Sevea, Iqbal Singh. 2009. "The Ahmadiyya Print Jihad in South and Southeast Asia." In *Islamic Connections: Muslim Societies in South and Southeast Asia*, edited by R. Michael Feener and Iqbal Singh Sevea, 134–48. Singapore: Institute of Southeast Asian Studies.

Shepard, William F. 1987. "Islam and Ideology: Towards a Typology." *International Journal of Middle East Studies* 19: 307–66.

Al-Shāṭibī, Abū Isḥāq. 1998. *Al-Muwāfaqāt fī 'Ulūm al-Sharī'a*. Beirut: Dār al-Kutub al-Islāmiyya.

Shihab, Moh. Quraish. 2004. *Jilbab, Pakaian Wanita Muslimah: Pandangan Ulama Masa Lalu & Cendekiawan Kontemporer*. Jakarta: Lentera Hati.

Sholeh, Asrorun Ni'am. 2011. "Agenda Konsolidasi Regulasi Negara: Pertarungan Nilai Dan Ideologi Belum Selesai." *Mimbar Ulama Indonesia*, January.

Sihombing, Uli Parulian. 2008. *Menggugat Bakor Pakem: Kajian Hukum Terhadap Pengawasan Agama Dan Kepercayaan Di Indonesia*. Jakarta: Indonesian Legal Resource Center.

Singh, David Emmanuel. 2010. "Integrative Political Ideology of Mawlana Mawdudi and Islamisation of the Muslim Masses in the Indian Subcontinent." *South Asia: Journal of South Asian Studies* XXIII (1): 129–148.

Sinha, Vineeta. 2010. *Religion and Commodification: "Merchandizing" Diasporic Hinduism*. New York: Routledge.

Sirry, Mun'im. 2013. "Fatwas and Their Controversy: The Case of the Council of Indonesien Ulama." *Journal of Southeast Asian Studies* 44 (1): 100–117.

Sjamsuddin, Nazaruddin. 1985. *The Republican Revolt: A Study of the Acehnese Rebellion*. Singapore: Institute of Southeast Asian Studies.

Sloane-White, Patricia. *Corporate Islam: Sharia and the Modern Workplace*. Cambridge: Cambridge University Press, 2017.

Snow, David A., and Robert Benford. 2005. "Clarifying The Relationship Between Framing and Ideology." In *Frames of Protest: Social Movements and the Framing Perspective*, edited by Hank Johnston and John A. Noakes, 205–212. Oxford: Rowman & Littlefield.

Soebijoto, Hertanto. 2010. "Kasus Ariel: MUI Akan Surati Presiden." *Kompas.Com*, July. http://entertainment.kompas.com/read/2010/07/06/15513890/Kasus.Ariel.MUI.Akan.Surati.Presiden, viewed on 29 December 2011.

Springer, Devin R. 2009. *Islamic Radicalism and Global Jihad*. Washington: Georgetown University Press.

Standard & Poor's Rating Service. 2012. *Islamic Finance Outlook September 2012*. New York: McGraw-Hill Publishing.

Stauth, Georg. 2002. *Politics and Cultures of Islamization in Southeast Asia, Indonesia and Malaysia in the Nineteen-Nineties*. Bielefeld: Transcript Verlag.

Steenbrink, Karel. 1988. "Indian Teachers and Their Indonesian Pupils: On Intellectual Relations Between Indonesia and India 1600–1800." In *India and Indonesia in the Ancient Regime*, 129–142. Leiden & New York: Brill.

Subhan, Arief. 2010. "The Indonesian Madrasah: Islamic Reform and Modernization of Indonesian Islam in Twentieth Century." In *Varieties of Religious Authority: Changes and Challenges in Twentieth-Century Indonesian Islam*, edited by Azyumardi Azra, Kees van Dijk, and Nico J.G. Kaptein, 126–136. Singapore: Institute of Southeast Asian Studies.

Sukardi, Rinakit. 2005. *The Indonesian Military after the New Order*. Copenhagen: NIAS Press.

Sukardja, Ahmad. 1995. *Piagam Madinah Dan Undang-Undang Dasar 1945: Kajian Perbandingan Tentang Dasar Hidup Bersama Dalam Masyarakat Yang Majemuk*. Jakarta: Penerbit Universitas Indonesia.

Suksi, Markku. 2011. *Sub-State Governance through Territorial Autonomy: A Comparative Study in Constitutional Law of Powers, Procedures and Institutions*. Heidelberg, Dordrecht, London & New York: Springer.

Sulaiman, M. Isa. 2006. "From Autonomy to Periphery: A Critical Evaluation of the Acehnese Nationalist Movement." In *Verandah of Violence: The Background to the Aceh Problem*, edited by Anthony Reid, 122–49. Singapore: NUS Press.

Sulaiman, Tasirun. 2009. *Wisdom of Gontor*. Vol. 19. Bandung: PT Mizan Publika.

Sunarwoto. 2013. "Dakwah Radio in Surakarta: An Contest for Islamic Identity." In *Islam in Indonesia: Contrasting Images and Interpretations*, edited by Jajat Burhanudin and Kees van Dijk, 195–214. Amsterdam: Amsterdam University Press.

Sunyoto, Agus. 2011. *Wali Songo: Rekonstruksi Sejarah Yang Disingkirkan*. Jakarta: Transpustaka.

Sunyoto, Agus. 2012. *Atlas Wali Songo*. Jakarta: Kerjasama Pustaka IIMaN, Trans Pustaka, dan LTN PBNU.

Suprapto, Rohmat. 2001. *Syariat "Kacapi Suling" & Syariat Progresif (Pergulatan Politik Dan Hukum Di Era Otonomi Daerah)*. Yogyakarta: Samudera Biru.

Suryanegara, Ahmad Mansur. 2009. *Api Sejarah*. Bandung: Salamadani Pustaka Semesta.

Sutiyono, and Ahmad Dzulfikar. 2010. *Benturan Budaya Islam: Puritan & Sinkretis*. Jakarta: Penerbit Buku Kompas.

Tagore, Saranindranath. 2010. "Rawlsian Liberalism, Secularism, and the Call for Cosmopolitanism." In *State and Securalism: Perspective from Asia*, edited by Michael Heng Siam-Heng and Ten Chin Liew, 37–59. Singapore: World Scientific Publishing Co. Pte. Ltd.

Tanjung, Akbar. 2007. *The Golkar Way: Survival Partai Golkar Di Tengah Turbulensi Politik Era Transisi*. Jakarta: Gramedia Pustaka Utama.

Tarrow, Sidney. 2005. *The New Transnational Activism*. Cambridge: Cambridge University Press.

Taymiyya, Ibn. 1989. *Sharḥ al-ʿAqīda al-Wasaṭiyya*. Riyadh: Dār al-Salām li al-Nashr.

Taylor, Charles. 2005. "Modes of Secularism." In *Secularism and its Critics*, edited by Rajeev Bhargava. Vol. 2. Oxford University Press, Incorporated.

The International Council on Human Rights Policy. 2009. *When Legal Worlds Overlap: Human Rights, State and Non-State Law*. Switzerland: ICHRP.

Tibi, Bassam. 2013. *The Sharia State: Arab Spring and Democratization*. New York: Routledge.

Tie, Warwick. 1999. *Legal Pluralism: Toward a Multicultural Conception of Law*. London: Ashgate/Dartmouth.

Tilly, Charles. 1978. *From Mobilization to Revolution*. New York: McGraw-Hill Publishing Company.

Tjandrasasmita, Uka. 2009. *Arkeologi Islam Nusantara*. Jakarta: Balai Pustaka.

Tremain, Shelley Lynn. 2005. *Foucault and the Government of Disability*. Michigan: University of Michigan Press.

Al-Ṭūfī, Najm al-Dīn. 1993. *Risāla fī Riʿāya al-Maṣlaḥa*. Cairo: Dar al-Miṣriyya al-Lubnāniyya.

Turmudi, Endang. 2006. *Struggling For The Umma: Changing Leadership Roles of Kiai in Jombang East Java*. Canberra: ANU E Press.

Turner, Bryan. 2003. *Islam: Islam, State and Politics*. London & New York: Routledge.

Turner, Bryan. 2011. *Religion and Modern Society: Citizenship, Secularisation and the State*. Cambridge: Cambridge University Press.

Ufen, Andreas. 2009. "Mobilising Political Islam: Indonesia and Malaysia Compared." *Commonwealth & Comparative Politics* 47 (3): 308–333.

Umam, Saiful. 1998. *Tokoh Dan Pemimpin Agama: Biografi Sosial-Intelektual*. Jakarta: Diterbitkan oleh Badan Litbang Agama, Departemen Agama RI dan Pusat Pengkajian Islam dan Masarakat [i.e. Masyarakat].

Van Bruinessen, Martin. 1992. "Gerakan Sempalan Di Kalangan Ummat Islam Indonesia: Latar Belakang Sosial-Budaya." *Ulumul Qur'an* III (1): 16–27.

Van Bruinessen, Martin. 2002. "Genealogies of Islamic Radicalism in Post-Suharto Indonesia." *South East Asian Research* 10 (2): 117–154.

Van Bruinessen, Martin. 2012. "Indonesian Muslims and Their Place in the Larger World of Islam." In *Indonesia Rising: The Repositioning of Asia's Third Giant*, edited by Anthony Reid, 117–40. Singapore: Institute of Southeast Asian Studies.

Van Dyke, Nella, and Holly J. McCammon, eds. 2010. *Strategic Alliances: Coalition Building and Social Movements*. Minneapolis: University of Minnesota Press.

Vickers, Adrian. 2013. *A History of Modern Indonesia*. Cambridge: Cambridge University Press.

Vogel, Frank E. 2011. "Saudi Arabia: Public, Civil and Individual Shariʿa in Law and Politics." In *Shariʿa Politics: Islamic Law and Society in the Modern World*, edited by Robert W. Hefner, 55–93. Indiana: Indiana University Press.

Vogel, Frank E. 2000. *Islamic Law and the Legal System of Saudi: Studies of Saudi Arabia*. Leiden: Brill.

Wagemakers, Joas. 2011. "The Transformation of a Radical Concept: Al-Wala' wa al-Bara' in the Ideology of Abu Muhammad al-Maqdisi." In *Global Salafism: Islam's New Religious Movement*, edited by Roel Meijer, 81–106. New York: Columbia University Press.

Watson, C.W. 2000. *Of Self and Nation: Autobiography and the Representation of Modern Indonesia*. Honolulu: University of Hawaii Press.

Weinata, Sairin, ed. 1994. *Himpunan Peraturan Di Bidang Keagamaan*. Jakarta: BPK Gunung Mulia.

Weiss, Bernard G. 2006. *The Spirit of Islamic Law*. Georgia: University of Georgia Press.

Whittier, Nancy. 2002. "Meaning and Structure in Social Movements." In *Social Movements, Identity, Culture and the State*, edited by David S. Meyer, Nancy Whittier, and Belinda Robnett. Oxford, New York: Oxford University Press.

Wicaksono, Agung. "Gubernur DKI Jakarta Dipilih Presiden: Sebuah Wacana Yang Patut Dipertimbangkan." *Jurnal PolGov* 1, no. 1 (2019): 35–56.

Wictorowicz, Quintan, ed. 2004. *Islamic Activism: a Social Movement Theory Approach*. Indiana: Indiana University Press.

William, Case. 2003. "Interlocking Elite in Southeast Asia." In *Elite Configuration at the Apex of Power*, edited by Mattei Dogan. Leiden: Brill.

Williams, Rhys H. 2002. "From the 'Beloved Community' to 'Family Values': Religious Language, Symbolic Repertoires, and Democratic Cultures." In *Social Movements, Identity, Culture, and the State*, edited by David S. Meyer, Nancy Whittier, and Belinda Robnet, 247–65. Oxford & New York: Oxford University Press.

Wuthnow, Robert. 2009. *Communities of Discourse: Ideology and Social Structure in the Reformation, the Enlightenment, and European Socialism*. Cambridge, MA: Harvard University Press.

Yayasan Amalbakti Muslim Pancasila. 2009. *999 Masjid : Yayasan Amalbakti Muslim Pancasila 1982–2009*. Jakarta: Yayasan Amalbakti Muslim Pancasila.

Zald, Mayer N. 2000. "Ideologically Structured Action: An Enlarged Agenda for Social Movement Research." *Mobilization: An International Quarterly* 5 (1): 1–16.

Zaman, Muhammad Qasim. 2006. "The 'Ulama of Contemporary Islam and Their Conceptions on the Common Good." In *Public Islam and the Common Good*, edited by Armando Salvatore and Dale F. Eickelman, 129–156. Leiden & Boston: Brill.

Zaman, Muhammad Qasim. 2009. "The Ulama and Contestations on Religious Authority." In *Islam and Modernity: Key Issues and Debates*, 206–236. Edinburgh: Edinburgh University Press.

Zollner, Barbara Z.E. 2009. *The Muslim Brotherhood: Hasan al-Hudaybi and Ideology*. London & New York: Routledge.

Al-Zuḥaylī, Wahba. 2003a. *Al-Tafsīr al-Munīr fī al-ʿAqīda wa al-Sharīʿa wa al-Manhaj*, Vol. IX. Damascus: Dār al-Fikr.

Al-Zuḥaylī, Wahba. 2003b. *Al-Tafsīr al-Munīr fī al-ʿAqīda wa al-Sharīʿa wa al-Manhaj, Vol. III*. Damascus: Dār al-Fikr.

Zuhri, Syaifudin. 2013. "Majelis Tafsir Al-Qur'ān and its Stuggle for Islamic Reformism." In *Islam in Indonesia: Contrasting Images and Interpretations*, edited by Jajat Burhanudin and Kees van Dijk, 227–241. Amsterdam: Amsterdam University Press.

Zulkarnain, Iskandar. 2005. *Gerakan Ahmadiyah Di Indonesia*. Vol. 8. Yogyakarta: PT LKiS Pelangi Aksara.

Index

212 ABI movement 359
'Abd al-Razzāq al-Sanhūrī 403
Abdul Halim 261, 263, 266
Abdulaziz Sachedina 317
Abdurrahman Wahid 6 *n.* 12, 12 *n.* 44, 78, 101 *n.* 27, 174, 175 *n.* 47, 282 *n.* 32, 324, 423
ABRI xiii, 173
ABRI Hijau 173
Abu al-A'la al-Mawdudi 12
Aceh x, xiii, xiv, xv, xvi, 17, 23, 40–41, 45, 52, 54, 60, 62 *n.* 85, 67 *n.* 107, 129 *n.* 113, 169–170, 172, 197 *n.* 142, 209, 219, 230–248, 250, 258 *n.* 97, 259, 261, 269–270, 295 *n.* 87, 310, 421, 423, 426–427, 429, 432, 436–437, 441, 444
Acehnese Council of Muslim 17
Acehnese Muslims 235, 242, 244–245
action 30–31, 44, 98, 125, 163, 191–192, 202, 205, 208, 234, 310, 338, 378, 383, 406
Adams 6 *n.* 14, 19–20, 22, 56 *n.* 59, 65 *n.* 99, 77 *n.* 143, 84 *n.* 168, 111 *n.* 54, 113 *nn.* 62, 64, 151 *n.* 185, 152, 155, 156 *n.* 204, 158, 159 *n.* 213, 160, 421
adilla al-aḥkām 112
ahl al-kitāb 196, 313–314
ahl al-sunna wa al-jamā'a 277
Ahmad Heryawan 260
Ahmadis 80 *n.* 153, 91, 181, 187, 226 *n.* 229, 267, 283, 288, 391
Ahmadiyah xiv, 80, 90–91, 106, 157, 177–178, 180–181, 183, 185–188, 197, 200, 222, 228, 260, 265–268, 283, 289, 345, 361, 391, 402, 406, 409, 431, 447
Aisjah Girindra 124 *n.* 100, 126 *nn.* 105–106, 127, 129–130
Ajinomoto 102, 110, 157, 324
AJMI xiii, 244
AKKBB xiii, 180, 181 *n.* 74, 187
al-aḥkām al-qaṭ'iyya 120
al-amr bi al-ma'rūf wa al-nahy 'an al-munkar 41, 194–195, 219, 403
al-Bannā 9–10
al-ḍarūriyyāt al-khamsa 122, 317
al-dīn wa al-dawla 14, 407
al-fiqh al-mu'āmala 336
al-Ghazālī 19, 373
Ali Shariati 12
Ali Yafie 78, 79 *nn.* 148–149, 100 *nn.* 22–23, 101, 128 *n.* 112
al-Ikhwān al-Muslimūn 9
al-Imam Muḥammad Ibn Sa'ūd Islamic University 217
aliran kebatinan 281
aliran sempalan 243
aliran sesat 183, 206, 228, 233, 242, 266, 268–269, 274, 277, 280, 284, 291, 374
al-Ittihadiyah 219 *n.* 211
al-Jābirī 37, 121
al-jam' wa al-tawfīq 121
al-kutūb al-mu'tabara 121
al-madhāhib al-arba'a 21
Almsgiving 16, 159, 298–300
Al-Nawawī 311
al-Na'im x, 317
al-qawā'id al-uṣūliyya 314
al-qawā'id al-fiqhiyya 121
al-Shāṭibī 37
Al-Shīrazi 311
al-Ṭūfī 37, 311
al-umma 84, 100, 105, 190, 196, 301–302
al-Washliyah 62, 87
Al-Zuḥaylī 305, 311 *n.* 139, 315, 447
al-'aql 122, 189, 317
AMAP xiii, 85
amar makruf nahi munkar 194–197
Amidhan x, 85 *n.* 174, 139, 186, 187 *n.* 101, 319, 324, 350
Amin Rais 3 *n.* 4, 299
amīr 172, 278
Amirmachmud 58–59, 65
Amman Message 290.–291
Annual Meeting of the DPS 147
Anwar Abbas 181, 378, 384, 387, 419
APBN xiii, 66, 85
Arab theory 44, 48
Armando Salvatore 4 *n.* 7, 26, 115 *n.* 74, 421, 442, 447
Arrival 45
asas tunggal 52, 96

Ash'ari 291
Attorney General 81, 181, 280, 288, 400, 402, 409
Autonomy 30, 169, 232, 235 *n.* 20, 237 *n.* 29, 239 *n.* 33, 241 *n.* 40, 248, 411, 444

Ba'asyir 172, 208
Bachtiar Nasir 384
Baharuddin Jusuf Habibie 166
Bahsul Masa'il 120, 339
baju koko 266
BAKORPAKEM xiii, 183, 280
Bangil 285
BASNAZ 300
Basri 62 *n.* 85, 71, 75–78, 124
Baswedan 347, 350, 355, 360, 380
Bayat 5 *n.* 11, 33, 81 *n.* 159, 94, 163, 250, 346, 366 *n.* 63, 400, 423
BKSPPI 176
blasphemy 105 *n.* 41, 281–282, 287, 357–358, 377, 405, 407
BMAU xiii, 259
BMI xiii, 77, 173, 177, 394
BNIS 393
Bobby Sayyid 9
BPH 148
BPJPH xiii, 128, 139, 326, 418
BPOM 133
Brawijaya University 124
BRIS 393
BSI 393
BSM 393
Bulukumba x, 40–41, 52, 169–170, 210, 230–232, 248, 250–258, 265, 269–270

CEDAW 304
Central Bank of Indonesia 144
Charles Tilly 29, 164, 429
China 45 *nn.* 15–16, 46, 266, 321, 353, 376, 378, 437
Chinese labels 321
Christian tradition 19
Christianisation 244
Christianity 34 *n.* 141, 269, 273 *n.* 6, 293, 305, 314, 434
Cianjur x, 40–41, 52, 169–170, 197 *n.* 142, 210, 230–233, 258–259, 261–270, 438
Cianjur MUI Chairman 263, 266
civil society 12 *n.* 45, 22, 32, 53, 82, 107, 139, 167, 215, 238, 299, 304, 339, 345 *n.* 10, 366
commanding right 35, 63, 83 *n.* 164, 194–197, 254, 349, 352, 403
Commission xiv, 20–21, 41, 71, 103, 109–112, 114, 117–119, 121, 123, 133–134, 149, 152, 154–160, 177 *n.* 57, 230, 239, 275–276, 283, 288, 343, 384, 398, 401
Commodification 36 *n.* 155, 233 *n.* 12, 319 *n.* 169, 322 *nn.* 187, 189, 412, 444
consolidated democracy 166, 169, 171
Constitution xiii, xvii, 1 *n.* 1, 49, 51, 63, 79, 96–97, 182, 184–185, 216–217, 230 *n.* 1, 261, 268, 293–294, 337, 402, 406, 411, 432
Council iii, x, xiii, xv, xvii, 1, 3 *n.* 5, 6 *n.* 14, 7 *n.* 15, 8 *n.* 19, 12, 17, 18 *nn.* 66, 69, 22 *n.* 91, 24, 48 *n.* 25, 54, 56 *n.* 59, 57–58, 61–63, 65 *n.* 99, 66–67, 69, 74 *n.* 130, 75, 78, 80–81, 84, 85 *n.* 173, 87–88, 90–93, 95 *n.* 8, 99, 101, 103, 110, 113 *nn.* 62, 66, 114 *n.* 69, 118 *n.* 83, 123, 129, 131 *nn.* 119, 120, 123, 127, 128, 132 *nn.* 130, 131, 133, 134, 135, 136, 145 *n.* 164, 152, 154, 156–157, 160, 163, 176, 178, 179 *n.* 64, 181, 183, 195, 203, 205–206, 210, 212, 222, 226, 235–236, 238, 263, 275 *nn.* 10, 9, 278 *n.* 19, 280 *n.* 27, 281, 283 *n.* 37, 292 *n.* 78, 324, 343 *n.* 1, 345 *n.* 8, 346 *n.* 12, 347 *n.* 14, 349, 357, 368 *n.* 70, 369 *nn.* 70, 71, 73, 375 *n.* 93, 385 *n.* 111, 386 *n.* 114, 410 *n.* 23, 429–431, 435, 437, 444–445
culturalisation 2

Dale Eickelman 26
dalīl 329, 332
Darul Arqam 117, 277, 279
Darul Hadits 278
Darul Islam 56 *n.* 58, 236, 248 *n.* 66, 259, 426, 433
ḍarūra 395
Dawam Rahardjo 282 *n.* 32
dawla 163, 200, 318 *n.* 166, 337
da'wa organisation 178
DDII xiii, 12, 48 *n.* 25, 88–90, 102 *n.* 31, 107, 176, 178–179, 184, 218 *n.* 208, 247
Decentralisation 30, 169

Decree No. 18/1998 97
deviant sects 34, 183, 243, 268, 276, 282 *n.* 33, 357, 386, 399
Dewan Dakwah Islamiyah Indonesia (DDII, Council of Indonesian Islamic Propagation) 12
Din Syamsuddin x, 39–40, 208, 282–283, 285, 287, 290 *n.* 76, 292, 337, 339, 353, 377, 384–385, 388, 419
DMI xiii, 62, 89
Dompet Du'afa 299
Donald L. Horowitz 6 *n.* 12, 287
Doug McAdam 29, 86 *n.* 175, 94 *n.* 4, 164 *n.* 12, 165 *n.* 14, 171 *n.* 34, 193 *n.* 121, 422, 424, 436, 440
Douglas Davies 319
DPRA xiii, 246–247
DPS xiii, 144–147, 151, 326 *n.* 205, 422
Dress Code 311
DSN xiii, 24, 41, 84–85, 92, 104, 108, 140, 142–151, 326–328, 331, 333–335, 339, 398, 403, 409, 422
dunyā 163, 200, 220
Dutch 19, 48, 55, 58 *n.* 65, 63, 157, 232 *n.* 9, 274, 405 *nn.* 16–17, 439

Egypt 9–10, 12 *n.* 40, 13 *n.* 47, 20, 81 *nn.* 158–159, 82, 89 *n.* 181, 179, 200, 202, 306–307, 327, 368, 373, 375, 403, 404 *n.* 12, 416, 423, 434–435, 441–442
electoral politics 41, 345, 366
Electoral politics 345
El-Nahdah 200
Ernest Gellner 45, 302, 303 *n.* 109, 435

fahm al-wāqiʿ 143
Farzana Shaikh 4
fatwa 13, 17–22, 24–25, 27–28, 34–35, 36–38, 41, 55 *n.* 55, 59, 63, 65–67, 71, 73, 75, 77, 80 *n.* 153, 84–85, 90–91, 93, 100, 102–103, 105–106, 108–111, 112 *n.* 59, 113 *n.* 66, 114, 115 *n.* 73, 116–117, 119, 120 *nn.* 88–90, 121–123, 129, 134, 139, 143, 145–146, 148–152, 156–157, 176–178, 180–182, 184–186, 188, 191, 197, 199, 206, 210–213, 221–225, 226 *n.* 229, 227–228, 231, 236, 239–242, 243 *n.* 47, 244, 245 *n.* 55, 250, 259, 265–266, 268, 271–274, 276–282, 286–287, 290–294, 297–305, 307–308, 309 *n.* 134, 310–311, 313, 315–318, 320–325, 327–328, 331–334, 337, 339, 346, 347–350, 352, 357, 359, 361–362, 367, 371, 398–402, 406–409, 412, 414, 416–419
Fatwa Commission 20–21, 41, 68 *n.* 109, 71, 74, 92, 103, 107–121, 123, 130 *n.* 117, 133–134, 148–149, 152, 156, 158–159, 224, 239, 276, 324, 349, 357, 384, 398, 401
Felicitas Opwis 27 *n.* 108, 38, 116, 314, 317
female circumcision 110, 302, 304–305, 400, 409
fiqh or fiqhiyya 5
firqa 277
forbid wrong 59, 194, 196, 236, 306
FPI xiv, 13, 98, 160, 176, 180, 181 *n.* 74, 184, 187, 194, 197, 199, 212, 230, 232, 247, 267–268, 283, 318, 337, 339, 351, 354 *n.* 33, 361, 377, 382, 391
Frame 162
Frank E. Vogel 38, 116 *n.* 77, 404 *n.* 13, 435
Free Aceh Movement 209, 238–239, 246
Free Papua Movement 209
FUI xiii, 50, 52, 88 *n.* 178, 98, 160, 179, 196–197, 214, 249, 339, 354, 382
FURKON xiii, 216

GAM xiv, 17, 239, 246–247
GARIS xiv, 259
Garis-Garis Besar Haluan Negara (GBHN, the Guidelines of National Development) 20
Gerakan Aceh Merdeka (GAM, Free Aceh Movement) 17
Gerbang Marhamah 264–265, 270
gereja liar 157
ghayr al-muʿtabar 279
Gillespie 8 *n.* 19, 22–23, 429
GNPF-MUI 357–359, 377
GSK 323
GUI 187
GUPPI xiv, 62

Habibie 6 *n.* 12, 77 *n.* 142, 82, 97, 126, 167–168, 173, 175 *n.* 48, 188, 216, 357, 422
ḥajj 24, 257
ḥalāl 314, 318, 325

Halal xiii, xiv, xvi, xvii, 36 *n.* 154, 111, 118, 123, 124 *nn.* 100–101, 126 *nn.* 105–106, 127 *n.* 109, 128, 129, 130, 131 *n.* 119–130, 132 *n.* 131, *n.* 133, 133–137, 139, 159, 191, 221, 224, 225 *n.* 228, 226–227, 318–320, 322, 325 *n.* 199, 326 *nn.* 203–204, 391 *n.* 125, 379, 391–392, 396, 403, 412–413, 418, 426–430, 435
halal certificate 128, 130, 132–136, 139, 320 *n.* 179, 324, 326
halal food 127–128, 326, 339, 393, 406
halal life-style 320
halal movement 123
halal tourism 393
ḥalal wa ṭayyib 201
Halim x, 40, 261–262, 264, 265 *n.* 116, 266
HAMAS 200
Hamka 12, 18, 45, 58–59, 62 *n.* 85, 65–67, 71–74, 95 *n.* 8, 102, 222, 355, 430
Ḥanafī 290–290, 311 *n.* 140
Ḥanbalī 68
ḥarām 212, 303, 318, 324
Ḥasan al-Bannā 32, 373
Hashim Kamali 44 *n.* 8, 325 *n.* 199, 404, 437
Henri Lefebvre 27, 424
heresy 207, 268, 274, 278, 282–283, 285–286, 291, 317, 385
ḥifẓ al-dīn 189, 317
Himpunan Fatwa Dewan Syariah Nasional MUI 143 *n.* 161, 145 *n.* 166, 146 *nn.* 168, 170, 150 *nn.* 180, 183, 226, 328 *nn.* 211–212, 329 *nn.* 215–217, 330 *n.* 219, 331 *n.* 223, 332 *n.* 225, 333 *n.* 229, *n.* 231, 334 *n.* 234, 335 *n.* 235, 426
Himpunan Fatwa MUI Sejak 1975 8 *n.* 20, 52 *n.* 42, 111 *n.* 58, 113 *n.* 66, 118 *n.* 83, 121 *n.* 93, 170 *n.* 31, 189 *n.* 105, 207 *n.* 170, 208 *n.* 172, 209 *nn.* 176–177, 179–180, 211 *n.* 185, 226, 278 *nn.* 16, 18–19, 279 *n.* 20, *n.* 23, 284 *n.* 44, 286 *n.* 57, 296 *n.* 92, 298 *n.* 98, 308 *n.* 131, 309 *n.* 133, 310 *nn.* 136–138, 311 *n.* 141, 316 *n.* 160, 318 *nn.* 165–166, 320 *n.* 179, 322 *n.* 187, 323 *n.* 192, 324 *n.* 195, 325 *nn.* 197–198, 202, 328 *nn.* 210, 213, 348 *n.* 18, 349 *n.* 19, 367 *n.* 65, 371 *n.* 79, 401 *n.* 5, 438
ḥisba 194, 197, 273
Hizbut Tahrir Indonesia (HTI, Liberation Party of Indonesia) 13
Howard Federspiel 60
HTI xiv, 8 *n.* 22, 13, 50, 52, 88 *n.* 178, 89, 98, 153, 160, 176–178, 184, 194, 196–197, 199, 202, 212, 218 *n.* 208, 219, 230, 232, 308, 309 *n.* 135, 337, 339, 370, 373, 377, 391, 404
ḥudūd 122, 251, 257
human rights 40, 105, 143, 166, 182 *n.* 81, 205, 246, 284, 288, 292, 300 *n.* 103, 305, 313, 316, 318, 341, 399, 405, 407, 409–410

IAIN x, xiv, 59
Ibn Kathīr 314, 315 *n.* 156
Ibn Qāsim al-ʿIbbādī 19
Ibn Qayyim al-Jawziyya 19
Ibrahim Hosen 21 *n.* 82, 107, 114, 118, 128 *n.* 112, 130 *n.* 117
ICAS 218
Ichwan Sam x, 39–40, 85, 90 *n.* 186, 93, 97 *n.* 15, 107, 117 *n.* 80, 130 *n.* 118, 137 *n.* 143, 144 *n.* 162, 147, 200, 215 *n.* 197, 294 *n.* 84, 319, 340 *n.* 251
ICIP xiv, 122 *n.* 95, 178, 181, 183
ICMI xiv, 20, 32, 77, 89, 97, 141 *n.* 153, 173–177, 216, 227, 299, 378, 413, 431
ICPD Cairo 304
ICRP 158 *n.* 208, 178, 313
IDB 327
identity 9, 13–14, 31, 43–44, 88, 93, 100, 105 *n.* 41, 108, 111, 150, 157, 165, 174–175, 189, 192, 206, 249, 303, 351, 353, 355–356, 368, 382, 399, 404, 408
ideology 1 *n.* 2, 9, 15, 31, 40, 43, 48, 52, 67, 79, 82, 95–99, 152, 159, 162, 167–168, 172–173, 184, 185 *n.* 93, 201, 215, 217, 223, 236, 244, 246, 264, 292, 303, 342, 365, 404–406, 411
ifrāṭī 122
iḥsān 321
ijmāʿ 21, 37–38, 113, 208
ijtihād 19–21, 38, 114–117, 121–122, 149–150, 207, 305, 323
Ijtimāʿ Sanawī 146, 147 *nn.* 173–174, 149 *n.* 179, 150 *nn.* 181–182
IKADI xiv, 176, 219 *nn.* 209, 211

Ikatan Cendekiawan Muslim Indonesia (ICMI, the Association of Indonesian Muslim Intellectuals) 20
ikhtilāf 200
ikhtiyār 209
ilḥāqī 121
ILO xiv, 168
imāma 278, 348
Indonesia iii, ix, x, xiii, xiv, xv, xvi, xvii, 1, 1 *nn.* 1–2, 2 *n.* 3, 3 *n.* 5, 3 *n.* 6, 6 *n.* 12, 6 *n.* 14, 7 *n.* 15, 7 *n.* 16, 7 *n.* 17, 8 *n.* 19, 8 *n.* 22, 9, 14, 16–20, 22–30, 32–33, 36, 38, 40–44, 46–49, 51– 61, 63–69, 72–83, 85–87, 89, 91, 93–101, 103, 105–106, 108–112, 116, 118, 120, 123–125, 127–130, 133, 137, 139–140, 142–143, 145, 147–154, 156–160, 162–173, 175–183, 185–191, 194–205, 207–219, 221–223, 225–226, 228, 230–232, 234, 236–237, 239, 243, 247–248, 250–251, 256, 258, 260–261, 264, 266, 270, 271–273, 275, 277–288, 290–291, 293–297, 299, 302–304, 306–308, 310, 313, 316, 318–319, 321, 324, 326–327, 329, 331, 333, 335–337, 339–342, 344, 346–347, 349, 352, 354–359, 363–365, 368–369, 371, 373–374, 377, 380, 382–383, 385, 387, 393–394, 397–403, 405–416, 419, 421–447
Indonesia Masterplan 392
Indonesian Constitution 51, 294
Indonesian Islam 7 *n.* 16, 8 *n.* 19, 16, 22–23, 25, 45, 47–48, 50 *n.* 35, 89 *n.* 181, 108, 202, 208 *n.* 174, 277–278, 347 *n.* 14, 368 *n.* 70, 369 *nn.* 71, 73, 385 *n.* 111, 391, 404, 423, 429–430, 432, 441–442, 444
Inkar Sunnah 80, 279, 288, 291
institutionalisation 40, 53–54, 63, 143, 187–188, 235, 403
international certification bodies 130
IPB xiv, 127, 130 *n.* 117
Irwandi 246–247, 391 *n.* 125
Islam xiii, xiv, xv, xvi, 1, 2 *n.* 3, 3 *nn.* 4–5, 4 *nn.* 6–7, 9, 5 *n.* 11, 7 *nn.* 15–17, 8 *nn.* 18, 22, 9, 11–15, 17–26, 30, 32–34, 37, 40, 43–44, 46–50, 52, 53–54, 56, 59–60, 62, 63, 72, 75, 76, 79, 81, 82, 84, 87, 88–89, 92, 95, 97–100, 104–105, 115–119, 122, 127, 134, 138, 143, 146, 152–154, 157, 162, 168, 170, 172–174, 176–177, 181, 183–184, 186–187, 189, 194–197, 199, 201–202, 204, 208, 210–212, 214, 216, 222, 224–225, 227–228, 233–236, 240, 242–244, 248, 250–253, 256, 258–263, 268, 270, 272–274, 277–279, 281, 283–285, 287–291, 293, 295, 297, 303–305, 308, 313, 316–319, 327, 336, 338–340, 342–343, 348, 352, 354–359, 361, 363, 365–366, 368, 371, 373–376, 382, 385, 387, 400, 402–405, 407–409, 418, 421–447
Islam Jama'ah 80 *n.* 154, 277–278, 288, 290
Islamic activists 89, 137, 194
Islamic Brotherhood xiii, 77, 179, 214, 249
Islamic Finance 327 *nn.* 206–207, 393, 414 *n.* 27, 431, 444
Islamic jurisprudence 16, 21, 38, 63 *n.* 92, 73–74, 78, 82, 112, 118 *n.* 83, 136–137, 274, 294, 298, 311, 317, 321, 332, 335–336, 374
Islamic law 16, 18–19, 21, 37–38, 54, 68, 83 *n.* 164, 113–114, 116, 120–122, 130, 144, 150, 189, 209–210, 224, 235, 258, 299, 305, 309, 311 *n.* 140, 313–314, 320 *n.* 179, 344, 411
Islamic organisation 21 *n.* 84, 24, 55 *n.* 56, 65, 80 *n.* 153, 88 *n.* 178, 107, 139, 148, 175, 177, 196 *n.* 138, 251, 259, 301, 339, 362, 412–413
Islamic recommendations 34, 103, 108, 398, 407
Islamic state 4 *n.* 9, 11, 17, 32, 34, 48 *n.* 25, 49–50, 52–53, 56 *n.* 58, 79, 95, 152–153, 162, 169, 230, 250, 252–253, 315, 337, 363–364, 398–400
Islamic studies ix, 25, 38, 137
Islamisation 3 *n.* 4, 4 *nn.* 6, 8–9, 12–16, 18, 33, 40–41, 44, 47, 51 *n.* 39, 53, 82, 86, 91, 98, 108, 110, 148, 153, 157, 159–160, 172, 202, 205, 232, 237, 353 *n.* 29, 400, 404 *n.* 13, 405, 416, 427, 435, 443
Islamism 6 *n.* 13, 9–12, 14 *n.* 51, 32–33, 44 *n.* 6, 94, 162, 163 *nn.* 5–6, 179 *nn.* 66–67, 184 *n.* 88, 185 *nn.* 92, 94, 189 *n.* 108, 190 *n.* 111, 200 *n.* 151, 215, 230 *n.* 1, 233, 371, 400, 404, 431–432, 434, 439–440, 442

Islamist 4 *n.* 9, 5 *n.* 11, 8 *n.* 22, 9–16, 22–23, 30, 33, 50, 52, 56 *n.* 58, 66, 76 *n.* 139, 81, 88, 91, 98, 153–154, 162, 176 *n.* 52, 178, 181 *n.* 75, 184, 187, 190, 197, 200–202, 216 *n.* 202, 217–218, 228, 250 *n.* 76, 283, 293, 337, 339, 354–360, 364–365, 368, 373, 382, 396, 400 *n.* 3, 404, 423, 425
Ismail Yusanto 13, 52, 88, 89 *n.* 179, 176 *n.* 51, 177, 196, 218 *n.* 208, 219, 338 *n.* 241, 374
istaḥala 396
istiḥsān 322
istinbāṭī 121
istiṣlāḥī 121
iʿtiqādī 119

Jakarta x, 3 *n.* 4, 6 *n.* 14, 8 *n.* 20, 8 *n.* 21, 8 *n.* 22, 11 *n.* 36, 12 *n.* 44, 18 *n.* 66, 19 *n.* 74, 38, 41, 48 *nn.* 24–25, 49–51, 52 *n.* 42, 54 *n.* 48, 55 *n.* 57, 56, 59, 67, 77, 79, 88, 104, 108, 111, 118, 129–130, 154, 180, 182–185, 204, 207–208, 213, 215–216, 218–219, 231–232, 234–239, 242–243, 245, 247, 254–255, 266, 268, 276, 285, 313, 338, 343, 345, 349–351, 353–357, 360, 362, 363, 371, 380–382, 388, 421–423, 426, 428–430, 432, 433, 435–445, 446
Jakarta Charter 48 *n.* 24, 49–51, 182, 184–185, 219, 236
Jalaludin Rakhmat 299
Jama'ah Muslimin Hizbullah 277–278, 291
Jama'at-i Islami 12
JamaJat-i Islami 9
Jamal Badawi 306
Jaringan Islam Liberal (JIL, Liberal Islam Network) 23
JAT xiv, 50, 52, 153
Jaʿfariyya 290
Jema'ah Tarbiyah 14–15
JI 172
jihād 10, 73
jilbāb 233, 252, 256, 266
Jilbabisasi 265
Jinayat 246–247
Johan Fischer 36, 319
Jokowi 41, 108, 128, 188, 284, 342–345, 350–351, 353, 355, 358, 360–363, 368–369, 380–385, 388, 390–392, 417–419, 440
Judaism 32 *n.* 130, 305, 314, 424
Jurgen Habermas 26
Jurnal Halal 118 *n.* 82, 124 *n.* 100, 126 *n.* 105, 127 *n.* 109, 224, 426–427, 429
Jusuf Kalla 344, 347 *n.* 15, 382

kafir 279
kaum tua 215
kelompok kultural 174
kelompok struktural 174
khādim al-ḥukūma 100, 418
khādim al-umma 100
KHI 210, 214
khilāfiyya fī al-madhāhib 120
KISDI xiv, 176
KNKS 393
Komisi Hukum dan Perundangan 109
KOMNAS Perempuan 230
KORPRI 297
KPSSI 249
Kristenisasi 244–245
kuffār 199, 315
KUHP xv, 154, 157, 172, 220
KUII xv, 79–80, 82, 99, 154, 156, 173, 196, 198, 202, 215–218, 220, 227, 251 *n.* 80

Law and Legislation Commission 152, 156, 158, 160
lawmakers 27–28, 109–110, 152, 160, 164, 169, 179, 182, 186, 191, 201, 203, 208, 210, 212–213, 220, 227, 231, 247, 249, 251, 262, 274, 281, 300, 306, 325, 328, 338, 341, 391, 399, 401, 410, 412–413, 415
LAZIZ 299–300
LBH xv, 178
legislation 19–20, 24, 27, 51, 73, 84, 97, 109, 126, 144, 152–156, 158–159, 164, 168, 170, 176, 186, 211, 213, 217, 226, 232, 241, 247, 252, 255, 281, 338, 367, 391, 399–401, 403–405, 415
LGBT 391
Lia Aminuddin 279
liberalism 13, 22–24, 90–91, 120, 177–178, 180–181, 188, 196, 226 *n.* 229, 228, 291–292, 315, 344, 371, 377, 385
LKS xv, 327, 330–333

local minority 392
LoGA 239–240
lotteries 209
LPPI 228 *n.* 236, 263–264, 270
LPPOM xv, 41, 84, 85, 108, 118, 123–125, 127–130, 132–139, 148, 173, 177, 201, 224, 226, 228, 320, 325–326, 379, 398, 409, 412–413, 418, 435
Lucinda Peach 27, 111, 241

Ma'ruf Amin x, 8 *n.* 21, 40, 78 *n.* 145, 97 *n.* 15, 98 *n.* 16, 103 *n.* 37, 111 *nn.* 54, 56, 117 *n.* 80, 118 *n.* 81, 119 *n.* 86, 140 *nn.* 150–151, 142 *n.* 156, 143 *nn.* 158–159, 150 *n.* 182, 151 *n.* 185, 153 *n.* 191, 158 *n.* 209, 160 *n.* 216, 167 *n.* 21, 180 *n.* 72, 189 *nn.* 107, 110, 200 *n.* 150, 201 *n.* 152, 206 *n.* 167, 214 *n.* 194, 319 *n.* 171, 324, 340 *n.* 251, 360, 376 *n.* 94, 385
Madjid 256, 293, 303 *n.* 110, 312, 407
mafsada 302
Mahfud 355, 361, 382, 385, 402
Mahfudh x, 8 *n.* 21, 40, 82, 93, 97, 98 *n.* 16, 102–103, 107 *n.* 47, 130 *n.* 118, 152, 154 *n.* 197, 200 *n.* 150, 286, 337, 353
Majelis Ulama Daerah Tingkat I 67
Majelis Ulama Daerah Tingkat II 67
Majelis Ulama Indonesia 6 *n.* 14, 7 *n.* 15, 8 *n.* 22, 44 *n.* 8, 56 *n.* 60, 64 *n.* 93, 65 *n.* 99, 67, 68 *n.* 108, 74 *n.* 130, 78 *nn.* 144–145, 80 *n.* 155, 83 *n.* 164, 84 *n.* 168, 96 *nn.* 10, 13, 9, 97 *n.* 14, 99 *n.* 20, 103 *n.* 34, 113 *nn.* 62, 66, 143 *n.* 161, 155 *n.* 199, 158 *n.* 212, 181 *n.* 76, 198 *n.* 145, 204 *n.* 157, 207 *n.* 170, 208 *n.* 171, 212 *n.* 186, 215 *n.* 198, 217 *n.* 203, 225–226, 237, 275 *n.* 9, 280 *n.* 27, 291 *n.* 77, 292 *n.* 78, 366 *n.* 62, 369 *n.* 70, 375 *n.* 91, 385 *n.* 111, 423, 426, 433, 437–438
Majelis Ulama Indonesia (MUI, the Council of Indonesian Ulama) 1
Majlis Tarjih of Muhammadiyah 280
māl 122, 189, 329 *nn.* 216–217, 334
Malay negeri 54
Malaysia xiv, 11–12, 36, 51 *n.* 39, 54, 72, 80 *n.* 154, 82, 129, 131 *nn.* 119, 127, 137, 165 *n.* 17, 172, 202, 212, 222, 272, 279 *n.* 25, 318 *n.* 167, 327, 340, 368, 375, 427–428, 439, 444, 446
Malik Fadjar 173
Mālikī 290
maqāṣid al-sharī'a 122
Mary Douglas 36, 319
Marzuki Mustamar 395
Masā'il Asāsiyya Waṭaniyya 209, 212
Masā'il Qānūniyya 209–210, 213
Masā'il Wāqi'iyya Mu'āṣira 209
maṣlaḥa 27, 37–38, 115–117, 121–122, 298, 302, 313, 325
Masyumi party 48 *n.* 25, 178, 185
Mathla'ul Anwar 62, 87, 89 *n.* 181
Maulana Hasanuddin 114 *n.* 67, 224, 225 *nn.* 227–228
Mawdudi 12, 13 *n.* 47, 443
MAWI xv, 57
mechanical slaughtering 320
Meeting of Ulama 203, 207–208, 210–212
Megawati 6 *n.* 12, 51 *n.* 37, 80, 166, 174, 188, 206, 347 *n.* 15, 354, 357
MES 393
Michael Cook 27 *n.* 108, 35, 194 *n.* 130, 273 *n.* 4, 306
Miftachul Achyar 389
Mimbar Ulama 159 *n.* 214, 221, 224 *n.* 224, 443
Ministry of Finance 144, 148
Ministry of Religious Affairs 20, 56 *n.* 60, 57, 66, 73–74, 76, 96, 101, 102 *n.* 28, 125, 133, 139, 154 *n.* 195, 181, 209 *n.* 174, 222, 225, 245, 267, 281, 294 *n.* 85, 300, 324, 326, 338, 386, 400, 412–413, 418
Mirza Ghulam Ahmad 80 *n.* 153, 279, 283, 421
MK 115 *n.* 74, 272 *n.* 3, 282, 421, 436
MMI xv, 8 *n.* 22, 13, 50, 52, 98, 153, 160, 176, 182, 194, 197, 199, 212, 219, 232, 324, 337, 339, 373, 404, 435
mobilisation 29–31, 41, 94, 99, 162, 164, 179, 192, 197 *n.* 141, 203, 211, 214, 216, 222, 306, 343, 360, 377, 380, 398
Mohammad Natsir 12, 48, 426
MORA 59 *n.* 73, 281, 289, 294 *n.* 85, 300–301
morality 1, 15, 27, 35, 41, 81, 111, 117, 138, 146, 158, 190–191, 204, 207, 212, 217, 238, 250, 252–253, 257, 261, 263 *n.* 112, 265, 269, 272, 306–308, 352, 367, 391

movement 4 *n.* 9, 9, 11, 14, 29–32, 41, 56 *n.* 58, 73, 78, 81–82, 86, 93, 98–100, 123, 127, 140, 143, 150, 154, 160, 162–164, 170–171, 186, 191–193, 202–203, 216, 220, 228, 232–233, 245, 249, 251–252, 261, 264, 266, 274, 351, 355, 357–360, 377, 380, 399, 405, 407–408, 415
MPR xv, 51, 80, 96–97, 168, 182, 216, 230
MPU x, xv, 40, 67 *n.* 107, 235, 236 *n.* 23, 237–246, 270, 436
MSG 102, 324
MTA xv, 183, 184 *n.* 86
muḍāraba 329, 333–334, 336
Mudzhar 6 *n.* 14, 7 *n.* 15, 17–19, 22, 55 *n.* 57, 56 *n.* 59, 61 *n.* 81, 65, 74 *n.* 130, 75 *nn.* 137–138, 79 *n.* 150, 110 *n.* 52, 113 *nn.* 62, 66, 114 *n.* 69, 347 *n.* 14, 437
muftī 34, 54, 115, 123, 235
Muhammad Khathath 88
Muḥammad Saʿīd al-ʿAshmāwī 2
Muhammad Sukino 183
Muhammadiyah x, 14–15, 21, 40, 49, 61, 62 *n.* 85, 65, 72–73, 75, 85, 87, 89–92, 105 *n.* 42, 106–107, 112 *n.* 59, 116, 118, 120, 122 *n.* 95, 125, 153, 184, 194, 207–208, 215 *n.* 197, 249, 251–253, 257, 279–280, 282–283, 288, 290, 300 *n.* 102, 301, 328, 337, 339, 354, 362, 373, 378, 384, 387, 409, 413, 429
Muhammed Ayoob 9
Muhyiddin Junaidi 362, 387
MUI iii, x, xv, 1, 6 *n.* 14, 8 *nn.* 19–22, 13–14, 17–44, 48, 52–53, 56–69, 71–79, 81–113, 115–119, 122–125, 127–128, 132–133, 136–140, 142–143, 146–149, 152–165, 167, 169, 170, 172–191, 193–215, 217, 220–237, 242–328, 331–334, 337, 339–352, 354–360, 363, 366–369, 374, 377, 379–380, 382–386, 388, 391, 397–418, 421, 422, 426, 428, 430–431, 433, 435, 437–438, 444
MUIPDIA xv, 237
mujtahid 114, 116–117, 279
Mukti Ali 58–59, 66
MUNAS xv, 41, 61, 101 *n.* 26, 102 *n.* 32, 177 *n.* 57, 203, 225, 291, 385, 388
muqārana al-madhāhib 121
murābaḥa 330, 332
musāwā 199
Muslim ix, x, xiii, xiv, xv, xvi, xvii, 1, 3 *n.* 6, 8 *n.* 18, 9, 11 *n.* 39, 12–13, 15, 17, 21 *n.* 82, 22–26, 31–37, 39–40, 44, 46–47, 49, 51 *n.* 37, 52–56, 58–67, 69, 71–73, 75, 80 *n.* 154, 81, 83 *n.* 164, 84–90, 92, 94–96, 98–101, 103–108, 113–116, 118, 120 *n.* 89, 121–125, 129, 131 *nn.* 119, 122, 127, 132, 134–136, 140, 143, 148, 150, 153–155, 158–160, 162, 164–165, 170, 172 *n.* 37, 173–176, 178–180, 182–183, 187 *nn.* 102, 103, 189–190, 194–200, 202–204, 206–208, 210, 214–220, 223, 225–227, 231, 232 *n.* 9, 233 *n.* 11, 237 *nn.* 27, 30, 239–241, 244, 246 *n.* 57, 249, 250 *n.* 75, 251–254, 256, 259–264, 266, 269, 271–275, 278–280, 282–284, 286 *n.* 54, 287–293, 296, 298, 300 *nn.* 101, 103, 301 *n.* 105, 302–304, 306, 307 *n.* 123, 308, 311–314, 316, 318, 321 *n.* 180, 323, 327, 329, 331–332, 334, 336, 338, 340, 342, 347–360, 363–366, 368–369, 373–374, 376–379, 382, 386, 391, 393, 400, 402–403, 405 *n.* 17, 407–408, 410, 412, 415–417, 423–429, 431, 433–436, 438–443, 447
mustaftī 110, 149
muʿāmala sharʿiyya 149

Nadirsyah Hosen 7 *n.* 15, 20, 21 *n.* 87, 50 *n.* 32, 65 *n.* 99, 230 *n.* 1, 369 *n.* 70
Nahdlatul Ulama x, xvi, 49, 55, 61–62, 64 *n.* 95, 65, 82, 106, 112 *n.* 59, 174, 213 *n.* 190, 215, 223 *n.* 222, 236, 275, 280, 282–283, 299, 339
najs 134
Nancy Fraser 26
National Agency of Sharia Arbitration 84, 334
National Congress 41, 57, 59, 63, 70, 80 *n.* 152, 87, 89–90, 96–97, 101 *n.* 26, 102 *n.* 32, 111, 114, 119, 176–177, 183, 191, 203–207, 225, 227, 237, 340
national consensus 49, 51, 400
Nazri Adlani 90, 100 *nn.* 22–23, 117 *n.* 80, 143
Negara Islam 46 *n.* 21
Negara Kesatuan Republik Indonesia (NKRI) 1

New Conservatism 118
New Order 6 *n.* 12, 18 *n.* 68, 22, 24, 32, 49 *n.* 28, 50 *n.* 35, 51 *n.* 39, 71, 75, 87, 97, 100, 103, 110, 168 *n.* 25, 171, 172 *n.* 37, 173 *n.* 42, 174 *nn.* 43–44, 190–191, 205, 215, 239 *n.* 32, 299 *n.* 100, 422, 430, 432, 438, 442, 444
NGO x, 210, 260, 339
normalisation 26, 35, 313, 316
NU xvi, 14–15, 21, 55 *n.* 56, 62 *n.* 85, 64 *n.* 95, 65 *n.* 102, 74, 76, 78, 80 *n.* 152, 85, 87, 89–92, 99 *n.* 21, 107, 112 *n.* 59, 114, 116, 118, 120, 125, 153, 175, 194, 207–208, 213, 249, 251–253, 257, 277 *n.* 13, 287–288, 290, 301, 328, 337, 338 *n.* 244, 339, 354, 356, 358, 360–361, 373, 383–384, 387, 389, 409, 413, 426
Nurcholish Madjid 78 *n.* 145, 79, 256 *n.* 91, 407 *n.* 19, 428

Olivier Roy 4 *n.* 6, 34 *n.* 138
Omnibus law 387
Omnibus Law 387
Opportunity Structure 162

Pabokori 40, 250, 258 *n.* 96, 270
PAKEM xvi, 282
Pakistan x, 9, 11 *n.* 37, 12, 20, 35, 82, 130, 289, 302, 307, 330, 368, 375, 421, 433, 439
Pancasila xvi, 1 *nn.* 1, 2, 15, 48–52, 63, 79, 80 *n.* 154, 82, 95–99, 152, 167–168, 172, 180, 185 *n.* 93, 188, 201, 204, 217, 229, 236, 250, 271, 296, 303, 337, 365, 371, 373 *n.* 85, 374, 385, 398–400, 404–405, 411, 425, 432
Parmusi 106–107
Partabai Pobokori x
Partai Bulan Bintang (PBB, Crescent Star Party) 14
Partai Demokrat 107, 350
Partai Keadilan Sejahtera (PKS, the Prosperous Justice Party) 10
Partai Persatuan Pembangunan (PPP, United Development Party) 14
PBB xvi, 14, 50, 102 *nn.* 29, 31, 168, 173, 176, 182, 184, 399
PBNU 353
PDII xvi, 56–57
PDIP xvi, 107, 175, 350, 353–356, 361
pembangunan nasional 61, 195
Pemurtadan 244, 265
Perda xvi, 169, 230 *n.* 2, 250 *n.* 75, 251–252, 254–257, 263, 266 *n.* 119, 293 *n.* 83, 425, 433, 441
perda syariah 232, 251, 254, 264
Persia 46
Persis 106–107, 116, 208, 301, 362
Perti 21, 62, 236, 301, 362
pesantren 21, 40, 61 *n.* 81, 74, 82, 89, 173 *n.* 41, 208, 297
Pesantren Gontor 208
PGI xvi, 57, 282 *n.* 33
Piagam Jakarta 48 *n.* 24, 49, 50 *n.* 35, 219
Piagam Madinah 50, 184, 444
pig enzymes 324–325
pig fat 102, 124, 323
PKB 107, 350, 361
pluralism 13, 18, 22–25, 28, 90–91, 120, 169, 177–178, 180–181, 186, 199, 228, 260, 291–292, 307, 315, 344, 371, 410, 412, 416
political Islam 32–33, 53, 77 *n.* 140, 81–82, 162, 174, 201, 218, 349, 400, 405, 413
politicisation 12, 32, 47, 81, 233, 252, 269–270, 336, 412
politics of piety 35, 250
pornography xiii, 85, 103, 157 *n.* 207, 179, 197, 202, 205–208, 210, 262, 308, 310, 338, 341, 401, 405
post-Islamism 33–34
poverty alleviation 142
PPMI 217
PPP xvi, 14, 73, 102 *n.* 31, 107, 155, 167, 173, 176, 182, 184, 350, 361, 399
Prabowo 174 *n.* 44, 343–344, 347 *n.* 15, 350, 354, 363, 380–381, 384, 396, 439
Prabowo Subianto 347 *n.* 15, 350, 380
President Wahid 110, 157, 304, 325, 411
Presidential Decree 169, 210, 214, 304, 315, 321
Prophet Muhammad 50 *n.* 35, 62, 80 *n.* 154, 209 *n.* 180, 277, 279 *n.* 22, 292, 308, 324
public Islam 26
public morality 36, 253, 306–308
Public Morality 242, 252, 306
PUSA xvi, 235

Qanun Jinayat 246–247
Qanun of Aceh 240
Qāsim Amīn 311
qiyās 21, 113
qiyāsī 121
Quintan Wictorowicz 162, 194 *n.* 129
Qum 285
Qur'an xv, 8 *n.* 18, 10, 21, 46, 62, 72 *n.* 119, 80 *n.* 154, 113–114, 117, 120–122, 137, 148–150, 183, 184 *n.* 87, 194, 196, 204, 209 *n.* 180, 218, 228, 243, 251, 253–254, 257, 274, 279, 280 *n.* 27, 283, 292, 297, 306, 312, 314 *nn.* 151–152, 315 *n.* 156, 316, 332, 357, 421, 430, 433, 442, 446–447

Rakernas 68–69
reform era 16, 22, 32, 40, 52, 65 *n.* 100, 72, 78–79, 82–83, 85, 87–88, 90, 92, 97, 99–101, 105–110, 123, 152, 154, 156, 164, 165 *n.* 15, 167, 169, 171–173, 176, 186–188, 190–191, 201–202, 205, 207, 215, 221, 223, 225, 231, 233, 260, 271, 277, 280, 283, 287, 328, 345, 347, 361, 375, 385, 388, 398, 401, 403, 406–407, 410–411
reform era of Indonesia 100, 166, 388
reformasi 79, 165–167, 205
"Religious Opinion" 357
religious perda 254
religious relativism 292
Republika 227, 299 *n.* 99
resource 29, 31, 59, 218, 413
revivalism 9, 12, 223
ribā 36, 67, 326–328
Ridwan 8 *n.* 21, 39, 57, 73, 88–90, 93, 102, 119 *n.* 86, 179, 181, 184, 218, 285, 354
Rizieq Shihab 354
RUU-APP 338

ṣadīq al-ḥukūma 388, 390, 418
Saiq Aqil Siradj 40
Salafi-Wahhabi 396
Salwa Ismail 10, 15 *n.* 55, 34, 163
Sampang 285, 287 *n.* 59, 288–289
Samuel N. Eisenstandt 26
Sandiaga Uno 360, 380, 384
santri 173, 199 *n.* 147, 208
Sanusi Baco x, 40, 249, 250 *n.* 73, 252 *n.* 81
Saudi Arabia 20, 25, 38, 82, 88, 116 *n.* 77, 202, 205, 217, 326–327, 359, 405 *n.* 15, 416, 446
Sayyid Quṭb 10, 15 *n.* 55
SBY 128, 343, 350, 391
SDSB xvi, 78, 110
secularism 13, 22, 24, 90–91, 120, 177–178, 180–181, 197, 226 *n.* 229, 228, 291–292, 295, 315, 344, 371
Sepilis 292 *n.* 78, 315, 345 *n.* 8, 431
Setara Institute 109 *n.* 50, 260, 288, 398 *n.* 1, 443
Shāfiʿī 68, 113, 120–121, 290, 298, 309, 311 *n.* 140, 320 *n.* 179, 396
sharia xii, xvi, 1, 4 *n.* 9, 9–10, 12, 14–17, 23–27, 29–32, 35–38, 40–43, 46, 49, 50 *n.* 35, 51, 53 *n.* 44, 54, 77, 79, 81–82, 85, 87–88, 93, 95, 97–99, 102–103, 109, 112, 118, 119 *n.* 86, 121–122, 124, 134, 136–137, 142–160, 162, 165 *n.* 17, 166–173, 175, 177–180, 182–189, 191, 193–194, 196–198, 200–203, 207–214, 217, 219–221, 223–224, 226, 228, 230–234, 236–239, 241–242, 244–249, 251–266, 269–272, 275, 301, 304, 306–307, 309, 312–313, 316–321, 326–328, 330 *n.* 218, 331, 333–337, 339, 341, 353, 357–358, 360, 367–369, 379–380, 386, 391, 398–401, 403–411, 414–416, 419
Sharia Activism 162
Sharia Banking 51, 144, 149 *n.* 179, 159–160, 379
sharia economy 24, 143, 145, 172, 188–189, 213, 220, 226, 326–328, 333–334, 336, 339, 353, 381, 386, 403, 414, 419
Sharia Finance xv, 150, 393
sharia finance institution 24, 144
shariatisation 1, 3 *n.* 6, 12, 14, 16–17, 24, 26, 28, 30, 32–35, 40–44, 48, 51–53, 93, 97, 100, 106, 108–110, 118, 123, 137, 140, 146–147, 152–154, 156–157, 159–160, 162–165, 168–173, 183–184, 186, 188, 191, 194, 198, 200, 202–203, 207, 209, 214, 220–223, 226–228, 230–234, 238, 241, 248–249, 257, 259–261, 271–272, 293, 336–338, 340, 342, 353–356, 368–369, 371, 377, 379, 385, 390, 397–399, 401, 404–412, 414–419

Shariatisation iii, 1, 14, 30, 44, 93, 95, 108, 175, 191, 230, 261, 271, 342, 368, 390, 398, 411, 415
Shariatisation of Indonesia iii
sharʿī 119
shaykh al-Islām 54
Shihab 180, 256, 285, 290 *n.* 75, 293, 312, 354, 359, 383, 390, 443
Shīʿa 11, 106, 177, 195 *n.* 133, 200, 273, 277, 280–281, 284, 287 *n.* 59, 288–291, 340, 376, 385, 391, 402, 406, 409
Shīʿa Sampang 286–287
SI MPR 216
Sidang Isbat 300, 302
Sidney Tarrow 29, 163, 192, 429
silaturahmi 146, 151
SILMUI xvi, 263–264
Siradj x, 280, 281 *n.* 29, 287, 293, 358, 362
SJH xvi, 134
Slamet Effendi Yusuf x, 88 *n.* 176, 89, 92 *n.* 189, 93, 104 *n.* 39
Social Mass Organisations 97
social movements 29–30, 162, 192, 359
South Sulawesi x, 23, 40–41, 52, 62 *n.* 85, 78, 128 *n.* 113, 152 *n.* 188, 213, 219 *n.* 213, 231–233, 248–249, 251–253, 270, 340 *n.* 250, 433, 441
Standardisation of Halal Fatwa 320
State Islamic University x, 105 *n.* 42, 118, 155 *n.* 201, 313, 354
State law 33/2014 on Halal Product Assurance 111
State Law 44/2008 on Pornography 111
State Law No. 1/1974 on marriage 73
State Law No. 33/2014 128, 139, 326 *n.* 203, 379, 391, 396, 418
Suara Hidayatullah 227
sufism 47
Suharto 1, 13 *n.* 49, 15, 16 *n.* 59, 18, 20, 22, 24, 32, 46 *n.* 21, 56, 58 *n.* 68, 59–61, 63, 65–69, 71–73, 75, 77 *n.* 142, 78–79, 82, 85, 87, 95, 96 *n.* 11, 100, 102–103, 105–106, 108–110, 115, 126, 152 *n.* 188, 154, 157, 160, 165–168, 171–172, 174, 175 *n.* 48, 177, 178 *n.* 64, 190–191, 195, 202, 205–206, 215–216, 223, 237, 248 *n.* 65, 278, 280, 282, 287, 296, 297 *n.* 94, 301, 303, 315, 346–347, 354, 357, 361, 365, 369, 375, 403, 406–407, 409, 412–413, 431, 441, 443, 446
Sukarno 6 *n.* 12, 55, 72, 76, 166, 174, 185 *n.* 93, 281, 347 *n.* 15, 357
Sunna 80 *n.* 154, 113–114, 117, 120–122, 137, 148–149, 209 *n.* 180, 218, 251, 274, 277 *n.* 13, 279 *n.* 22, 291, 316
Sunnī 10–11, 116, 121, 123, 195, 199–200, 242, 267, 273, 275, 277, 284–287, 290, 303 *n.* 111, 340, 348–349, 374, 376, 386, 401–402, 441
Suryadharma Ali 128, 139, 185, 282–283, 287, 413
Syafi'i Ma'arif 293
syariah 41, 172 *n.* 38, 201–202, 211, 232–233, 250–255, 257, 264, 269–270, 401
Syarikat Islam 87, 176, 219 *n.* 211
Syukri Ghozali 58–59, 71, 74–75, 107, 436

Tabligh Akbar 176, 185–186, 428
tajdīd 79 *n.* 147, 84, 115, 303 *n.* 110
takāful 199, 328, 333
takfīr 41, 199, 274, 279, 290 *n.* 74
Talal Asad 34, 273, 318
taqlīd 114
Tarbiyah xvi, 10, 14, 16 *n.* 60, 21, 87, 301, 435
tasāmuḥ 83 *n.* 164, 199
tawassuṭ 199, 220
tawāzun 220
tawṣiya 13, 34, 41
taʿāwun 199
tenda besar 13, 41, 88, 93, 95, 105–107, 164, 175
Tengku Zulkarnaen 419
Terrorism xvii, 85
The framing theory 30
The Front Pembela Islam (FPI, the Islam Defender Front) 13
the Iranian Revolution 9, 11
The Majelis Mujahidin Indonesia (MMI, Indonesian Mujahidin Council) 13
the Muslim Brotherhood 9–10, 15, 200, 202
the National Peoplets Assembly 16
the positivisation of sharia 3
TPFKM xvii, 85
TPM xvii, 176
TPT xvii, 85
traders 45, 47, 380

tradition ix, 16, 21, 27, 32, 34, 39, 44, 53, 63 *n.* 92, 76, 80 *n.* 154, 83 *n.* 164, 93, 113, 116, 121 *n.* 92, 126, 153, 163, 179, 187, 190, 194, 195 *n.* 133, 196–197, 208 *n.* 173, 209 *n.* 180, 225, 234, 242, 252, 274, 279 *n.* 22, 292, 298, 303, 305, 312, 327, 331–332, 349, 359, 363, 373, 401–402, 409

ukhuwwa bashariyya 83 *n.* 164, 198
Ukhuwwa Islāmiyya 198
ukhuwwa waṭaniyya 83 *n.* 164, 198
ulama xii, 1, 17–18, 21, 37–38, 40, 46 *n.* 20, 53, 61 *n.* 80, 62–67, 71–72, 74–76, 78, 82, 87, 91, 95 *n.* 8, 96, 101 *n.* 27, 106, 108, 110, 112–113, 118, 121 *n.* 92, 122, 126, 128, 136, 145, 147–148, 150, 154, 164, 178, 197–198, 201, 204, 206–207, 209 *n.* 180, 213–214, 234–240, 243, 246, 247 *n.* 62, 258, 262, 270, 285, 299–300, 305, 314, 317, 319, 329, 346, 348 *n.* 17, 357, 359, 361, 383, 390, 412–413, 416
umarāʾ 59, 63, 71, 263
Universal Human Rights 316
unlawful animals 321
unlawful products 321
unregistered marriage 209
uṣūl al-fiqh 122

Vaccine 323
Vali Nasr 11–12
Vedi R. Hadiz 190, 369, 373
vilayat al-faqeh 54

wadah tunggal 60
Wael B. Hallaq 38, 322 *n.* 182
Wahba al-Zuḥaylī 19, 120 *n.* 89, 305, 311, 318 *n.* 166, 328
Wahhābī 291
Wahhabism 213, 228, 405
Wahid Hasyim 174
waqf 218
Wasidi Swastomo 263
West Java x, 13, 40–41, 46, 52, 55, 56 *n.* 58, 60, 62 *n.* 85, 67, 127, 128 *n.* 113, 187, 219 *n.* 211, 224, 231–233, 236, 258–261, 266 *n.* 119, 269, 285, 295 *n.* 87, 392, 439
William Shepard 9
Worship 273, 293, 296, 443

YDDP xvii, 77, 84
Yogyakarta x, 3 *n.* 4, 10 *nn.* 30, 34, 13, 46 *n.* 21, 47 *n.* 22, 62 *n.* 85, 65 *n.* 101, 80 *n.* 153, 109 *n.* 50, 129 *n.* 113, 155 *n.* 200, 157 *n.* 208, 174 *n.* 44, 182, 184 *n.* 90, 215, 219 *n.* 209, 259 *n.* 100, 281 *n.* 31, 324, 337 *n.* 239, 354 *n.* 32, 398 *n.* 1, 422–423, 425, 438–440, 445, 447
Yudoyono 6 *n.* 12, 128, 166, 180, 188, 247, 288, 347 *n.* 15, 349, 355, 357, 409
Yunahar Ilyas 89, 384
Yūsuf al-Qaraḍāwī 10 *n.* 33, 300

Zaitun Rasmin 384
zakat xii, 35, 233, 250, 255, 298–300
Zaydiyya 290

Printed in the United States
by Baker & Taylor Publisher Services